U0920911

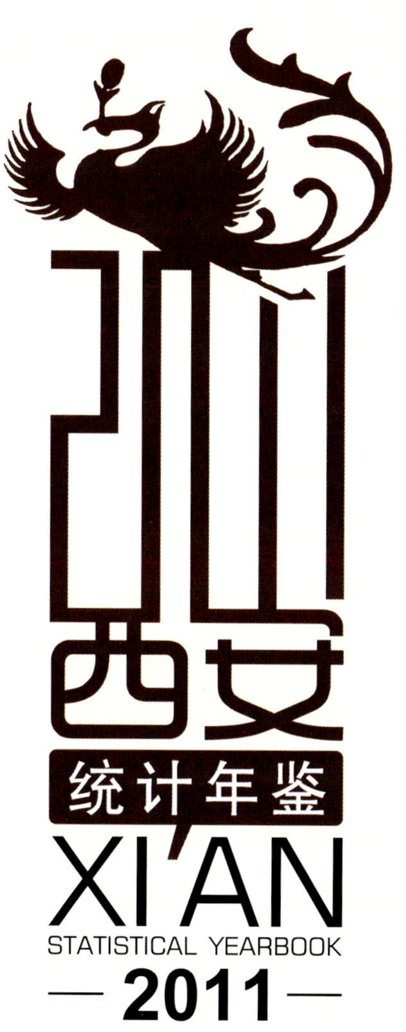

西安统计年鉴

XI'AN STATISTICAL YEARBOOK

— 2011 —

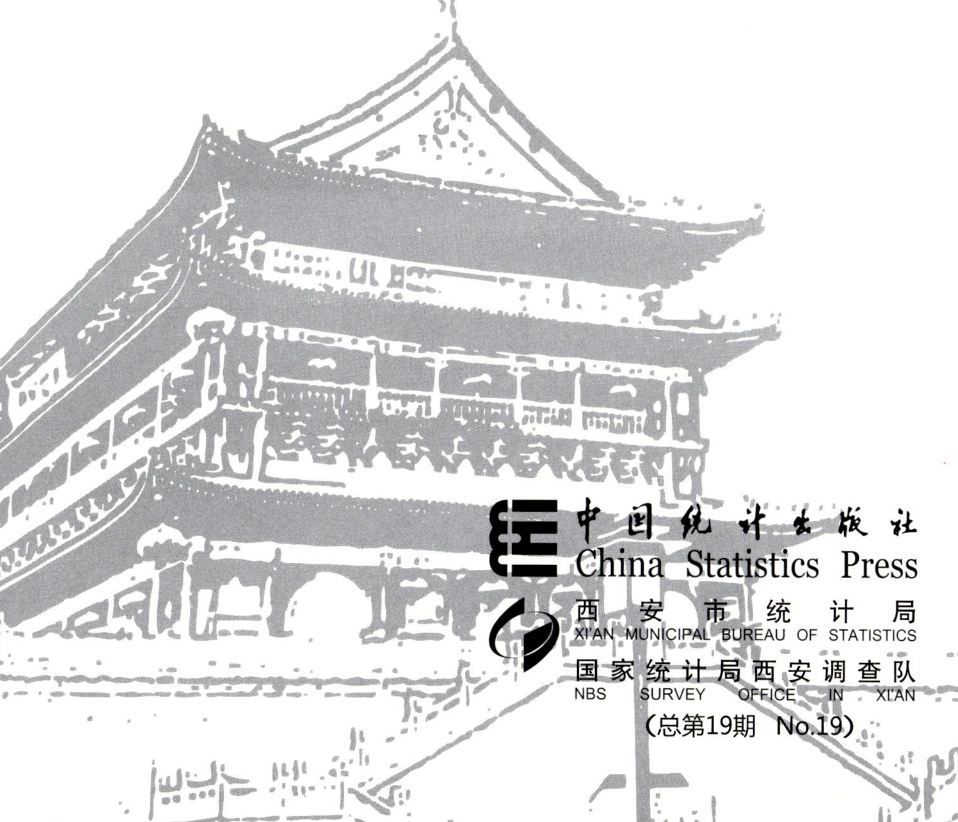

中国统计出版社
China Statistics Press
西安市统计局
XI'AN MUNICIPAL BUREAU OF STATISTICS
国家统计局西安调查队
NBS SURVEY OFFICE IN XI'AN
（总第19期 No.19）

（京）新登字 041 号

图书在版编目（CIP）数据

西安统计年鉴.2011：/西安市统计局，国家统计局西安调查队编.
—北京：中国统计出版社，2011.9
ISBN 978-7-5037-6321-2/C.2541

Ⅰ.①西…
Ⅱ.①西… ②国…
Ⅲ.统计资料-西安市-2011-年鉴
Ⅳ.①C832.411-54

中国版本图书馆CIP数据核字（2011）第164253号

西安统计年鉴—2011

作　　者/ 西安市统计局　国家统计局西安调查队
责任编辑/ 佘竞雄
责任校对/ 赵群洁
封面设计/ 西安市丰润广告有限责任公司
出版发行/ 中国统计出版社
通信地址/ 北京市西城区月坛南街57号
邮　　编/ 100826
电　　话/（010）63376907
E-mail / yearbook@gj.stats.cn
印　　刷/ 西安煤航信息产业有限公司
经　　销/ 新华书店
开　　本/ 890×1240毫米 1/16
字　　数/ 1326千字
印　　张/ 41.5
版　　别/ 2011年8月第1版
版　　次/ 2011年8月第1次印刷
书　　号/ ISBN 978-7-5037-6321-2/C·2541
定　　价/ 260.00元

《西安统计年鉴—2011》编辑部

XI'AN STATISTICAL YEARBOOK-2011

EDITORLAL STAFF

生产总值 [亿元]
Gross Dometic (100 million yuan)

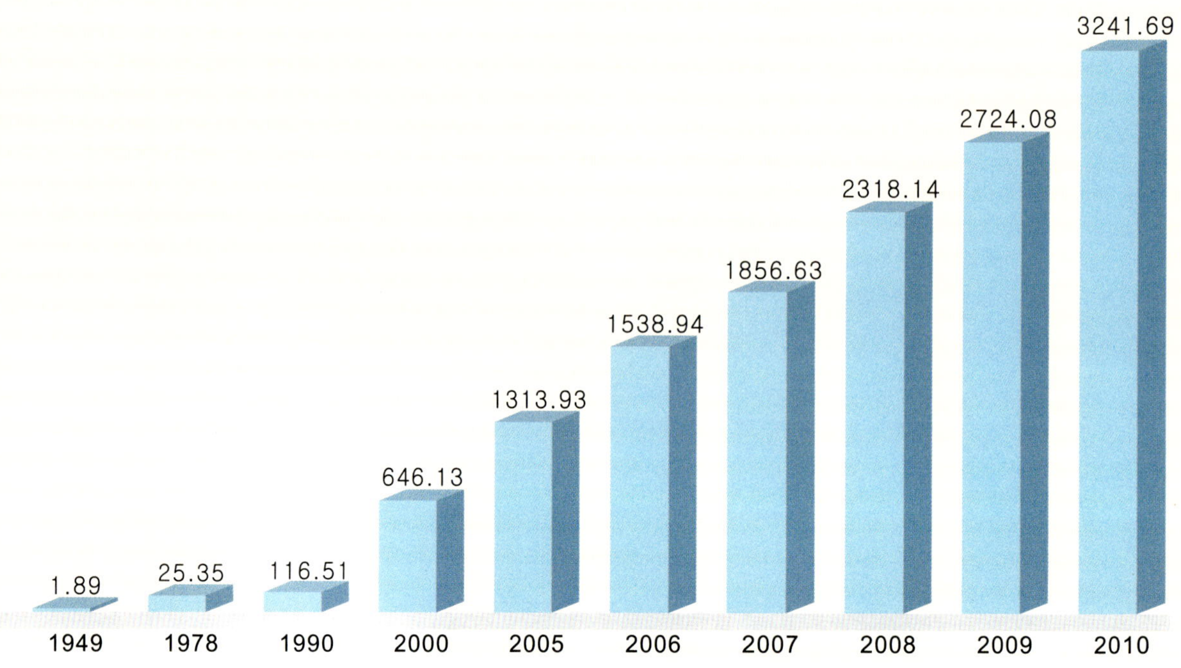

生产总值指数 [以上年为100]
Indices of Gross Domestic Product (perceding year=100)

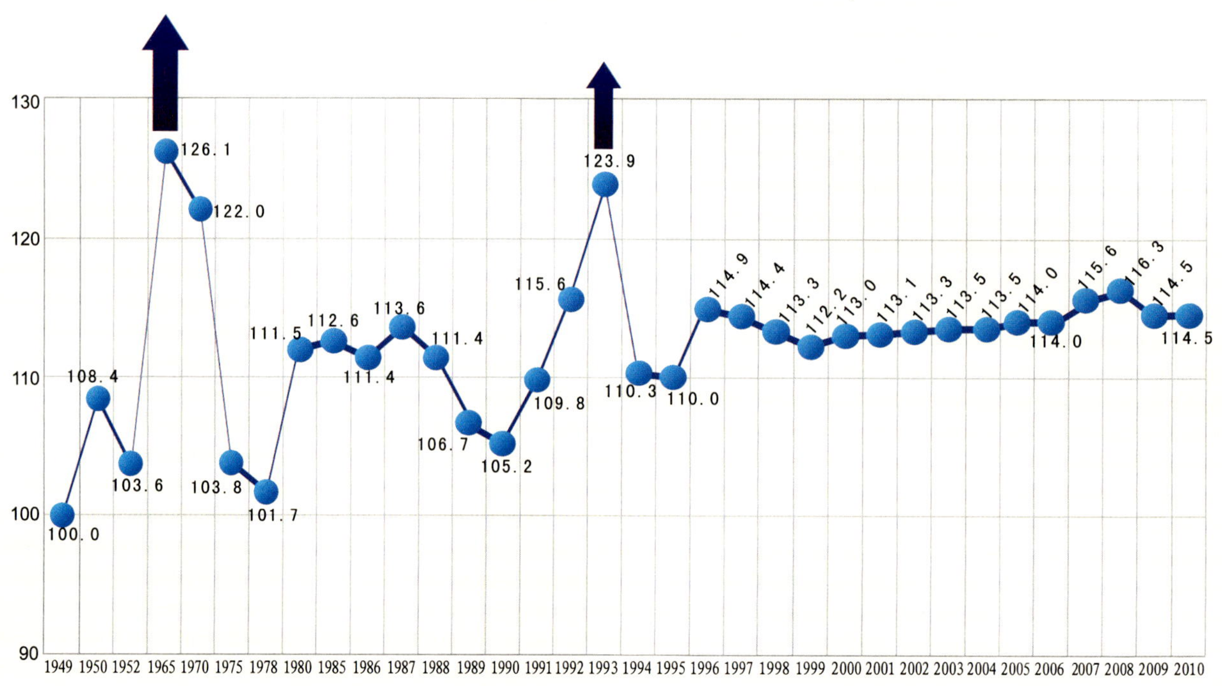

生产总值构成 [%]
Composition of Gross Domestic Product (%)

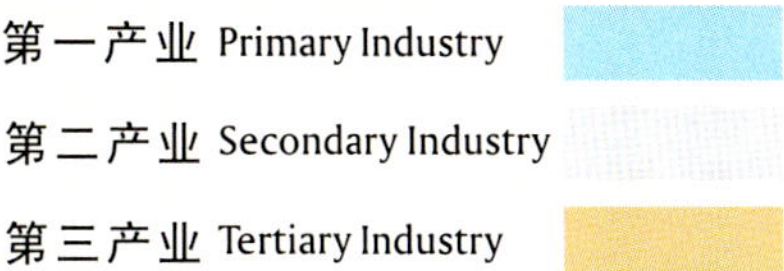

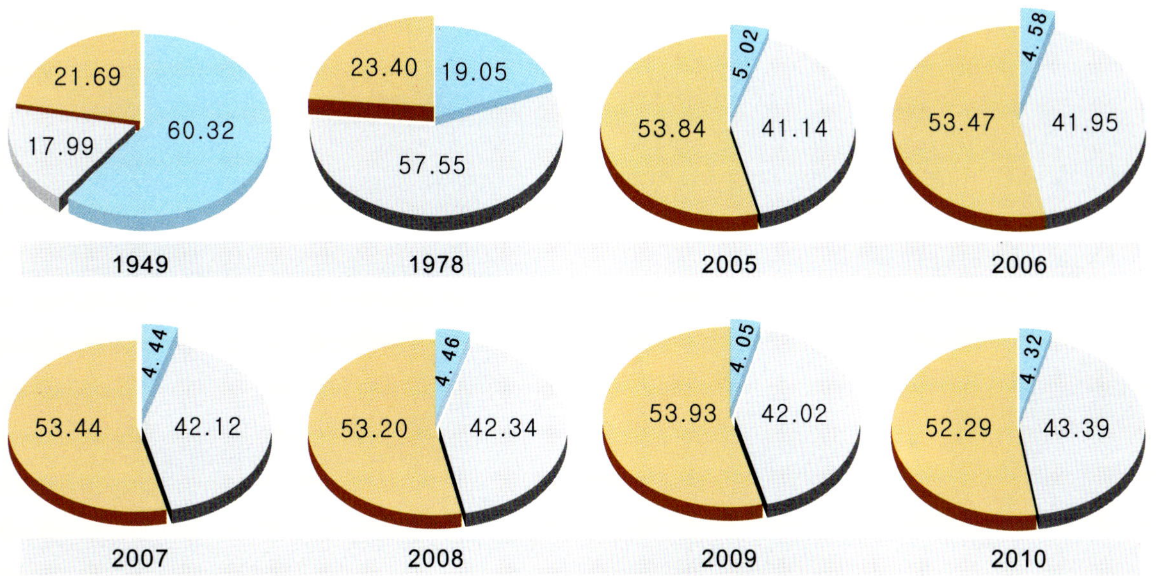

人均GDP [元/人]
Per Dapita GDF (yuan/person)

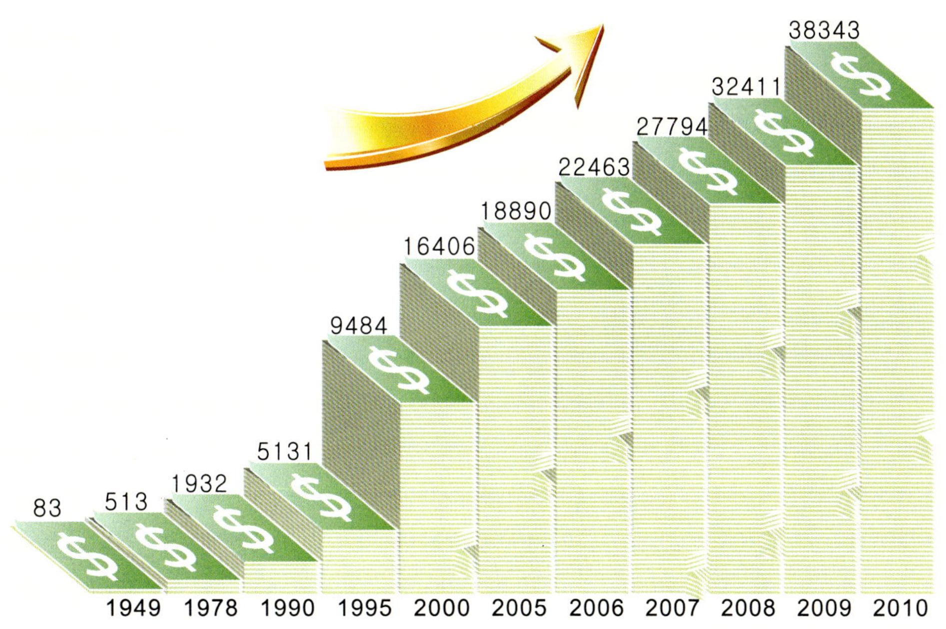

年末常住人口 [万人]
The Permanent Population(year-end) (10000 persons)

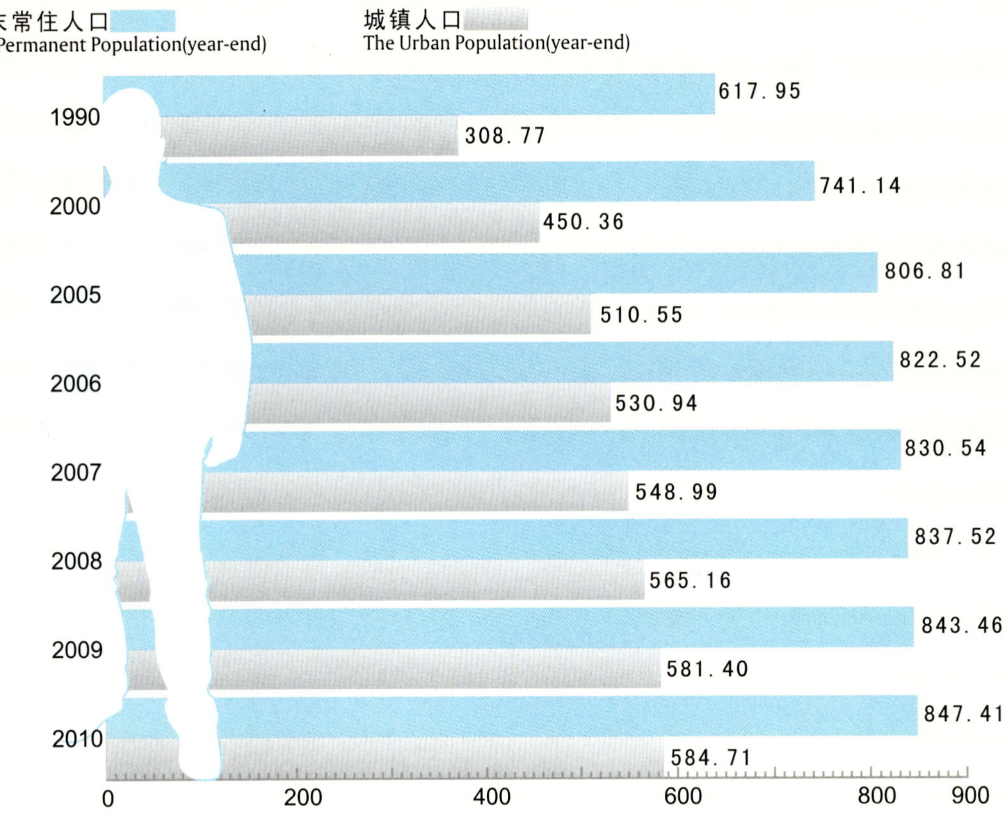

社会从业人数 [万人]
Social Workers(10000 persons)

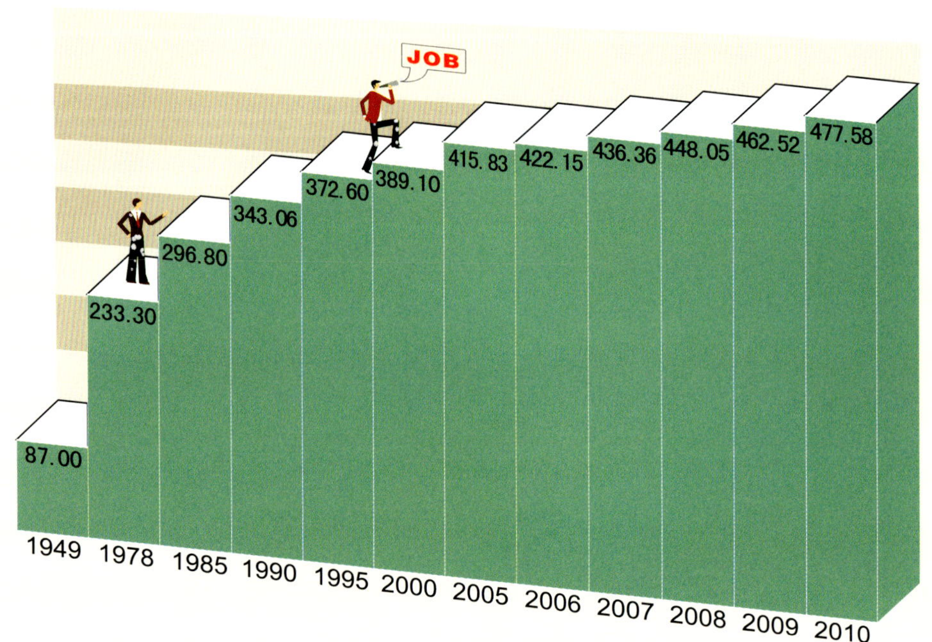

固定资产投资 [亿元]
Investment In Fixed Assets(100million yuan)

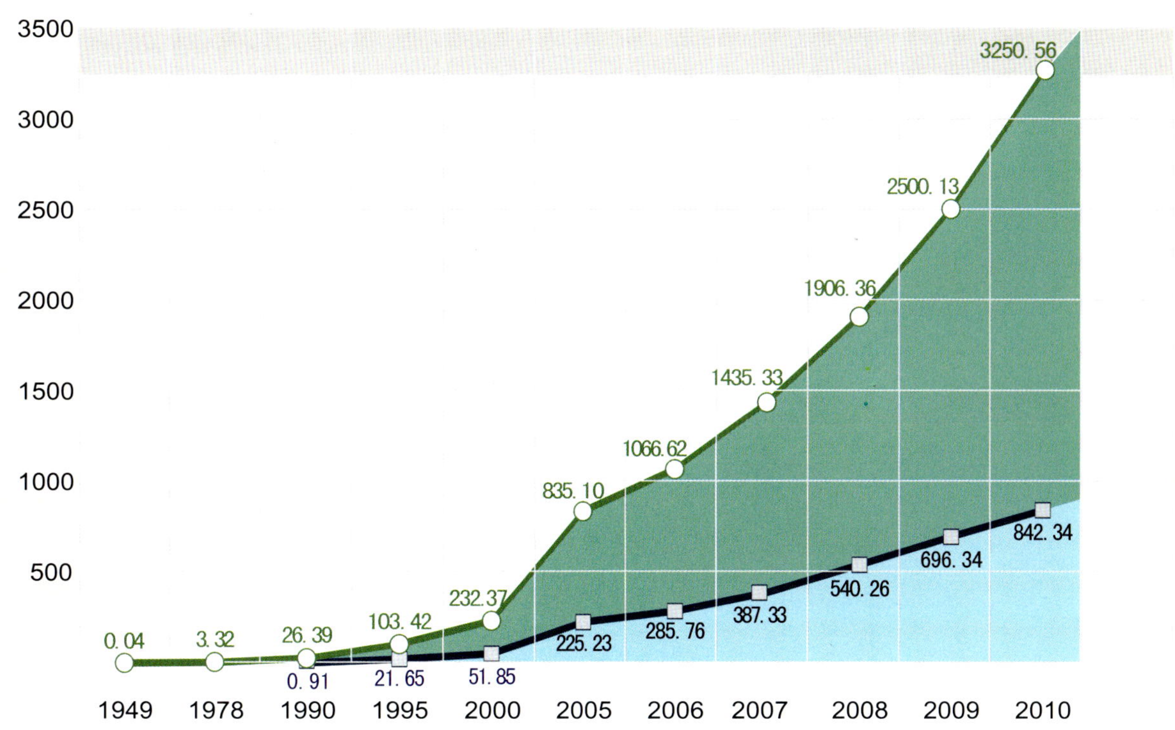

新增固定资产及住宅竣工面积
Newly Increased Fixed Assets and Residential Area of Completien

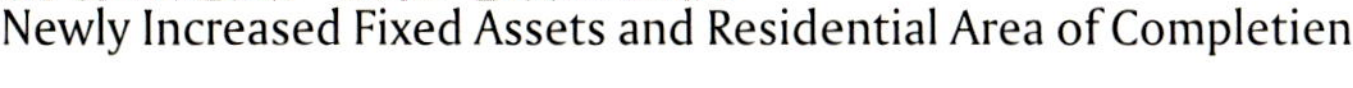

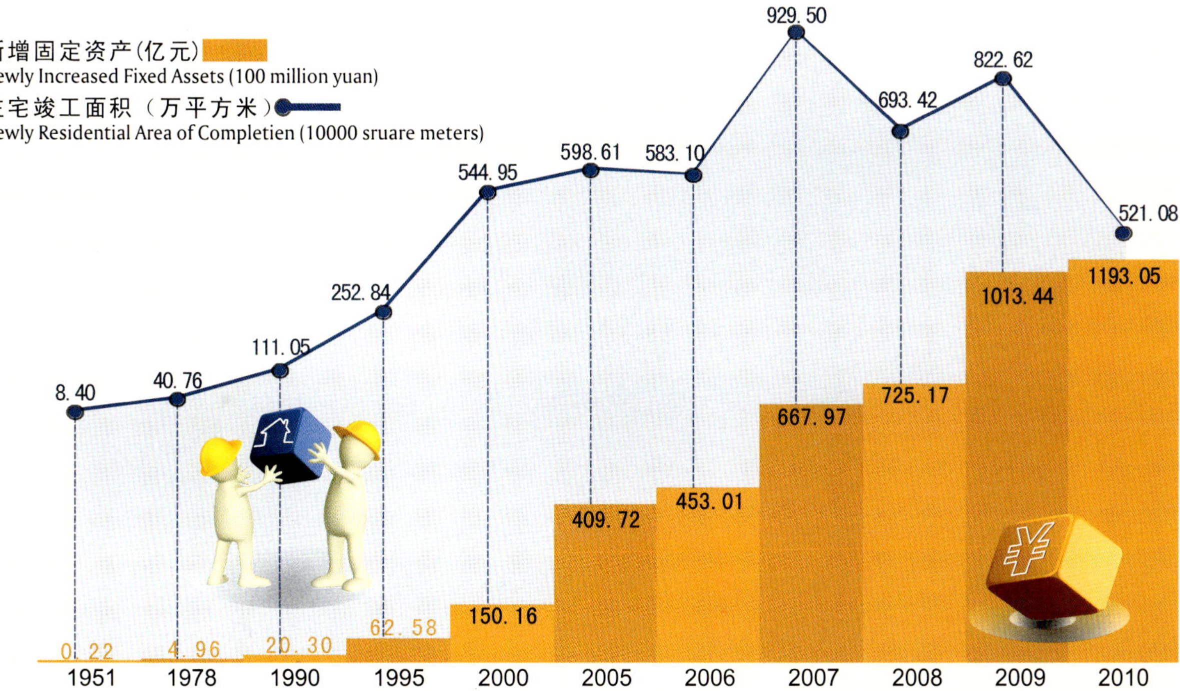

农林牧渔及服务业总产值［亿元］
Gross Output Value of Farming,Forestry,Animal Husbandry,Fishery,Service (100 milliion yuan)

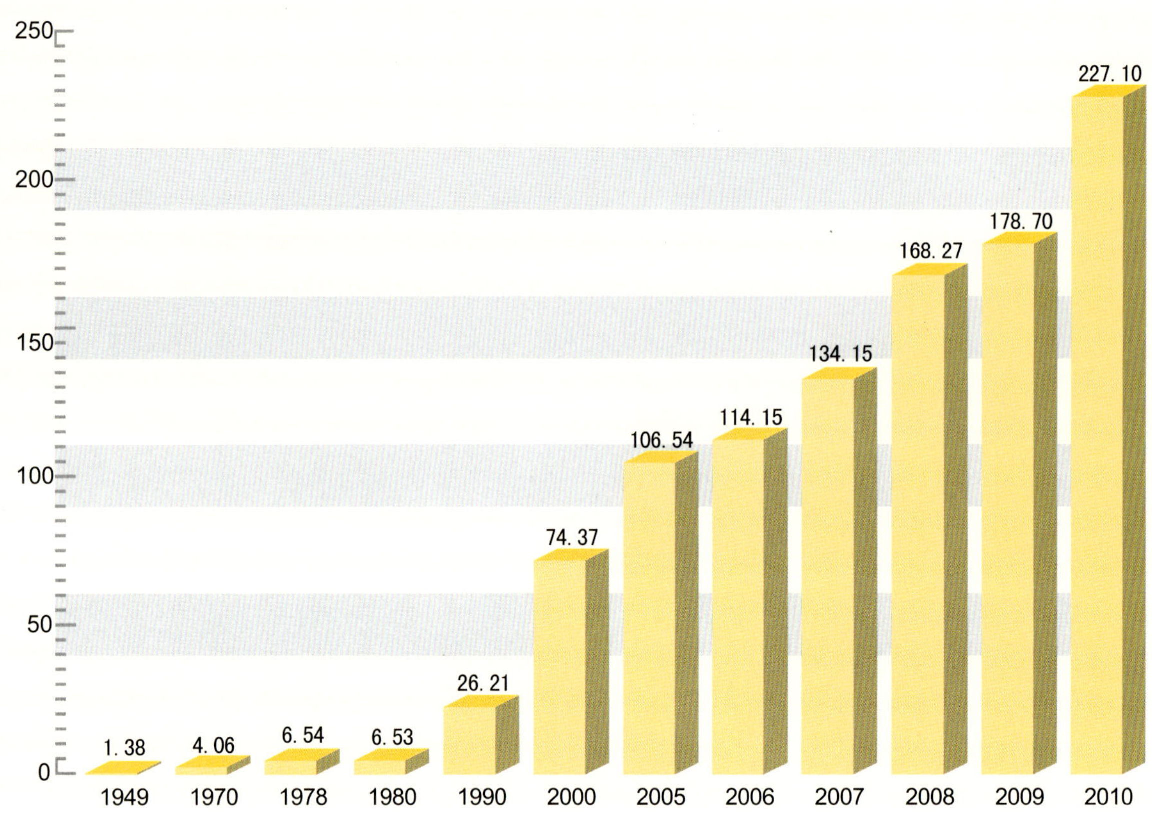

粮食、蔬菜产量［万吨］
Grain, vegetables Product (10,000 tons)

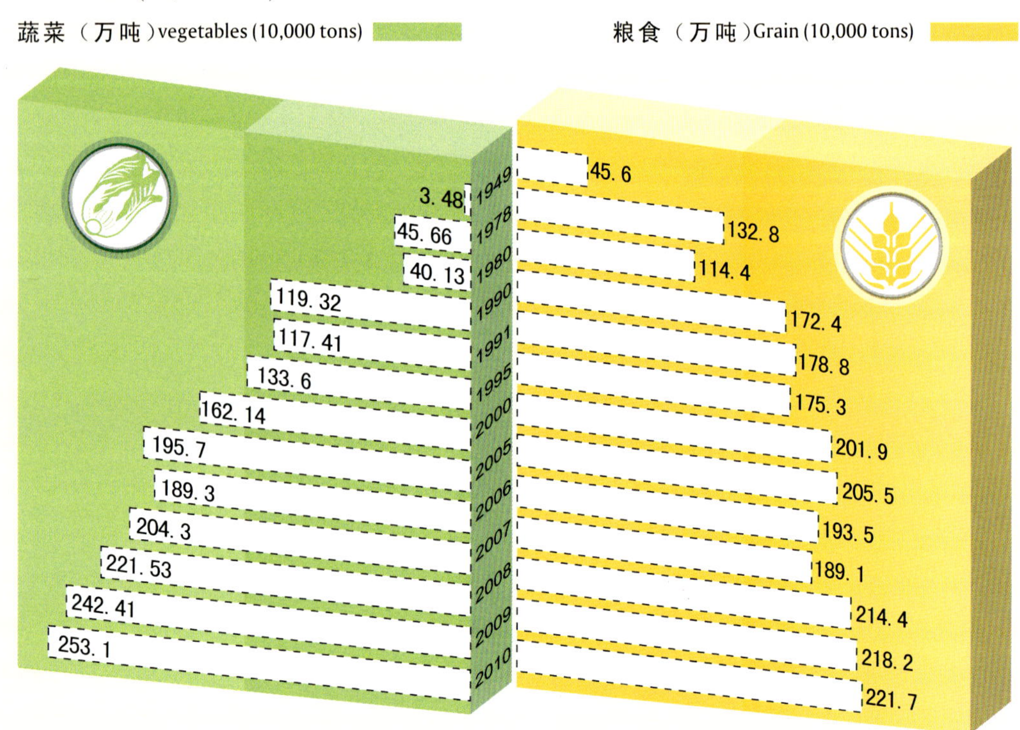

全部工业总产值及指数
Total Industrial Output Value and Index

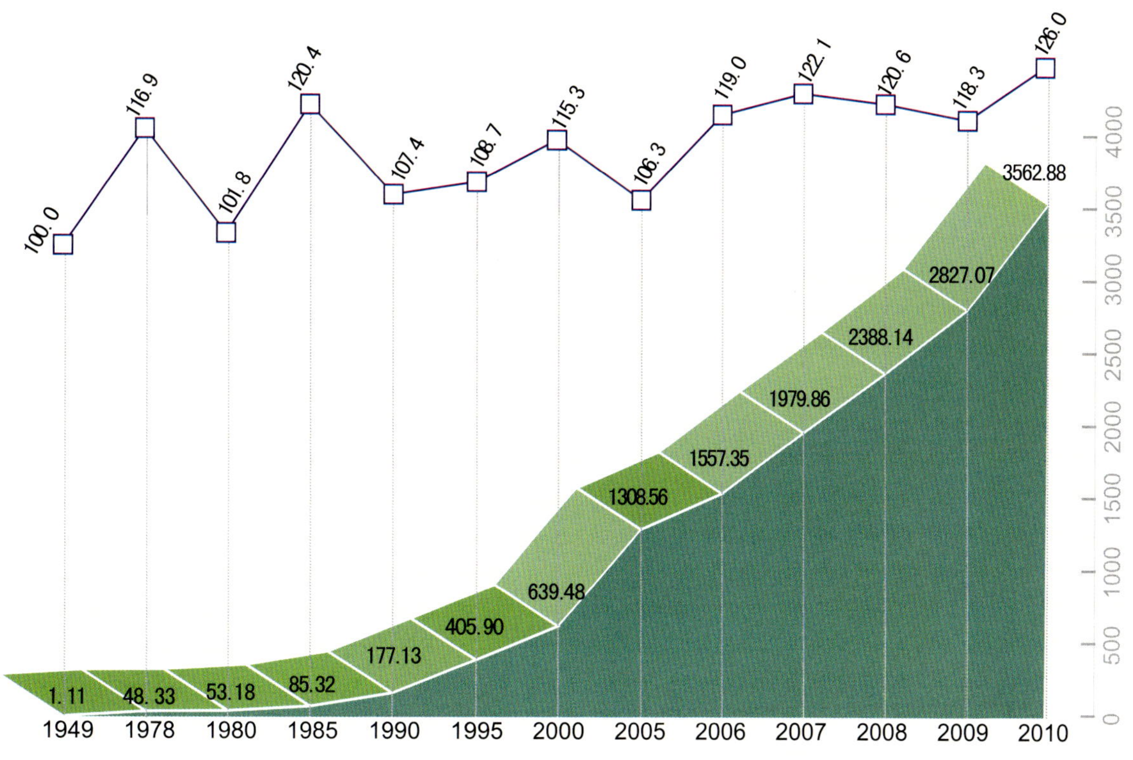

主要工业产品产量
Output of Major Industriat Products

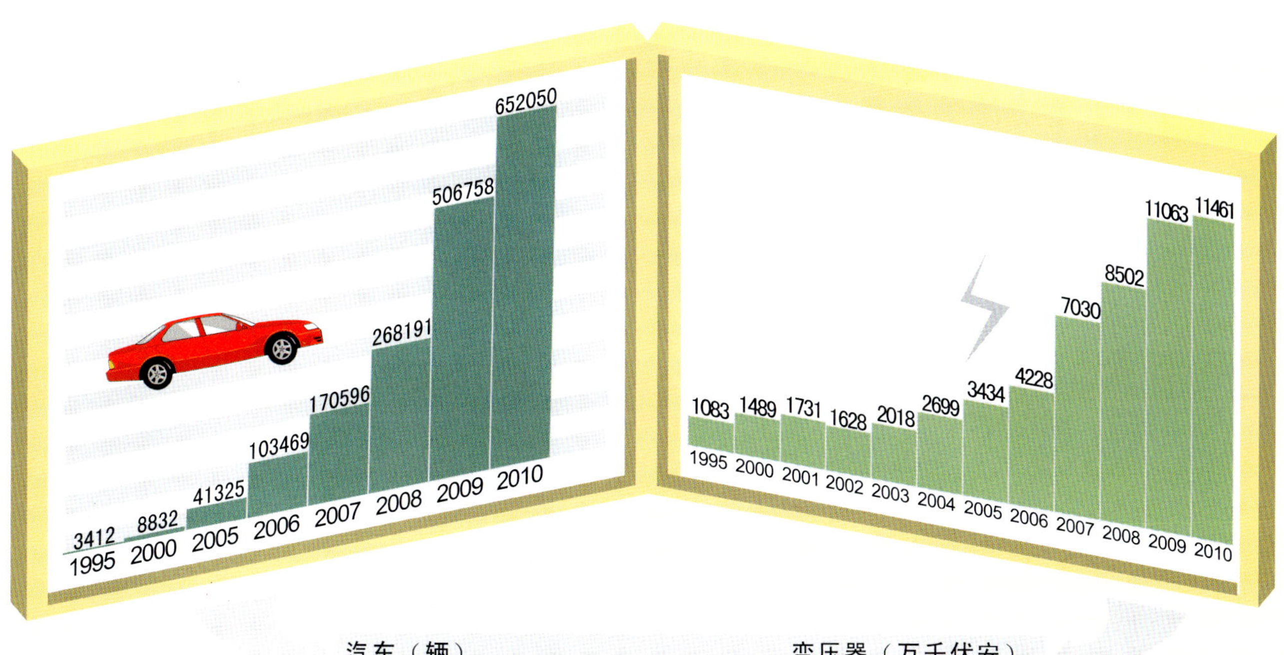

汽车（辆）
Motor Vehicle (unit)

变压器（万千伏安）
Transformer (10000Kva)

交通
Traffic

等级公路（公里）
Expressways and Class I to IV Highways(KM)

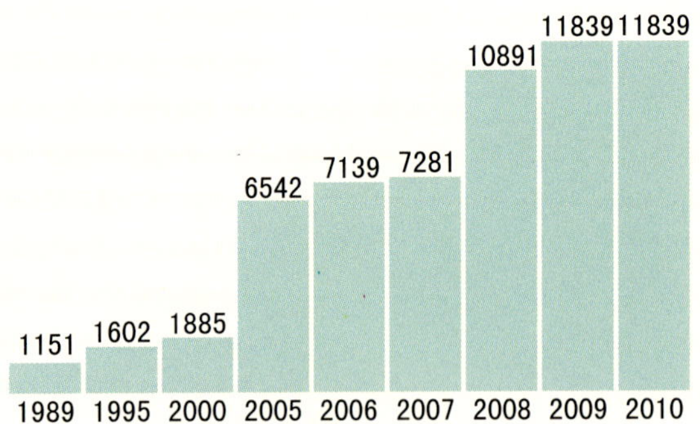

民航通航里程（公里）（重复航线）
Length of total Civil Aviation Routes(KM)

1995	2000	2005	2006	2007	2008	2009	2010
119753	139764	485749	418852	553355	515524	587904	742375

高速公路（公里）
High speed (KM)

2005	2006	2007	2008	2009	2010
252	252	286	374	377	377

全社会车辆数［万辆］
Possession of Civil Vehicles (10000 units)

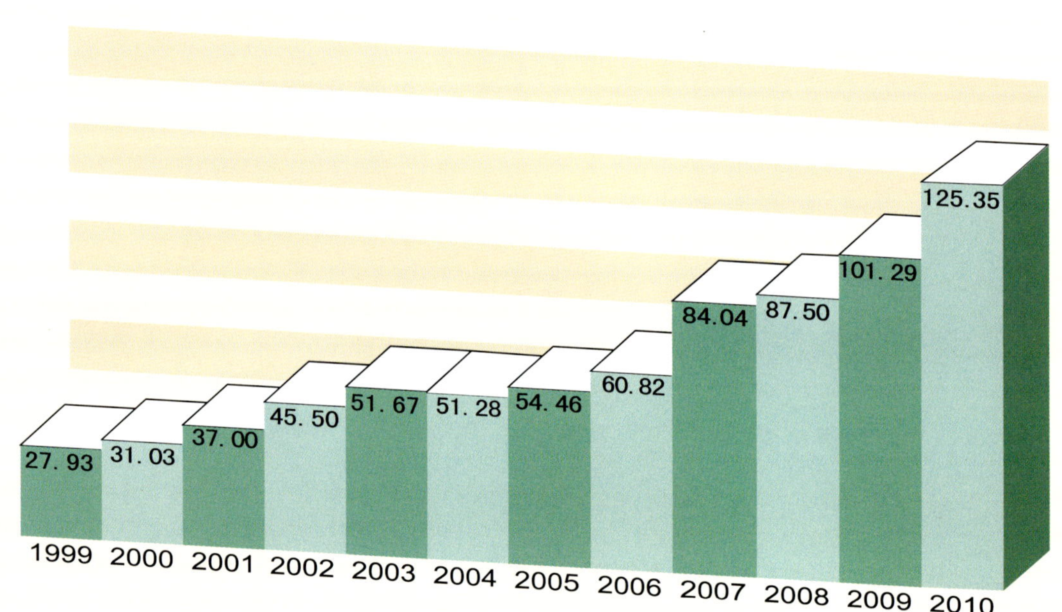

社会消费品零售总额［亿元］

Total Retail Sales of Consumer Goods (100million yuan)

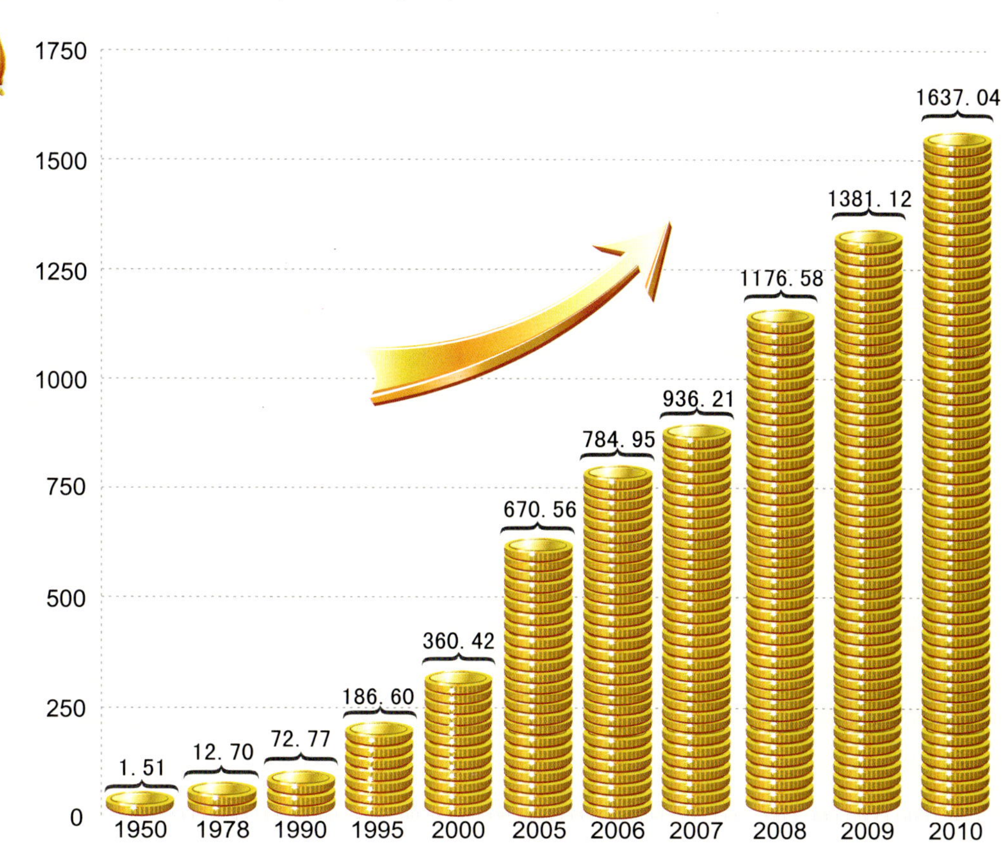

经营网点［个］

Bussiness Network (unit)

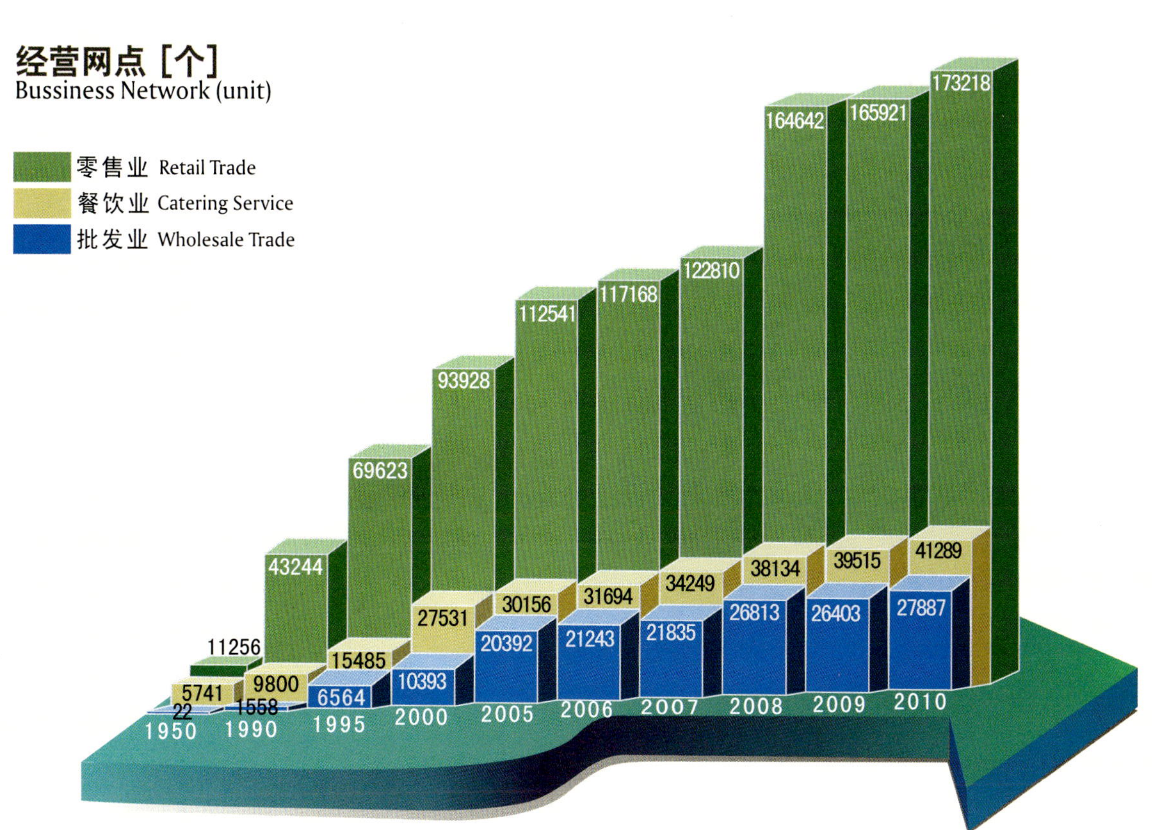

外商实际直接投资额 [亿美元]
Value of Foreign Direct Investment (USD 100million)

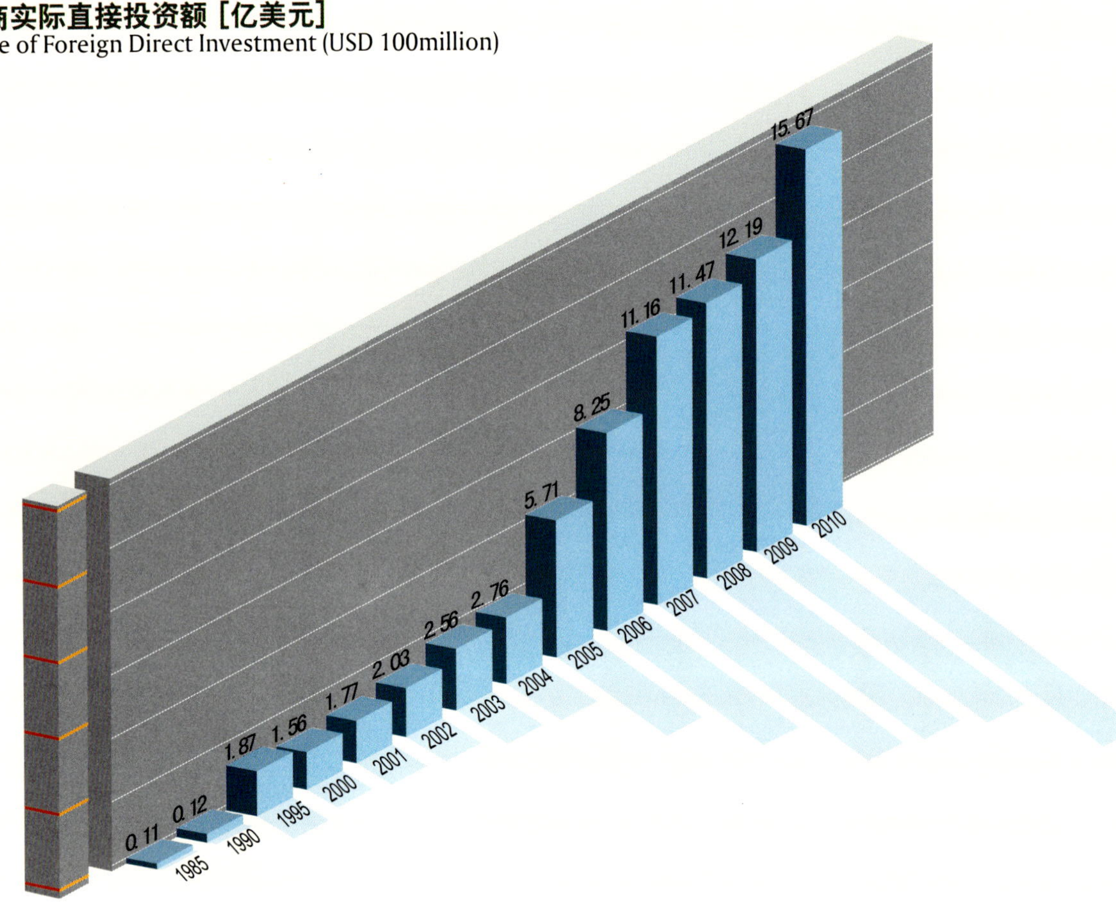

进出口总额 [亿美元]
Total Value of Imports and Exports (USD 100million)

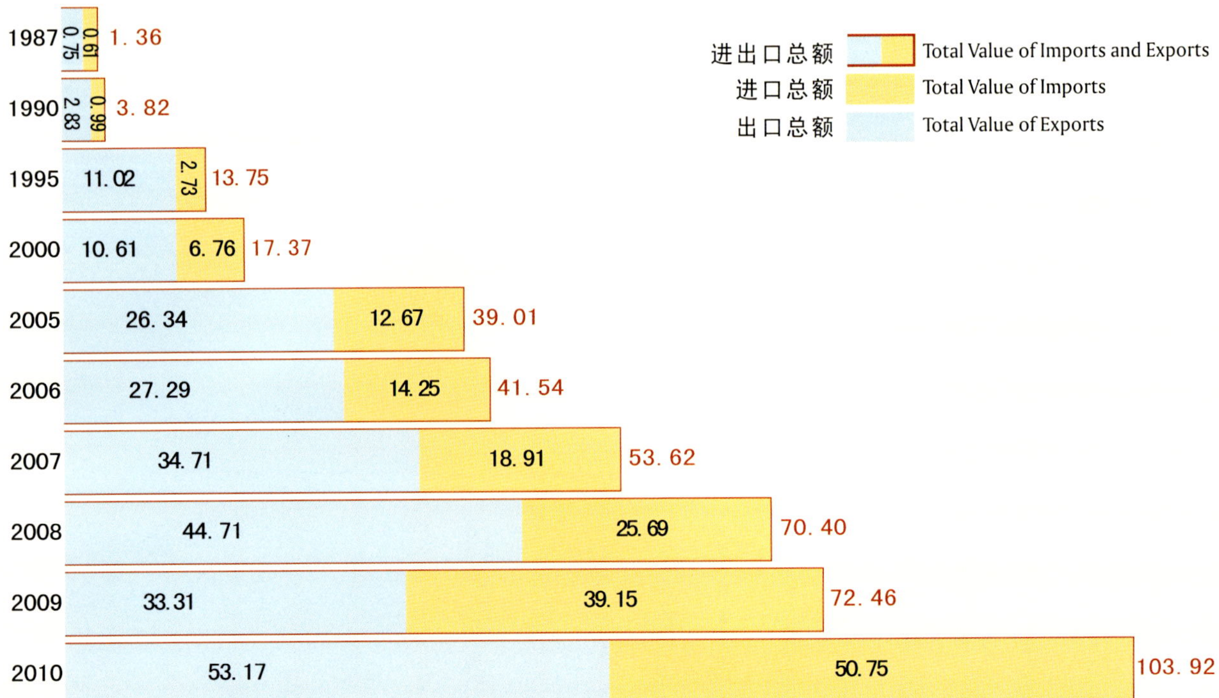

旅游人数及收入
Number of Tourists and Tourism Income

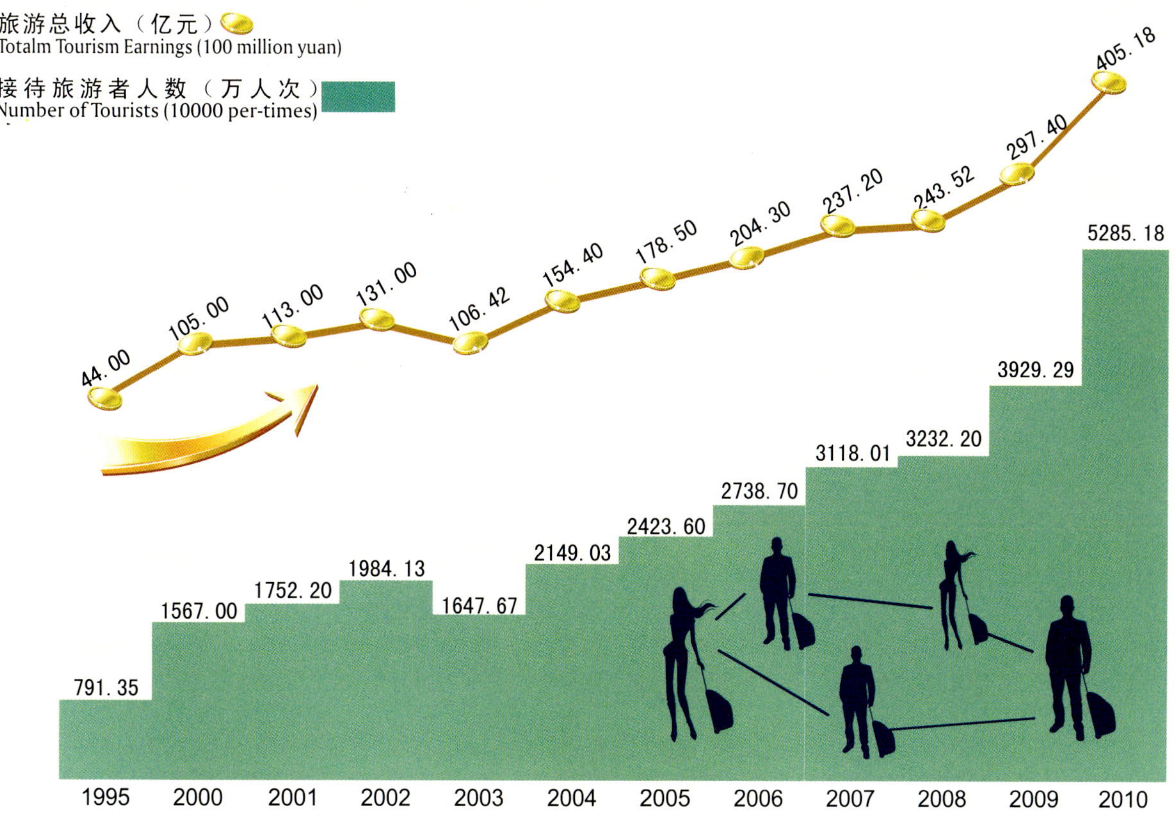

国际旅游人数及收入
Number of International Tourists and Tourism Income

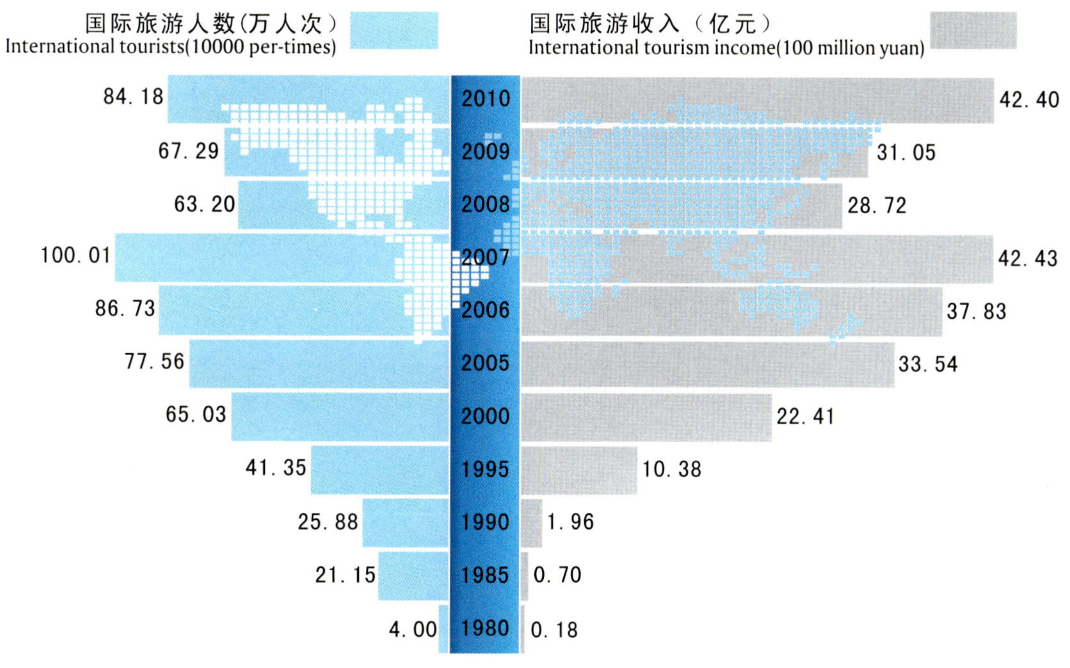

财政收支 [亿元]
Government Revenue and Expenditure (100 million yuan)

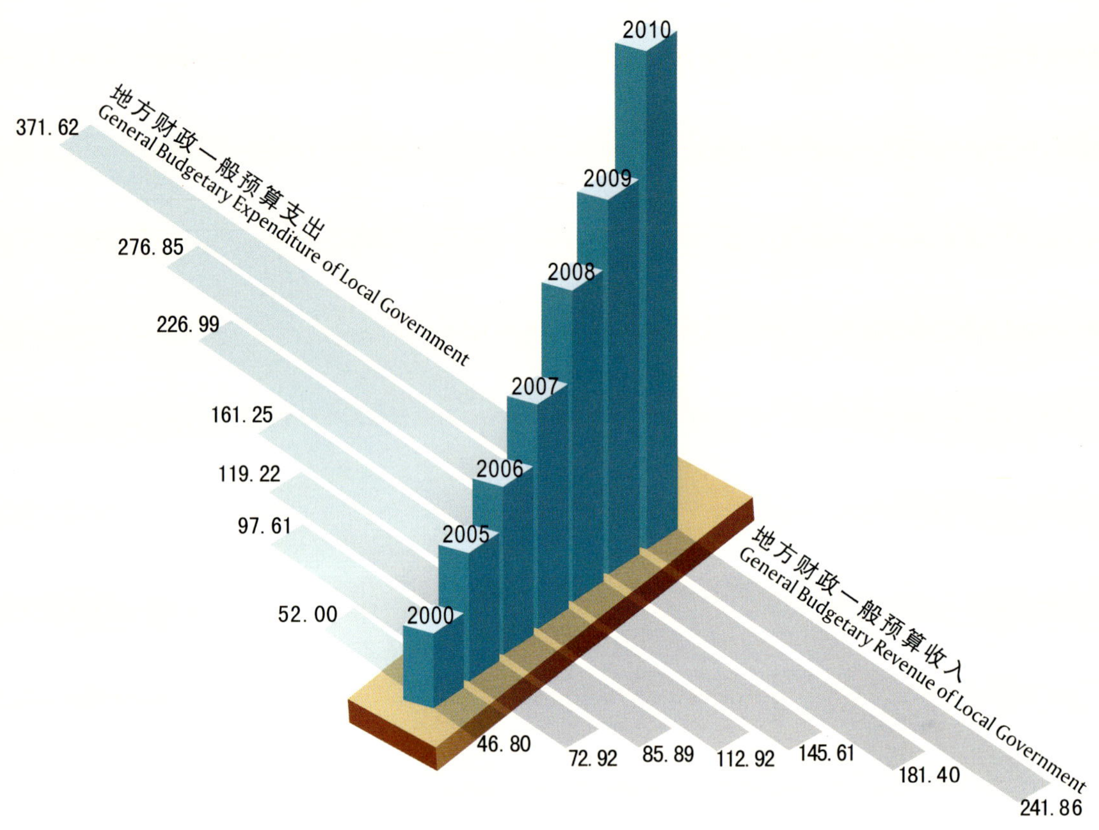

金融机构人民币存贷款年末余额 [亿元]
Balance of Deposit and Loans in Dmestic Funded Financial Institutions(100 million yuan)

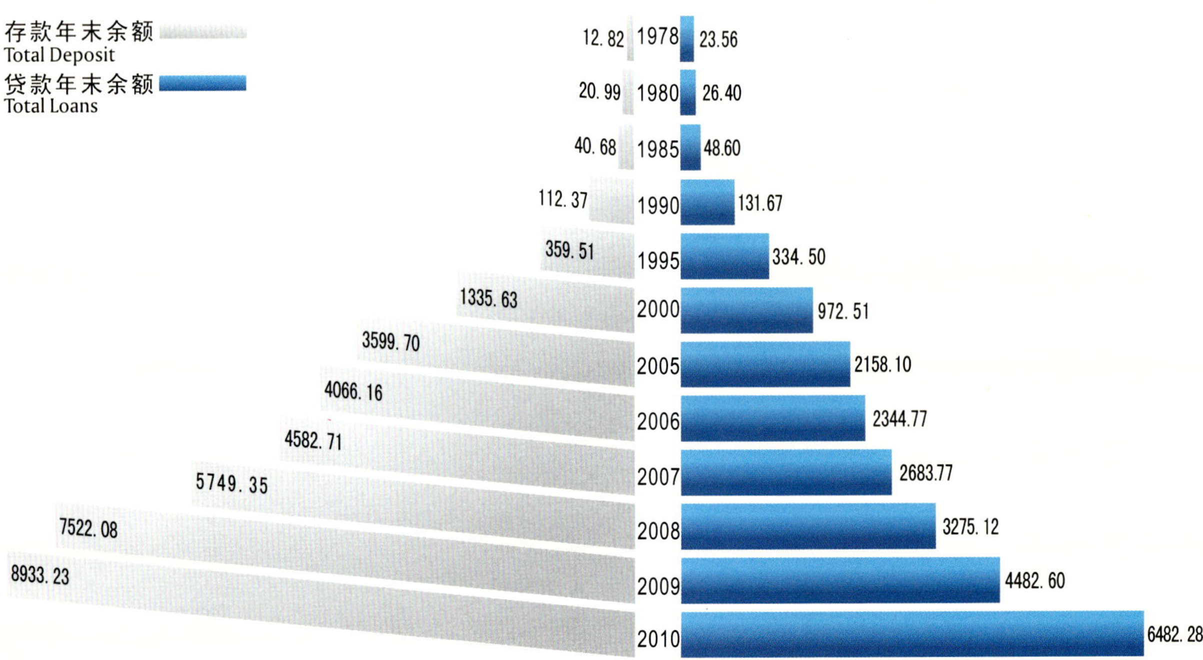

城市公共营运车辆［辆］
Operating Vehicles (unit)

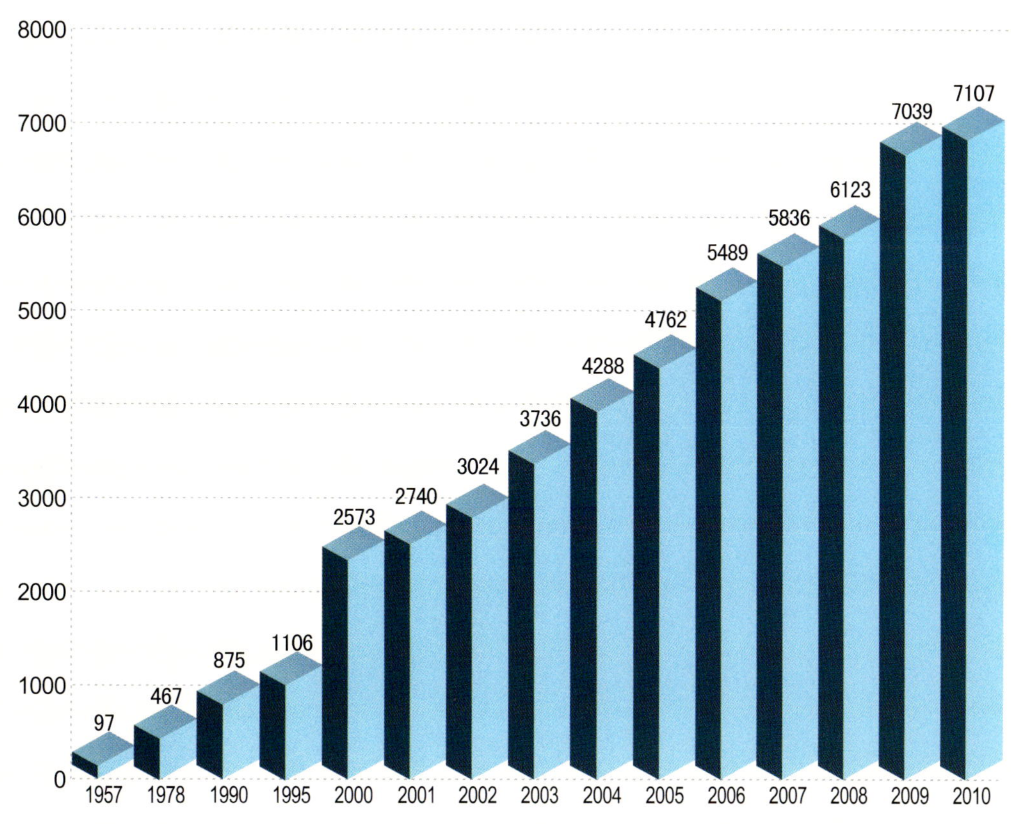

建成区面积［平方公里］
Area of the Regions Constructed (sq.km)

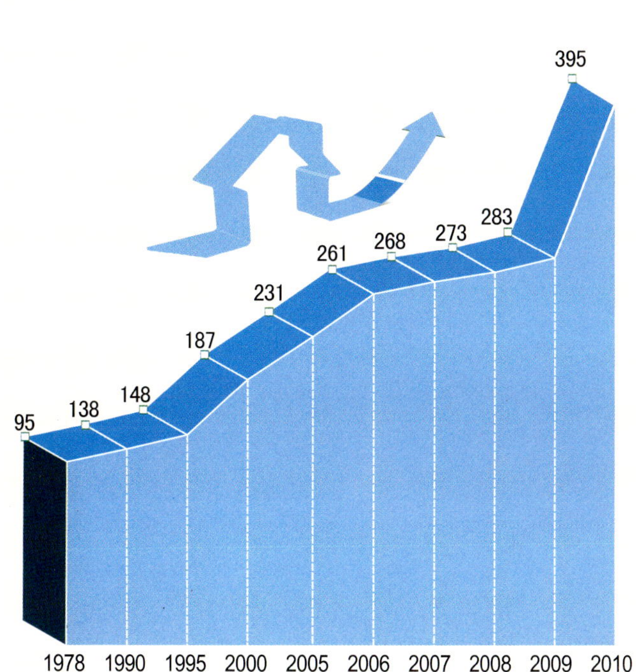

园林绿地总面积［公顷］
Total Area of Parks,Gardens and Green Area(hectare)

普通教育在校学生［万人］
Total Enrollments (10000 persons)

普通高等教育 Regular Instiutions of Higher Education　普通中学 Regular Secondary Schools　小学 Primary Schools

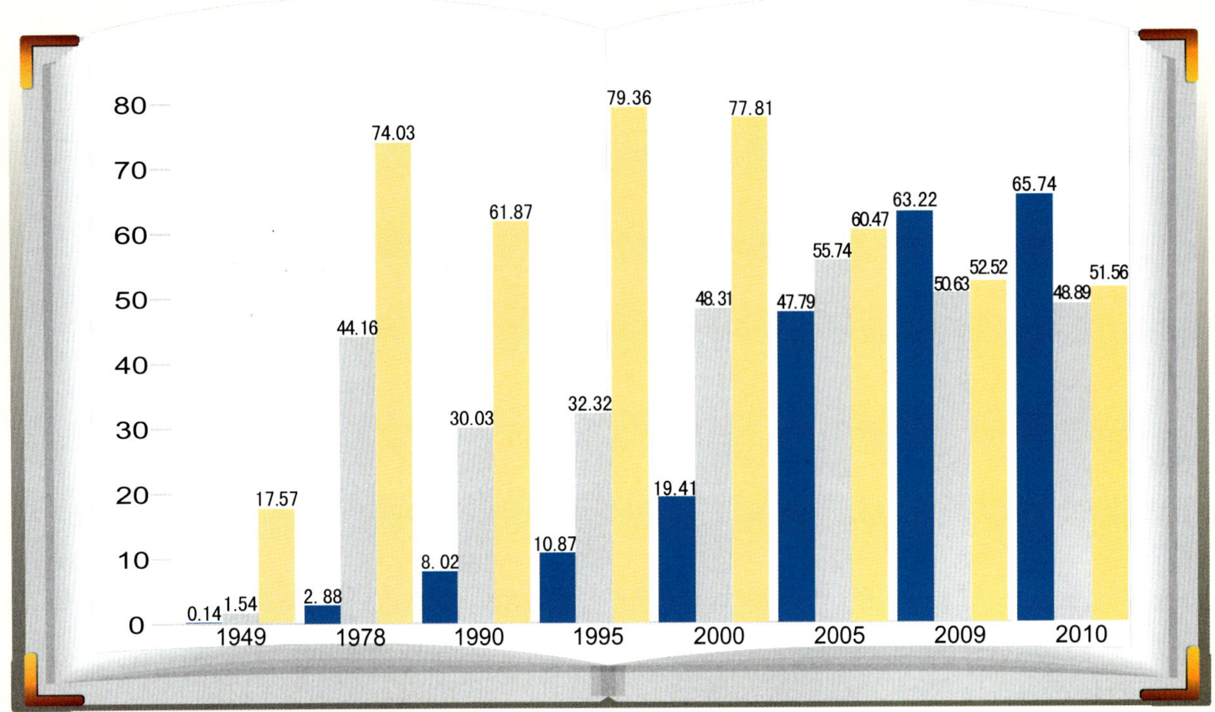

专任教师(万人)
Number of Full-time Teachers (10000 persons)

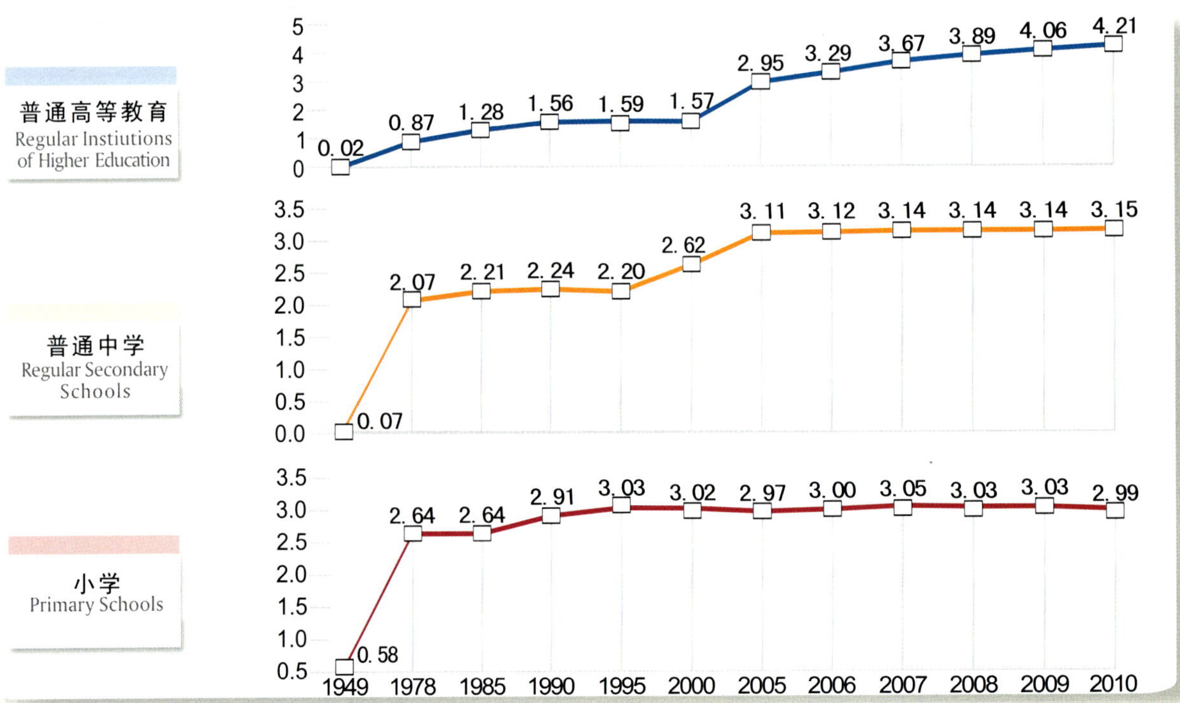

城乡居民收入 [元]
The Income of Urban and Rural residents (yuan)

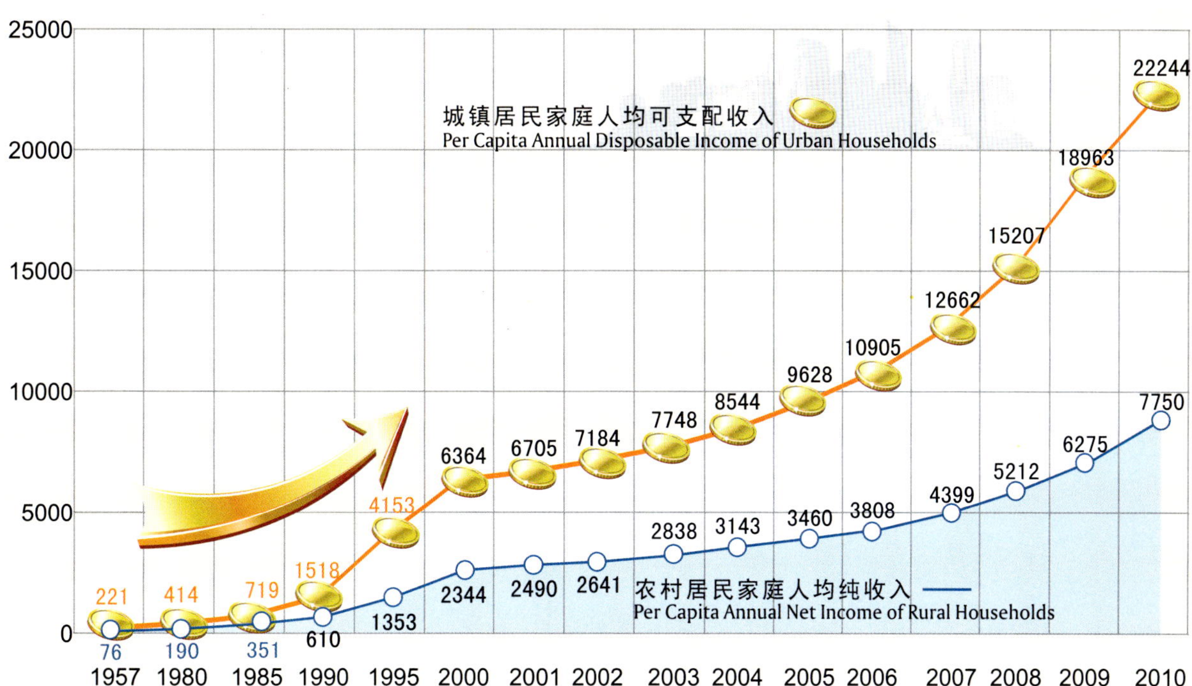

价格指数 [以上年价格为100]
Various Price Indices (Price of Preceding year =100)

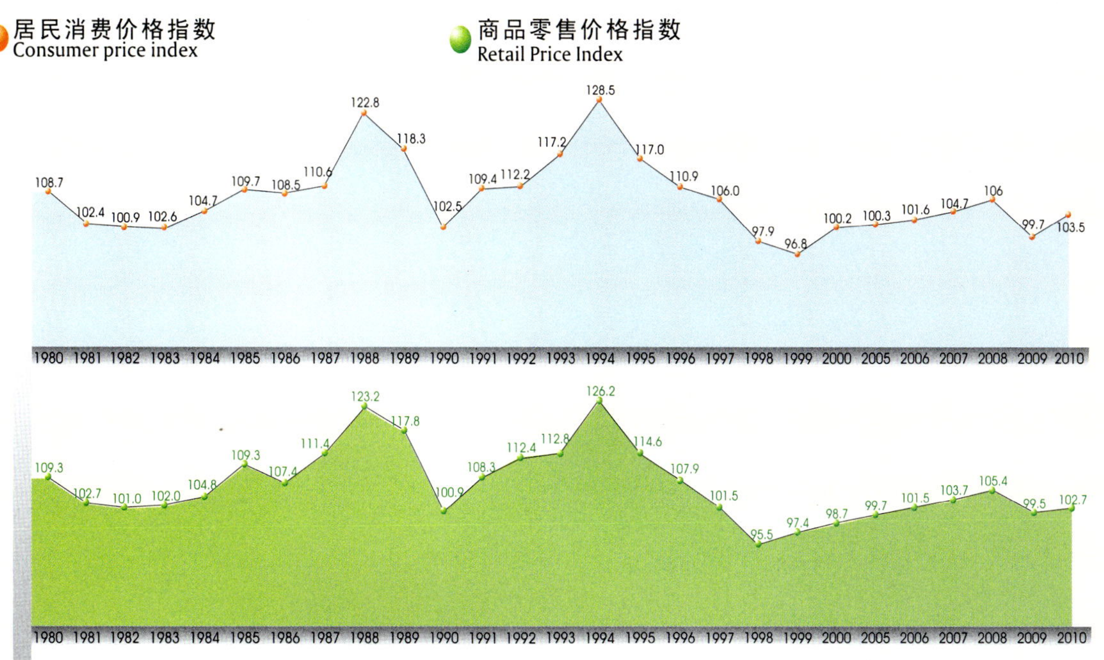

西安
统计年鉴
XI'AN
STATISTICAL YEARBOOK
2011

目　录

西安市2010年国民经济和社会发展统计公报……1

一、综　合

1-1　行政区划（2010年底）……1
1-2　土地面积和常住人口密度（2010年）……2
1-3　自然状况和资源（2010年）……3
1-4　气象情况（2010年）……3
1-5　国有土地使用权出让、划拨情况……4
1-6　按登记注册类型分法人单位（2010年）……5
1-7　按行业分法人单位（2010年）……6
1-8　各区县法人单位（2010年）……10
1-9　按登记注册类型分产业活动单位（2010年）……11
1-10　按行业分产业活动单位（2010年）……13
1-11　各区县产业活动单位（2010年）……17
1-12　国民经济和社会发展总量与速度指标……18
1-13　国民经济和社会发展结构指标……28
1-14　国民经济和社会发展比例和效益指标……32
1-15　平均每天主要社会经济活动……38
1-16　各区县国民经济和社会发展主要指标（2010年）……40
主要统计指标解释……42

二、国民经济核算

2-1　主要年份生产总值……49
2-2　主要年份生产总值指数（上年=100）……50
2-3　主要年份生产总值指数（1952年=100）……51
2-4　主要年份生产总值构成……52
2-5　全市各区县生产总值（2010年）……53
2-6　全市各区县生产总值指数（2010年）（上年=100）……54
2-7　全市各区县生产总值构成（2010年）……55
2-8　主要年份分行业增加值……56
2-9　主要年份分行业增加值指数（上年=100）……56
2-10　主要年份支出法生产总值……57

2-11　主要年份支出法生产总值指数（上年=100）……58
2-12　按支出法计算的生产总值及指数（2010年）……59
2-13　分行业资本形成总额（2010年）……59
2-14　最终消费支出（2010年）……60
2-15　居民总消费水平（2010年）……61
2-16　非公有制经济增加值（2010年）……61
2-17　五大主导产业增加值……62
2-18　五大主导产业增加值比重……62
主要统计指标解释……63

三、人口、从业人员与职工工资

3-1　主要年份人口、人口密度和人口发展情况……71
3-2　主要年份人口变动情况……72
3-3　各区县人口和户数（2010年）……73
3-4　各区县人口变动情况（2010年）……74
3-5　主要年份常住人口……74
3-6　主要年份社会从业人数……75
3-7　分行业从业人数（2010年）……76
3-8　全部单位从业人员情况（2010年）……78
3-9　国有单位从业人员情况（2010年）……80
3-10　城镇集体单位从业人员情况（2010年）……82
3-11　其他经济类型单位从业人员情况（2010年）……84
3-12　全部单位从业人员劳动报酬（2010年）……86
3-13　国有单位从业人员劳动报酬（2010年）……88
3-14　城镇集体单位从业人员劳动报酬（2010年）……90
3-15　其他经济类型单位从业人员劳动报酬（2010年）……92
3-16　城镇非私营单位在岗职工平均工资……94
3-17　城镇登记失业人数及失业率……96
主要统计指标解释……97

四、固定资产投资

4-1　主要年份按城乡分全社会固定资产投资……103
4-2　主要年份按经济类型分全社会固定资产投资……104
4-3　主要年份按产业分全市固定资产投资……105
4-4　全市固定资产投资（2010年）……106
4-5　按行业分全市固定资产投资（2010年）……109
4-6　主要年份按资金来源及建设性质分全市固定资产投资……110

4-7 主要年份国有经济单位固定资产投资……112
4-8 农村集体固定资产投资（2010年）……114
4-9 主要年份农村集体固定资产投资……115
4-10 主要年份市属固定资产投资……118
4-11 市属固定资产投资（2010年）……120
4-12 按行业分市属固定资产投资（2010年）……122
4-13 按资金来源及建设性质分市属固定资产投资（2010年）……123
4-14 按登记注册类型及隶属关系分市区固定资产投资（2010年）……124
4-15 按行业分市区固定资产投资（2010年）……125
4-16 按资金来源及建设性质分市区固定资产投资（2010年）……126
4-17 全市固定资产投资资金来源（2010年）……127
4-18 市属固定资产投资资金来源（2010年）……127
4-19 全市固定资产投资效果（2010年）……128
4-20 市属固定资产投资效果（2010年）……128
4-21 分区县、开发区全社会固定资产投资额（2010年）……129
4-22 全市分行业房屋建筑面积（2010年）……130
4-23 市属分行业房屋建筑面积（2010年）……132
4-24 主要年份全市新增固定资产及房屋竣工面积……134
4-25 主要年份市属新增固定资产及房屋竣工面积……135
4-26 各区县、开发区新增固定资产及房屋施工、竣工面积（2010年）……136
4-27 全市分行业施工项目（2010年）……138
4-28 市属分行业施工项目（2010年）……140
4-29 主要年份房地产开发投资主要指标……142
4-30 分区县、开发区房地产开发主要指标（2010年）……144
4-31 房地产开发投资主要指标（2010年）……146
4-32 商品房销售情况（2010年）……147
4-33 房地产开发投资资金来源（2010年）……148
4-34 房地产开发经营情况（2010年）……149
主要统计指标解释……150

五、财　　政

5-1 主要年份地方财政一般预算收入及支出……155
5-2 财政收入（2010年）……156
5-3 财政支出（2010年）……157
5-4 各区县、开发区一般预算财政收入（2010年）……158
5-5 各区县、开发区一般预算支出（2010年）……162
主要统计指标解释……167

六、物价指数

6-1　主要年份各种价格指数……175
6-2　居民消费价格指数（2010年）……176
6-3　商品零售价格指数（2010年）……178
6-4　主要年份工业品出厂价格指数……180
6-5　主要年份原材料、燃料、动力购进价格指数……182
6-6　土地交易价格指数（2010年）……183
6-7　房屋销售价格指数（2010年）……183
6-8　房屋租赁价格指数（2010年）……184
6-9　主要年份固定资产投资价格指数……184
6-10　主要年份建筑安装工程价格指数……184
主要统计指标解释……185

七、人民生活

7-1　主要年份城乡居民家庭人均收入及恩格尔系数……189
7-2　主要年份城乡居民人民币储蓄存款……190
7-3　分区县城乡居民人均收入……191
7-4　主要年份城镇居民家庭及收支基本情况……192
7-5　城镇居民家庭基本情况表（2010年）……195
7-6　城镇居民家庭年人均收入情况（2010年）……196
7-7　城镇居民家庭年人均支出情况（2010年）……197
7-8　城镇居民家庭年人均消费性支出情况（2010年）……198
7-9　主要年份城镇居民家庭年人均购买主要商品数量……202
7-10　城镇居民家庭居住情况（2010年）……204
7-11　主要年份城镇居民家庭平均每百户年末拥有主要耐用消费品数量……206
7-12　主要年份农民家庭基本情况……208
7-13　主要年份农村居民家庭人均总收入和纯收入……210
7-14　农村居民家庭平均每人总收入和纯收入（2010年）……212
7-15　农村居民家庭基本情况（2010年）……214
7-16　农村居民家庭平均每人全年总支出（2010年）……216
7-17　农村居民家庭平均每人生活消费支出（2010年）……216
7-18　农村居民家庭人均生产情况（2010年）……218
7-19　农村居民家庭人均出售产品情况（2010年）……218
7-20　农村居民家庭人均粮食收支情况（2010年）……220
7-21　农村居民家庭平均每人购买商品（2010年）……220
7-22　农村居民家庭人均主要食品消费量（2010年）……222
7-23　农村居民家庭每百户耐用消费品年末拥有量（2010年）……224

7-24 农村居民家庭人均住房情况（2010年）……224
主要统计指标解释……226

八、城市公用事业

8-1 城市供水……231
8-2 城市售电……231
8-3 城市供燃气……232
8-4 城市供热……232
8-5 城市公共交通……233
8-6 市政设施……233
8-7 城市设施水平……234
8-8 城市规模及用地情况……234
8-9 城市园林绿化……235
8-10 城市环境卫生……235
8-11 市区及县供水（2010年）……236
8-12 市区及县供燃气（2010年）……236
8-13 市区及县供热（2010年）……237
8-14 市区及县市政设施（2010年）……237
主要统计指标解释……238

九、环境保护

9-1 城市环境保护（2010年）……243
9-2 主要年份工业“三废”排放及处理利用情况……244
9-3 工业污染排放及处理利用情况（2010年）……246
9-4 城市污水处理情况（2010年）……247
9-5 危险废物集中处置情况（2010年）……248
9-6 生活及其他污染情况（2010年）……248
9-7 工业污染治理项目建设情况（2010年）……249
9-8 各区县环境保护基本情况（2010年）……250
主要统计指标解释……252

十、农　　业

10-1 农村基层组织、乡村户数、人口及劳动力情况……257
10-2 各区县农村基层组织、乡村户数及人口（2010年）……258
10-3 各区县从业人员数（2010年）……258
10-4 主要年份耕地面积……259

10-5 各区县耕地面积（2010年）……260
10-6 主要年份农业机械拥有量（年末数）……262
10-7 各区县农业机械拥有量（2010年）……264
10-8 主要年份农业机械、化肥、水利、水电情况……266
10-9 各区县农业机械、化肥、水利、水电情况（2010年）……268
10-10 主要年份农林牧渔及服务业总产值及指数……270
10-11 主要年份农林牧渔及服务业总产值指数……271
10-12 各区县农林牧渔及服务业总产值（2010年）……271
10-13 各区县农林牧渔及服务业总产值指数及构成（2010年）……272
10-14 主要年份农林牧渔及服务业增加值……273
10-15 主要年份农林牧渔及服务业增加值指数……274
10-16 各区县农林牧渔及服务业增加值（2010年）……274
10-17 各区县农林牧渔及服务业增加值指数（2010年）……275
10-18 主要年份农作物播种面积……276
10-19 各区县主要农作物播种面积（2010年）……277
10-20 主要年份农作物产品产量……278
10-21 各区县主要农作物产品产量（2010年）……279
10-22 主要年份农作物单位面积产量……280
10-23 各区县主要农作物单位面积产量（2010年）……280
10-24 主要年份林业生产情况……281
10-25 各区县林业生产情况（2010年）……282
10-26 主要年份果业生产情况……282
10-27 各区县果业生产情况（2010年）……283
10-28 主要年份畜牧业生产情况……284
10-29 各区县畜牧业生产情况（2010年）……285
10-30 主要年份畜产品和水产品产量……286
10-31 各区县主要畜产品和水产品产量（2010年）……288
10-32 主要年份农产品人均占有量……289
10-33 主要年份农村经济效益主要指标……290
主要统计指标解释……291

十一、工　业

11-1 主要年份全部工业总产值……297
11-2 各区县、开发区规模以上工业总产值（2010年）……299
11-3 规模以上工业企业主要产品产量……301
11-4 主要年份规模以上工业企业主要经济指标……305
11-5 各区县规模以上工业企业主要经济指标（2010年）……306
11-6 主要年份规模以上工业企业经济效益指标（2010年）……309

11-7　规模以上工业企业主要经济指标（2010年）……310
11-8　规模以上国有及国有控股工业企业主要经济指标（2010年）……322
11-9　规模以上股份制工业企业主要经济指标（2010年）……334
11-10　规模以上外商及港澳台商工业企业主要经济指标（2010年）……346
11-11　规模以上大中型工业企业主要经济指标（2010年）……358
11-12　规模以上工业高技术产业企业主要经济指标（2010年）……370
11-13　规模以上工业企业主要经济效益指标（2010年）……376
主要统计指标解释……380

十二、能　源

12-1　规模以上工业企业能源购进、消费及库存（2010年）……389
12-2　规模以上工业分行业主要能源品种消费量（2010年）……392
12-3　规模以上工业分行业综合能源消费量（2010年）……394
12-4　主要年份单位GDP能耗……395
12-5　各区县单位GDP能耗……395
12-6　主要年份规模以上工业单位增加值能耗……395
12-7　各区县规模以上工业单位增加值能耗……396
12-8　主要年份单位GDP电耗……396
12-9　各区县单位GDP电耗……397
12-10　规模以上工业企业用水情况……397
12-11　规模以上工业企业分行业用水量（2010年）……398
主要统计指标解释……400

十三、建筑业

13-1　主要年份建筑业总产值……405
13-2　全市建筑施工企业基本情况（2010年）……405
13-3　施工总承包和专业承包建筑业企业生产情况（2010年）……406
13-4　施工总承包和专业承包建筑业企业财务状况（2010年）……410
13-5　劳务分包建筑业企业基本情况（2010年）……412
13-6　分区县建筑业主要经济指标（2010年）……413
13-7　分区县建筑业房屋施工及竣工面积（2010年）……414
13-8　分区县建筑业企业主要经济效益指标（2010年）……415
主要统计指标解释……416

十四、运输和邮电

14-1　主要年份各种交通线路和桥梁……421
14-2　各种交通线路里程和桥梁数……423

14-3 主要年份全社会车辆数……424
14-4 全社会车辆数……425
14-5 主要年份交通运输量及周转量……426
14-6 交通运输量及运输周转量……427
14-7 主要年份邮政电信情况……428
14-8 邮政业务及服务网点……430
14-9 电信业务情况……430
主要统计指标解释……431

十五、国内贸易

15-1 主要年份社会消费品零售总额……437
15-2 社会消费品零售总额（2010年）……438
15-3 各区县社会消费品零售总额（2010年）……439
15-4 主要年份批发零售贸易业、餐饮业网点和人员……441
15-5 批发贸易业机构、网点、人员（2010年）……442
15-6 零售贸易业机构、网点、人员（2010年）……444
15-7 餐饮业机构、网点、人员（2010年）……446
15-8 各区县批发、零售、餐饮业机构、网点、人员（2010年）……448
15-9 限额以上批发零售贸易企业财务状况（2010年）……450
15-10 限额以上住宿和餐饮业企业主要财务状况（2010年）……462
15-11 限额以上批发和零售业商品购进、销售和库存总额（2010年）……470
15-12 限额以上住宿和餐饮业经营情况（2010年）……474
15-13 限额以上批发和零售业主要商品分类销售额（2010年）……476
15-14 亿元以上商品交易市场成交情况（2010年）……477
15-15 批发和零售业连锁经营情况（2010年）……478
15-16 住宿和餐饮业连锁经营情况（2010年）……479
15-17 成品油批发企业（单位）能源购进、销售与库存（2010年）……480
15-18 成品油零售企业（单位）能源商品销售与库存（2010年）……480
主要统计指标解释……481

十六、对外经济贸易和旅游

16-1 主要年份外资、外贸和国际旅游基本情况……487
16-2 主要年份利用外资情况……489
16-3 外国和港澳台地区在西安直接投资（2010年）……490
16-4 各区县、开发区外商直接投资（2010年）……491
16-5 主要年份进出口总额……492
16-6 外贸商品进出口总额分国别和地区（2010年）……493

16-7　主要商品分大类出口金额……494
16-8　主要商品分大类进口金额……497
16-9　主要年份旅游人数及收入……498
16-10　主要年份国际旅游收入……499
16-11　主要年份涉外星级宾馆接待海外旅游者情况……500
16-12　主要年份旅行社及A级景点……500
主要统计指标解释……501

十七、金融业

17-1　西安银行系统机构、人员数……507
17-2　金融机构（含外资）本外币存贷款年末余额（2010年）……508
17-3　金融机构（不含外资）本外币存贷款年末余额（2010年）……509
17-4　主要年份金融机构（含外资）人民币存款年末余额……510
17-5　主要年份金融机构（含外资）人民币贷款年末余额……511
17-6　金融机构（含外资）人民币存贷款年末余额（2010年）……512
17-7　金融机构（不含外资）人民币存贷款年末余额（2010年）……513
17-8　金融机构现金收入、支出（2010年）……514
17-9　保险业务情况……515
17-10　西安证券期货系统机构、人员数（2010年）……516
17-11　证券期货市场基本情况（2010年）……517
主要统计指标解释……518

十八、教育和科技

18-1　主要年份各类普通教育基本情况……523
18-2　各级普通教育基本情况（2010年）……524
18-3　主要年份普通高等教育基本情况……525
18-4　主要年份研究生情况……525
18-5　普通高等学校分学校研究生（2010年）……526
18-6　全市普通高等学校分学校情况（2010年）……527
18-7　主要年份博士后、博士、硕士流动站情况……529
18-8　主要年份普通中等专业学校基本情况……530
18-9　中等技术（中等专业）学校分学校基本情况（2010年）……531
18-10　主要年份普通中学基本情况……532
18-11　各区县普通中学基本情况（2010年）……533
18-12　主要年份职业中学基本情况……533
18-13　各区县职业中学基本情况（2010年）……534
18-14　主要年份小学基本情况……534

18-15 各区县小学基本情况（2010年）……535
18-16 主要年份幼儿园基本情况……535
18-17 主要年份特殊教育学校基本情况……536
18-18 主要年份小学、初中升学率……537
18-19 主要年份小学学龄儿童入学率……538
18-20 主要年份平均每万人口在校学生数和大中小学生构成……539
18-21 成人教育情况（2010年）……541
18-22 研究与试验发展（R&D）情况……543
18-23 科研院所研究与试验发展（R&D）情况……544
18-24 大专院校研究与试验（R&D）情况……545
18-25 大中型企业研究与试验发展（R&D）情况……546
18-26 主要年份企事业单位知识产权情况……547
18-27 主要年份高新技术产业开发区情况……548
18-28 高新技术产业开发区发展规模（2010年）……549
18-29 主要年份高新技术产业开发区建设与集资情况……549
主要统计指标解释……550

十九、文化、体育、卫生、社会福利和其他

19-1 文化事业机构和人数（2010年）……557
19-2 文化事业发展情况……558
19-3 群众艺术馆、文化馆（站）活动情况……558
19-4 文物保护业基本情况（2010年）……559
19-5 广播电台及节目制作情况……559
19-6 电视台及节目制作情况……560
19-7 体育事业基本情况（市属）（2010年）……560
19-8 少年儿童分项业余体校情况（市属）（2010年）……561
19-9 卫生机构、床位及人员数（2010年）……562
19-10 各区县卫生机构、床位及人员数（2010年）……566
19-11 卫生机构各类人员数……567
19-12 医院、卫生院诊疗人次及诊疗情况（2010年）……568
19-13 医院、卫生院床位及病人治疗情况（2010年）……570
19-14 县（区）村卫生室基本情况（2010年）……572
19-15 社会福利事业单位基本情况（2010年）……574
19-16 社会福利事业单位机构、人员数……574
19-17 各区县优抚对象人员情况（2010年）……575
19-18 计划生育和婚姻情况（2010年）……576
19-19 律师、公证及调解基本情况……577
19-20 共青团组织情况……578

19-21 妇联组织状况……578
19-22 妇联工作情况……579
19-23 交通事故情况……580
19-24 火灾情况……580
19-25 安全生产情况……581
19-26 刑事案件情况……582
19-27 治安案件情况……582
19-28 分区县刑事、治安案件情况（2010年）……583
19-29 西安市人民检察院案件受理情况……584
19-30 西安市中级人民法院案件基本情况（2010年）……585
主要统计指标解释……588

二十、企业调查

20-1 企业景气指数（2010年）……595
20-2 企业家信心指数（2010年）……596
主要统计指标解释……597

CONTENTS

Statistical Communique of Xi'an City on the 2010 National Economic and Social Development······1

CHAPTER 1 GENERAL SURVEY

1-1 Administrative Division (End of 2010) ······1
1-2 Statistics on Land Area and Density of Permanent Population (2010) ······2
1-3 Nature Conditions and Resources (2010) ······3
1-4 Climate Condition (2010) ······3
1-5 Basic Statistics on Lease and Administrative Allocation of Use Right of State-Owned Land······ 4
1-6 Impersonal Entities Grouped by Status of Registion (2010) ······5
1-7 Impersonal Entities by Sector (2010) ······6
1-8 Impersonal Entities by Region (2010) ······10
1-9 Industrial Active Units by Status of Registion (2010) ······11
1-10 Industrial Active Units by Sector (2010) ······13
1-11 Industrial Active Units by Region (2010) ······17
1-12 Principal Aggregate Indicators on National Economic and Social Development and Their Related Indices and Growth Rates······18
1-13 Structural Indicators on National Economic and Social Development······28
1-14 Indicators on Proportions and Efficiency in National Economic and Social Development······32
1-15 Selected Indicators on Average Daily Social and Economic Activities······38
1-16 Principal Indicators of National Economy and Social Development by Region (2010) ······40
Explanatory Notes on Main Statistical Indicators······42

CHAPTER 2 NATIONAL ECONOMIC ACCOUNTS

2-1 Gross Domestic Product in Representative Years······49
2-2 Indices of Gross Domestic Product in Representative Years (preceding year = 100) ······50
2-3 Indices of Gross Domestic Product in Representative Years (1952=100) ······51
2-4 Composition of Gross Domestic Product in Representative Years······52
2-5 Gross Domestic Product by Region (2010) ······53
2-6 Indices of Gross Domestic Product by Region (2010) (preceding year = 100) ······54
2-7 Composition of Gross Domestic Product by Region (2010) ······55
2-8 Value-added by Sector in Representative Years······56

2-9 Indices of Value-added by Sector in Representative Years (preceding year=100) ······56
2-10 Gross Domestic Products by Expenditure Approach in Representative Years······57
2-11 Indices of Gross Domestic Product by Expenditure Approach
in Representative Years (preceding year = 100) ······58
2-12 Gross Domestic Product and Indices by Expenditure Approach (2010) ······59
2-13 Gross Capital Formation by Sector (2010) ······59
2-14 Final Consumption Expenditures (2010) ······60
2-15 Consumption of Residents (2010) ······61
2-16 The Added Value of Non-public-owned Economic (2010) ······61
2-17 Value-added of the Five Leading Industries······62
2-18 Proportions of Value-added of the Five Leading Industries······62
Explanatory Notes on Main Statistical Indicator······63

CHAPTER 3 POPULATION, EMPLOYMENT AND WAGES

3-1 Population, Population Density and Population Development in Representative years······71
3-2 Population Changes in Representative Years ······72
3-3 Population and Households by Region (2010) ······73
3-4 Population Changes by Region (2010) ······74
3-5 Permanent population in Representative Years······74
3-6 Number of Social Laborers in Representative Years······75
3-7 Number of Employed Persons by Sector (2010) ······76
3-8 Basic Facts on All Employed Persons (2010) ······78
3-9 Basic Facts on Persons Employed by State-owned Units (2010) ······80
3-10 Basic Facts on Persons Employed by Urban Collective-owned Units (2010) ······82
3-11 Basic Facts on Persons Employed by Other Units (2010) ······84
3-12 Remuneration of All Employed Persons (2010) ······86
3-13 Remuneration of Persons Employed by State-owned Units (2010) ······88
3-14 Remuneration of Persons Employed by Urban Collective-owned Units in Towns and Cities (2010) ······90
3-15 Remuneration of Persons Employed by Other Units (2010) ······92
3-16 Remuneration of Persons Employed by Non-private Units······94
3-17 Registered Unemployed Persons and Unemployment Rate in Urban Area ······96
Explanatory Notes on Main Statistical Indicator······97

CHAPTER 4 INVESTMENT IN FIXED ASSETS

4-1 Total Investment in Fixed Assets in the Whole Country by Rural and Urban Areas
in Representative Years······103

4-2 Total Investment in Fixed Assets in the Whole Country by Registration Status in Representative Years······104
4-3 Total Investment in Fixed Assets in the Whole City by Three Strata of Industry in Representative Years······105
4-4 Total Investment in Fixed Assets in the Whole City (2010) ······106
4-5 Total Investment in Fixed Assets in the Whole City by Sector (2010) ······109
4-6 Total Investment in Fixed Assets in the Whole City by Sources of Funds and Type of Construction in Representative Years······110
4-7 Investment in Fixed Assets of State-owned Units in Representative Years······112
4-8 Investment in Fixed Assets of Rural Collective Owned Units (2010) ······114
4-9 Investment in Fixed Assets of Rural Collective Owned Units in Representative Years······115
4-10 Investment in Fixed Assets of Municipal Units in Representative Years······118
4-11 Investment in Fixed Assets of Municipal Units (2010) ······120
4-12 Investment in Fixed Assets of Municipal Units by Sector (2010) ······122
4-13 Investment in Fixed Assets of Municipal Units by Sources of Funds and Type of Construction (2010) ······123
4-14 Investments in Fixed Assets of Urban Districts by Registration Status and Jurisdiction of Management (2010) ······124
4-15 Investments in Fixed Assets of Urban Districts by Sector (2010) ······125
4-16 Investment in Fixed Assets of Urban Area by Sources of Funds and Type of Construction (2010) ······126
4-17 Source of Funds for Total Fixed Assets Investment of Whole City (2010) ······127
4-18 Source of Funds for Fixed Estate of Municipal Units (2010) ······127
4-19 Achievements of Total Assets Investment of Whole City (2010) ······128
4-20 Achievement of Fixed Assets Investment of Municipal Units (2010) ······128
4-21 Investment Fulfilled In Fixed Assets by Region (2010) ······129
4-22 Floor Space of Buildings Construction by Sector (2010) ······130
4-23 Floors Space of Buildings Construction of Municipal Units by Sector (2010) ······132
4-24 Value of Newly Added Fixed Assets and Floor Spaces Completed of Whole City in Representative Years······134
4-25 Value of Newly Added Fixed Assets and Floor Spaces Completed of Municipal Units in Representative Years······135
4-26 Newly Added Fixed Assets and Floor Space of Constructing and Completed Buildingsby Region (2010) ···136
4-27 Construction Projects of Whole City by Sector (2010) ······138
4-28 Construction Projects of Municipal Units by Sector (2010) ······140
4-29 Main Indicators of Investment in Real Estate Development in Representative Years ······142
4-30 Main Indicators of Real Estate Development by Region (2010) ······144
4-31 Main Indicators of Investment in Real Estate Development (2010) ······146
4-32 Sales of Commercial Houses (2010) ······147
4-33 Source of Funds for Investment in Real Estate Development (2010) ······148
4-34 Running of Real Estate Development (2010) ······149
Explanatory Notes on Main Statistical Indicator······150

CHAPTER 5 GOVERNMENT FINANCE

5-1 General Budgetary Local Government Revenue and Expenditure in Representative Years……155
5-2 Government Revenue (2010)……156
5-3 Government Expenditures (2010)……157
5-4 Financial Revenue of Local Government by Region (2010)……158
5-5 Financial Expenditures of Local Government by Region (2010)……162
Explanatory Notes on Main Statistical Indicator……167

CHAPTER 6 PRICE INDICES

6-1 Price Indices in Representative Years……175
6-2 Residents Consumer Price Indices (2010)……176
6-3 Retail Price Indices (2010)……178
6-4 Producer Price Index for Manufacture in Representative Years……180
6-5 Purchase Price Indices of Major Raw Materials, Fuels and Power in Representative Years……182
6-6 Transactions Price Indices of Land (2010)……183
6-7 Selling Price Indices of Real Estate (2010)……183
6-8 Renting Price Indices of Houses (2010)……184
6-9 Price Indices for Investment in Fixed Assets in Representative Years……184
6-10 Price Indices of Construction and Installation in Representative Years……184
Explanatory Notes on Main Statistical Indicator……185

CHAPTER 7 PEOPLE'S LIVELIHOOD

7-1 Per Capita Annual Income and Engel's Coefficient of Urban and Rural Households in Representative Years……189
7-2 Savings Deposit of Urban and Rural Households in Representative Years……190
7-3 Per Capita Income of Urban and Rural Households by Region……191
7-4 Basic Conditions of Urban Households in Representative Years……192
7-5 Basic Conditions of Urban Households (2010)……195
7-6 Statistics on Per Capital Annual Income of Urban Residents (2010)……196
7-7 Statistics on Per Capital Annual Living Expenditure of Urban Households (2010)……197
7-8 Statistics on Per Capita Annual Consumption Expenditure of Urban Households (2010)……198
7-9 Per Capita Annual Purchases of Principal Goods in Urban Household in Representative Years……202
7-10 Conditions of Dwellings of Urban Households (2010)……204
7-11 Number of Durable Consumer Goods Owned Every 100 Urban Households in Representative Years……206
7-12 Basic Indicators of Rural Households in Representative Years……208

7-13 Per Capita Annual Total Revenue and Net Income of Rural Households in Representative Years ······210
7-14 Per Capita Annual Total Revenue and Net Income of Ruval Households (2010) ······212
7-15 Basic Conditions of Rural Households (2010) ······214
7-16 Per Capita Annual Total Expenditure of Rural Households (2010) ······216
7-17 Per Capita Living Expenditure of Rural Households (2010) ······216
7-18 Output of Major Farm Crops Per Capita by Rural Households (2010) ······218
7-19 Per Capita Product Sold by Rural Households (2010) ······218
7-20 Per Capita Annual Income and Expenditure of Grains of Rural Households (2010) ······220
7-21 Per Capita Purchase of Commodities in Rural Households (2010) ······220
7-22 Per Capita Average Food Consumption of Rural Households (2010) ······222
7-23 Year-end Possession of Durable Consumer Goods Per 100 Rural Households (2010) ······224
7-24 Per Capita Housing Conditions of Rural Households (2010) ······224
Explanatory Notes on Main Statistical Indicator ······226

CHAPTER 8 URBAN PUBLIC UTLITIES

8-1 Urban Water Supply ······234
8-2 Urban Consumption of Electricity ······231
8-3 Gas Supply in Urban Area ······232
8-4 Heating in Urban Area ······232
8-5 Urban Public Traffic ······233
8-6 Municipal Facilities ······233
8-7 Urban Municipal Facilities ······234
8-8 City Scale and Land Use ······234
8-9 Urban Parks, Gardens and Green Areas in Cities ······235
8-10 Urban Environment Sanitation ······235
8-11 Urban Water Supply (2010) ······236
8-12 Gas Supply in Urban Area (2010) ······236
8-13 Heating in Urban Area (2010) ······237
8-14 Municipal Facilities in Urban Area (2010) ······237
Explanatory Notes on Main Statistical Indicator ······238

CHAPTER 9 ENVIRONMENT PROTECTION

9-1 Urban Environmental Protection (2010) ······243
9-2 Discharge and Treatment of Waste Gas, Water & Solid Wastes in Representative Years ······244
9-3 Discharge and Treatment of Industrial Pollution (2010) ······246
9-4 Urban Sewage Disposal (2010) ······247

9-5 Condition of Collected Dangerous Wastes Treated (2010) ……248
9-6 Domestic Pollution and Other conditions (2010) ……248
9-7 Condition of Anti-Industrial-Pollution Projects (2010) ……249
9-8 Condition of Environment Protection by Regions (2010) ……250
Explanatory Notes on Main Statistical Indicator ……252

CHAPTER 10 AGRICULTURE

10-1 Grass-root Organizations, Households, Population and Labor Resources in Rural Area ……257
10-2 Grass-root Organizations, Households and Population in Rural Area by Region (2010) ……258
10-3 Number of Labors Families by Region (2010) ……258
10-4 Area of Cultivated Land in Representative Years ……259
10-5 Area of Cultivated Land by Region (2010) ……260
10-6 Possession of Agricultural Machinery in Representative Years (Number of year-end) ……262
10-7 Possession of Agricultural Machinery by Region (2010) ……264
10-8 Agricultural Machinery, Chemical Fertilizers, Water Conservancy, Hydropowerin Representative Years ……266
10-9 Agricultural Machinery, Chemical Fertilizers, Water Conservancy and Hydropower by Region (2010) ……268
10-10 Gross Output Value of Farming, Forestry, Animal Husbandry, Fishery, Service and Related Indices in Representative Years ……270
10-11 Related Indices of Gross Output Value of Farming, Forestry, Animal Husbandry, Fishery, Service and Related Indices in Representative Years ……271
10-12 Gross Output Value of Farming, Forestry, Animal Husbandry, Fishery and Service by Region (2010) ……271
10-13 Gross Output Value and Its Composition of Farming, Forestry, Animal Husbandry, Fishery and Service at Current Price by Region (2010) ……272
10-14 Value-Added of Farming, Forestry, Animal Husbandry, Fishery and Service in Representative Years ……273
10-15 Indices of Value-Added of Farming, Forestry, Animal Husbandry, Fishery and Service in Representative Years ……274
10-16 Value-Added of Farming, Forestry, Animal Husbandry, Fishery and Service by Region (2010) ……274
10-17 Indices of Value-Added of Farming Forestry, Animal Husbandry, Fishery and Service by Region (2010) ……275
10-18 Sown Areas of Farm Crops in Representative Years ……276
10-19 Sown Areas of Major Farm Crops by Region (2010) ……277
10-20 Yield of Major Farm Crops in Representative Years ……278
10-21 Yield of Major Farm Crops by Region (2010) ……279

10-22 Yield of Farm Crops per Hectare in Representative Years······280
10-23 The Output of Main Crops per Hectare by Region (2010) ······280
10-24 Statistics on Forestry in Representative Years······281
10-25 Statistics On Forestry by Region (2010) ······282
10-26 Statistics on Fruits in Representative Years······282
10-27 Area and Output of Fruits by Region (2010) ······283
10-28 Statistics on Livestock Husbandry in Representative Years······284
10-29 Statistics On Livestock, Animal Husbandry by Region (2010) ······285
10-30 Output of Livestock Products and Aquatic Products in Representative Years······286
10-31 Output of Major Livestock Products and Aquatic Products by Region (2010) ······288
10-32 Per Capita Output of Major Farm Products in Representative Years······289
10-33 Main Indicators of Rural Economic Benefit in Representative Years······290
Explanatory Notes on Main Statistical Indicator······291

CHAPTER 11 INDUSTRY

11-1 Gross Output Value of Industry in Representative Years······297
11-2 Gross Output Value of Industrial Enterprises Above Designated Size by Region (2010) ······299
11-3 Output of Major Industrial Products of Enterprises above Designated Size ······301
11-4 Main Economic Indicators of All Industrial Enterprises above Designated Size In Representative Years······305
11-5 Main Economic Indicators of All Industrial Enterprises Above Designated Size (2010) ······306
11-6 Indicators of Economic Benefit of Industrial Enterprises Above Designated Size in Representative Years (2010) ······309
11-7 Main Economic Indicators of All Industrial Enterprises Above Designated Size (2010) ······310
11-8 Economic Indicators of all State-owned and State-holding Share Industrial Enterprises Above Designated size (2010) ······322
11-9 Main Indicators of Share-holding Corporation Industrial Enterprises Above Designated Size (2010) ······334
11-10 Economic Indicators of Foreign Fund Industrial Enterprises Above Designated Size (2010) ······346
11-11 Economic Indicators of Large and Medium-sized Industrial Enterprises Above Designated size by Region (2010) ······358
11-12 Economic Indicators of High Technology Industry Industrial Enterprises Above Designated Size (2010) ······370
11-13 Main Indicators of Economic Benefit of Industrial Enterprises Above Designated Size (2010) ······376
Explanatory Notes on Main Statistical Indicator······380

CHAPTER 12 ENERGY

12-1 Energy Purchases Consumption and Inventory of Industrial Enterprises Above Designated size (2010) ···389

12-2 Major Energy Consumption above Designated Size by Sector (2010)……392
12-3 Comprehensive Energy Consumption by Sector above Designated Size (2010)……394
12-4 Energy Consumption per Unit of GDP in Representative Years ……395
12-5 Energy Consumption per Unit of GDP by Region……395
12-6 Energy Consumption per Unit of Industrial Value-added above Designated Size in Representative Years ……395
12-7 Energy Consumption per Unit of Industrial Value-added above Designated Size by Region……396
12-8 Electricity Consumption per Unit of GDP in Representative Years ……396
12-9 Electricity Consumption per Unit of GDP by Region……397
12-10 Statistics on Water Use of Industrial Enterprises above Designated Size……397
12-11 Volume of Water Use of Industrial Enterprises above Designated Size by Sector (2010) ……398
Explanatory Notes on Main Statistical Indicator……400

CHAPTER 13 CONSTRUCTION

13-1 Total Output Value of Construction in Representative Year……405
13-2 Main Indicators on Construction Enterprise of Xi'an (2010) ……405
13-3 Main Indicators on Overall Constructing Contractors and Professional Contractors by Registration Status (2010) ……406
13-4 Financial Status of Overall Constructing Contractors and Professional Contractors (2010) ……410
13-5 Basic Statistic on Enterprises of Work Subcontractors (2010) ……412
13-6 Main Indicators of Construction Enterprises by Region (2010) ……413
13-7 Floor Space of Buildings under Construction & Completed by Region (2010) ……414
13-8 Main Economic Benefit Indicators on Construction Enterprises by Region (2010) ……415
Explanatory Notes on Main Statistical Indicator……416

CHAPTER 14 TRANSPORT, POSTAL AND TELECOMMUNICATION SERVICES

14-1 Transportation Routes and Number of Bridges in Representative Years……421
14-2 Length of Transportation Routes and Number of Bridges……423
14-3 Possession of Civil Vehicles in Representative Years……424
14-4 Possession of Civil Vehicles……425
14-5 Passenger Traffic and Kilometers and Freight Traffic and Ton-kilometers in Representative Years……426
14-6 Passenger Traffic and Kilometers and Freight Traffic and Ton-kilometers……427
14-7 Basic Statistic on Postal and Telecommunication Service……428

14-8 Postal service and branch post office······430
14-9 Telecommunication service······430
Explanatory Notes on Main Statistical Indicator······431

CHAPTER 15 DOMESTIC TRADE

15-1 Total Retail Sales of Consumer Goods in Representative Year······437
15-2 Total Retail Sales of Consumer Goods (2010)······438
15-3 Total Retail Sales of Consumer Goods by Region (2010)······439
15-4 Wholesale and Retail Trade, Catering Outlets and Staff in Representative Years······441
15-5 Organizations, Establishments and Persons Engaged in Whole-sale Trade (2010)······442
15-6 Organizations, Establishments and Persons Engaged in Retail Trade (2010)······444
15-7 Organizations Staff and Branch Shops of Catering Trade (2010)······446
15-8 Organizations, Branch Shops and Staff of Wholesale,Retail and Catering Trade by Region (2010)······448
15-9 Financial Status of Enterprises Above Designated Size in Wholesale and Retail (2010)······450
15-10 Financial Status of Catering Enterprises Above Designated Size (2010)······462
15-11 Total Sales of Enterprises Above Designated Size in Wholesale and Retail Trades Grouped by Category of Commodities (2010)······470
15-12 Statistic on Hotel Services and Catering Services above Designed Size (2010)······474
15-13 Sale Values of Enterprises above Designated Size of Wholesale and Retail Trades by Category of Main Commodities (2010)······476
15-14 Basic Statistics on Commodity Exchange Markets of Transaction Value over 100 Million Yuan (2010)······477
15-15 Basic Statistics on Chain Business of Wholesale and Retail Trades (2010)······478
15-16 Basic Statistics on Chain Business of Hotels and Catering Services (2010)······479
15-17 Purchases, Sales and Stock of Refined Oil Wholesale Enterprises (2010)······480
15-18 Purchases, Sales and Stock of Refined Oil Retail Enterprises (2010)······480
Explanatory Notes on Main Statistical Indicator······481

CHAPTER 16 FOREIGN TRADE AND ECONOMIC COOPERATION, TOURISM

16-1 Main Indicators on Foreign Investments, International Trading and International Tourism in Representative Years······487
16-2 Utilization of Foreign Capital in Representative Years······489
16-3 Direct Investments from Foreign Countries and Hong Kong, Macao and Taiwan in Xi'an (2010)······490
16-4 Direct Investment by Foreign Entrepreneurs by Region and Economic Zone (2010)······491
16-5 Total Imports and Exports In Representative Years······492

16-6 Total Value of Imports and Exports by Country and Region (2010) ······493
16-7 Export Value of Major Merchandise by Type ······494
16-8 Import Value of Major Merchandise by Type······497
16-9 Number of Tourists and Tourism Earnings In Representative Years ······498
16-10 Earning of International Tourism In Representative Years······499
16-11 Mainly Concerning Oversea Tourists Reception in Star-rated Hotels······500
16-12 Statistics of Travel Agencies and Level-A Scenic Spots······500
Explanatory Notes on Main Statistical Indicator······501

CHAPTER 17 Financial Intermediation

17-1 Number of Institution and Employed Person in Finance System in Xi'an······507
17-2 Financial Institution Including Foreign-funded Balance of Basic Currencyand Foreign Currency at Year-end (2010) ······508
17-3 Domestic Funded Financial Institution Balance of Basic Currency and Foreign Currency At Year-end (2010) ······509
17-4 Year-end Balance of Deposit in Financial Institutions Including Foreign-funded in Representative Years······510
17-5 Year-end Balance of Loans in Financial Institutions Including Foreign-funded in Representative Years······511
17-6 Year-end Balance of Deposit and Loans in Financial Institutions Including Foreign-funded (2010) ······512
17-7 Year-end Balance of Deposit and Loans in Financial Institutions Not Including Foreign-funded (2010) ······513
17-8 Cash Income and Expenditure of Domestic Funded Financial Institutions (2010) ······514
17-9 Indicators of Insurance Business······515
17-10 Number of Institution and Employed Person in Securities and Futures System in Xi'an (2010) ······516
17-11 Basic Facts on Securities and Futures Markets (2010) ······517
Explanatory Notes on Main Statistical Indicator······518

CHAPTER 18 EDUCATION, SCIENCE AND TECHNOLOGY

18-1 Basic Statistics on Regular Education in Representative Years······523
18-2 Basic Facts on Regular Education by School Type (2010) ······524
18-3 Basic Statistics on Regular Institutions in Representative Years······525
18-4 Basic Situation of the major Year on Post-graduates in Representative Years······525
18-5 Post-graduates in Regular Institutions of Higher Education (2010) ······526
18-6 Basic Facts on Regular Higher Education by Unit (2010) ······527
18-7 Mobile Research Centers for Post-doctors, Doctors and Masters in Representative Years······529

18-8 Basic Statistics on Specialized Secondary Schools in Representative Years……530
18-9 Situation of Every Secondary Technical and Specialized Secondary school (2010) ……531
18-10 Basic Statistics on Regular Secondary Schools in Representative Years……532
18-11 Basic Statistics on Regular Secondary Schools by Region (2010) ……533
18-12 Basic Statistics on Vocational Secondary Schools in Representative Years……533
18-13 Basic Statistics on Vocational Secondary Schools by Region (2010) ……534
18-14 Basic Statistics on Primary Schools in Representative Years……534
18-15 Basic Statistics on Primary Schools by Region (2010) ……535
18-16 Basic Statistics on Kindergartens in Representative Years……535
18-17 Basic Statistics on Special Education Schools in Representative Years……536
18-18 Rate of Graduates from Junior Schools and Primary Schools Entering Higher Level Schools in Representative Years……537
18-19 Percentage of School-Age Children Enrolled in Representative Years……538
18-20 Student Enrollment Per 10000 Populations and Composition of Students Enrolled in Representative Years……539
18-21 Adult Education (2010) ……541
18-22 Research and Experiment Development Facts……543
18-23 Research and Experiment Development Facts in Scientific Research Institutions……544
18-24 Research and Experiment Development Facts in Universities ……545
18-25 Research and Experiment Development Facts in Large-size and Medium-size Industrial Enterprises……546
18-26 Intellectual Property Right of Enterprises and Institutions in Representative Years……547
18-27 Basic Statistics of Hi-Tech Development Zone in Representative Years……548
18-28 Development Status of Hi-Tech Development Zone (2010) ……549
18-29 Capital Construction and Funds-Raising of Hi-Tech Development Zone in Representative Years……549
Explanatory Notes on Main Statistical Indicator……550

CHAPTER 19 CULTURES, SPORTS, PUBLIC HEALTH, SOCIAL WELFARE INSTITUTIONS AND OTHER SOCIAL ACTIVITIES

19-1 Number of Institutions and Personnel in Culture and Art (2010) ……557
19-2 Basic Statistics on Culture Development……558
19-3 Basic Statistics on Activities of Mass Art Centers and Cultural Centers……558
19-4 Basic Statistics on Cultural Relics Protection (2010) ……559
19-5 Basic Statistics of Broadcasting Stations and Program Production……559
19-6 Basic Statistics of TV Stations and Production of TV Program……560
19-7 The Basic Situations of Sports (Under Municipality) (2010) ……560
19-8 Basic Statistics of Youth Part-time Physical Training School (2010) ……561
19-9 Number of Health Care Institutions, Beds and Employed Persons in Health Care Institutions (2010) ……562

19-10 Number of Health Care Institutions , Beds and Employed Persons
in Health Care Institutions by Region (2010) ……566
19-11 Number of Employed Persons in Health Care Institutions……567
19-12 Number of Visits and Inpatients in Medical Institutions (2010) ……568
19-13 Beds and Patients Treated Conditions in Health Care Institutions (2010) ……570
19-14 Basic Statistics on Clinics in Counties and Villages (2010) ……572
19-15 Basic Statistics on Social Welfare Institutions (2010) ……574
19-16 Number of Social Welfare Institutions and Employed Persons……574
19-17 Statistics on Persons Enjoying Favoured Treatment by Region (2010) ……575
19-18 Conditions of Birth Control and Marriage Registration (2010) ……576
19-19 Basic Statistics on Lawyers、Notaries and Mediation……577
19-20 Basic Facts on Communist Youth League……578
19-21 Women's Organizations Status……578
19-22 Basic Facts on Women's Federation……579
19-23 Statistics on Traffic Accidents……580
19-24 Statistics on Fires……580
19-25 Data on Safety in Production……581
19-26 Data on Criminal Cases……582
19-27 Data on Public Order Cases……582
19-28 Data on Criminal Cases and Public Order Cases Grouped by Districts and Counties (2010) ……583
19-29 Data on Acceptance of Cases of Xi'an People's Procuratorate……584
19-30 Xi'an Intermediate People's Court Basic Data of the Law Cases (2010) ……585
Explanatory Notes on Main Statistical Indicator……588

CHAPTER 20 ENTERPRISES INVESTIGATION

20-1 Business Climate Index (2010) ……595
20-2 Entrepreneur Expectation Indicator (2010) ……596
Explanatory Notes on Main Statistical Indicator……597

西安市2010年国民经济和社会发展统计公报

西安市统计局　国家统计局西安调查队

2011年3月21日

2010年，是“十一五”的收官之年，面对极为复杂的国内外经济形势，市委、市政府带领全市人民，深入贯彻科学发展观，紧紧抓住国家深入推进西部大开发和实施《关中天水经济区发展规划》等历史机遇，坚持以人文西安、活力西安、和谐西安和建设人民满意城市为目标，转变发展方式，破解发展难题，全市经济保持了回升向好、较快增长的基本态势，圆满完成了“十一五”规划目标任务，西安进入了建设国际化大都市的新阶段。

一、综合

初步核算，全年实现生产总值（GDP）3241.49亿元，比上年增长14.5%。分产业看，第一产业增加值140.06亿元，增长6.9%；第二产业增加值1409.53亿元，增长18.0%；第三产业增加值1691.90亿元，增长12.5%。第一产业增加值占国内生产总值的比重为4.3%，第二产业增加值比重为43.5%，第三产业增加值比重为52.2%。

全年居民消费价格比上年上涨3.5%，其中食品价格上涨7.0%。商品零售价格上涨2.7%，工业品出厂价格上涨2.3%，原材料、燃料、动力购进价格上涨6.3%。

2010年全市居民消费价格指数比上年涨跌幅度

单位：%

指　　标	2010年
居民消费价格总水平	3.5
食品	7.0
#粮食	15.7
烟酒及用品	0.7
衣着	-1.1
家庭设备用品及维修服务	4.8
医疗保健和个人用品	4.0
交通和通讯	-0.3
娱乐教育文化用品及服务	1.0
居住	2.7

全市城镇新增就业人数12.02万人，下岗失业人员再就业4.69万人，就业困难人员实现再就业1.35万人。城镇登记失业率4.2%。全市农村劳动力实现转移就业人员73.26万人。

全年财政总收入510.69亿元，比上年增长27.6%。地方财政一般预算收入241.86亿元，增长33.3%，其中，营业税、增值税、企业所得税和个人所得税分别增长39.8%、10.3%、35.9%和28.8%。全年地方财政一般预算支出371.62亿元，比上年增长34.2%，其中，医疗卫生支出增长49.7%；农林水事务支出增长44.7%；教育支出增长35.3%；社会保障和就业支出增长23.1%；一般公共服务支出增长15.1%；环境保护支出增长6.9%。

二、农业

全年粮食播种面积621.71万亩，比上年减少7.0万亩；油料播种面积8.98万亩，增加0.39万亩；蔬菜播种面积95.71万亩，增加0.88万亩；园林水果实有面积74.95万亩，增加3.87万亩。全年粮食产量221.65万吨，较上年增长1.6%，创历史最高水平，其中，夏粮产量106.60万吨，增长3.5%，秋粮115.05万吨，下降0.1%。

2010年全市农业主要产品产量

产品名称	计量单位	绝对数	比上年增长（%）
油　料	万吨	1.17	4.5
蔬　菜	万吨	253.10	4.4
园林水果	万吨	84.78	7.4
肉　类	万吨	13.65	8.2
奶　类	万吨	63.37	2.5
禽　蛋	万吨	12.38	6.1
大牲畜年末存栏数	万头	21.60	3.7
猪年末存栏数	万头	94.32	2.7
羊年末存栏数	万只	29.45	5.4
家禽年末存栏数	万只	1034.20	5.4

全市农用机械总动力267.73万千瓦，比上年增长2.3%；农田有效灌溉面积281.28万亩，增长3.0%；全年农用化肥施用量（实物量）78.11万吨，增长0.6%。

三、工业和建筑业

全年全部工业增加值1006.38亿元，比上年增长18.1%。规模以上工业增加值增长19.7%。其中，轻工业增加值增长13.2%，重工业增加值增长21.9%。

全年规模以上工业中，农副食品加工业增加值比上年增长16.6%；通用设备制造业增长28.8%；专用设备制造业增长19.8%；交通运输设备制造业增长25.9%；通信设备、计算机及其他电子设备制造业增长26.8%。六大高耗能行业比上年增长25.3%，其中，非金属矿物制品业增长25.3%；化学原料及化学制品制造业增长16.0%；有色金属冶炼及压延加工业增长25.4%；黑色金属冶炼及压延加工业增长32.6%；电力、热力的生产和供应业增长36.4%；石油加工、炼焦及核燃料加工业增长10.3%。

2010年全市规模以上工业主要产品产量

产品名称	计量单位	产量	比上年增长（%）
发电量	亿千瓦小时	96.94	17.1
原油加工量	万吨	174.17	3.1
乳制品	万吨	102.07	28.9
液体乳	万吨	95.33	29.6
商品混凝土	万立方米	1441.51	28.5
机制纸及纸板	万吨	49.6	4.1
缝纫机	万架	58.17	80.8
配合饲料	万吨	20.2	46.4
合成洗涤剂	万吨	8.34	5.1
水泥	万吨	678.34	42.0
风机	台	1656	132.3
汽车	万辆	65.21	28.7
#轿车	万辆	52.12	21.9
低压开关板	面	23527	55.8
变压器	万千伏安	11461.13	3.6
电力电缆	千米	6205.4	40.0
气体压缩机	万台	538.5	169.7
电子元件	亿只	13.89	217.3

全市规模以上工业企业经济效益综合指数为234.2，比上年提高26.1个百分点。规模以上工业企业主营业务收入3006.18亿元，增长27.6%。全市规模以上工业企业实现利税总额319.73亿元，同比增长21.5%，其中，利润总额213.37亿元，同比增长27.8%。

全年建筑业实现增加值403.15亿元，比上年增长17.6%。全年具有资质等级的总承包和专业承包建筑企业328家。房屋建筑施工面积4852.94万平方米，比上年增长16.3%。按建筑业总产值计算，全员劳动生产率28.15万元/人。

四、固定资产投资

全年全社会固定资产投资3250.56亿元，比上年增长30.0%，扣除价格因素，实际增长25.2%。其中，城镇投资3101.06亿元，增长31.0%；非公有制单位投资1588.31亿元，增长24.3%。

在城镇投资中，第一产业投资39.82亿元，增长62.8%；第二产业投资559.53亿元，增长16.0%，其中，工业投资501.78亿元，增长13.6%；第三产业投资2501.70亿元，增长34.4%。

2010年重点行业城镇固定资产投资及其增长速度

单位：亿元

指　标	绝对数	比上年增长（%）
农林牧渔业	39.82	62.8
制造业	409.24	8.2
交通运输、仓储及邮政业	175.09	16.5
信息传输、计算机服务和软件业	50.99	140.2
批发和零售业	53.99	-13.2
住宿和餐饮业	38.96	-12.3
水利、环境和公共设施管理业	509.39	45.4
教　育	77.93	1.9
卫生、社会保障和社会福利业	19.73	19.1
公共管理和社会组织	218.26	-1.9

全年房地产开发投资842.34亿元，增长21.0%；商品房销售面积1587.81万平方米，增长26.4%。

2010年房地产开发和销售主要指标

指　标	计量单位	绝对数	比上年增长（%）
房地产开发投资	亿元	842.34	21
#住宅	亿元	670.26	17.9
商品房施工面积	万平方米	6697.39	17.3
#住宅	万平方米	5777.71	17.9
新开工面积	万平方米	2043.82	20.7
#住宅	万平方米	1771.33	20.7
商品房竣工面积	万平方米	463.65	-14.6
#住宅	万平方米	412.44	-9.1
商品房销售面积	万平方米	1587.81	26.4
#住宅	万平方米	1523.24	26.7

全年新增固定资产949.79亿元，固定资产交付使用率29.2%。各类房屋竣工面积775.16万平方米，竣工率69.4%。共有1220个城镇建设项目建成投产，项目建成投产率55.7%。

五、国内贸易

全年社会消费品零售总额1611.04亿元，比上年增长18.9%，扣除价格因素，实际增长15.8%。按经营单位所在地统计，城镇消费品零售额1544.16亿元，增长19.2%；乡村消费品零售额66.88亿元，增长11.9%。按消费形态统计，商品零售额1436.91亿元，增长19.5%；餐饮收入额174.13亿元，增长14.2%。

在限额以上企业商品零售额中，食品、饮料、烟酒类零售额比上年增长16.8%，服装鞋帽、针纺织品类增长30.0%，体育娱乐用品类增长28.9%，书报杂志类增长7.3%，日用品类增长27.9%，家用电器和音像器材类增长27.3%，通讯器材类下降0.2%，文化办公用品类增长17.1%，金银珠宝类增长39.1%，汽车类增长29.6%。

六、对外经济

全年进出口总额103.82亿美元，比上年增长43.2%。其中，出口53.17亿美元，增长59.5%；进口50.65亿美元，增长29.2%。

分贸易方式看，一般贸易进出口54.89亿美元，增长15.0%；加工贸易进出口39.75亿美元，增长94.9%。分经营主体看，国有企业进出口36.92亿美元，增长16.5%；外商投资企业进出口44.08亿美元，增长1倍；私营企业进出口22.71亿美元，增长18.8%。

主要进出口商品中，机电产品出口38.52亿美元，增长80.2%，进口34.56亿美元，增长40.4%；农产品出口3.05亿美元，增长7.2%，进口1.02亿美元，增长3.5倍；矿产品出口3.58亿美元，增长43.2%，进口6.03亿美元，增长9.3%；纺织服装出口1.86亿美元，增长11.9%，进口483万美元，增长55.9%。

全年批准外商直接投资项目82个，合同利用外商直接投资11.97亿美元，比上年增长99.4%；实际利用外商直接投资15.67亿美元，增长28.5%。

七、交通、邮电和旅游

全年货物运输周转量430.17亿吨公里，比上年增长14.3%。其中，铁路180.01亿吨公里，增长9.5%；公路248.77亿吨公里，增长17.8%；民航1.39亿吨公里，增长45.6%。

全年铁路旅客发送量2781.35万人次，比上年增长7.4%，货物发送量705.87万吨，增长14.9%；公路客运量26536万人次，增长5.0%，货运量33610万吨，增长12.1%；民航旅客吞吐量1801.03万人次，增长17.8%，货物吞吐量15.81万吨，增长24.6%。

年末全市民用汽车保有量达到96万辆，比上年末增长26.9%，其中私人汽车保有量78.28万辆，增长31.2%。全市轿车保有量49.20万辆，增长31.3%，其中私人轿车42.86万辆，增长33.8%。

全年邮政业务收入6.31亿元，增长10.6%；电信业务收入103.89亿元，增长9.2%。全市固定电话年末用户261.77万户。移动电话用户1423.08万户，其中，电信和联通3G移动电话用户33.40万户。电信互联网用户146.18万户。

全年共接待国内游客5201万人次，比上年增长34.7%；海外游客84.18万人次，增长25.1%。全年实现旅游总收入405.18亿元，增长36.4%，其中外汇收入5.30亿美元，增长35.8%。

八、金融

年末全市金融机构本外币各项存款余额9044.15亿元，比上年末增长16.5%。人民币存款余额8933.23亿元，增长16.6%，其中，企事业单位存款余额3556.78亿元，增长10.6%；城乡居民储蓄存款余额3641.09亿元，增长18.1%。金融机构本外币贷款余额6591.73亿元，比上年末增长19.0%。人民币贷款余额6482.28亿元，增长18.7%，其中，短期贷款1097.60亿元，下降15.8%；中长期贷款5075.98亿元，增长35.7%。全年金融机构现金收入10880.23亿元，比上年增长19.3%；现金支出10610.74亿元，比上年增长20.0%；货币净回笼296.48亿元，比上年下降3.3%。

全年证券市场各类证券成交额12105.51亿元，比上年下降12.5%。其中，股票成交额11909.24亿元，基金成交额47.47亿元，债券成交额8.75亿元。年末全市拥有上市股份公司28家，上市总股本184.38亿股，总市值2718.74亿元。年末股票市场累计开户数152.25万户，比上年末增长3.2%。

截止2010年底，全市共有保险机构432家，其中，财产险178家，人寿险254家。保险专业中介机构95家。全年保费收入158.01亿元，比上年增长29.4%。其中，财产险保费收入33.86亿元，增长30.7%；人身险保费收入124.14亿元，增长29.0%。全年支付各类保险赔款及给付27.03亿元，比上年增长7.5%。其中财产险、人身险分别为14.10亿元和12.93亿元，分别比上年增长11.8%和3.1%。

九、教育和科学技术

全市研究生培养单位46个，招收研究生2.60万人，在学研究生7.70万人；普通高校50所，在校学生65.74万人，毕业生16.33万人；普通中学436所，在校学生48.89万人，毕业生17.01万人；小学1531所，在校学生51.56万人，毕业生9.61万人。小学、初中学龄人口入学率分别为99.96%和99.61%。

全年实施市级科技计划项目333项（含高新技术专项26项），其中科技创新和成果转化项目176项。重点扶持高新技术企业152家，支持建设农业科技示范园11家，科技示范乡镇10个，实施区县工业科技引导项目15个。全年争取国家、省资金1.86亿元。全年技术市场交易额57.3亿元。全年申请专利量19485件，专利授权量8037件。

十、文化、体育和卫生

全市艺术表演团体11个，公共图书馆15个，文化馆15个，文化站184个，博物馆55个。全年组织开展各类群众文化活动1562场次。全市拥有电视台2座、广播电台2座、广播电视台6座，电视人口覆盖率和广播人口覆盖率分别达98.6%、99.4%。

全年举办各类群众体育展示表演和竞赛活动共计260项次，体育社团举办和承办体育赛事306项次，其中国际性和全国性赛事16项次，累计参与群众超过300万人次。新建城市社区全民健身器材配送工程50个、乡镇农民体育健身工程5个、乡镇体育示范站30个、社区全民健身路径70个，更新30个。全市已有社会体育指导员7579名，晨晚练点1600个，健身气功站点122个、在册练功人数4890人。

我市培养输送的运动员参加国际比赛取得3金、1银、1铜的好成绩，参加全国比赛取得11个第一名、11个第二名、7个第三名的成绩。在陕西省第十四届运动会上，我市代表团共获673枚奖牌，其中金牌349枚。

年末全市共有各类卫生机构5632个，其中医院、卫生院412个；各类卫生技术人员5.66万人，其中执业（助理）医师2.19万人；卫生机构床位3.94万张。

十一、人民生活和社会保障

全市城镇居民人均可支配收入22244元，剔除价格因素，比上年实际增长13.3%；农民人均纯收入7750元，实际增长18.0%。城镇居民家庭食品消费支出占家庭消费总支出的比重为31.3%，农村为32.5%。城镇居民人均住房建筑面积28.7平方米，农村居民人均住房面积66.7平方米。

全市城镇基本医疗保险参保人数365.49万人；城镇企业职工养老保险参保人数190.12万人；失业保险参保人数130.51万人；工伤保险参保人数109.52万人，职工生育保险参保人数87.90万人。参加农村新型合作医疗的农民人数达387.55万人，实际参合率97%，覆盖率100%。

十二、城市建设、环境和安全生产

全年完成市政公用设施投资246.8亿元，新增人行天桥3座，建设公交港湾6处，新增城区集中供热面积815.3万平方米，新建改造绿地广场147个，新增城市园林绿化面积1245万平方米。

城市环境空气质量全年好于国家二级标准（良好）以上的天数304天，与上年持平。全年建成并投入运行污水处理厂14家，污水处理能力达到121.6万吨/日，比上年增加27.6万吨/日；可吸入颗粒物年均值较上年上升11.5%，环境空气中二氧化硫年均值较上年下降10.4%。全市集中式饮用水源地的水质达标率为100%。区域环境噪声等效声级均值为55.2分贝，道路交通噪声等效声级均值为68.0分贝。

全年共发生各类安全生产事故4173起，比上年减少52起，下降1.2%；死亡568人，比上年减少18人，下降3.1%；受伤2529人，比上年增加265人，上升11.7%；经济损失3666.8万元，比上年增加537.89万元，上升17.2%。

注：

1.本公报数据为初步统计数。

2.国内生产总值、各产业增加值绝对数按现价计算，增长速度按不变价格计算。

3.六大高耗能行业分别为：化学原料及化学制品制造业、非金属矿物制品业、黑色金属冶炼及压延加工业、有色金属冶炼及压延加工业、石油加工炼焦及核燃料加工业、电力热力的生产和供应业。

4.从2010年起，社会消费品零售总额统计采用新的分组，即将经营单位所在地分组由“市”、“县”、“县以下”改为“城镇”、“乡村”；取消按行业分组，新设按“商品零售额”和“餐饮收入额”两种消费形态的分组。

5.鉴于第六次全国人口普查正在进行数据审核工作，因此本公报不公布人口数据和人均指标，人口数据待第六次全国人口普查公报正式公布。

资料来源：本公报中物价数据来自国家统计局西安调查队；城镇新增就业、登记失业率、社会保障数据来自西安市人力资源和社会保障局；财政数据来自市财政局；进出口数据来自西安海关；利用外资数据来自市商务局；铁路运输数据来自西安铁路局；公路运输数据来自市交通运输局；民航运输数据来自西安咸阳国际机场；民用汽车数据来自市车管所；邮政业务数据来自市邮政局；电信数据来自中国移动西安分公司、中国电信西安分公司、中国联通西安分公司、陕西铁通西安分公司；旅游数据来自市旅游局；货币金融数据来自中国人民银行西安分行营业管理部；上市公司数据、保险业数据来自市金融办；教育数据来自市教育局；科技数据来自市科技局；艺术表演团体、公共图书馆、文化馆、广播、电视数据来自市文化广电新闻出版局；博物馆数据来自市文物局；体育数据来自市体育局；卫生、新农合数据来自市卫生局；集中供热面积、建成区绿化面积来自市城乡建设委员会；城市污水处理、环境监测数据来自市环境保护局；安全生产数据来自市安全生产监督管理局；其他数据均来自市统计局。

Statistical Communique of Xi'an City on the 2010 National Economic and Social Development

Xi'an Municipal Bureau of Statistics and NBS Survey Office in xi'an

Mar.21st, 2011

In 2010, the last year of 'leventh Five-Year Plan', facing with complex domestic and international economic environment, the municipal party committee and municipal government of Xi'an leaded the people to apply 'Scientific Outlook on Development', seize the historical opportunity brought by the extensive promotion of the Western Development Strategy and the 'Guan zhong- Tian shui economic zone development planning', insist on aiming at the construction of Humanistic Xi'an、Vigor Xi'an、Harmonious Xi'an and People's satisfaction city, transform the mode of economic development, crack development problem. As a result of these above, the economy of the whole city maintained steady and rapid development, which met the goal of 'Eleventh Five-Year Plan' successfully. Xi'an has step into a new period, in which we are constructing an international metropolis.

I. General Outlook

In 2010, the gross domestic product (GDP) preliminarily estimated was 324.149 billion Yuan, up by 14.5 percent against the previous year. Analyzed by different industries, the value added of the primary industry was 14.006 billion Yuan, up by 6.9 percent; the value added of the secondary industry was 140.953 billion Yuan, a rise of 18.0 percent; and the value added of the tertiary industry was 169.19 billion Yuan, up by 12.5 percent. The value added of the primary industry accounted for 4.3 percent of the GDP, that of the secondary industry accounted for 43.5 percent, and that of the tertiary industry accounted for 52.2 percent.

The general level of consumer prices in Xi'an was up by 3.5 percent against the previous year. Of this total, the prices for food went up by 7.0 percent; the retail prices for commodities up by 2.7percent; the producer prices for manufactured goods were up by 2.3 percent; the purchasing price for raw materials, fuels and power went up by 6.3 percent.

Up and fall extent of Residents Consumer Price Indices with previous year (2010)

unit:%

Item	2010
General Level of Residents Consumer Price	3.5
Food	7.0
#Grain	15.7
Tobaccos and Alcohols	0.7
Clothing	-1.1
Household facilities and maintaining services	4.8
Medical, Health and Personal Articles	4.0
Transportation and Communication	-0.3
Recreation, Education and Cultural articles and Services	1.0
Residence	2.7

In 2010, the newly increased employed people in urban areas in Xi'an numbered 120.2 thousand. The number of reemployment of laid-off workers was 46.9 thousand, and the number of reemployment of people who were difficult to find job was 13.5 thousand. The urban unemployment rate through unemployment registration was 4.2 percent at the end of 2010. The transfer of surplus agricultural labor force employment in Xi'an numbered 732.6 thousand.

The financial revenue totaled 51.069 billion Yuan, an increase of 27.6 percent as compared with the previous year. The General Budget Revenue of Regional Finance reached 24.186 billion Yuan, up by 33.3 percent. Of this, business tax, value added tax, income tax of enterprises and individual income tax were up by 39.8 percent, 10.3 percent, 35.9 percent and 28.8 percent respectively. The General Budget Expenditure of Regional Finance totaled 37.162 billion Yuan, up by 34.2 percent. Of this total expenditure, the expenditure on health care was up by 49.7 percent; that on agriculture, forestry and water affairs was up by 44.7 percent; that on education was up by 35.3 percent; that on social security and employment was up by 23.1

percent; that on general public service was up by 15.1 percent; that on environmental protection was up by 6.9 percent.

II. Agriculture

In 2010, the sown area of grain was 414.47 thousand hectares, a decrease of 4.67 thousand hectares as against previous year; the sown area of oil-bearing crops was 5.99 thousand hectares, a rise of 0.26 thousand hectares; the sown area of vegetables was 63.81 thousand hectares, an increase of 0.59 thousand hectares; the sown area of garden and fruits was 49.97 thousand hectares, an increase of 2.58 thousand hectares. The total output of grain in 2010 was 2.2165 million tons, up by 1.6 percent over the previous year, setting historical high. Of this, the output of summer crops was 1.066 million tons, up by 3.5 percent, and that of the autumn grain was 1.1505 million tons, a decrease of 0.1 percent.

Main products of agricultural production in 2010

Name of Products	Unit	Output	Increase over the last year (%)
Edible	10,000 ton	1.17	4.5
Vegetable	10,000 ton	253.10	4.4
Fruit	10,000 ton	84.78	7.4
Meat	10,000 ton	13.65	8.2
Milk	10,000 ton	63.37	2.5
Egg	10,000 ton	12.38	6.1
Year-end Cattle on hand	10,000 head	21.60	3.7
Year-end Pig on hand	10,000 head	94.32	2.7
Year-end Sheep on hang	10,000 head	29.45	5.4
Year-end Fowl on hand	10,000 head	1034.20	5.4

The total power of agricultural machinery was 2.6773 million kilowatts, up by 2.3 percent against the previous year; over 187.52 thousand hectares of farmland was with effective irrigation systems, up by 3.0 percent; the total of fertilizer utilized (physical quantity) was 781.1 thousand tons, up by 0.6 percent.

III. Industry and Construction

In 2010, the value added by the industrial sector was 100.638 billion Yuan, up by 18.1 percent over the previous year. The value added of industrial enterprises above the designated size was up by 19.7 percent. Of this, the value added of the light industry was up by 13.2 percent; that of the heavy industry was up by 21.9 percent.

In 2010, of the industrial enterprises above designated size, the growth of value added for processing of food from agricultural products was up by 16.6 percent over the previous year; for manufacture of general machinery up by 28.8 percent; for manufacture of special purpose machinery up by 19.8 percent; for manufacture of transport equipment up by 25.9 percent; for manufacture of communication equipment, computers and other electronic equipment up by 26.8 percent; The growth of the value added for the major six high energy consuming industries were 25.3 percent, of which, that of the manufacture of non-metallic mineral products was 25.3 percent, manufacture of raw chemical materials and chemical products 16.0 percent, smelting and pressing of ferrous metals 25.4 percent, smelting and pressing of non-ferrous metals 32.6 percent, production and supply of electric power and heat power 36.4 percent and 10.3 percent for processing of petroleum, coking, processing of nuclear fuel

Output of Major Industrial Products above designated size in Xi'an(2010)

Name of Products	Unit	Output	Increase over the last year (%)
Electricity	100 million kilowatt-hour	96.94	17.1
Crude Oil Processing	10,000 tons	174.17	3.1
Dairy	10,000 tons	102.07	28.9
Liquid mil	10,000 tons	95.33	29.6
Commerical ready -mixed concrete	10,000 cubic meter	1441.51	28.5
Machine Made Paper	10,000 tons	49.6	4.1
Sewing Machine	10,000 tons	58.17	80.8
Mixed-feed	10,000 tons	20.2	46.4
Detergent	10,000 tons	8.34	5.1
Cement	10,000 tons	678.34	42.0
Draught fan	unit	1656	132.3
Motor Vehicle	10,000 units	65.21	28.7
#Car	10,000 units	52.12	21.9
Low voltage shifter plate	unit	23527	55.8
Transformer	10,000 kilovolt amperes	11461.1	3.6
Electric Cable	Km	6205.4	40.0
Gas compressor	10,000 units	538.5	169.7
Electronic component	100 million units	13.89	217.3

The composite index on economic benefits of the industrial enterprises above the designated size in 2010 was 234.2, an increase of 26.1 percent over the previous year. The main business income of the industrial enterprises above designated size is 300.618

billion Yuan, up by 27.6 percent over the previous year. The profit and tax from the industrial enterprises above the designated size in 2010was 31.973 billion Yuan, up by 21.5 percent. Of this, the profit was 21.337 billion Yuan, up by 27.8 percent.

In 2010, the value added by the construction enterprises in Xi'an was 40.315 billion Yuan, up by 17.6 percent over the previous year, and 328 construction enterprises qualified for general contracts and specialized contracts. Total floor space of building was 48.5294 million square meters, up by 16.3 percent. Calculated by the total output value of construction, the overall labor productivity was 281.5 thousand Yuan per person.

IV. Investment in Fixed Assets

The completed investment in fixed assets of the city in 2010 was 325.056 billion Yuan, up by 30.0 percent over the previous year. The real growth was 25.2 percent after deducting the price factors. Of the total investment in urban areas was 310.106 billon Yuan, up by 31.0 percent, and that in non-public sector economy was 158.831 billon Yuan, up by 24.3 percent.

In urban areas, the investment in the primary industry was 3.982 billion Yuan, up by 62.8 percent against the previous year; in the secondary industry, it was 55.953 billion Yuan, up by 16.0 percent, of which industrial investment was 50.178 billion Yuan, up by 13.6 percent; in the tertiary industry, it was 250.17 billion Yuan, up by 34.4 percent.

Total and growth rate of investments in fixed assets in urban areas of important industries in 2010

Unit:100 million yuan

Item	Investment	Increase over the last year （%）
Farming ,Forestry,Animal Husbandry and Fishery	39.82	62.8
Manufacturing	409.24	8.2
Transport,Storage and Postal Service	175.09	16.5
Information Transmission,Computer Service and Software Service	50.99	140.2
Wholesale and Retail Trade	53.99	-13.2
Accommodation and Catering Trade	38.96	-12.3
Water conservancy,environment and public facilities administration industry	509.39	45.4
Education	77.93	1.9
Sanition,social insurance and social welfare industry	19.73	19.1
Public administration	218.26	-1.9

In 2010, the investment in real estate development was 84.234 billion Yuan, up by 21.0 percent; the sold area of commercial housing was 15.8781 million square meters, up by 26.4 percent.

Main Indicators of Real estate development and sales in 2010

Item	Unit	Absolute Number	Increase over the last year （%）
Investment in Real Estate Deelopment	100 million yuan	842.34	21.0
#Residential Buildings	100 million yuan	670.26	17.9
Floor Spaces of Commercial Houses Under Construction	10,000 sq.m	6697.39	17.3
#Residential Buildings	10,000 sq.m	5777.71	17.9
Floor Spaces of Newly Constructed	10,000 sq.m	2043.82	20.7
#Residential Buildings	10,000 sq.m	1771.33	20.7
Floor Spaces of Commercial Houses Completed	10,000 sq.m	463.65	-14.6
#Residential Buildings	10,000 sq.m	412.44	-9.1
Floor Spaces of Commercial Houses Sold	10,000 sq.m	1587.81	26.4
#Residential Buildings	10,000 sq.m	1523.24	26.7

The value of fixed assets increased in 2010, was 94.979 billion Yuan, and the rate of projects delivered of fixed assets was 29.2 percent. The completed area of various kinds of buildings was 7.7516 million square meters, and the rate of completed area was 69.4 percent. 1220 projects of urban construction were completed and put into use this year, and the rate of construction projects completed and put into use was 55.7 percent.

V. Domestic Trade

In 2010, the total retail sales of consumer goods reached 161.104 billion Yuan, a growth of 18.9 percent over the previous year, or a real growth of 15.8 percent after deducting price factors. An analysis on different areas showed that the retail sales of consumer goods in urban areas stood at 154.416 billion Yuan, up by 19.2 percent, and that in rural areas reached 6.688 billion Yuan, up by 11.9 percent. Grouped by consumption patterns, the income of retail sales of commodities was 143.691 billion Yuan, up by 19.5 percent; that of catering industry was 17.413 billion Yuan, up by 14.2 percent.

Of the total retail sales by wholesale and retail enterprises above designated size, the sales of food, beverage, wine and cigarette was up by 16.8 percent; clothing ,shoes, hats, and needle textiles up by 30.0

percent; sports-recreation up by 28.9 percent; books, newspapers and magazines up by 7.3 percent; daily necessities up by 27.9 percent; electric and electronic appliances for household use and audio-video equipment up by 27.3 percent; telecommunication equipment down by 0.2 percent; cultural and office goods up by 17.1 percent; gold, silver and jewelry up by 39.1 percent and motor vehicles up by 29.6 percent.

VI. Foreign Economic Relations

In 2010, the total value of imports and exports reached 10.382 billion US Dollars, up by 43.2 percent over the previous year. Of this, the value of exports was 5.317 billion US Dollars, up by 59.5 percent, and that of imports was 5.065 billion US Dollars, up by 29.2 percent.

Analyzed by different trade modes, the value of imports and exports of general trade was 5.489 billion US Dollars, up by 15.0 percent, and that of processing trade was 3.975 billion US Dollars, up by 94.9 percent. Analyzed by different management bodies, the value of imports and exports of state-owned enterprises was 3.692 billion US Dollars, up by 16.5 percent; that of foreign-invested enterprises was 4.408 billion US Dollars, up by 100.0 percent; that of private enterprises was 2.271 billion US Dollars, up by 18.8 percent.

Of the main import and export commodities, the value of exports of electromechanical products was 3.852 billion US Dollars, up by 80.2 percent; that of imports of electromechanical products was 3.456 billion US Dollars, up by 40.4 percent. The value of exports of agricultural product was 0.305 billion US Dollars, up by 7.2 percent; that of imports of agricultural products was 0.102 billion US Dollars, up by 350.0 percent. The value of exports of mineral products was 0.358 billion US Dollars, up by 43.2 percent; that of imports of mineral products was 0.603 billion US Dollars, up by 9.3 percent. The value of exports of textile products was 0.186 billion US Dollars, up by 11.9 percent; that of imports of textile products was 4.83 million US Dollars, up by 55.9 percent.

In 2010, there were 82 Foreign Direct Investment projects approved in Xi'an; the contracted Foreign Direct Investment was 1.197 billion US dollars, up by 99.4 percent over the pervious year; the realized Foreign Direct Investment was 1.567 billion US dollars, up by 28.5 percent.

VII. Transportation, Post, Telecommunications and Tourism

In 2010, the total freight traffic reached 43.017 billion ton-kilometers, up by 14.3 percent over the previous year. Of this that by railway transportation was 18.001 billion ton-kilometers, up by 9.5 percent; that by highway transportation was 24.877 billion ton-kilometers, up by 17.8 percent; that by airway transportation was 0.139 billion ton-kilometers, up by 45.6 percent.

By railway, the transport total of passengers and goods was 27.8135 million person-times and 7.0587 million tons respectively, up by 7.4 percent and 14.9 percent over the previous year respectively. By highway, the transport total of passengers and goods was 265.36 million person-times and 336.10 million tons respectively, up by 5.0 percent and 12.1 percent respectively. By airway, the transport total of passengers and goods was 18.0103 million person-times and 158.1 thousand tons respectively, up by 17.8 and 24.6 percent respectively.

The total number of motor vehicles for civilian use reached 960 thousand by the end of 2010, up by 26.9 percent, of which private-owned vehicles numbered 782.8 thousand, up 31.2 percent. The total number of cars for civilian use stood at 492 thousand, up by 31.3 percent, of which private-owned cars numbered 428.6thousand, up by 33.8 percent.

The revenue of post services totaled 0.631 billion Yuan, up by 10.6 percent over the previous year; that of telecommunication services was 10.389 billion Yuan, up by 9.2 percent. At the end of 2010, there were 2.6177 million fixed telephone users; there were 14.2308 million mobile phone users, of which the number of telecom and China Unicom 3G mobile phone was 334 thousand, and that of telecom Internet was 1.4618 million.

The total of domestic tourists was 52.01 million person-times, up by 34.7 percent; that of oversea tourists was 841.8 thousand person-times, up by 25.1

percent. The revenue from tourism totaled 40.518 billion Yuan, up by 36.4 percent. Of this, the revenue from foreign exchange was 0.53 billion US Dollars, up by 35.8 percent.

VIII. Financial Intermediation

Savings deposit in Renminbi and foreign currencies in all items of financial institutions totaled 904.415 billion Yuan at the end of 2010, an increase of 16.5 percent as compared with the end of the previous year. The savings deposit in Renminbi stood at 893.323 billion Yan, an increase of 16.6 percent, of which the savings deposit of enterprises was 355.678 billion Yuan, up by 10.6 percent, and that of urban and rural residents was 364.109 billion Yuan, up by 18.1 percent. Loans in all items of financial institutions in Renminbi and foreign currencies reached 659.173 billion Yuan, an increase of 19.0 percent as compared with the end of the previous year. The loans in Renminbi stood at 648.228 billion Yuan, an increase of 18.7 percent, of which the short-term loans totaled 109.76 billion Yuan, down by 15.8 percent, and medium -and- long term loans reached 507.598 billion Yuan, up by 35.7 percent. Cash income in all items of financial institutions was 1088.023 billion Yuan, up by 19.3 percent over the previous year; cash expenditure was 1061.074 billion Yuan, up by 20.0 percent; net withdrawal of currency was 29.648 billion Yuan, down by 3.3 percent.

The trading volume of stock exchange market was 1210.551 billion Yuan in 2010, a decrease of 12.5 percent as compared with the previous year. Of the total trading volume, stock was 1190.924 billion Yuan; fund was 4.747 billion Yuan; bond was 0.875 billion Yuan. There were 28 listed companies in Xi'an at the end of 2010, of which the total capital stock was 18.438 billion Yuan, and the total market value was 271.874 billion Yuan. The were 1.5225 million accounts in stock market at the end of 2010, an increase of 3.2 percent as compared with the end of the previous year.

By the end of 2010, there were 432 insurance institutions, of which the number of property insurance was 178, and that of life insurance was 254. There were 95 intermediary organs of insurance. The received by the insurance companies totaled 15.801 billion Yuan in 2010, up by 29.4 percent. Of this, the revenue from property insurance was 3.386 billion Yuan, up by 30.7 percent; that from life insurance was 12.414 billion Yuan, up by 29.0 percent. In total, insurance companies paid an indemnity worth of 2.703 billion Yuan, up by 7.5 percent over the previous year, of which the worth of property insurance and life insurance were 1.41 billion Yuan and 1.293 billion Yuan respectively, up by 11.8 percent and 3.1 percent respectively.

IX. Education and Science and Technology

There were 46 post-graduate training units, with 77 thousand post-graduate education enrollments, including 26 thousand new students; there were 50 general universities and colleges, with 657.4 thousand general tertiary education enrollments, including 163.3 thousand graduates; there were 436 general middle schools and high schools, with 488.9 thousand junior high education enrollments and 170.1 thousand graduates; there were 1531 primary schools, with 515.6 thousand primary education enrollments and 96.1 thousand graduates. The enrollment rates for school-age population of primary school and junior high school were 99.96 percent and 99.61 percent respectively.

333 science and technology projects were carried out in 2010 (including 26 projects of high technology). Of this, there were 176 projects carried out for technology innovation and achievements transfer. There were 152 high-tech enterprises major supported, 11 demonstration gardens of agricultural science and technology supported for construction, 10 technology demonstration towns and 15 important direction projects of industry science and technology in districts and counties implemented. 0.186 billion Yuan was strived from the national and the province. The turnover in technology market reached 5.73 billion Yuan. 19,485 patents were applied and 8,307 were approved in 2010.

X. Culture, Sports and Public Health

By the end of 2010, there were 11 art-performing groups, 15 public libraries, 184

culture stations, 55 museums. 1562 various kinds of mass cultural activities were organized in 2010.

There were 2 television stations, 2 radio broadcasting stations, and 6 radio broadcasting and television stations. The coverage rate of television broadcasting and radio broadcasting were 98.6 percent and 99.4 percent respectively.

260 mass sports performances and competition activities were organized in 2010, and 306 sports competition were organized and host by sports associations, including 16 international and national sports competition, with more than 3 million people per time taking part in these sports above. In 2010, there were 50 fitness equipment delivery projects of urban communities, 5 fitness projects for township farmers, 30 sports demonstration stations of villages and towns, and 70 public national fitness paths of community built, and 30 were updated. There were 7,759 social sport instructors, 1600 sites for morning and evening exercise and 122 sites for fitness Qigong, with 4,890 taking part in fitness Qigong.

In 2010, athletes from our city won 3 gold medals, 1 silver medal and 1 bronze medal in the national games, and obtained good results for 11 first, 11 second, 7 third.

In the fourteenth Games of Shaanxi province, the delegation of Xi'an won 637 medals, including 349 gold medals.

At the end of 2010, there were 5,632 health institutions in Xi'an, including 412 general hospitals and health centers. There were all 56.6 thousand health care workers, including 21.9 thousand practicing (assistant) doctors. General health centers in Xi'an possessed 39.4 thousand beds.

XI. Living Conditions and Social Security

In 2010, the annual per capita disposable income of urban households was 22,244 Yuan, or a real increase of 13.3 percent over the previous year when the factors of price increase were deducted, and that of rural households was 7,750 Yuan, or a real increase of 18.0 percent. The proportion of expenditure on food to the total expenditure of households was 31.3 percent for urban households and 32.5 percent for rural households. The annual per capita building area of urban households was 28.7 square meters, and annual per capita living space of rural households was 66.7 square meters.

By the end of 2010, a total of 3.6549 million people participated in urban basic health insurance program; a total of 1.9012 million people participated in basic pension program for staff and workers of enterprises; a total of 1.3051 million people participated in unemployment insurance programs; a total of 1.0952 million people participated in work accident insurance; a total of 879 thousand people participated in maternity insurance programs for staff and workers. The number of farmers taking part in the new cooperative medical care system in rural areas reached 3.8755 million, with a participation rate of 97.0 percent, 100% covered.

XII. Urban Construction, Environment and Work Safety

The total investment of municipal utilities was 24.68 billion Yuan.3 pedestrian bridges and 6 bus harbour were newly built. 8.153 million square meters area for centralized heating in urban areas was newly added. 147 green squares were reformed and newly built. 12.45 million square meters area for landscaping in urban was newly added.

In 2010, there were 304 days with air quality better than standard Grade II, the same as last year. 14 sewage treatment plants were built and put into use in 2010, and sewage treatment capacity reached 1.216 million tons per day, up by 0.276 million tons per day as compared with the previous year. The daily average value of inhaled particle was up 11.5 percent over the previous year, maintained the same level of the previous year; the annual average value of sulfur dioxide in air was down by 10.4 percent. All of water quality of reference water source reached the state standard. The average value of sound level equivalent of regional environmental noises was 55.2 decibel, and the average value of sound level equivalent of transportation noises was 68.0 decibel.

In 2010, various kinds of work accidents amounted to 4,173, a decrease of 52 as compared with the previous year, down by 1.2 percent. Of this, there ware 568 people dead, a decrease of 18, down by 3.1 percent; there were 2,529 people injured, an increase of

265, up by 11.7 percent; the property losses was 36.668 million Yuan, an increase of 5.3789 million Yuan, up by 17.2 percent.

Notes:

1. All figures in this Communique are preliminary statistics.

2. Gross domestic product (GDP) and value added as quoted in this Communique are calculated at current prices, whereas their growth rates are at constant prices.

3. Six highly energy-consuming industries are: manufacture of raw chemical materials and chemical products, manufacture of non-metallic mineral products, smelting and pressing of ferrous metals, smelting and pressing of non-ferrous metals, oil processing, coking and nuclear fuel processing, and production and supply of electricity and heat.

4. From 2010, new grouping method is adopted for the statistics on the total retail sales of consumer goods: grouping according to operation location changes from city, county and below county level to urban and rural areas; grouping according to industries is cancelled and new grouping according to retail sales of commodities and earnings of catering is added.

5. In view of the data for the sixth national census being reviewed, this communique does not publish population data and per capita indicators. The population data will be officially published in the sixth national population census communique.

Data Sources:

In this communique, data of price are from NBS Survey Office in Xi'an ;data of newly increased employed people, unemployment rate through unemployment registration and social security are from the Xi'an Municipal Bureau of Human Resources and Social Security; financial data are from the Xi'an Municipal Bureau of Finance; data of imports and exports are from the Xi'an Customs; data of utilizing foreign capital are from the Xi'an Municipal Bureau of Business; data of railway transportation are from the Xi'an Municipal Bureau of Railways; data of highway transportation are from the Xi'an Municipal Bureau of Transport; data of air transport are from the Xi'an-Xian yang International Airport; data of motor vehicles for civilian use are from the Xi'an vehicle administration; data of post services are from the Xi'an Municipal Bureau of post; data of telecommunications are from Xi'an branch of China Mobile、China Unicom、China Telecom, and Shaanxi CTT; data of tourism are from the Xi'an Tourism Administration; data of monetary and financial are from business management department for Xi'an branch of the People's Bank of China; data of listed companies and insurance are from Xi'an Municipal Finance Office; data of education are from the Xi'an Municipal Bureau of Education; data of technology are from Xi'an Municipal Bureau of Technology; data of art-performing groups, public libraries, culture centers, radio and television are from the Xi'an Municipal Bureau of Culture, Radio, Press and Publication; data of museum are from Xi'an Municipal Bureau of Heritage; data of sports are from the Xi'an Municipal Bureau of Sport; data of health and new cooperative medical care system in rural areas are from the Xi'an Municipal Bureau of Health; data of central heating area and green area are from Xi'an Municipal Urban and Rural Construction Committee; data of sewage treatment in urban and environment monitoring are from the Xi'an Municipal Bureau of Environmental Protection; data of work safety are from the State Administration of Work Safety; all the other data are from Xi'an Municipal Bureau of Statistics.

1 综 合

GENERAL SURVEY

资料整理：张小文　刘　婷　张利民　张　奇
Data management:Zhang Xiaowen Liu Ting Zhang Limin Zhang Qi

第一部分　综合

一、简要说明

本章资料主要包括西安市行政区划、自然地理、自然资源、气象、国民经济和社会发展等综合资料，由西安市统计局综合处根据局内各专业处及有关部门统计资料进行整理和编辑。

二、主要指标

生产总值（亿元）	3241.69	比上年增长	14.5%
工业增加值（亿元）	1003.57	比上年增长	18.1%
农林牧渔业总产值（亿元）	227.10	比上年增长	7.4%
全社会固定资产投资额（亿元）	3250.56	比上年增长	30.0%
社会消费品零售总额（亿元）	1637.04	比上年增长	18.5%
地方财政一般预算收入（亿元）	241.86	比上年增长	33.3%
地方财政一般预算支出（亿元）	371.62	比上年增长	34.2%
商品出口总额（亿美元）	53.17	比上年增长	59.6%
城镇居民人均可支配收入（元）	22244	比上年增长	17.3%
农村居民人均纯收入（元）	7750	比上年增长	23.5%

1 GENERAL SURVEY

Ⅰ.Brief Introduction

This chapter consists of mainly unified data of administrative divisions, natural geography, natural resources, meteorology, national economy and social development of Xi'an city. It is compiled by Integration Division of Xi'an Bureau of Statistics according to the reported data from other divisions of the Xi'an Bureau of Statistics and other departments of the municipal government.

Ⅱ.Major Indicators

		Increase over Preceding Year
Gross Domestic Product(100 mil. yuan)	3241.69	14.5%
Gross Industrial Added Value(100 mil. yuan)	1003.57	18.1%
Gross Output Value of Farming, Forestry, Animal Husbandry and Fishery(100 mil. yuan)	227.10	7.4%
Investment Fulfilled In Fixed Assets(100 mil. yuan)	3250.56	30.0%
Total Retail Sales of Consumer Goods(100 mil. yuan)	1637.04	18.5%
Local Government Revenue(100 mil. yuan)	241.86	33.3%
Local Government Expenditures(100 mil. yuan)	371.62	34.2%
Total Value of Exports(USD 100 mil.)	53.17	59.6%
Per Capita Annual Disposable Income of Urban Households (yuan)	22244	17.3%
Per Capita Net Income of Rural Residents(yuan)	7750	23.5%

1-1 行政区划（2010年底）

Administrative Division （End of 2010）

单位:个 (unit)

区县名称	Name of District and County	乡镇及街道办 Township and Urban Subdistrict Office	镇数 Town	乡数 Township	街道办事处 Urban Subdistrict Office	村民委员会 Villagers' Committee	社区居委会 Neighbourhood Committee
西安市	**Xi'an**	**176**	**36**	**42**	**98**	**3063**	**701**
(一)市区	**Urban Districts**	**108**	**2**	**8**	**98**	**1562**	**650**
新城区	Xincheng	9			9	1	104
碑林区	Beilin	8			8		103
莲湖区	Lianhu	9			9	5	129
灞桥区	Baqiao	9			9	226	35
未央区	Weiyang	10			10	192	71
雁塔区	Yanta	8			8	103	118
阎良区	Yanliang	7	2		5	80	23
临潼区	Lintong	23		3	20	284	38
长安区	Chang'an	25		5	20	671	29
(二)四县	**Four Counties**	**68**	**34**	**34**		**1501**	**51**
蓝田县	Lantian	22	10	12		519	9
周至县	Zhouzhi	22	9	13		376	14
户　县	Huxian	16	11	5		518	20
高陵县	Gaoling	8	4	4		88	8

注：本表数据来自2010年市民政部门报表。

Note:Figures in the table are from the 2010 report of civil administration department.

1-2 土地面积和常住人口密度（2010年）

Statistics on Land Area and Density of Permanent Population （2010）

区县名称	Name of District and County	土地面积 Area 绝对数（平方公里) Absolute Value (sq.km)	比重(%) Proportion (%)	常住人口（万人） Total of Permanent Population (10 000 persons)	常住人口密度 (人/平方公里) Density of Permanent Population (person/ sq.km)
西 安 市	**Xi 'an**	**10108**	**100.0**	**847.41**	**838**
(一)市区	**Urban Districts**	**3582**	**35.4**	**650.70**	**1817**
新城区	Xincheng	30	0.3	59.01	19670
碑林区	Beilin	24	0.2	61.62	25675
莲湖区	Lianhu	43	0.4	69.86	16247
灞桥区	Baqiao	325	3.2	59.56	1833
未央区	Weiyang	262	2.6	80.72	3081
雁塔区	Yanta	149	1.5	117.98	7918
阎良区	Yanliang	244	2.4	27.87	1142
临潼区	Lintong	915	9.1	65.60	717
长安区	Chang'an	1590	15.7	108.48	682
(二)四县	**Four Counties**	**6526**	**64.6**	**196.71**	**301**
蓝田县	Lantian	2008	19.9	51.42	256
周至县	Zhouzhi	2949	29.2	56.29	191
户　县	Huxian	1282	12.7	55.65	434
高陵县	Gaoling	287	2.8	33.35	1162

注：本表土地面积数据来自2011年市土地部门报表。

Note: Figures in the table are from the 2011 report of department in charge of land.

1-3 自然状况和资源（2010年）

Nature Conditions and Resources（2010）

指 标	Item	2010
一、自然状况	**Nature Conditions**	
土地总面积(平方公里)	Total Land Area (sq.km)	10108
# 市区面积	Urban Area	3582
气候（市区）	Climate (Urban Area)	
平均气温(℃)	Average Annual Temperature (℃)	15.3
年降水量(毫米)	Total Annual Precipitation (mm)	504.4
日照时数(小时)	Total Sunshine Time (hour)	1847.6
平均风速(米/秒)	Average Wind-speed (m/sec.)	1.4
二、自然资源	**Natural Resources**	
年末实有耕地面积（万亩）	Cultivated Area Year-end (10 000 mu)	383.32
林业用地面积（千公顷）	Area of Forestry (1 000 hectare)	508.39
全市水面面积 (万亩)	Whole Water Area (10 000 mu)	4.30
# 可养殖面积	Area for Aquatics Breeding	2.24
水资源总量(亿立方米)	Total Water Resource (0.1 billion cu.m)	24.10
# 天然地表水资源总量	Total Savageness Surface Water Resource	20.20
地下水资源总量(亿立方米)	Total Ground Water Resource (0.1 billion cu.m)	14.70

注：1.本表数据来自2010年气象、林业、水务等部门报表。

2.全市水面面积包括湖泊、水库、鱼塘、城市段河流面积等。

Note:1.Figures in the table are from the 2010 reports of departments in charge of meteorology, forestry and water affairs.

2.The whole water area of Xi'an includes the water area of lakes,reservoirs,fish ponds city sections of river,etc.

1-4 气 象 情 况（2010年）

Climate Condition （2010）

区县名称	Name of District and County	平均气温 (℃) Average Temperature (℃)	日照时数 (小时) Sunshine Time (hour)	降水天数 (天) Raining days (day)	年降水量 (毫米) Total Annual Precipitation (mm)	平均风速 (米/秒) Average Wind-speed (m/second)
市 区	Urban Districts	15.3	1847.6	79	504.4	1.4
临潼区	Lintong	14.5	1583.1	97	618.5	1.7
长安区	Chang'an	13.5	1769.1	100	735.4	1.2
蓝田县	Lantian	13.6	1977.8	116	682.2	1.5
周至县	Zhouzhi	14.1	1715.6	118	624.8	1.0
户 县	Huxian	14.8	2196.6	112	642.9	0.7
高陵县	Gaoling	14.4	1717.8	99	546.4	1.8

注：本表数据来自2010年市气象部门报表。

Note:Figures in the table are from the 2010 report of meteorological department.

1-5 国有土地使用权出让、划拨情况

Basic Statistics on Lease and Administrative Allocation of Use Right of State-Owned Land

项　　目	Item	2000	2005	2006	2007	2008	2009	2010
国有土地使用权出让	**Lease of the Use Right of State-owned Land**							
出让地块(宗)	Land leased (item)	202	312	316	333	278	297	386
协议	Agreement	200	241	225	171	119	100	173
招标	Invitation for Bid				1	3		3
拍卖	Auction	2	8	7	3	5	1	11
挂牌交易	Listed Transaction		63	84	158	149	196	199
出让面积（公顷）	Area of Totally Leased Land (hectare)	3115	986	1208	843	809	1047	1364
土地使用权出让总收入（万元）	**Total Revenue from Leasing of the Use Right (10 000 yuan)**	**38428**	**89039**	**156231**	**267666**	**309181**	**284405**	**358098**
国有土地使用权划拨	**Administrative Allocation of the Use Right of State-owned Land**							
划拨地块（宗）	Land Allocated (item)	113	100	90	100	102	79	108
划拨面积（公顷）	Area of Land Allocated(hectare)	12543	835	259	388	455	1721	1027

注：本表数据来自2010年市土地部门报表。

Note:Figures in the table are from the 2010 report of meteorological department.

1-6 按登记注册类型分法人单位（2010年）

Impersonal Entities Grouped by Status of Registion （2010）

单位：个 (unit)

分组	Item	法人单位数 Number of Enterprises	企业 Enterprises
总计	**Total**	**70269**	**56860**
按登记注册类型分	Grouped by Status of Registion		
内资企业	Domestic Funded Enterprises	69525	56122
国有企业	State-owned Enterprises	7160	1874
集体企业	Collective-owned Enterprises	3153	1787
股份合作企业	Cooperative Enterprises	412	378
联营企业	Joint Ownership Enterprises	181	153
国有联营企业	State Joint Ownership Enterprises	37	27
集体联营企业	Collective Joint Ownership Enterprises	89	82
国有与集体联营企业	Joint State-collective Ownership Enterprises	17	14
其他联营企业	Other Joint Ownership Enterprises	38	30
有限责任公司	Limited Liability Corporations	17197	17177
国有独资公司	State Sole Funded Corporations	128	128
其他有限责任公司	Other Limited Liability Corporations	17069	17049
股份有限公司	Share-holding Corporations Limited	947	938
私营企业	Private Enterprises	31999	31376
私营独资企业	Private-funded Enterprises	11197	10713
私营合伙企业	Private Partnership Enterprises	2069	1980
私营有限责任公司	Private Limited Liability Corporations	16414	16372
私营股份有限公司	Private Share-holding Corporations Ltd.	2319	2311
其他企业	Other Enterprises	8476	2439
港、澳、台商投资企业	Enterprises with Funds from Hong Kong, Macao and Taiwan	250	247
与港澳台商合资经营	Joint-venture with Funds from Hong Kong, Macao and Taiwan	98	97
与港澳台商合作经营	Cooperative Enterprises with Funds from Hong Kong Macau and Taiwan	14	14
港澳台商独资	Enterprises with Sole Investment from Hong Kong Macau and Taiwan	118	116
港澳台商投资股份有限公司	Share-holding Corporations Ltd. with funds from Hong Kong, Macao & Taiwan	20	20
外商投资企业	Foreign Funded Enterprises	494	491
中外合资营企业	Sino-foreign Joint Ventures	193	193
中外合作企业	Sino-Foreign Cooperation Enterprises	19	17
外资企业	Foreign Owned Enterprises	250	249
外商投资股份有限公司	Limited Company Funded by Foreign Investment	32	32
按控股情况分	Grouped by Controlling Share Hold		
国有控股	Controlling Share Hold by the State	2741	2741
集体控股	Controlling Share Hold by the Collective	2145	2145
私人控股	Controlling Share Hold by the Private	36446	36446
港澳台控股	Controlling Share Hold by the Hong Kong,Macao and Taiwan	209	209
外商控股	Controlling Share Hold by the Foreign Investment	348	348
其他	Others	14971	14971

1-7 按行业分法人单位（2010年）

Impersonal Entities by Sector（2010）

单位：个 (unit)

分 组	Item	法人单位数 Number of Enterprises	企 业 Enterprises
总 计	**Total**	**70269**	**56860**
（一）农、林、牧、渔业	Agriculture,Forestry,Animal Husbandry and Fishery	1054	767
农 业	Farming	325	255
林 业	Forestry	146	125
畜牧业	Animal Husbandry	312	248
渔 业	Fishery	15	12
农、林、牧、渔服务业	Services in Support of Agriculture	256	127
（二）采矿业	Mining	207	207
煤炭开采和洗选业	Mining and Washing of Coal	6	6
石油和天然气开采业	Extraction of Petroleum and Natural Gas	28	28
黑色金属矿采选业	Mining of Ferrous Metal Ores	1	1
有色金属矿采选业	Mining of Non-ferrous Metal Ores	26	26
非金属矿采选业	Mining and Processing of Nonmetal Ores	125	125
其他采矿业	Mining of Other Ores	21	21
（三）制造业	Manufacturing	11038	11038
农副食品加工业	Processing of Food from Agricultural Products	355	355
食品制造业	Manufacture of Foods	380	380
饮料制造业	Manufacture of Beverages	107	107
烟草制品业	Manufacture of Tobacco	4	4
纺织业	Manufacture of Textile	151	151
纺织服装、鞋、帽制造业	Manufacture of Textile Wearing Apparel, Footware and Caps	168	168
皮革、毛皮、羽毛（绒）及其制品业	Manufacture of Leather, Fur, Feather and Related Products	20	20
木材加工及木、竹、藤、棕、草制品业	Processing of Timber,Manufacture of Wood,Bamboo,Rattan, Plam and Straw Products	142	142
家具制造业	Manufacture of Furniture	272	272
造纸及纸制品业	Manufacture of Paper and Paper Products	445	445
印刷业和记录媒介的复制	Printing,Reproduction of Recording Media	468	468
文教体育用品制造业	Manufacture of Articles For Culture,Education and Sport Activities	31	31
石油加工、炼焦及核燃料加工业	Processing of Petroleum, Coking, Processing of Nuclear Fuel	37	37
化学原料及化学制品制造业	Manufacture of Raw Chemical Materials and Chemical Products	557	557

1-7 续表1 continued 1

单位：个 （unit）

分　组	Item	法人单位数 Number of Enterprises	企业 Enterprises
医药制造业	Manufacture of Medicines	274	274
化学纤维制造业	Manufacture of Chemical Fibers	16	16
橡胶制品业	Manufacture of Rubber	97	97
塑料制品业	Manufacture of Plastics	306	306
非金属矿物制品业	Manufacture of Non-metallic Mineral Products	1076	1076
黑色金属冶炼及压延加工业	Smelting and Pressing of Ferrous Metals	106	106
有色金属冶炼及压延加工业	Smelting and Pressing of Non-ferrous Metals	129	129
金属制品业	Manufacture of Metal Products	791	791
通用设备制造业	Manufacture of General Purpose Machinery	1463	1463
专用设备制造业	Manufacture of Special Equipment	1039	1039
交通运输设备制造业	Manufacture of Transport Equipment	435	435
电气机械及器材制造业	Manufacture of Electric Equipment and Machinery	984	984
通信设备、计算机及其他电子设备制造业	Manufacture of Communication Equipment, Computers and other Electronic Equipment	497	497
仪器仪表及文化办公用	Manufacture of Measuring Instruments and Machinery for Cultural Activity and Office Work	388	388
工艺品及其他制造业	Manufacture of Artwork and Other Manufacturing	254	254
废弃资源和废旧材料回收加工业	Recycling and Disposal of Waste	46	46
（四）电力、燃气及水的生产和供应业	Production and Distribution of Electricity,Gas and Water	169	168
电力、热力的生产和供应业	Production and Supply of Electric Power and Heat Power	90	90
燃气生产和供应业	Gas mining and supplying industry	29	29
水的生产和供应业	Production and Supply of Water	50	49
（五）建筑业	Construction	4040	4040
房屋和土木工程建筑业	Construction of Building & Civil Engineering	1154	1154
建筑安装业	Architectural Installation	921	921
建筑装饰业	Architectural Decoration	1463	1463
其他建筑业	Other Construction	502	502
（六）交通运输、仓储和邮政业	Traffic, Transport, Storage and Post	1264	1232
铁路运输业	Transport Via Railway	18	18
道路运输业	Transport Via Road	633	609
城市公共交通业	Urban Public Traffic	98	97

1-7 续表2 continued 2

单位：个 (unit)

分组	Item	法人单位数 Number of Enterprises	企业 Enterprises
水上运输业	Water Transport	1	1
航空运输业	Air Transport	18	17
管道运输业	Transport Via Pipeline	6	6
装卸搬运和其他运输服务业	Loading, Unloading, Portage and Other Transport Services	294	291
仓储业	Storage	164	161
邮政业	Post	32	32
（七）信息传输、计算机服务和软件业	Information Transmission, Computer Services and Software	2110	2094
电信和其他信息传输服务业	Telecom & Other Information Transmission Services	326	323
计算机服务业	Computer Services	942	931
软件业	Software Industry	842	840
（八）批发和零售业	Wholesale and Retail Trades	20951	20951
批发业	Wholesale Trade	11844	11844
零售业	Retail Trade	9107	9107
（九）住宿和餐饮业	Hotels and Catering Services	2167	2156
住宿业	Hotels	819	814
餐饮业	Catering Services	1348	1342
（十）金融业	Financial Intermediation	362	353
银行业	Bank	70	67
证券业	Security Activities	40	40
保险业	Insurance	109	107
其他金融活动	Other Financial Intermediation	143	139
（十一）房地产业	Real Estate	3566	3544
房地产业	Real Estate	3566	3544
（十二）租赁和商务服务业	Leasing and Business Services	5405	5203
租赁业	Leasing	491	489
商务服务业	Business Services	4914	4714
（十三）科学研究、技术服务和地质勘查业	Scientific Research, Technical Sevice and Geologic Prospecting	2663	2126
研究与试验发展	Research and Experimental Development	282	186
专业技术服务业	Professional Technical Services	1238	1068
科技交流和推广服务业	Services of Science and Technology Exchanges and Promotion	1058	816
地质勘查业	Geologic Prospecting	85	56

1-7 续表3 continued 3

单位：个 (unit)

分 组	Item	法人单位数 Number of Enterprises	企 业 Enterprises
（十四）水利、环境和公共设施管理业	Management of Water Conservancy, Environment and Public Facilities	468	287
水利管理业	Management of Water Conservancy	98	22
环境管理业	Environmental Management	106	63
公共设施管理业	Management of Public Facilities	264	202
（十五）居民服务和其他服务业	Services to Households and Other Services	1902	1841
居民服务业	Services to Households	765	717
其他服务业	Other Services	1137	1124
（十六）教育	Education	3288	207
教 育	Education	3288	207
（十七）卫生、社会保障和社会福利业	Health, Social Security and Social Welfare	2384	62
卫 生	Health	2267	55
社会保障业	Social Security	34	2
社会福利业	Social Welfare	83	5
（十八）文化、体育和娱乐业	Culture, Sports and Entertainment	836	584
新闻出版业	Journalism and Publishing Activities	110	66
广播、电视、电影和音像业	Broadcasting, Movies, Television and Audiovisual Activities	168	142
文化艺术业	Cultural and Art Activities	303	154
体 育	Sports Activities	48	19
娱乐业	Entertainment	207	203
（十九）公共管理和社会组织	Public Management and Social Organizaion	6395	
中国共产党机关	Organs of Communist Party of China	193	
国家机构	Government Agencies	1647	
人民政协和民主党派	People's Political Consultative Conference and Democratic Parties	27	
群众团体、社会团体和宗教组织	Non-Government Organizations, Social Organizations and Religion Organizations	920	
基层群众自治组织	Grass-roots Mass Self-Government Organizations	3608	
（二十）国际组织	International Organizations		
国际组织	International Organizations		

1-8 各区县法人单位（2010年）

Impersonal Entities by Region（2010）

单位：个 (unit)

分　组	Item	法人单位数 Number of Enterprises	企　业 Enterprises
合　计	**Total**	**70269**	**56860**
新城区	Xincheng	5103	4332
碑林区	Beilin	8858	8059
莲湖区	Lianhu	7927	7084
灞桥区	Baqiao	3294	2362
未央区	Weiyang	11395	10774
雁塔区	Yanta	15782	14740
阎良区	Yanliang	1163	769
临潼区	Lintong	2238	1249
长安区	Chang'an	4073	2522
蓝田县	Lantian	2790	937
周至县	Zhouzhi	2453	959
户　县	Huxian	3813	2128
高陵县	Gaoling	1380	945

1-9 按登记注册类型分产业活动单位（2010年）

Industrial Active Units by Status of Registion （2010）

单位：个 (unit)

分组	Item	产业活动单位数 Number of Industrial Active Units	企业 Enterprises
总计	**Total**	**78692**	**62106**
按登记注册类型分	Grouped by Status of Registion		
内资企业	Domestic Funded Enterprises	77642	61062
国有企业	State-owned Enterprises	10385	2735
集体企业	Collective-owned Enterprises	3760	2117
股份合作企业	Cooperative Enterprises	807	772
联营企业	Joint Ownership Enterprises	224	192
国有联营企业	State Joint Ownership Enterprises	44	33
集体联营企业	Collective Joint Ownership Enterprises	102	93
国有与集体联营企业	Joint State-collective Ownership Enterprises	21	17
其他联营企业	Other Joint Ownership Enterprises	57	49
有限责任公司	Limited Liability Corporations	18341	18317
国有独资公司	State Sole Funded Corporations	151	151
其他有限责任公司	Other Limited Liability Corporations	18190	18166
股份有限公司	Share-holding Corporations Limited	2073	2062
私营企业	Private Enterprises	32921	32282
私营独资企业	Private-funded Enterprises	11318	10819
私营合伙企业	Private Partnership Enterprises	2092	2003
私营有限责任公司	Private Limited Liability Corporations	17124	17081
私营股份有限公司	Private Share-holding Corporations Ltd.	2387	2379
其他企业	Other Enterprises	9131	2585

1-9 续表 continued

单位：个 (unit)

分组	Item	产业活动单位数 Number of Industrial Active Units	企业 Enterprises
港、澳、台商投资企业	Enterprises with Funds from Hong Kong, Macao and Taiwan	342	339
与港澳台商合资经营	Joint-venture with Funds from Hong Kong, Macao and Taiwan	106	105
与港澳台商合作经营	Cooperative Enterprises with Funds from Hong Kong Macau and Taiwan	16	16
港澳台商独资	Enterprises with Sole Investment from Hong Kong Macau and Taiwan	198	196
港澳台商投资股份有限公司	Share-holding Corporations Ltd. with funds from Hong Kong, Macao & Taiwan	22	22
外商投资企业	Foreign Funded Enterprises	708	705
中外合资营企业	Sino-foreign Joint Ventures	223	223
中外合作企业	Sino-Foreign Cooperation Enterprises	21	19
外资企业	Foreign Owned Enterprises	424	423
外商投资股份有限公司	Limited Company Funded by Foreign Investment	40	40

1-10 按行业分产业活动单位（2010年）

Industrial Active Units by Sector（2010）

单位：个　　(unit)

分组	Item	产业活动单位数 Number of Industrial Active Units	企业 Enterprises
总　计	**Total**	**78692**	**62106**
（一）农、林、牧、渔业	Agriculture,Forestry,Animal Husbandry and Fishery	1081	772
农　业	Farming	326	256
林　业	Forestry	147	126
畜牧业	Animal Husbandry	315	251
渔　业	Fishery	15	12
农、林、牧、渔服务业	Services in Support of Agriculture	278	127
（二）采矿业	Mining	214	214
煤炭开采和洗选业	Mining and Washing of Coal	6	6
石油和天然气开采业	Extraction of Petroleum and Natural Gas	35	35
黑色金属矿采选业	Mining of Ferrous Metal Ores	1	1
有色金属矿采选业	Mining of Non-ferrous Metal Ores	26	26
非金属矿采选业	Mining and Processing of Nonmetal Ores	125	125
其他采矿业	Mining of Other Ores	21	21
（三）制造业	Manufacturing	11264	11264
农副食品加工业	Processing of Food from Agricultural Products	372	372
食品制造业	Manufacture of Foods	383	383
饮料制造业	Manufacture of Beverages	110	110
烟草制品业	Manufacture of Tobacco	4	4
纺织业	Manufacture of Textile	154	154
纺织服装、鞋、帽制造业	Manufacture of Textile Wearing Apparel, Footware and Caps	170	170
皮革、毛皮、羽毛（绒）及其制品业	Manufacture of Leather, Fur, Feather and Related Products	20	20
木材加工及木、竹、藤、棕、草制品业	Processing of Timber,Manufacture of Wood,Bamboo,Rattan, Plam and Straw Products	145	145
家具制造业	Manufacture of Furniture	279	279
造纸及纸制品业	Manufacture of Paper and Paper Products	449	449
印刷业和记录媒介的复制	Printing,Reproduction of Recording Media	476	476
文教体育用品制造业	Manufacture of Articles For Culture,Education and Sport Activities	33	33
石油加工、炼焦及核燃料加工业	Processing of Petroleum, Coking, Processing of Nuclear Fuel	37	37
化学原料及化学制品制造业	Manufacture of Raw Chemical Materials and Chemical Products	568	568

1-10 续表1 continued 1

单位：个 (unit)

分组	Item	产业活动单位数 Number of Industrial Active Units	企业 Enterprises
医药制造业	Manufacture of Medicines	280	280
化学纤维制造业	Manufacture of Chemical Fibers	18	18
橡胶制品业	Manufacture of Rubber	97	97
塑料制品业	Manufacture of Plastics	309	309
非金属矿物制品业	Manufacture of Non-metallic Mineral Products	1091	1091
黑色金属冶炼及压延加工业	Smelting and Pressing of Ferrous Metals	106	106
有色金属冶炼及压延加工业	Smelting and Pressing of Non-ferrous Metals	130	130
金属制品业	Manufacture of Metal Products	799	799
通用设备制造业	Manufacture of General Purpose Machinery	1488	1488
专用设备制造业	Manufacture of Special Equipment	1061	1061
交通运输设备制造业	Manufacture of Transport Equipment	460	460
电气机械及器材制造业	Manufacture of Electric Equipment and Machinery	1011	1011
通信设备、计算机及其他电子设备制造业	Manufacture of Communication Equipment, Computers and other Electronic Equipment	508	508
仪器仪表及文化办公用	Manufacture of Measuring Instruments and Machinery for Cultural Activity and Office Work	402	402
工艺品及其他制造业	Manufacture of Artwork and Other Manufacturing	257	257
废弃资源和废旧材料回收加工业	Recycling and Disposal of Waste	47	47
（四）电力、燃气及水的生产和供应业	Production and Distribution of Electricity,Gas and Water	185	182
电力、热力的生产和供应业	Production and Supply of Electric Power and Heat Power	96	94
燃气生产和供应业	Gas mining and supplying industry	34	34
水的生产和供应业	Production and Supply of Water	55	54
（五）建筑业	Construction	4212	4212
房屋和土木工程建筑业	Construction of Building & Civil Engineering	1271	1271
建筑安装业	Architectural Installation	942	942
建筑装饰业	Architectural Decoration	1480	1480
其他建筑业	Other Construction	519	519
（六）交通运输、仓储和邮政业	Traffic, Transport, Storage and Post	1611	1554
铁路运输业	Transport Via Railway	21	21
道路运输业	Transport Via Road	726	681
城市公共交通业	Urban Public Traffic	105	104

1-10 续表2 continued 2

单位：个 (unit)

分　组	Item	产业活动单位数 Number of Industrial Active Units	企 业 Enterprises
水上运输业	Water Transport	2	1
航空运输业	Air Transport	20	19
管道运输业	Transport Via Pipeline	7	7
装卸搬运和其他运输服务业	Loading, Unloading, Portage and Other Transport Services	313	310
仓储业	Storage	177	173
邮政业	Post	240	238
（七）信息传输、计算机服务和软件业	Information Transmission, Computer Services and Software	2258	2234
电信和其他信息传输服务业	Telecom & Other Information Transmission Services	450	441
计算机服务业	Computer Services	955	943
软件业	Software Industry	853	850
（八）批发和零售业	Wholesale and Retail Trades	22488	22488
批发业	Wholesale Trade	12053	12053
零售业	Retail Trade	10435	10435
（九）住宿和餐饮业	Hotels and Catering Services	2453	2435
住宿业	Hotels	879	869
餐饮业	Catering Services	1574	1566
（十）金融业	Financial Intermediation	2161	2134
银行业	Bank	1515	1500
证券业	Security Activities	72	72
保险业	Insurance	426	419
其他金融活动	Other Financial Intermediation	148	143
（十一）房地产业	Real Estate	3676	3642
房地产业	Real Estate	3676	3642
（十二）租赁和商务服务业	Leasing and Business Services	5660	5338
租赁业	Leasing	503	501
商务服务业	Business Services	5157	4837
（十三）科学研究、技术服务和地质勘查业	Scientific Research, Technical Sevice and Geologic Prospecting	2794	2163
研究与试验发展	Research and Experimental Development	289	191
专业技术服务业	Professional Technical Services	1277	1094
科技交流和推广服务业	Services of Science and Technology Exchanges and Promotion	1142	821
地质勘查业	Geologic Prospecting	86	57

1-10 续表3 continued 3

单位：个 (unit)

分组	Item	产业活动单位数 Number of Industrial Active Units	企业 Enterprises
（十四）水利、环境和公共设施管理业	Management of Water Conservancy, Environment and Public Facilities	585	291
水利管理业	Management of Water Conservancy	133	22
环境管理业	Environmental Management	158	64
公共设施管理业	Management of Public Facilities	294	205
（十五）居民服务和其他服务业	Services to Households and Other Services	2360	2271
居民服务业	Services to Households	1187	1123
其他服务业	Other Services	1173	1148
（十六）教育	Education	3605	225
教　育	Education	3605	225
（十七）卫生、社会保障和社会福利业	Health, Social Security and Social Welfare	2800	78
卫　生	Health	2656	71
社会保障业	Social Security	54	2
社会福利业	Social Welfare	90	5
（十八）文化、体育和娱乐业	Culture, Sports and Entertainment	907	609
新闻出版业	Journalism and Publishing Activities	124	73
广播、电视、电影和音像业	Broadcasting, Movies, Television and Audiovisual Activities	174	145
文化艺术业	Cultural and Art Activities	336	155
体　育	Sports Activities	52	22
娱乐业	Entertainment	221	214
（十九）公共管理和社会组织	Public Management and Social Organizaion	8378	
中国共产党机关	Organs of Communist Party of China	208	
国家机构	Government Agencies	3084	
人民政协和民主党派	People's Political Consultative Conference and Democratic Parties	28	
群众团体、社会团体和宗教组织	Non-Government Organizations, Social Organizations and Religion Organizations	1437	
基层群众自治组织	Grass-roots Mass Self-Government Organizations	3621	
（二十）国际组织	International Organizations		
国际组织	International Organizations		

1-11 各区县产业活动单位（2010年）

Industrial Active Units by Region（2010）

单位：个 （unit）

分组	Item	产业活动单位数 Number of Industrial Active Units	企业 Enterprises
合计	**Total**	**78692**	**62106**
新城区	Xincheng	5964	4988
碑林区	Beilin	9985	9017
莲湖区	Lianhu	8821	7816
灞桥区	Baqiao	3622	2639
未央区	Weiyang	12052	11293
雁塔区	Yanta	16981	15627
阎良区	Yanliang	1480	917
临潼区	Lintong	2813	1411
长安区	Chang'an	4436	2752
蓝田县	Lantian	3182	1067
周至县	Zhouzhi	3297	1113
户县	Huxian	4348	2444
高陵县	Gaoling	1711	1022

1-12 国民经济和社会发展总量与速度指标

指　　标	Item	总量指标				
		1995	2000	2005	2006	2007
人口与就业	**Population and Employment**					
人口	**Population**					
年底总人口(万人)	Population at the Year-end (10 000 persons)	648.21	688.01	741.73	753.11	764.25
非农业人口	Non-agricultural Population	255.71	285.79	333.14	343.78	353.85
农业人口	Agriculturral Population	392.50	402.22	408.59	409.33	410.40
男性人口	Male	334.75	355.18	382.02	387.37	392.41
女性人口	Female	313.46	332.83	359.71	365.74	371.84
就业	**Employment**					
就业人员数(万人)	Employment(10 000 persons)	372.60	389.10	415.83	422.15	436.36
#全部单位在岗职工人数	Number of Employed Staff and Workers	141.17	109.62	119.73	121.06	125.56
城镇登记失业人数(万人)	Registered Unemployed in Urban Areas(10 000 persons)	5.92	3.85	8.45	8.74	8.77
宏观经济	**Macroeconomic Indicator**					
国民经济核算	**National Accounts**					
生产总值(亿元)	Gross Domestic Product(100 mil. yuan)	330.35	646.13	1313.93	1538.94	1856.63
第一产业	Primary Industry	41.40	44.65	66.01	70.44	82.51
第二产业	Secondary Industry	135.33	277.13	540.50	645.65	781.94
工业	Industry	112.50	218.44	420.00	494.22	594.95
第三产业	Tertiary Industry	153.62	324.35	707.42	822.85	992.18
#最终消费	Total Consumption	239.64	413.43	766.62	870.93	995.22
资本形成总额	Total Investment	151.55	287.82	839.01	1045.27	1451.47
固定资产投资	**Investment in Fixed Assets**					
全社会固定资产投资总额(亿元)	Total Investment in Fixed Assets(100 mil. yuan)	103.42	232.37	835.10	1066.62	1435.33
一、城镇	Urban Area	88.50	203.01	776.33	971.84	1340.59
#房地产	Real Estate	21.65	51.85	225.23	285.76	387.33
二、农村	Rural Area	14.92	29.36	58.77	94.78	94.74
在固定资产投资中：国有经济	State-Owned	69.08	159.60	373.70	401.14	476.78
集体经济	Collective-Owned	9.78	14.65	59.23	110.68	207.08
个体经济	Self-employed Individual	11.13	24.40	79.04	107.33	183.09
财政	**Public Finance**					
地方财政一般预算收入(亿元)	General Budgetary Revenue of Local Government (100 mil. yuan)	18.21	46.80	72.92	85.89	112.92
地方财政一般预算支出(亿元)	General Budgetary Expenditure of Local Government (100 mil. yuan)	18.42	52.00	97.61	119.22	161.25
物价指数(上年=100)	**Price Indices(preceding year=100)**					
商品零售价格指数	Retail Price Index	114.6	98.7	99.7	101.5	103.7
居民消费价格指数	Consumer Price Index	117.0	100.2	100.3	101.6	104.7
工业品出厂价格指数	Ex-Factory Price Indices of Industrial Products	110.8	99.4	103.9	103.2	101.9
利用外资签订协议金额	**Utilization of Foreign Capital**					
利用外资签定协议额(万美元)	Amount of Foreign Capital for Utilization Through Signed Contracts or Agreements(USD 10 000)	28956	54123	121499	182525	143978
外商实际直接投资额(万美元)	Amount of Foreign Capital Actually Utilized (USD 10 000)	18653	15633	57113	82463	111567

注：1.国民经济核算2004-2008年为全国第二次经济普查修订数据。

2.2009年及以前年份财政收支为一般预算收支与基金预算收支之和。

Principal Aggregate Indicators on National Economic and Social Development and Their Related Indices and Growth Rates

Aggregate Data			速度指标(%) Indices and Growth Rates						
2008	2009	2010	指数 Index (2010比以下各年) (2010 as percentage of the following years)			平均增长速度 Average Annual Growth Rate			
			2000	2005	2009	1996-2005	1996-2000	2001-2005	2006-2010
772.30	781.67	782.73	113.8	105.5	100.1	1.4	1.2	1.5	1.1
363.87	370.66	374.64	131.1	112.5	101.1	2.7	2.2	3.1	2.4
408.43	411.01	408.09	101.5	99.9	99.3	0.4	0.5	0.3	-0.03
395.54	399.28	398.80	112.3	104.4	99.9	1.3	1.2	1.5	0.9
376.76	382.39	383.93	115.4	106.7	100.4	1.4	1.2	1.6	1.3
448.05	462.52	477.58	122.7	114.8	103.3	1.1	0.9	1.3	2.8
126.89	129.62	130.70	119.2	109.2	100.8	-1.7	-4.9	1.8	1.8
9.40	10.02	10.46	271.7	123.8	104.4	3.6	-8.2	17.0	4.4
2318.14	2724.08	3241.69	378.1	200.9	114.5	13.5	13.6	13.5	15.0
103.45	110.38	140.06	168.9	136.8	106.7	4.4	4.6	4.3	6.5
981.58	1144.75	1406.72	417.7	206.0	118.0	16.0	16.8	15.2	15.5
721.40	816.92	1003.57	393.0	196.9	118.1	15.3	15.5	14.3	14.5
1233.11	1468.95	1694.91	374.4	203.2	112.5	11.9	10.9	13.0	15.2
1182.61	1403.10	1598.51	280.5	183.2	110.5	9.4	9.9	8.9	12.9
1837.86	2281.91	2835.42	756.6	283.8	118.7	16.6	11.8	21.5	23.2
1906.36	2500.13	3250.56	1398.9	389.2	130.0	23.2	17.6	29.2	31.2
1786.60	2367.58	3104.92	1529.4	399.9	131.1	24.3	18.1	30.8	31.9
540.26	696.34	842.34	1624.6	374.0	121.0	26.4	19.1	34.1	30.2
119.76	132.55	145.64	496.0	247.8	109.9	14.7	14.5	14.9	19.9
694.89	932.91	1348.76	845.1	360.9	144.6	18.4	18.2	18.5	29.3
246.89	289.91	326.44	2228.3	551.1	112.6	19.7	8.4	32.2	40.7
50.43	97.86	54.73	224.3	69.2	55.9	21.7	17.0	26.5	-7.1
145.61	181.40	241.86	516.8	331.7	133.3	13.4	20.8	9.3	27.1
226.99	276.85	371.62	714.7	380.7	134.2	18.8	23.1	13.4	30.7
105.4	99.5	102.70							
106.0	99.7	103.50							
103.7	99.9	102.30							
118230	60027	119689	221.1	98.5	199.4	15.4	13.3	17.6	-0.3
114738	121872	156653	1002.1	274.3	128.5	11.8	-3.5	29.6	22.4

Note:1.The data of national account between 2004 and 2008 was from the second national economic census.

2.Government revenue and expenditure in 2009 and before 2009 was the sum of ordinary budgetary revenue and expenditure plus fund budgetary revenue and expenditure.

1–12 续表1

指标	Item	总量指标				
		1995	2000	2005	2006	2007
产业	**Industry**					
农业	**Agriculture**					
耕地面积(万亩)	Cultivated Areas(10 000 hectares)	464.0	443.4	400.2	395.8	390.8
乡村劳动力资源总数（万人）	Total Number of Rural Labor Source (10 000 persons)	213.8	240.8	255.9	257.7	254.1
农林牧渔及服务业总产值(亿元)	Gross Output Value of Farming Forestry, Animal Husbandry and Fishery(100 mil yuan)	75.46	74.37	106.54	114.15	134.15
主要农产品产量(万吨)	Output of Major Farm Products(10 000 tons)					
粮　食	Grain	175.3	201.9	205.5	193.5	189.1
奶　类	Milk	13.3	24.6	42.2	47.1	52.8
油　料	Oil-bearing Crops	2.2	1.3	1.2	1.1	1.0
蔬　菜	Vegetables	133.6	162.1	195.7	189.3	204.4
水　果	Fruits	24.1	34.4	51.3	55.3	60.5
肉　类	Meat	12.8	14.8	18.2	10.9	10.2
水产品	Aquatic Products	0.9	1.1	0.9	1.2	1.2
工业	**Industry**					
全部工业总产值（亿元）	Gross industrial Output Value(100 mil. yuan)	405.90	639.48	1308.56	1557.35	1979.86
规模以上工业企业主要经济指标（亿元）	Principal Indicators of Industrial Enterprises of State Ownership and Non-state-owned Above Designated Size(100 mil. yuan)					
资产总计	Total Assets		958.05	1503.85	1651.67	1940.52
主营业务收入	Revenue from Principal Business		420.42	980.97	1183.51	1561.25
利润总额	Profits		16.11	28.72	61.46	106.22
从业人员年平均人数（万人）	Annual Average Employers(10 000 persons)		43.25	37.92	37.94	38.55
主要工业产品产量	Output of Major Industrial Products					
布(万米)	Cloth(10 000 m)	30332	24818	27012	26508	27995
机制纸及纸板(吨)	Machine-Made Paper(tons)	364400	54711	221865	325107	426520
家用电冰箱(台)	Household Refrigerators(unit)	13000	5860	25407	69199	94090
发电量(亿千瓦时)	Electricity(100 million kwh)	22.00	19.00	48.00	67.00	71.00
钢材(吨)	Steel Products(ton)	314400	100000	240182	715303	787274
汽车(万辆)	Motor Vehicle (10 000 units)	0.3	0.9	4.1	10.3	17.1
建筑业	**Construction**					
建筑业企业从业人数(人)	Number of Employed Persons(person)		136718	158311	172179	296538
建筑业总产值(亿元)	Gross Output Value(100 mil. yuan)	42.55	105.93	326.65	416.48	604.75
房屋建筑施工面积(万平方米)	Floor Space of Buildings under Construction (10 000 sq.m)	601.70	793.30	1801.20	2140.10	2802.00
房屋建筑竣工面积(万平方米)	Floor Space of Buildings Completed (10 000 sq.m)	177.15	336.80	569.01	594.20	835.95

continued 1

Aggregate Data			速度指标(%)			Indices and Growth Rates			
			指数 Index (2010比以下各年) (2010 as percentage of the following years)			平均增长速度 Average Annual Growth Rate			
2008	2009	2010	2000	2005	2009	1996-2005	1996-2000	2001-2005	2006-2010
390.8	387.9	383.3	86.5	95.8	98.8	-1.5	-0.9	-2.0	-9.0
256.2	255.0	256.4	106.5	100.2	100.5	1.8	2.4	1.2	0.04
168.27	178.70	227.10	174.6	139.2	107.4	4.8	4.9	5.1	6.8
214.4	218.2	221.7	109.8	107.9	101.6	1.6	2.9	0.4	1.5
59.0	61.8	63.4	257.6	150.2	102.5	12.3	13.1	11.4	8.5
1.2	1.1	1.2	92.3	100.0	107.1	-5.9	-10.0	-1.6	
221.5	242.4	253.1	156.1	129.3	104.4	3.9	3.9	3.8	5.3
71.7	79.0	84.8	246.5	165.3	107.4	7.8	7.4	8.3	10.6
11.5	12.6	13.7	92.2	75.0	108.2	3.6	2.9	4.2	-5.6
1.2	1.3	1.2	108.2	132.2	91.5	1.0	4.1	-3.9	5.7
2388.14	2827.07	3562.88	510.0	261.2	126.0	17.5	16.4	14.3	21.2
2426.13	2913.56	3592.13	374.9	238.9	123.3			9.4	19.0
1928.05	2384.52	3011.09	716.2	307.0	126.3			18.5	25.1
84.89	177.20	245.37	1523.1	854.4	138.5			12.3	53.6
40.17	43.42	47.11	108.9	124.2	108.5			-2.6	4.4
22721	22202	23810	95.9	88.1	107.2	-1.2	-3.9	1.7	-2.5
442758	476258	495966	906.5	223.5	104.1	-4.8	-31.6	32.3	17.5
100854	92146	107571	1835.7	423.4	116.7	6.9	-14.7	34.1	33.5
71.69	83.21	96.94	510.2	202.0	117.1	8.0	-2.9	20.4	15.1
478819	1105074	1107663	25640.3	461.2	100.2	-2.7	-57.6	123.4	35.8
26.8	50.7	65.2	7245.6	1590.5	128.7	28.3	24.6	35.4	73.9
400740	461080	539000	394.5	340.5	116.9			3.0	27.8
915.19	1296.58	1820.35	1718.4	557.3	140.4	22.6	20.0	25.3	41.0
3133.90	3947.01	4592.57	578.9	255.0	116.4	11.6	5.7	17.8	20.6
1056.53	1209.88	1391.91	413.3	244.6	115.0	12.4	13.7	11.1	19.6

1-12 续表2

指　　标	Item	总量指标				
		1995	2000	2005	2006	2007
交通运输	**Transportation**					
货运量(万吨)	Freight Traffic(10 000 tons)	9590	6999	12051	11832	15124
铁　路	Railways	3317	3101	540	573	589
公　路	Highways	6268	3890	11505	11254	14530
民用航空	Civil Aviation	5	8	6	5	5
客运量(万人次)	Passenger Traffic(10 000 persons-times)	9069	8068	10479	11245	12466
铁　路	Railways	2678	2130	1796	2066	2380
公　路	Highways	6128	5578	8294	8682	9466
民用航空	Civil Aviation	263	360	389	497	620
邮电通信业	**Post and Telecommunication Services**					
邮电业务总量(亿元)	Total Business Revenue(100 mil. yuan)	7.65	46.16	132.04	186.76	226.76
函　件(万件)	Number of Letters Delivered(10 000 pieces)	14647	8230	9526	9328	5544
本地电话局用交换机容量(万门)	Capacity of Local Office Telephone Exchanges (10 000 line)	58.3	204.8	457.3	474.7	479.7
本地电话年末用户(万户)	Number of Subscribers of Local Telephone at Year-end(10 000 subscribers)	25.95	124.26	321.48	315.96	314.58
城市电话用户	Urban Telephone Subscribers	29.15	107.24	271.40	269.21	272.64
乡村电话用户	Rural Telephone Subscribers	0.84	17.02	50.08	46.75	41.94
移动电话用户(万户)	Number of Mobile Telephone Subscribers (10 000 subscribers)		73.10	419.96	551.07	664.59
互联网年末宽带用户(万户)	Number of Subscribers of Internet Services (10 000 subscribers)			33.93	50.88	58.62
国内商业	**Domestic Trade**					
社会消费品零售总额(亿元)	Total Retail Sales of Consumer Goods (100 mil. yuan)	186.60	360.42	670.56	784.95	936.21
对外经济贸易	**Foreign Trade**					
进出口总额(万美元)	Total Exports and Imports(USD 10 000)	137510	173696	390146	415403	536162
出口额	Exports	110163	106062	263441	272862	347133
进口额	Imports	27347	67634	126705	142541	189029
国际旅游	**International Tourism**					
国际旅游者人数(万人次)	Number of International Tourists(10 000 persons)	41.35	65.03	77.56	86.73	100.01
国际旅游收入(亿元)	Foreign Exchange Earnings from Tourism (10 000 yuan)	10.38	22.41	33.54	37.83	42.43
金融业	**Financial Intermediation**					
金融机构（不含外资）人民币存款余额(亿元)	Balance of Deposits in Domestic Funded Financial Institutions (100 mil. yuan)	359.51	1335.63	3599.70	4066.16	4582.71
金融机构（不含外资）人民币贷款余额 (亿元)	Balance of Loans in Domestic Funded Financial Institutions (100 mil. yuan)	334.50	972.52	2158.10	2344.77	2683.77

注：1.2006年铁路数据按新口径统计；

2.2006年国际互联网络用户改为互联网宽带用户。

continued 2

Aggregate Data			速度指标(%)			Indices and Growth Rates			
			指数 Index (2010比以下各年) (2010 as percentage of the following years)			平均增长速度 Average Annual Growth Rate			
2008	2009	2010	2000	2005	2009	1996-2005	1996-2000	2001-2005	2006-2010
27560	30606	34323	490.4	284.8	112.1	2.3	-6.1	11.5	23.3
605	614	706	22.8	130.7	115.0	-16.6	-1.3	-29.5	5.5
26949	29986	33610	864.0	292.1	112.1	6.3	9.1	24.2	23.9
6	6	7	87.5	116.7	116.7	1.8	9.9	-5.6	3.1
26501	28693	30294	375.5	289.1	105.6	-2.3	-2.3	5.4	23.7
2680	2585	2781	130.6	154.8	107.6	-4.5	-4.5	-3.4	9.1
23175	25271	26536	475.7	319.9	105.0	-1.9	-1.9	8.3	26.2
646	837	977	271.4	251.2	116.7	6.5	6.5	1.6	20.2
264.67	298.92	323.11	700.0	244.7	108.1	43.3	43.3	23.4	19.6
5638	6128	8176	99.3	85.8	133.4	-10.9	-10.9	3.0	-3.0
462.5	441.1	449.0	219.3	98.2	101.8	28.6	28.6	17.4	-0.4
306.88	289.10	261.77	210.7	81.4	90.5	35.6	32.9	20.9	-4.0
268.49	253.28	228.27	212.9	84.1	90.1	32.9	29.8	20.4	-3.4
38.39	35.82	33.50	196.8	66.9	90.5	82.6	82.5	24.1	-7.7
737.76	1120.06	1423.08	1946.8	338.9	127.1			41.9	27.6
81.40	116.79	146.18		430.8	125.2				33.9
1176.58	1381.12	1637.04	454.2	244.1	118.5	13.6	14.1	13.2	19.5
704029	724618	1039273	598.3	266.4	143.4	11.0	4.8	17.6	21.6
447113	333114	531729	501.3	201.8	159.6	9.1	-0.8	20.0	15.1
256916	391504	507544	750.4	400.6	129.6	16.6	19.9	13.4	32.0
63.20	67.29	84.18	129.4	108.5	125.1	6.5	9.5	3.6	1.7
28.72	31.05	42.40	189.2	126.4	136.6	12.4	16.6	8.4	4.8
5788.43	7457.71	8863.36	663.6	246.2	118.8	25.9	30.0	21.9	19.7
3267.89	4436.50	6420.72	660.2	297.5	144.7	20.5	23.8	17.3	24.4

Note:1. The railway data is added up according to new aperture in 2006.

2. The number of broadband internet subscribers changed from Internet subscribers in 2006.

1–12 续表3

指　　标	Item	总量指标			
		1995	2000	2005	2006
保险公司保险金额(亿元)	Insurance Coverage of Insurance Companies (100 mil. yuan)	1155.01	1586.67	3598.63	8152.93
保险公司保费收入(亿元)	Insurance Premium of Insurance Companies (100 mil. yuan)	4.70	13.58	44.94	52.51
保险公司赔款及付给金额(亿元)	Indemnity Expenditure and Payment of Insurance Companies (100 mil. yuan)	1.70	1.39	9.50	11.80
教育、科技、文化	**Education, Science and Technology and Culture**				
教育	**Education**				
专任教师数(人)	Full-time Teachers(person)	74905	78973	98561	100308
普通高等学校	Institutions of Higher Education	15914	15679	29498	32891
中等学校	Secondary Schools	28721	32923	39416	37399
小 学	Primary Schools	30270	30215	29647	30018
在校学生数(万人)	Students Enrollment(10 000 person)	131.66	156.16	186.34	187.43
普通高等学校	Institutions of Higher Education	11.67	19.41	53.06	57.10
中等学校	Secondary Schools	41.43	58.75	72.81	76.70
小 学	Primary Schools	79.36	77.81	60.47	59.33
科技	**Science and Technology**				
高新技术企业(个)	Hi-tech Enterprises (unit)		632	1029	1062
企事业单位累计授权专利数（件）	Accumulated patents awarded(unit)	3164	6139	11670	13442
文化	**Culture**				
图书馆总藏量(千册件)	Total Collections in Library (1000 Volume-time)	2830	3214	3671	3807
文化馆、站（个)	Cultural Centers or Stations (unit)	201	251	192	193
电视节目制作时间(小时)	Time for TV Programs Production(hours)	5738	11871	27377	36337
家庭、生活、环境	**Family, People's Livelihood and Environment**				
家庭	**Family**				
家庭总户数 (万户)	Total Number of Households(10 000 households)	171.25	187.08	203.04	207.04
城镇居民平均每户家庭人口(人)	Average Household Size in Urban Areas(person)	3.88	2.99	2.93	2.90
农村居民平均每户家庭人口(人)	Average Household Size in Rural Areas(person)	4.60	4.30	4.22	4.19
婚姻	**Marriages and Divorces**				
结婚对数(对)	Register Number of Marriages(couples)	47236	46415	49962	67018
离婚对数(对)	Number of Divorces(couples)	4296	5161	12747	12708
居住	**Housing**				
城镇居民人均现住房总建筑面积(平方米)	Per Capita Total Building Area of Urban Residents' Houses(sq.m)	13.05	14.82	16.38	23.15
农村居民人均居住面积(平方米)	Per Capita Net Floor Space of Rural Residents(sq.m)	21.77	28.31	36.73	40.05

注：1.2008年及以前图书馆总藏量为图书馆藏书量。
2.2005年以前城镇居民人均现住房总建筑面积为城镇人均住房使用面积。

continued 3

Aggregate Data				速度指标(%)			Indices and Growth Rates			
				指数 Index (2010比以下各年) (2010 as percentage of the following years)			平均增长速度 Average Annual Growth Rate			
2007	2008	2009	2010	2000	2005	2009	1996-2005	1996-2000	2001-2005	2006-2010
10244.24	30224.55	18999.60	30066.78	1895.0	835.5	158.2	12.0	6.6	17.8	52.9
72.33	101.45	122.11	162.27	1194.9	361.1	132.9	24.6	23.6	27.0	29.3
19.91	25.92	25.16	28.80	2071.9	303.2	114.5	18.8	-3.9	46.9	24.8
105863	110629	115076	115864	146.7	117.6	100.7	2.8	1.1	4.5	3.3
36717	38926	40605	42098	268.5	142.7	103.7	6.4	-0.3	13.5	7.4
38613	41321	44137	43822	133.1	111.2	99.3	3.2	2.8	3.7	2.1
30533	30382	30334	29944	99.1	101.0	98.7	-0.2		-0.4	0.2
196.34	199.73	203.49	202.80	129.9	108.8	99.7	3.5	3.5	3.6	1.7
62.31	66.68	70.31	73.30	377.6	138.1	104.3	16.4	10.7	22.3	6.7
77.2	78.39	80.66	77.90	132.6	107.0	96.6	5.8	7.2	4.4	1.4
56.83	54.66	52.52	51.60	66.3	85.3	98.2	-2.7	-0.4	-4.9	-3.1
1311	1324	592	672	106.3	65.3	113.5			10.2	-8.2
15971	19256	23962	31999	521.2	274.2	133.5	13.7	14.2	13.7	22.4
3893	4040	4324	4465	138.9	121.6	103.3	2.6	2.6	2.7	4.0
197	197	197	197	78.1	103.2	99.5	-0.6	4.5	-5.4	0.6
25883	26897	27131	29626	249.6	108.2	109.2	16.9	15.6	18.2	1.6
211.12	216.52	221.51	226.71	121.2	111.7	102.3	1.7	1.8	1.7	2.2
2.91	2.82	2.84	2.81	94.0	95.9	98.9	-2.8	-5.1	-0.4	-0.8
4.48	4.03	4.07	3.94	90.7	92.4	95.8	-0.9	-1.3	-0.4	-1.6
67637	77912	88138	83645	180.2	167.4	94.9	0.6	-0.4	1.5	10.9
15536	15722	15796	19060	369.3	149.5	120.7	11.5	3.7	19.8	8.4
23.63	26.32	28.40	28.70	193.7	175.2	101.1	2.3	2.6	2.0	11.9
42.92	54.97	56.73	66.73	235.7	181.7	117.6	5.4	5.4	5.3	12.7

Note:1.'Total collections in libraries' was the 'number of collections in libraries' in 2008 and before.

2.The per capital total building area of urban residents' houses was replaced as the per Capital dwelling area of urban residents before 2005.

1-12 续表4

指　　标	Item	总量指标			
		1995	2000	2005	2006
生活	**People's Livelihood**				
城镇居民人均可支配收入(元)	Per Capita Annual Disposable Income of Urban Households (yuan)	4153	6364	9628	10905
农村居民人均纯收入(元)	Per Capita Net Income of Rural Residents(yuan)	1353	2344	3460	3808
城乡储蓄存款余额(亿元)	Outstanding Amount of Saving Deposits in Urban and Rural Areas(100 mil yuan)	230.63	675.83	1716.76	1950.53
工资	**Wages and Welfare**				
在岗职工工资总额(亿元)	The Gross Salary of Workers (100 mil yuan)	67.23	101.68	211.14	246.43
城镇非私营单位在岗职工年平均工资(元)	Aunual Average Wage of Stuff and Workers in Urban Non-privite Enterprises(yuan)	4763	9179	17728	20475
卫生	**Health Care**				
医院、卫生院(个)	Number of Hospitals(unit)	368	426	479	475
执业（助理）医师（人）	Licensed（Assistant） Doctors (person)	18846	18750	17730	18007
医院、卫生院床位数(张)	Number of Hospital Beds(unit)	28265	28697	30087	30840
市政建设	**City Construction**				
自来水供应量(万立方米)	Volume of Tap Water Supply(10 000 cu.m)	35885	30273	35776	28762
自来水供水管道长度(公里)	Length of Water Supply Pipelines(km)	1066	2237	2315	1529
城市天然气供气量(万立方米)	Volume of Natural Gas Supply in Urban Areas (10 000 cu.m)	8419	11513	53202	68631
公交运营汽(电)车总数(辆)	Total Number of Public Buses and Trolley Buses(unit)	977	2573	4762	5489
道路长度(公里)	Length of Paved Roads(km)	835	975	1382	1480
绿地面积(公顷)	Areas of Green Land(hectare)	5603	4116	4867	8106
环境、灾害	**Environment and Disaster**				
工业废水排放量(万吨)	Volume of Waste Water up to the Standard for Discharge(10 000 tons)	12479	9145	16969	16389
工业废水排放达标量（万吨）	Volume of Waste Water up to the Standard for Discharge(10 000 tons)	8408	6130	16215	15267
火灾发生数(起)	Number of Fire Disasters(case)	426	1040	2664	2310
火灾事故损失额（万元）	Fire Loss(10 000 yuan)	742.1	472.4	1565.5	1376.0
交通事故发生数（起）	Number of Traffic Accidents(case)	3065	4099	4903	3709
交通事故损失额（万元）	Loss of Traffic Accidents(10 000 yuan)	1103.2	1116.1	2024.4	1328.3

continued 4

Aggregate Data				速度指标(%)			Indices and Growth Rates			
				指数 Index (2010比以下各年) (2010 as percentage of the following years)			平均增长速度 Average Annual Growth Rate			
2006	2007	2008	2010	2000	2005	2009	1996-2005	1996-2000	2001-2005	2006-2010
12662	15207	18963	22244	349.5	231.0	117.3	8.8	8.9	8.6	18.2
4399	5212	6275	7750	330.6	224.0	123.5	9.8	11.6	8.1	17.5
2002.38	2513.70	3084.20	3641.09	536.8	211.1	118.1	19.4	24.0	20.5	16.2
313.40	373.24	439.74	501.76	493.5	237.6	114.1	12.1	8.6	15.7	18.9
25012	29749	34032	37870	412.6	213.6	111.3	14.1	14.0	14.1	16.4
459	432	415	412	96.7	86.0	99.3	2.7	3.0	2.4	-3.0
17266	18066	19284	18763	100.1	105.8	97.3	-0.6	-0.1	-1.1	1.1
30823	32998	34904	36796	128.2	122.3	105.4	0.6	0.3	1.0	4.1
32959	36471	38307	41089	135.7	114.9	107.3		-3.3	3.4	2.8
2424	2385	1985	2416	108.0	104.4	121.7	8.1	16.0	0.7	0.9
72253	84874	95885	109052	947.2	205.0	113.7	20.5	6.5	35.8	15.4
5836	6123	7039	7107	276.2	149.2	101.0	17.2	21.4	13.1	8.3
1842	2115	2296	2662	273.0	192.6	115.9	5.2	3.1	7.2	14.0
8670	9199	9553	12140	294.9	249.4	127.1	-1.4	-6.0	3.4	20.1
19069	18304	13168	13840	151.3	81.6	105.1	3.1	-6.0	13.2	-4.0
18352	17862	12106	13269	216.5	81.8	109.6	6.8	-6.1	21.5	-3.9
2009	1537	1485	1825	175.5	68.5	122.9	20.1	19.5	20.7	-7.3
773.9	1907.7	1850.6	2224.2	470.8	142.1	120.2	7.8	-8.6	27.1	7.3
3647	2576	2702	2323	56.7	47.4	86.0	4.8	6.0	3.6	-13.9
1038.0	522.8	851.7	736.6	66.0	36.4	86.5	6.3	0.2	12.6	-18.3

1-13 国民经济和社会发展结构指标

Structural Indicators on National Economic and Social Development

单位: % (%)

指　　标	Item	1995	2000	2005	2006	2007	2008	2009	2010
人口与就业	**Population and Employment**								
人口	**Population**								
农业与非农业结构	Structure								
农业	Agriculture	60.55	58.46	55.09	54.40	53.70	52.88	52.58	52.14
非农业	Non-Agriculture	39.45	41.54	44.91	45.60	46.30	47.12	47.42	47.86
性别结构	Sexual Structure								
男	Male	51.64	51.62	51.50	51.40	51.35	51.22	51.08	50.95
女	Female	48.36	48.38	48.50	48.60	48.65	48.78	48.92	49.05
就业	**Employment**								
产业结构	Industrial Structure								
第一产业	Primary Industry	41.17	37.78	32.78	32.00	30.55	28.50	26.40	25.65
第二产业	Secondary Industry	29.43	27.57	27.46	27.50	28.66	29.10	28.45	29.65
第三产业	Tertiary Industry	29.40	34.65	39.76	40.50	40.79	42.40	45.15	44.70
宏观经济	**Macro Economy**								
国民经济核算	**National Accounting**								
生产总值产业结构	Industrial Structure								
第一产业	Primary Industry	12.53	6.91	5.02	4.58	4.44	4.46	4.05	4.32
第二产业	Secondary Industry	40.97	42.89	41.14	41.95	42.12	42.34	42.02	43.39
第三产业	Tertiary Industry	46.50	50.20	53.84	53.47	53.44	53.20	53.93	52.29
生产总值支出结构	Structure of Gross Domestic by Expenditures								
最终消费	Total Consumption	72.54	63.99	58.35	56.59	53.60	51.02	51.51	49.31
资本形成总额	Total Investment	45.88	44.55	63.85	67.92	78.18	79.28	83.77	87.47
货物和服务净出口	Net Export of Goods and Services	-18.42	-8.54	-22.20	-24.51	-31.78	-30.30	-35.28	-36.78
投　资	**Investment**								
全社会固定资产投资结构	Structure of Total Investment in Fixed Assets								
城乡结构	Urban and Rural Composition								
城镇	Urban Area	85.57	87.36	92.96	91.11	93.40	93.72	94.70	95.52
#房地产	Real Estate	20.93	22.31	27.00	26.80	26.09	28.34	27.85	25.91
农村	Rural Area	14.43	12.64	7.04	8.89	6.60	6.28	5.30	4.48
经济类型结构	Registion Status Composition								
国有单位	State-owned Enterprises Investment	66.80	68.68	44.75	37.61	33.22	36.45	37.31	41.49
集体单位	Collective-owned Enterprises Investment	9.46	6.30	7.09	10.38	14.43	12.95	11.60	10.04
个体经济	Self-employed Individual	10.76	10.50	9.46	10.06	12.75	2.65	3.91	1.68
其他单位投资	Other Investment	12.99	14.51	38.69	41.95	39.60	47.95	47.18	46.70

1-13 续表1 continued 1

单位:% (%)

指　　标	Item	1995	2000	2005	2006	2007	2008	2009	2010
财　政	**Government Finance**								
财政收入结构	Structure of Government Revenue								
中　央	Central Government		31.94	58.30	59.40	60.40	39.49	39.68	37.28
地　方	Local Governments		68.06	41.70	40.60	39.60	44.87	45.32	47.36
产　业	**Industrial**								
农　业	**Agriculture**								
农林牧渔及服务业总产值结构	Structure of Gross Output Value of Farming,Forestry,Animal Husbandry, Fishery and Service								
农　业	Farming	68.03	69.23	61.69	60.93	59.50	56.85	59.42	63.36
林　业	Forestry	0.96	1.14	1.23	1.33	1.18	1.13	1.27	1.18
牧　业	Animal Husbandry	30.29	28.58	30.96	31.48	30.58	33.52	30.56	27.72
渔　业	Fishery	0.72	1.05	0.69	0.61	0.68	0.66	0.66	0.56
农林牧渔服务业	Farming,Forestry,Animal Husbandry and Fishery			5.43	5.65	8.06	7.84	8.09	7.18
工　业	**Industry**								
工业总产值经济类型结构	Structure of Gross Output Value of Industry by Registion Status								
国有经济	State-owned Enterprises	51.04	43.00	45.21	48.34	51.41	52.26	51.07	51.52
集体经济	Collective-owned Enterprises	40.98	32.76	5.16	3.31	1.85	1.85	1.38	1.22
其他经济类型	Others	7.98	24.24	49.63	48.35	46.74	45.89	47.55	47.26
工业总产值轻重结构	Structure of Gross Output Value of Industry by Ligth Industry and Heavy Industry								
轻工业	Light Industry	40.31	48.81	31.17	28.97	37.03	25.17	23.47	22.01
重工业	Heavy Industry	59.69	51.19	68.83	71.03	62.97	74.83	76.53	77.99
工业总产值规模结构	Structure of Gross Output Value of Industry by Size of Enterprises								
大型企业	Large Enterprises	38.80	36.29	35.46	38.34	42.18	43.85	43.54	42.11
中型企业	Medium-sized Enterprises	9.14	5.14	24.67	21.93	21.07	20.96	21.88	23.96
小型企业	Small Enterprises	52.06	58.57	39.87	39.73	36.75	35.19	34.58	33.93

注：本表2008年以后财政收入结构中地方指地方财政一般预算收入。

Note:Composition of government revenue after 2008 in this table refers to local government ordinary bugdetaty revenue.

1-13 续表2 continued 2

单位: % (%)

指标	Item	1995	2000	2005	2006	2007	2008	2009	2010
建筑业	**Construction**								
建筑业总产值结构	Structure of Gross Output Value of Construction Industry								
土木工程建筑业	Civil Engineering Construction	86.27	88.50	56.59	57.81	57.78	59.14	67.14	68.61
房屋工程建筑	Building Construction	12.84	9.28	34.05	34.58	32.44	29.80	25.50	24.63
建筑安装业	Installation of Construction								4.39
装修装饰业	Decoration	0.89	2.21	1.08	1.13	1.74	1.67	1.50	0.82
其 他	Others		0.01	8.28	6.48	8.04	9.39	5.86	1.55
交通运输业	**Transportation**								
客运量结构	Structure of Freight Traffic								
铁 路	Railways	29.13	26.40	17.14	18.37	19.09	10.11	9.01	9.18
公 路	Highways	67.57	69.14	79.15	77.31	75.93	87.45	88.07	87.59
民 航	Civil Aviation	2.90	4.46	3.71	4.42	4.97	2.44	2.92	3.23
货运量结构	Structure of Freight Traffic								
铁 路	Railways	34.59	44.30	26.92	4.84	3.90	2.20	2.01	2.06
公 路	Highways	65.36	55.58	73.04	95.12	96.07	97.78	97.97	97.92
民 航	Civil Aviation	0.05	0.12	0.04	0.04	0.03	0.02	0.02	0.02
国内商业	**Domestic Trade**								
社会消费品零售总额结构	Composition of Retail Sales of Consumer Goods								
城镇	Urban Area	88.95	87.99	90.17	90.24	90.32	90.43	90.49	95.91
农村	Rural Area	11.05	12.01	9.83	9.76	9.68	9.57	9.51	4.09
国际旅游	**International Tourism**								
国际旅游人数结构	Structure of Tourists								
外国人	Foreigners	89.76	84.03	84.91	84.63	85.09	84.78	87.81	86.97
华侨及港澳台同胞	Overseas Chinese and Compatriots form Hong Kong, Macao and Taiwan	10.24	15.97	15.09	15.37	14.91	15.22	12.19	13.03
教育文化、卫生、人民生活	**Education and Culture，Health Care，People's Livelihood**								
教 育	**Education**								
在校学生结构	Structure of Student Enrollment								
普通高等学校	Regular Institutions of Higher Schools	8.81	12.44	28.48	29.57	31.74	33.38	34.55	36.15
中等学校	Secondary Schools	31.28	37.67	39.07	39.71	39.32	39.25	39.64	38.41
小学	Primary Schools	59.91	49.89	32.45	30.72	28.94	27.37	25.81	25.44

1-13 续表3 continued 3

单位: % (%)

指　　标	Item	1995	2000	2005	2006	2007	2008	2009	2010
专任教师结构	Full-time Teachers by Type								
普通高等学校	Regular Institutions of Higher Schools	21.25	19.89	29.92	32.79	34.68	35.19	35.29	36.33
中等学校	Secondary Schools	38.34	41.77	39.98	37.28	36.48	37.35	38.35	37.82
小学	Primary Schools	40.41	38.34	30.10	29.93	28.84	27.46	26.36	25.85
人民生活	**People's Livelihood**								
城镇居民消费结构	Consumption Structure of Urban Residents								
食　品	Food	44.68	36.46	37.04	34.42	36.61	36.40	32.43	31.29
衣　着	Clothing	12.67	8.13	9.03	8.72	9.41	10.25	10.98	11.11
家庭设备用品及服务	Household facilities,Articles and Services	13.75	11.33	4.73	6.49	5.91	6.33	7.28	7.56
医疗保健	Health Care	3.27	7.23	9.45	7.73	8.40	9.67	9.65	9.50
交通和通信	Transportation and Communication	5.58	6.93	9.67	10.27	11.35	10.37	11.33	12.06
教育文化娱乐服务	Recreation,Education and Culture Articles	9.05	13.74	17.18	18.55	14.52	14.35	14.34	14.66
居　住	Residence	6.49	11.23	9.10	10.54	10.18	8.81	8.86	9.33
杂项商品和服务	Articles for Daily Use and Others	4.51	4.95	3.80	3.28	3.62	3.82	5.13	4.49
农村居民消费结构	Consumption Structure of Rural Residents								
食品消费支出	Food	50.31	36.63	36.34	36.80	38.15	36.95	35.81	32.54
衣　着	Clothing	8.39	6.65	6.11	6.45	6.09	6.52	6.40	6.55
居　住	Residence	5.92	21.41	17.76	18.03	22.72	19.39	19.47	24.41
家庭设备用品及服务	Household facilities,Articles and Services	5.17	5.47	5.11	5.64	5.66	7.02	6.97	6.53
医疗保健	Health Care	1.78	6.93	8.19	8.00	7.61	8.05	8.50	8.54
交通和通讯	Transportation and Communication	8.09	4.21	8.19	8.75	7.58	7.84	9.83	8.45
文化娱乐用品及服务	Recreation,Education and Culture Articles	18.53	14.49	16.15	14.31	10.44	12.43	11.13	11.20
其它商品及服务	Articles for Daily Use and Others	1.81	4.21	2.15	2.02	1.75	1.80	1.89	1.78
卫　生	**Health Care**								
卫生技术人员结构	Medical Technical Personnel by Types								
执业（助理）医师	Licensed（Assistant） Doctors	45.42	44.82	41.96	41.05	39.51	38.09	37.34	33.16
注册护士	Registered Nurses	32.68	34.29	33.14	35.42	35.09	36.23	39.05	40.01
药　师	Junior Paramedics	8.78	8.31	7.30	6.81	6.19	5.74	5.45	5.36
技　师	Technicians	5.21	5.21	5.33	5.11	6.97	6.68	6.49	8.11
其　他	Others	7.91	7.37	12.27	11.61	12.24	13.26	11.67	13.36

1-14 国民经济和社会发展比例和效益指标

指 标	Item	1995
人口与就业	**Population and Employment**	
人口	**Population**	
出生率(‰)	Birth Rate(‰)	11.95
死亡率(‰)	Death Rate(‰)	4.98
自然增长率(‰)	Natural Growth Rate(‰)	6.97
就业	**Employment**	
就业者负担人口	Dependency Ratio	1.7
三次产业就业者比例	Employment Ratio by Type of Industry	
(以第一产业为100)	(Employment in primary industry=100)	
第一产业	Primary Industry	100.0
第二产业	Secondary Industry	71.5
第三产业	Tertiary Industry	71.4
城镇登记失业率(%)	Unemployment Rate in Urban Areas(%)	3.1
宏观经济	**Macro Economy**	
国民核算	**National Accounting**	
三次产业增加值比例	Ratio of Value-added by Type of Industry	
(以第一产业为100)	(Employment in primary industry=100)	
第一产业	Primary Industry	100.0
第二产业	Secondary Industry	326.9
第三产业	Tertiary Industry	371.1
全社会劳动生产率(元/人)	Overall Labor Productivity(yuan/person)	8963
第一产业	Primary Industry	2698
第二产业	Secondary Industry	12404
第三产业	Tertiary Industry	14488
人均生产总值(元)	Per Capita GDP(yuan)	5131
固定资产投资	**Investment in Fixed Assets**	
全社会固定资产投资相当于生产总值比例(%)	Proportion of Investment in fixed Assets to GDP(%)	31.3
房屋建筑面积竣工率(%)	Rate of Floor Space of Buildings Completed in Construction(%)	33.4
固定资产交付使用率(%)	Rate of Fixed Assets Completed in Capital Construction and Put into Use(%)	70.7
建设项目建成投产率(%)	Rate of Projects Completed in Capital Construction and Put into Use(%)	43.7
财政	**Finance**	
地方财政总收入相当于生产总值比例(%)	Proportion of Local Government Revenue to GDP(%)	5.5
地方财政一般预算支出相当于生产总值比例(%)	Proportion of Local Government Expenditures to GDP(%)	5.6
利用外资	**Utilization of Foreign Capital**	
外商实际直接投资额相当于利用外资协议金额比例(%)	Proportion of Foreign Capital Actually Used to Total Amount of Foreign Capital for Utilization by Signed Contracts or Agreements (%)	64.42

注：本表财政收入数据2009年及以前为一般预算财政收入和基金收入之和。

Indicators on Proportions and Efficiency in National Economic and Social Development

2000	2003	2004	2005	2006	2007	2008	2009	2010
13.07	8.48	9.19	9.58	9.98	10.00	10.15	10.08	9.73
5.96	4.68	5.87	5.16	5.46	5.48	5.57	5.63	5.34
7.11	3.80	3.32	4.42	4.52	4.52	4.58	4.45	4.39
1.8	1.8	1.8	1.8	1.8	1.9	1.9	1.9	1.8
100.0	100.0	100.0	100.0	100.0	100.0	100.0	100.0	100.0
73.0	74.4	78.8	83.8	85.9	93.8	101.9	107.7	115.6
91.7	101.7	110.1	121.3	126.5	133.5	148.6	171.0	174.3
3.4	4.5	4.3	4.3	4.3	4.3	4.2	4.3	4.2
100.0	100.0	100.0	100.0	100.0	100.0	100.0	100.0	100.0
620.7	803.2	792.1	818.8	916.6	947.7	948.8	1037.1	1004.4
726.4	963.3	938.8	1071.7	1168.2	1202.5	1192.0	1330.8	1210.1
16367	23605	27069	31837	36730	43252	52422	59832	68965
2960	3501	4174	4747	5191	6148	7921	8830	11452
25443	36914	43199	47853	56073	64851	76899	87452	102992
24024	33502	37040	44024	48938	56870	67031	73674	80267
9484	13341	15294	16406	18890	22463	27794	32411	38343
36.0	50.5	58.7	65.8	72.4	81.4	82.2	91.8	100.3
42.0	33.8	24.4	28.1	26.1	29.0	16.9	16.0	6.9
74.0	62.7	42.8	52.8	46.6	49.8	40.5	42.8	38.4
44.2	39.9	41.5	54.2	47.0	40.6	53.3	72.5	53.9
7.3	7.7	7.8	6.6	6.5	7.1	10.9	12.2	15.8
8.0	8.2	8.1	8.1	9.1	9.9	14.5	15.4	11.5
28.88	26.52	35.24	47.01	45.18	77.49	97.05	203.03	130.9

Note:Figures of government revenue for 2009 and before are sum of general budgetary revenue and fund revenue.

1-14 续表1

指　　标	Item	1995
能　源	**Energy**	
单位生产总值能耗降低率（%）	Decreasing Rate of Energy Consumption per Unit GDP(%)	
规模以上工业单位增加值能耗降低率（%）	Decreasing Rate of Energy Consumption per Unit Industrial value-added Above Designated Size(%)	
单位生产总值电耗降低率（%）	Decreasing Rate of Electricity Consumption per Unit GDP(%)	
产　业	**Industries**	
农业	**Agriculture**	
人均耕地面积(公顷)	Per Capita Cultivated Land(hectare)	0.08
农业从业者人均耕地面积(公顷)	Cultivated Land per Agricultural Laborer(hectare)	0.20
每公顷耕地农业机械总动力(千瓦)	Total Power of Agricultural Machinery per Hectare of Cultivated Land(kw)	5.23
每公顷耕地化肥施用量(公斤)	Chemical Fertilizer Consumption per Hectare of Cultivated Land(kg)	536
每公顷耕地生产的农业产值(元)	Agricultural Output Value per Hectare of Cultivated Land(yuan)	24396
每个农林牧渔及服务业劳动力农产品生产量(公斤)	Output of Farm Products per Farming,Forestry,Animal Husbandry,Fishery and Service Husbandry and Fishery Laborer (kg)	
粮食	Grain	1150
蔬菜	Vegetables	877
禽蛋	Poultry Eggs	93
肉类	Meat	84
水产品	Aquatic Products	6
每公顷播种面积农产品产量(公斤)	Output of Farm Crops per Hectare of Sown Area(kg)	
粮食	Grain	3806
油料	Oil-bearing Crops	1753
蔬菜	Vegetables	34800
规模以上工业企业效益	Economic Benefit of Industrial Enterprises above Designated Size	
总资产贡献率（%）	Ratio of Total Assets to Industrial Output Value (%)	
资产负债率（%）	Assets-Liability Ratio (%)	
流动资产周转次数（次/年）	Rate of Annual Turnover Working Capitals(times/year)	
成本费用利润率（%）	Ratio of Profits to Cost (%)	
产品销售率（%）	Proportion of Industrial Products Sold(%)	
全员劳动生产率（元/人）	Overall Labor Productivity (yuan/person)	
建筑业	**Construction**	
机械装备率(元／人)	Value of Machinery per Laborer(yuan/person)	5990
产值利税率(%)	Ratio of Per-tax Profits to Gross Output Value (%)	3.5
全员劳动生产率(元／人)(按总产值计算)	Overall Labor Productivity(yuan/person) (in terms of gross output value per employee)	37689
邮电通信业	**Post and Communication Services**	
电话普及率(含移动电话）(部/百人)	Access to Telephones, National(include mobilphone) (set/100 persons)	7.9
移动电话普及率(部/百人)	Access to Mobilphones (set/100 persons)	0.48
国内商业	**Domestic Trade**	
人均批发零售和住宿餐饮业消费品零售额(元)	Per Capita Retail Sales of Wholesale,Retail Trade and Accommodation Catering Trade (yuan)	1979

continued 1

2000	2003	2004	2005	2006	2007	2008	2009	2010
				4.15	5.75	6.65	5.56	2.06
				3.04	12.56	13.43	10.48	12.18
				4.48	6.94	6.93	5.33	1.00
0.07	0.07	0.07	0.07	0.06	0.06	0.06	0.06	0.06
0.20	0.19	0.19	0.22	0.23	0.25	0.21	0.21	0.22
6.78	7.54	7.93	8.39	8.63	8.99	10.41	10.12	10.48
664	725	780	794	819	843	867	891	922
25161	30357	35862	39937	43261	51361	64593	69106	88869
1382	1213	1392	1493	1569	1433	1695	1792	1901
1110	1167	1287	1421	1536	1549	1752	1990	2171
95	89	84	86	92	74	86	96	106
101	114	122	132	145	77	91	104	117
8	7	7	7	7	9	10	11	10
4342	4182	4656	4796	5025	4452	5102	5206	5349
1526	1532	1758	1821	1880	1934	2008	1956	2004
37797	36657	35002	35231	35916	33677	35723	38344	39667
	7.0	6.9	8.4	7.8	10.2	8.6	11.3	12.2
65.0	61.3	65.2	65.0	64.3	64.6	62.6	61.1	57.6
4.2	5.7	5.0	3.1	5.5	7.3	4.6	8.1	8.8
1.0	1.1	1.2	1.3	1.4	1.6	1.5	1.7	1.6
97.1	96.3	97.9	97.5	98.2	96.8	96.1	97.6	97.1
29496	58801	66752	82815	97561	129706	150641	161289	188483
6805	9453	13240	13332	13502	9079	12026	11928	9461
3.4	4.1	4.4	4.8	4.5	5.2	6.0	6.3	4.4
74347	132981	163414	206337	241887	203994	226669	285854	321340
31.2	69.1	88.8	100.0	111.1	117.9	124.7	167.1	199.0
10.62	33.67	48.29	56.62	66.99	80.02	88.09	132.79	168
4027	6956	7859	8795	9437	10932	13840	16432	19363

1-14 续表2

指　　标	Item	1995
对外经济贸易	**Foreign Trade**	
进出口总额相当于生产总值比例(%)	Proportion of Total Imports & Exports to GDP(%)	34.76
国际旅游	**International Tourism**	
每一来华游客花费(元)	Expenditure per International Tourist in China(yuan)	2511
金融	**Finance and Insurance**	
金融机构存款相当于生产总值比例(%)	Bank Deposits as Percentage of GDP(%)	108.83
金融机构贷款相当于生产总值比例(%)	Bank Loans as Percentage of GDP(%)	101.26
金融机构现金支出相当于收入比例(%)	Proportion of Cash Outlay to Cash Receipt in Bank(%)	88.84
教育、科技、文化	**Education, Science and Technology and Culture**	
教育	**Education**	
学龄儿童入学率(%)	Rate of School-age Children Enrollment(%)	99.69
小学升学率(%)	Rate of Graduates of Primary Schools Entering Junior Secondary Schools(%)	94.85
初中升学率(%)	Rate of Graduates of Junior Secondary Schools Entering Senior Secondary Schools(%)	72.35
学校教师负担系数	Student-teacher Ratio(in percentage)	
高等学校	Colleges and Universities	6.83
中等学校	Secondary Schools	14.42
小学	Primary Schools	26.22
文化(个)	**Culture (unit)**	
每百万人有艺术表演团体	Number of Troupes per Million Persons	3.39
每百万人有公共图书馆	Number of Public Libraries per Million Persons	2.31
家庭、生活、环境	**Family, People's Livelihood and Environment**	
家庭	**Family**	
城市居民家庭	Urban Households	
平均每户就业面（%）	Percentage of Employees Per Household (%)	55.90
每一就业者负担人数(人)	Persons Supported by Each Laborer (person)	1.79
农村居民家庭	Rural Households	
平均每一劳动力负担人口（人）	Persons Supported by Each Laborer(person)	1.58
卫生	**Health Care**	
每千人医院数(个)	Number of Hospitals per 1000 Persons(unit)	0.06
每千人医生数(人)	Number of Doctors per 1000 Persons(person)	2.91
每千人医院床位数(张)	Number of Hospital Beds per 1000 Persons(unit)	4.36
市政建设	**City Construction**	
城市自来水普及率(%)	Percentage of Households with Access to Tap Water(%)	
城市用气普及率(%)	Percentage of Households with Access to Tap Gas (%)	
人均公园绿地面积(平方米)	Public Green Areas per 10 000 Persons(hectare)	3.80

continued 2

2000	2003	2004	2005	2006	2007	2008	2009	2010
22.25	20.19	23.29	24.79	22.01	22.21	21.97	18.17	21.20
3445	3584	4212	4324	4353	4242	4544	4614	5037
206.71	281.61	277.73	283.41	275.92	259.80	264.31	279.84	278.99
150.51	206.43	186.17	169.91	159.11	152.16	149.22	166.65	203.30
94.78	95.54	95.43	96.78	97.29	96.98	97.00	96.95	97.50
99.85	99.88	99.87	99.90	99.92	99.94	99.95	99.96	99.96
97.21	97.26	96.79	99.31	104.23	102.70	103.81	101.76	102.48
80.50	80.26	81.60	81.39	86.06	88.70	90.03	90.09	90.67
12.38	19.87	16.69	17.99	17.36	16.97	17.13	17.32	17.41
17.84	18.52	18.78	18.47	20.51	19.99	18.97	18.27	17.78
25.75	22.69	21.71	20.38	19.78	18.61	17.99	17.32	17.22
3.20	3.07	3.03	2.56	2.31	2.16	2.15	2.13	1.53
2.18	1.95	2.07	2.02	1.82	1.81	1.79	1.78	1.77
45.73	48.00	48.80	47.44	48.30	47.77	47.87	53.20	53.70
2.19	2.08	2.05	2.11	2.07	2.09	2.09	1.88	1.86
1.57	1.56	1.56	1.60	1.59	1.57	1.50	1.50	1.50
0.03	0.04	0.04	0.04	0.04	0.04	0.03	0.03	0.03
2.35	2.02	2.04	2.39	2.19	2.08	2.16	2.29	2.20
3.83	3.94	3.91	3.75	3.46	3.42	3.65	3.84	4.10
98.95	99.04	99.09	99.00	99.09	100.01	111.22	100.00	98.77
81.51	91.23	91.20	91.30	92.62	98.60	97.66	98.15	97.02
5.12	5.35	5.03	5.63	7.59	7.61	7.80	7.90	9.11

1-15 平均每天主要社会经济活动

指　　标	Item	1995	2000
一、每天创造的财富	**Daily Production**		
生产总值(万元)	Gross Domestic Product(10 000 yuan)	9050.7	17702.2
第一产业	Primary Industry	1134.3	1223.3
第二产业	Secondary Industry	3707.7	7592.6
工业	Industry	3082.2	5984.7
建筑业	Construction	625.5	1608.0
第三产业	Tertiary Industry	4208.8	8886.3
#交通运输、仓储及邮政业	Transport, Storage, Post & Telecommunication Services	674.0	1709.3
批发和零售贸易餐饮业	Wholesale and Retail Trade & Catering Services	909.6	2164.4
财政总收入(万元)	Total Government Revenue(10 000 yuan)	498.8	1304.0
财政一般预算支出(万元)	Government General Budgetary Expenditures(10 000 yuan)	504.7	1274.1
粮食(吨)	Grain(ton)	4801	5532
奶类(吨)	Milk(ton)	364	674
蔬菜(吨)	Vegetables(ton)	3660	4442
肉类(吨)	Meat(ton)	350	404
水产品(吨)	Aquatic Products(ton)	23	31
布(万米)	Cloth(10 000 m)	83.0	77.0
发电量(万千瓦小时)	Electricity(10 000 kwh)	610.0	534.0
钢材(吨)	Steel(ton)	861	274
汽车(辆)	Motor Vehicle(unit)	8	25
二、每天消费量	**Daily National Consumption**		
最终消费(万元)	Final Consumption Expenditure(10 000 yuan)	6565.5	11326.9
社会消费品零售总额(万元)	Total Retail Sales of Consumer Goods (10 000 yuan)	5112.3	9874.5
三、每天其他经济活动	**Other Daily Economic Activities**		
资本形成总额(万元)	Gross Capital Formation(10 000 yuan)	4152.1	7885.5
固定资本形成	Fixed Capital Formation		
存货增加	Changes in Stock		
竣工住宅面积(平方米)	Floor Space of Buildings Completed (sq.m)	6927	14930
货运量(万吨)	Freight Traffic(10 000 tons)	26.3	19.2
客运量(万人)	Passenger Traffic(10 000 persons)	24.8	22.1
邮电业务总量(万元)	Business Volume of Postal and Telecommunications Services(10 000 yuan)	209.6	1264.7
进出口总额(万美元)	Total Value of Imports and Exports (USD 10 000)	110.2	475.9
出口额	Exports	82.5	290.6
进口额	Imports	27.7	185.3
外商实际直接投资额(万美元)	Foreign Capital Actually Used(USD 10 000)	51.1	42.8
国际旅游人数(人次)	Number of Tourists from Abroad(person-time)	1133.8	1781.9
城乡居民储蓄额(万元)	Outstanding Amount of Savings Deposit (10 000 yuan)	1546.3	2450.3
四、每天人口变动和婚姻	**Daily Population Changes and Marriages**		
出　生(人)	Births(person)	211	247
死　亡(人)	Deaths(person)	88	113
结　婚(对)	Marriages(couple)	129	129
离　婚(对)	Divorces(couple)	12	14

注：本表财政收入数据2009年及以前为一般预算财政收入和基金收入之和。

Selected Indicators on Average Daily Social and Economic Activities

2005	2006	2007	2008	2009	2010
35998.1	42162.7	50866.6	63510.7	74632.3	88813.4
1808.5	1929.9	2260.6	2834.3	3024.1	3837.3
14808.2	17689.0	21423.0	26892.6	31363.0	38540.3
11506.9	13540.3	16300.0	19764.4	22381.4	27495.1
3301.4	4148.8	5123.0	7128.2	8981.6	11045.2
19381.4	22543.8	27183.0	33783.8	40245.2	46435.9
1816.4	2029.6	2307.1	2716.7	3030.1	3416.2
5414.8	5998.6	7276.7	9001.6	10605.5	12094.3
2300.6	2638.6	3433.6	6517.8	9080.0	13991.5
2819.6	3689.0	4771.4	8679.2	11509.0	10181.4
5631	5831	5180	5874	5978	6074
1157	1292	1447	1616	1694	1736
5362	5709	5601	6069	6641	6934
499	538	280	316	346	374
26	27	34	34	36	33
74.0	72.6	76.7	62.3	60.8	65.2
1316.3	1830.1	1946.3	1964.1	2279.7	2655.9
658	1960	2157	1312	3028	3035
112	282	468	734	1389	1787
21003.3	23861.1	27266.3	32400.3	38441.1	43794.8
18371.5	21505.5	25649.6	32235.1	37838.9	44850.4
22986.6	28637.5	39766.3	50352.3	62518.1	77682.7
20918.4	26404.9	34795.6	45315.3	58878.9	72237.8
2068.2	2232.6	4970.7	5037.0	3639.2	5444.9
16400	15975	25466	18998	22537	12287
33.0	32.4	41.4	75.5	83.9	94.0
28.7	30.8	34.2	72.6	78.6	83.0
3617.7	5116.7	6212.7	7256.4	8189.6	8852.3
1068.9	1138.1	1468.9	1928.9	1985.3	2847.3
721.8	747.6	951.0	1225.0	912.6	1456.8
347.1	390.5	517.9	703.9	1072.6	1390.5
156.5	225.9	305.7	314.4	333.9	429.2
2125.0	2376.1	2739.9	1731.5	1843.6	2306.3
47034.5	53439.1	54727.7	68614.0	84175.6	99318.4
210	223	226	232	232	225
63	122	124	127	130	124
137	184	185	213	241	229
35	35	43	43	43	52

Note: Figures of government revenue for 2009 and before are sum of general budgetary revenue and fund revenue.

1-16 各区县国民经济和社会发展主要指标（2010年）

指　　标	Item	新城区 Xincheng	碑林区 Beilin	莲湖区 Lianhu
一、年底总人口（常住人口）（万人）	Population at the Year-end Permanent population(10 000 persons)	59.01	61.62	69.86
二、生产总值(亿元)	Gross Domestic Product(100 mil. yuan)	326.02	358.90	376.99
第一产业	Primary Industry			
第二产业	Secondary Industry	132.45	85.08	174.84
工　业	Industry	81.77	33.42	126.29
第三产业	Tertiary Industry	193.57	273.82	202.15
三、全社会固定资产投资总额(亿元)	Total Investment in Fixed Assets(100 mil. yuan)	263.73	279.06	347.93
#城镇	Urban Area	263.73	279.06	347.93
#房地产	Real Estate	68.22	141.13	62.47
四、财政一般预算收入(亿元)	Local Financial Revenue(100 mil. yuan)	16.36	21.66	22.35
财政一般预算支出(亿元)	Local Financial Expenditure(100 mil. yuan)	12.61	13.30	15.20
五、农林牧渔及服务业总产值(亿元)	Gross Output Value of Farming Forestry, Animal Husbandry and Fishery(100 mil yuan)			
主要农产品产量(万吨)	Output of Major Farm Products(10 000 tons)			
粮　食	Grain			
蔬　菜	Vegetables			
水　果	Fruits			
肉　类	Meat			
奶　类	Milk			
六、规模以上工业总产值(亿元)	Gross industrial Output Value(100 mil. yuan)	272.13	108.14	458.30
七、建筑业总产值(亿元)	Gross Output Value(100 mil. yuan)	2072.91	2971.02	1491.04
房屋建筑施工面积 (万平方米)	Floor Space of Buildings under Construction (10 000 sq.m)	664.29	1644.51	828.95
房屋建筑竣工面积(万平方米)	Floor Space of Buildings Completed(10 000 sq.m)	151.72	490.12	166.26
八、社会消费品零售总额(亿元)	Total Retail Sales of Consumer Goods (100 mil. yuan)	285.04	285.18	234.58
九、城镇居民人均可支配收入(元)	Per Capita Annual Disposable Income of Urban Households (yuan)	22554	22998	22940
农村居民人均纯收入(元)	Per Capita Net Income of Rural Residents(yuan)			
十、医疗机构数(个)	Number of Health Care Institutions(unit)	300	327	337
卫生技术人员(人)	Number of Medical Technical Personnel（person）	10393	8575	7192
床位数(张)	Number of Beds(unit)	6422	5846	4740

Principal Indicators of National Economy and Social Development by Region（2010）

灞桥区 Baqiao	未央区 Weiyang	雁塔区 Yanta	阎良区 Yanliang	临潼区 Lintong	长安区 Chang'an	蓝田县 Lantian	周至县 Zhouzhi	户 县 Huxian	高陵县 Gaoling
59.56	80.72	117.98	27.87	65.60	108.48	51.42	56.29	55.65	33.35
170.94	403.89	600.38	100.15	150.61	273.24	70.18	53.16	105.78	149.10
11.50	2.48	2.13	14.26	25.58	24.50	16.64	15.27	15.59	12.12
97.54	218.78	211.34	50.33	79.15	136.07	26.33	13.88	58.56	119.88
83.91	156.63	105.00	41.56	72.12	110.92	17.44	10.62	50.61	110.79
61.90	182.63	386.91	35.56	45.88	112.67	27.21	24.01	31.63	17.10
162.90	438.59	810.20	117.83	108.45	302.26	68.29	67.28	109.64	174.41
154.70	426.14	808.17	108.10	98.02	275.67	46.30	40.69	86.34	170.07
22.27	134.34	332.13	5.66	3.76	58.31	2.02	1.83	3.12	7.09
10.02	14.46	20.37	4.95	4.59	13.22	1.54	1.02	3.39	5.20
10.50	12.83	13.08	9.00	15.41	24.46	13.26	14.27	13.23	10.04
17.83	4.08	3.01	21.42	41.11	38.22	28.68	26.27	26.03	20.44
7.28	2.68	0.06	9.60	40.10	41.49	33.53	28.86	37.15	20.90
27.82	5.55	4.22	52.53	36.82	51.25	14.86	15.68	25.88	18.49
8.56	1.58	1.19	5.31	6.41	6.53	11.80	29.84	8.57	5.00
0.69	0.36	0.31	0.50	3.68	1.78	1.56	2.47	1.69	0.61
6.36	2.45	0.13	7.53	33.91	2.02	3.61	1.29	3.37	2.69
242.15	499.88	286.19	163.55	222.01	334.89	31.93	11.11	96.89	402.98
195.35	4501.67	5892.21	161.68	78.13	234.01	94.56	37.43	98.74	374.71
56.67	386.65	277.70	80.12	93.31	183.82	65.21	18.22	120.38	172.75
28.26	77.07	224.93	32.02	63.73	58.47	47.55	10.95	53.37	163.47
38.30	232.17	316.17	19.28	40.30	91.07	29.60	19.79	32.34	13.22
22184	23517	21162	22927	18213	19557	14874	14877	16761	17377
9712	9863	8849	8969	7156	7389	5316	5238	6549	7106
304	142	375	70	92	157	72	67	83	59
3239	3793	10146	1511	1877	3491	1247	1611	2436	1068
2373	2585	7490	1323	1439	2413	1179	779	1962	856

主要统计指标解释

行政区划 指国家对行政区域的划分。根据宪法规定，我国的行政区域划分如下:⑴全国分为省、自治区、直辖市;⑵省、自治区分为自治州、县、自治县、市;⑶自治州分为县、自治县、市;⑷县、自治县分为乡、民族乡、镇;⑸直辖市和较大的市分为区、县;⑹国家在必要时设立的特别行政区。

自然资源 指人类可以直接从自然界获得，并用于生产和生活的物质资源。自然资源一般可以分成可再生资源和非再生资源两大类。可再生资源指在较短时间内可以再生、可以循环利用的资源，包括土地资源、水资源、气候资源、生物资源和海洋资源等。非再生资源指在使用后不能再生的资源，包括矿产资源和地热能源。

土地资源 土地指陆地的表层部分，它主要由岩石、岩石的风化物和土壤构成。土地资源按利用类型可以分为农用地、建筑用地和未利用地。农用地包括耕地、园地、林地、牧草地和水面。建筑用地包括居民点及工矿用地、交通用地和水利设施用地。未利用地指农用地和建筑用地以外的土地，包括滩涂、荒漠、戈壁、冰川和石山等。

耕地面积 指经过开垦用以种植农作物并经常进行耕耘的土地面积。包括种有作物的土地面积、休闲地、新开荒地和抛荒未满三年的土地面积。

林业用地面积 指生长乔木、竹类、灌木、沿海红树林等林木的土地面积，包括有林地、灌木林、疏林地、未成林造林地、迹地、苗圃等。

草地面积 指牧区和农区用于放牧牲畜或割草，植被盖度在5%以上的草原、草坡、草山等面积。包括天然的和人工种植或改良的草地面积。

水资源 水在自然界中以固体、液体和气态三种聚集状态存在，分布于海洋、陆地（包括土壤）以及大气之中，通过水循环形成水资源。水资源包括经人类控制并直接可供灌溉、发电、给水、航运、养殖等用途的地表水和地下水，以及江河、湖泊、井、泉、潮汐、港湾和养殖水域等。水资源是发展国民经济不可缺少的重要自然资源。

气温 指空气的温度，我国一般以摄氏度（℃）为单位表示。气象观测的温度表是放在离地面约1.5米处通风良好的百叶箱里测量的，因此，通常说的气温指的是离地面1.5米处百叶箱中的温度。其统计计算方法为:

月平均气温是将全月各日的平均气温相加，除以该月的天数而得。

年平均气温是将12个月的月平均气温累加后除以12而得。

降水量 指从天空降落到地面的液态或固态（经融化后）水，未经蒸发、渗透、流失而在地面上积聚的深度。其统计计算方法为:

月降水量是将全月各日的降水量累加而得。

年降水量是将12个月的月降水量累加而得。

日照时数 指太阳实际照射地面的时间。其统计方法与降水量相同。

现行价格 指计算各种总量指标所采用的价格，按报告期实际销售平均单价计算。

平均增长速度 我国计算平均增长速度有两种方法:一种是习惯上经常使用的"水平法"，又称几何平均法，是以间隔期最后一年的水平同基期水平对比来计算平均每年增长（或下降）速度;另一种是"累计法"，又称代数平均法或方程法，是以间隔期内各年水平的总和同基期水平对比来计算平均每年增长（或下降）速度。在一般正常情况下，两种方法计算的平均每年增长速度比较接近;但在经济发展不平衡、出现大起大落时，两种方法计算的结果差别较大。

法人单位 指依法成立，有自己的名称、组织机构和场所，能够独立承担民事责任；独立拥有和使用（或授权使用）资产，承担负债，有权与其他单位签定合同；会计上独立核算，能够编制资产负债表的单位。包括企业法人、事业单位法人、机关法人、社会团体法人和经法定程序批准设立的其他法人，包括民办非企业单位、基金会、居委会、村委会及其他组织机构。

产业活动单位 指在一个场所从事一种或主要从事一种社会经济活动，能够相对独立地组织生产经营或业务活动，并能够掌握收入等业务核算资料的单位。

企业（单位）登记注册类型 是以在工商行政管理机关登记注册的各类企业为划分对象，以工商行政管理部门对企业登记注册的类型为依据，将企业登记注册类型分为内资企业、港澳台商投资企业和外商投资企业三大类。内资企业包括国有企业、集体企业、股份合作企业、联营企业、有限责任公司、股份有限公司、私营公司和其他企业;港澳台商投资企业和外商投资企业分别包括合资经营企业、合作经营企业、独资经营企业和股份有限公司。对不在工商行政管理部门进行登记注册的行政机关、事业单位和社会团体，主要按其经费来源和管理方式进行划分。

国有企业 指企业全部资产归国家所有，并按《中华人民共和国企业法人登记管理条例》规定登记注册的非公司制的经济组织。不包括有限责任公司中的国有独资公司。

集体企业 指企业资产归集体所有，并按《中华人民共和国企业法人登记管理条例》规定登记注册的经济组织。

股份合作企业 指以合作制为基础，由企业职工共同出资入股，吸收一定比例的社会资产投资组建，实行自主经营，自负盈亏，共同劳动，民主管理，按劳分配与按股分红相结合的一种集体经济组织。

联营企业 指两个及两个以上相同或不同所有制性质的企业法人或事业单位法人，按自愿、平等、互利的原则，共同投资组成的经济组织。联营企业包括国有联营企业、集体联营企业、国有与集体联营企业和其他联营企业。

有限责任公司 指根据《中华人民共和国公司登记管理条例》规定登记注册，由两个以上、五十个以下的股东共同出资，每个股东以其所认缴的出资额对公司承担有限责任，公司以其全部资产对其债务承担责任的经济组织。有限责任公司包括国有独资公司以及其他有限责任公司。

股份有限公司 指根据《中华人民共和国公司登记管理条例》规定登记注册，其全部注册资本由等额股份构成并通过发行股票筹集资本，股东以其认购的股份对公司承担有限责任，公司以其全部资产对其债务承担责任的经济组织。

私营企业 指由自然人投资设立或由自然人控股，以雇佣劳动为基础的营利性经济组织。包括按照《公司法》、《合伙企业法》、《私营企业暂行条例》规定登记注册的私营有限责任公司、私营股份有限公司、私营合伙企业和私营独资企业。

其他企业 指上述企业之外的其他内资经济组织。

中外合资经营企业 指外国企业或外国人与中国内地企业依照《中华人民共和国中外合资经营企业法》及有关法律的规定，按合同规定的比例投资设立、分享利润和分担风险的企业。

中外合作经营企业 指外国企业或外国人与中国内地企业依照《中华人民共和国中外合作经营企业法》及有关法律的规定，依照合作合同的约定进行投资或提供条件设立、分配利润和分担风险的企业。

外资企业 指依照《中华人民共和国外资企业法》及有关法律的规定，在中国内地由外国投资者全额投资设立的企业。

外商投资股份有限公司 指根据国家有关规定，经外经贸部依法批准设立，其中外资的股本占公司注册资本的比例达25%以上的股份有限公司。凡其中外资股本占公司注册资本的比例小于25%的，属于内资企业中的股份有限公司。

Explanatory Notes on Main Statistical Indicators

Administrative Division refers to the division of administrative areas by the state. The Constitution of the People's Republic of China stipulates that the administrative areas in China are divided as: 1) The whole country is divided into provinces, autonomous regions and municipalities directly under the central government; 2) Provinces and autonomous regions are divided into autonomous prefectures, counties, autonomous counties and cities; 3) Autonomous prefectures are divided into counties, autonomous counties and cities; 4) Counties and autonomous counties are divided into townships, nationality townships and towns; 5) Municipalities and large cities are divided into districts and counties, 6) The state shall, when necessary, establish special administrative regions.

Natural Resources refer to material resources that could be obtained from the nature by human being and used for production and living. Natural resources in general can be classified as renewable resources and non-renewable resources. Renewable resources refer to resources that could be renewed and recycled during a relatively short period of time, including land resource, water resource, climate resource, biology resource and marine resource. Non-renewable resources include resources that could not be renewed, such as minerals and geothermal resource.

Land Resource Land refers to the surface of the earth, consisting of mainly rocks and its whethering and earth. Land resource can be classified, by its utilization, as land for agriculture, land for construction and unused land. Land for agriculture includes cultivated land, plantation land, forestland, grassland and waters. Land for construction includes land for residential purpose, for manufacturing and mining, for transportation and for water-conservancy projects. Unused land refers to land other than land for agriculture and construction, including beaches, deserts, Gobi, glaciers and rock mountains.

Area of Cultivated Land refers to area of land reclaimed for the regular cultivation of various farm crops, including crop-cover land, fallow, newly reclaimed land and land laid idle for less than 3 years.

Area of Afforested Land refer to land for trees bamboo, bushes and mangrove, including forest-cover land, bush-covered land, sparse forest land, land planned for afforestation and nurseries of young trees.

Area of Grassland refers to areas of grassland, grass-slopes and grass-covered hills with a vegetation-covering rate of over 5% that are used for animal husbandry or harvesting of grass. It includes natural, cultivated and improved grassland areas.

Water Resource Water exists in the nature in solid, liquid and gaseous states, is distributed in the ocean, land (including earth) and air, and constitutes the water resource through the circulation of water. Water resource includes the surface water and underground water that is controlled by the human being for irrigation, power-generation, water supply, navigation and cultivation. It also includes rivers, lakes, wells, springs, tides, gulf and water area for cultivation. Water resource as an important natural resource is indispensable for the development of the national economy.

Temperature refers to the air temperature. China uses centigrade as the unit. The thermometry used for weather observation is put in a breezy shutter, which is 1.5 meters high from the ground. Therefore, the commonly used temperature refers to the temperature in the breezy shutter 1.5 meters away from the ground. The calculation method is as follows:

Monthly average temperature is the summation of average daily temperature of one month divided by the actual days of that particular month.

Annual average temperature is the summation of monthly average of a year divided by 12 months.

Volume of Precipitation refers to the deepness of liquid state or solid state (thawed) water falling from the sky to the ground that has not been evaporated, infiltrated or run off. The calculation method is as follows:

Monthly precipitation is the summation of daily precipitation of a month.

Annual precipitation is the summation of 12 months precipitation of a year.

Sunshine Hours refer to the actual hours of sunirradiating the earth. The calculation method is the same as that of the precipitation.

Current Prices refer to prices that used to caculate kinds of tatol amount indexes on the average unit prices of effective sale in report period.

Average Annual Growth Rate Two methods for calculating average annual growth rate are applied in China, one is often called level approach, or the method of calculating geometric average, which is derived by comparing the level of the last year of the interval with

uneven economic development occurred with striking fluctuations in growth.

Impersonal entities refer to organizations that are established by law, have their own names, organizations and locations, and are able to independently bear civil liability; and that own and use (or authorize)their assets and undertake liabilities independently, and have the right to sign contracts with other units; and that account and compile the balance sheet independently. Impersonal entities include business entities, public institutions, official organ institutions and social organizations as legal persons and other entities established under the admission of legal procedure, including private non-enterprise units, foundations, neighborhood committees, village committees and other organizations.

Industrial active unit refer to that defined as a unit that engages in one or primarily one socio-economic activity at a certain place. It is able to organize productive and administrative activities independently, and to get hold of the accounting data of revenue and other business activities.

Registration Status of Enterprises Enterprises are classified into 3 categories, namely domestic-funded enterprises, enterprises with investment from Hong Kong, Macau and Taiwan, and enterprises with foreign investment, in the light of the registration status of an enterprise in industrial and commercial administration agencies. Domestic-funded enterprises include state-owned enterprises, collective-owned enterprises, cooperative enterprises, joint ownership enterprises, limited liability corporations, share-holding corporations Ltd., private enterprises and other enterprises. Included in the enterprises with investment from Hong Kong, Macau and Taiwan and enterprises with foreign investment are joint-venture enterprises, cooperative enterprises, sole investment enterprises and share-holding corporations Ltd. For government agencies, institutions and social organizations which are not requested to be registered in industrial and commercial administration agencies, they are classified mainly by their sources of funds and way of management.

State-owned Enterprises refer to non-corporationeconomic units where the entire assets are owned by the state and which have registered in accordance with the *Regulation of the Peoples Republic of China on the Management of Registration of Corporate Enterprises*. Excluded from this category are sole state-funded corporations in the limited liability corporations.

Collective-owned Enterprises refer to economic units where the assets are owned collectively and which have registered in accordance with the *Regulation of the Peoples Republic of China on the Management of Registration of Corporate Enterprises*.

Cooperative Enterprises refer to a form of collective economic units (enterprises) where capitals come mainly from employees as their shares, with certain proportion of capital from the outside, where production is organized on the basis of independent operation, independent accounting for profits and losses, joint work, democratic management, and a distribution system that integrates remuneration according to work with dividend according to capital share.

Joint Ownership Enterprises refer to economic units established by two or more corporate enterprises or corporate institutions of the same or different ownership, through joint investment on the basis of equality, voluntary participation and mutual benefits. They include state jointownership enterprises, collective joint ownership enterprises, joint state-collective enterprises, other joint ownership enterprises.

Limited Liability Corporations refer to economic units established with investment from 2-50investors and registered in accordance with the *Regulation of the Peoples Republic of China on the Management of Registration of Corporations*, each investor bearing limited liability to the corporation depending on its share of investment, and the corporation bearing liability to its debt to the maximum of its total assets. Limited liability corporations include exclusive state-funded limited liability corporations and other limited liability corporations.

Share-holding Corporations Ltd. refer to economic units registered in accordance with the*Regulation of the Peoples Republic of China on the Management of Registration of Corporations*, with total registered capitals divided into equal shares and raised through issuing stocks. Each investor bears limited liability to the corporation depending on the holding of shares, and the corporation bears liability to its debt to the maximum of its total assets.

Private Enterprises refer to profit-making economic units invested and established by natural persons, or controlled by natural persons using employed labour. Included in this category are private limited liability corporations, private share-holding corporations Ltd., private partnership enterprises and private-fundedenterprises registered in accordance with the *Corporation Law*, *Partnership Enterprises Law* and

Interim Regulations on Private Enterprises.

Other Domestic-funded Enterprises refer to domestic-funded economic units other than those mentioned above.

Joint-venture Enterprises with Foreign Investment refer to enterprises jointly established by foreign enterprises or foreigners with enterprises in the mainland of China in accordance with the *Law of the Peoples Republic of China on Sino-foreign Joint Venture Enterprises* and other relevant laws, where the share of investment, profits and risks is stipulated in the contract.

Cooperation Enterprises with Foreign Investment refer to enterprises jointly established by foreign enterprises or foreigners with enterprises in the mainland of China in accordance with the *Law of the Peoples Republic of China on Sino-foreign Cooperative Enterprises* and other relevant laws, where the investment or provision of facilities, and the share of profits and risks is stipulated in the cooperative contract.

Enterprises with Sole (exclusive) Foreign Investment refer to enterprises established in the mainland of China with exclusive investment from foreign investors in accordance with the *Law of the Peoples Republic of China on Foreign-Funded Enterprises* and other relevant laws.

Share-holding Corporations Ltd. with Foreign Investment refer to share-holding corporations Ltd. established with the approval from the Ministry of Foreign Trade and Economic Relations in line with relevant state regulations, where the share of investment from foreign investors exceeds 25% of the total registered capital of the corporation. In case the share of foreign investment is less than 25% of the total registered capital, the enterprise is to be classified as domestic-funded share-holding corporation Ltd.

2

国民经济核算

NATIONAL ECONOMIC ACCOUNTS

资料整理：连　鹏　马秋娟　吴　羽
Data management: Lian Peng Ma Qiujuan Wu Yu

第二部分 国民经济核算

一、简要说明

本章资料包括西安生产总值、构成和指数，分区县生产总值等。根据国家统计局的统一要求，为保持GDP数据的历史可比性，根据国家统计局和陕西省统计局《年度GDP历史数据修订办法》，对2005—2007年度GDP历史数据进行了修订；人均GDP按户籍人口计算，2005年以后按常住人口计算。资料由西安市统计局国民经济核算处提供。

二、主要指标

生产总值（亿元）	3241.69	比上年增长 14.5%
第一产业	140.06	比上年增长 6.9%
第二产业	1406.72	比上年增长 18.0%
第三产业	1694.91	比上年增长 12.5%
人均生产总值（元/人）	38343	比上年增长 13.8%

2 NATIONAL ECONOMIC ACCOUNTS

Ⅰ.Brief Introduction

The data in this chapter consists of composition and indices of the GDP in Xi'an and GDP by region, etc. According to the request of National Bureau of Statistic, in order to keep the history GDP data comparable, the GDP of 2005 - 2007 had been adjusted based on Adjusting Method of yearly GDP released by National Bureau of Statistic and Shaan'xi Provincial Bureau of Statistic. Per capital GDP had been calculated on register population, and after 2005 was calculated on permanent population. Data in this chapter is provided by National Economic Accounting Division of the Xi'an Bureau of Statistics.

Ⅱ.Major Indicators

		Increase over Preceding Year
Gross Domestic Product(100 mil. yuan)	3241.69	14.5%
Primary Industry	140.06	6.9%
Secondary Industry	1406.72	18.0%
Tertiary Industry	1694.91	12.5%
Per Capita Gross Domestic Product（yuan/person)	38343	13.8%

2-1 主要年份生产总值

Gross Domestic Product in Representative Years

（本表按当年价格计算） (Data in the table are calculated at current prices)

单位：亿元 (100 million yuan)

年 份 Year	生产总值 Gross Domestic Product	第一产业 Primary Industry	第二产业 Secondary Industry	第三产业 Tertiary Industry	人均GDP（元/人） Per Capita Gross Domestic Product （yuan/person)
1952	3.37	1.59	0.88	0.90	135
1965	12.76	2.62	7.22	2.92	323
1970	17.76	3.13	10.96	3.67	412
1975	21.33	4.14	12.63	4.56	448
1978	25.35	4.83	14.59	5.93	513
1980	31.66	4.73	18.69	8.24	623
1983	35.89	5.22	20.14	10.53	674
1984	44.14	7.45	24.17	12.52	817
1985	57.58	8.76	30.83	17.99	1049
1986	65.78	9.59	33.86	22.33	1178
1987	80.16	10.73	37.69	31.74	1409
1988	99.22	11.47	46.58	41.17	1711
1989	109.38	12.78	48.91	47.69	1861
1990	116.51	13.94	50.15	52.42	1932
1991	136.14	17.17	57.06	61.91	2224
1992	164.85	18.78	69.22	76.85	2662
1993	229.56	22.58	110.88	96.10	3661
1994	289.82	31.68	128.27	129.87	4563
1995	330.35	41.40	135.33	153.62	5131
1996	406.95	46.94	161.63	198.38	6246
1997	488.82	51.33	197.97	239.52	7424
1998	525.85	51.91	216.32	257.62	7906
1999	577.29	45.53	243.35	288.41	8599
2000	646.13	44.65	277.13	324.35	9484
2001	734.86	45.87	312.90	376.09	10628
2002	826.68	47.77	353.58	425.33	11831
2003	946.66	50.72	407.38	488.56	13341
2004	1102.39	60.21	476.92	565.26	15294
2005	1313.93	66.01	540.50	707.42	16406
2006	1538.94	70.44	645.65	822.85	18890
2007	1856.63	82.51	781.94	992.18	22463
2008	2318.14	103.45	981.58	1233.11	27794
2009	2724.08	110.38	1144.75	1468.95	32411
2010	3241.69	140.06	1406.72	1694.91	38343

注：2005年以后人均GDP按平均常住人口计算。根据全国第二次经济普查结果，对2005-2007年生产总值及人均GDP进行了修订。

Note:Per capital GDP after 2005 was calculated on permanent population,according to the second national census,we made adjustments to the GDP , the value-added of the primary industry and per capital local GDP of 2005-2007.

2-2 主要年份生产总值指数（上年=100）

Indices of Gross Domestic Product in Representative Years(preceding year = 100)

（本表按可比价格计算） (Data in the table are calculated at constant prices)

年 份	Year	生产总值 Gross Domestic Product	第一产业 Primary Industry	第二产业 Secondary Industry	第三产业 Tertiary Industry	人均生产总值 Per Capita Gross Domestic Product
1952		103.6	92.2	137.5	123.7	
1965		126.1	134.1	133.0	106.7	
1970		122.0	109.4	140.0	100.1	
1975		103.8	92.6	107.1	107.5	
1978		101.7	101.6	99.4	108.2	
1980		111.5	83.3	119.7	116.5	
1985		112.6	107.5	111.8	116.9	
1986		111.4	107.7	108.4	118.8	
1987		113.6	100.8	109.1	126.6	
1988		111.4	81.2	115.5	114.7	
1989		106.7	103.0	104.5	110.8	
1990		105.2	103.0	102.5	109.6	
1991		109.8	118.6	108.6	108.6	108.2
1992		115.6	109.4	118.1	115.0	114.3
1993		123.9	112.5	142.7	108.4	122.3
1994		110.3	98.4	110.6	113.2	108.8
1995		110.0	104.5	112.1	108.6	108.5
1996		114.9	106.8	118.8	111.7	113.5
1997		114.4	109.1	116.7	112.4	113.2
1998		113.3	106.5	117.5	108.8	112.1
1999		112.2	97.4	115.7	110.1	111.2
2000		113.0	103.5	115.1	111.5	111.4
2001		113.1	102.5	115.3	112.6	111.4
2002		113.3	103.1	115.0	113.0	112.1
2003		113.5	101.8	117.5	111.2	111.7
2004		113.5	106.7	115.9	112.0	111.7
2005		114.0	107.5	112.3	116.3	112.2
2006		114.0	107.1	113.7	114.9	112.9
2007		115.6	104.5	115.7	116.4	113.9
2008		116.3	107.6	116.4	116.9	115.3
2009		114.5	106.3	114.0	115.5	113.7
2010		114.5	106.9	118.0	112.5	113.8
平均每年增长	**Yearly Average Growth Rates**					
"一五"时期	**The First Five-Year Plan Period**	**15.8**	**5.9**	**37.7**	**16.9**	
"二五"时期	**The Second Five-Year Plan Period**	**2.0**	**-3.7**	**2.4**	**8.4**	
1963--1965年	**Readjust Period**	**14.2**	**16.2**	**23.3**	**0.3**	
"三五"时期	**The Third Five-Year Plan Period**	**7.1**	**0.1**	**11.7**	**5.4**	
"四五"时期	**The Fourth Five-Year Plan Period**	**5.0**	**4.0**	**5.3**	**5.0**	
"五五"时期	**The Fifth Five-Year Plan Period**	**6.0**	**-0.7**	**6.5**	**10.1**	
"六五"时期	**The Sixth Five-Year Plan Period**	**10.7**	**7.9**	**10.4**	**12.9**	
"七五"时期	**The Seventh Five-Year Plan Period**	**9.6**	**-1.3**	**7.9**	**16.0**	
"八五"时期	**The Eighth Five-Year Plan Period**	**13.8**	**8.5**	**17.8**	**10.7**	**12.3**
"九五"时期	**The Ninth Five-Year Plan Period**	**13.5**	**4.6**	**16.8**	**10.9**	**12.3**
"十五"时期	**The Tenth Five-Year Plan Period**	**13.5**	**4.3**	**15.2**	**13.0**	**11.8**
"十一五"时期	**The Eleventh Five-Year Plan Period**	**15.0**	**6.5**	**15.5**	**15.2**	**13.9**

注：根据全国第二次经济普查结果，对2005-2007年生产总值指数进行了修订。

Note:according to the second national census,we made the Indices to the GDP , the value-added of the primary industry and per capital local GDP of 2005-2007.

2-3 主要年份生产总值指数（1952年=100）

Indices of Gross Domestic Product in Representative Years(1952=100)

（本表按可比价格计算） (Data in the table are calculated at constant prices)

年份 Year	生产总值 Gross Domestic Product	第一产业 Primary Industry	第二产业 Secondary Industry	第三产业 Tertiary Industry
1952	100.0	100.0	100.0	100.0
1965	341.6	173.3	1048.3	329.2
1970	481.6	174.3	1821.0	428.6
1975	614.2	211.9	2362.5	547.9
1978	678.7	231.3	2560.8	643.8
1980	821.4	204.2	3237.2	885.2
1985	1366.8	299.1	5310.6	1632.4
1986	1523.1	322.3	5756.7	1928.9
1987	1730.0	324.9	6280.6	2441.6
1988	1926.3	263.7	7256.6	2801.2
1989	2054.8	271.6	7583.1	3104.6
1990	2162.5	279.7	7772.7	3403.6
1991	2374.4	331.7	8441.2	3696.3
1992	2744.8	362.9	9969.1	4250.7
1993	3400.8	408.2	14225.9	4607.8
1994	3751.1	401.8	15733.8	5216.0
1995	4126.2	419.9	17637.6	5664.6
1996	4741.0	448.5	20953.5	6327.4
1997	5423.7	489.3	24452.7	7112.0
1998	6145.1	521.1	28731.9	7737.9
1999	6894.8	507.6	33242.8	8519.4
2000	7791.1	525.4	38262.5	9499.1
2001	8811.7	538.5	44116.7	10696.0
2002	9983.7	555.2	50734.2	12086.5
2003	11331.5	265.2	59612.7	13440.2
2004	12861.3	603.1	69091.1	15053.0
2005	14661.9	648.3	77589.3	17506.6
2006	16714.6	694.3	88219.0	20115.1
2007	19322.1	725.5	102069.4	23414.0
2008	22471.6	780.6	118808.8	27371.0
2009	25730.0	829.8	135442.0	31613.5
2010	29460.9	950.1	155081.1	36197.5

2-4 主要年份生产总值构成

Composition of Gross Domestic Product in Representative Years

（本表按当年价格计算） (Data in the table are calculated at current prices)

单位：% (%)

年 份	Year	生产总值 Gross Domestic Product	第一产业 Primary Industry	第二产业 Secondary Industry	第三产业 Tertiary Industry
1952		100	47.18	26.11	26.71
1965		100	20.53	56.58	22.89
1970		100	17.62	61.71	20.67
1975		100	19.41	59.21	21.38
1978		100	19.05	57.55	23.40
1980		100	14.94	59.03	26.03
1985		100	15.22	53.54	31.24
1986		100	14.58	51.47	33.95
1987		100	13.38	47.02	39.60
1988		100	11.56	46.95	41.49
1989		100	11.68	44.72	43.60
1990		100	11.96	43.05	44.99
1991		100	12.61	41.91	45.48
1992		100	11.39	41.99	46.62
1993		100	9.84	48.30	41.86
1994		100	10.93	44.26	44.81
1995		100	12.53	40.97	46.50
1996		100	11.53	39.72	48.75
1997		100	10.50	40.50	49.00
1998		100	9.87	41.14	48.99
1999		100	7.89	42.15	49.96
2000		100	6.91	42.89	50.20
2001		100	6.24	42.58	51.18
2002		100	5.78	42.77	51.45
2003		100	5.36	43.03	51.61
2004		100	5.46	43.26	51.28
2005		100	5.02	41.14	53.84
2006		100	4.58	41.95	53.47
2007		100	4.44	42.12	53.44
2008		100	4.46	42.34	53.20
2009		100	4.05	42.02	53.93
2010		100	4.32	43.39	52.29
"一五"时期	**The First Five-Year Plan Period**	**100**	**32.88**	**43.92**	**23.20**
"二五"时期	**The Second Five-Year Plan Period**	**100**	**18.08**	**58.63**	**23.29**
1963-1965年	**Readjust Period**	**100**	**19.36**	**55.37**	**25.27**
"三五"时期	**The Third Five-Year Plan Period**	**100**	**18.60**	**57.33**	**24.07**
"四五"时期	**The Fourth Five-Year Plan Period**	**100**	**20.46**	**59.59**	**19.95**
"五五"时期	**The Fifth Five-Year Plan Period**	**100**	**18.40**	**57.69**	**23.91**
"六五"时期	**The Sixth Five-Year Plan Period**	**100**	**16.03**	**55.01**	**28.96**
"七五"时期	**The Seventh Five-Year Plan Period**	**100**	**12.42**	**46.11**	**41.47**
"八五"时期	**The Eighth Five-Year Plan Period**	**100**	**11.44**	**43.52**	**45.04**
"九五"时期	**The Ninth Five-Year Plan Period**	**100**	**9.09**	**41.45**	**49.46**
"十五"时期	**The Tenth Five-Year Plan Period**	**100**	**5.49**	**42.47**	**52.04**
"十一五"时期	**The Eleventh Five-Year Plan Period**	**100**	**4.34**	**42.47**	**53.19**

2-5 全市各区县生产总值（2010年）

Gross Domestic Product by Region（2010）

单位：亿元 (100 million yuan)

区县名称	Name of District and County	生产总值 Gross Domestic Product	第一产业 Primary Industry	第二产业 Secondary Industry	工业 Industry	第三产业 Tertiary Industry
新城区	Xincheng	326.02		132.45	81.77	193.57
碑林区	Beilin	358.90		85.08	33.42	273.82
莲湖区	Lianhu	376.99		174.84	126.29	202.15
灞桥区	Baqiao	170.94	11.50	97.54	83.91	61.90
未央区	Weiyang	403.89	2.48	218.78	156.63	182.63
雁塔区	Yanta	600.38	2.13	211.34	105.00	386.91
阎良区	Yanliang	100.15	14.26	50.33	41.56	35.56
临潼区	Lintong	150.61	25.58	79.15	72.12	45.88
长安区	Chang'an	273.24	24.50	136.07	110.92	112.67
蓝田县	Lantian	70.18	16.64	26.33	17.44	27.21
周至县	Zhouzhi	53.16	15.27	13.88	10.62	24.01
户 县	Huxian	105.78	15.59	58.56	50.61	31.63
高陵县	Gaoling	149.10	12.12	119.88	110.79	17.10

2-6 全市各区县生产总值指数（2010年）（上年=100）

Indices of Gross Domestic Product by Region（2010）（preceding year = 100）

区县名称	Name of District and County	生产总值 Gross Domestic Product	第一产业 Primary Industry	第二产业 Secondary Industry	工业 Industry	第三产业 Tertiary Industry
新城区	Xincheng	114.3		117.9	117.8	112.2
碑林区	Beilin	114.5		118.1	117.1	113.7
莲湖区	Lianhu	114.5		118.3	117.8	111.3
灞桥区	Baqiao	116.1	107.3	118.6	118.1	114.0
未央区	Weiyang	115.0	96.8	116.2	115.0	113.9
雁塔区	Yanta	114.3	95.4	116.1	115.1	113.4
阎良区	Yanliang	115.8	107.6	119.2	119.7	113.6
临潼区	Lintong	114.5	106.9	119.0	119.1	111.1
长安区	Chang'an	116.1	107.5	119.2	119.4	114.8
蓝田县	Lantian	112.8	106.8	116.0	118.0	112.5
周至县	Zhouzhi	110.3	108.0	109.9	109.0	111.7
户　县	Huxian	112.5	107.3	114.6	115.5	111.1
高陵县	Gaoling	125.1	107.7	129.2	130.0	112.2

2–7 全市各区县生产总值构成（2010年）

Composition of Gross Domestic Product by Region（2010）

单位：% (%)

区县名称	Name of District and County	生产总值 Gross Domestic Product	第一产业 Primary Industry	第二产业 Secondary Industry	第三产业 Tertiary Industry
新城区	Xincheng	100.0		40.6	59.4
碑林区	Beilin	100.0		23.7	76.3
莲湖区	Lianhu	100.0		46.4	53.6
灞桥区	Baqiao	100.0	6.7	57.1	36.2
未央区	Weiyang	100.0	0.6	54.2	45.2
雁塔区	Yanta	100.0	0.4	35.2	64.4
阎良区	Yanliang	100.0	14.2	50.3	35.5
临潼区	Lintong	100.0	17.0	52.6	30.4
长安区	Chang'an	100.0	9.0	49.8	41.2
蓝田县	Lantian	100.0	23.7	37.5	38.8
周至县	Zhouzhi	100.0	28.7	26.1	45.2
户　县	Huxian	100.0	14.7	55.4	29.9
高陵县	Gaoling	100.0	8.1	80.4	11.5

2-8 主要年份分行业增加值

Value-added by Sector in Representative Years

单位：亿元 (100 million yuan)

指 标	Item	2004	2005	2006	2007	2008	2009	2010
生产总值	**Gross Domestic Product**	**1102.39**	**1313.93**	**1538.94**	**1856.63**	**2318.14**	**2724.08**	3241.69
第一产业	Primary Industry	60.21	66.01	70.44	82.51	103.45	110.38	140.06
第二产业	Secondary Industry	476.92	540.50	645.65	781.94	981.58	1144.75	1406.72
工业	Industry	383.46	420.00	494.22	594.95	721.40	816.92	1003.57
建筑业	Construction	93.46	120.50	151.43	186.99	260.18	327.83	403.15
第三产业	Tertiary Industry	565.26	707.42	822.85	992.18	1233.11	1468.95	1694.91
交通运输、仓储及邮政业	Transportation,Storage,Post and Telecommunications	55.10	66.30	74.08	84.21	99.16	110.60	124.69
批发和零售业	Wholesale and Retail Trades	125.12	147.20	166.72	195.51	242.91	293.05	337.85
住宿和餐饮业	Accommodation and Catering Trade	35.89	50.44	52.23	70.09	85.65	94.05	103.58
金融保险业	Banking and Insurance	61.49	75.00	96.50	128.50	160.84	198.47	226.42
房地产业	Real Estate	39.05	52.48	62.32	75.26	92.97	124.98	158.86
其他服务业	Others Services	248.61	316.00	371.00	438.61	551.58	647.80	743.51

2-9 主要年份分行业增加值指数（上年=100）

Indices of Value -added by Sector in Representative Years(preceding year=100)

（本表按可比价格计算） (Data in the table are calculated at constant prices)

指 标	Item	2005	2006	2007	2008	2009	2010
生产总值	**Gross Domestic Product**	**114.0**	**114.0**	**115.6**	**116.3**	**114.5**	114.5
第一产业	Primary Industry	107.5	107.1	104.5	107.6	106.3	106.9
第二产业	Secondary Industry	112.3	113.7	115.7	116.4	114.0	118.0
工业	Industry	110.3	112.3	114.9	115.7	111.7	118.1
建筑业	Construction	120.0	118.7	118.4	118.9	121.2	117.6
第三产业	Tertiary Industry	116.3	114.9	116.4	116.9	115.5	112.5
交通运输、仓储及邮政业	Transportation,Storage,Post and Telecommunications	113.2	112.3	110.3	108.4	105.0	111.5
批发和零售业	Wholesale and Retail Trades	112.7	112.5	112.9	115.0	119.7	112.3
住宿和餐饮业	Hotels and Catering Services	136.1	116.6	117.3	111.6	106.6	107.2
金融保险业	Banking and Insurance	109.3	107.3	126.7	113.6	121.4	110.7
房地产业	Real Estate	112.9	117.5	119.7	107.6	131.6	118.6
其他服务业	Others Services	117.7	117.7	116.3	122.5	113.2	112.7

2-10 主要年份支出法生产总值

Gross Domestic Product by Expenditure Approach in Representative Years

（本表按当年价格计算） (Data in the table are calculated at current prices)

单位：亿元 (100 million yuan)

年 份 Year	生产总值 Gross Domestic Product	最终消费支出 Final Consumption Expenditures	资本形成总额 Total Investment	货物和服务净出口 Net Export of Goods and Services
1992	164.85	148.09	68.61	-51.85
1993	229.56	172.60	113.48	-56.52
1994	289.82	200.88	131.97	-43.03
1995	330.35	239.64	151.55	-60.84
1996	406.95	272.46	170.35	-35.86
1997	488.82	317.61	182.30	-11.09
1998	525.85	343.15	200.96	-18.26
1999	577.29	377.89	257.65	-58.25
2000	646.13	413.43	287.82	-55.12
2001	734.86	456.78	328.59	-50.51
2002	826.68	505.57	385.45	-64.34
2003	946.66	541.73	507.87	-102.94
2004	1102.39	689.24	649.93	-236.78
2005	1313.93	766.62	839.01	-291.70
2006	1538.94	870.93	1045.27	-377.26
2007	1856.63	995.22	1451.47	-590.06
2008	2318.14	1182.61	1837.86	-702.33
2009	2724.08	1403.10	2281.91	-960.93
2010	3241.69	1598.51	2835.42	-1192.24

2-11 主要年份支出法生产总值指数（上年=100）

Indices of Gross Domestic Product by Expenditure Approach in Representative Years（preceding year = 100）

年 份 Year	生产总值 Gross Domestic Product	最终消费 Final Consumption Expenditures	资本形成总额 Total Investment
1992	115.6	114.4	116.0
1993	123.9	103.1	124.9
1994	110.3	104.9	116.4
1995	110.0	110.0	114.6
1996	114.9	102.1	105.8
1997	114.4	108.2	106.6
1998	113.3	114.9	108.1
1999	112.2	114.8	123.6
2000	113.0	109.9	116.2
2001	113.1	108.5	111.2
2002	113.3	109.7	117.1
2003	113.5	108.8	129.6
2004	113.5	109.8	123.7
2005	114.0	107.7	127.0
2006	114.0	109.4	120.1
2007	115.6	109.5	135.2
2008	116.3	116.9	120.2
2009	114.5	118.4	122.6
2010	114.5	110.5	118.7

2-12 按支出法计算的生产总值及指数（2010年）

Gross Domestic Product and Indices by Expenditure Approach（2010）

单位：亿元 (100 million yuan)

指 标	Item	2010	指数（以上年为100） Indices (preceding year=100)
生产总值	**Gross Domestic Product**	**3241.69**	**114.5**
（一）最终消费支出	Final Consumption Expenditures	1598.51	110.5
1.居民消费支出	Resident Consumption Expenditures	1185.94	113.0
农村居民	Village Residents	152.93	107.7
城镇居民	Urban Residents	1033.01	113.8
2.政府消费支出	Government Consumption Expenditures	412.57	103.8
（二）资本形成总额	Gross Total Capital Formation	2835.42	118.7
1.固定资本形成总额	Fixed Capital	2636.68	117.1
2.存货增加	Change of Goods in Stock	198.74	143.8
（三）货物和服务净出口	Net Export of Goods and Services	-1192.24	117.9

2-13 分行业资本形成总额（2010年）

Gross Capital Formation by Sector （2010）

单位：亿元 (100 million yuan)

指 标	Item	2010
资本形成总额	**Total Investment**	**2835.42**
一、固定资本形成总额	**Gross Fixed Capital Formation**	**2636.68**
1.住宅	Residential Buildings	948.07
2.非住宅建筑物	Non-residential Buildings	1302.53
3.机器和设备	Machinery and Equipment	195.56
4.土地改良支出	Land Reform Expenditure	2.49
5.矿藏勘探费	Cost of Mineral Deposits Prospecting	0.24
6.计算机软件	Computer Softwares	59.38
7、其他	Others	128.41
二、存货增加	**Change of Goods in Stock**	**198.74**
1.农林牧渔业	Agriculture, Forestry, Animal Husbandry and Fishery	1.45
2.工业	Industry	90.85
3.建筑业	Construction	22.07
4.交通运输、仓储及邮政业	Transportation, Storage and Post	2.66
5.批发和零售业	Wholesale and Retail Trades	18.47
6.住宿和餐饮业	Hotels and Catering Services	0.22
7.房地产	Real Estate	61.42
8.其他	Others	1.60

2-14 最 终 消 费 支 出（2010年）

Final Consumption Expenditures（2010）

单位：亿元　　(100 million yuan)

指　　标	Item	2010
最终消费支出	**Final Consumption Expenditures**	**1598.51**
一、居民消费支出	**Resident Consumption Expenditures**	**1185.94**
（一）农村居民	Rural Residents	152.93
1.食品类支出	Food Expenditures	48.16
2.衣着类支出	Clothing Expenditures	9.70
3.居住类支出	Residence Expenditures	15.55
4.家庭设备、用品及服务类支出	Household Facilities、Articles and Services Expenditures	9.68
5.医疗保健类支出	Medical Care Expenditures	14.59
6.交通和通信类支出	Transportion and Communication Expenditures	12.49
7.文教娱乐用品及服务类支出	Culture、Education and Entertainment Expenditures	16.59
8.银行中介服务支出	Indirect Calculated Expenditures of Financial Intermediation Services	6.72
9.保险服务消费支出	Insurance Services Consumption Expenditures	0.36
10.自有住房服务虚拟类支出	Virtual Expenditures of Private Housing Services	16.47
11.其它商品和服务类支出	Other goods and services Expenditures	2.62
（二）城镇居民	Urban Residents	1033.01
1.食品类支出	Food Expenditures	301.82
2.衣着类支出	Clothing Expenditures	107.13
3.居住类支出	Residence Expenditures	95.78
4.家庭设备、用品及服务类支出	Household Facilities、Articles and Services Expenditures	75.85
5.医疗保健类支出	Medical Care Expenditures	98.76
6.交通和通信类支出	Transportion and Communication Expenditures	116.33
7.文教娱乐用品及服务类支出	Culture、Education and Entertainment Expenditures	141.36
8.银行中介服务支出	Indirect Calculated Expenditures of Financial Intermediation Services	28.18
9.保险服务消费支出	Insurance Services Consumption Expenditures	3.53
10.自有住房服务虚拟类支出	Virtual Expenditures of Private Housing Services	22.92
11.实物收入消费支出	Physical goods Consumption Expenditures	6.74
12.其它商品和服务类支出	Other goods and services Expenditures	34.61
二、政府消费支出	**Government Consumption Expenditures**	**412.57**

2-15 居民总消费水平（2010年）

Consumption of Residents （2010）

指　　标	Item	2010	指数（%）(上年=100) Indices (preceding year=100)
一、按当年价格计算 (元/人)	**Calculated at Current Prices (yuan/person)**		
全体居民消费水平	Per Capita Consumption of All Residents	14027	115.9
农村居民	Farmer	5829	114.6
城镇居民	Non-Farmer	17717	115.2
二、按可比价格计算 (元/人)	**Calculated at Comparable Prices (yuan/person)**		
全体居民消费水平	Per Capita Consumption of All Residents	12420	112.3
农村居民	Farmer	4989	109.7
城镇居民	Non-Farmer	15763	111.8
三、常住居民年平均人口(万人)	**Average Annual Population of Residents (10 000 persons)**	**845.44**	**100.6**

2-16 非公有制经济增加值（2010年）

The Added Value of Non-public-owned Economic （2010）

单位：亿元　　(100 million yuan)

产　业	Industry	生产总值 Gross Domestic Product	非公有制经济增加值 the Added Value of Non-public-owned Economic	非公有制经济增加值占GDP比重(%) the Added Value of Non-public-owned Economic Percentage to GDP
总　计	**Gross Domestic Product**	**3241.69**	**1611.28**	**49.70**
第一产业	Primary Industry	140.06	42.66	30.46
第二产业	Secondary Industry	1406.72	665.90	47.34
第三产业	Tertiary Industry	1694.91	902.72	53.26

2-17 五大主导产业增加值

Value-added of the Five Leading Industries

单位：亿元 (100 million yuan)

产业 Industries	五大主导产业增加值（剔除重复） Value-added of Five Leading Industries	高新技术产业增加值 High-Tech Industry	装备制造业增加值 Manufacture of Equipment	旅游业增加值 Tourism	文化产业增加值 Culture Industry	现代服务业增加值 Modern Services
2004	429.37	78.70	154.28	83.14	46.01	209.23
2005	536.08	100.46	179.88	99.90	60.46	272.51
2006	654.05	119.37	218.10	120.37	77.93	332.65
2007	839.20	142.45	280.12	148.53	99.98	416.26
2008	1084.89	199.23	344.61	189.86	127.44	734.95
2009	1324.33	296.68	392.27	226.82	151.02	881.20
2010	1622.99	361.92	485.53	275.35	184.03	1056.73

注：五大主导产业增加值为剔除产业间重复计算部分；

各产业增加值为包含产业间重复计算部分。

Note: 'Value-added of Five Leading Industries' excludes the overlaps between different industries.

Value-added of each industry includes the overlaps.

2-18 五大主导产业增加值比重

Proportions of Value-added of the Five Leading Industries

单位：% (%)

产业 Industries	五大主导产业增加值（剔除重复） Value-added of Five Leading Industries	高新技术产业增加值 High-Tech Industry	装备制造业增加值 Manufacture of Equipment	旅游业增加值 Tourism	文化产业增加值 Culture Industry	现代服务业增加值 Modern Services
2004	38.9	7.1	14.0	7.5	4.2	19.0
2005	40.8	7.6	13.7	7.6	4.6	20.7
2006	42.5	7.8	14.2	7.8	5.1	21.6
2007	45.2	7.7	15.1	8.0	5.4	22.4
2008	46.8	8.6	14.9	8.2	5.5	31.7
2009	48.6	10.9	14.4	8.3	5.5	32.3
2010	50.1	11.2	15.0	8.5	5.7	32.6

注：五大主导产业增加值为剔除产业间重复计算部分，各产业增加值为包含产业间重复计算部分。根据全国第二次经济普查结果，对2005-2008年各产业增加值数据进行了修订。

Note: 'Value-added of Five Leading Industries' excludes the overlaps between different industries,Value-added of each industry includes the overlaps.According to the second national census,Data of value-added of each industry from 2005 to 2008 was revided.

主要统计指标解释

生产总值（GDP）是按市场价格计算的一个地区（或国家）所有常住单位在一定时期内生产活动的最终成果。生产总值有三种表现形态，即价值形态、收入形态和产品形态。从价值形态看，它是所有常住单位在一定时期内生产的全部货物和服务价值超过同期中间投入的全部非固定资产货物和服务价值的差额，即所有常住单位的增加值之和;从收入形态看，它是所有常住单位在一定时期内创造并分配给常住单位和非常住单位的初次收入分配之和;从产品形态看，它是所有常住单位在一定时期内最终使用的货物和服务价值与货物和服务净出口价值之和。在实际核算中，生产总值有三种计算方法，即生产法、收入法和支出法。三种方法分别从不同的方面反映生产总值及其构成。

三次产业是根据社会生产活动历史发展的顺序对产业结构的划分，产品直接取自自然界的部门称为第一产业，对初级产品进行再加工的部门称为第二产业，为生产和消费提供各种服务的部门称为第三产业。它是世界上较为通用的产业结构分类，但各国的划分不尽一致。

我国的三次产业划分是:

第一产业:农业（包括农业、林业、畜牧业、渔业和农林牧渔服务业）。

第二产业:工业（包括采矿业，制造业，电力、燃气及水的生产和供应业）和建筑业。

第三产业:除第一、第二产业以外的其他各业。

支出法生产总值指一个地区（或国家）所有常住单位在一定时期内用于最终消费、资本形成总额，以及货物和服务的净出口总额，它反映本期生产的生产总值的使用及构成。

最终消费指常住单位在一定时期内对于货物和服务的全部最终消费支出，也就是常住单位为满足物质、文化和精神生活的需要，从本国经济领土和国外购买的货物和服务的支出;不包括非常住单位在本国经济领土内的消费支出。最终消费分为居民消费和政府消费。

居民消费指常住住户对货物和服务的全部最终消费支出。居民消费按市场价格计算，即按居民支付的购买者价格计算。购买者价格是购买者取得货物所支付的价格，包括购买者支付的运输和商业费用。居民消费除了直接以货币形式购买货物和服务的消费之外，还包括以其他方式获得的货物和服务的消费支出，即所谓的虚拟消费支出。居民虚拟消费支出包括以下几种类型：单位以实物报酬及实物转移的形式提供给劳动者的货物和服务；住户生产并由本住户消费了的货物和服务，其中的服务仅指住户的自有住房服务；金融机构提供的金融媒介服务；保险公司提供的保险服务。

政府消费指政府部门为全社会提供公共服务的消费支出和免费或以较低价格向住户提供的货物和服务的净支出。前者等于政府服务的产出价值减去政府单位所获得的经营收入的价值，政府服务的产出价值等于它的经常性业务支出加上固定资产折旧;后者等于政府部门免费或以较低价格向住户提供的货物和服务的市场价值减去向住户收取的价值。

资本形成总额指常住单位在一定时期内获得的减去处置的固定资产加存货的变动，包括固定资本形成总额和存货增加。

固定资本形成总额指常住单位购置、转入和自产自用的固定资产，扣除固定资产的销售和转出后的价值，分有形固定资产形成总额和无形固定资产形成总额。有形固定资产形成总额包括一定时期内完成的建筑工程、安装工程和设备工器具购置（减处置）价值，以及土地改良、新增役、种、奶、毛、娱乐用牲畜和新增经济林木价值。无形固定资产形成总额包括矿藏的勘探、计算机软件、娱乐和文学艺术品原件等获得减处置。

存货增加　指常住单位存货实物量变动的市场价值，即期末价值减期初价值的差额。存货增加可以是正值，也可以是负值；正值表示存货上升，负值表示存货下降。它包括生产单位购进的原材料、燃料和储备物资等存货，以及生产单位生产的产成品、在制品等存货等。

货物和服务净出口　指货物和服务出口减货物和服务进口的差额。出口包括常住单位向非常住单位出售或无偿转让的各种货物和服务的价值；进口包括常住单位从非常住单位购买或无偿得到的各种货物和服务的价值。由于服务活动的提供与使用同时发生，因此服务的进出口业务并不发生出入境现象，一般把常住单位从国外得到的服务作为进口，非常住单位从本国得到的服务作为出口。货物的出口和进口都按离岸价格计算。

劳动者报酬　指劳动者因从事生产活动所获得的全部报酬。包括劳动者获得的各种形式的工资、奖金和津贴，既包括货币形式的，也包括实物形式的；还包括劳动者所享受的公费医疗和医药卫生费、上下班交通补贴和单位支付的社会保险费等。对于个体经济来说，其所有者所获得的劳动报酬和经营利润不易区分，这两部分统一作为劳动者报酬处理。

生产税净额 指生产税减生产补贴后的余额。生产税指政府对生产单位生产、销售和从事经营活动以及因从事生产活动使用某些生产要素（如固定资产、土地、劳动力）所征收的各种税、附加费和规费。生产补贴与生产税相反，指政府对生产单位的单方面收入转移，因此视为负生产税，包括政策亏损补贴、粮食系统价格补贴、外贸企业出口退税收入等。

固定资产折旧 指一定时期内为弥补固定资产损耗按照核定的固定资产折旧率提取的固定资产折旧，或按国民经济核算统一规定的折旧率虚拟计算的固定资产折旧。它反映了固定资产在当期生产中的转移价值。各类企业和企业化管理的事业单位的固定资产折旧是指实际计提并计入成本费中的折旧费；不计提折旧的政府机关、非企业化管理的事业单位和居民住房的固定资产折旧是按照统一规定的折旧率和固定资产原值计算的虚拟折旧。原则上，固定资产折旧应按固定资产的重置价值计算，但是目前我国尚不具备对全社会固定资产进行重估价的基础，所以暂时只能采用上述办法。

营业盈余 指常住单位创造的增加值扣除劳动者报酬、生产税净额和固定资产折旧后的余额。它相当于企业的营业利润加上生产补贴，但要扣除从利润中开支的工资和福利等。

Explanatory Notes on Main Statistical Indicators

Gross Domestic Product (GDP) refers to the final products of all resident units in a oregin (or a country) during a certain period at market price. Gross domestic product is expressed in three different forms, i.e. value, income, and products respectively. The form of value refers to the total value of all products and services produced by all resident units during a certain period of time minus total value of intimidate input of materials and services of the nature of non-fixed assets or the summation of the value-added of all resident units; the form of income includes all the income created by all resident units and distributed primarily to all resident and non-resident units; the form of products refers to the value of all final goods and services for final use by all resident units plus the value of net exports of goods and services during a given period of time. In the practice of national accounting, gross domestic product is calculated with three approaches, i.e. production approach, income approach, and expenditure approach, which reflect gross domestic product and its composition from different aspects.

Three Industries Industry structure has been classified according to the historical sequence of development. Primary industry refers to extraction of natural resources; secondary industry involves processing of primary products; and tertiary industry provides services of various kinds for production and consumption. The above classification is universal although it varies to some extent form country to country.

Industry in China comprises:

Primary industry: agriculture (including farming, forestry, animal husbandry and fishery).

Secondary industry: industry (including mining and quarrying, manufacturing, production and supply of electricity, water and gas) and construction.

Tertiary industry: all other industries not included in primary or secondary industry.

GDP Calculated with Expenditure Approach refers to total expenditure on final consumption, total capital formation and net export of goods and services by resident units of a country in a certain period of time. It reflects the composition of GDP by its use.

Final Consumption refers to the total expenditure of resident units on final consumption of goods and services in a certain period, namely the expenditure of the resident units for purchases of goods and services from domestic economic territory and abroad to meet the requirements of material, cultural and spiritual life. It excludes the expenditure of non-resident units on consumption in the economic territory of the country. The final consumption is classified into household consumption and government consumption.

Households Consumption refers to the total expenditure of resident households on the final consumption of goods and services. The households consumption is calculated at market prices, namely the purchasers prices which the households pay; the purchasers prices of goods are the prices the households pay when they obtain the goods, including the transport and commercial expenses paid by the households. In addition to the consumption of goods and services bought by the households directly with money, the expenditure on goods and services obtained by the households in other ways, i.e. the so-called imputed expenditure on consumption, is also included in the households consumption. The imputation expenditure of the households on consumption includes the following types: (a) the goods and services provided to the households by the units in the form of payment in kind and transfer in kind; (b) the goods and services produced and consumed by the households themselves, in which the services refer only to the services provided by the residential buildings owned by the households; (c) the services of financial intermediary provided by the financial institutions; (d) theinsurance services provided by the insurance companies.

Government Consumption refers to the expenditure on the consumption of the public services provided by the government to the whole society and the net expenditure on the goods and services provided by the government to the households at free charge or lower prices. The former equals to the output value of the government services minus the value of operating income obtained by the government departments. (The output Value of the government services equals to its current operating expenditure plus depreciation of fixed assets).

The latter equals to the market value of the goods and services provided by the government free of charge or at low prices to the households minus the value received by the government from the households.

Total Capital Formation refers to the fixed assets acquired minus those disposed and the change in inventory, including the total fixed assets formation and the increase in inventory.

Total Fixed Capital Formation refers to the value of fixed assets purchased, transferred in by the resident units and those produced and used by themselves deducting the value of fixed assets sold and transferred out. It can be classified into total tangible assets formation and total intangible assets formation. The total tangible assets Formation include the value of the construction projects, installation projects completed and the equipment, apparatus and instruments purchased as well as the value of land improved, the value of draught animals, breeding stock, milk, wool and recreational animals and the newly increased economic forest in a certain period. The total intangible assets formation includes the prospecting of minerals, the acquisition of computer software, theoriginals of recreational works and works of literature and arts minus the disposal of them.

Increase in Inventory refers to the market value of the change in inventory, i.e. the difference of value between the beginning and the end of the period. The increase in inventory can be positive or negative. A positive value indicates the increase in inventory while a negative value indicates the decrease in stock. The inventory includes the raw materials, fuels and reserve materials purchased by the production units as well as the inventory of finished products, semi-finished products, work-in-progress, etc.

Net Export of Goods and Services refers to the difference of the exports of goods and services minus the imports of goods and services. The imports include the value of various goods and services sold or gratuitously transferred by the resident units to the non-resident units. The imports include the value of various goods and services purchased or gratuitously acquired by the resident units from the non-resident units. Because the provision of services and the use of them happen simultaneously, the import and export of services do not appear to have the phenomena of crossing the border of the country. The acquisition of services by the resident units from abroad is usually treated as import while the acquisition of services by non-resident units in this country is usually treated as export. The export and import of goods are calculated at FOB.

Labourers Remuneration refers to the whole payment of various forms earned by the labourers from the productive activities they are engaged in. It includes wages, bonuses and allowances the labourers earned in monetary form and in kind. It also includes the free medical services provided to the labourers and the medicine expenses, traffic subsidies and social insurance fee paid by the labourers working units for them. As the individual economy is concerned, since the labourers remuneration is not easily distinguished from the operating profit, both are treated as labourers remuneration.

Net Taxes on Production refers to the residual of the taxes on production minus the subsidies on production. The taxes on production refers to the various taxes, extra charges and fees levied on the production units on theirproduction, sale and business activities as well as on some factors of production, such as fixed assets, land and labour force, used in the production activities they are engaged in. In contrast to the taxes on production, the subsidies on production refer to the unilateral transfer of part of the governments revenue to the production units and is therefore regarded as negative taxes on production. They include subsidies on the loss due to implementation of government policies, price subsidies to the grain institutions, foreign trade corporations receipts from drawback, etc.

Depreciation of Fixed Assets refers to the depreciation of fixed assets of a given period, drawn in accordance with the stipulated depreciation rate for the purpose of compensating the wear loss of the fixed assets or the depreciation of fixed assets calculated in a fictitious way in accordance with the stipulated unified depreciation rate in the national economic accounting system. It reflects the value of transfer of the fixed assets in the production of the current period. The depreciation of fixed assets in various enterprises and institutions managed as enterprisesrefers to the depreciation expenses actually drawn and calculated as part of the cost. In government agencies and institutions not managed as enterprises which do not draw the depreciation expenses, as well as for the houses of residents, the depreciation of Fixed assets is the imputed depreciation, which is calculated in accordance with the stipulated unified depreciation rate. In principle, the depreciation of fixedassets should be calculated on the basis of the repurchased value of the fixed assets. However, there is no actual condition to re-evaluate all the fixed assets in China. Therefore, the above-mentioned methods are temporarily adopted at present.

Operating Surplus refers to the balance of the value added created by the resident units deducting the labourers remuneration, net taxes on production and the depreciation of fixed assets. It is equivalent to the business profit of the enterprises plus subsidies on production, but the wages and welfare expenses paid from the profits should be deducted.

3 人口、从业人员与职工工资

POPULATION，EMPLOYMENT AND WAGES

资料整理：王义龙　张　静
Data management:Wang Yilong　Zhang Jing

第三部分　人口、从业人员与职工工资

一、简要说明

本章资料包括主要年份人口、分区县户籍和常住人口及变动、从业人员及劳动报酬等。户籍人口数为公安年报数，1991年以前年份市区数未包括临潼、长安。主要数据由西安市统计局人口就业处提供。

二、主要指标

年末户籍人口（万人）	782.73	比上年增长	0.1%
人口自然增长率（‰）	4.39	比上年下降	0.1个千分点
常住人口（万人）	847.41	比上年增长	0.5%
男女性别比（以女性为100）	105.18	比上年下降	1.71个百分点
户籍人口密度（人/平方公里）	774	比上年增加	1人/平方公里
城镇非私营单位在岗职工年平均工资（元）	37870	比上年增长	11.3%

3　POPULATION,EMPLOYMENT AND WAGES

Ⅰ.Brief Introduction

This chapter consists of the data about the population of consequent years, population of all the districts and counties and the correspondent changes, the employed and their wages. Thc population data are from the annual report of the Xi'an Bureau of Public Security, with Lintong, Chang'an not included before 1991. The population data is provided primarily by Population & Employment Division of the Xi'an Bureau of Statistics.

Ⅱ.Major Indicators

		Increase over Preceding Year
Total Population of Year-end(10 000 persons)	782.73	0.1%
Natural Gorwth Rate(‰)	4.39	-0.1thousands of points
Permanent Population(10 000 persons)	847.41	
Sex Ratio (female = 100)	105.18	
Density of Population (person/sq.km)	774	0.5%
Aunual Average Wage of Stuff and Workers	37870	-1.71percentage points
in Urban Non-privite Enterprises(yuan)		1
		11.3%

3-1 主要年份人口、人口密度和人口发展情况

Population, Population Density and Population Development in Representative years

单位：万人 (10 000 persons)

年 份 Year	总人口 Total population	市区 Urban Area	女性人口数 Number of Female	非农业人口数 Non-Agricultural Population	人口密度（人/平方公里) Density of Population (person/sq.km)	总人口指数(上年为100) Total Population Index (100 for preceding year) 全市 Whole City	市区 Urban Area
1952	252.92	92.42	118.81	57.61	254	102.6	103.1
1965	400.05	179.88	190.72	136.39	401	102.5	103.4
1970	435.12	188.12	210.47	139.12	436	101.9	101.4
1978	498.10	210.15	241.82	159.98	499	101.7	102.7
1980	511.91	221.19	249.26	172.85	513	101.4	102.6
1985	553.11	245.76	268.40	201.90	554	101.6	102.2
1986	563.97	251.80	273.30	205.92	565	102.0	102.5
1987	574.46	257.69	278.12	210.25	575	101.9	102.3
1988	585.85	264.94	283.68	216.99	587	102.0	102.8
1989	597.36	270.80	289.44	222.54	598	102.0	102.2
1990	608.89	275.69	295.29	226.98	610	101.9	101.8
1991	615.48	419.29	298.13	230.85	617	101.1	152.1
1992	623.20	429.54	301.92	236.45	624	101.3	102.4
1993	630.91	435.41	305.30	240.85	632	101.2	101.4
1994	639.45	442.30	309.17	248.35	641	101.4	101.6
1995	648.21	448.65	313.46	255.71	645	101.4	101.4
1996	654.87	454.68	316.60	261.28	653	101.0	101.3
1997	662.06	461.17	320.18	267.52	663	101.1	101.4
1998	668.22	466.31	323.20	271.75	669	100.9	101.1
1999	674.50	463.56	326.12	276.14	676	100.9	99.4
2000	688.01	483.10	332.83	285.79	689	102.0	104.2
2001	694.84	489.88	336.04	292.62	696	101.0	101.4
2002	702.59	497.38	339.51	300.05	704	101.1	101.5
2003	716.58	510.26	346.26	312.88	718	102.0	102.6
2004	725.01	516.30	350.85	318.50	717	101.2	101.2
2005	741.73	533.21	359.71	333.14	734	102.3	103.3
2006	753.11	540.97	365.74	343.78	745	101.5	101.5
2007	764.25	549.19	371.84	353.85	756	101.5	101.5
2008	772.30	554.73	376.76	363.87	764	101.1	101.0
2009	781.67	561.58	382.39	370.66	773	101.2	101.2
2010	782.73	562.65	383.93	374.64	774	100.1	100.2

注:人口部分均为公安年报数据，系户籍人口。1991年以前年份，市区数未包括临潼、长安。

Note: The population data are taken from annual reports of pulic recurity, namely the registered household population..The population of urban area before 1991 doesn't include Lintong and Chang'an.

3-2 主要年份人口变动情况

Population Changes in Representative Years

单位：万人 （10 000 persons）

年份 Year	出生 Birth 人数 Population	出生率(‰) Birth Rate (‰)	死亡 Death 人数 Population	死亡率(‰) Death Rate (‰)	自然增长率(‰) Natural Gorwth Rate (‰)	迁入人口 Immigrant population	迁出人口 Emigrant population
1952	7.68	30.74	2.21	8.86	21.88		
1965	11.53	29.19	3.36	8.50	20.69	13.11	10.83
1970	12.05	27.96	2.34	5.44	22.52	6.88	8.39
1978	7.81	19.04	3.17	6.66	12.38	8.98	9.16
1980	6.59	12.96	3.19	6.28	6.68	13.36	9.64
1985	8.95	16.30	3.01	5.48	10.82	11.60	8.74
1986	10.14	18.15	2.78	4.97	13.18	11.79	8.39
1987	9.76	17.14	2.83	4.97	12.17	12.58	9.26
1988	9.42	16.24	2.89	4.98	11.26	13.54	8.97
1989	11.78	19.92	3.04	5.13	14.79	12.73	10.15
1990	12.40	20.55	3.45	5.72	14.83	11.82	9.86
1991	8.73	14.25	3.26	5.33	8.92	8.98	6.09
1992	8.98	14.49	3.39	5.48	9.01	13.94	9.54
1993	9.25	14.75	3.37	5.38	9.37	11.50	8.33
1994	8.08	12.71	3.16	4.97	7.74	13.40	8.59
1995	7.69	11.95	3.21	4.98	6.97	14.41	8.85
1996	7.26	11.15	3.41	5.24	5.91	11.94	8.88
1997	6.84	10.38	3.12	4.75	5.63	12.58	8.62
1998	6.40	9.62	3.10	4.66	4.96	10.89	8.36
1999	6.19	9.22	3.88	5.78	3.44	12.58	9.23
2000	8.90	13.07	4.06	5.96	7.11	17.12	9.23
2001	5.11	7.39	2.89	4.19	3.20	15.16	10.83
2002	5.34	7.64	3.08	4.41	3.23	13.90	9.41
2003	6.02	8.48	3.32	4.68	3.80	20.60	9.15
2004	6.63	9.19	4.23	5.87	3.32	15.56	10.19
2005	7.67	9.58	4.13	5.16	4.42	22.61	9.46
2006	8.13	9.98	4.45	5.46	4.52	17.23	11.75
2007	8.27	10.00	4.53	5.48	4.52	19.90	14.01
2008	8.47	10.15	4.65	5.57	4.58	18.49	15.04
2009	8.47	10.08	4.73	5.63	4.45	16.84	13.14
2010	8.23	9.73	4.51	5.34	4.39	14.09	13.50

注：2004年以前为公安年报数据。2005−2009年出生、死亡、自然增长率为人口变动抽样调查数据。2010年出生、死亡、自然增长率根据第六次人口普查数据推算得出。

Note:Before 2004, the data were taken from annual reports of public security. The data of birthrate, death rate and the natural population growth rate in 2005-2009 were taken from the statistics from spot check on population changes.The data of rate for birth、death and naturally increase in 2010 is inferred according to the data of he sixth national population.

3-3 各区县人口和户数（2010年）

Population and Households by Region（2010）

单位：万人 (10 000 person)

区县 District and County	总户数(万户) Number of Households (10 000 households)	总人口 Total Population	非农业人口 Non-agriculture	按性别分 Grouped by Sex 男 Male	女 Female	常住人口 Permanent population 2000	2010
合　计 Total	**226.71**	**782.73**	**374.64**	**398.80**	**383.93**	**741.14**	**847.41**
新城区 Xincheng	16.61	50.36	50.36	25.61	24.75	53.63	59.01
碑林区 Beilin	20.31	73.25	73.25	38.13	35.12	71.16	61.62
莲湖区 Lianhu	21.41	64.09	64.09	32.49	31.60	64.32	69.86
灞桥区 Baqiao	16.21	50.86	23.24	25.29	25.57	50.38	59.56
未央区 Weiyang	15.82	51.70	33.84	25.84	25.86	46.91	80.72
雁塔区 Yanta	21.55	79.31	63.43	39.84	39.47	81.00	117.98
阎良区 Yanliang	7.21	25.24	8.82	12.76	12.48	24.01	27.87
临潼区 Lintong	18.92	69.76	11.64	35.29	34.47	65.14	65.60
长安区 Chang'an	26.82	98.08	13.76	49.26	48.82	87.99	108.48
蓝田县 Lantian	17.88	64.36	5.86	33.37	30.99	57.07	51.42
周至县 Zhouzhi	17.14	66.56	6.25	35.13	31.43	60.87	56.29
户　县 Huxian	18.07	59.71	11.46	31.03	28.68	56.01	55.65
高陵县 Gaoling	8.76	29.45	8.64	14.76	14.69	22.65	33.35

注：2010年常住人口为年末常住人口数，根据第六次人口普查数据推算得出。

Note:The data of inhabitant in 2010 is the data for the end of 2010, and that is inferred according to the data of the sixth national population.

3-4 各区县人口变动情况（2010年）

Population Changes by Region（2010）

区 县	District and County	出生率(‰) Birth Rate (‰)	死亡率(‰) Death Rate (‰)	自然增长率(‰) Natural Gorwth Rate (‰)	迁入人口(人) Immigrant population (person)	迁出人口(人) Emigrant population (person)
合 计	**Total**	**9.73**	**5.34**	**4.39**	**140932**	**135012**
新城区	Xincheng	6.62	3.40	3.22	4638	3054
碑林区	Beilin	7.64	4.44	3.20	16341	31186
莲湖区	Lianhu	8.79	5.36	3.43	8010	7186
灞桥区	Baqiao	10.70	6.28	4.42	7799	5053
未央区	Weiyang	10.86	5.26	5.60	18250	7330
雁塔区	Yanta	8.41	4.08	4.33	37296	46631
阎良区	Yanliang	9.03	4.61	4.42	3516	2129
临潼区	Lintong	10.22	4.90	5.32	4277	2606
长安区	Chang'an	10.83	6.27	4.56	11742	9064
蓝田县	Lantian	11.45	6.78	4.67	4800	5316
周至县	Zhouzhi	12.97	7.53	5.44	6095	5454
户 县	Huxian	9.96	5.87	4.09	6855	7271
高陵县	Gaoling	9.85	5.33	4.52	11313	2721

注：出生、死亡、自然增长率根据第六次人口普查数据推算得出。

Note:The data of rate for birth、death and naturally increase is inferred according to the data of he sixth national population.

3-5 主要年份常住人口

Permanent population in Representative Years

单位：万人 (10 000 persons)

年 份 Year	年末常住人口 Permanent population (year-end)	城镇 Urban	农村 Rural
2000	741.14	450.36	290.78
2005	806.81	510.55	296.26
2006	822.52	530.94	291.58
2007	830.54	548.99	281.55
2008	837.52	565.16	272.36
2009	843.46	581.40	262.06
2010	847.41	584.71	262.70

注：2000年常住人口为人口普查数据。2005–2009年常住人口为人口变动抽样调查数据。2010年常住人口为年末常住人口数，根据第六次人口普查数据推算得出。

Note:Data in 2000 were taken from population census, The permanent population in 2005-2009 were taken from sample survey on population changing.The data of inhabitant in 2010 is the data for the end of 2010, and that is inferred according to the data of the sixth national population.

3-6 主要年份社会从业人数

Number of Social Laborers in Representative Years

单位：万人 (10 000 persons)

年 份 Year	合 计 Total	一、按城乡分 Grouped by Urban area and Rural area					二、按三次产业分 Grouped by Industry		
		1.城镇 Urban	国有经济 State-owned Enterprises	集体经济 Collective-owned Enterprises	其他经济 Others	2.乡村 Village	第一产业 Primary Industry	第二产业 Secondary Indusyry	第三产业 Tertiary Industry
1985	296.80	129.07	96.80	29.07	3.20	167.73	135.89	98.61	62.30
1986	299.45	132.82	101.28	28.43	3.11	166.63	127.46	100.61	71.38
1987	312.16	138.56	104.58	30.72	3.26	173.60	130.36	107.75	74.05
1988	327.76	142.24	106.46	30.73	5.05	185.52	138.87	108.12	80.77
1989	332.65	145.65	108.80	30.44	6.41	187.00	142.21	106.40	84.04
1990	343.06	147.93	110.95	29.78	7.20	195.13	149.64	106.74	86.68
1991	347.65	149.48	111.87	29.80	7.81	198.17	152.24	108.19	87.22
1992	357.51	151.67	113.19	29.97	8.51	205.84	154.75	110.22	92.54
1993	363.70	155.72	112.98	29.77	12.97	207.98	154.02	114.02	95.66
1994	364.56	154.88	113.39	27.97	13.52	209.68	153.51	108.53	102.52
1995	372.60	158.80	113.79	25.58	19.43	213.80	153.39	109.67	109.54
1996	379.29	164.54	113.29	24.82	26.43	214.75	153.43	109.17	116.69
1997	385.14	169.52	112.44	23.52	33.56	215.62	153.23	109.46	122.45
1998	393.95	177.20	106.06	21.50	49.64	216.75	153.00	110.45	130.50
1999	400.43	180.27	105.08	20.50	54.69	220.16	154.64	110.58	135.21
2000	389.10	176.45	103.46	18.40	54.59	212.65	147.03	107.26	134.81
2001	389.30	177.94	100.47	17.10	60.37	211.36	145.09	108.96	135.25
2002	397.16	181.85	100.54	16.90	64.41	215.31	143.04	111.62	142.50
2003	404.92	183.23	94.51	16.78	71.94	221.69	146.67	109.09	149.16
2004	409.57	187.53	93.43	15.41	78.69	222.04	141.81	111.70	156.06
2005	415.83	192.53	93.27	14.47	84.79	223.30	136.31	114.20	165.32
2006	422.15	196.16	84.46	14.41	97.29	225.99	135.10	116.09	170.96
2007	436.36	214.27	90.58	11.88	111.81	222.09	133.33	125.06	177.97
2008	448.05	224.20	90.17	10.60	123.43	223.85	127.87	130.23	189.95
2009	462.52	239.39	90.83	7.63	140.93	223.13	122.13	131.57	208.82
2010	477.58	252.54	94.01	5.48	153.05	225.04	117.27	145.40	214.91

3-7 分行业从业人数（2010年）

单位：万人

行　业	Sector	合计 Total
总　计	**Total**	**477.58**
一、按国民经济行业分组	**Grouped by Sector**	
（一）农、林、牧、渔业	Agriculture ,Forestry,Animal Husbandry and Fishery	117.27
（二）采矿业	Mining	0.37
（三）制造业	Manufacturing	92.75
（四）电力、燃气及水的生产和供应业	Production and Distribution of Electricity,Gas and Water	3.26
（五）建筑业	Construction	49.02
（六）交通运输、仓储和邮政业	Traffic,Transport,Storage and Post	31.80
（七）信息传输、计算机服务和软件业	Information Transmission,Computer Service and Software	7.19
（八）批发和零售业	Wholesale and Retail Trades	60.01
（九）住宿和餐饮业	Hotels and Catering Services	22.50
（十）金融业	Financial Intermediation	6.71
（十一）房地产业	Real Estate	3.82
（十二）租赁和商务服务业	Leasing and Business Services	9.14
（十三）科学研究、技术服务和地质勘察业	Scientific Research,Technical Service and Geologic Prospecting	11.36
（十四）水利、环境和公共设施管理业	Management of Water Conservancy, Environment and Public Facilities	2.31
（十五）居民服务和其他服务业	Services to Households and Other Services	12.80
（十六）教育	Education	20.96
（十七）卫生、社会保障和社会福利业	Health,Social Security and Social Welfare	11.46
（十八）文化、体育和娱乐业	Culture, Sports and Entertainment	3.21
（十九）公共管理和社会组织	Public Management and Social Organization	11.64
二、按三次产业分	**Guroped by Industry**	
第一产业	Primary Industry	117.27
第二产业	Secondary Industry	145.40
第三产业	Tertiary Industry	214.91

Number of Employed Persons by Sector（2010）

(10 000 persons)

国有经济 State-owned Enterprises	集体经济 Collective-owned Enterprises	城镇其他经济 Urban Other Enterprises	城镇私营经济及个体劳动者 Urban Private Enterprises and Individual Labors	乡镇劳动者 Rural and Urban Labourer
94.01	**5.48**	**48.16**	**104.89**	**225.04**
0.42		0.01	0.26	116.58
0.05		0.32		
22.62	1.44	20.99	23.76	23.94
2.95	0.02	0.29		
8.14	1.65	3.04	6.99	29.20
8.03	0.10	2.41	9.35	11.91
2.56	0.03	2.37	0.85	1.38
2.52	0.55	3.93	34.10	18.91
1.16	0.06	3.01	13.07	5.20
1.27	0.19	4.63		0.62
1.08	0.37	2.37		
0.98	0.44	0.39	5.45	1.88
8.28	0.05	1.06		1.97
2.13	0.03	0.15		
0.35	0.36	0.85	6.35	4.89
15.07	0.02	1.10	2.45	2.32
5.32	0.14	0.19	1.69	4.12
1.56	0.03	1.05	0.57	
9.52				2.12
0.42		0.01	0.26	116.58
33.76	3.11	24.64	30.75	53.14
59.83	2.37	23.51	73.88	55.32

3-8 全部单位从业人员情况（2010年）

单位：人

分　组	Classify	单位从业人员 Employed Persons	女性 Female
总　计	**Total**	**1403797**	**523751**
一、按企业、事业、机关分组	**Groped by Enterprises,Insitutions and Agencies**		
1.企业	Enterprises	1073530	378310
2.事业	Institutions	232779	119220
3.机关	Agencies and Organizations	96174	25518
4.民间非盈利组织	Non-profit NGO	1314	703
5.其他	Others		
二、按国民经济行业分组	**Grouped by Sector**		
（一）农、林、牧、渔业	Agriculture ,Forestry,Animal Husbandry and Fishery	3965	1076
（二）采矿业	Mining	3674	1056
（三）制造业	Manufacturing	420074	142382
（四）电力、燃气及水的生产和供应业	Production and Distribution of Electricity,Gas and Water	32291	9797
（五）建筑业	Construction	116209	19908
（六）交通运输、仓储和邮政业	Traffic,Transport,Storage and Post	99961	27650
（七）信息传输、计算机服务和软件业	Information Transmission,Computer Service and Software	49149	23370
（八）批发和零售业	Wholesale and Retail Trades	61974	31666
（九）住宿和餐饮业	Hotels and Catering Services	41566	24492
（十）金融业	Financial Intermediation	58926	26682
（十一）房地产业	Real Estate	34025	11912
（十二）租赁和商务服务业	Leasing and Business Services	16537	4590
（十三）科学研究、技术服务和地质勘察业	Scientific Research,Technical Services and Geological Prospecting	90767	28458
（十四）水利、环境和公共设施管理业	Management of Water Conservancy, Environment and Public Facilities	22693	9784
（十五）居民服务和其他服务业	Services to Households and Other Services	14706	6401
（十六）教育	Education	161492	83810
（十七）卫生、社会保障和社会福利业	Health,Social Security and Social Welfare	55816	34692
（十八）文化、体育和娱乐业	Culture, Sports and Entertainment	25273	10876
（十九）公共管理和社会组织	Public Management and Social Organization	94699	25149

Basic Facts on All Employed Persons（2010）

(person)

在岗职工合计 Total Fully Employed Staff and Workers	专业技术人员 Scientific and Technical Personnel	专业技术人员 / 女性 Female	其他从业人员 Other Employed Persons	单位从业人员平均人数 Average Employment	单位从业人员平均人数 / 在岗职工 Fully Employed Staff and Workers	单位从业人员平均人数 / 其他从业人员 Other Employed Persons
1306962	**457222**	**176245**	**96835**	**1412771**	**1324947**	**87824**
996441	312212	94908	77089	1084318	1013761	70557
220939	138716	78832	11840	232264	222778	9486
88348	6217	2453	7826	94735	87045	7690
1234	77	52	80	1454	1363	91
3915	990	376	50	3976	3926	50
3641	307	58	33	3667	3626	41
405888	127794	30893	14186	431033	419542	11491
31650	10316	2421	641	32887	32260	627
106135	29663	7618	10074	123496	113534	9962
88792	10268	3789	11169	96794	85692	11102
41089	25271	5908	8060	50801	43464	7337
58460	6748	2621	3514	60583	57785	2798
41037	4724	1979	529	39358	38895	463
41481	17959	9649	17445	54629	37383	17246
32303	7474	2522	1722	34324	32923	1401
15542	4443	980	995	17664	16933	731
85627	48648	15262	5140	90519	86086	4433
20659	3128	1729	2034	22590	20676	1914
14556	1617	689	150	15227	15061	166
153068	110243	60226	8424	160703	153731	6972
51545	34518	23651	4271	56034	53140	2894
24357	7409	3416	916	25172	24368	804
87217	5702	2458	7482	93314	85922	7392

3-9 国有单位从业人员情况（2010年）

单位：人

分组	Classify	单位从业人员 Employed Persons	女性 Female
合　计	**Total**	**888420**	**328062**
一、按企业、事业、机关分组	**Groped by Enterprises,Insitutions and Agencies**		
1.企业	Enterprises	564865	185634
2.事业	Institutions	227381	116910
3.机关	Agencies and Organizations	96174	25518
4.民间非盈利组织	Non-profit NGO		
5.其他	Others		
二、按国民经济行业分组	**Grouped by Economic Sector**		
(一)农、林、牧、渔业	Agriculture ,Forestry,Animal Husbandry and Fishery	3886	1045
(二)采矿业	Mining	486	2
(三)制造业	Manufacturing	205244	65345
(四)电力、燃气及水的生产和供应业	Production and Distribution of Electricity,Gas and Water	29184	8797
(五)建筑业	Construction	70377	13153
(六)交通运输、仓储和邮政业	Traffic,Transport,Storage and Post	75800	19957
(七)信息传输、计算机服务和软件业	Information Transmission,Computer Service and Software	25154	13779
(八)批发和零售业	Wholesale and Retail Trades	21073	9930
(九)住宿和餐饮业	Hotels and Catering Services	10963	5760
(十)金融业	Financial Intermediation	12643	5904
(十一)房地产业	Real Estate	8266	3468
(十二)租赁和商务服务业	Leasing and Business Services	8800	2944
(十三)科学研究、技术服务和地质勘察业	Scientific Research,Technical Service and Geologic Prospecting	79910	25650
(十四)水利、环境和公共设施管理业	Management of Water Conservancy, Environment and Public Facilities	20864	8920
(十五)居民服务和其他服务业	Services to Households and Other Services	3395	1199
(十六)教育	Education	150331	78577
(十七)卫生、社会保障和社会福利业	Health,Social Security and Social Welfare	52527	32787
(十八)文化、体育和娱乐业	Culture, Sports and Entertainment	14818	5696
(十九)公共管理和社会组织	Public Management and Social Organization	94699	25149

Basic Facts on Persons Employed by State-owned Units （2010）

(person)

在岗职工合计 Total Fully Employed Staff and Workers	专业技术人员 Scientific and Technical Personnel	女性 Female	其他从业人员 Other Employed Persons	单位从业人员平均人数 Average Employment	在岗职工 Fully Employed Staff and Workers	其他从业人员 Other Employed Persons
830940	**331831**	**137263**	**57480**	**910819**	**859626**	**51193**
526370	189071	57144	38495	589660	555057	34603
216222	136543	77666	11159	226424	217524	8900
88348	6217	2453	7826	94735	87045	7690
3836	981	374	50	3895	3845	50
486				486	486	
197589	70247	17098	7655	220750	214790	5960
28544	9636	2330	640	29826	29200	626
63415	21834	5889	6962	76796	69637	7159
67002	7401	2881	8798	75557	66681	8876
21677	13495	2248	3477	27880	25443	2437
20658	2437	1006	415	21875	21333	542
10514	705	258	449	10913	10500	413
11136	5033	2320	1507	12370	10821	1549
6988	1902	726	1278	7869	6883	986
8042	2382	584	758	8816	8217	599
75505	42027	13676	4405	79686	75858	3828
19146	2956	1666	1718	20655	19054	1601
3350	199	112	45	3514	3470	44
143071	105783	58121	7260	149518	143571	5947
48545	32787	22501	3982	52242	49598	2644
14219	6324	3015	599	14857	14317	540
87217	5702	2458	7482	93314	85922	7392

3-10 城镇集体单位从业人员情况（2010年）

单位：人

分　组	Classify	单位从业人员 Employed Persons	女性 Female
总　计	**Total**	**47531**	**13206**
一、按企业、事业、机关分组	**Groped by Enterprises,Insitutions and Agencies**		
1.企业	Enterprises	46210	12576
2.事业	Institutions	1321	630
3.机关	Agencies and Organizations		
4.民间非盈利组织	Non-profit NGO		
5.其他	Others		
二、按国民经济行业分组	**Grouped by Sector**		
(一)农、林、牧、渔业	Agriculture ,Forestry,Animal Husbandry and Fishery		
(二)采矿业	Mining		
(三)制造业	Manufacturing	12113	4214
(四)电力、燃气及水的生产和供应业	Production and Distribution of Electricity,Gas and Water	171	26
(五)建筑业	Construction	15616	2622
(六)交通运输、仓储和邮政业	Traffic,Transport,Storage and Post	778	200
(七)信息传输、计算机服务和软件业	Information Transmission,Computer Service and Software	302	36
(八)批发和零售业	Wholesale and Retail Trades	3147	1245
(九)住宿和餐饮业	Hotels and Catering Services	618	379
(十)金融业	Financial Intermediation	1792	878
(十一)房地产业	Real Estate	2503	931
(十二)租赁和商务服务业	Leasing and Business Services	4322	128
(十三)科学研究、技术服务和地质勘察业	Scientific Research,Technical Service and Geologic Prospecting	453	109
(十四)水利、环境和公共设施管理业	Management of Water Conservancy, Environment and Public Facilities	332	117
(十五)居民服务和其他服务业	Services to Households and Other Services	3607	1570
(十六)教育	Education	169	110
(十七)卫生、社会保障和社会福利业	Health,Social Security and Social Welfare	1383	592
(十八)文化、体育和娱乐业	Culture, Sports and Entertainment	225	49
(十九)公共管理和社会组织	Public Management and Social Organization		

Basic Facts on Persons Employed by Urban Collective-owned Units（2010）

(person)

在岗职工合计 Total Fully Employed Staff and Workers	其他从业人员 Other Employed Persons	单位从业人员平均人数 Average Employment	在岗职工 Fully Employed Staff and Workers	其他从业人员 Other Employed Persons
46485	**1046**	**55598**	**54664**	**934**
45375	835	53864	53029	835
1110	211	1734	1635	99
11930	183	13949	13779	170
171		171	171	
15465	151	16408	16271	137
776	2	1089	1086	3
302		319	319	
2844	303	3642	3327	315
618		653	653	
1558	234	2385	2269	116
2500	3	3774	3771	3
4322		5408	5408	
444	9	452	443	9
332		443	443	
3533	74	4133	4039	94
169		170	170	
1296	87	2016	1929	87
225		586	586	

3-11 其他经济类型单位从业人员情况（2010年）

单位：人

分组	Classify	单位从业人员 Employed Persons	女性 Female
合　计	**Total**	**467846**	**182483**
一、按登记注册类型分组	**Grouped by Registion Status**		
（一）内资	Domestic Investment	375962	143912
1.股份合作	Share-holding Cooperative	6646	2535
2.联营	Joint Ownership	6703	2793
3.有限责任公司	Limited Liability Corporations	278817	104219
#国有独资	Sole State-funded	11023	4858
4.股份有限公司	Share-holding Corperation Ltd.	82080	33617
5.其他	Others	1716	748
（二）港、澳、台商投资	Enterprises with Funds from Hong Kong, Macao and Taiwan	18741	9316
（三）外商投资	Enterprises with Foreign Funded	73143	29255
二、按企业、事业分组	**Grouped by Enterprise and Instilution**		
1.企业	Enterprises	462455	180100
2.事业	Institutions	4077	1680
3.民间非盈利组织	Non-profit NGO	1314	703
4.其他	Others		
三、按国民经济行业分组	**Grouped by Sector**		
（一）农、林、牧、渔业	Agriculture,Forestry,Animal Husbandry and Fishery	79	31
（二）采矿业	Mining	3188	1054
（三）制造业	Manufacturing	202717	72823
（四）电力、燃气及水的生产和供应业	Production and Distribution of Electricity,Gas and Water	2936	974
（五）建筑业	Construction	30216	4133
（六）交通运输、仓储和邮政业	Traffic,Transport,Storage and Post	23383	7493
（七）信息传输、计算机服务和软件业	Information Transmission,Computer Service and Software	23693	9555
（八）批发和零售业	Wholesale and Retail Trades	37754	20491
（九）住宿和餐饮业	Hotels and Catering Services	29985	18353
（十）金融业	Financial Intermediation	44491	19900
（十一）房地产业	Real Estate	23256	7513
（十二）租赁和商务服务业	Leasing and Business Services	3415	1518
（十三）科学研究、技术服务和地质勘察业	Scientific Research,Technical Service and Geologic Prospecting	10404	2699
（十四）水利、环境和公共设施管理业	Management of Water Conservancy, Environment and Public Facilities	1497	747
（十五）居民服务和其他服务业	Services to Households and Other Services	7704	3632
（十六）教育	Education	10992	5123
（十七）卫生、社会保障和社会福利业	Health,Social Security and Social Welfare	1906	1313
（十八）文化、体育和娱乐业	Culture, Sports and Entertainment	10230	5131
（十九）公共管理和社会组织	Public Management and Social Organization		

Basic Facts on Persons Employed by Other Units（2010）

(person)

在岗职工合计 Fully Employed Staff and Workers	其他从业人员 Other Employed Persons	单位从业人员平均人数 Average Employment	在岗职工 Fully Employed Staff and Workers	其他从业人员 Other Employed Persons
429537	**38309**	**446354**	**410657**	**35697**
339790	36172	360074	325696	34378
6543	103	6524	6395	129
6447	256	6565	6202	363
261728	17089	269179	253046	16133
10163	860	10456	9662	794
63361	18719	76071	58323	17748
1711	5	1735	1730	5
18636	105	18573	18466	107
71111	2032	67707	66495	1212
424696	37759	440794	405675	35119
3607	470	4106	3619	487
1234	80	1454	1363	91
79		81	81	
3155	33	3181	3140	41
196369	6348	196334	190973	5361
2935	1	2890	2889	1
27255	2961	30292	27626	2666
21014	2369	20148	17925	2223
19110	4583	22602	17702	4900
34958	2796	35066	33125	1941
29905	80	27792	27742	50
28787	15704	39874	24293	15581
22815	441	22681	22269	412
3178	237	3440	3308	132
9678	726	10381	9785	596
1181	316	1492	1179	313
7673	31	7580	7552	28
9828	1164	11015	9990	1025
1704	202	1776	1613	163
9913	317	9729	9465	264

3-12 全部单位从业人员劳动报酬（2010年）

Remuneration of All Employed Persons（2010）

单位:万元 (1 0000yuan)

行　　业	Sector	单位从业人员劳动报酬 Remuneration of Employment	在岗职工工资总额 Total Wages of Employed Staff and Workers
总　计	**Total**	**5208781**	**5017637**
一、按企业、事业、机关分组	**Groped by Character of Unit**		
1.企业	Enterprises	3708831	3546199
2.事业	Institutions	1118109	1102751
3.机关	Agencies and Organizations	377652	364628
4.民间非盈利组织	Non-profit NGO	4188	4059
5.其他	Others		
二、按国民经济行业分组	**Grouped by Sector**		
（一）农、林、牧、渔业	Agriculture ,Forestry,Animal Husbandry and Fishery	8524	8482
（二）采矿业	Mining	11791	11716
（三）制造业	Manufacturing	1149281	1120412
（四）电力、燃气及水的生产和供应业	Production and Distribution of Electricity, Gas and Water	129929	129236
（五）建筑业	Construction	331893	314148
（六）交通运输、仓储和邮政业	Traffic,Transport,Storage and Post	403989	380540
（七）信息传输、计算机服务和软件业	Information Transmission,Computer Service and Software	233199	209781
（八）批发和零售业	Wholesale and Retail Trades	152079	146997
（九）住宿和餐饮业	Hotels and Catering Services	77326	76649
（十）金融业	Financial Intermediation	349361	308986
（十一）房地产业	Real Estate	155395	152561
（十二）租赁和商务服务业	Leasing and Business Services	53464	51609
（十三）科学研究、技术服务和地质勘察业	Scientific Research,Technical Service and Geologic Prospecting	501981	491143
（十四）水利、环境和公共设施管理业	Management of Water Conservancy, Environment and Public Facilities	57202	55766
（十五）居民服务和其他服务业	Services to Households and Other Services	40264	40110
（十六）教育	Education	853075	839283
（十七）卫生、社会保障和社会福利业	Health,Social Security and Social Welfare	246745	240987
（十八）文化、体育和娱乐业	Culture, Sports and Entertainment	80362	79104
（十九）公共管理和社会组织	Public Management and Social Organization	372922	360129

3-12 续表 continued

单位:万元 (10 000 yuan)

行业	Sector	其他从业人员劳动报酬 Remuneration of Other Employed Persons	在岗职工平均工资（元） Average Wages of Employed Staff and Workers (yuan)
总 计	**Total**	**191144**	**37870**
一、按企业、事业、机关分组	**Groped by Character of Unit**		
1.企业	Enterprises	162632	34981
2.事业	Institutions	15358	49500
3.机关	Agencies and Organizations	13024	41890
4.民间非盈利组织	Non-profit NGO	129	29779
5.其他	Others		
二、按国民经济行业分组	**Grouped by Sector**		
（一）农、林、牧、渔业	Agriculture ,Forestry,Animal Husbandry and Fishery	42	21604
（二）采矿业	Mining	75	32311
（三）制造业	Manufacturing	28869	26706
（四）电力、燃气及水的生产和供应业	Production and Distribution of Electricity, Gas and Water	693	40061
（五）建筑业	Construction	17745	27670
（六）交通运输、仓储和邮政业	Traffic,Transport,Storage and Post	23449	44408
（七）信息传输、计算机服务和软件业	Information Transmission,Computer Service and Software	23418	48265
（八）批发和零售业	Wholesale and Retail Trades	5082	25439
（九）住宿和餐饮业	Hotels and Catering Services	678	19707
（十）金融业	Financial Intermediation	40375	82654
（十一）房地产业	Real Estate	2835	46339
（十二）租赁和商务服务业	Leasing and Business Services	1855	30478
（十三）科学研究、技术服务和地质勘察业	Scientific Research,Technical Service and Geologic Prospecting	10838	57053
（十四）水利、环境和公共设施管理业	Management of Water Conservancy, Environment and Public Facilities	1436	26971
（十五）居民服务和其他服务业	Services to Households and Other Services	154	26632
（十六）教育	Education	13791	54594
（十七）卫生、社会保障和社会福利业	Health,Social Security and Social Welfare	5758	45349
（十八）文化、体育和娱乐业	Culture, Sports and Entertainment	1258	32462
（十九）公共管理和社会组织	Public Management and Social Organization	12793	41913

3–13 国有单位从业人员劳动报酬（2010年）

Remuneration of Persons Employed by State-owned Units （2010）

单位:万元　　　　(1 0000yuan)

行　业	Sector	单位从业人员劳动报酬 Remuneration of Employment	在岗职工工资总额 Total Wages of Employed Staff and Workers
总　计	**Total**	**3379632**	**3277041**
一、按隶属关系分组	**Grouped by Administrative Relationship**		
1.中央	Central	1419566	1368241
2.省、自治区、直辖市	Provincial	606447	595250
3.地区	District	580256	567979
4.县及县以下	County and Below	679419	653917
5.其他	Others	93945	91654
二、按企业、事业、机关分组	**Groped by Character of Unit**		
1.企业	Enterprises	1908538	1832994
2.事业	Institutions	1093441	1079419
3.机关	Agencies and Organizations	377652	364628
4.民间非盈利组织	Non-profit NGO		
5.其他	Others		
三、按国民经济行业分组	**Grouped by Sector**		
（一）农、林、牧、渔业	Agriculture ,Forestry,Animal Husbandry and Fishery	8364	8322
（二）采矿业	Mining	865	865
（三）制造业	Manufacturing	488440	474206
（四）电力、燃气及水的生产和供应业	Production and Distribution of Electricity, Gas and Water	116665	115974
（五）建筑业	Construction	213044	200286
（六）交通运输、仓储和邮政业	Traffic,Transport,Storage and Post	296527	279081
（七）信息传输、计算机服务和软件业	Information Transmission,Computer Service and Software	101824	93252
（八）批发和零售业	Wholesale and Retail Trades	50646	49927
（九）住宿和餐饮业	Hotels and Catering Services	20255	19672
（十）金融业	Financial Intermediation	60590	57515
（十一）房地产业	Real Estate	20712	18776
（十二）租赁和商务服务业	Leasing and Business Services	36478	35080
（十三）科学研究、技术服务和地质勘察业	Scientific Research,Technical Service and Geologic Prospecting	444919	435689
（十四）水利、环境和公共设施管理业	Management of Water Conservancy, Environment and Public Facilities	52051	50934
（十五）居民服务和其他服务业	Services to Households and Other Services	11498	11462
（十六）教育	Education	794970	783314
（十七）卫生、社会保障和社会福利业	Health,Social Security and Social Welfare	239447	233986
（十八）文化、体育和娱乐业	Culture, Sports and Entertainment	49415	48569
（十九）公共管理和社会组织	Public Management and Social Organization	372922	360129

3-13 续表 continued

单位:万元 (10 000 yuan)

行业	Sector	其他从业人员劳动报酬 Remuneration of Other Employed Persons	在岗职工平均工资（元） Average Wages of Employed Staff and Workers (yuan)
总 计	**Total**	**102591**	**38122**
一、按隶属关系分组	**Grouped by Administrative Relationship**		
1.中央	Central	51325	35969
2.省、自治区、直辖市	Provincial	11197	41777
3.地区	District	12277	42345
4.县及县以下	County and Below	25503	36384
5.其他	Others	2291	40043
二、按企业、事业、机关分组	**Groped by Character of Unit**		
1.企业	Enterprises	75544	33024
2.事业	Institutions	14022	49623
3.机关	Agencies and Organizations	13024	41890
4.民间非盈利组织	Non-profit NGO		
5.其他	Others		
三、按国民经济行业分组	**Grouped by Sector**		
（一）农、林、牧、渔业	Agriculture ,Forestry,Animal Husbandry and Fishery	42	21644
（二）采矿业	Mining		17798
（三）制造业	Manufacturing	14234	22078
（四）电力、燃气及水的生产和供应业	Production and Distribution of Electricity, Gas and Water	691	39717
（五）建筑业	Construction	12758	28761
（六）交通运输、仓储和邮政业	Traffic,Transport,Storage and Post	17446	41853
（七）信息传输、计算机服务和软件业	Information Transmission,Computer Service and Software	8572	36651
（八）批发和零售业	Wholesale and Retail Trades	719	23404
（九）住宿和餐饮业	Hotels and Catering Services	583	18736
（十）金融业	Financial Intermediation	3074	53151
（十一）房地产业	Real Estate	1936	27279
（十二）租赁和商务服务业	Leasing and Business Services	1397	42692
（十三）科学研究、技术服务和地质勘察业	Scientific Research,Technical Service and Geologic Prospecting	9230	57435
（十四）水利、环境和公共设施管理业	Management of Water Conservancy, Environment and Public Facilities	1117	26731
（十五）居民服务和其他服务业	Services to Households and Other Services	36	33033
（十六）教育	Education	11656	54559
（十七）卫生、社会保障和社会福利业	Health,Social Security and Social Welfare	5461	47177
（十八）文化、体育和娱乐业	Culture, Sports and Entertainment	846	33924
（十九）公共管理和社会组织	Public Management and Social Organization	12793	41913

3-14 城镇集体单位从业人员劳动报酬（2010年）

Remuneration of Persons Employed by Urban Collective-owned Units in Towns and Cities（2010）

单位:万元 (1 0000yuan)

分组	Classify	单位从业人员劳动报酬 Remuneration of Employment	在岗职工工资总额 Total Wages of Employed Staff and Workers
总计	**Total**	**69840.7**	**68357**
一、按企业、事业、机关分组	**Groped by Character of Unit**		
1.企业	Enterprises	66742	65733
2.事业	Institutions	3099	2624
3.机关	Agencies and Organizations		
4.民间非盈利组织	Non-profit NGO		
5.其他	Others		
二、按国民经济行业分组	**Grouped by Sector**		
（一）农、林、牧、渔业	Agriculture ,Forestry,Animal Husbandry and Fishery		
（二）采矿业	Mining		
（三）制造业	Manufacturing	20431	20207
（四）电力、燃气及水的生产和供应业	Production and Distribution of Electricity, Gas and Water	288	288
（五）建筑业	Construction	22034	21847
（六）交通运输、仓储和邮政业	Traffic,Transport,Storage and Post	1825	1823
（七）信息传输、计算机服务和软件业	Information Transmission,Computer Service and Software	899	899
（八）批发和零售业	Wholesale and Retail Trades	4822	4480
（九）住宿和餐饮业	Hotels and Catering Services	870	870
（十）金融业	Financial Intermediation	3860	3335
（十一）房地产业	Real Estate	3416	3411
（十二）租赁和商务服务业	Leasing and Business Services	1961	1961
（十三）科学研究、技术服务和地质勘察业	Scientific Research,Technical Service and Geologic Prospecting	436	422
（十四）水利、环境和公共设施管理业	Management of Water Conservancy, Environment and Public Facilities	262	262
（十五）居民服务和其他服务业	Services to Households and Other Services	4645	4576
（十六）教育	Education	195	195
（十七）卫生、社会保障和社会福利业	Health,Social Security and Social Welfare	3434	3320
（十八）文化、体育和娱乐业	Culture, Sports and Entertainment	464	464
（十九）公共管理和社会组织	Public Management and Social Organization		

3-14 续表 continued

单位:万元 (1 0000yuan)

分组	Classify	其他从业人员劳动报酬 Remuneration of Other Employed Persons	在岗职工平均工资（元） Average Wages of Employed Staff and Workers (yuan)
总 计	**Total**	**1483.4**	**12505**
一、按企业、事业、机关分组	**Groped by Character of Unit**		
1.企业	Enterprises	1009	12396
2.事业	Institutions	475	16050
3.机关	Agencies and Organizations		
4.民间非盈利组织	Non-profit NGO		
5.其他	Others		
二、按国民经济行业分组	**Grouped by Sector**		
（一）农、林、牧、渔业	Agriculture ,Forestry,Animal Husbandry and Fishery		
（二）采矿业	Mining		
（三）制造业	Manufacturing	224	14665
（四）电力、燃气及水的生产和供应业	Production and Distribution of Electricity, Gas and Water		16836
（五）建筑业	Construction	187	13427
（六）交通运输、仓储和邮政业	Traffic,Transport,Storage and Post	2	16790
（七）信息传输、计算机服务和软件业	Information Transmission,Computer Service and Software		28176
（八）批发和零售业	Wholesale and Retail Trades	342	13464
（九）住宿和餐饮业	Hotels and Catering Services		13315
（十）金融业	Financial Intermediation	525	14696
（十一）房地产业	Real Estate	6	9045
（十二）租赁和商务服务业	Leasing and Business Services		3626
（十三）科学研究、技术服务和地质勘察业	Scientific Research,Technical Service and Geologic Prospecting	14	9515
（十四）水利、环境和公共设施管理业	Management of Water Conservancy, Environment and Public Facilities		5910
（十五）居民服务和其他服务业	Services to Households and Other Services	69	11329
（十六）教育	Education		11447
（十七）卫生、社会保障和社会福利业	Health,Social Security and Social Welfare	115	17210
（十八）文化、体育和娱乐业	Culture, Sports and Entertainment		7923
（十九）公共管理和社会组织	Public Management and Social Organization		

3-15 其他经济类型单位从业人员劳动报酬（2010年）

Remuneration of Persons Employed by Other Units（2010）

单位: 万元 (1 0000yuan)

分组	Classify	单位从业人员劳动报酬 Remuneration of Employment	在岗职工工资总额 Total Wages of Employed Staff and Workers
总计	**Total**	**1759308**	**1672239**
一、按登记注册类型分组	**Grouped by Registion Status**		
（一）内资	Domestic Investment	1394704	1311683
1.股份合作	Share-holding Cooperative	21778	21666
2.联营	Joint Ownership	32379	31375
3.有限责任公司	Limited Liability Corporations	962490	923025
4.股份有限公司	Share-holding Corperation Ltd.	367186	324754
5.其他	Others	10871	10864
（二）港、澳、台商投资	Enterprises with Funds from Hong Kong, Macao and Taiwan	77298	77069
（三）外商投资	Enterprises with Foreign Funded	287306	283487
二、按企业、事业分组	**Grouped by Enterprise and Instilution**		
1.企业	Enterprises	1733551	1647472
2.事业	Institutions	21569	20708
3.民间非盈利组织	Non-profit NGO	4188	4059
4.其他	Others		
三、按国民经济行业分组	**Grouped by Sector**		
（一）农、林、牧、渔业	Agriculture,Forestry,Animal Husbandry and Fishery		
（二）采矿业	Mining	160	160
（三）制造业	Manufacturing	10926	10851
（四）电力、燃气及水的生产和供应业	Production and Distribution of Electricity, Gas and Water	640409	625998
（五）建筑业	Construction	12975	12973
（六）交通运输、仓储和邮政业	Traffic,Transport,Storage and Post	96814	92014
（七）信息传输、计算机服务和软件业	Information Transmission,Computer Service and Software	105637	99636
（八）批发和零售业	Wholesale and Retail Trades	130477	115630
（九）住宿和餐饮业	Hotels and Catering Services	96611	92591
（十）金融业	Financial Intermediation	56202	56107
（十一）房地产业	Real Estate	284912	248137
（十二）租赁和商务服务业	Leasing and Business Services	131267	130374
（十三）科学研究、技术服务和地质勘察业	Scientific Research,Technical Service and Geologic Prospecting	15025	14568
（十四）水利、环境和公共设施管理业	Management of Water Conservancy, Environment and Public Facilities	56626	55032
（十五）居民服务和其他服务业	Services to Households and Other Services	4889	4570
（十六）教育	Education	24121	24072
（十七）卫生、社会保障和社会福利业	Health,Social Security and Social Welfare	57910	55775
（十八）文化、体育和娱乐业	Culture, Sports and Entertainment	3864	3681
（十九）公共管理和社会组织	Public Management and Social Organization	30483	30071

3-15 续表 continued

单位: 万元 (1 0000yuan)

分组	Classify	其他从业人员劳动报酬 Remuneration of Other Employed Persons	在岗职工平均工资（元） Average Wages of Employed Staff and Workers (yuan)
总　计	**Total**	**87070**	**40721**
一、按登记注册类型分组	**Grouped by Registion Status**		
（一）内资	Domestic Investment	83022	40273
1.股份合作	Share-holding Cooperative	113	33879
2.联营	Joint Ownership	1005	50588
3.有限责任公司	Limited Liability Corporations	39465	36477
4.股份有限公司	Share-holding Corperation Ltd.	42433	55682
5.其他	Others	7	62798
（二）港、澳、台商投资	Enterprises with Funds from Hong Kong, Macao and Taiwan	229	41736
（三）外商投资	Enterprises with Foreign Funded	3819	42633
二、按企业、事业分组	**Grouped by Enterprise and Instilution**		
1.企业	Enterprises	86079	40611
2.事业	Institutions	861	57220
3.民间非盈利组织	Non-profit NGO	129	29779
4.其他	Others		
三、按国民经济行业分组	**Grouped by Sector**		
（一）农、林、牧、渔业	Agriculture,Forestry,Animal Husbandry and Fishery		
（二）采矿业	Mining		19691
（三）制造业	Manufacturing	75	34558
（四）电力、燃气及水的生产和供应业	Production and Distribution of Electricity, Gas and Water	14411	32779
（五）建筑业	Construction	2	44906
（六）交通运输、仓储和邮政业	Traffic,Transport,Storage and Post	4800	33307
（七）信息传输、计算机服务和软件业	Information Transmission,Computer Service and Software	6002	55585
（八）批发和零售业	Wholesale and Retail Trades	14846	65320
（九）住宿和餐饮业	Hotels and Catering Services	4020	27952
（十）金融业	Financial Intermediation	95	20225
（十一）房地产业	Real Estate	36775	102143
（十二）租赁和商务服务业	Leasing and Business Services	893	58545
（十三）科学研究、技术服务和地质勘察业	Scientific Research,Technical Service and Geologic Prospecting	457	44039
（十四）水利、环境和公共设施管理业	Management of Water Conservancy, Environment and Public Facilities	1594	56241
（十五）居民服务和其他服务业	Services to Households and Other Services	319	38763
（十六）教育	Education	50	31874
（十七）卫生、社会保障和社会福利业	Health,Social Security and Social Welfare	2135	55831
（十八）文化、体育和娱乐业	Culture, Sports and Entertainment	183	22821
（十九）公共管理和社会组织	Public Management and Social Organization	412	31770

3-16 城镇非私营单位在岗职工平均工资

单位: 元

分　组	Classify	全部单位 All Units 2009	全部单位 All Units 2010
合　计		**34032**	**37870**
一、按企业、事业分组	**Grouped by Enterprise and Instilution**		
1.企业	Enterprises	31322	34981
2.事业	Institutions	44689	49500
3.机关	Government Agencies	40510	41890
4.民间非盈利组织	Non-profit NGO	24340	29779
5.其他	Others		
二、按国民经济行业分组	**Grouped by Sector**		
（一）农、林、牧、渔业	Agriculture,Forestry,Animal Husbandry and Fishery	23498	21604
（二）采矿业	Mining	15065	32311
（三）制造业	Manufacturing	24784	26706
（四）电力、燃气及水的生产和供应业	Production and Distribution of Electricity, Gas and Water	36865	40061
（五）建筑业	Construction	25970	27670
（六）交通运输、仓储和邮政业	Traffic,Transport,Storage and Post	38838	44408
（七）信息传输、计算机服务和软件业	Information Transmission,Computer Service and Software	42965	48265
（八）批发和零售业	Wholesale and Retail Trades	20628	25439
（九）住宿和餐饮业	Hotels and Catering Services	18307	19707
（十）金融业	Financial Intermediation	71348	82654
（十一）房地产业	Real Estate	41133	46339
（十二）租赁和商务服务业	Leasing and Business Services	35704	30478
（十三）科学研究、技术服务和地质勘察业	Scientific Research,Technical Service and Geologic Prospecting	45931	57053
（十四）水利、环境和公共设施管理业	Management of Water Conservancy, Environment and Public Facilities	25694	26971
（十五）居民服务和其他服务业	Services to Households and Other Services	24274	26632
（十六）教育	Education	49335	54594
（十七）卫生、社会保障和社会福利业	Health,Social Security and Social Welfare	42789	45349
（十八）文化、体育和娱乐业	Culture, Sports and Entertainment	30056	32462
（十九）公共管理和社会组织	Public Management and Social Organization	40392	41913

Remuneration of Persons Employed by Non-private Units

(yuan)

国有单位 State-owned Units		集体单位 Collective-Owned Units		其它单位负责人 Other Units Responsible Persons	
2009	2010	2009	2010	2009	2010
34662	**38122**	**11492**	**12505**	**37307**	**40721**
30233	33024	11434	12396	37236	40611
45140	49623	12396	16050	45263	57220
40510	41890				
		12063		24825	29779
				33950	
23688	21644			11520	19691
16696	17798			14255	34558
19651	22078	11427	14665	36525	32779
34845	39717	16702	16836	54085	44906
31327	28761	9159	13427	26219	33307
37931	41853	13683	16790	47842	55585
43790	36651	14056	28176	42065	65320
26047	23404	11190	13464	20844	27952
17082	18736	16265	13315	19141	20225
62224	53151		14696	77528	102143
32296	27279	17479	9045	46882	58545
44442	42692	13198	3626	22852	44039
44721	57435	11562	9515	67657	56241
25975	26731	17144	5910	26227	38763
33186	33033	13402	11329	27024	31874
50203	54559	12816	11447	42454	55831
45708	47177	10783	17210	26143	22821
30500	33924	8797	7923	31878	31770
40392	41913				

3-17 城镇登记失业人数及失业率

Registered Unemployed Persons and Unemployment Rate in Urban Area

年　份 Year	年末实有城镇登记失业人数（万人） Real Number of Registered Unemployed Persons by Year-end (10 000 persons)	城镇登记失业率 (%) Registered Unemployment in Urban Area (%)
2002		3.7
2003		4.5
2004	8.29	4.3
2005	8.45	4.3
2006	8.74	4.3
2007	8.77	4.3
2008	9.40	4.2
2009	10.02	4.3
2010	10.46	4.2

主要统计指标解释

人口数 指一定时点、一定地区范围内的有生命的个人的总和。年度统计的年末人口数，指每年12月31日24时的人口数。

出生率（又称粗出生率） 指在一定时期内（通常为一年）平均每千人所出生的人数的比率，一般用千分率表示。其计算公式为:

出生率=年出生人数/年平均人数*1000‰

式中：出生人数指活产婴儿，即胎儿脱离母体时（不管怀孕月数），有过呼吸或其他生命现象。年平均人数指年初、年底人口数的平均数，也可用年中人口数代替。

死亡率（又称粗死亡率） 指在一定时期内（通常为一年）一定地区的死亡人数与同期内平均人数（或期中人数）之比，一般用千分率表示。本资料中的死亡率指年死亡率，其计算公式为:

死亡率=年死亡人数/年平均人数*1000‰

人口自然增长率 指在一定时期内（通常为一年）人口自然增加数（出生人数减死亡人数）与该时期内平均人数（或期中人数）之比，一般用千分率表示。计算公式为:

人口自然增长率=（本年出生人数-本年死亡人数）/年平均人数*1000‰

单位从业人员 指在各级国家机关、政党机关、社会团体及企业、事业单位中工作，取得工资或其他形式的劳动报酬的全部人员。包括在岗职工、再就业的离退休人员、民办教师以及在各单位中工作的外方人员和港澳台方人员、兼职人员、借用的外单位人员和第二职业者。不包括离开本单位仍保留劳动关系的职工。各单位的就业人员反映了各单位实际参加生产或工作的全部劳动力。

城镇私营和个体就业人员 城镇私营就业人员指在工商管理部门注册登记，其经营地址设在县城关镇（含城关镇）以上的私营企业就业人员; 包括私营企业投资者和雇工。城镇个体就业人员指在工商管理部门注册登记，并持有城镇户口或在城镇长期居住，经批准从事个体工商经营的就业人员; 包括个体经营者和在个体工商户劳动的家庭帮工和雇工。

城镇登记失业人员 指有非农业户口，在一定的劳动年龄内，有劳动能力，无业而要求就业，并在当地就业服务机构进行求职登记的人员。

城镇登记失业率 指城镇登记失业人数同城镇从业人数与城镇从业人数与城镇登记失业人数之和的比。计算公式为:

城镇登记失业率=城镇登记失业人数/（城镇单位就业人数+城镇私营企业及个体就业人数+城镇登记失业人数）*100%

职工 指在国有经济、城镇集体经济、联营经济、股份制经济、外商和港、澳、台投资经济、其他经济单位及其附属机构工作，并由其支付工资的各类人员，不包括返聘的离退休人员、民办教师、在国有经济单位工作的外方人员和港、澳、台人员。

(1998年以后的的职工数据均为在岗职工，其他相关指标如职工工资总额，职工平均工资等指标也从1998年按此口径进行了相应调整。)

国有单位职工 指在国有经济单位及其附属机构工作，并由其支付工资的各类人员。

城镇集体单位职工 指在城镇集体经济单位及其管理部门工作，并由其支付工资的各类人员。

其他单位职工 指在联营经济、股份制经济、外商投资经济、港、澳、台投资经济单位工作，并由其支付工资的各类人员。

在岗职工 指在本单位工作并由单位支付工资的人员，以及有工作岗位，但由于学习、病伤产假等原因暂未工作，仍由单位支付工资的人员。

职工工资总额 指各单位在一定时期内直接支付给本单位全部职工的劳动报酬总额。工资总额的计算原则应以直接支付给职工的全部劳动报酬为根据。各单位支付给职工的劳动报酬以及其他根据有关规定支付的工资，不论是计入成本的还是不计入成本的，不论是按国家规定列入计征奖金税项目的，还是未列入计征奖金税项目的，不论是以货币形式支付的还是以实物形式支付的，均包括在工资总额内。

职工平均工资 指企业、事业、机关单位的职工在一定时期内平均每人所得的货币工资额。它表明一定时期职工工资收入的高低程度，是反映职工工资水平的主要指标。计算公式为:

职工平均工资=报告期实际支付的全部职工工资总额/报告期全部职工平均人数

Explanatory Notes on Main Statistical Indicators

Total Population refers to the total number of people alive at a certain point of time within a given area.Annual statistics on the total population is taken at midnight, the 31st of December.

Birth Rate or (Crude Birth Rate) refers to the ratio of the number of births to the average population (or mid-period population) during a certain period of time (usually a year) which is often expressed in ‰. Birth rate in the chapter refers to annual birth rate. The following formula is used:

Birth Rate = Number of Births/Average Number of Population×1000‰

Number of births refers to live births i.e. the births when babies had showed any vital phenomena regardless of the length of pregnancy.Annual Average Number of Population is the average of the number of population at the beginning of the year and that at the end of the year. Sometimes it is substituted for with the mid year population.

Death Rate (or Crude Death Rate) refers to the ratio of the number of deaths to the average population (or mid-period population) during a certain period of time (usually a year) which is often expressed in ‰. Death rate in the chapter refers to annual death rate. The following formula is used:

Death Rate= Number of Deaths/Annual Average Number of Population×1000‰

Natural Growth Rate of Population refers to the ratio of natural increase in population (number of births minus number of deaths) in a certain period of time (usually a year) to the average population (or mid-period population) of the same period which is often expressed in ‰. The following formulas are applied:

Natural Growth of Population = (Number of Births-Number of Deaths)/Average Number of Population× 1000‰

Persons Employed in Various Units refer to all the persons working in government agencies of various levels, political and party organizations, social organizations, enterprises and institutions, and receiving wages or other forms of payment. They include fully-employed staff and workers, re-employed retirees, teachers in schools run by the local people, foreigners and Chinese compatriots from Hong Kong, Macao, and Taiwan working in various units, part-time employees, employees of other units working temporarily at current posts, and employees holding the second job, but exclude staff and workers who have left their working units while keeping their labour contract (employment relation) unchanged. This indicator reflects the total number of laborers actually engaged in production or other operations in various units.

Persons Employed in Private Enterprises and Self-Employed Individuals in Urban Areas Persons employed in private enterprises refer to the persons employed in the private enterprises which have been registered at the departments of industrial and commercial administration and are situated at a county town (i.e. a town where the county government is located) for business operation or at urban areas with the level higher than a county town. The self-employed individuals in urban areas refer to persons who hold the certificates of residence in urban areas or have resided in the urban areas for a long time and have been registered at the departments of industrial and commercial administration and approved to be engaged in individual industrial or commercial business, including self-employed persons as well as helpers and hired labourers who work in the individual households engaged in industrial or commercial business.

Registered Urban Unemployed Persons The registered unemployed persons in urban areas refer to the persons who are registered as permanent residents in the urban areas engaged in non-agricultural activities, aged within the range of working age, capable to labour, unemployed but desirous to be employed and have been registered at the local employment service agencies to apply for a job.

Registered Urban Unemployment Rate Registered unemployment rate in urban areas refers to the ratio of the number of the registered unemployed persons to the sum of the number of persons employed in various units and in private enterprises in urban areas, urban self-employed individuals and the registered urban unemployed persons . The formula is as follows:

Registered urban unemployment rate = number of registered urban unemployed persons÷ (number of persons employed in urban units + number of persons employed in urban private enterprises + and self-employed individuals in urban Areas + number ofregistered urban unemployed persons) × 100%.

Staff and Workers refer to the persons who work in (and receive payment therefrom) enterprises and institutions of state ownership, collective ownership, joint ownership, share holding, foreign ownership, and ownership by entrepreneurs from Hong Kong, Macao, and Taiwan, and other types of ownership and their affiliated units, excluding the retired persons invited to work in the units again, teachers in the schools run by the local people and foreigners and persons coming from Hong Kong, Macao and Taiwan and working in the state-owned economic units.

(Number of staff and workers in this yearbook include only fully employed staff and workers, excluding those who have left their working units while keeping their labour contract/employment relation unchanged).

Staff and Workers in State-owned Economic Units refer to the persons who work in the state-owned economic units or their attached units and are listed in their payrolls.

Staff and Workers of Collective Owned Units in Urban Areas refer to the persons who work in collective owned units in urban areas and their administration departments and receive payment therefrom.

Staff and Workers in Units of Other types of Ownership refer to those who work in (and receivepayment therefrom) enterprises and institutions of joint ownership, share holding, foreign ownership, and ownership by entrepreneurs from Hong Kong, Macao, and Taiwan.

Fully Employed Staff and Workers refer to persons who work in, and receive wages from their working units, as well as persons who have their work posts, but are temporarily absent from work for reasons of study or on sick, injury or maternal leave and still receive wages from their working units.

Total Wages of Staff and Workers refer to the total remuneration payment to staff and workers in various units during a certain period of time. The calculation of total wages is based on the total remuneration payment to the staff and workers. Therefore, all the wages and salaries and other payments to staff and workers are included in the total wages regardless of their sources, category, and forms (in kind or cash). (Total wages of staff and workers in this yearbook include only total wages of fully employed staff and workers, excluding the living allowances distributed to those who have left their working units while keeping their labour contract/employment relation unchanged).

Average Wage of Staff and Workers refers to the average wage in money terms per person during a certain period of time for staff and workers in enterprises, institutions, and government agencies, which reflects the general level of wage income during a certain period of time and is calculated as follows:

Average Wage of Staff and Workers = Total Wages of Staff and Workers at the Report/Average Number of Staff and Workers at the Report Period.

4 固定资产投资

INVESTMENT IN FIXED ASSETS

资料整理：种亚莉　王　峰　令润翠
Data management:Zhong Yali Wang Feng Ling Runcui

第四部分　固定资产投资

一、简要说明

本章资料主要包括全社会固定资产投资、城镇投资、房地产开发投资、城乡集体固定资产投资和城乡私人建房投资以及分区县情况，由西安市统计局固定资产投资处提供。

二、主要指标

全社会固定资产投资（亿元）	3250.56	比上年增长	30.0%
#国有经济单位	1348.76	比上年增长	44.6%
集体经济单位	326.44	比上年增长	12.6%
#城镇投资	3104.92	比上年增长	31.1%
房地产开发	842.34	比上年增长	21.0%
全市新增固定资产（亿元）	1193.05	比上年增长	17.7%
全市竣工住宅面积（万平方米）	521.08	比上年下降	36.7%

4 INVESTMENT IN FIXED ASSETS

Ⅰ.Brief Introduction

This chapter consists of primarily the data on fixed asset investment, Investment of Urban Units, real estate development investment, urban and rural area collective fixed asset investment, urban and rural area private housing investment and the classified Data of the districts and the counties on real estate development investment, provided by Fixed Asset Investment Division of the Xi'an Bureau of Statistics.

Ⅱ.Major Indicators

		Increase over Preceding Year
Investment Fulfilled In Fixed Assets(100 mil. yuan)	3250.56	30.0%
State-owned Enterprises	1348.76	44.6%
Collective-owned Enterprises	326.44	12.6%
Investment of Urban Units	3104.92	31.1%
Real Estate Development	842.34	21.0%
Investment Fulfilled Newly Increased Fixed Assets(100 mil. yuan)	1193.05	17.7%
Total Floor Space of Building Completed(10 000 sq.m)	521.08	-36.7%

4-1 主要年份按城乡分全社会固定资产投资

Total Investment in Fixed Assets in the Whole Country by Rural and Urban Areas in Representative Years

单位：亿元 (100 million yuan)

年份 Year	合计 Total	城镇 Urban Area	房地产开发 Real Estate	农村 Rural Area
1979	4.08	3.01		1.07
1980	6.12	4.48		1.64
1981	5.59	4.56		1.03
1982	9.49	8.02		1.47
1983	10.46	9.17		1.29
1984	12.89	10.69		2.20
1985	18.44	14.44		4.00
1986	22.15	18.54		3.61
1987	27.05	23.15		3.90
1988	29.14	24.43		4.71
1989	28.30	23.85		4.45
1990	26.39	23.10	0.91	3.29
1991	30.76	25.55	2.01	5.21
1992	38.48	32.85	3.32	5.63
1993	75.06	66.65	7.39	8.41
1994	85.57	73.47	12.02	12.10
1995	103.42	88.50	21.65	14.92
1996	114.38	96.98	24.66	17.40
1997	116.90	95.17	24.68	21.73
1998	154.80	138.68	38.21	16.12
1999	197.31	172.64	44.30	24.67
2000	232.37	203.01	51.85	29.36
2001	287.72	256.95	67.42	30.77
2002	338.15	307.24	79.37	30.91
2003	478.10	445.74	124.82	32.36
2004	646.69	612.03	169.67	34.66
2005	835.10	776.33	225.23	58.77
2006	1066.62	971.84	285.76	94.78
2007	1435.33	1340.59	387.33	94.74
2008	1906.36	1786.60	540.26	119.76
2009	2500.13	2367.58	696.34	132.55
2010	3250.56	3104.92	842.34	145.64

4-2 主要年份按经济类型分全社会固定资产投资

Total Investment in Fixed Assets in the Whole Country by Registion Status in Representative Years

单位：亿元　　(100 million yuan)

年 份 Year	合 计 Total	国有经济 State-owned	集体经济 Collective-owned	个体经济 Self-employed Individual	其他经济 Others
1985	18.44	13.96	1.36	3.12	
1986	22.15	18.05	0.97	3.13	
1987	27.05	22.18	1.50	3.37	
1988	29.14	23.72	1.86	3.56	
1989	28.30	23.22	1.46	3.62	
1990	26.39	22.21	1.44	2.74	
1991	30.76	24.42	2.26	4.08	
1992	38.48	32.04	1.45	4.99	
1993	75.06	59.66	3.03	6.55	5.82
1994	85.57	64.71	4.14	10.09	6.63
1995	103.42	69.08	9.78	11.13	13.43
1996	114.38	80.66	8.73	12.50	12.49
1997	116.90	77.46	10.21	15.11	14.12
1998	154.80	113.07	7.89	10.59	23.25
1999	197.31	136.50	13.62	16.22	30.97
2000	232.37	159.60	14.65	24.40	33.72
2001	287.72	175.58	14.67	38.57	58.90
2002	338.15	200.06	13.70	44.68	79.71
2003	478.10	264.83	22.33	73.43	117.51
2004	646.69	329.14	40.06	48.95	228.54
2005	835.10	373.70	59.23	79.04	323.13
2006	1066.62	401.14	110.68	107.33	447.47
2007	1435.33	476.78	207.08	183.09	568.38
2008	1906.36	694.89	246.89	50.43	914.15
2009	2500.13	932.91	289.91	97.86	1179.45
2010	3250.56	1348.76	326.44	54.73	1520.63

注：集体经济：包括城镇集体和农村集体。

个体经济：包括私营个体投资及城镇工矿区私人建房和农村私人建房。

Note: Collective-owned: Including Urban Collective-owned and Rural Collective-owned.

Individual: Including Individual Investment, Private Building Construction in Urban Industrial and Mining Regions and Rural Areas.

4-3 主要年份按产业分全市固定资产投资

Total Investment in Fixed Assets in the Whole City by Three Strata of Industry in Representative Years

单位：亿元 (100 million yuan)

年 份 Year	合 计 Total	第一产业 Primary Industry	第二产业 Secondary Industry	工业 Industry	第三产业 Tertiary Industry
1979	3.01	0.06	1.24	1.20	1.71
1980	4.48	0.06	2.09	1.99	2.33
1981	4.56	0.11	2.10	1.83	2.35
1982	8.02	0.04	4.07	3.63	3.91
1983	9.17	0.11	4.97	4.41	4.09
1984	10.69	0.19	4.56	3.99	5.94
1985	14.44	0.18	7.22	6.45	7.04
1986	18.54	0.16	8.98	8.37	9.40
1987	23.15	0.19	11.81	11.26	11.15
1988	24.43	0.15	11.95	11.20	12.33
1989	23.85	0.13	11.94	11.50	11.78
1990	23.10	0.25	11.03	10.59	11.82
1991	25.55	0.27	12.48	11.95	12.80
1992	32.85	0.10	15.60	14.73	17.15
1993	66.65	0.07	24.50	22.44	42.08
1994	73.47	0.03	27.04	25.85	46.40
1995	88.50	0.14	28.80	27.71	59.56
1996	96.98	0.13	25.96	24.24	70.89
1997	95.17	0.24	23.65	21.66	71.28
1998	138.68	0.48	35.33	29.86	102.87
1999	172.64	0.94	39.88	36.40	131.82
2000	203.01	0.76	57.21	54.37	145.04
2001	256.95	0.86	63.31	61.28	192.78
2002	307.24	4.29	74.34	68.45	228.61
2003	445.74	3.34	83.25	78.41	359.15
2004	612.03	3.38	97.69	95.67	510.96
2005	776.33	5.26	144.25	140.44	626.82
2006	971.84	10.04	213.43	206.48	748.37
2007	1340.59	10.20	297.53	286.61	1032.86
2008	1786.60	23.75	369.74	356.12	1393.11
2009	2367.58	24.46	458.44	442.70	1884.68
2010	3104.92	39.83	556.10	498.62	2508.99

4-4 全市固定资产投资（2010年）

Total Investment in Fixed Assets in the Whole City（2010）

单位：万元 (10 000 yuan)

分　组	Classify	合计 Total	房地产开发 Real Estate
一、本年完成投资	**Investment Completed This Year**	**31049184**	**8423447**
按登记注册类型分	**Grouped by Registion Status**		
内资	Domestic Funded	29939235	7839547
国有	State-owned Enterprises	13119098	827930
集体	Collective-owned Enterprises	2113520	276426
股份合作	Share-holding Corperative	199205	91999
国有联营	State Joint Ownership Enterprises	1142	
集体联营	Collective Joint Ownership Enterprises	1700	
国有与集体联营	Joint State-collective Enterprises	13122	9152
其他联营	Other Joint Ownership Enterprises	51265	32765
国有独资公司	State Sole-funded Corporations	367380	181183
其他有限责任公司	Other Limited Liability Corporations	9303905	4133707
股份有限公司	Share-holding Corperation Ltd.	775082	174983
私营及个体	Private and Individual	3425261	1898606
其他	Others	568555	212796
港澳台商投资	Enterprises with Funds from Hong Kong,Macao and Taiwan	571212	220650
合资经营企业(港或澳、台资)	Joint Venture	268870	29478
合作经营企业(港或澳、台资)	Cooperation	37034	37034
独资企业	Sole-funded	256308	154138
股份有限公司	Share-Holding Corporations Ltd.	9000	

4-4 续表1 continued 1

单位：万元 (10 000 yuan)

指 标	Item	合计 Total	房地产开发 Real Estate
外商投资	Enterprises with Foreign Investment	538737	363250
合资经营企业(港或澳、台资)	Joint Venture	156133	125414
合作经营企业(港或澳、台资)	Cooperation	214614	189598
独资企业	Sole-Funded	166979	48238
股份有限公司	Share-Holding Corporations Ltd.	1011	
按隶属关系分	**Grouped by Jurisdiction of Management**		
中央	Central	1814042	63264
省属	Provincial	3760288	339290
市属	Municipal	25474854	8020893
按建设性质分	**Grouped by Type of Construction**		
#新建	New Construction	14292899	
扩建	Expansion	2649749	
改建和技术改造	Reconstruction	2620997	
按构成分	**Grouped by Composition**		
1.建筑工程	Construction Projects	19583638	6034071
2.安装工程	Installment Projects	2106567	780008
3.设备、工器具购置	Purchasing of Equipment and Instruments	3094336	174597
4.其他	Others	6264643	1434771
按工程用途分	**Grouped by Purpose of Project**		
#住宅	Residential Buildings	9143236	6704066

4-4 续表2 continued 2

指 标	Item	合计 Total	房地产开发 Real Estate
二、构成（%）	**Proportion (%)**		
按登记注册类型分	**Grouped by Status**		
#国有经济	State-owned	43.4	12.0
集体经济	Collective-owned	7.5	4.4
按隶属关系分	**Grouped by Jurisdiction of Management**		
中央	Central	5.8	0.8
省属	Provincial	12.1	4.0
市属	Municipal	82.0	95.2
按建设性质分	**Grouped by Type of Construction**		
#新建	New Construction	46.0	
扩建	Expansion	8.5	
改建和技术改造	Reconstruction	8.4	
按构成分	**Grouped by Composition of Funds**		
1.建筑工程	Construction Projects	63.1	71.6
2.安装工程	Installation Projects	6.8	9.3
3.设备工器具购置	Purchasing of the Equipment and Instruments	10.0	2.1
4.其他费用	Others	20.2	17.0
按工程用途分	**Grouped by Purpose of Project**		
#住宅	Residential Buildings	29.4	79.6
三、房屋面积(平方米)	**Floor Space (sq.m)**		
本年施工房屋面积	Floor Space of Buildings Under Construction This Year	111661874	66973869
#住宅	Residential Buildings	80598742	57777112
本年竣工房屋面积	Floor Space of Buildings Completed This Year	7751562	4636472
#住宅	Residential Buildings	5210847	4124392
四、本年新增固定资产(万元）	**Newly Increase in Fixed Assets(10 000 yuan)**	**11930457**	**1682023**

4-5 按行业分全市固定资产投资（2010年）

Total Investment in Fixed Assets in the Whole City by Sector （2010）

指　标	Item	2010
本年完成投资（万元）	**Grouped by Sector (10 000 yuan)**	**31049184**
（一）农、林、牧、渔业	Agriculture,Forestry,Animal Husbandry and Fishery	398240
（二）采矿业	Mining	290955
（三）制造业	Manufacturing	4069216
农副食品加工业	Processing of Food from Agricultural Products	128749
食品制造业	Manufacture of Foods	174352
饮料制造业	Manufacture of Beverages	
石油加工、炼焦及核燃料加工业	Processing of Petroleum, Coking,Processing of Nuclear Fuel	20665
化学原料及化学制品制造业	Manufacture of Raw Chemical Materials and Chemical Products	53698
医药制造业	Manufacture of Medicines	106766
金属制品业	Manufacture of Metal Products	111837
通用设备制造业	Manufacture of General Purpose Machinery	258725
专用设备制造业	Manufacture of Special Purpose Machinery	799620
交通运输设备制造业	Manufacture of Transport Equipment	645384
电气机械及器材制造业	Manufacture of Electrical Machinery and Equipment	294786
通信设备、计算机及其他电子设备制造业	Manufacture of Communication Equipment, Computers and Other Electronic Equipment	700801
仪器仪表及文化办公用机械制造业	Manufacture of Measuring Instruments and Machinery for Cultural Activity and Office Work	88993
（四）电力、燃气及水的生产和供应业	Production & Supply of Electricity,Gas & Water	625986
（五）建筑业	Construction	574873
（六）交通运输、仓储和邮政业	Transport,Storage and Post	1769356
（七）信息传输、计算机服务和软件业	Information Transmission,Computer Service and Software	509902
（八）批发和零售业	Wholesale and Retail Trades	547444
（九）住宿和餐饮业	Hotels and Catering Services	389667
（十）金融业	Financial Intermediation	12868
（十一）房地产业	Real Estate	12543310
（十二）租赁和商务服务业	Leasing and Business Services	435042
（十三）科学研究、技术服务和地质勘察业	Scientific Research,Technical Service and Geologic Prospecting	370377
（十四）水利、环境和公共设施管理业	Management of Water Conservancy, Environment and Public Facilities	5115257
（十五）居民服务和其他服务业	Services to Households and Other Services	80836
（十六）教育	Education	779341
（十七）卫生、社会保障和社会福利业	Health,Social Security and Social Welfare	197291
（十八）文化、体育和娱乐业	Culture, Sports and Entertainment	156596
（十九）公共管理和社会组织	Public Management and Social Organization	2182627

4-6 主要年份按资金来源及建设性质分全市固定资产投资

指　　标	Item	1995	2000
一、投资总额(万元)	**Total Investment (10 000 yuan)**	**884994**	**2030122**
（一）按资金来源分	Grouped by Funds Source		
1.国家预算内资金	State Budgetary Funds	69185	160982
2.国内贷款	Domestic Loans	216565	432282
3.债券	Bonds	873	32460
4.利用外资	Utilization of Foreign Funds	80792	31622
5.自筹资金	Self-raising Funds	385047	875352
6.其他资金	Others	132532	497424
（二）按构成分	Grouped by Composition of Funds		
1.建筑安装工程	Construction and Installation Projects	527220	1404184
2.设备、工器具购置	Purchasing of Equipment and Instruments	233730	382495
3.其它费用	Others	124044	243443
（三）按建设性质分	Grouped by Type of Construction		
#新　建	New Construction	210926	533058
扩　建	Expansion	180210	542510
改　建	Reconstruction	157457	263657
二、房屋施工面积(万平方米)	**Floor Space Under Construction**	**1070.58**	**1702.58**

Total Investment in Fixed Assets in the Whole City by Sources of Funds and Type of Construction in Representative Years

2001	2002	2003	2004	2005	2006	2007	2008	2009	2010
2569496	**3072442**	**4457381**	**6120324**	**7763283**	**9718418**	**13405920**	**17865977**	**23675759**	**31049184**
256403	355960	365263	436496	728885	677145	670592	1555809	2562756	1649563
672379	666146	1219234	1565246	1257175	1631689	1619218	2162957	3301919	4288663
6753	766	3278							
54907	15192	47509	47401	40583	165390	183422	261325	144124	126802
1121502	1392915	1733132	2629720	4001700	5538393	8565573	12771844	15776565	18279153
457552	641463	1088965	1441461	1734940	1705801	2367115	1114042	1890395	6705003
1698777	2119151	3067309	4127677	5086664	6486233	9165668	12864657	16337466	21690205
452602	552251	577240	708988	1021079	1409589	1858720	2024631	2619783	3094336
418117	401040	812832	1283659	1655540	1822596	2381532	2976689	4718510	6264643
723957	874392	1294032	1874116	2907551	3511432	5123975	6356716	8567540	14292899
581138	868603	1102914	1169537	1208430	1101740	994841	2118013	3054929	2649749
344879	343184	447944	670229	782953	1099304	1548130	1921664	2738799	2620997
1767.13	2396.89	2716.18	3177.36	4030.38	4589.39	5759.28	6570.94	9571.25	11166.19

4–7 主要年份国有经济单位固定资产投资

指　　标	Item	1985	1990	1995
一、投资总额(万元)	**Total Investment (10 000 yuan)**	**139567**	**222084**	**690806**
1.按资金来源分	Grouped by Funds Source			
国家预算内投资	State Budgetary Funds	45815	48770	67426
国内贷款	Domestic Loans	27102	58602	145108
债 券	Bonds			
利用外资	Utilization of Foreign Funds	2244	9970	46811
自筹资金	Self-raising Funds	56758	91527	330333
其它资金	Others	7648	13215	101128
2.按构成分	Grouped by Composition of Funds			
建筑安装工程	Construction and Installation Projects	83542	130615	405057
设备、工具、器具购置	Purchasing of Equipment and Instruments	36328	72043	209351
其它费用	Others	19697	19426	76398
3.按建设性质分	Grouped by Type of Construction			
#新　建	New Construction	33366	55242	165793
扩　建	Expansion	55370	60641	162796
改　建	Reconstruction	33505	63253	145783
4.按国民经济行业分	Grouped by Sector			
#农林牧渔业	Agriculture,Forestry,Animal Husbandry and Fishery	1736	1888	1127
工业建筑业	Industry and Construction	61634	101407	240665
运输邮电业	Transportation,Post and Telecommunications	4949	28180	
二、新增固定资产(万元)	**Newly Increased in Fixed Assets (10 000 yuan)**	**83030**	**195429**	**509328**
三、房屋建筑面积(万平方米)	**Floor Space of Buildings (10 000 sq.m)**			
施工面积	Floor Space Under Construction	586	509	841
竣工面积	Floor Space Completed	214	203	304
#住 宅	Residential Building	125	108	214

Investment in Fixed Assets of State-owned Units in Representative Years

2000	2001	2002	2003	2004	2005	2006	2007	2008	2009	2010
1596002	**1755787**	**2000636**	**2648283**	**3291356**	**3736992**	**4011446**	**4767827**	**6948899**	**9329071**	**13487620**
165304	255860	351540	268537	361654	722673	699765	655259	1034930	1367405	1312512
280585	471506	453958	823374	858396	850554	882295	664703	1175473	1766395	2305605
32886	6865		2310							
15276	20815	6617	4846	10851	9900	73830	58711	65209	29033	24222
689732	715351	840082	803648	779205	1405167	1968662	2830256	4055904	5047734	8335268
412219	285390	348439	745568	1281250	748698	386894	558898	617383	1118504	1510013
1102548	1177790	1449583	1897323	2197052	2394409	2532743	2925696	4973312	5596104	8591043
328432	334174	347647	335454	333272	384157	536340	865951	728554	1131474	1522615
165022	243823	203406	415506	761032	958426	942363	976180	1247033	2601493	3373962
390119	486585	537537	883859	1157470	1740071	1737828	1893488	2881551	4358755	7363825
460381	436404	672297	726753	965832	907723	884083	658048	1617290	1670225	1685886
254860	328685	272499	377060	514870	617680	642848	950958	1005897	1484559	1715761
4077	3666	24087	25034	14908	26132	66279	67049	6422942	8694113	12325705
408234	361954	358027	427632	410907	571954	572491	989275	1565134	1541388	2421783
360779	472278	375131	312306	407674	147961	317144	292019	4795642	7114717	9863058
1220632	**1120240**	**1134623**	**1732895**	**1733550**	**1988546**	**1799515**	**2651549**	**1963274**	**3743856**	**3859619**
1342	1155	1590	1331	1041	1397	1331	1546	1367	2384	2765
577	492	452	514	255	518	390	552	266	312	189
475	392	311	343	162	234	219	350	151	226	112

4-8 农村集体固定资产投资（2010年）

Investment in Fixed Assets of Rural Collective Owned Units（2010）

单位：万元 (10 000 yuan)

指　　标	Item	2010
一、本年完成投资	**Investment Completed This Year**	**949949**
建筑工程	Constrution Projects	725624
安装工程	Installment Projects	41428
设备购置	Purchasing of Equipment	49680
其他	Others	133217
二、本年新增固定资产	**Newly Increased Fixed in Assets This Year**	**671743**
三、本年资金来源合计	**Total of Sources of Funds This Year**	**1026065**
上年末结余资金	**Balance of Last Year**	**300**
本年资金来源小计	**Subtotal Funds This Year**	**1025765**
国家资金	State Funds	56321
国内贷款	Domestic Loans	59338
利用外资	Utilization of Foreign Funds	
自筹资金	Self-raising Funds	892713
其他资金	Others	17393
四、房屋建筑面积(平方米)	**Floor Space of Buildings(sq.m)**	
施工面积	Floor Space Under Construction	1314577
#住宅	Residential Buildings	426675
竣工面积	Floor Space Completed	539987
#住宅	Residential Buildings	128075

4-9 主要年份农村集体固定资产投资

Investment in Fixed Assets of Rural Collective Owned Units in Representative Years

指　　标	Item	1995	2000	2001	2002
一、投资总额(万元)	**Total Investment (10 000 yuan)**	**37892**	**89626**	**82623**	**68610**
1.按资金来源分	Grouped by Funds Source				
国家资金	State Funds	1442	9388	994	2369
国内贷款	Domestic Loans	10925	2977	5596	1818
利用外资	Utilization of Foreign Funds	5021	5394	70	8973
自筹资金	Self-raising Funds	12220	53338	58911	41183
群众集资	Mass Fund-raising	3732	7413	8248	10647
其他资金	Others	4552	11116	8804	3620
2.按行业划分	Grouped by Sector				
农林牧渔业	Ariculture, Forestry, Animal Husbandry, Fishery	170	9075	4452	4358
工业	Industry	20286	32437	21155	16998
建筑业	Construction	2475	12309	8523	5243
交通运输、仓储和邮政业	Transport,Storage,and Post	668	2444	1023	1057
信息传输、计算机服务和软件业	Information Transmission,Computer Service and Software				
批发和零售贸易业	Wholesale and Retail Trade	3749	8444	26611	9273
住宿和餐饮业	Hotels and Catering Services				
金融业	Financial Intermediation		10	700	
房地产业	Real Estate	2338	12519	8260	10286
租赁和商务服务业	Leasing and Business Services				
居民服务和其他服务	Services to Households and Other Services				
卫生体育社会福利业	Health Care,Sports and Social Welfare	3054	126	107	281
教育文化艺术及广播电影电视业	Education,Culture and Arts,Radio, Film and Television	4642	6110	7973	9713
科学研究和综合技术服务业	Scientific Research and Polytechnical Services		500	790	
水利、环境和公共设施管理业	Management of Water Conservancy, Environment and Public Facilities	350	5017	1170	8747
国家机关政党机关和社会团体	Governmental and Party Agencies and Social Organizations	160	635	1859	2654
二、竣工房屋建筑面积(万平方米)	**Floor Space of the Building Completed (10 000 sq.m)**	**16.08**	**83.96**	**41.1**	**43.31**
#住宅	Residential Buildings	0.92	21.33	10.82	8.35
三、本年新增固定资产(万元)	**Newly Increase Fixed Assets This Year (10 000 yuan)**	**32405**	**89626**	**75732**	**55215**

4-9 续表1 continued 1

指　　标	Item	2003	2004	2005	2006
一、投资总额(万元)	**Total Investment (10 000 yuan)**	**79216**	**132614**	**324932**	**704576**
1.按资金来源分	Grouped by Funds Source				
国家资金	State Funds	3198	3388	4295	14889
国内贷款	Domestic Loans	742	981	10994	19415
利用外资	Utilization of Foreign Funds	3887	41		21
自筹资金	Self-raising Funds	52946	95820	212297	576709
群众集资	Mass Fund-raising	6256			
其他资金	Others	12187	32384	97346	93542
2.按行业划分	Grouped by Sector				
农林牧渔业	Ariculture, Forestry, Animal Husbandry, Fishery	3632	3174	17663	11684
工业	Industry	5228	19382	21023	72083
建筑业	Construction	10248	17442	1591	2437
交通运输、仓储和邮政业	Transport,Storage,and Post	220	3188	21479	17576
信息传输、计算机服务和软件业	Information Transmission,Computer Service and Software			390	905
批发和零售贸易业	Wholesale and Retail Trade	2760	6819	12528	33516
住宿和餐饮业	Hotels and Catering Services			15182	15160
金融业	Financial Intermediation	25			
房地产业	Real Estate	19315	1400		70
租赁和商务服务业	Leasing and Business Services			300	
居民服务和其他服务	Services to Households and Other Services			1049	1760
卫生体育社会福利业	Health Care,Sports and Social Welfare	326	150	55	3595
教育文化艺术及广播电影电视业	Education,Culture and Arts,Radio, Film and Television	4831	6160	10054	21602
科学研究和综合技术服务业	Scientific Research and Polytechnical Services			10571	641
水利、环境和公共设施管理业	Management of Water Conservancy, Environment and Public Facilities	20001	62016	212007	61173
国家机关政党机关和社会团体	Governmental and Party Agencies and Social Organizations	12630	12883	1040	462374
二、竣工房屋建筑面积(万平方米)	**Floor Space of the Building Completed (10 000 sq.m)**	**48.26**	**55.62**	**46.04**	**215.98**
#住宅	Residential Buildings	23.2	34.46	25.89	86.45
三、本年新增固定资产(万元)	**Newly Increase Fixed Assets This Year (10 000 yuan)**	**72862**	**87865**	**148210**	**432586**

4-9 续表2 continued 2

指　　标	Item	2007	2008	2009	2010
一、投资总额(万元)	**Total Investment (10 000 yuan)**	**666887**	**785921**	**861851**	**949949**
1.按资金来源分	Grouped by Funds Source				
国家资金	State Funds	26924	35800	53406	52158
国内贷款	Domestic Loans	42216	79031	31422	54952
利用外资	Utilization of Foreign Funds	2029	3058		
自筹资金	Self-raising Funds	528735	590202	766778	826731
群众集资	Mass Fund-raising				
其他资金	Others	66983	77830	10245	16108
2.按行业划分	Grouped by Sector				
农林牧渔业	Ariculture, Forestry, Animal Husbandry, Fishery	27578	30115	69950	349761
工业	Industry	136203	184342	142060	64821
建筑业	Construction	1200	5400		7705
交通运输、仓储和邮政业	Transport,Storage,and Post	55138	42731	30990	8070
信息传输、计算机服务和软件业	Information Transmission,Computer Service and Software	670	650		800
批发和零售贸易业	Wholesale and Retail Trade	62206	19691	10740	12060
住宿和餐饮业	Hotels and Catering Services	5631	19178	27580	58330
金融业	Financial Intermediation			1600	
房地产业	Real Estate	900	7256	8330	96900
租赁和商务服务业	Leasing and Business Services	1300	1000	250	
居民服务和其他服务	Services to Households and Other Services	5390	500	3630	
卫生体育社会福利业	Health Care,Sports and Social Welfare	200	795	7613	
教育文化艺术及广播电影电视业	Education,Culture and Arts,Radio, Film and Television	32247	12294	21622	
科学研究和综合技术服务业	Scientific Research and Polytechnical Services	930		900	
水利、环境和公共设施管理业	Management of Water Conservancy, Environment and Public Facilities	49418	133369	218661	280703
国家机关政党机关和社会团体	Governmental and Party Agencies and Social Organizations	287876	328600	317925	70799
二、竣工房屋建筑面积(万平方米)	**Floor Space of the Building Completed (10 000 sq.m)**	**192.01**	**46.89**	**207.69**	**539987**
#住宅	Residential Buildings	37.06	11.8	11.08	128075
三、本年新增固定资产(万元)	**Newly Increase Fixed Assets This Year (10 000 yuan)**	**586012**	**376378**	**792448**	**671743**

4–10 主要年份市属固定资产投资

单位：万元

指　　标	Item	1985	1990	1995	2000	2001
一、投资总额	**Total Investment**	**38896**	**80958**	**432451**	**1263023**	**1539717**
1.按经济类型分	Grouped by Type of Enterprises					
国有经济	State-owned Enterprises	34313	72078	258545	890546	894700
集体经济	Collective-owned Enterprises	4583	8880	5720	52893	62895
其他经济	Others			168186	319584	582122
2.按管理渠道分	Grouped by Management					
城镇投资	Investment of Urban Units	38896	80958	432451	1263023	1539717
房地产开发	Real Estate		5485	171291	473787	566557
二、新增固定资产	**Newly Increased Fixed Assets**	**27872**	**69434**	**273324**	**953173**	**1159980**
三、房屋竣工面积	**Floor Space of the**	**98.62**	**95.02**	**202.52**	**509.48**	**535.98**
(万平方米)	**Building Completed(10000sq.m)**					
#住　宅	Residential Buildings	45.11	50.12	143.30	373.51	396.01

Investment In Fixed Assets of Municipal Units in Representative Years

(10 000 yuan)

2002	2003	2004	2005	2006	2007	2008	2009	2010
1848833	**2978747**	**4355271**	**5788693**	**7835681**	**10555849**	**14648360**	**19063075**	**25474854**
1006245	1586057	1884624	2198836	2591184	2972840	4480627	6527566	9306901
63877	142849	257226	258327	363909	1366567	1646111	1614290	2253851
778711	1249841	2213421	3331530	4880588	6216442	8521622	10921219	13914102
1848833	2978747	4355271	5788693	7835681	10555849	14648360	19063075	25474854
702233	1114809	1492693	2062940	2641871	3515719	4938202	6575526	8020893
1295389	**1812099**	**1962795**	**3011104**	**3495179**	**5279938**	**6488364**	**8380033**	**10423906**
537.4374	**631.8902**	**606.2317**	**767.7031**	**914.7989**	**1343.8785**	**987.0482**	**1359.4584**	**668.49**
331.45	387.82	388.79	436.43	432.43	734.05	602.69	727.41	448.46

4-11 市属固定资产投资（2010年）

Investment in Fixed Assets of Municipal Units（2010）

单位：万元 (10 000 yuan)

分类	Classify	城镇 Urban Area	房地产开发 Real Estate
一、本年完成投资	**Accomplished Investment This Year**	**25474854**	**8020893**
区县属	District and County		
按登记注册类型分	**Grouped by Registion Status**		
内资	Domestic Funded	24322574	7436993
国有	State-owned Enterprises	9046580	751492
集体	Collective-owned Enterprises	2093956	276426
股份合作	Share-holding Corperative	158195	91999
国有联营	State Joint Ownership Enterprises	1142	
集体联营	Collective Joint Ownership Enterprises	1700	
国有与集体联营	State-owned and Collective-owned Joint Enterprises	13122	9152
其他联营	Other Joint Ownership Enterprises	51265	32765
国有独资公司	Sole State-funded Corporations	259179	148605
其他有限责任公司	Other Limited Liability Corporations	8069228	3864717
股份有限公司	Share-holding Corperation Ltd.	718000	174983
私营及个体	Private and Individual	3382740	1898606
其他	Others	527467	188248
港澳台商投资	Enterprises with Investment from Hong Kong, Macao and Taiwan	571022	220650
合资经营企业(港或澳、台资)	Joint Venture	268680	29478
合作经营企业(港或澳、台资)	Cooperation	37034	37034
独资企业	Sole-Funded	256308	154138
股份有限公司	Share-Holding Corporations Ltd.	9000	
外商投资	Enterprises with Foreign Investment	538737	363250
合资经营企业(港或澳、台资)	Joint Venture	156133	125414
合作经营企业(港或澳、台资)	Cooperation	214614	189598
独资企业	Sole-funded	166979	48238
股份有限公司	Share-holding Corporations Ltd.	1011	
按建设性质分	**Grouped by Type of Construction**		
#新建	New Construction	11298771	
扩建	Expansion	2466831	
改建和技术改造	Reconstruction	2080075	
按构成分	**Grouped by Composition**		
1.建筑工程	Construction Projects	16710897	5810966
2.安装工程	Installment Projects	1495256	707857
3.设备工器具购置	Purchasing of Equipment and Instruments	1604764	152492
4.其他费用	Others	5663937	1349578
按工程用途分	**Grouped by Purpose of Project**		
#住宅	Residential Buildings	8583905	6410821

4-11 续表 continued

指　　标	Item	城镇 Urban Area	房地产开发 Real Estate
二、构成（%）	**Proportion (%)**		
按登记注册类型分	**Grouped by Status**		
#国有经济	State-owned	36.5	11.2
集体经济	Collective-owned	8.8	4.6
按建设性质分	**Grouped by Type of Construction**		
#新建	New Construction	44.4	
扩建	Expansion	9.7	
改建和技术改造	Reconstruction	8.2	
按构成分	**Grouped by Composition of Funds**		
1.建筑工程	Construction Projects	65.6	72.4
2.安装工程	Installation Projects	5.9	8.8
3.设备工器具购置	Purchasing of the Equipment and Instruments	6.3	1.9
4.其他费用	Others	22.2	16.8
按工程用途分	**Grouped by Purpose of Project**		
#住宅	Residential Buildings	33.7	79.9
三、房屋面积(平方米)	**Floor Space (sq.m)**		
本年施工房屋面积	Floor Space of Buildings Under Construction This Year	99569250	63180362
#住宅	Residential Buildings	74224014	54543746
本年竣工房屋面积	Floor Space of Buildings Completed This Year	6684868	4202356
#住宅	Residential Buildings	4484575	3739462
四、本年新增固定资产(万元)	**Newly Increase in Fixed Assets(10 000 yuan)**	**10423906**	**1562592**

4-12 按行业分市属固定资产投资（2010年）

Investment in Fixed Assets of Municipal Units by Sector（2010）

指　标	Item	2010
本年完成投资（万元）	**Grouped by Sector (10 000 yuan)**	**25474854**
（一）农、林、牧、渔业	Agriculture,Forestry,Animal Husbandry and Fishery	398240
（二）采矿业	Mining	34377
（三）制造业	Manufacturing	2778579
#农副食品加工业	Processing of Food from Agricultural Products	128749
食品制造业	Manufacture of Foods	174352
饮料制造业	Manufacture of Beverages	60686
石油加工、炼焦及核燃料加工业	Processing of Petroleum, Coking,Processing of Nuclear Fuel	
化学原料及化学制品制造业	Manufacture of Raw Chemical Materials and Chemical Products	53698
医药制造业	Manufacture of Medicines	106576
金属制品业	Manufacture of Metal Products	111837
通用设备制造业	Manufacture of General Purpose Machinery	188981
专用设备制造业	Manufacture of Special Purpose Machinery	288804
交通运输设备制造业	Manufacture of Transport Equipment	410432
电气机械及器材制造业	Manufacture of Electrical Machinery and Equipment	265170
通信设备、计算机及其他电子设备制造业	Manufacture of Communication Equipment, Computers and Other Electronic Equipment	469923
仪器仪表及文化办公用机械制造业	Manufacture of Measuring Instruments and Machinery for Cultural Activity and Office Work	12196
（四）电力、燃气及水的生产和供应业	Production & Supply of Electricity,Gas & Water	308549
（五）建筑业	Construction	227296
（六）交通运输、仓储和邮政业	Transport,Storage and Post	932387
（七）信息传输、计算机服务和软件业	Information Transmission,Computer Service and Software	98901
（八）批发和零售业	Wholesale and Retail Trades	443454
（九）住宿和餐饮业	Hotels and Catering Services	323073
（十）金融业	Financial Intermediation	12075
（十一）房地产业	Real Estate	11914643
（十二）租赁和商务服务业	Leasing and Business Services	311166
（十三）科学研究、技术服务和地质勘察业	Scientific Research,Technical Service and Geologic Prospecting	64523
（十四）水利、环境和公共设施管理业	Management of Water Conservancy, Environment and Public Facilities	4791687
（十五）居民服务和其他服务业	Services to Households and Other Services	80836
（十六）教育	Education	343175
（十七）卫生、社会保障和社会福利业	Health,Social Security and Social Welfare	165510
（十八）文化、体育和娱乐业	Culture, Sports and Entertainment	126198
（十九）公共管理和社会组织	Public Management and Social Organization	2120185

4-13 按资金来源及建设性质分市属固定资产投资（2010年）

Investment in Fixed Assets of Municipal Units by Sources of Funds and Type of Construction（2010）

指 标	Item	2010
投资总额(万元)	**Total Investment (10 000 yuan)**	25474854
一、按资金来源分	**Grouped by Funds Sources**	
1.国家预算内资金	State Budgetary Funds	1244332
2.国内贷款	Domestic Loans	2698424
3.债 券	Bonds	
4.利用外资	Utilization of Foreign Funds	124492
5.自筹资金	Self-raising Funds	15220575
6.其他资金	Others	6187031
二、按建设性质分	**Grouped by Type of Construction**	
#新 建	New Construction	11298771
扩 建	Expansion	2466831
改 建	Reconstruction	2080075
三、按构成分	**Grouped by Composition of Funds**	
1.建筑工程	Construction Project	16710897
2.安装工程	Installation Projects	1495256
3.设备、工器具购置	Purchasing of Equipment and Instruments	1604764
4.其它费用	Others	5663937

4-14 按登记注册类型及隶属关系分市区固定资产投资（2010年）

Investments in Fixed Assets of Urban Districts by Registration Status and Jurisdiction of Management（2010）

分　组	Classify	2010
本年完成投资（万元）	**Investment Completed This Year (10 000yuan)**	**27816952**
一、按登记注册类型分	**Grouped by Registion Status**	
内资	Domestic Funded	26716860
国有	State-owned Enterprises	11502967
集体	Collective-owned Enterprises	1883219
股份合作	Share-holding Corperative	166437
国有联营	State Joint Ownership Enterprises	1142
集体联营	Collective Joint Ownership Enterprises	
国有与集体联营	Joint State-collective Enterprises	13122
其他联营	Other Joint Ownership Enterprises	51265
国有独资公司	State Sole-funded Corporations	367380
其他有限责任公司	Other Limited Liability Corporations	8691328
股份有限公司	Share-holding Corperation Ltd.	507572
私营及个体	Private and Individual	2993399
其他	Others	539029
港澳台商投资	Enterprises with Funds from Hong Kong,Macao and Taiwan	562366
合资经营企业(港或澳、台资)	Joint Venture	260024
合作经营企业(港或澳、台资)	Cooperation	37034
独资企业	Sole-funded	256308
股份有限公司	Share-Holding Corporations Ltd.	9000
外商投资	Enterprises with Foreign Investment	537726
合资经营企业(港或澳、台资)	Joint Venture	156133
合作经营企业(港或澳、台资)	Cooperation	214614
独资企业	Sole-Funded	166979
股份有限公司	Share-Holding Corporations Ltd.	
二、按隶属关系分	**Grouped by Jurisdiction of Management**	
中央	Central	1752940
省属	Provincial	3534178
市属	Municipal	22529834

4-15 按行业分市区固定资产投资（2010年）

Investments in Fixed Assets of Urban Districts by Sector（2010）

指　标	Item	2010
本年完成投资（万元）	**Grouped by Sector (10 000 yuan)**	**27816952**
（一）农、林、牧、渔业	Agriculture,Forestry,Animal Husbandry and Fishery	110574
（二）采矿业	Mining	251028
（三）制造业	Manufacturing	3118879
农副食品加工业	Processing of Food from Agricultural Products	66059
食品制造业	Manufacture of Foods	132627
饮料制造业	Manufacture of Beverages	43938
石油加工、炼焦及核燃料加工业	Processing of Petroleum, Coking,Processing of Nuclear Fuel	20665
化学原料及化学制品制造业	Manufacture of Raw Chemical Materials and Chemical Products	39118
医药制造业	Manufacture of Medicines	53197
金属制品业	Manufacture of Metal Products	77754
通用设备制造业	Manufacture of General Purpose Machinery	154854
专用设备制造业	Manufacture of Special Purpose Machinery	656262
交通运输设备制造业	Manufacture of Transport Equipment	373839
电气机械及器材制造业	Manufacture of Electrical Machinery and Equipment	256561
通信设备、计算机及其他电子设备制造业	Manufacture of Communication Equipment, Computers and Other Electronic Equipment	679627
仪器仪表及文化办公用机械制造业	Manufacture of Measuring Instruments and Machinery for Cultural Activity and Office Work	88993
（四）电力、燃气及水的生产和供应业	Production & Supply of Electricity,Gas & Water	545981
（五）建筑业	Construction	477820
（六）交通运输、仓储和邮政业	Transport,Storage and Post	1619851
（七）信息传输、计算机服务和软件业	Information Transmission,Computer Service and Software	505832
（八）批发和零售业	Wholesale and Retail Trades	494921
（九）住宿和餐饮业	Hotels and Catering Services	347188
（十）金融业	Financial Intermediation	12868
（十一）房地产业	Real Estate	12160624
（十二）租赁和商务服务业	Leasing and Business Services	430242
（十三）科学研究、技术服务和地质勘察业	Scientific Research,Technical Service and Geologic Prospecting	365928
（十四）水利、环境和公共设施管理业	Management of Water Conservancy, Environment and Public Facilities	4333738
（十五）居民服务和其他服务业	Services to Households and Other Services	53536
（十六）教育	Education	608476
（十七）卫生、社会保障和社会福利业	Health,Social Security and Social Welfare	122027
（十八）文化、体育和娱乐业	Culture, Sports and Entertainment	125777
（十九）公共管理和社会组织	Public Management and Social Organization	2131662

4-16 按资金来源及建设性质分市区固定资产投资（2010年）

Investment in Fixed Assets of Urban Area by Sources of Funds and Type of Construction（2010）

指　　标	Item	2010
投资总额(万元)	**Total Investment (10 000 yuan)**	**27816952**
一、按资金来源分	**Grouped by Funds Sources**	
1.国家预算内资金	State Budgetary Funds	1359640
2.国内贷款	Domestic Loans	4123094
3.债 券	Bonds	
4.利用外资	Utilization of Foreign Funds	116907
5.自筹资金	Self-raising Funds	16089927
6.其他资金	Others	6127384
二、按建设性质分	**Grouped by Type of Construction**	
#新 建	New Construction	12154229
扩 建	Expansion	2177534
改 建	Reconstruction	2240817
三、按构成分	**Grouped by Composition of Funds**	
1.建筑工程	Construction Project	17707754
2.安装工程	Installation Projects	1896723
3.设备、工器具购置	Purchasing of Equipment and Instruments	2760304
4.其它费用	Others	5452171

4-17 全市固定资产投资资金来源（2010年）

Source of Funds for Total Fixed Assets Investment of Whole City（2010）

单位：万元 (10 000 yuan)

指　标	Item	城镇 Urban Area	房地产开发 Real Estate
一、本年资金来源合计	**Total of Sources of Funds This Year**	**42608976**	**15435198**
1.上年末结余资金	Balance of Last Year	3604489	2538734
2.本年资金来源小计	Subtotal Funds This Year	39004487	12896464
(1) 国家预算内资金	State Budgetary Funds	2072208	
(2) 国内贷款	Domestic Loans	5387488	1861610
(3) 债券	Bonds		
(4) 利用外资	Utilization of Foreign Funds	159290	55561
(5) 自筹资金	Self-raising Funds	22962568	4261600
(6) 其他资金	Others	8422933	6717693
二、本年各项应付款合计	**Total Sums of Money to be Paid This Year**	**2749121**	**837605**

4-18 市属固定资产投资资金来源（2010年）

Source of Funds for Fixed Estate of Municipal Units（2010）

单位：万元 (10 000 yuan)

指　标	Item	城镇 Urban Area	房地产开发 Real Estate
一、本年资金来源合计	**Total of Sources of Funds This Year**	**35911882**	**14662443**
1.上年末结余资金	Balance of Last Year	3316167	2345659
2.本年资金来源小计	Subtotal Funds This Year	32595715	12316784
(1) 国家预算内资金	State Budgetary Funds	1592154	
(2) 国内贷款	Domestic Loans	3452701	1722685
(3) 债券	Bonds		
(4) 利用外资	Utilization of Foreign Funds	159290	55561
(5) 自筹资金	Self-raising Funds	19475109	4062534
(6) 其他资金来源	Others	7916461	6476004
二、本年各项应付款合计	**Total Sums of Money to be Paid This Year**	**2514102**	**787426**

4-19 全市固定资产投资效果（2010年）

Achievements of Total Assets Investment of Whole City（2010）

指　　标	Item	城镇 Urban Area	房地产开发 Real Estate
一、建设项目投产率(%)	**Rate of Projects Put Into use(%)**	**53.9**	
施工项目个数（个）	Number of Constructing Projects (unit)	2130	
本年投产项目个数（个）	Number of Projects Put into Use (unit)	1149	
二、固定资产交付使用率(%)	**Rate of Fixed Assets Put into Use(%)**	**38.4**	**45.3**
本年新增固定资产（万元）	Newly Increased Fixed Assets This Year (10000.yuan)	11930457	10248434
本年完成投资（万元）	Investment Completed This Year (10000.yuan)	31049184	22625737
三、建设周期(年)	**Construction Period (year)**	**3.2**	**2.7**
计划总投资（万元）	Total Planned Investment (10000.yuan)	97989545	61038506
本年完成投资（万元）	Investment Completed This Year (10000.yuan)	31049184	22625737
四、房屋建筑面积竣工率(%)	**Completion Rate of Buildings (%)**	**6.9**	**7.0**
本年施工房屋面积（平方米）	Floor Space of the Constructing Buildings This Year (sq.m)	111661874	44688005
本年竣工房屋面积（平方米）	Floor Space of the Buildings Completed This Year (sq.m)	7751562	3115090

4-20 市属固定资产投资效果（2010年）

Achievement of Fixed Assets Investment of Municipal Units（2010）

指　　标	Item	城镇 Urban Area	房地产开发 Real Estate
一、建设项目投产率(%)	**Rate of Projects Put Into use(%)**	**57.3**	
施工项目个数(个)	Number of Constructing Projects (unit)	1861	
本年投产项目个数(个)	Number of Projects Put into Use (unit)	1066	
二、固定资产交付使用率(%)	**Rate of Fixed Assets Put into Use(%)**	**40.9**	**50.8**
本年新增固定资产（万元）	Newly Increased Fixed Assets This Year (10000.yuan)	10423906	8861314
本年完成投资（万元）	Investment Completed This Year (10000.yuan)	25474854	17453961
三、建设周期(年)	**Construction Period (year)**	**3.3**	**2.9**
计划总投资（万元）	Total Planned Investment (10000.yuan)	85038253	49863043
本年完成投资（万元）	Investment Completed This Year (10000.yuan)	25474854	17453961
四、房屋建筑面积竣工率(%)	**Completion Rate of Buildings (%)**	**6.7**	**6.8**
本年施工房屋面积（平方米）	Floor Space of the Constructing Buildings This Year (sq.m)	99569250	36388888
本年竣工房屋面积（平方米）	Floor Space of the Buildings Completed This Year (sq.m)	6684868	2482512

4–21 分区县、开发区全社会固定资产投资额（2010年）

Investment Fulfilled In Fixed Assets By Region （2010）

单位：万元 (10 000 yuan)

区县名称	Name of District and County	全社会固定资产投资 Investment Fulfilled In Fixed Assets	城 镇 Urban Area	房地产 Real Estate	农村集体 Rural Collective-owned Units	农村私人建房 Private Housing in Country
区 县	**Region**					
新城区	Xincheng	2637266	2637266	682245		
碑林区	Beilin	2790607	2790607	1411307		
莲湖区	Lianhu	3479335	3479335	624653		
灞桥区	Baqiao	1629018	1546964	222717	46431	35623
未央区	Weiyang	4385921	4261393	1343391	97130	27398
雁塔区	Yanta	8101966	8081699	3321282		20267
阎良区	Yanliang	1178258	1081008	56619	77221	20029
临潼区	Lintong	1084539	980217	37608	34403	69919
长安区	Chang'an	3022567	2756662	583083	163481	102424
蓝田县	Lantian	682881	462963	20157	149335	70583
周至县	Zhouzhi	672797	406887	18292	191488	74422
户 县	Huxian	1096427	863435	31207	173128	59864
高陵县	Gaoling	1744059	1700748	70886	17332	25979
开发区	**Development Zones**					
高新区	GaoXin	3445495	3445495	821770		
经开区	JingKai	2818100	2818100	441810		
曲江新区	Qujiang	2511281	2511281	846775		
浐灞生态区	Chanba Eco-District	752196	752196	145045		
航空基地	Aviation Industry Base	333140	333140			
航天基地	Aerospace Base	402704	402704	208402		
国际港务区	International Trade&Logistic Park	156012	156012			
沣渭新区	FengWei					

4-22 全市分行业房屋建筑面积（2010年）

单位：平方米

行　　业	Item	本年施工房屋面积 Floor Space of Buildings Under Construction This Year	住宅 Residential Buildings
合　计	**Total**	**111661874**	**80598742**
（一）农、林、牧、渔业	Agriculture, Forestry, Animal Husbandry and Fishery	93715	945
（二）采矿业	Mining	148025	
（三）制造业	Manufacturing	4684106	930784
（四）电力、燃气及水的生产和供应业	Generation and Supply of Electricity, Production and Supply of Gas and Water	87213	
（五）建筑业	Construction	816922	415441
（六）交通运输、仓储和邮政业	Transportation, Storage and Post	542527	
（七）信息传输、计算机服务和软件业	Information Transmission, Computer Service and Software	197019	
（八）批发和零售业	Wholesale and Retail Trades	873981	202423
（九）住宿和餐饮业	Hotels and Catering Services	519480	116600
（十）金融业	Financial Intermediation	2500	
（十一）房地产业	Real Estate	83770676	69855140
（十二）租赁和商务服务业	Leasing and Business Services	929128	228502
（十三）科学研究、技术服务和地质勘查业	Scientific Research, Technical Service and Geologic Prospecting	916227	227962
（十四）水利、环境和公共设施管理业	Management of Water Conservancy, Environment and Public Facilities	3594201	2450125
（十五）居民服务和其他服务业	Services to Households and Other Services	96375	3200
（十六）教育	Education	5639421	1324342
（十七）卫生、社会保障和社会福利业	Health,Social Security and Social Welfare	717859	134808
（十八）文化、体育和娱乐业	Culture, Sports and Entertainment	579519	43050
（十九）公共管理和社会组织	Public Management and Social Organization	7452980	4665420

Floor Space of Buildings Construction by Sector（2010）

(sq.m)

本年竣工房屋面积 Floor Space of Buildings Completed This Year	住宅 Residential Buildings	竣工房屋价值（万元） Value of Buildings Completed(10 000yuan)	住宅 Residential Buildings
7751562	**5210847**	**2139352**	**1562093**
64063	945	3734	132
2125		130	
915915	204687	194513	78815
3810		762	
57300	49000	7196	5996
71423		17225	
142896	4048	22664	1380
106300		38780	
5176770	4536665	1594889	1402924
165977	100636	43010	16980
78105	14000	34291	6740
30218		9184	
626437	246366	127854	42456
171871	41000	22211	4670
30103		8741	
108249	13500	14168	2000

4-23 市属分行业房屋建筑面积（2010年）

单位：平方米

行业	Item	本年施工房屋面积 Floor Space of Buildings Under Construction This Year	住宅 Residential Residence
合计	**Total**	**99569250**	**74224014**
（一）农、林、牧、渔业	Agriculture, Forestry, Animal Husbandry and Fishery	93715	945
（二）采矿业	Mining	148025	
（三）制造业	Manufacturing	3594302	339346
（四）电力、燃气及水的生产和供应业	Generation and Supply of Electricity, Production and Supply of Gas and Water	67213	
（五）建筑业	Construction	534770	198440
（六）交通运输、仓储和邮政业	Transportation, Storage and Post	501310	
（七）信息传输、计算机服务和软件业	Information Transmission, Computer Service and Software	181626	
（八）批发和零售业	Wholesale and Retail Trades	741009	178813
（九）住宿和餐饮业	Hotels and Catering Services	189280	16600
（十）金融业	Financial Intermediation		
（十一）房地产业	Real Estate	79230864	66095619
（十二）租赁和商务服务业	Leasing and Business Services	835832	165206
（十三）科学研究、技术服务和地质勘查业	Scientific Research, Technical Service and Geologic Prospecting	254401	
（十四）水利、环境和公共设施管理业	Management of Water Conservancy, Environment and Public Facilities	3443051	2450125
（十五）居民服务和其他服务业	Services to Households and Other Services	96375	3200
（十六）教育	Education	2548747	63340
（十七）卫生、社会保障和社会福利业	Health,Social Security and Social Welfare	610461	54200
（十八）文化、体育和娱乐业	Culture, Sports and Entertainment	297726	27760
（十九）公共管理和社会组织	Public Management and Social Organization	6200543	4630420

Floors Space of Buildings Construction of Municipal Units by Sector（2010）

(sq.m)

本年竣工房屋面积 Floor Space of Buildings Completed This Year	住　宅 Residential Residence	竣工房屋价值(万元) Value of Buildings Completed (10 000 yuan)	住　宅 Residential Residence
6684868	**4484575**	**1879464**	**1410875**
64063	945	3734	132
2125		130	
897915	186687	186953	71255
3810		762	
49000	49000	5996	5996
68213		16525	
108198	4048	16264	1380
96100		33380	
4703654	4112735	1488586	1309136
102681	37340	38030	12000
1000		591	
30218		9184	
277566	39320	42339	4306
160175	41000	19831	4670
13800		3141	
106350	13500	14018	2000

4-24 主要年份全市新增固定资产及房屋竣工面积

Value of Newly Added Fixed Assets and Floor Spaces Completed of Whole City in Representative Years

年 份 Year	新增固定资产(万元) Newly Increased Fixed Assets (10 000 yuan)	房屋竣工面积(平方米) Floor Space of Buildings Completed (sq.m)	住 宅 Residential Residence
1978	49582	990996	407554
1980	46377	1648691	1001544
1985	86174	2224195	1290728
1986	134037	2729528	1559067
1987	167160	2414751	1192115
1988	168152	2118312	1024255
1989	165811	1784546	877691
1990	203000	2118777	1110535
1991	178572	1853384	958364
1992	223270	2047478	1126628
1993	416963	2578987	1448829
1994	553714	2829057	1844859
1995	625803	3576699	2528435
1996	600353	3321838	2495208
1997	628819	3744631	2865398
1998	802337	3828026	2756265
1999	1189176	6810370	5508336
2000	1501585	7148313	5449502
2001	1677665	6925619	5022617
2002	1989689	7732772	4861279
2003	2794439	9179629	5780646
2004	2619467	7765905	4983286
2005	4097225	11314125	5986051
2006	4530136	11994519	5830981
2007	6679699	16721647	9295019
2008	7251721	11133098	6934222
2009	10134370	15291263	8226162
2010	11930457	7751562	5210847

4-25 主要年份市属新增固定资产及房屋竣工面积

Value of Newly Added Fixed Assets and Floor Spaces Completed of Municipal Units in Representative Years

年 份 Year	新增固定资产 (万元) Newly Increased Fixed Assets (10 000 yuan)	房屋竣工面积 (平方米) Floor Space of Buildings Completed (sq.m)	住 宅 Residential Buildings
1978	7529	249793	103060
1980	10664	497472	284022
1985	27872	986197	451128
1986	47827	1077660	690965
1987	56953	937402	417050
1988	50175	717169	351330
1989	69817	713432	315937
1990	69434	950215	501234
1991	67392	788184	377550
1992	108469	981637	417800
1993	181449	1384411	689602
1994	314996	1351075	894704
1995	273324	2025223	1433005
1996	296898	1984330	1487837
1997	374318	2264862	1666509
1998	521350	2383041	1691699
1999	859070	5012547	4074889
2000	953173	5094751	3735111
2001	1159980	5359752	3960060
2002	1295389	5374374	3314467
2003	1812099	6318902	3878178
2004	1962795	6062317	3887867
2005	3011104	7677031	4364275
2006	3495179	9147989	4324291
2007	5279938	13438785	7340515
2008	6488361	9870482	6026891
2009	8380033	13594584	7274105
2010	10423906	6684868	4484575

4-26 各区县、开发区新增固定资产及房屋施工、竣工面积（2010年）

区县名称	Name of District and County	新增固定资产（亿元）Increased Fixed Assets (10 000 yuan)	房屋施工面积（平方米）Floor Space of Buildings Under Construction(sq.m)	住　宅 Residenctial Buildings
区　县	**Region**			
新城区	Xincheng	71.72	7055189	5286395
碑林区	Beilin	66.57	15147730	12160294
莲湖区	Lianhu	55.98	12922282	10970853
灞桥区	Baqiao	53.15	5783407	4120881
未央区	Weiyang	258.74	19225285	13980419
雁塔区	Yanta	111.45	30588398	23144742
阎良区	Yanliang	42.37	2753003	990715
临潼区	Lintong	29.50	1821107	1184868
长安区	Chang'an	327.00	8629403	5450624
蓝田县	Lantian	32.71	925179	665736
周至县	Zhouzhi	17.90	715383	333233
户　县	Huxian	33.48	2442835	993460
高陵县	Gaoling	65.97	3652673	1316522
开发区	**Development Zones**			
高新区	GaoXin	249.77	9269268	6000314
经开区	JingKai	214.45	8188357	3985286
曲江新区	Qujiang	53.66	6604861	5887963
浐灞生态区	Chanba Eco-District	9.12	1337153	1268224
航空基地	Aviation Industry Base			
航天基地	Aerospace Base	5.72	3509659	2782455
国际港务区	International Trade&Logistic Park	2.58		
沣渭新区	FengWei			

Newly Added Fixed Assets and Floor Space of Constructing and Completed Buildings by Region （2010）

房屋竣工面积 （平方米） Floor Space of Buildings Completed(sq.m)	住 宅 Residenctial Buildings	商品房销售面积 （平方米） Floor Space of Houses Sales(sq.m)	商品房销售额 （万元） Sales Income of Commercial Houses(10 000 yuan)
197569	163139	1260747	537197
1260272	995696	817573	411504
236163	176204	1269316	589230
183958	152269	677906	258606
1682045	1404858	3827477	1759582
1115947	986215	5699601	2672897
144245	118288	212344	59210
309036	169101	75321	18281
1370249	678728	1352392	575859
62351	22995	111120	23547
49000	49000	75133	13033
741393	143516	141728	32818
399334	150838	357418	118252
140338	99457	1639349	809918
328953	249476	1014890	511224
742037	676764	1521356	873945
		337057	206211
140015	87878	207095	127347

4-27 全市分行业施工项目（2010年）

行　业	Item	本年新增固定资产（万元）Increased Fixed Assets This Year(10 000 yuan)
合　计	**Total**	**11930457**
（一）农、林、牧、渔业	Agriculture, Forestry, Animal Husbandry and Fishery	212405
（二）采矿业	Mining	7500
（三）制造业	Manufacturing	3727750
（四）电力、燃气及水的生产和供应业	Generation and Supply of Electricity, Production and Supply of Gas and Water	321295
（五）建筑业	Construction	121969
（六）交通运输、仓储和邮政业	Transportation, Storage and Post	459263
（七）信息传输、计算机服务和软件业	Information Transmission, Computer Service and Software	254975
（八）批发和零售业	Wholesale and Retail Trades	220534
（九）住宿和餐饮业	Hotels and Catering Services	327165
（十）金融业	Financial Intermediation	868
（十一）房地产业	Real Estate	3353614
（十二）租赁和商务服务业	Leasing and Business Services	109600
（十三）科学研究、技术服务和地质勘查业	Scientific Research, Technical Service and Geologic Prospecting	160490
（十四）水利、环境和公共设施管理业	Management of Water Conservancy, Environment and Public Facilities	1215020
（十五）居民服务和其他服务业	Services to Households and Other Services	26440
（十六）教育	Education	380879
（十七）卫生、社会保障和社会福利业	Health,Social Security and Social Welfare	135077
（十八）文化、体育和娱乐业	Culture, Sports and Entertainment	96125
（十九）公共管理和社会组织	Public Management and Social Organization	799488

Construction Projects of Whole City by Sector（2010）

施工项目个数（个） Number of Constructing Projects（unit）	本年新开工 Newly Started This Year	投产项目个数（个） Projects put into Use (unit)
2130	**1481**	**1149**
137	128	105
5	3	3
529	363	283
83	40	39
57	44	28
111	71	67
22	10	9
97	68	60
78	62	42
3	2	2
198	117	60
49	32	14
42	18	9
363	253	230
24	21	11
113	83	72
53	40	34
38	19	19
128	107	62

4-28 市属分行业施工项目（2010年）

行　　业	Item	本年新增固定资产（万元） Increased Fixed Assets This Year(10 000 yuan)
合　计	**Total**	**10423906**
（一）农、林、牧、渔业	Agriculture, Forestry, Animal Husbandry and Fishery	212405
（二）采矿业	Mining	7500
（三）制造业	Manufacturing	3566289
（四）电力、燃气及水的生产和供应业	Generation and Supply of Electricity, Production and Supply of Gas and Water	313365
（五）建筑业	Construction	59763
（六）交通运输、仓储和邮政业	Transportation, Storage and Post	217533
（七）信息传输、计算机服务和软件业	Information Transmission, Computer Service and Software	12604
（八）批发和零售业	Wholesale and Retail Trades	185273
（九）住宿和餐饮业	Hotels and Catering Services	205965
（十）金融业	Financial Intermediation	75
（十一）房地产业	Real Estate	3169314
（十二）租赁和商务服务业	Leasing and Business Services	104620
（十三）科学研究、技术服务和地质勘查业	Scientific Research, Technical Service and Geologic Prospecting	9950
（十四）水利、环境和公共设施管理业	Management of Water Conservancy, Environment and Public Facilities	1121151
（十五）居民服务和其他服务业	Services to Households and Other Services	26440
（十六）教育	Education	216863
（十七）卫生、社会保障和社会福利业	Health,Social Security and Social Welfare	127711
（十八）文化、体育和娱乐业	Culture, Sports and Entertainment	73234
（十九）公共管理和社会组织	Public Management and Social Organization	793851

Construction Projects of Municipal Units by Sector（2010）

施工项目个数（个） Number of Constructing Projects（unit）	本年新开工 Newly Started This Year	投产项目个数（个） Projects put into Use (unit)
1861	**1369**	**1066**
137	128	105
5	3	3
487	350	275
59	37	37
44	41	22
84	59	52
15	6	5
86	61	53
69	56	40
2	2	1
175	107	55
43	28	13
13	8	4
348	247	225
24	21	11
76	61	60
46	37	32
30	17	14
118	100	59

4-29 主要年份房地产开发投资主要指标

单位：万元

指　　标	Item	1997	1998	1999	2000	2001
本年完成投资额	Investment Completed This Year	246817	382142	442982	518460	674211
本年施工面积（平方米）	Floor Space of Buildings Under Construction This Year(sq.m)	4514661	6788737	7934602	7631791	7437846
#住宅	Residential Buildings	3311624	5523667	6495345	6198502	5804332
本年竣工面积（平方米）	Floor Space of Buildings Completed This Year(sq.m)	1356154	1561710	3777862	3210975	3162449
#住宅	Residential Buildings	1203270	1333330	3522764	2955463	2696055
竣工价值	Value of Floor Space of Buildings Completed	119557	143620	382245	269408	372040
#住宅	Residential Buildings	96347	109982	330190	229708	286154
商品房销售面积（平方米）	Floor Space of Commercialized Buildings sold(sq.m)	784514	1171051	2969705	2129156	2253468
#住宅	Residential Buildings	726872	1086108	2849545	2007741	1921961
商品房销售额	Total Sales of Commercialized Buildings	128058	177389	351861	325193	472204
#住宅	Residential Buildings	113917	154614	323482	294562	355310
商品房预售面积（平方米）	Floor Space of Commercialized Buildings Presold(sq.m)	263531	2520176	302513	2530349	674407
#住宅	Residential Buildings	232660	2467716	273431	2530349	651990
商品房空置面积（平方米）	Floor Space of Vacant Commercialized Buildings(sq.m)	587064	325156	623796	364097	508233
#住宅	Residential Buildings	502608	228149	523181	240212	341836
商品房出租面积（平方米）	Floor Space of Commercialized Buildings Recenting(sq.m)	256918	10365	18780	11673	91889
#住宅	Residential Buildings	228672	120	1461	200	970
本年新增固定资产	Newly Increased Fixed Assets This Year	143616	199261	430985	383811	507658

Main Indicators of Investment in Real Estate Development in Representative Years

(10 000 yuan)

2002	2003	2004	2005	2006	2007	2008	2009	2010
793689	1248177	1696685	2252303	2857605	3873342	5402617	6963350	8423447
11725803	13431222	16336814	21742931	23835612	29159540	36328733	57086279	66973869
9646770	9436123	12040107	17833558	18902667	23768164	30791305	49015888	57777112
3297069	3396721	3808406	3616231	3996417	4832987	4439585	5428145	4636472
2902965	2895565	3080577	3165164	3421533	4224701	4124612	4534926	4124392
369347	547322	737507	805820	820227	1011283	1064984	1680809	1456187
304553	440117	555753	681123	657982	771267	960167	1374229	1286907
2528958	2527368	3054710	4973421	6215019	8339198	7607224	12560212	15878076
2370397	2302824	2799011	4763928	5840605	7829108	7157617	12021163	15232412
513468	542851	813529	1712897	2061450	2817880	2964440	4885458	7070016
454597	442468	712650	1580322	1794716	2517411	2689174	4507051	6612683
610198	523516	1764049	3000743	4282029	4910694	5692237	11254387	15102031
557343	491159	1590960	2871309	4081064	4575415	5411982	10951690	14522025
571417	638528	1085214	1235881	1124943	454242	554012	406750	343153
446968	523449	727633	991685	858896	386193	354024	287267	262250
157455	105608	111812	173178	85334	108370	349432	382331	286016
11326	54250	57799	40863	37400	53554	45294	65549	7013
484349	621336	833564	927832	1002244	1431710	1240156	1957125	1682023

4-30 各区县、开发区房地产开发主要指标（2010年）

单位：万元

区县名称	Name of District and County	企业（单位）个数（个） Number of Enterprises (Unit)	本年完成投资 Investment Completed This Year	本年新增固定资产 Increased Fixed Assets This Year(10 000 yuan)
区　县	**Region**			
新城区	Xincheng	42	682245	111400
碑林区	Beilin	56	1409039	245732
莲湖区	Lianhu	51	607998	51100
灞桥区	Baqiao	26	251717	44018
未央区	Weiyang	90	1343391	474002
雁塔区	Yanta	151	3332495	458404
阎良区	Yanliang	19	56619	25055
临潼区	Lintong	3	37608	10163
长安区	Chang'an	49	561793	211115
蓝田县	Lantian	8	20157	5595
周至县	Zhouzhi	6	18292	3165
户　县	Huxian	9	31207	10120
高陵县	Gaoling	12	70886	32154
开发区	**Development Zones**			
高新区	GaoXin	47	736690	55660
经开区	JingKai	38	441805	118500
曲江新区	Qujiang	28	846775	380653
浐灞生态区	Chanba Eco-District	9	145045	
航空基地	Aviation Industry Base			
航天基地	Aerospace Base	11	196869	34801
国际港务区	International Trade&Logistic Park			
沣渭新区	FengWei	1	10400	

Main Indicators of Real Estate Development by Region（2010）

(10 000 yuan)

房屋施工面积（平方米）Floor Space of Buildings Under Construction(sq.m)	住宅 Residenctial Buildings	房屋竣工面积（平方米）Floor Space of Buildings Completed(sq.m)	住宅 Residenctial Buildings	竣工房屋价值（万元）Value of Buildings Completed(10 000yuan)	住宅 Residenctial Buildings
5042295	4381622	161644	158344	36900	34260
8612928	6852232	792262	674934	212347	172268
6555064	5539508	159165	136016	51080	40153
2538488	2305354	173451	141762	38099	29146
13413267	11898221	1596605	1394858	427631	352711
22898331	19697166	580942	576115	418511	411497
1134677	990715	144245	118288	25055	23423
341227	341227	55276	55276	10050	10050
4570520	4031467	740583	647953	194237	172536
300646	294916	20999	17975	3595	3292
344173	266433				
344555	320911	60462	52033	7872	6761
877698	857340	150838	150838	30810	30810
7551539	5202813	140338	99457	53931	36599
4365208	3660704	322480	249476	100500	75540
6212108	5628063	455237	451764	380639	374423
1280153	1268224				
3000659	2720492	87878	87878	34801	34801
54000	52000				

4-31 房地产开发投资主要指标（2010年）

Main Indicators of Investment in Real Estate Development（2010）

单位：万元 (10 000 yuan)

指　标	Item	全市合计 Total	国有 State-owned	市区 Urban Area	市属 Municipal
企业(单位)个数(个)	Number of Enterprises(unit)	522	37	487	453
本年完成投资	Investment Completed This Year	8423447	1009113	8282905	8020893
#土地开发投资额	Investments in Land Development				
按工程用途分	Grouped by Function				
住宅	Residential Buildings	6704066	808367	6596687	6410821
#别墅、高档公寓	Villas and Top-Grade Apartments	215263	27708	215263	208535
经济适用房	Economically Affordable Housing	226086	29810	226086	226086
办公楼	Office Buildings	337207	33930	335710	301139
商业营业用房	Houses for Business Use	809745	65746	801132	784676
其他	Others	572429	101070	549376	524257
本年新增固定资产	Increased Fixed Assets This Year	1682023	198407	1630989	1562592
房屋建筑面积及竣工价值	Floor Space of Buildings and Value of Buildings Completed				
施工房屋面积(平方米)	Floor Space of Buildings Under Construction (sq.m)	66973869	9512761	65106797	63180362
#住宅	Residential Buildings	57777112	8257606	56037512	54543746
经济适用房	Economically Affordable Housing	2158822	249055	2158822	2158822
竣工房屋面积(平方米)	Floor Space of Buildings Completed (sq.m)	4636472	733059	4404173	4202356
#住宅	Residential Buildings	4124392	638036	3903546	3739462
经济适用房	Economically Affordable Housing	393970		393970	393970
竣工房屋价值	Value of Buildings Completed	1456187	183379	1413910	1352926
#住宅	Residential Buildings	1286907	142768	1246044	1196161
经济适用房	Economically Affordable Housing	86067		86067	86067
商品房销售面积(平方米)	Floor Space of Commercialized Buildings Sold(sq.m)	15878076	1858096	15196110	15063624
商品房销售额(万元)	Sales Income of Commercialized Buildings	7070016	776433	6883496	6699951
年平均从业人员数(人)	Annual Average Number of Employed Persons(person)	25506	4061	24069	24343
本年应付工资总额	Total Income of Working Staff Engaged	98928	13975	95514	92903
本年应付福利费总额	Total Welfare Expense payable	9737	2062	9398	8945

4-32 商品房销售情况（2010年）

Sales of Commercial Houses（2010）

指标	Item	全市合计 Total	国有 State Owned	市区 Urban Area	市属 municipal
商品房销售面积(平方米)	**Floor Space of Commercialized Buildings Sold(sq.m)**	**15878076**	**1858096**	**15196110**	**15063624**
现房销售面积	**Floor Space of Completed Apartment Sales**	**776045**	**64201**	**715725**	**652516**
期房销售面积	**Floor Space of Forward Delivery Housing Sales**	**15102031**	**1793895**	**14480385**	**14411108**
住宅	Residential Buildings	15232412	1806202	14556078	14431666
#别墅、高档公寓	Villas and High-grade Apartments	330782		330782	307658
经济适用房	Economically Affordable Housing	798510	119923	798510	798510
办公楼	Office Buildings	354554		354554	354554
商业营业用房	Houses for Business Use	227959	40207	222327	216322
其他	Others	63151	11687	63151	61082
商品房销售额(万元)	**Sales Income of Commercialized Buildings (10 000 yuan)**	**7070016**	**776433**	**6883496**	**6699951**
现房销售额(万元)	**Floor Space of Completed Apartment Sales**	**337730**	**36483**	**323223**	**276079**
期房销售额(万元)	**Floor Space of Forward Delivery Housing Sales**	**6732286**	**739950**	**6560273**	**6423872**
住宅	Residential Buildings	6612683	735377	6428488	6256732
#别墅、高档公寓	Villas and High-grade Apartments	303092		303092	293942
经济适用房	Economically Affordable Housing	203228	40447	203228	203228
办公楼	Office Buildings	212919		212919	212919
商业营业用房	Houses for Business Use	214649	35801	212324	201891
其他	Others	29765	5255	29765	28409
商品房空置面积(平方米)	**Vacancy of Commercialized Buildings(sq.m)**	**343153**	**32290**	**294493**	**297657**
#待售一年以上	Being Idle for One Year	179121	32290	150187	139867
待售三年以上(含三年)	Being Idle for One Year	20393		20393	20393
住宅	Residence	262250	8624	222019	236189
#别墅、高档公寓	Villas and High-grade Apartments	48160		48160	37898
经济适用房	Economically Affordable Housing	10707		10707	10707
办公楼	Office Buildings	9605	7205	9605	2400
商业营业用房	Houses for Business Use	42390	7134	37892	39487
其他	Others	28908	9327	24977	19581
商品房出租面积(平方米)	**Floor Space of Commercialized Leased Buildings(sq.m)**	**286016**	**2630**	**277669**	**283386**
住宅	Residential Buildings	7013		7013	7013
办公楼	Office Buildings	227781		227781	227781
商业营业用房	Houses for Business Use	51222	2630	42875	48592
其他	Others				

4–33 房地产开发投资资金来源（2010年）

Source of Funds for Investment in Real Estate Development（2010）

单位：万元 (10 000 yuan)

指　标	Item	全市合计 Total	国有 State-owned	市区 Urban Area	市属 Municipal
一、本年资金来源合计	**Total**	**15435198**	**1744608**	**15181569**	**14662443**
1.上年末结余资金	Balance of Last Year	2538734	433943	2501150	2345659
2.本年资金来源小计	Total Funds This Year	12896464	1310665	12680419	12316784
(1) 国内贷款	Domestic Loans	1861610	295639	1849498	1722685
#银行贷款	Bank Loan	1764173	278699	1752893	1628258
非银行金融机构贷款	Loans from financial Institutions except Bank	97437	16940	96605	94427
(2) 利用外资	Utilization of Foreign Funds	55561		55561	55561
#外商直接投资	Foreign Direct Investment	55550		55550	55550
(3) 自筹资金	Self-raising Funds	4261600	222336	4157680	4062534
#企事业单位自有资金	Funds at the disposal of Enterprises	1920637	101708	1868400	1740192
(4) 其他资金	Others	6717693	792690	6617680	6476004
#定金及预付款	Earnest Money and Advance payment	4148413	527699	4103898	3975813
个人按揭贷款	Personal Mortgage loan	2030037	115566	1992111	1960957
二、本年各项应付款合计	**Total Sums of Money to be Paid This Year**	**837605**	**54590**	**790112**	**787426**
#工程款	Project Fund	505946	47033	471218	466058

4-34 房地产开发经营情况（2010年）

Running of Real Estate Development（2010）

单位：万元 (10 000 yuan)

指 标	Item	全市合计 Total	国有 State-owned	市区 Urban Area	市属 Municipal
一、资产总计	**Total Assets**	**22619691**	**2661250**	**22270624**	**21487817**
负债总计	Total Liabilities	17364118	2212802	17067056	16542487
所有者权益合计	Total Creditor's Equity	5259987	448448	5203568	4945330
#实收资本	Held Capital	3456754	336298	3407320	3236840
国家资本	State Capital	196851	64011	196665	158851
集体资本	Collectively Owned Capital	37708		36351	32708
法人资本	Corporation Capital	2144674	267955	2124289	2006734
个人资本	Individual Capital	698167	4332	670661	659193
港澳台资本	Capital from Hong Kong,Maocao and Taiwan	185447		185447	185447
外商资本	Foreign Capital	193907		193907	193907
二、损益情况	**Total Revenue**				
1.主营业务收入	Revenue from Principal Business	6854478	681464	6688583	6540297
土地转让收入	Revenue of Land Transferred	68506	5781	68506	68506
商品房屋销售收入	Revenue of Commercial Houses Sold	6612687	659396	6446806	6308249
房屋出租收入	Revenue of Houses Leased	86852	3978	86852	86735
其他收入	Other Revenue	86432	12309	86419	76807
2.主营业务成本	Cost of Principal Business	5281915	543620	5156484	5055236
3.主营业务税金及附加	Taxes and Other Charges on Principal Business	462937	44267	454718	437692
4.主营业务利润	Principal Business Profit	1069311	92558	1039186	1008679
5.其他业务收入	Other Business Revenue	10828	1216	10505	9755
6.其他业务利润	Other Business Profit	14126	2990	13828	10726
7.销售费用	Sales Expenditures	218721	19919	213792	209880
8.管理费用	Management Cost	211837	19689	204916	199749
#税金	Tax	21863	2300	21707	20483
差旅费	Travel Expense	5925	347	5535	5697
工会经费	Labor Union Expenditure	941	113	913	885
9.财务费用	Fiscal Expenditure	41901	-1537	41300	40747
#利息支出	Interest Exchange	-1040	-2334	-1376	-1592
10.营业利润	Operating Profit	650395	60704	630550	610346
投资收益	Investment Revenue	3206	2719	3215	3088
营业外收入	Non-business Revenue	8702	4760	8672	8640
营业外支出	Non-business Expenditures	12480	890	12216	12169
11.利润总额	Total Profit	851551	62562	832281	814347

主要统计指标解释

全社会固定资产投资 即固定资产投资额是以货币表现的建造和购置固定资产活动的工作量，它是反映固定资产投资规模、速度、比例关系和使用方向的综合性指标。全社会固定资产投资按登记注册类型可分为国有、集体、个体、联营、股份制、外商、港澳台商、其他等。按照报表种类，全社会固定资产投资总额分为城镇固定资产投资、房地产开发投资和农村农户和非农户投资等。

房地产开发投资 指房地产开发公司、商品房建设公司及其他房地产开发法人单位和附属于其他法人单位实际从事房地产开发或经营的活动单位统一开发的包括统代建、拆迁还建的住宅、厂房、仓库、饭店、宾馆、度假村、写字楼、办公楼等房屋建筑物和配套的服务设施，土地开发工程（如道路、给水、排水、供电、供热、通讯、平整场地等基础设施工程）的投资;不包括单纯的土地交易活动。

施工项目 指报告期内曾进行建筑或安装工程施工活动的建设项目，包括报告期内新开工项目、报告期以前开工跨入报告期继续施工的项目以及报告期施过工并在报告期内全部建成投产或停缓建的项目。

全部建成投产项目 工业项目是指设计文件规定形成生产能力的主体工程及其相应配套的辅助设施全部建成，经负荷试运转，证明具备生产设计规定合格产品的条件，并经过验收鉴定合格或达到竣工验收标准，与生产性工程配套的生活福利设施可以满足近期正常生产的需要，正式移交生产的建设项目。非工业项目是指设计文件规定的主体工程和相应的配套工程全部建成，能够发挥设计规定的全部效益，经验收鉴定合格或达到竣工验收标准，正式移交使用的建设项目。

新增生产能力 指通过固定资产投资活动而增加的设计能力或工程效益，它是用实物形态表示的固定资产投资的成果。新增生产能力的计算，是以能独立发挥生产能力或工程效益的单项工程（或项目）为对象。当单项工程（或项目）建成，经有关部门鉴定合格，正式移交投入生产，即可计算新增生产能力。

新增生产能力或工程效益有以下几种表现形式:

（1）以建设项目或单项工程建成后的年产能力表示，如煤炭开采、石油开采等。

（2）以建设项目或单项工程建成后处理原料的能力表示，如选矿工程的年处理矿石能力、洗煤厂年洗原煤能力等。

（3）以新增的主要设备数量或容量表示，如棉纺锭锭数、发电机组容量等。

（4）以建筑物容积、容量、面积或长度表示，如水库容量、铁路公路里程等。

新增生产能力的数量一般按设计能力计算。设计能力是指设计文件中规定的在正常情况下能够达到的生产能力，而不论投产后的实际产量如何。以设备数量、建筑物容积、面积、长度等表示生产能力或工程效益，则按建成的实际数量计算。

房屋建筑面积 指从房屋外墙线算起的各层平面面积的总和，包括可供使用的有效面积和房屋结构（如柱、墙）占用的面积。多层建筑按各层（包括地下室）面积总和计算。

住宅建筑面积 指施工和竣工房屋建筑面积中供居住用的施工和竣工房屋建筑面积。

施工面积 指报告期内施工的全部房屋建筑面积。包括本期新开工的面积、上期跨入本期继续施工的房屋面积、上期停缓建在本期恢复施工的房屋面积、本期竣工的房屋面积及本期施工后又停缓建的房屋面积。

竣工面积 指在报告期内房屋建筑按照设计要求已全部完工，达到住人和使用条件，经验收鉴定合格，正式移交使用单位的建筑面积。

房屋建筑面积竣工率 指一定时期内房屋竣工面积占同期房屋施工面积的比率。它是从房屋建筑施工速度的角度反映投资效果和建筑业经济效益的指标。

新增固定资产 指通过投资活动所形成的新的固定资产价值，包括已经建成投入生产或交付使用的工程价值和达到固定资产标准的设备、工具、器具的价值及有关应摊入的费用。它是以价值形式表示的固定资产投资成果的综合性指标，可以综合反映不同时期、不同部门、不同地区的固定资产投资成果。

建设项目投产率 指一定时期内全部建成投入生产项目个数与同期正式施工项目个数的比率。它是从项目建设速度的角度反映投资效果的指标。

固定资产交付使用率 指一定时期新增固定资产与同期完成投资额的比率。它是反映各个时期固定资产动用速度，衡量建设过程中投资效果的一个综合性指标。

Explanatory Notes on Main Statistical Indicators

Total Investment in Fixed Assets in the Whole Country Total investment in fixed assets refers to the volume of activities in construction and purchases of fixed assets in monetary terms. It is a comprehensive indicator which shows the size, pace, proportional relations and use orientation of the investment in fixed assets. Total investment in fixed assets in the whole country includes, by registration type of ownership, the investment by the state-owned units, collective units, individuals, joint ownership units, share-holding units, as well as investment by businessmen from foreign countries and from Hong Kong, Macau and Taiwan, and by other units. According to category of report form, total investment in Fixed Assets in whole country includes urban investment in fixed Assets, investment in real estate development, rural households and non-rural households investment, etc.

Investment in Real Estate Development It includes the investment by the real estate development companies, commercial buildings construction companies and other real estate development units of various types of ownership in the construction of house buildings, such as residential buildings, factory buildings, warehouses, hotels, guesthouses, holiday villages, office buildings, and the complementary service facilities and land development projects, such as roads, water supply, water drainage, power supply, heating, telecommunications, land leveling and other projects of infrastructure. It excludes the activities in simple land transactions.

Projects under Construction refer to projects having construction and installation activities undertaken in the reference period, including projects started in the reference period, or continued from the previous period, or completed and put into production or suspended in the reference period.

Projects Completed and Put into Use Industrial projects refer to the major projects and accessory facilities completed which result in forming production capacity and have been checked and accepted while the living and welfare facilities have been completed and can ensure normal production and formally put into production. Non-industrial projects refer to the major projects and accessory facilities completed which possess the designed capacity and have been checked, accepted and formally put into production.

Newly Increased Production Capacity refers to the increase of designed capacity and project efficiency through investment in fixed assets, which reflects the accomplishment of investment in fixed assets in kind. The calculation of newly increased production capacity is based on individual project which operates independently and efficiently. When an individual project is completed and checked and accepted and put into production, it is counted as newly increased production capacity.

The newly increased production capacity and project efficiency are usually expressed in one of the following forms:

(1)annual production capacity, such as extraction of coal and petroleum;

(2)raw material processing capacity, such as ore dressing capacity of ore dressing projects, the dressing capacity of a coal washery;

(3)number or capacity of major equipment increased, such as the number of cotton spindles increased and the capacity of generating sets increased;

(4)physical measures of construction, such as volume, capacity, area, and length, for instance, the capacity of reservoirs, the length of railways or highways.

Newly increased production capacity in terms of quantity is calculated in designed capacity in general, which refers to the production capacity of a project under normal conditions designed in construction documents regardless of the actual output.

Floor Space of Buildings under Construction andCompleted refers to total floor space in each story of buildings calculated from the outside line of building walls, including both usable space and the space occupied by constructions like pillars or walls. The floor space of multi-story buildings includes the total floor space of each story (including basement).

Floor Space of Residential Buildings refers to the floor space of the residential buildings under construction and completed among the total space of buildings under construction and completed.

Floor Space under Construction refers to total floor space of all buildings under construction during the reference period, including floor space of newly started buildings during the reference period, floor space of construction extended from the previous period to the current period, floor space of construction suspended during the previous period and resumed in the current period, floor space of construction completed in the current period, and floor space of construction started and then suspended in the current period.

Floor Space of Buildings Completed refers to the floor space of buildings completed in the reference period, which have come up to the designed standards and have been put into use.

Completion Rate of Floor Space of Buildings refers to the ratio of the floor space of buildings completed in certain period of time to the floor space of buildings under construction in the same period which reflects the investment result and economic efficiency of the construction industry from the angle of the speed of project construction.

Newly Increased Fixed Assets refer to the newly increased value of fixed assets through investment, including the value of projects completed and put into production, the value of equipment, tools, and vessels considered as fixed assets, as well as the relevant expenses as investment in fixed assets. This is a comprehensive indicator of investment in fixed assets, reflecting the achievements of investment in fixed assets in different periods, different sectors, and different regions.

Rate of Construction Projects Completed and Put into Use refers to the ratio of the number of construction projects completed and put into use in certain period of time to the number of projects under construction in the same period. this reflects the investment efficiency from the angle of the speed of projects construction.

Rate of Projects of Fixed Assets Completed and Put into Operation refers to the ratio of the newly increased fixed assets to the total investment made in the same period. This is a comprehensive indicator, reflecting the speed of the employment of fixed assets and the investment efficiency.

5 财　政

GOVERNMENT FINANCE

资料整理：刘　婷

Data management:Liu Ting

第五部分　财政

一、简要说明

本章资料主要包括地方财政收入、支出总额构成及分区县情况，由西安市统计局综合处根据西安市财政局提供资料整理。

二、主要指标

财政总收入（亿元）	510.69	比上年增长 27.6%
一般预算收入（亿元）	241.86	比上年增长 33.3%
一般预算支出（亿元）	371.62	比上年增长 34.2%

5 GOVERNMENT FINANCE

Ⅰ.Brief Introduction

This chapter consists primarily of data on regional revenue, expenditure of the municipal government, regional revenue and expenditure of the districts and the counties. The data are provided by the Xi'an Bureau of Finance and are compiled by Integration division of the Xi'an Bureau of Statistics.

Ⅱ.Major Indicators

		Increase over Preceding Year
Total Government Revenue(100 mil. Yuan)	510.69	27.6%
General Budgetary Revenue(100 mil. Yuan)	241.86	33.3%
Ordinary Budgetary Expenditures(100 mil. Yuan)	371.62	34.2%

5-1 主要年份地方财政一般预算收入及支出

General Budgetary Local Government Revenue and Expenditure in Representative Years

单位：亿元　　　　(100 million yuan)

年　份 Year	地方财政一般预算收入 General Budgetary Revenue of Local Government	地方财政一般预算支出 General Budgetary Expenditure of Local Government
2000	46.80	52.00
2001	51.45	57.30
2002	54.50	63.80
2003	72.90	76.60
2004	75.30	87.30
2005	72.92	97.61
2006	85.89	119.22
2007	112.92	161.25
2008	145.61	226.99
2009	181.40	276.85
2010	241.86	371.62

5-2 财政收入（2010年）

Government Revenue（2010）

单位：万元 （10 000 yuan）

指　　标	Item	2010
财政总收入	**Total Government Revenue**	**5106899**
# 一般预算	**General Budgetary**	**2418567**
一、税收收入	**Total Tax Revenue**	**2072713**
1.增值税	Value Added Tax	211325
2.营业税	Business Tax	860373
3.企业所得税	Corporate Income Tax	188436
4.企业所得税退税	Return for Corporate Income Tax	-148
5.个人所得税	Individual Income Tax	81405
6.资源税	Resource Tax	475
7.固定资产投资方向调节税	Tax on Adjustment of the Orientation of Investment in Fixed Assets	
8.城市维护建设税	City Maintenance and Construction Tax	144678
9.房产税	House Property Tax	67463
10.印花税	Stamp Tax	55235
11.城镇土地使用税	Urban Land Use Tax	59900
12.土地增值税	Land Appreciation Tax	112809
13.车船税（款）	Tax on the Use of Vehicles and Ships	29129
14.耕地占用税（款）	Farm Land Occupatian Tax	96788
15.契税（款）	Deed Tax	164749
16.其他税收收入	Other Tax Revenue	96
二、非税收收入	**Total Non-tax Revenue**	**345854**
1.专项收入	Special Program Receipts	66438
2.行政事业性收费收入	Charge of Adminnistrative and Institutional Units	144929
3.罚没收入	Penalty Receipts	65332
4.国有资本经营收入	State-owned Assets Profit	22443
5.国有资源（资产）有偿使用收入	Revenue for the use of State-owned Assets（Resources）	45801
6.其他收入	Other Revenue	911
基金预算收入	**Fund Budgetary**	**2526715**

5-3 财政支出（2010年）

Government Expenditures（2010）

单位:万元 (10 000 yuan)

指　　标	Item	2010
一、基金预算	**Fund Budgetary**	**2484087**
二、一般预算	**General Budgetary**	**3716175**
1.一般公共服务	Expenditure for General Public Services	453381
2.外交支出	Expenditure for Foreign Affairs	
3.国防支出	Expenditure for National Defense	3450
4.公共安全支出	Expenditure for Public Security	232607
5.教育支出	Expenditure for Education	530805
6.科学技术支出	Expenditure for Science and Technology	43550
7.文化体育与传媒支出	Expenditure for Cultural, sports and the media	63127
8.社会保障和就业支出	Expenditure for Social Safety Net and Employment Effort	522072
9.医疗卫生支出	Expenditure for Medical and Health Care	270981
10.环境保护支出	Expenditure for Environment Protection	55273
11.城乡社区事务支出	Expenditure for Urban and Rural Community Affairs	475627
12.农林水事务支出	Expenditure for Agriculture, Forestry and Water Conservancy	251423
13.交通运输支出	Expenditure for Transportation	150841
14.资源勘探电力信息等事务	Expenditure for Mining ,Electricity and Information	193190
15.商业服务业等事务	Expenditure for Commerce and Services	71475
16.金融监管支出	Expenditure for Financial Supervision	13863
17.地震灾后恢复重建支出	Expenditure for Post-earthquake Recovery and Reconstruction	2514
18.国土资源气象等事务	Expenditure for Land Recources and Meteorological Affairs	21150
19.住房保障支出	Expenditure for Housing Support	91749
20.粮油物资储备管理等事务	Material Reserves Management Affairs Spending	17680
21.国债还本付息支出	Expenditure for National Debt and Interest(10 000yuan)	101094
22.其它支出	Other Expenditure	150323

5-4 各区县、开发区一般预算财政收入（2010年）

Financial Revenue of Local Government by Region（2010）

单位：万元 （10 000 yuan）

区　县	Region	一般预算收入 General Budgetary Revenue	税收收入 Tax Revenue	增值税 Value Added Tax	营业税 Business Revenue	企业所得税 Corporate Income Tax
全市	**Total**	**2418567**	**2072713**	**211325**	**860373**	**188436**
市本级	**Sum of city level**	**453708**	**318153**	**18970**	**32183**	**38559**
区、县合计	**Region**	**1391457**	**1222526**	**127769**	**592281**	**99048**
新城区	Xincheng	163588	136783	10813	69105	20700
碑林区	Beilin	216601	193210	18040	98305	22277
莲湖区	Lianhu	223533	178707	28256	87117	16719
雁塔区	Yanta	203716	195637	12278	130383	11887
灞桥区	Baqiao	100245	92078	5719	46611	1824
未央区	Weiyang	144600	133663	20104	62491	9581
阎良区	Yanliang	49530	40435	2152	11808	2692
临潼区	Lintong	45908	40435	9344	8500	2849
长安区	Chang'an	132207	118894	7907	41973	7155
蓝田县	Lantian	15401	12192	1625	6870	758
周至县	Zhouzhi	10169	6984	517	4585	65
户　县	Huxian	33948	27617	4029	10929	768
高陵县	Gaoling	52011	45891	6985	13604	1773
开发区合计	**Sum of Development Zones**	**573402**	**532034**	**64586**	**235909**	**50829**
高新区	GaoXin	330631	301461	41719	120348	36706
经开区	JingKai	123065	116187	21651	52007	10497
曲江新区	Qujiang	71202	68732	319	40520	2101
浐灞生态区	Chanba Eco-District	36739	34571	743	18147	1117
航空基地	Aviation Industry Base	1831	1726	207	456	96
航天基地	Aerospace Base	7903	7377	-72	3744	304
国际港务区	International Trade&Logistic Park	2031	1980	19	687	8
沣渭新区	FengWei					

5-4 续表1 continued 1

单位：万元 (10 000 yuan)

区　县	Region	税收收入 Tax Revenue 个　人所得税 Individual Income Tax	资源税 Resource Tax	城市维护建设税 City Maintenance and Construction Tax	耕地占用税 Farm Land Occupation Tax	契税 Deed Tax	其他各项税收收入 Other Tax Revenue
全市	**Total**	**81405**	**475**	**144678**	**96788**	**164749**	**324484**
市本级	**Sum of city level**	**12647**		**3554**		**74565**	**137675**
区、县合计	**Region**	**49184**	**473**	**99191**	**96788**	**22729**	**135063**
新城区	Xincheng	7227		12487	107		16344
碑林区	Beilin	15606		15693			23289
莲湖区	Lianhu	6632	3	18388	720		20872
雁塔区	Yanta	8889		17003			15197
灞桥区	Baqiao	1082	1	6938	21050		8853
未央区	Weiyang	3429	1	11604	11076		15377
阎良区	Yanliang	2497		1784	9466	4658	5378
临潼区	Lintong	1141	8	4234	5989	3868	4502
长安区	Chang'an	1514	4	4501	32800	8607	14433
蓝田县	Lantian	129	387	629	260	420	1114
周至县	Zhouzhi	69	36	389	230	415	678
户　县	Huxian	377	33	1659	5080	1530	3212
高陵县	Gaoling	592		3882	10010	3231	5814
开发区合计	**Sum of Development Zones**	**19574**	**2**	**41933**		**67455**	**51746**
高新区	GaoXin	14610		24805		33425	29848
经开区	JingKai	3683	2	9941		4641	13765
曲江新区	Qujiang	669		4628		15738	4757
浐灞生态区	Chanba Eco-District	453		1747		9924	2440
航空基地	Aviation Industry Base	36		238		340	353
航天基地	Aerospace Base	106		496		2310	489
国际港务区	International Trade&Logistic Park	17		78		1077	94
沣渭新区	FengWei						

5-4 续表2

单位：万元

区　县	Region	非税收入 Non-tax Revenue	专项收入 Special Program Receipts	行政事业性收费收入 Charge of Adiministrative and Institutional Units
全市	**Total**	**345854**	**66438**	**144929**
市本级	**Sum of city level**	**135555**	**5813**	**63379**
区、县合计	**Region**	**168931**	**42584**	**64153**
新城区	Xincheng	26805	5128	4958
碑林区	Beilin	23391	6746	11010
莲湖区	Lianhu	44826	7793	22388
雁塔区	Yanta	8079	7301	
灞桥区	Baqiao	8167	2982	2795
未央区	Weiyang	10937	4316	1410
阎良区	Yanliang	9095	767	6604
临潼区	Lintong	5473	1633	1268
长安区	Chang'an	13313	1927	9078
蓝田县	Lantian	3209	353	484
周至县	Zhouzhi	3185	259	1756
户　县	Huxian	6331	1109	1500
高陵县	Gaoling	6120	2270	902
开发区合计	**Sum of Development Zones**	**41368**	**18041**	**17397**
高新区	GaoXin	29170	10655	15501
经开区	JingKai	6878	4285	445
曲江新区	Qujiang	2470	1985	201
浐灞生态区	Chanba Eco-District	2168	767	1023
航空基地	Aviation Industry Base	105	102	
航天基地	Aerospace Base	526	213	227
国际港务区	International Trade&Logistic Park	51	34	
沣渭新区	FengWei			

continued 2

(10 000 yuan)

罚没收入 Penalty Receipts	国有资本经营收入 State-owned Assets Profit	国有资源(资产)有偿使用收入 The Revenues of the Compensation for the Use of State-owned Resoures(Assants)	其他收入 Other Income	基金收入 Fund Revenue
65332	**22443**	**45801**	**911**	**2526715**
39081	**21230**	**5750**	**302**	**458718**
23147	**1213**	**37225**	**609**	**307504**
3922	68	12729		
2613		3022		
2844		11249	552	73595
747		31		
942		1448		57838
1369		3842		
773	105	846		3160
2111		404	57	28459
1786		522		44681
1955		417		34288
799		371		3728
1707		2015		7120
1579	1040	329		54635
3104		**2826**		**1760493**
757		2257		127836
1940		208		279822
83		201		623965
238		140		513614
		3		37989
72		14		157019
14		3		20248

5–5 各区县、开发区一般预算支出（2010年）

单位:万元

区　县	Region	一般预算支出 Ordinary Budgetary Expenditures	一般公共服务支出 General Public Services	国防支出 Expenditure for National Defense	公共安全支出 Expenditure for Public Safety
合　计	**Total**	**3716175**	**453381**	**3450**	**232607**
市本级	**Sum of city level**	**1448293**	**142730**	**1790**	**99272**
区、县合计	**Region**	**1771955**	**236711**	**1630**	**127694**
新城区	Xincheng	126076	22424	181	13546
碑林区	Beilin	133034	18413	280	17634
莲湖区	Lianhu	152009	23939	98	13964
雁塔区	Yanta	130818	19227	174	14049
灞桥区	Baqiao	104972	15921	144	9429
未央区	Weiyang	128260	25059	262	11150
阎良区	Yanliang	90044	10824		6105
临潼区	Lintong	154060	15123		7391
长安区	Chang'an	244637	32671	183	10366
蓝田县	Lantian	132634	11743	94	6147
周至县	Zhouzhi	142652	11247	64	4905
户　县	Huxian	132347	13427	67	7387
高陵县	Gaoling	100412	16693	83	5621
开发区合计	**Sum of Development Zones**	**495927**	**73940**	**30**	**5641**
高新区	GaoXin	202744	27343	30	2126
经开区	JingKai	162694	15457		2310
曲江新区	Qujiang	65477	17923		385
浐灞生态区	Chanba Eco-District	36209	9532		
航空基地	Aviation Industry Base	11215	787		20
航天基地	Aerospace Base	7935	1585		800
国际港务区	International Trade&Logistic Park	9653	1313		
沣渭新区	FengWei				

Financial Expenditures of Local Government by Region（2010）

(10 000 yuan)

教育支出 Expenditure for Education	科学技术支出 Expenditure for Science and Technology	文化体育与传媒支出 Expenditure for Culture,Sport and Media	社会保障和就业支出 Expenditure for Social Safety Net and Employment Effort	医疗卫生支出 Expenditure for Medical and Health Care	环境保护支出 Expenditure for Environment Protection
530805	**43550**	**63127**	**522072**	**270981**	**55273**
103773	**21411**	**19584**	**234971**	**94060**	**27907**
419732	**11097**	**15856**	**286501**	**176841**	**18775**
29754	906	290	27625	7987	3
28918	1027	751	32446	10234	345
32269	1292	979	31038	9513	
29234	1558	969	21943	10384	311
31936	732	619	19857	9938	722
32509	1420	701	16274	11375	483
20969	593	802	12434	11761	708
39668	302	2007	19878	20885	1839
56099	1313	2801	45486	23345	1394
37771	230	1099	16269	18041	5241
32139	193	1446	17957	16719	5080
28321	549	1787	13987	13885	2424
20145	982	1605	11307	12774	225
7300	**11042**	**27687**	**600**	**80**	**8591**
5059	11002	1766	350		1381
1873	30		250		1086
368		25921		80	360
	10				1110
					124
					30
					4500

5-5 续表1

单位:万元

区　县	Region	一般预算支出 Ordinary Budgetary Expenditures 城乡社区事务支出 Expenditure for Urban and Rural Community Affairs	农林水事务支出 Expenditure for Agriculture,Foresty Water Conservancy	交通运输支出 Expenditure for Industry,Commerce and Banking	资源勘探电力信息等事务支出 Expenditure for Mining,Electricity and Information
合　计	**Total**	**475627**	**251423**	**150841**	**193190**
市本级	**Sum of city level**	**166009**	**85546**	**94593**	**99554**
区、县合计	**Region**	**157159**	**161649**	**56248**	**15701**
新城区	Xincheng	15135	152	638	1855
碑林区	Beilin	15709	128	602	245
莲湖区	Lianhu	31923	186	555	742
雁塔区	Yanta	20180	3949	701	201
灞桥区	Baqiao	2722	5530	3968	228
未央区	Weiyang	15114	5528	2273	3006
阎良区	Yanliang	9101	9161	2950	2095
临潼区	Lintong	8633	21864	9243	542
长安区	Chang'an	15728	34093	11213	414
蓝田县	Lantian	2846	18891	5643	1978
周至县	Zhouzhi	4706	26543	6462	1106
户　县	Huxian	10864	22455	6745	2684
高陵县	Gaoling	4498	13169	5255	605
开发区合计	**Sum of Development Zones**	**152459**	**4228**		**77935**
高新区	GaoXin	102188	48		50685
经开区	JingKai	6927	382		20371
曲江新区	Qujiang	12481	3318		
浐灞生态区	Chanba Eco-District	17567			3511
航空基地	Aviation Industry Base	7156			1128
航天基地	Aerospace Base	3240	80		2200
国际港务区	International Park Trade&Logistic Park	2900	400		40
沣渭新区	FengWei				

continued 1

(10 000 yuan)

商业服务业等事务 Expenditure for Commerce and Services	金融监管支出 Expenditure for Financial Supervision	地震灾后恢复重建支出 Expenditure for Post-earthquake Reconstruction	国土资源气象等事务 Expenditure for Land Recources and Meteorological Affairs	住房保障支出 Expenditure for Housing Support	粮油物资储备管理等事务支出 Material Reserves Management Affairs Spending
71475	**13863**	**2514**	**21150**	**91749**	**17680**
34477	**13848**		**6606**	**67346**	**14760**
31940	**15**	**2514**	**14163**	**24403**	**2420**
1351			1532	2686	10
2481		6	631	350	25
1864			513	2666	
2337			1951		
1817			212	1094	91
1378			1495	190	41
1450			439	287	174
3368			779	1713	493
3691		7	2411	2904	454
2374	15		646	2820	220
3983		2501	1407	3592	251
2513			919	3623	325
3333			1228	2478	336
5058			**381**		**500**
1			17		
1					500
4556			85		
			279		
500					

5-5 续表2 continued 2

单位:万元 (10 000 yuan)

区 县	Region	一般预算支出 Ordinary Budgetary Expenditure 国债还本付息支出 Expenditure for National Debt and Interst	其他支出 Other Expenditure	基金支出 Fund Expenditure
合 计	**Total**	**101094**	**150323**	**2484087**
市本级	**Sum of city level**	**100513**	**19543**	**431348**
区、县合计	**Region**	**448**	**10458**	**300676**
新城区	Xincheng	1		865
碑林区	Beilin		2809	2358
莲湖区	Lianhu	3	465	79225
雁塔区	Yanta		3650	812
灞桥区	Baqiao	12		28551
未央区	Weiyang	2		18376
阎良区	Yanliang	85	106	5577
临潼区	Lintong	25	307	32416
长安区	Chang'an	9	55	30387
蓝田县	Lantian	201	365	31858
周至县	Zhouzhi	29	2322	8144
户 县	Huxian	41	344	5458
高陵县	Gaoling	40	35	56649
开发区合计	**Sum of Development Zones**	**133**	**120322**	**1752063**
高新区	GaoXin	88	660	127926
经开区	JingKai	45	113462	270912
曲江新区	Qujiang			624268
浐灞生态区	Chanba Eco-District		4200	513704
航空基地	Aviation Industry Base		2000	37986
航天基地	Aerospace Base			157019
国际港务区	International Trade&Logistic Park			20248
沣渭新区	FengWei			

主要统计指标解释

财政收入 指国家财政参与社会产品分配所取得的收入，是实现国家职能的财力保证。主要包括：

（1）各项税收：包括国内增值税、国内消费税、进口货物增值税和消费税、出口货物退增值税和消费税、营业税、企业所得税、个人所得税、资源税、城市维护建设税、房产税、印花税、城镇土地使用税、土地增值税、车船税、船舶吨税、车辆购置税、关税、耕地占用税、契税、烟叶税等。

（2）非税收入：包括专项收入、行政事业性收费、罚没收入和其他收入。

财政支出 指国家财政将筹集起来的资金进行分配使用，以满足经济建设和各项事业的需要。主要包括：

（1）一般公共服务：指政府提供基本公共管理与服务的支出，包括人大事务、政协事务、政府办公厅（室）及相关机构事务、发展与改革事务、统计信息事务、财政事务、税收事务、审计事务、海关事务、人力资源事务、纪检监察事务、人口与计划生育事务、商贸事务、知识产权事务、工商行政管理事务、国土资源事务、海洋管理事务、测绘事务、地震事务、气象事务、民族事务、宗教事务、港澳台侨事务、档案事务、共产党事务、民主党派事务及工商联事务、群众团体事务、彩票事务等。

（2）外交：指政府外交事务支出，包括外交行政管理、驻外机构、对外援助、国际组织、对外合作与交流、边界勘界联检等方面的支出。

（3）国防：指政府用于国防方面的支出，包括用于现役部队、预备役部队、民兵、国防科研事业、专项工程、国防动员等方面的支出。

（4）公共安全：指政府维护社会公共安全方面的支出，包括武装警察、公安、国家安全、检察、法院、司法行政、监狱、劳教、国家保密、缉私警察等。

（5）教育：指政府教育事务支出，包括教育行政管理、学前教育、小学教育、初中教育、普通高中教育、普通高等教育、初等职业教育、中专教育、技校教育、职业高中教育、高等职业教育、广播电视教育、留学生教育、特殊教育、干部继续教育、教育机关服务等。

（6）科学技术：指用于科学技术方面的支出，包括科学技术管理事务、基础研究、应用研究、技术研究与开发、科技条件与服务、社会科学、科学技术普及、科技交流与合作等。

（7）文化教育与传媒：指政府在文化、文物、体育、广播影视、新闻出版等方面的支出。

（8）社会保障和就业：指政府在社会保障与就业方面的支出，包括社会保障和就业管理事务、民政管理事务、财政对社会保险基金的补助、补充全国社会保障基金、行政事业单位离退休、企业改革补助、就业补助、抚恤、退役安置、社会福利、残疾人事业、城市居民最低生活保障、其他城镇社会救济、农村社会救济、自然灾害生活救助、红十字事务等。

（9）医疗卫生：指政府医疗卫生方面的支出，包括医疗卫生管理事务支出、医疗服务支出、医疗保障支出、疾病预防控制支出、卫生监督支出、妇幼保健支出、农村卫生支出等。

（10）环境保护：指政府环境保护支出，包括环境保护管理事务支出、环境监测与监察支出、污染治理支出、自然生态保护支出、天然林保护工程支出、退耕还林支出、风沙荒漠治理支出、退牧还草支出、已垦草原退耕还草、能源节约利用、污染减排、可再生能源和资源综合利用等支出。

（11）城乡社区事务：指政府城乡社区事务支出，包括城乡社区管理事务支出、城乡社区规划与管理支出、城乡社区公共设施支出、城乡社区住宅支出、城乡社区环境卫生支出、建设市场管理与监督支出等。

（12）农林水事务：指政府农林水事务支出，包括农业支出、林业支出、水利支出、扶贫支出、农业综合开发支出等。

（13）交通运输：指政府交通运输和邮政业方面的支出，包括公路运输支出、水路运输支出、铁路运输支出、民用航空运输支出、邮政业支出等。

（14）工业商业金融等事务：指政府对工业、商业及金融等方面的支出，包括采掘业支出、制造业支出、建筑业支出、工业和信息产业监管支出、国有资产监管支出、商业流通事务支出、金融业监管支出、旅游业管理与服务支出等。

中央财政收入和地方财政收入 指按现行分税制财政体制划分的中央本级收入和地方本级收入。属于中央财政的收入包括关税，进口货物增值税和消费税，出口货物退增值税和消费税，消费税，铁道部门、各银行总行、各保险公司总公司等集中交纳的营业税和城市维护建设税，增值税75%部分，纳入共享范围的企业所得税60%部分，未纳入共享范围的中央企业所得税、中央企业上交的利润，个人所得税60%部分，车辆购置税，船舶吨税，证券交易印花税97%部分，海洋石油资源税，中央非税收入等。属于地方财政的收入包括营业税（不含铁道部门、各银行总行、各保险公司总公司集中交纳的营业税），地方企业上交利润，城市维护建设税（不含铁道部门、各银行总行、各保险公司总公司集中交纳的部分），房产税，城镇土地使用税，土地增值税，车船税，耕地占用税，契税，烟叶税，印花税，增值税25%部分，纳入共享范围的企业所得税40%部分，个人所得税40%部分，证券交易印花税3%部分，海洋石油资源税以外的其他资源税，地方非税收入等。

中央财政支出和地方财政支出 指根据政府在经济和社会活动中的不同职责，划分中央和地方政府的责权，按照政府的责权划分确定的支出。中央财政支出包括一般公共服务，外交支出，国防支出，公共安全支出，以及中央政府调整国民经济结构、协调地区发展、实施宏观调控的支出等。地方财政支出包括一般公共服务，公共安全支出，地方统筹的各项社会事业支出等。

Explanatory Notes on Main Statistical Indicators

Government Revenue refers to income for the government finance through participating in the distribution of social products. It is the financial guarantee to ensure government functioning. The contents of government revenue include the following main items:

(1) Various tax revenues, including domestic value added tax (VAT), domestic consumption tax, VAT and consumption tax from imports, VAT and consumption tax rebate for exports, business tax, corporate income tax, individual income tax, resource tax, city maintenance and construct tax, house property tax, stamp tax, urban land use tax, land appreciation tax, tax on vehicles and boat operation, ship tonnage tax, vehicle purchase tax, tariffs, farm land occupation tax, deed tax, and tobacco leaf tax, etc.

(2) Non-tax revenue, including special program receipts, charge of administrative and institutional units, penalty receipts and others non-tax receipts.

Government Expenditure refers to the distribution and use of the funds which the government finance has raised, so as to meet the needs of economic construction and various causes. It includes the following main items:

(1) Expenditure for general public services: It refers to the spending on the basic public management and services which provided by governments, including the expense on affairs of People' s Congress, affairs of People' s Political Consultative Conference, affairs of government general office and relative institutions, affairs of development and reform, affairs of statistics, affairs of finance, affairs of taxation, affairs of audit, affairs of customs, affairs of human resources and social security, affairs of discipline inspection and supervision, affairs of population and family planning, affairs of commerce and trade, affairs of intellectual property, affairs of administration for industry and commerce, affairs of land and resources, affairs of oceanic administration, affairs of surveying and mapping, affairs of earthquake, ethnic affairs, religious affairs, affairs of Hong Kong, Macao, Taiwan, and Overseas Chinese, affairs of archives administration, affairs of Chinese Communist Party, affairs of democratic parties and federation of industry and commerce, affairs of mass organization, and affairs of lottery, etc.

(2) Expenditure for foreign affairs: It refers to the spending of government on foreign affairs, including the expense on administration of foreign affairs, missions overseas, external assistance, international organizations, foreign cooperation and communication, surveying and joint inspection on borderline, etc.

(3) Expenditure for national defence: It refers to the spending of government on national defence, including the expense on active force, reserve force, militia, scientific research on national defence, special projects, mobilization of national defence, etc.

(4) Expenditure for public security: It refers to the spending of government on maintaining social and public security, including the expense on armed police force, public security, state security, prosecution, courts, justice, prison, labour education and rehabilitation, protection of state secrecy, anti-smuggling police, etc.

(5) Expenditure for education: It refers to the spending of government on education, including the expense on the administration of education, pre-primary education, primary education, secondary education, high school education, regular higher education, primary vocational education, secondary vocational education, technical school education, vocational high school education and higher vocational education, radio and television education, student abroad education, special education, on the job training of cadres, education authorities services, etc.

(6) Expenditure for science and technology: It refers to the spending of government on science and technology (S&T), including the expense on the administration of S&T, basic research, applied research, research and development, conditions and services of S&T, popularization of social science, science and technology, exchanges and cooperation of S&T, etc.

(7) Expenditure for culture, sport and media: It refers to the spending of government on culture, cultural heritage, sports, radio, film, television, press and publication, etc.

(8) Expenditure for social safety net and employment effort: It refers to the spending of government on social

safety net and employment, including the expense on administration of social safety net and employment, civil affairs, budgetary subsidy on the social insurance funds, subsidy on National Social Security Fund, retirees of administrative units and institutions, subsidy on enterprise reform, subsidy on employment effort, pension, placement of ex-serviceman, social welfare, the handicapped undertakings, the system of cost of living allowances for urban residents, other urban social relief, rural social relief, living relief of natural disasters, affairs of Red Cross Society, etc.

(9) Expenditure for medical and health care: It refers to the spending of government on medical and health care, including the expense on administration of medical and health care, medical services, health care, disease prevention and control, health inspection and supervision, women and children's health, rural health care, etc.

(10) Expenditure for environment protection: It refers to the spending of government on environment protection, including the expense on administration of environment protection, environment monitoring and supervision, pollution control, natural ecology protection, project of virgin forests protection, reforesting farmland, controlling the sources of dust storms, returning pastureland to grassland, returning pastureland to grassland, returning cultivated land to grassland, energy conservation, emissions reduction, comprehensive utilization of renewable energy and resources, etc.

(11) Expenditure for urban and rural community affairs: It refers to the spending of government on urban and rural community affairs, including the expense on administration of urban and rural community, planning and management of urban and rural community, public facilities of urban and rural community, housing of urban and rural community, sanitation of urban and rural community, management and supervision on the construction market, etc.

(12) Expenditure for agriculture, forestry and water conservancy: It refers to the spending of government on agriculture, forestry and water conservancy, including the expense on agriculture, forestry, water conservancy, poverty alleviation, comprehensive agricultural development, etc.

(13) Expenditure for transportation: It refers to the spending of government on transportation and postal services, including the expense on road transportation, waterway transportation, railway transportation, civil aviation transportation, and postal services.

(14) Expenditure for industry, commerce and banking: It refers to the spending of government on industry, commerce and banking, including the expense on mining, manufacturing, construction, industry and information technology supervision and administration, State-owned assets supervision and administration, commerce and circulation affairs, financial intermediation supervision and administration, tourism administration and service, etc.

Revenue of the Central Government and Revenue of the Local Governments refers to the revenue collected by the Central Government and that by the local governments as defined by the decentralized taxation system. In accordance with this system, the revenue of the Central Government includes tariff, VAT and consumption tax from imports, VAT and consumption tax rebate for exports, consumption tax, business tax and city maintenance and construct tax from the Ministry of Railways, head offices of banks, head offices of insurance company, which are handed over to the government in a centralized way, 75% of the value added tax, 60% the share part of the corporate income tax, unshared part of corporate income tax of the central enterprises, profit handed in by the central enterprises, 60% of individual income tax, vehicle purchase tax, ship tonnage tax, 97% of stamp tax on securities transactions, resource tax on the offshore petroleum resources. The revenue of the local governments includes business tax (excluding the part of the Ministry of Railways, head offices of banks, head offices of insurance company, which are handed over to the government in a centralized way), profit handed in by the local enterprises, city maintenance and construct tax (excluding the part of the Ministry of Railways, head offices of banks, head offices of insurance company, which are handed over to the government in a centralized way), house property tax, urban land use tax, land appreciation tax, tax on vehicles and boat operation, farm land occupation tax, deed tax, and tobacco leaf tax, stamp tax, 25% of the value added tax, 40% the share part of the corporate income tax, 40% of individual income tax, 3%

of stamp tax on securities transactions, resource tax other than the tax on offshore petroleum resources, local non-tax revenue, etc.

Expenditure of the Central Government and Expenditure of the Local Governments according to the different functions of the Central Government and local governments in economic and social activities, the rights of affairs administration are demarcated between those of the Central Government and those of local governments; and the classification of the expenditure between the Central Government and local governments are made on the basis of the classification of the rights of affairs administration between them. The expenditure of the Central Government includes the expenditure for general public services, expenditure for foreign affairs, expenditure for public security, and the expenditure of the Central Government for adjusting the national economic structure; coordinating the development among different regions; and exercising macroeconomic regulation. The expenditure of the local governments includes mainly the expenditure for general public services, expenditure for public security, and expenditures for social development which are planed by local governments, etc.

6 物价指数

PRICE INDICES

资料整理：李 欣 刘 青 郭菁媛
Data management:Li Xin Liu Qing Guo Jingyuan

第六部分　物价指数

一、简要说明

本章资料主要包括居民消费、零售、工业产品出厂、主要原材料购进、土地交易、房地产销售、租赁以及固定资产投资和建筑安装工程等价格指数，由国家统计局西安调查队提供。

二、主要指标

商品零售价格总指数（上年=100）	102.7	比上年提高 3.2个百分点
居民消费价格总指数（上年=100）	103.5	比上年提高 3.8个百分点

6 PRICE INDICES

Ⅰ.Brief Introduction

This chapter consists primarily of data on price indices of residents consumption, retail, industrial products dispatching sales, primary raw material purchasing, land deal, real estate selling, leasing, fixed asset investment and construction installation projects, provided by Fixed Asset Investment Division of the NBS Survey Office in Xi'an.

Ⅱ.Major Indicators

		Increase over Preceding Year
Retail Price Index(the price Preceding year=100)	102.7	3.2 percentage points
Consumer Price Index(the price Preceding year=100)	103.5	3.8 percentage points

6-1 主要年份各种价格指数

Price Indices in Representative Years

(以上年价格为100) (the price of Preceding year=100)

年 份 Year	居民消费价格指数 Consumer Price Index	商品零售价格指数 Retail Price Index	工业品出厂价格指数 Producer Price Index for Manufactured Goods	原材料，燃料，动力购进价格指数 Purchasing Price Index for Raw Material, Fuel and Power	固定资产投资价格指数 Price Index for Investment in Fixed Assets
1980	108.7	109.3			
1981	102.4	102.7			
1982	100.9	101.0			
1983	102.6	102.0			
1984	104.7	104.8			
1985	109.7	109.3			
1986	108.5	107.4			
1987	110.6	111.4			
1988	122.8	123.2			
1989	118.3	117.8			
1990	102.5	100.9			
1991	109.4	108.3			
1992	112.2	112.4			
1993	117.2	112.8	102.5	104.3	
1994	128.5	126.2	132.2	115.0	
1995	117.0	114.6	110.8	113.1	
1996	110.9	107.9	100.7	103.8	
1997	106.0	101.5	98.6	102.5	
1998	97.9	95.5	94.4	97.5	
1999	96.8	97.4	97.5	96.9	100.8
2000	100.2	98.7	99.4	102.4	102.1
2001	99.9	98.9	99.3	101.0	101.3
2002	98.6	98.5	98.2	98.4	101.2
2003	100.5	100.0	101.5	105.3	102.4
2004	102.3	101.9	102.7	110.4	103.3
2005	100.3	99.7	103.9	109.6	102.4
2006	101.6	101.5	103.2	106.1	102.0
2007	104.7	103.7	101.9	106.2	103.5
2008	106.0	105.4	103.7	108.5	110.5
2009	99.7	99.5	99.9	100.7	97.9
2010	103.5	102.7	102.3	106.3	103.8

6-2 居民消费价格指数（2010年）

Residents Consumer Price Indices（2010）

(以上年价格为100) (the price of Preceding year=100)

类　别	Item	2010
居民消费价格总指数	**Consumer Price Index**	**103.5**
非食品价格指数	Non-foodstuff Price Index	101.9
服务项目价格指数	Price Index of Service	104.1
工业品价格指数	Ex-factory Price Indices of Industrial Products	100.2
扣除食品和能源价格指数	Price Index with Food and Energy Excluded	101.7
扣除鲜菜鲜果总指数	Price Index with Fresh Vegetables and Fruits Excluded	102.9
消费品价格指数	Price Index of Consumer Goods	103.3
一、食品	**Food**	**107.0**
1.粮食	Grain	115.7
2.淀粉	Starches	104.0
3.干豆类及豆制品	Beans and Bean Products	100.6
4.油脂	Oil or Fat	105.1
5.肉禽及其制品	Meat,Poultry and Processed Products	105.2
6.蛋	Eggs	104.6
7.水产品	Aquatic Products	107.3
8.菜	Vegetables	115.9
9.调味品	Flavouring	110.2
10.糖	Carbohydrate	108.4
11.茶及饮料	Tea and Beverages	101.0
12.干鲜瓜果	Dried and Fresh Melons and Fruits	110.3
13.糕点饼干	Cake and Biscuit	102.6
14.液体乳及乳制品	Milk and Its Product	101.2
15.在外用膳食品	Dining Out	102.0
16.其他食品	Other Food	101.6
二、烟酒及用品	**Tobacco,Liquor and Articles**	**100.7**
1.烟草	Tobacco	99.8
2.酒	Liquor	102.6
3.吸烟、饮酒用品	Articles for Smoking and Drinking	102.5
三、衣着	**Clothing**	**98.9**
1.服装	Garments	96.7
2.衣着材料	Clothing Material	101.2
3.鞋袜帽	Footgear and Hats	103.8
4.衣着加工服务费	Clothing Manufacturing Services	100.7

6-2 续表 continued

(以上年价格为100) (the price of Preceding year=100)

类　　别	Item	2010
四、家庭设备用品及维修服务	**Household facilities,Articles and Services**	**104.8**
1.耐用消费品	Durable Consumer Goods	99.4
2.室内装饰品	Interior Decorations	96.8
3.床上用品	Bed Articles	93.5
4.家庭日用杂品	Daily Use Household Articles	100.6
5.家庭服务及加工维修服务	Household Service and Maintenance Renovation	112.6
五、医疗保健和个人用品	**Health Care and Personal Articles**	**104.0**
1.医疗保健	Health Care	103.7
（1）医疗器具及用品	Medical Instrument Articles	104.2
（2）中药材及中成药	Traditional Chinese Medicine	113.8
（3）西药	Western Medicine	102.1
（4）保健器具及用品	Health Care Appliances and Articles	101.6
（5）医疗保健服务	Health Care Services	100.0
2.个人用品及服务	Personal Articles and Services	104.4
六、交通和通信	**Transportation and Communication**	**99.7**
1.交通	Transportation	102.1
（1）交通工具	Transportation Facility	96.9
（2）车用燃料及零配件	Fuels and Parts	113.2
（3）车辆使用及维修费	Fees for Vehicles Use and Maintenance	100.7
（4）市区公共交通费	Incity Traffic Fare	101.1
（5）城市间交通费	Intercity Traffic Fare	105.1
2.通信	Communication	97.3
（1）通信工具	Telecommunication Facility	82.7
（2）通信服务	Telecommunication Service	100.0
七、娱乐教育文化用品及服务	**Recreation,Education and Culture Articles**	**101.0**
1.文娱用耐用消费品及服务	Durable Consumer Goods for Cultural and Recreational Use and Services	91.7
2.教育	Education	101.3
3.文化娱乐	Cultural and Recreational Articles	100.4
4.旅游	Touring	109.9
八、居住	**Residence**	**102.7**
1.建房及装修材料	Building and Building Decoration Materials	100.6
2.租房	Renting	106.3
3.自有住房	Private Housing	106.6
4.水、电、燃料	Water, Electricity and Fuels	101.3

6-3 商品零售价格指数（2010年）

Retail Price Indices（2010）

(以上年价格为100)　　(the price of Preceding year=100)

类　　别	Item	2010
商品零售价格总指数	**Retail Price Indices**	**102.7**
一、食品	**Food**	**107.1**
1.粮食	Grain	114.6
2.淀粉	Starches	104.0
3.干豆类及豆制品	Beans and Bean Products	106.8
4.油 脂	Oil or Fat	105.1
5.肉禽及其制品	Meat,Poultry and Processed Products	104.6
6.蛋	Eggs	104.7
7.水产品	Aquatic Products	107.9
8.菜	Vegetables	115.6
9.调味品	Flavouring	106.6
10.糖	Carbohydrate	112.5
11.干鲜瓜果	Dried and Fresh Melons and Fruits	110.4
12.糕点饼干面包	Cake,Biscuit and Bread	102.5
13.液体乳及乳制品	Milk and Its Product	101.1
14.在外用膳食品	Dining Out	102.6
15.其它食品	Other Food and Manufacturing Services	101.6
二、饮料、烟酒	**Beverages,Tobacco and Liquor**	**101.2**
1.茶及饮料	Tea and Beverages	102.4
2.烟草	Tobacco	100.1
3.酒	Liquor	102.2
三、服装、鞋帽	**Garments,Shoes and Hats**	**99.0**
1.服装	Garments	96.9
2.鞋袜帽	Footgear and Hats	103.8
四、纺织品	**Textiles**	**93.7**
1.衣着材料	Cotton Cloth	101.6
2.床上用品	Blend Cloth	93.5
五、家用电器及音像器材	**Household Appliances,Music and Video Equipment**	**92.9**
1.家庭设备	Household facility	96.0
2.文娱用耐用消费品	Durable Consumer Goods on Cultural and Recreational Use	90.4
3.音像器材	Music and Video Equipment	98.1
六、文化办公用品	**Cultural and Office Appliances**	**97.5**

6-3 续表 continued

(以上年价格为100) (the price of Preceding year=100)

类　　别	Item	2010
七、日用品	**Articles for Daily Use**	**101.7**
1.日用百货	General Merchandise for Daily Use	101.9
2.日用杂品	Miscellaneous for Daily Use	97.3
3.洗涤用品	Daily Use Articles For Washing	101.8
4.其它日用品	Other Daily Articles	102.9
八、体育娱乐用品	**Sports and Recreation Articles**	**96.0**
1.体育用品	Sports Goods	101.5
2.娱乐用品	Receration Goods	94.0
九、交通、通信用品	**Transportation and Communication Goods**	**96.0**
1.交通运输机械	Transportation Machinery	98.3
2.通信器材	Communication Machinery	85.4
十、家具	**Furniture**	**109.7**
十一、化妆品	**Cosmetics**	**102.3**
十二、金银珠宝	**Gold,Silver and Jewelry**	**113.5**
十三、中西药品及医疗保健用品	**Traditional Chinese and Western Medicines And Health Care Articles**	**104.6**
1.医疗器具及用品	Medical Apparatus and Article	104.2
2.中药材及中成药	Traditional Chinese Medicinal Materials and Medicines	113.3
3.西药	Western Medicine	101.8
4.保健品及器具	Health Care Apparatus and Article	101.4
十四、书报杂志及电子出版物	**Books,Newspapers,Magazines and Electronic Publications**	**101.3**
1.教材及参考书	Teaching Materials and Reference Books	102.3
2.书报杂志	Books, Newspapers and Magazines	100.0
3.电子音像制品	Electronic Audio-video Products	99.8
十五、燃料	**Fuel**	**109.3**
1.煤炭及制品	Coal and Its Products	101.5
2.石油及制品	Oil and Its Products	110.2
十六、建筑材料及五金电料	**Building Materials and Hardware**	**103.6**
1.建筑装潢材料	Building Decoration Materials	102.6
2.五金电料	Hardware	105.1

6-4 主要年份工业品出厂价格指数

（上年价格=100）

类　　别	Classify	1997	1998	1999	2000
全部工业品	**Total Industry Products**	**98.63**	**94.37**	**97.49**	**99.43**
按轻重工业分	Grouped by Light Industry and Heavy Industry				
轻工业	Light Industry	98.17	91.11	95.87	97.82
以农产品为原料	Using Farm Products as Raw Materials	99.21	89.47	95.19	99.18
以非农产品为原料	Using Non-farm Products as Raw Materials	96.79	93.41	96.97	95.45
重工业	Heavy Industry	98.98	97.30	98.92	100.75
采掘工业	Mining and Quarrying Industry		104.14	101.52	97.48
原料工业	Raw Materials Industry	100.96	100.70	102.27	107.74
加工工业	Processing Industry	97.86	95.63	98.00	98.36
按用途分	Grouped by Use				
生产资料	Means of Production	99.58	96.57	98.28	100.50
采掘工业	Mining & Quarrying Industry		104.14	101.52	97.48
原料工业	Raw Materials Industry	100.89	100.57	100.20	106.38
加工工业	Processing Industry	98.87	94.67	97.59	98.67
生活资料	Consumer Goods	97.03	91.36	96.46	97.27
（1）食品	Food	108.21	97.75	95.79	94.40
（2）衣着	Clothing	92.96	83.88	95.19	101.56
（3）一般日用品	Articles for Daily Use	91.63	95.06	97.62	96.89
（4）耐用消费品	Durable Consumer Goods	99.65	95.41	98.02	95.93
按工业部门分	Grouped by Industrial Sector				
1.冶金工业	Metallurgical Industry	99.17	97.50	91.20	98.20
2.电力工业	Power Industry	111.29	111.23	109.33	109.63
3.煤炭及炼焦工业	Coal and Coking Industry	98.87	98.48	96.30	100.54
4.石油工业	Petroleum Industry			107.09	134.24
5.化学工业	Chemical Industry	91.77	92.93	96.61	96.69
6.机械工业	Machine Manufacturing Industry	98.76	94.59	98.09	98.02
7.建筑材料工业	Building Materials Industry	98.19	99.30	96.71	98.51
8.森林工业	Timber Industry	107.55	104.47	97.94	98.90
9.食品工业	Food Industry	106.80	95.27	95.45	94.32
10.纺织工业	Textiles Industry	94.32	82.58	93.65	103.35
11.缝纫工业	Tailoring Industry	100.14	97.29	99.10	103.50
12.皮革工业	Leather Industry	91.18	96.78	98.00	99.20
13.造纸工业	Paper Industry			95.33	96.68
14.文教艺术用品工业	Cultural,Educational & Handicrafts Articles			96.65	96.36
15.其他工业	Other Industry	109.51	109.22	98.89	104.84

Producer Price Index for Manufacture in Representative Years

(the price of Preceding year=100)

2001	2002	2003	2004	2005	2006	2007	2008	2009	2010
99.30	**98.20**	**101.45**	**102.67**	**103.89**	**103.22**	**101.90**	**103.72**	**99.85**	**102.25**
99.60	98.40	101.27	103.40	99.93	100.16	101.80	103.68	100.64	102.50
99.00	98.40	104.45	108.67	97.30	100.06	103.32	106.02	98.91	104.00
100.60	98.60	99.89	100.80	101.19	100.22	100.81	102.12	101.79	101.41
99.20	98.20	101.64	101.92	107.86	105.52	101.92	103.77	99.32	102.19
94.80	101.30	103.38	140.50	107.88	100.63	111.56	122.27	89.99	150.21
101.10	101.30	111.18	108.95	114.23	111.77	104.88	110.75	99.52	108.90
98.50	97.70	100.09	100.56	106.66	104.19	101.19	101.94	99.35	100.83
99.10	98.00	101.84	102.74	105.34	104.19	101.27	103.38	99.33	102.21
94.80	101.30	103.38	140.50	107.88	100.63	111.56	122.27	89.99	105.21
101.10	101.00	108.13	106.62	111.27	111.56	104.76	110.17	99.73	109.00
98.50	97.40	100.89	102.03	104.34	102.98	100.62	102.00	99.31	101.00
99.90	99.10	100.50	102.54	100.36	100.36	103.54	104.74	101.43	102.53
99.60	101.20	101.02	103.55	100.31	100.43	105.31	106.57	100.26	103.29
99.40	100.80	99.43	102.68	101.97	103.34	104.56	105.05	102.68	101.23
101.90	97.90	101.22	101.17	101.29	100.79	100.09	102.67	102.64	101.20
97.00	98.10	97.18	98.30	99.07	99.39	100.73	100.74	103.89	101.90
97.20	98.70	103.77	107.12	103.91	106.47	103.20	104.77	91.98	105.77
102.40	100.00	103.19	104.05	110.55	107.85	105.53	109.95	108.97	101.19
110.30	106.70	136.75	131.38	97.06	95.36	106.83	104.80	101.69	110.56
96.60	100.70	118.63	110.52	121.74	117.61	104.82	115.64	96.73	114.18
100.50	99.20	100.16	100.80	103.23	100.77	101.10	104.11	102.60	100.83
98.30	97.60	99.83	100.61	104.94	103.43	100.98	101.65	99.93	100.94
100.60	99.60	99.69	99.95	98.61	98.88	98.85	101.75	101.91	99.93
98.10	98.90	100.08	100.21	101.63	101.61	101.10	101.10	101.10	101.68
99.80	101.10	102.78	107.52	98.27	99.00	106.10	109.29	98.33	104.30
97.50	94.90	117.34	119.08	89.92	102.42	98.38	99.66	97.51	108.90
100.00	101.10	100.22	103.57	100.84	103.52	104.64	105.10	102.61	101.31
101.00	101.80	98.68	99.59	101.16	100.00	99.04	99.57	99.68	99.62
102.30	95.00	96.91	100.15	101.16	100.04	100.13	104.46	98.43	100.37
101.10	103.40	97.52	96.47	98.10	100.08	99.08	99.15	102.24	99.94
107.10	99.40	103.26	105.02	103.42	105.65	111.37	104.31	99.66	100.51

6–5 主要年份原材料、燃料、动力购进价格指数

Purchase Price Indices of Major Raw Materials,Fuels and Power in Representative Years

(上年价格=100) (the price of Preceding year=100)

类　别	Item	2000	2001	2002	2003	2004
全部原材料	**Total of Raw Materials**	**102.38**	**101.00**	**98.40**	**105.29**	**110.39**
(一)燃料、动力类	Fuel and Power	105.01	101.80	100.90	105.65	109.36
(二)黑色金属材料类	Ferrous Metals	102.69	102.10	98.50	107.43	117.38
#钢材	Steel	103.35	102.40	97.90	105.97	114.76
(三)有色金属材料和电线类	Non-ferrous Metals and Electric Wires	105.17	95.50	96.80	105.80	114.08
(四)化工原料类	Raw Chemical Materials	104.55	102.50	97.90	102.43	106.30
(五)木材及纸浆类	Timber and Paper Pulp	101.21	102.80	99.40	101.19	100.27
(六)建筑材料及非金属矿类	Building Materials and Non-metal ores	100.28	99.70	98.60	99.62	110.42
(七)其它工业原材料及半成品类	Other Industrial Raw Materials and Semi-Products	98.75	100.80	98.90	102.50	111.17
(八)农副产品类	Agricultural Products	100.42	102.80	98.20	113.72	112.74
(九)纺织原料类	Textile Materials	98.03	96.80	90.60	103.44	103.88

6–5 续表 continued

(上年价格=100) (the price of Preceding year=100)

类　别	Item	2005	2006	2007	2008	2009	2010
全部原材料	**Total of Raw Materials**	**109.62**	**106.08**	**106.17**	**108.50**	**100.74**	**106.30**
(一)燃料、动力类	Fuel and Power	123.50	112.55	106.96	109.83	105.08	108.58
(二)黑色金属材料类	Ferrous Metals	107.56	99.17	104.78	111.27	99.17	103.11
#钢材	Steel	107.46	98.48	104.90	111.65	98.71	103.47
(三)有色金属材料和电线类	Non-ferrous Metals and Electric Wires	107.82	116.46	110.71	99.13	93.86	113.56
(四)化工原料类	Raw Chemical Materials	106.06	101.57	105.59	111.36	94.96	103.93
(五)木材及纸浆类	Timber and Paper Pulp	108.18	111.66	105.90	106.50	102.60	101.07
(六)建筑材料及非金属矿类	Building Materials and Non-metal ores	99.27	100.69	104.01	104.82	106.84	102.08
(七)其它工业原材料及半成品类	Other Industrial Raw Materials and Semi-Products	106.09	104.34	108.84	110.62	101.41	108.10
(八)农副产品类	Agricultural Products	100.89	107.19	107.17	108.87	99.57	106.54
(九)纺织原料类	Textile Materials	97.62	101.53	100.52	99.81	97.58	104.57

6-6 土地交易价格指数（2010年）

Transactions Price Indices of Land（2010）

(上年价格=100) (the price of Preceding year=100)

项　　目	Item	2010
土地交易总计	**Transactions Price Indices of Land**	**103.50**
一、居住用地	**Land for Residential Building Use**	**104.60**
（一）经济适用房用地	Economically Affordable Housing	
（二）商品住宅用地	Commercialized Housing	104.60
1.普通住宅用地	General Residential Buildings	104.40
2.高档住宅用地	Luxury Residential Buildings	101.90
二、工业用地	**Land for Industry and Storage Use**	**101.10**
三、商业营业用地	**Land for Business,Tourism and Entertainment**	**102.30**
四、其他用地	**Land for Other Uses**	**103.90**

6-7 房屋销售价格指数（2010年）

Selling Price Indices of Real Estate（2010）

(上年价格=100) (the price of Preceding year=100)

项　　目	Item	2010
房屋销售总计	**Selling Price Indices of Houses**	**112.1**
一、新建房	**Newly Commercial Houses**	**113.3**
（一）住宅	Residential Buildings	112.9
按房屋类型分	By Type of Housing	
1.经济适用房	Economically Affordable Housing	102.2
2.商品住宅	Commercialized Houses	114.0
（1）普通住宅	General Residential Buildings	114.2
①多层住宅	Multi-storey Buildings	120.3
②高层住宅	High-layer Buildings	114.1
③其他住宅	Other Buildings	
（2）高档住宅	Luxury Residential Buildings	113.3
①别墅	Villas	115.3
②高档公寓	High-grade Apartments	117.1
按套型分	By Dwelling Size Classification	
#90平方米以下	#90 Square Meters Below	112.9
（二）非住宅	Non-residential Buildings	117.0
1.办公楼	Office Buildings	111.8
2.商业营业用房	Houses for Business Use	125.8
3.其他用房	Others	109.8
二、二手房	**Second-hand Houses**	**107.3**
（一）住宅	Residential Buildings	108.1
1.普通住宅	General Residential Buildings	107.4
（1）多层住宅	Multi-storey Buildings	103.0
（2）高层住宅	High-layer Buildings	111.5
（3）其他住宅	Others Buildings	106.3
2.高档住宅	High-Rise Buildings	113.3
（1）别墅	Villas	
（2）)高档公寓	High-grade Apartments	113.3
（二）非住宅	Non-residential Buildings	103.1

6-8 房屋租赁价格指数（2010年）

Renting Price Indices of Houses（2010）

(上年价格=100) (the price of Preceding year=100)

项　　目	Item	2010
房屋租赁价格指数	**Renting Price Indices of Houses**	**106.1**
一、住　宅	**Residential Buildings**	**106.3**
（一）经济适用房	Economical Affordable Housing	
（二）廉租房	Tenement House	100.0
（三）商品住宅	Commercialized Residential Buildings	106.4
1.普通住宅	General Residential Buildings	105.8
2.高档住宅	Luxury Residential Buildings	109.3
（1）别墅	Villas	
（2）高档公寓	High-grade Apartment	**109.3**
二、非住宅	**Non-residential Buildings**	105.9
（一）办公楼	Office Buildings	101.5
（二）商业营业用房	Commercial Business Buildings	108.5
（三）其他	Others Buildings	101.5

6-9 主要年份固定资产投资价格指数

Price Indices for Investment in Fixed Assets in Representative Years

(上年价格=100) (the price of Preceding year=100)

项　　目	Item	2000	2004	2005	2006	2007	2008	2009	2010
固定资产投资价格指数	**Price Indices for Investment in Fixed Assets**	**102.1**	**103.3**	**102.4**	**102.0**	**103.5**	**110.5**	**97.9**	**103.8**
建筑安装、装饰工程	Construction,Installation and Decoration	103.9	104.6	102.3	102.6	104.9	114.9	97.1	105.5
设备、工器具购置	Purchase of Equipment and Instruments	97.9	100.5	104.5	100.8	100.7	101.0	98.6	100.0
其他费用	Others	100.0	100.6	100.5	100.5	100.6	101.9	100.9	100.8

6-10 主要年份建筑安装工程价格指数

Price Indecies of Construction and Installation in Representative Years

(上年价格=100) (the price of Preceding year=100)

项　　目	Item	2000	2004	2005	2006	2007	2008	2009	2010
建筑安装工程价格指数	**Expenditure of Construction and Installation**	**103.9**	**104.6**	**102.3**	**102.6**	**104.9**	**114.9**	**97.1**	**105.5**
#人工费	Labor-hour Expense	103.6	105.2	106.9	108.3	109.1	114.5	110.6	111.9
材料费	Material Expense	104.4	105.1	101.4	101.1	104.3	117.6	94.1	105.2
机械使用费	Machinery Use Expense	103.9	102.8	102.5	104.5	104.5	106.5	99.3	103.3

主要统计指标解释

商品零售价格指数 是反映一定时期内城乡商品零售价格变动趋势的一种经济指数。零售物价的调整变动直接影响到城乡居民的生活支出和国家的财政收入，影响居民购买力和市场供需平衡，影响消费与积累的比例。因此，计算零售价格指数，可以从一个侧面对上述经济活动进行观察和分析。

居民消费价格指数 是反映一定时期内城乡居民所购买的生活消费品价格和服务项目价格变动趋势和程度的相对数，是对城市居民消费价格指数和农村居民消费价格指数进行综合汇总计算的结果。利用居民消费价格指数，可以观察和分析消费品的零售价格和服务价格变动对城乡居民实际生活费用支出的影响程度。

工业品出厂价格指数 是反映全部工业产品出厂价格总水平的变动趋势和程度的相对数，包括工业企业售给本企业以外所有单位的各种产品和直接售给居民用于生活消费的产品。通过工业品出厂价格指数能观察出厂价格变动对工业总产值的影响。

固定资产投资价格指数 是反映固定资产投资价格变动趋势和程度的相对数。固定资产投资额是由建筑安装工程投资完成额、设备、工器具购置投资完成额和其他费用投资完成额三部分组成的。编制固定资产投资价格指数应首先分别编制上述三部分投资的价格指数，然后采用加权算术平均法求出固定资产投资价格总指数。

编制固定资产投资价格指数可以准确地反映固定资产投资中涉及的各类商品和取费项目价格变动趋势和变动幅度，消除按现价计算的固定资产投资指标中的价格变动因素，真实地反映固定资产投资的规模、速度、结构和效益，为国家科学地制定、检查固定资产投资计划并提高宏观调控水平，为完善国民经济核算体系提供科学的、可靠的依据。

房地产价格指数 包括房屋销售价格指数、房屋租赁价格指数和土地交易价格指数。这三套指数的计算方法相似，均采用由下到上逐级汇总的方法。即由细项到小类，由小类到中类，再由中类到大类，最后由大类汇出总指数。对没有细项或小类的部分，其起始类就是小类或中类。中类以下（含中类）指数采用样本资料作权数的加权调和平均公式计算，大类和总指数采用固定权数加权的算术平均公式计算。

Explanatory Notes on Main Statistical Indicators

Retail Price Index it is an economic index which reflects the trend of commodity retail price changes of urban and rural area in an period of time. The change and adjustment in retail prices directly affect the living expenditure of urban and rural residents, government revenue, purchasing power of residents and the equilibrium of market supply and demand, and the ratio of consumption to accumulation. Therefore, the calculation of retail price index is useful to analyze the changes of the above economic activities.

Consumer Price Index reflects the trend and degree of changes in prices of consumer goods and services purchased by urban and rural residents, and is a composite index derived from the urban consumer price index and the rural consumer price index. Consumer price index can be used to analyze the impact of consumer price change on actual expenditure for living cost of urban and rural residents.

Ex-factory Price Index of Industrial Products reflects the trend and degree of changes in general ex-factory prices of all industrial products, including sales of industrial products by an industrial enterprise to all units outside the enterprise, as well as sales of consumer goods to residents. It can be used to analyze the impact of ex-factory prices on gross industrial output value.

Price Index of Investment in Fixed Assets reflects the trend and degree of changes in prices of investment in fixed assets. The investment in fixed assets consists of three components, namely the investment in construction and installation, the investment in purchases of equipment and instrument, and the investment in other items. Price index of investment in fixed assets is calculated as the weighted arithmetic mean of the price indices of the three components of investment in fixed assets. Removing the factor of price change in the aggregates of investment at current prices, this indicator shows the changes in the prices of commodities and fees involved in the investment of fixed assets, and can be used to observe the actual size, growth, structure, and efficiency of investment in fixed assets and provides reliable and scientific data for government planning, management, decision making, and further improving the current national accounting system.

Price Indices for Real Estate include price index for selling houses and buildings, price index for leasing houses and buildings and price index for land transaction. The methods for the compilation of the three sets of indices are similar in that they all use bottom-up approach, under which indices for the item groups are compiled first, and then indices for the major groups, categories, major categories and finally the overall indices are compiles. The indices for item groups, major groups and categories are calculated using the formulae of weighted harmonic mean with sample data as the weights, and the indices for the major categories and the overall indices are calculated using the arithmetic mean with fixed weights.

7 人民生活

PEOPLE'S LIVELIHOOD

资料整理：冯军魁　贾薪蓉　赵兰莉
Data management:Feng Junkui Jia Xinrong Zhao Lanli

第七部分　人民生活

一、简要说明

本章资料主要内容包括城乡居民家庭基本情况、主要商品购买数量、耐用消费品拥有数量等，由西安市统计局人口就业处提供。

二、主要指标

城镇居民人均可支配收入（元）	22244	比上年增长 17.3%
城镇居民人均消费性支出（元）	16543	比上年增长 16.1%
农村居民人均纯收入（元）	7750	比上年增长 23.5%
农村居民人均生活消费支出（元）	5633	比上年增长 18.1%

7 PEOPLE'S LIVELIHOOD

Ⅰ.Brief Introduction

Data in this chapter reflects situation of the people's daily life of Xi'an city. It consists of mainly basic condition of urban and rural households, volume of primary commodity purchasing, possession of endurable goods, etc. The data come from Population & Employment Division of the Xi'an Bureau of Statistics.

Ⅱ.Major Indicators

		Increase over Preceding Year
Per Capita Annual Disposable Income of Urban Households (yuan)	22244	17.3%
Per Capita Annual Consumption Expenditure of Urban Households (yuan)	16543	16.1%
Per Capita Living Expenditure Built(yuan)	7750	23.5%
Per Capita Net Income of Rural Residents(yuan)	5633	18.1%

7-1 主要年份城乡居民家庭人均收入及恩格尔系数

Per Capita Annual Income and Engel's Coefficient of Urban and Rural Households in Representative Years

年 份 Year	城镇居民家庭人均可支配收入 Per Capita Annual Disposable Income of Urban Households		农村居民家庭人均纯收入 Per Capita Annual Net Income of Rural Households		城镇居民家庭恩格尔系数（%）Engel's Coefficient of Urban Households	农村居民家庭恩格尔系数（%）Engel's Coefficient of Rural Households
	绝对数（元）Value(yuan)	指数（1980年=100）Indax (preceding year=100)	绝对数（元）Value(yuan)	指数（1980年=100）Index (preceding year=100)		
1978			140	100.0		
1979						
1980	414		190	135.7	53.3	53.3
1981	446	107.7	207	147.9	52.9	53.7
1982	479	115.6	254	181.4	55.1	56.7
1983	509	122.9	245	175.0	55.1	58.4
1984	540	130.3	299	213.6	54.9	51.7
1985	719	173.5	351	250.7	49.5	48.5
1986	911	219.8	390	278.6	49.9	47.9
1987	1034	249.7	434	310.0	50.6	50.3
1988	1142	275.6	482	344.3	44.9	47.5
1989	1344	324.3	530	378.6	51.7	48.2
1990	1518	366.5	610	435.7	53.1	49.5
1991	1619	390.9	707	505.0	51.6	46.7
1992	1992	481.0	783	559.3	52.5	50.9
1993	2661	642.5	870	621.4	46.4	46.0
1994	3517	849.1	1078	770.0	45.2	50.1
1995	4153	1002.5	1353	966.4	44.7	50.3
1996	5023	1212.6	1586	1132.9	42.6	49.9
1997	5344	1290.1	1846	1318.6	40.7	49.2
1998	5670	1368.7	2052	1465.7	39.8	42.4
1999	5999	1448.3	2203	1573.6	36.3	39.1
2000	6364	1536.5	2344	1674.3	36.5	36.6
2001	6705	1618.8	2490	1778.6	34.8	33.9
2002	7184	1734.3	2641	1886.4	34.4	31.1
2003	7748	1870.7	2838	2027.1	34.8	37.6
2004	8544	2062.8	3143	2245.0	36.1	35.7
2005	9628	2324.5	3460	2471.4	37.0	36.3
2006	10905	2632.9	3808	2720.0	34.4	36.8
2007	12662	3057.0	4399	3142.1	36.6	38.2
2008	15207	3671.4	5212	3722.9	36.4	37.0
2009	18963	4578.2	6275	4482.3	32.4	35.8
2010	22244	5370.4	7750	5535.7	31.3	32.5

7-2 主要年份城乡居民人民币储蓄存款

Savings Deposit of Urban and Rural Households in Representative Years

单位：亿元 (100 million yuan)

年 份 Year	年末余额 Balance at Year-end
1978	3.72
1979	4.85
1980	5.48
1981	6.36
1982	7.76
1983	10.02
1984	14.70
1985	16.70
1986	23.10
1987	32.13
1988	32.51
1989	45.78
1990	62.23
1991	78.64
1992	96.09
1993	124.61
1994	174.19
1995	230.63
1996	394.02
1997	358.78
1998	499.68
1999	586.40
2000	675.83
2001	800.86
2002	988.04
2003	1210.56
2004	1432.86
2005	1716.76
2006	1950.53
2007	2002.38
2008	2513.70
2009	3084.20
2010	3641.09

7-3 分区县城乡居民人均收入

Per Capita Income of Urban and Rural Households by Region

单位：元 （yuan）

区 县	District	城镇居民人均可支配收入 Per Capita Disposable Income of Urban Households			农民人均纯收入 Per Capita net Income of Rural Households		
		2008	2009	2010	2008	2009	2010
全 市	**Total**	**15207**	**18963**	**22244**	**5212**	**6275**	**7750**
新城区	Xincheng	15213	19049	22554			
碑林区	Beilin	15508	19424	22998			
莲湖区	Lianhu	15471	19375	22940			
雁塔区	Yanta	14195	17843	21162	5844	7136	8849
灞桥区	Baqiao	14883	18721	22184	6441	7826	9712
未央区	Weiyang	15695	19762	23517	6585	7948	9863
阎良区	Yanliang	15534	19512	22927	5939	7233	8969
临潼区	Lintong	12489	15527	18213	4828	5794	7156
长安区	Chang'an	13108	16490	19557	4926	5965	7389
蓝田县	Lantian	10202	12713	14874	3611	4315	5316
周至县	Zhouzhi	10229	12715	14877	3537	4248	5238
户 县	Huxian	11496	14313	16761	4408	5307	6549
高陵县	Gaoling	11890	14827	17377	4708	5735	7106

7-4 主要年份城镇居民家庭及收支基本情况

Basic Conditions of Urban Households in Representative Years

指　标	Item	2001	2002	2004
一、平均每户家庭人口(人)	**Average Household Size(person)**	**3.03**	**3.01**	**2.99**
二、平均每户就业人口(人)	**Average Number of Employed Persons Per Housedhold (person)**	**1.38**	**1.47**	**1.46**
三、平均每户就业面(%)	**Proportion Percentage of Employment Per Housedhold (%)**	**45.6**	**48.8**	**48.8**
四、平均每一就业者负担人数(人)	**Number of Dependents per Emplyee(person)**	**2.19**	**2.05**	**2.05**
五、年人均家庭总收入(元)	**Per Capita Annual Income(yuan)**	**6743.12**	**7670.67**	**9150.65**
#可支配收入	Disposable Income	6704.86	7183.54	8544.03
（一）工资性收入	Income from Wages and Salaries	4288.09	5075.62	6050.38
（二）经营性收入	Net Business Income	135.27	159.03	251.36
（三）财产性收入	Income from Properties	49.35	60.90	186.95
（四）转移性收入	Income from Transfer	2270.41	2375.12	2661.95
六、年人均家庭总支出(元)	**Annual Actual Expenditure Per Capita (yuan)**	**6678.56**	**7819.74**	**9312.05**
1.消费性支出	Consumption Expenditure	5815.66	6419.21	7427.82
(1)食品	Food	2023.91	2205.38	2685.10
(2)衣着	Clothing	485.93	540.52	611.03
(3)家庭设备用品及服务	Facilities,Articles and Services	628.91	467.36	493.33
(4)医疗保健	Health Care and Medical Services	406.13	535.52	641.77
(5)交通和通信	Transport and Communication Services	453.12	567.96	688.22
(6)教育和文化娱乐服务	Education,Receration and Cultural Services	908.07	1126.68	1252.55
(7)居住	Residence	531.45	783.56	813.14
(8)杂项商品和服务	Miscellaneous Goods and Services	378.14	192.23	242.68
2.购房与建房支出	Purchase and Construction Expenditure of Houses	289.23	415.08	590.33
3.转移性支出	Transfer Expenditure	573.59	567.81	768.01
4.财产性支出	Property Expenditure			
5.社会保障支出	Social Services Expenditure		417.64	525.89
七、人均期末手存现金(元)	**Cash Reserves at Hand at the end of Year Per Capita (yuan)**	**550.39**	**587.82**	**882.65**

7-4 续表1 continued 1

指　　标	Item	2005	2006	2007
一、平均每户家庭人口(人)	**Average Household Size(person)**	**2.93**	**2.90**	**2.91**
二、平均每户就业人口(人)	**Average Number of Employed Persons Per Housedhold (person)**	**1.39**	**1.40**	**1.39**
三、平均每户就业面(%)	**Proportion Percentage of Employment Per Housedhold (%)**	**47.4**	**48.3**	**47.8**
四、平均每一就业者负担人数(人)	**Number of Dependents per Emplyee(person)**	**2.11**	**2.07**	**2.09**
五、年人均家庭总收入(元)	**Per Capita Annual Income(yuan)**	**10387.44**	**11708.43**	**13421.45**
#可支配收入	Disposable Income	9627.89	10905.39	12662.03
（一）工资性收入	Income from Wages and Salaries	6926.28	7622.92	8897.30
（二）经营性收入	Net Business Income	163.66	345.70	375.68
（三）财产性收入	Income from Properties	193.20	317.87	208.83
（四）转移性收入	Income from Transfer	3104.30	3421.93	3939.67
六、年人均家庭总支出(元)	**Annual Actual Expenditure Per Capita (yuan)**	**10030.64**	**12033.94**	**12257.69**
1.消费性支出	Consumption Expenditure	7899.81	8986.87	10097.95
(1)食品	Food	2926.32	3093.12	3696.57
(2)衣着	Clothing	712.98	783.93	950.50
(3)家庭设备用品及服务	Facilities,Articles and Services	373.36	582.84	597.11
(4)医疗保健	Health Care and Medical Services	746.67	695.09	847.80
(5)交通和通信	Transport and Communication Services	763.55	922.99	1145.90
(6)教育和文化娱乐服务	Education,Receration and Cultural Services	1357.50	1666.93	1466.55
(7)居住	Residence	719.00	946.87	1027.90
(8)杂项商品和服务	Miscellaneous Goods and Services	300.42	295.09	365.62
2.购房与建房支出	Purchase and Construction Expenditure of Houses	722.35	1273.52	524.62
3.转移性支出	Transfer Expenditure	745.23	1043.44	933.52
4.财产性支出	Property Expenditure		1.89	9.33
5.社会保障支出	Social Services Expenditure	663.24	728.23	692.27
七、人均期末手存现金(元)	**Cash Reserves at Hand at the end of Year Per Capita (yuan)**	**1121.29**	**15251.31**	**1563.41**

7-4 续表2 continued 2

指　标	Item	2008	2009	2010
一、平均每户家庭人口(人)	**Average Household Size(person)**	**2.82**	**2.84**	**2.81**
二、平均每户就业人口(人)	**Average Number of Employed Persons Per Housedhold (person)**	**1.35**	**1.51**	**1.51**
三、平均每户就业面(%)	**Proportion Percentage of Employment Per Housedhold (%)**	**47.87**	**53.20**	**53.70**
四、平均每一就业者负担人数(人)	**Number of Dependents per Emplyee(person)**	**2.09**	**1.88**	**1.86**
五、年人均家庭总收入(元)	**Per Capita Annual Income(yuan)**	**16365.67**	**20299.12**	**23879.86**
#可支配收入	Disposable Income	15206.89	18963.31	22243.63
（一）工资性收入	Income from Wages and Salaries	10944.90	13562.24	15733.57
（二）经营性收入	Net Business Income	410.70	715.99	979.21
（三）财产性收入	Income from Properties	241.24	357.26	506.47
（四）转移性收入	Income from Transfer	4768.83	5663.63	6660.60
六、年人均家庭总支出(元)	**Annual Actual Expenditure Per Capita (yuan)**	**14380.69**	**17619.36**	**20597.76**
1.消费性支出	Consumption Expenditure	12015.81	14250.78	16543.21
(1)食品	Food	4374.24	4621.40	5176.55
(2)衣着	Clothing	1232.12	1564.44	1837.40
(3)家庭设备用品及服务	Facilities,Articles and Services	761.01	1037.98	1542.77
(4)医疗保健	Health Care and Medical Services	1161.86	1375.57	1250.86
(5)交通和通信	Transport and Communication Services	1246.34	1614.68	1572.40
(6)教育和文化娱乐服务	Education,Receration and Cultural Services	1724.63	2043.52	1995.20
(7)居住	Residence	1058.11	1262.81	2424.51
(8)杂项商品和服务	Miscellaneous Goods and Services	457.49	730.36	743.53
2.购房与建房支出	Purchase and Construction Expenditure of Houses	262.31	606.42	639.82
3.转移性支出	Transfer Expenditure	1042.50	1517.15	1907.40
4.财产性支出	Property Expenditure	23.30	23.09	53.55
5.社会保障支出	Social Services Expenditure	1036.78	1221.92	1453.77
七、人均期末手存现金(元)	**Cash Reserves at Hand at the end of Year Per Capita (yuan)**	**1296.10**	**2553.73**	**4727.95**

注：2007年因统计制度变化，部分数据有调整。

Note:As statistical system was changed in 2007, some data was adjusted.

7-5 城镇居民家庭基本情况表（2010年）

Basic Conditions of Urban Households（2010）

指　　标	Item	合计 Total
一、可支配收入(新算法)(元)	**Disposable Income (New Algorithm)(yuan)**	**22243.63**
二、家庭人口数(人/户)	**Number of Family Members (Person/Household)**	**2.81**
（一）有收入者人数	Family Members Earning Income	2.14
1.就业人口数	Family Members Employed	1.51
（1）国有经济单位职工人数	Employed by State-Owned Enterprises	0.89
（2）城镇集体经济单位职工人数	Employed by Urban Collective Enterprises	0.05
（3）其他各种经济类型单位职工	Employed by Other Units	0.09
（4）城镇个体经营者人员数	Personnel of Urban Individual Business	0.08
（5）城镇个体被雇人员数	Employed by Self-Employers	0.24
（6）离退休再就业人员数	Re-Employed Resigned and Retired Personnel	0.07
（7）其他就业人员数	Others	0.09
2.离退休人数	Resigned and Retired	0.60
3.其他有收入者人数	Others	0.03
（二）无收入者人数	Family Members Without Income	0.67
三、非家庭人口在家用餐人次数	**None-Family Members Eating At Home**	**4.66**
(人次/户)	**(Person-Times/Household)**	
四、家庭人口在外用餐人次数	**Family Members Eating Outside**	**11.46**
(人次/户)	**(Person-Times/Household)**	

7-6　城镇居民家庭年人均收入情况（2010年）

Statistics on Per Capital Annual Income of Urban Residents （2010）

单位：元　　(yuan)

项　目	Item	总平均 Total
一、家庭总收入	**Total Family Income**	**23879.86**
#可支配收入	Disposable Income	22243.63
（一）工薪收入	Income from Wages and Salaries	15733.57
#工资及补贴收入	Wages and Subsidies	15494.65
（二）经营性收入	Net Income from Business	979.21
（三）财产性收入	Income from Properties	506.47
#利息收入	Interest Income	44.77
出租房屋收入	House Rents	203.29
（四）转移性收入	Transfer Income	6660.60
#养老金或离退休金	Pensions	5351.76
提取住房公积金	Withdrawal of Housing Funds	74.54
记账补贴	Book-Keeping Allowances	120.08
二、出售财物收入	**Income from Sales Of Property**	**160.80**
1.出售住房收入	Sales of Housing	141.87
2.出售其他物品收入	Sales of Other Properties	18.93
三、借贷收入	**Income For Savings and Credit**	**5647.57**

7-7 城镇居民家庭年人均支出情况（2010年）

Statistics on Per Capital Annual Living Expenditure of Urban Households（2010）

单位:元 (yuan)

项　目	Item	总平均 Total
一、家庭总支出	**Total Expenditures**	**20597.76**
（一）消费支出	Consumption Expenditures	16543.21
#服务性消费支出	Consumption on Service	4834.04
1.食品	Food	5176.55
2.衣着	Clothing	1837.40
3.家庭设备用品及服务	Household Facilities,Articles and Service	1250.86
4.医疗保健	Health Care and Medical Service	1572.40
5.交通和通信	Transport and Communications	1995.20
6.教育文化娱乐服务	Education,Receration and Cultural Services	2424.51
7.居住	Residence	1542.77
8.杂项商品和服务	Miscellaneous Goods and Services	743.53
（二）购房与建房支出	Expenditures on House Purchasing/Construction	639.82
（三）转移性支出	Transfer Expenditures	1907.40
（四）财产性支出	Property Expenditures	53.55
（五）社会保障支出	Expenditures on Social Security	1453.77
二、借贷支出	**Expenditures on Loans and Debts**	**7316.69**

7-8 城镇居民家庭年人均消费性支出情况（2010年）

Statistics on Per Capita Annual Consumption Expenditure of Urban Households（2010）

单位:元 (yuan)

项　目	Item	总平均 Total
消费支出	**Consumption Expenditures**	**16543.21**
#服务性消费支出	Consumption on services	4834.04
食品	**Food**	**5176.55**
（一）粮油类	Grains and oil	731.05
1.粮食	Grain	472.18
2.淀粉及薯类	Starches and Tubers	44.43
3.干豆类及豆制品	Bean and Bean Products	80.25
4.油脂类	Oil or Fats	134.19
（二）肉禽蛋水产品类	Meat,Poultry,Egg and Aquatic Products	871.50
1.肉类	Meat	509.42
2.禽类	Poultry	123.02
3.蛋类	Egg	93.73
4.水产品类	Aquatic Products	145.33
（三）蔬菜类	Vegetables	494.38
1.鲜菜	Fresh Vegetables	445.00
2.干菜	Dried Vegetables	30.01
3.菜制品	Vegetable Products	19.38
（四）调味品	Flavouring	87.72
（五）糖烟酒饮料类	Sugar,Tobacco,Liquor and Beverage	722.51
1.糖类	Sugar	48.65
2.烟草类	Tobacco	314.84
3.酒类	Liquor	199.09
4.饮料	Beverage	159.93
（六）干鲜瓜果类	Dried and Fresh Melons &Fruits	467.96

7-8 续表1 continued 1

单位:元 (yuan)

项　目	Item	总平均 Total
（七）糕点、奶及奶制品	Cakes, Milk and Processed Products	411.36
1.糕点	Cakes	143.53
2.奶及奶制品	Milk and Its Products	267.83
（八）其他食品	Other Food	119.65
（九）饮食服务	Catering Services	1270.41
1.食品加工服务费	Charge for Food Processing Services	1.10
2.在外饮食	Foods Consumed outside	1269.31
非食品类	**Non-food**	
一、衣着	**Clothing**	**1837.40**
（一）服装	Garments	1249.82
（二）衣着材料	Cloth Materials	14.22
（三）鞋类	Shoes	489.69
（四）其他衣着用品	Others	74.07
（五）衣着加工服务费	Tailoring and Laundering	9.60
二、家庭设备用品及服务	**Household Facilities,Articles and Services**	**1250.86**
（一）耐用消费品	Durable Consumer Goods	476.34
1.家具	Furniture	137.05
2.家庭设备	Household Facilities	339.29
（二）室内装饰品	Interior Decorations	48.16
（三）床上用品	Bed Articles	110.90
（四）家庭日用杂品	Daily Use Household Articles	517.99
（五）家具材料	Furniture Materials	53.06
（六）家庭服务	Household Services	44.41

7-8 续表2 continued 2

单位:元 (yuan)

项　目	Item	总平均 Total
三、医疗保健	**Medicine and Medical Services**	**1572.40**
（一）医疗器具	Medical Appliances and Articles	13.40
（二）保健器具	Health Care Articles	20.79
（三）药品费	Medicines	613.17
（四）滋补保健品	Tonic	163.15
（五）医疗费	Medical Care Services	713.24
（六）其他	Others	48.65
四、交通和通讯	**Transportation ,Post and Telecommumication Services**	**1995.20**
（一）交通	Trasportation	1269.67
1.家庭交通工具	Family Vehicles	645.01
2.车辆用燃料及零配件	Fuel and Accessories	196.60
3.交通工具服务支出	Expenditure on Maintenance of Vehicles	112.58
4.交通费	Transport Servi	315.47
（二）通信	Telecommumication	725.53
1.通信工具	Telecommunication Tools	153.62
2.通信服务	Telecommunication Services	571.90
五、教育文化娱乐服务	**Recreation,Culture and Education Services**	**2424.51**
（一）文化娱乐用品	Recreating Goods	516.67
（二）文化娱乐服务	Recreation and Culture Services	903.78
（三）教育	Education	1004.07

7-8 续表3 continued 3

单位:元 (yuan)

项　目	Item	总平均 Total
六、居住	**Residence**	**1542.77**
（一）住房	Housing	627.37
1.租赁房房租	House Renting	94.17
2.住房装潢支出	Home Decorate Expenditure	354.48
3.维修用建筑材料	Building Material for Repair	121.50
4.其他	Others	57.22
（二）水电燃料及其他	Water,Electricity,Fuel and Others	778.87
1.水	Water	75.69
2.电	Electricity	313.58
3.燃料	Fuel	163.59
4.取暖费		208.17
5.其他	Others	17.84
（三）居住服务费	Cost on Housing Service	136.54
1.物业管理费	Housing Management	79.87
2.维修服务费	Expenditures on House Maintenance	17.37
3.其他	Others	39.29
七、杂项商品和服务	**Miscellaneous Commodities and Services**	**743.53**
（一）杂项商品	Miscellaneous Commodities	540.99
1.金银珠宝饰品	Jewel	134.25
2.手表	Watches	23.05
3.理发美容用具	Hair-care	10.65
4.化妆品	Cosmetics	182.13
5.其他杂品	Others	190.90
（二）服务	Services	202.54
1.旅馆住宿费	Rent for Hotels	19.24
2.理发洗澡费	Hair-cutting and Bathing	52.62
3.美容费	Cosmetic	49.22
4.其他服务	Others	81.46

7-9 主要年份城镇居民家庭年人均购买主要商品数量

商品名称	Name of Commodities	2000	2001	2002
植物油（市斤）	Vegetable Oil(500g)	10.0	9.1	9.9
猪　肉（市斤）	Pork (500g)	13.7	12.0	12.9
牛　肉（市斤）	Beef(500g)	1.7	1.6	1.4
羊　肉（市斤）	Mutton (500g)	0.7	0.5	0.8
鸡　（市斤）	Chicken (500g)	4.4	3.6	3.7
鲜　蛋（市斤）	Eggs (500g)	12.3	10.8	11.4
鱼（市斤）	Fish(500g)	3.7	3.8	4.5
鲜　菜（市斤）	Fresh Vegetables (500g)	107.0	104.5	112.3
白　酒（市斤）	Liquor(500g)	0.9	1.0	1.0
果　酒（市斤）	Fruit Wine (500g)	0.2	0.3	0.3
啤　酒（市斤）	Beer (500g)	3.0	3.6	4.7
糕　点（市斤）	Cake(500g)	4.6	4.2	4.8
鲜乳品（市斤）	Fresh Dairy Products (500g)	12.0	12.8	18.9
奶　粉（市斤）	Milk Powder (500g)	0.6	0.6	0.6
服　装（件）	Clothes(unit)	5.1	5.6	6.6
鞋（双）	Shoes(pair)	2.4	2.5	2.6
水（吨）	Water(ton)	25.7	24.5	28.6
电（度）	Electricity (degree)	307.5	309.7	390.8
煤　炭（公斤）	Coal (kg)	62.0	61.7	51.8
罐装液化石油气（公斤）	Liquified Petroleum Gas (kg)	17.9	14.5	13.3
管道天燃气（立方米）	Piping Gas (cu.m)	26.1	26.4	35.1

Per Capita Annual Purchases of Principal Goods in Urban Household in Representative Years

2003	2004	2005	2006	2007	2008	2009	2010
9.4	9.4	12.3	10.1	10.2	11.5	10.2	9.5
13.6	12.5	15.0	13.6	12.8	19.0	12.6	13.1
1.5	2.0	2.6	2.4	1.9	2.1	2.7	3.2
1.0	1.1	1.1	0.8	0.8	0.7	1.0	1.1
4.0	3.5	5.0	3.8	4.1	6.3	4.2	4.4
11.9	10.4	14.1	11.8	11.1	13.2	10.7	11
5.2	4.3	5.6	4.6	5.3	6.1	5.0	5.1
109.7	113.4	132.5	110.9	113.9	126.5	111.7	111.7
1.0	1.4	1.3	1.3	1.5	0.9	1.1	1.2
0.2	0.2	0.2	0.3	0.2	0.2	0.3	0.4
4.0	4.0	6.5	6.3	4.6	3.8	5.2	5.3
5.3	5.4	6.6	5.9	6.5	11.3	8.1	8.2
21.8	20.4	28.0	25.0	25.3	16.9	19.6	20.2
0.7	0.7	0.6	0.5	0.7	0.9	0.6	0.6
6.5	6.8	6.9	7.1	9.0	6.9	8.7	9.2
2.7	2.8	2.8	2.8	2.8	3.2	4.2	3.7
28.8	26.5	26.1	22.9	22.8	22.2	27.1	28.4
385.3	435.6	449.5	444.9	460.6	439.3	523.1	589.9
45.1	51.4	33.9	46.0	66.5	70.4	34.3	30.5
12.2	12.7	9.8	7.5	6.9	8.1	7.5	5.6
39.0	38.4	58.2	46.4	38.8	33.2	45.2	54.2

7–10　城镇居民家庭居住情况（2010年）

Conditions of Dwellings of Urban Households （2010）

住房情况	Accommodation data	2010
一、家庭居住人口（人/户）	**Number of Persons Per Household(person/household)**	**2.81**
二、现住房总建筑面积（平方米/人）	**Building Area of Living Houses(sq.m/person)**	**28.70**
三、房屋产权(合计)（%）	**Proportion of Property Right of Houses(%)**	
租赁公房	Public Houses Rent	8.13
租赁私房	Private Houses Rent	4.64
原有私房	Originally Self-owned Houses	3.48
房改私房	Present Self-owned Houses	53.23
商品房	Commercial Houses	16.17
其 他	Others	14.34
四、住宅建筑式样(合计)（%）	**Proportion of Patterns of Residential Building(%)**	
单栋住宅	Flats With Complete Facilities (%)	1.08
四居室	4 Rooms	2.82
三居室	3 Rooms	25.70
二居室	2 Rooms	61.86
一居室	1 Rooms	3.40
普通楼房	Ordinary Storeyed Building	3.57
平房及其他	Single-storey Houses and Others	1.58
五、装修状况(合计)（%）	**Proportion of Decoration Condition(%)**	
有装修	Decorated	67.14
未装修	Undecorated	32.86
如果装修过,最近一次装修花费（元/户）	Expenditure of Latest Decoration(yuan/household)	19154.59
六、现有住房按市场价估计值（元/户）	**Estimated Market Price of Present Houses(yuan/household)**	**191053.55**
七、租赁房房租（元/户）	**Expenditure of Rent Houses(yuan/household)**	**391.78**
八、自有房房租折算（元/户）	**Rent of Self-owned Houses(yuan/household)**	**6137.53**
九、购房总金额（元/户）	**Total Expenditure on Purchase of Houses(yuan/household)**	**66653.55**
购房实际支出金额	Expenditure on Purchase Practice of Houses(yuan/household)	64107.59
十、饮水情况(合计)（%）	**Proportion of Water Drinking(%)**	
自来水	Tap Water	90.88
矿泉水	Mineral Water	4.56
纯净水	Pure Water	4.56
井、河水	Well Water and River Water	
其 他	Others	

7-10 续表 continued

住房情况	Accommodation data	2010
十一、用水情况(合计)（%）	**Proportion of Water Use Condition(%)**	
独用自来水	Moloply Use of Tap Water	98.01
公用自来水	Public Tap Water	1.99
井、河水	Well Water and River Water	
其 他	Others	
十二、卫生设备(合计)（%）	**Proportion of Sanitary Facilities(%)**	
无卫生设备	Without Sanitary Facilities	0.08
有厕所浴室	With Bathroom and Lavatory	81.09
有厕所无浴室	With Lavatory but without Bathroom	15.17
公 用	Common-used Sanitary Facilities	3.65
十三、取暖设备(合计)（%）	**Proportion of Heating Facilities(%)**	
无取暖设备	Without Heating Facilities (%)	8.13
空调设备	Air-conditioner	12.52
暖 气	Central Heating	63.27
其 他	Others	16.09
十四、炊用燃料使用情况(合计)（%）	**Proportion of Cooking Fuels(%)**	
管道天煤气	Pipeline Gas	31.18
罐装液化石油气	Liquefied Gas	61.44
煤 炭	Coal	3.90
其他燃料	Others	3.48
十五、除了现住房，还有几处其他住房（套/户）	**Other Living Houses besides Present Living House(unit/household)**	**0.13**
①出租房（套/户）	Houses for Rent(unit/household)	0.09
②偶尔居住房（套/户）	Houses Seldom Living in (unit/household)	0.03
③其它用途房（套/户）	Houses for other Purposes(unit/household)	0.01

7-11 主要年份城镇居民家庭平均每百户年末拥有主要耐用消费品数量

商品名称	Commodity Names	2000	2001	2002
摩托车（辆）	Motorcycle (unit)	5.0	6.0	8.7
家用汽车（辆）	Car (unit)			0.3
洗衣机（台）	Washing Machine (unit)	96.7	97.7	97.3
电冰箱（台）	Refrigerator (unit)	91.0	91.3	95.7
彩色电视机（台）	Color TV Set (unit)	124.0	123.7	128.3
家用电脑（台）	Computer (unit)	11.7	15.7	19.0
组合音响（套）	Hi-Fi System (set)	16.7	19.3	23.0
摄像机（台）	Pick-up Camera (unit)	1.0	0.3	1.0
照相机（架）	Camera (set)	46.3	47.3	48.0
钢琴（架）	Piano (set)	1.3	0.3	1.7
其它中高档乐器（件）	Other High-Grade Musical Instruments (unit)	2.3	3.7	6.7
微波炉（台）	Oven (unit)	18.0	27.7	39.3
空调器（台）	Air Conditioner (unit)	51.3	54.3	75.0
淋浴热水器（台）	Shower(unit)	52.3	52.3	63.7
健身器材（件）	Health Care Equipment (unit)	3.3	3.0	1.7
消毒碗柜（台）	Disinfecting Cupboard(unit)			1.7
洗碗机（台）	Dishwasher (unit)			
固定电话（部）	Telephone (unit)	81.3	86.0	88.0
移动电话（部）	Hand Telephone (unit)	7.6	19.3	48.3

Number of Durable Consumer Goods Owned Every 100 Urban Households in Representative Years

2003	2004	2005	2006	2007	2008	2009	2010
10.2	9.1	8.6	8.9	5.4	7.9	7.6	8.0
0.3	0.3	0.6	0.9	2.0	4.0	9.0	13.3
95.7	98.3	101.1	101.1	98.9	95.3	98.8	100.3
91.8	91.2	90.9	94.4	95.7	89.2	95.0	97.1
127.0	134.0	134.0	136.0	134.5	119.9	126.7	128.7
23.9	31.7	20.3	37.1	45.6	54.0	68.8	76.1
22.9	20.0	34.0	20.6	24.8	19.0	25.2	27.7
1.7	1.1	3.1	4.3	4.8	7.7	9.7	11.1
48.3	44.3	49.7	47.7	50.1	39.9	52.1	57.7
2.0	2.0	1.4	1.7	1.1	2.4	2.4	2.7
5.9	7.1	11.4	12.9	6.0	4.7	5.3	5.3
42.2	47.1	52.0	52.9	56.4	52.7	62.1	66.4
82.4	92.6	99.7	102.9	116.0	104.0	119.7	129.5
70.0	74.9	110.3	71.4	74.1	70.9	79.9	82.3
2.6	2.9	6.9	3.4	4.0	4.3	4.8	5.0
4.7	7.1	29.4	6.0	7.4	5.5	7.8	8.5
				0.6	0.6	0.3	0.8
87.1	85.7	88.0	79.1	75.2	67.4	72.8	71.5
74.4	102.0	119.7	144.3	162.3	162.1	185.3	196.4

7-12 主要年份农民家庭基本情况

项　　目	Item	1998	1999
一、调查户数（户）	**Households Surveyed(household)**	**460**	**460**
二、调查人口（人）	**Residents Sueveyed(person)**		
1.常住人口	Average Number of Permanent Residents	2028	2024
2.整半劳动力	Average Number Able-bodied and Semi-able-bodied Laborers Per Households	1279	1296
3.平均每个劳动力负担人口	Persons Supported by Each Laborers	1.59	1.56
三、平均每人全年收入(元)	**Per Capita Annual Income(yuan)**		
1.总收入	Total Revenue	2597.24	2711.55
2.纯收入	Net Income	2052.07	2202.73
3.现金收入	Cash Income	2087.96	2288.00
4.可支配收入	Disposable Income		
四、按人均纯收入分组（%）	**Grouped by Per Capita Annual Net Income(%)**		
户数占总户数比重	Percentage of Households		
1000元以下	Below 1000 yuan		
1000-2000元	1000-2000 yuan		
2000-3000元	2000-3000 yuan		
3000-4000元	3000-4000 yuan		
4000-5000元	4000-5000 yuan		
5000元以上	Over 5000 yuan		
五、农民家庭房屋情况	**Rural Household Housing Condition**		
1.年末人均住房价值(元)	Average Value of Living House Per Capita of Year-end(yuan)	4813.50	4850.32
2.年末人均住房面积(m^2)	Average Floor Space of Living House Per Capita at Year-end(sq.m)	27.32	26.80
3.年内人均新建房屋面积(m^2)	Percapita Space of Building Newly Built Within the year (sq.m)	1.33	2.03
4.年内人均新建房屋价值(元)	Percapita Value of Building Newly Built Within the Year(yuan)	308.01	304.40
六、生活消费支出总计（元）	**Living Expenditure Built(yuan)**	**1564.81**	**1492.43**
食品消费支出	Food	663.75	584.18
衣着	Clothing	120.76	112.83
居住	Residence	327.56	247.45
家庭设备用品及服务	Household Facilities,Articles and Services	87.43	97.79
医疗保健	Medical and Health Care Services	72.72	94.60
交通通讯	Transport and Communications	51.99	62.45
文化娱乐用品及服务	Culture,Educational and Recreational Articles and Services	196.96	230.09
其它商品及服务	Other Commodities and Services	43.64	63.04

Basic Indicators of Rural Households In Representative Years

2000	2001	2002	2003	2004	2005	2006	2007	2008	2009	2010
500	**770**	**770**	**750**	**710**	**720**	**700**	**700**	**900**	**940**	**940**
2147	3214	3212	3102	2920	3040	2935	2924	3628	3828	3704
1371	2008	2017	1993	1873	1904	1841	1863	2422	2557	2469
1.57	1.60	1.59	1.56	1.56	1.60	1.59	1.57	1.50	1.50	1.50
2929.23	3185.54	3370.82	3571.71	3889.12	4495.44	4968.93	5605.12	6746.04	7961.26	9737.00
2343.76	2490.27	2641.44	2837.83	3142.78	3459.60	3808.38	4398.64	5212.14	6275.22	7750.00
2513.14	2747.00	2965.92	3042.02	3299.16	3940.24	4466.49	4969.58	6249.34	7297.58	9265.00
2225.13	2357.30	2560.58	2729.88	3021.25	3353.43	3562.80	4167.18	4983.23	6008.41	7369.00
		11.69	10.00	5.49	5.14	3.57	2.57	1.89	1.70	1.06
		28.57	26.67	22.40	18.33	14.57	7.57	7.33	3.83	2.45
		27.92	26.00	28.45	25.00	22.43	15.14	13.78	7.98	5.74
		15.45	16.13	19.30	20.70	19.43	21.00	13.00	12.55	6.91
		5.97	10.00	9.01	11.94	13.57	17.72	14.00	12.87	11.28
		10.40	11.20	15.35	18.89	26.43	36.00	50.00	61.07	72.55
5398.21	6286.53	6883.06	7354.40	7780.97	9052.30	10878.22	13145.27	20476.11	24500.32	32059.00
28.31	29.72	32.54	33.90	34.66	36.73	40.05	42.92	54.97	56.73	67.00
1.58	1.81	2.20	0.98	1.13	1.13	1.82	2.03	1.80	2.62	4.00
408.07	475.33	484.18	239.47	309.07	365.97	746.64	787.03	784.68	1349.27	2380.00
1605.36	**1676.42**	**1782.14**	**1802.75**	**2276.65**	**2602.68**	**2708.87**	**3380.80**	**3938.09**	**4771.06**	**5633.00**
587.97	567.62	553.78	677.03	812.47	945.76	996.75	1289.61	1455.22	1708.35	1833.00
106.80	105.53	115.02	113.15	133.97	159.09	174.81	205.85	256.92	305.46	369.00
343.71	409.90	444.92	314.04	478.37	462.21	488.47	768.16	763.44	928.87	1375.00
87.89	74.29	83.64	98.59	104.93	133.11	152.83	191.26	276.61	332.52	368.00
111.25	115.92	136.18	128.47	173.89	213.04	216.67	257.14	316.95	405.62	481.00
67.51	88.83	115.14	143.45	191.89	213.12	236.97	256.27	308.85	469.06	476.00
232.61	241.31	275.38	296.80	340.88	420.45	387.51	352.98	489.68	531.23	631.00
67.62	73.02	58.08	31.22	40.25	55.90	54.86	59.53	70.42	89.95	100.00

7-13 主要年份农村居民家庭人均总收入和纯收入

单位：元

指　标	Item	2005
一、全年总收入	Annul Total Revenue	**4495.44**
1.工资性收入	Wages Income	1292.69
2.家庭经营收入	Household Business Income	2612.18
3.财产性收入	Property Income	330.42
4.转移性收入	Transfer Income	260.15
二、全年纯收入	Annul Net Income	**3459.60**
1.工资性收入	Wages Income	1292.69
2.家庭经营纯收入	Household Business Net Income	1629.54
（1）第一产业收入	'Income from Primary Industry	982.81
（1）第二产业收入	Income from Secondary Industry	143.16
（1）第三产业收入	Income from Tertiary Industry	503.57
3.财产性收入	Property Income	330.42
4.转移性收入	Transfer Income	206.95

Per Capita Annual Total Revenue and Net Income of Rural Households In Representative Years

(yuan)

2006	2007	2008	2009	2010
4968.92	**5605.13**	**6746.04**	**7961.25**	**9736.93**
1498.79	1751.84	2161.42	2587.24	3307.61
2799.09	3063.28	3595.63	4109.86	4734.60
388.00	449.52	553.35	738.95	1025.49
283.04	340.49	435.64	525.20	669.23
3808.38	**4398.64**	**5212.14**	**6275.22**	**7750.35**
1498.79	1751.84	2161.42	2587.24	3307.61
1661.10	1887.68	2092.35	2469.83	2826.61
992.79	1168.79	1232.01	1431.38	1532.79
166.33	177.99	241.48	257.74	290.73
502.00	540.90	618.86	780.71	1003.09
388.00	449.52	553.35	738.95	1025.49
260.46	309.60	405.02	479.20	590.64

7-14 农村居民家庭平均每人总收入和纯收入（2010年）

单位：元

项　　目	Item	西安市 Xi'an	灞桥区 Baqiao	未央区 Weiyang
一、全年总收入	**Annual Total Revenue**	**9737**	**9811**	**10469**
（一）工资性收入	Income from Wages and Salaries	3308	4049	4857
（二）家庭经营收入	Income from Household Operations	4735	3223	1560
（三）财产性收入	Income from Properties	1025	1459	3272
（四）转移性收入	Income from Transfers	669	1080	780
二、全年纯收入	**Annual Net Income**	**7750**	**8849**	**9712**
（一）工资性收入	Wages Income	3308	4049	4857
（二）家庭经营纯收入	Household Business Net Income	2827	2375	1000
1.第一产业收入	Income from Primary Industry	1533	618	172
2.第二产业收入	Income from Secondary Industry	291	225	173
3.第三产业收入	Income from Tertiary Industry	1003	1532	655
（三）财产性收入	Property Income	1025	1459	3272
（四）转移性收入	Transfer Income	591	966	582
三、可支配收入	**Disposable Income**	**7369**	**8376**	**9488**

Per Capita Annual Total Revenue and Net Income of Rural Households（2010）

（yuan)

雁塔区 Yanta	阎良区 Yanliang	临潼区 Lintong	长安区 Chang'an	蓝田县 Lantian	周至县 Zhouzhi	户 县 Huxian	高陵县 Gaoling
10438	**14319**	**9655**	**8662**	**6417**	**8377**	**9361**	**9163**
3838	2280	2959	3421	2197	1924	3383	2916
2102	10568	5513	4027	3809	5944	5481	5054
4205	601	185	404	57	168	26	665
293	870	997	810	355	340	470	529
9863	**8969**	**7156**	**7389**	**5316**	**5238**	**6549**	**7106**
3838	2280	2959	3421	2197	1924	3383	2916
1567	5354	3117	2759	2727	2868	2771	3028
1	3286	2271	732	1754	1954	1929	1988
584	667	576	31	26	275	424	70
982	1402	270	1995	948	639	418	969
4205	601	185	404	57	168	26	665
253	734	895	805	336	277	369	499
9523	**8661**	**6906**	**6961**	**4955**	**4807**	**6176**	**6518**

7-15 农村居民家庭基本情况（2010年）

项　目	Item	西安市 Xi'an	灞桥区 Baqiao	未央区 Weiyang
一、调查户数（户）	**Number of Households Surveyed (household)**	**940**	**100**	**80**
二、常住人口（人）	**Permanent Residents(person)**	**3704**	**400**	**346**
6岁及以下	6 Year-old and Below	202	20	24
7-15岁人口	7-15 Year-old	333	22	26
16-60岁人口	16-60 Year-old	2682	311	248
61岁以上人口	61 Year-old and Above	487	47	48
三、整半劳动力（人）	**Able-bodied and Semi-able-bodied Labourer(person)**	**2469**	**297**	**206**
四、常住人口外出从业人数（人）	**Permanent Residents Employed in Other Places Outside(person)**	**539**	**87**	**42**
五、劳动力文化程度（人）	**Labourer Literacy(person)**	**2469**	**297**	**206**
1.不识字或识字很少	Illiterates or Semi-illiterates	23	1	0
2.小学文化程度	Primary Schools	181	11	5
3. 初中文化程度	Junior Secondary Schools	1431	188	117
4. 高中程度	Senior Secondary Schools	628	70	50
5.中专程度	Specialized Secondary Schools	96	7	18
6. 大专及以上	Universities and Colleges and Above	110	20	16
六、人均耕地经营面积（亩）	**Area of Cultivated Land Managed per Capita(mu)**	**0.97**	**0.44**	**0.05**

Basic Conditions of Rural Households（2010）

雁塔区 Yanta	阎良区 Yanliang	临潼区 Lintong	长安区 Chang'an	蓝田县 Lantian	周至县 Zhouzhi	户 县 Huxian	高陵县 Gaoling
80	**80**	**100**	**120**	**90**	**90**	**100**	**100**
309	**301**	**406**	**485**	**362**	**297**	**423**	**375**
20	6	20	26	20	24	22	20
26	23	41	44	49	33	43	26
227	230	296	335	254	199	298	284
36	42	49	80	39	41	60	45
219	**219**	**253**	**293**	**251**	**202**	**270**	**259**
10	**82**	**76**	**63**	**53**	**5**	**59**	**62**
219	**219**	**253**	**293**	251	202	270	259
	3	4		9	4	2	
3	8	23	15	38	40	20	18
102	119	141	193	165	85	159	162
69	79	74	62	31	58	77	58
21	8	5	17	4	3	1	12
24	2	6	6	4	12	11	9
0.01	0.87	1.34	0.85	2.15	1.62	1.07	1.23

7-16 农村居民家庭平均每人全年总支出（2010年）

单位：元

项目	Item	西安市 Xi'an	灞桥区 Baqiao	未央区 Weiyang
全年总支出	**Annual Total Expenditure**	**8003**	**7645**	**9369**
一、家庭经营费用支出	**Expenditure for Household Business**	**1703**	**578**	**428**
#农业支出	Farming	733	120	12
牧业支出	Animal Husbandry	624	293	312
二、购置生产用固定资产支出	**Purchasing Productive Fixed Assets**	**197**	**279**	
三、建造生产性固定资产雇工支出	**Expenditure on labor hiring on building of productive fixed assets**	**6**		
四、税费支出	**Expenditure for Tax and Fee**	**5**	**4**	
五、生活消费支出	**Expenditure for Living Consumption**	**5633**	**6198**	**8519**
六、财产性支出	**Expenditure for Property**	**16**		**29**
七、转移性支出	**Expenditure for Transfer**	**443**	**587**	**393**

7-17 农村居民家庭平均每人生活消费支出（2010年）

单位：元

项目	Item	西安市 Xi'an	灞桥区 Baqiao	未央区 Weiyang
生活消费支出总计	**Living Expenditure**	**5633**	**6198**	**8519**
一、食品消费支出	**Food**	**1833**	**1908**	**1906**
二、衣着	**Clothing**	**369**	**493**	**538**
三、居住	**Residence**	**1375**	**1349**	**3607**
四、家庭设备用品及服务	**Household Facilities,Articles and Service**	**368**	**390**	**337**
五、医疗保健	**Medical and Health Care Services**	**481**	**534**	**586**
六、交通通讯	**Transport,Post and Telecommunication Services**	**476**	**551**	**732**
七、文化娱乐用品及服务	**Cultural,Educational and Recreational Articles and Services**	**631**	**836**	**719**
八、其它商品及服务	**Other Commodities and Services**	**100**	**137**	**95**
附：人均生活消费现金支出	Per Capita Cash Expenditure for Living Consumption	5452	6131	8499

Per Capita Annual Total Expenditure of Rural Households（2010）

（yuan)

雁塔区 Yanta	阎良区 Yanliang	临潼区 Lintong	长安区 Chang'an	蓝田县 Lantian	周至县 Zhouzhi	户 县 Huxian	高陵县 Gaoling
7874	**10927**	**8830**	**7604**	**5252**	**8702**	**7921**	**6700**
404	**4752**	**2154**	**1149**	**958**	**3029**	**2421**	**1789**
1	4654	612	352	239	808	592	711
	18	1289	62	122	1941	1587	633
	17	**396**	**526**	**59**	**378**	**42**	**119**
1		**6**			**7**	**31**	**12**
17	**1**		**5**	**3**		**15**	**1**
7073	**5713**	**5923**	**5491**	**3851**	**4794**	**4936**	**4159**
	20	**10**	**14**	**85**			**6**
379	**424**	**342**	**419**	**296**	**495**	**474**	**612**

Per Capita Living Expenditure of Rural Households（2010）

（yuan)

雁塔区 Yanta	阎良区 Yanliang	临潼区 Lintong	长安区 Chang'an	蓝田县 Lantian	周至县 Zhouzhi	户 县 Huxian	高陵县 Gaoling
7073	**5713**	**5923**	**5491**	**3851**	**4794**	**4936**	**4159**
2893	**2109**	**1550**	**1688**	**1522**	**1549**	**1690**	**1775**
568	**421**	**303**	**285**	**241**	**349**	**312**	**262**
1046	**684**	**1641**	**1417**	**920**	**905**	**1349**	**664**
492	**761**	**444**	**366**	**208**	**297**	**253**	**219**
502	**363**	**650**	**659**	**307**	**386**	**394**	**335**
448	**582**	**716**	**365**	**233**	**476**	**389**	**311**
1004	**762**	**573**	**602**	**327**	**663**	**487**	**454**
119	**32**	**45**	**110**	**92**	**171**	**64**	**141**
7073	5689	5740	5370	3270	4688	4443	4037

7-18 农村居民家庭人均生产情况（2010年）

单位：公斤

项　　目	Item	西安市 Xi'an	灞桥区 Baqiao	未央区 Weiyang
粮食产量	Output of Grain	640.59	142.77	4.62
#1.小麦	Wheat	324.29	113.03	4.62
2.玉米	Corn	303.44	29.36	
3.大豆	Soybean	1.19		
棉花产量	Output of Cotton	0.34		
油料产量	Output of Oil-bearing Crops	0.54	0.53	
蔬菜产量	Output of Vegetables	239.24	8.00	
水果产量	Output of Fruits	100.21	21.94	

7-19 农村居民家庭人均出售产品情况（2010年）

单位：公斤

项　　目	Item	西安市 Xi'an	灞桥区 Baqiao	未央区 Weiyang
粮食	Grain	330.52	50.90	4.41
棉花	Cotton	0.33		
油料	Oil-bearing Corps	0.06	0.25	
蔬菜	Vegetables	225.48	2.87	
水果	Fruits	173.90	20.69	
肉猪及猪肉	Fattened Hogs & Pork	25.07	5.32	
菜牛及牛肉	Beef Cattle & Beef	0.61		
菜羊及羊肉	Mutton Sheep & Mutton	0.35		
蛋类	Poultry Eggs	6.15		
奶类	Milks	73.88	48.77	121.68

Output of Major Farm Crops Per Capita by Rural Households（2010）

（kg）

雁塔区 Yanta	阎良区 Yanliang	临潼区 Lintong	长安区 Chang'an	蓝田县 Lantian	周至县 Zhouzhi	户　县 Huxian	高陵县 Gaoling
	1484.32	816.89	549.40	785.76	745.37	909.69	1009.43
	849.53	396.31	280.77	324.89	419.88	438.58	463.34
	634.78	345.83	267.55	431.35	322.12	469.90	534.36
			0.06	11.76		0.31	
	3.92			0.21			
				0.44	5.45		
	1766.59	187.79	39.92	12.42	128.22	159.56	388.09
	45.93	18.86	0.05	65.01	955.75	74.26	5.60

Per Capita Product Sold by Rural Households（2010）

（kg）

雁塔区 Yanta	阎良区 Yanliang	临潼区 Lintong	长安区 Chang'an	蓝田县 Lantian	周至县 Zhouzhi	户　县 Huxian	高陵县 Gaoling
	518.09	481.55	454.95	241.77	498.16	390.87	611.81
	3.92			0.15			
				0.30			
	1689.91	176.67	40.33	7.89	149.84	143.64	335.91
	47.24	16.77	0.05	63.00	1905.17	57.99	4.29
	3.32	10.71	6.47	4.16	70.29	109.23	36.48
		0.35		2.00	4.67		
		0.09	0.10	2.46	0.38	0.47	
				0.99	0.05	38.72	16.09
	192.72	267.05		1.06			120.57

7-20 农村居民家庭人均粮食收支情况（2010年）

单位：公斤

项　目	Item	西安市 Xi'an	灞桥区 Baqiao	未央区 Weiyang
一、粮食收入合计	**Total Grain Income**	**745.67**	**255.23**	**148.54**
1.家庭经营生产	Self-produced	640.59	142.77	4.62
2.购入	Purchased	101.92	112.46	142.10
3.借入	Borrowed	0.43		
4.收回借出粮	Grains Taken Back	2.31		
5.其它粮食收入	Other Grain Income	0.42		1.82
二、粮食支出合计	**Total Grain Expenditure**	**552.56**	**200.31**	**158.38**
1.主食用粮	Staple Food	158.62	130.38	96.71
2.其它生活用粮	Other Living Uses			
3.出售	Sold Out	332.27	50.90	4.41
4.种籽	Seeds	8.16	1.51	0.03
5.饲料	Fodder	53.41	17.52	57.23
6.借出	Lent Out			
7.归还借粮	Grains Returned			
8.其它粮食支出	Other Grain Expenditure	0.10		
三、年末粮食结存调查数	**Year-end Grain Deposite Balance**	**374.01**	**49.16**	**4.65**

7-21 农村居民家庭平均每人购买商品（2010年）

单位：元

商品名称	Commodity Names	西安市 Xi'an	灞桥区 Baqiao	未央区 Weiyang
一、食品类	**Food**	**1304.87**	**1493.14**	**1575.91**
二、衣着类	**Clothing**	**367.94**	**491.37**	**536.27**
三、居住类	**Residence**	**979.97**	**1044.05**	**3015.02**
四、家用设备和日用品	**Household Facilities and Articles**	**352.32**	**376.06**	**324.61**
五、交通、通讯类	**Transport,post and Telecommunication**	**281.49**	**257.67**	**538.60**
六、文教类	**Cultural and Edueation**	**153.50**	**129.81**	**173.75**
七、医疗保健类	**Health Care and Medical Services**	**167.52**	**159.01**	**280.85**
八、其他杂项商品	**Other Commodities and Services**	**59.03**	**78.68**	**48.47**

Per Capita Annual Income and Expenditure of Grains of Rural Households（2010）

（kg)

雁塔区 Yanta	阎良区 Yanliang	临潼区 Lintong	长安区 Chang'an	蓝田县 Lantian	周至县 Zhouzhi	户 县 Huxian	高陵县 Gaoling
163.36	**1569.27**	**955.78**	**616.99**	**846.12**	**844.22**	**982.49**	**1135.33**
	1484.32	816.89	549.4	785.76	745.37	909.69	1009.43
163.33	84.95	134.02	51.93	60.36	98.51	72.8	122.2
		1.23					2.93
		1.67	15.66				0.77
0.03		1.97			0.34		
163.33	**615.64**	**766.05**	**578.45**	**625.55**	**661.27**	**739.63**	**929.83**
163.33	79.45	126.14	113.94	328.94	139.23	292.24	98.67
	518.09	481.56	455.01	259.41	498.46	390.87	611.81
	11.56	8.55	8.68	5.09	16.15	13.38	16.38
	6.54	149.8	0.82	31.12	7.43	43.14	202.97
				0.99			
	204.42	**784.95**	**644.53**	**609.02**	**309.36**	**382.27**	**525.88**

Per Capita Purchase of Commodities in Rural Househlods（2010）

（yuan)

雁塔区 Yanta	阎良区 Yanliang	临潼区 Lintong	长安区 Chang'an	蓝田县 Lantian	周至县 Zhouzhi	户 县 Huxian	高陵县 Gaoling
2319.4	**1979.84**	**975.99**	**1082.22**	**709.15**	**1112.03**	**872.92**	**1335.29**
563.84	**420.56**	**302.13**	**283.39**	**240.14**	**348.04**	**311.39**	**260.8**
326.43	**444.63**	**1212.72**	**889.34**	**686.37**	**711.39**	**1022.46**	**315.62**
436.49	**750.14**	**434.68**	**359.8**	**203.65**	**257.7**	**245.05**	**204.55**
104.44	**421.61**	**542.6**	**202.07**	**104.84**	**316.9**	**207.37**	**149.23**
241.51	**360.45**	**112.34**	**144.59**	**94.87**	**149.84**	**133.25**	**59.88**
199.45	**175.75**	**140.61**	**216.57**	**94.74**	**178.17**	**162.08**	**72.72**
70.71	**16.97**	**25.63**	**74.28**	**57.07**	**67.05**	**53.72**	**89.93**

7-22 农村居民家庭人均主要食品消费量（2010年）

单位：公斤

食品名称	Food Names	西安市 Xi'an	灞桥区 Baqiao	未央区 Weiyang
一、粮食	**Grain**	**158.62**	**130.38**	**96.71**
#小麦	Wheet	103.41	62.90	37.26
二、油脂类	**Oil or Fat**	**11.62**	**13.27**	**6.79**
三、蔬菜及菜制品	**Vegetable and Its Products**	**1531.79**	**95.92**	**80.40**
四、瓜果类	**Melons and Fruits**	**11.49**	**11.48**	**12.22**
五、水果类	**Fruits**	**17.97**	**21.43**	**17.32**
六、肉禽及制品	**Meat,Poultry and Their Products**	**13.62**	**14.58**	**12.29**
七、蛋类及蛋制品	**Eggs and Its Products**	**6.43**	**8.54**	**7.05**
八、奶和奶制品	**Milk and Dairy Products**	**8.99**	**7.63**	**11.17**
九、酒	**Liquor**	**4.72**	**4.59**	**3.48**

Per Capita Average Food Consumption of Rural Households（2010）

（kg）

雁塔区 Yanta	阎良区 Yanliang	临潼区 Lintong	长安区 Chang'an	蓝田县 Lantian	周至县 Zhouzhi	户 县 Huxian	高陵县 Gaoling
163.33	**79.45**	**126.13**	**113.94**	**328.94**	**139.23**	**292.24**	**98.67**
28.57	42.97	102.76	79.98	270.37	74.26	221.32	77.8
10.41	**37.26**	**8.38**	**7.84**	**5.95**	**11.08**	**9.3**	**11.61**
17596.92	**75.7**	**58.64**	**60.33**	**55.99**	**37.88**	**48.72**	**112.33**
8.73	**12.46**	**11.48**	**9.42**	**5.53**	**8.65**	**15**	**19**
20.98	**27.53**	**16.57**	**13.18**	**7.49**	**18.38**	**24.33**	**15.05**
15.49	**43.32**	**5.89**	**11.05**	**5.46**	**15.02**	**12.6**	**8.02**
6.08	**9.02**	**5.16**	**4.83**	**7.53**	**5.25**	**6.1**	**5.5**
9.39	**10.02**	**10.64**	**11.99**	**6.3**	**10.83**	**6.37**	**5.67**
3.45	**4.98**	**6.54**	**6.08**	**5.95**	**3.62**	**2.82**	**4.93**

7-23 农村居民家庭每百户耐用消费品年末拥有量（2010年）

品　　名	Item	西安市 Xi'an	灞桥区 Baqiao	未央区 Weiyang
大型家具(件)	Large Furnitures (unit)			
洗衣机(台)	Washing Machine(unit)	99	105	104
电风扇(台)	Electric Fan(unit)			
电冰箱(台)	Refrigerator(unit)	63	81	101
空调机(台)	Air Conditioner(unit)	48	61	86
热水器(台)	Water Heater(unit)	47	62	89
自行车(辆)	Bicycle (unit)	133	122	128
摩托车(辆)	Motorcycle(unit)	43	29	11
生活用汽车(辆)	Automobile(unit)	10	10	16
电话机(部)	Telephone (unit)	59	52	55
移动电话(部)	Mobile Phone(unit)	193	228	203
彩色电视机(台)	Color TV Set(unit)	133	150	136
黑白电视机(台)	Black-white TV Set(unit)	3		
影碟机(台)	Video Disc Player (unit)	58	95	13
照相机(架)	Camera(set)	18	24	31
家用计算机(台)	Computer(unit)	23	23	40

7-24 农村居民家庭人均住房情况（2010年）

指　　标	Item	西安市 Xi'an	灞桥区 Baqiao	未央区 Weiyang
一、年末住房面积 (平方米)	**Floor Space of Houses at the End of Year (sq.m)**	**66.73**	**87.58**	**109.77**
二、住房类型 (平方米)	**Pattern of Houses(sq.m)**			
1. 楼房面积	Floor Space of Storied Building	39.06	79.20	109.78
2. 砖瓦平房面积	Floor Space of Single-storey Building	12.83	8.39	0.17
3. 其他	Others	1.29		
三、年末住房价值(元)	**Value of Houses at the End of Year (yuan)**	**32059.43**	**44693.50**	**49002.77**
四、年内新建（购）房屋面积(平方米)	**Floor Space Of Newly-Built Purchased Houses (sq.m)**	**3.68**	**2.50**	**15.21**
年内新建（购）房屋价值(元)	Value of Houses of Newly-Built Purchased (yuan)	2379.52	1275.00	6358.38

Year-end Possession of Durable Consumer Goods Per 100 Rural Households（2010）

雁塔区 Yanta	阎良区 Yanliang	临潼区 Lintong	长安区 Chang'an	蓝田县 Lantian	周至县 Zhouzhi	户 县 Huxian	高陵县 Gaoling
104	100	109	96	77	100	93	104
100	91	45	45	37	33	30	82
114	55	32	25	11	14	18	83
84	53	29	12	12	39	30	77
98	123	160	125	74	141	197	148
9	70	68	21	67	76	24	57
19	13	6	9	6	4	2	17
90	49	64	75	57	39	73	37
241	163	186	126	152	263	179	208
148	133	136	112	117	142	138	127
		5	13	1	4	1	
99	49	51	58	84	37	33	57
90	14	2	6	3	10	5	10
78	23	13	8	4	6	12	37

Per Capita Housing Conditions of Rural Households（2010）

雁塔区 Yanta	阎良区 Yanliang	临潼区 Lintong	长安区 Chang'an	蓝田县 Lantian	周至县 Zhouzhi	户 县 Huxian	高陵县 Gaoling
138.55	**63.68**	**43.52**	**41.13**	**34.18**	**56.44**	**48.98**	**65.87**
34.26	11.69	13.56	27.16	16.59	41.04	42.05	16.68
0.52		29.74	13.47	12.85	15.02	6.70	35.75
	6.42	0.22	0.49	4.74	0.74	0.22	1.33
89147.25	**36754.15**	**14806.11**	**11616.29**	**16495.86**	**37367.00**	**19476.60**	**22274.67**
6.52		**3.71**	**0.33**	**1.95**	**0.81**	**2.96**	**4.00**
12233.01		1701.35	144.33	919.89	336.70	1252.96	1600.00

主要统计指标解释

一、城镇住户

城镇家庭总收入 指调查户中生活在一起的所有家庭成员在调查期得到的工资性收入、经营净收入、财产性收入、转移性收入的总和，不包括出售财物和借贷收入。

城镇家庭可支配收入 指调查户可用于最终消费支出和其他非义务性支出以及储蓄的总和，即居民家庭可以用来自由支配的收入。它是家庭总收入扣除交纳的个人所得税、个人交纳的社会保障支出以及调查户的记账补贴后的收入。

城镇家庭消费性支出 指调查户用于本家庭日常生活的全部支出，包括食品、衣着、居住、家庭设备用品及服务、医疗保健、交通和通信、娱乐教育文化服务、其他商品和服务八大类等。包括用于赠送的商品或服务。

二、农村住户

整、半劳动力 整劳动力指男子18周岁到50周岁，女子18周岁到45周岁；半劳动力指男子16周岁到17周岁，51周岁到60周岁；女子16周岁到17周岁，46周岁到55周岁，同时具有劳动能力的人。虽然在劳动年龄之内，但已丧失劳动能力的人，不应算为劳动力；超过劳动年龄，但能经常参加劳动，计入半劳动力数内。常住人口中的职工，若这些职工为劳动力，就包括在本户的整半劳动力中。

总收入 指调查期内农村住户和住户成员从各种来源渠道得到的收入总和。按收入的性质划分为工资性收入、家庭经营收入、财产性收入和转移性收入。

纯收入 指农村住户当年从各个来源得到的总收入相应地扣除所发生的费用后的收入总和。计算方法：

纯收入=总收入-税费支出-家庭经营费用支出-生产性固定资产折旧-赠送农村内部亲友支出

纯收入主要用于再生产投入和当年生活消费支出，也可用于储蓄和各种非义务性支出。“农民人均纯收入”是按人口平均的纯收入水平，反映的是一个地区农村居民的平均收入水平。

总支出 指农村住户用于生产、生活和再分配的全部支出。包括家庭经营费用支出、购置生产性固定资产支出、税费支出、生活消费支出、财产性支出和转移性支出。

Explanatory Notes on Main Statistical Indicators

I. Urban Households

Total Income of Urban Households refers to the sum of wage and salary; net business income; income from properties; and income from transfers of members of the households. Income from selling of properties and income from borrowing are not included..

Disposable Income of Urban Households refers to the actual income at the disposal of members of the households which can be used for final consumption, other non-compulsory expenditure and savings. This equals to total income minus income tax, personal contribution to social security and subsidy for keeping diaries in being a sample household. The following formula is used:

Disposable income = total household income - income tax - personal contribution to social security - subsidy for keeping diaries for a sampled household

Consumption Expenditure of Urban Households refers to total expenditure of households for consumption in daily life, including expenditure on the eight categories of food; clothing; housing; household appliances and services; health care and medical services; transport and communications; recreation, education and cultural services; and miscellaneous goods and services.

II. Rural Household

Full/Semi Labour Force Full labour force refers to persons capable of work, aged 18-50 for males and 18-45 for females. Semi labour force refers to persons capable of work, aged 16-17 and 51-60 for males and 16-17 and 46-55 for females. Persons at their working ages but not capable of work are not to be included as labour force. Persons not at working ages but participating regularly in work are included in semi labour force. For staff and workers who are usual residents, are included as full or semi labour force of the household if they are in the labour force.

Total Income refers to the sum of income earned from various sources by the rural households and their members during the reference period, and is classified as income from wages and salaries, income from household operations, income from properties and income from transfers.

Net Income refers to the total income of rural households from all sources minus all corresponding expenses. The formula for calculation is as follows:

Net income = total income - taxes and fees paid - household operation expenses - taxes and fees depreciation of fixed assets for production - gifts to non-rural relatives

Net income is mainly used as input for reinvestment in production and as consumption expenditure of the year, and also used for savings and non-compulsory expenses of various forms. "Per capita net income of farmers" is the level of net income averaged by population, reflecting the average income level of rural households in a given area.

Total Expenditure refers to total expenses of rural households on production, consumption and redistribution, including expenditure on household operations; purchase of productive fixed assets; taxes and fees; expenses on household consumption; expenses on properties; and expenses on transfers.

8 城市公用事业

URBAN PUBLIC UTILITIES

资料整理：陈超毅

Data management:Chen Chaoyi

第八部分 城市公用事业

一、简要说明

本章资料主要包括城市供水、售电、供燃气、供热、公共交通、市政设施、市政设施水平、城市规模及用地状况、园林绿地、环境卫生等情况，由西安市统计局社会科技处根据西安市城建委和西安市供电局等部门提供的数据整理。

二、主要指标

人均公园绿地面积（平方米）	9.11	比上年同口径增长	19.9%
人均城市道路面积（平方米）	15.40	比上年同口径增长	5.3%
用水普及率（%）	98.77	比上年同口径下降	1.2个百分点
燃气普及率（%）	97.02	比上年同口径增加	2.3个百分点
每万人拥有公共交通车辆（标台）	23.77	比上年增长	3.7%

8 URBAN PUBLIC UTILITIES

Ⅰ.Brief IntroductionData in this chapter reflects basic condition of urban public utilities of Xi'an City. Data on public utilities primarily consist of urban water supply, electricity sales, gas sales, urban heating, public transportation, municipal facilities, level of municipal construction, scale of the city, condition of land utilization, parks, greenbelt and environmental sanitation. Data in this chapter is compiled by Social Science & Technology Division of Xi'an Bureau of Statistics according to the data provided by Committee of Urban Construction and Bureau of Electricity Supply of Xi'an, and other department concerned.

Ⅱ.Major Indicators

		Increase over Preceding Year
Per Capita Public Green Areas (sq.m)	9.11	19.9%
Per Captia Area of Roads (sq.m)	15.40	5.3%
Water-Consuming Popularization (%)	98.77	-1.2 percentage points
Gas-Consuming Popularization (%)	97.02	2.3 percentage points
Number of Public Transport Vehicles Per 10 000 Population (unit)	23.77	3.7%

8-1 城市供水

Urban Water Supply

指　标	Item	2000	2007	2008	2009	2010
年末水厂个数（个）	Number of Water Factory at Year-end (unit)	8	9	9	9	18
供水综合生产能力（万立方米/日）	Total Volume of Water Supply (10 000 cu.m/day)	139.9	180.7	180.5	190.0	248.1
#地下水	Groundwater	73.9	53.7	52.4	55.3	106.8
年末供水管道总长度（公里）	Length of Water Supply Pipelines at Year-end (km)	2237	2424	2385	1985	2416
全年供水总量（万立方米）	Total Annual Volume of Water Supply (10 000 cu.m)	30273	32959	36471	38307	41089
#生产运营用水	For Productive Use	6486	5570	6292	6414	6267
居民家庭用水	For Residential Use	10949	13931	17510	18513	20944
用水人口（万人）	Population with Access to Tap Water (10 000 persons)	257.0	331.3	374.1	357.6	410.9

注：1.2009年部门统计制度变化，年末供水管道总长度和用水人口数调整；
2.2010年数据口径变化，为全市口径，与往年不可比。

Note:1.Departmental statistical system was changed in 2009,length of water supply pipelines at year-end and population with access to tap water were adjusted.
2.Statistic caliber of 2010 has changed to city data, not comparable with that of former years.

8-2 城市售电

Urban Consumption of Elecricity

单位:万千瓦时　　(10 000kwh)

分　类	Classify	2000	2007	2008	2009	2010
总　计	**Total**	**732373**	**1482896**	**1605089**	**1724067**	**1993751**
#行业用电合计	Total Electricity Consumed	599855	1215799	1293574	1358483	1499903
1.第一产业	Primary Industry	77579	120134	127054	99083	108720
2.第二产业	Secondary Industry	354245	700026	724852	766029	883259
3.第三产业	Tertiary Industry	168031	395639	441668	493371	507924
一、农、林、牧、渔业	**Farming,Forestry,Animal Husbandry and Fishery**	**77579**	**120134**	**127054**	**99083**	**108720**
二、工业	**Industry**	**345175**	**674990**	**696291**	**724920**	**838317**
1.轻工业用电	Light Industrial	152125	187323	182176	167144	177362
2.重工业用电	Heavy Industrial	193050	487667	514115	557776	660955
三、信息传输、计算机服务和软件业	**Information Transmission,Computer Service and Software Service**		**21938**	**26680**	**29328**	**30760**
四、建筑业	**Construction**	**9070**	**25036**	**28561**	**41108**	**44942**
五、交通运输、仓储和邮政业	**Transport,Storage and Postal Service**	**22904**	**53825**	**56614**	**62031**	**58509**
六、公共事业及管理组织	**Public Administration and Non-profit Institution**		**144859**	**165024**	**177409**	**154074**
七、商业、住宿和餐饮业	**Accommodation and Catering Trade**		**107343**	**111676**	**122203**	**148418**
八、金融、房地产、商务及居民服务业	**Banking,Real Estate Trade and Resident Services**		**67674**	**81674**	**102400**	**116163**
九、城乡居民生活用电	**Residential Electricity Consumption**	**132518**	**267097**	**311515**	**365585**	**493848**
1.乡村	In Rural Areas	31281	38395	63072	99941	142059
2.城市	In Urban Areas	101237	228702	248443	265644	351789

8-3 城市供燃气

Gas Supply in Urban Area

指 标	Item	2000	2007	2008	2009	2010
一、天然气	**Natural Gas**					
管道长度（公里）	Total Length of Gas Pipelines (km)	480	3121	3540	3932	4488.3
供气总量（万立方米）	Total Gas Supply(10 000 cu.m)	11513	72253	84874	95884	109052
#家庭用量	Residential Households	2808	9854	13767	15473	20989.5
用气人口（万人）	Population with Access to Gas (10 000 persons)	79.5	233.6	246.7	285.0	333.1
二、液化石油气	**Liquefied Petroleum Gas**					
供气总量（吨）	Total Gas Supply (ton)	43304	73081	74164		11469.2
#家庭用量	Residential Households	43303	46051	46342		7376
用气人口（万人）	Population with Access to Gas (10 000 persons)	101.6	93.0	81.9		31.2

注：1.2009年部门统计制度变化，无液化石油气相关统计指标；

2.2010年数据为全市口径，2009年以前数据为市区口径。

Note:1.Departmental statistical system was changed in 2009,statistical indicators about liquefied petroeum gas were canceled.

2.Statistic caliber of 2010 has changed to data of city,while it was downtown data before 2009.

8-4 城市供热

Heating in Urban Area

指 标	Item	2000	2007	2008	2009	2010
供热能力	Heating Capacity					
蒸气（吨/小时）	Steam (ton/hour)	766	1680	1063	2118	2235
热水（兆瓦）	Hot Water (1 billion kw)	405	1627	2935	3088	3531
供热总量	Volume Supplied					
蒸气（万吉焦）	Steam (10 000 gigajoules)	126	1510	1192	1541	1674
热水（万吉焦）	Hot Water (10 000 gigajoules)	202	1075	896	1220	2570
管道长度（公里）	Length of Pipelines (km)					
蒸气	Steam	221	296	240	209	180
热水	Hot Water	133	263	179	289	361
供热面积（万平方米）	Heated Area (10 000sq.m)	854	2811	3179	5178	6094
#住宅	Residential Buildings	536	2098	2616	4325	5009

注：2010年数据为全市口径，2009年以前数据为市区口径。

Note:Statistic Aperture of 2010 has changed to data of city,while it was downtown data before 2009.

8–5 城市公共交通

Urban Public Traffic

指　　标	Item	2000	2007	2008	2009	2010
运营车辆(辆)	Operating Vehicles (unit)	2573	5836	6123	7039	7107
1.汽车	Bus	2488	5772	6059	7004	7107
2.电车	Trolley	85	64	64	35	
标准运营车辆（标台）	Standard Vehicles (unit)	2509	5969	6416	7833	8139
运营线路网长度（公里）	Length of Routes (km)	434	734	856	940	
客运总量(万人次)	Number of Passengers carried (10 000 persons)	44570	114859	139924	161782	162400
出租汽车数（辆）	Number of Taxis (unit)	10277	11879	11879	12786	12786

注：2010年“运营线路网长度”统计单位发生变更，故无数据。

Note:Since the unit of "length of operating routes" has changed, statistics are not available in 2010.

8–6 市政设施

Municipal Facilities

指　　标	Item	2000	2007	2008	2009	2010
一、道路长度（公里）	**Length of Roads (km)**	**975**	**1842**	**2115**	**2296**	**2662**
二、道路面积（万平方米）	**Area of Roads (10 000 sq.m)**	**1263**	**4190**	**4722**	**5057**	**5965**
三、人行道面积（万平方米）	**Area of Sidewalks (10 000 sq.m)**	**636**	**1337**	**1470**	**1517**	**1834**
四、桥梁数（座）	**Number of Bridges (unit)**	**79**	**259**	**305**	**314**	**347**
#立交桥	Overpasses	22	48	71	71	71
五、路灯盏数（万盏）	**Number of Street Lights (10000unit)**	**2.75**	**26.00**	**26.64**	**27.14**	**29.18**
六、排水管道长度（公里）	**Length of Drainage Pipelines (km)**	**835**	**1964**	**2562**	**2848**	**3765**
七、污水年排放量（万立方米）	**Annual Discharge Volume of Sewage (10 000 cu.m)**	**23543**	**24719**	**21886**	**31394**	**34706**
八、污水处理厂日处理能力（万立方米/日）	**Daily Disposal Capacity of Sewage (10 000 cu.m/day)**	**29.0**	**43.5**	**77.5**	**80.0**	**106.5**
九、污水处理厂年处理量（万立方米）	**Yearly Disposal Capacity of Sewage Disposal Plant (10 000 cu.m)**	**5441**	**12338**	**13003**	**20386**	**25088**
十、防洪堤长度（公里）	**Length of Flood Control Dikes (km)**	**2**	**39**	**119**	**119**	**168**

注：2010年数据为全市口径，2009年以前数据为市区口径。

Note:Statistic Aperture of 2010 has changed to data of city,while it was downtown data before 2009.

8-7 城市设施水平

Urban Municipal Facilities

指　标	Item	2000	2007	2008	2009	2010
一、人均日生活用水量（升）	**Per Capita Daily Consumption of Tap Water For Residential Use (liter)**	**241.54**	**187.01**	**179.74**	**198.36**	**186.23**
二、用水普及率（%）	**Water-Consuming Popularization (%)**	**98.95**	**100.01**	**111.22**	**100.00**	**98.77**
三、每万人拥有公共交通车辆（标台）	**Number of Public Transport Vehicles Per 10 000 Population (unit)**	**10.17**	**18.02**	**19.07**	**22.92**	**23.77**
四、燃气普及率（%）	**Gas-Consuming Popularization (%)**	**81.51**	**98.60**	**97.66**	**98.15**	**97.02**
五、人均拥有道路面积（平方米）	**Per Captia Area of Roads (sq.m)**	**5.12**	**12.65**	**14.04**	**14.80**	**15.40**
六、排水管道密度（公里/平方公里）	**Density of Drainage Pipelines (km/sq.km)**	**4.47**	**6.26**	**8.04**	**10.06**	**9.53**
七、污水处理率（%）	**Rate of Sewerage Disposal (%)**	**23.11**	**61.56**	**65.12**	**80.97**	**83.96**
八、园林绿化	**Afforestation and Parks and Gardens**					
#人均公园绿地面积（平方米）	Per Capita Public Green Areas (sq.m)	5.12	7.61	7.80	7.90	9.11
建成区绿地率（%）	Rate of Green Areas in Developed Areas (%)	19.67	31.11	31.89	40.42	29.18
九、垃圾无害化处理率（%）	**Rate of No Harm Disposal of Garbage (%)**	**90.89**	**81.23**	**90.35**	**90.30**	**93.87**

注：1.由于用水人口包括不在城市辖区内但已经使用城市供水的人口，故有些年份用水普及率有大于100%；
2.2010年数据为全市口径，2009年以前数据为市区口径。

Note:1.As population with access to tap water contained the people who were out of urban area but had used tap water, water-consuming popularization was over 100% in some year.
2.Statistic Aperture of 2010 has changed to data of city,while it was downtown data before 2009.

8-8 城市规模及用地情况

City Scale and Land Use

指　标	Item	2000	2007	2008	2009	2010
建成区面积（平方公里）	Area of the Constructed Regions (sq.km)	187	268	273	283	395
城市建设用地（平方公里）	Land use for Construction (sq.km)	175	277	370	277	336
#工业用地	Industrial	35	61	64	61	61
仓储用地	Storage	8	12	4	12	12
对外交通用地	External Transportation	10	8	8	8	8
生活居住用地	Residential Area	73	66	122	122	122

注：2010年数据为全市口径，2009年以前数据为市区口径。

Note:Statistic Aperture of 2010 has changed to data of city,while it was downtown data before 2009.

8-9 城市园林绿化

Urban Parks,Gardens and Green Areas in Cities

指　　标	Item	2000	2007	2008	2009	2010
一、公园个数（个）	**Number of Parks (unit)**	**47**	**50**	**54**	**55**	**68**
二、公园面积（公顷）	**Area of Parks (hectare)**	**880**	**1129**	**1233**	**1241**	**1335**
三、园林绿地总面积（公顷）	**Total Area of Parks,Gardens and Green Areas (hectare)**	**4116**	**8670**	**9199**	**9553**	**12140**
#公园绿地面积	Public Green Areas	1263	2520	2625	2700	3526
四、年末绿化覆盖面积（公顷）	**Coverage Space of Green Areas at year-end (hectare)**	**6542**	**11087**	**11616**	**12059**	**15646**
五、建成区绿化覆盖率（%）	**Coverage of Green Areas in Developed Areas (%)**	**33.29**	**39.71**	**40.33**	**40.42**	**37.5**

注：1.2006年统计口径发生变化，原“公共绿地面积”改为“公园绿地面积”；
2.2010年数据为全市口径，2009年以前数据为市区口径。

Note:1.As regulations of 2006 were changed, 'public green area' was replaced by 'park green area'.
2.Statistic Aperture of 2010 has changed to data of city,while it was downtown data before 2009.

8-10 城市环境卫生

Urban Environment Sanitation

指　　标	Item	2000	2007	2008	2009	2010
清扫面积(万平方米)	Area Under Cleaning Program (10 000 sq.m)	1739	3646	4218	5285	6290
清运生活垃圾（万吨）	Volume of Residential Garbage Disposal (10 000 tons)	98	147	152	179	237
清运粪便（万吨）	Volume of Excrement and Urine Disposal (10 000 tons)	5	4	4	3	3
公共厕所（座）	Number of Public Lavatories (unit)	430	962	1131	1131	1257
市容环卫专用车辆（台）	Special Vehicles of Environmental Sanitation (unit)	330	768	716	939	1042

注：2010年数据为全市口径，2009年以前数据为市区口径。

Note:Statistic Aperture of 2010 has changed to data of city,while it was downtown data before 2009.

8-11 市区及县供水（2010年）

Urban Water Supply（2010）

指　　标	Item	西安 Xi'an	市区 City	蓝田县 Lantian	周至县 ZhouZhi	户县 Huxian	高陵县 GaoLing
年末水厂个数（个）	Number of Water Factory at Year-end (unit)	18	11	2	2	2	1
供水综合生产能力	Total Volume of Water Supply						
（万立方米/日）	(10 000 cu.m/day)	188.9	180.8	0.6	1.0	2.5	4.0
#地下水	Groundwater	49.8	46.8				3.0
年末供水管道总长度	Length of Water Supply Pipelines	2258.8	1903.4	49.5	38.0	75.1	192.8
（公里）	at Year-end (km)						
全年供水总量（万立方米）	Total Annual Volume of Water Supply	40205.3	38535.7	192.0	244.7	522.0	710.9
	(10 000 cu.m)						
#生产运营用水	For Productive Use	6000.3	5564.9	45.0	1.5	86.0	302.9
居民家庭用水	For Residential Use	20599.5	19739.1	106.0	205.0	278.0	271.4
用水人口（万人）	Population with Access to Tap Water	401.3	365.4	6.0	7.7	11.0	11.2
	(10 000 persons)						

注：2009年部门统计制度变化，年末供水管道总长度和用水人口数调整。

Note:Departmental statistical system was changed in 2009,length of water supply pipelines at year-end and population with access to tap water were adjusted.

8-12 市区及县供燃气（2010年）

Gas Supply in Urban Area（2010）

指　　标	Item	西安 Xi'an	市区 City	蓝田县 Lantian	周至县 ZhouZhi	户县 Huxian	高陵县 GaoLing
一、天然气	**Natural Gas**						
管道长度（公里）	Total Length of Gas Pipelines (km)	4488.3	4337.9	10.1	20.3	41.3	78.6
供气总量（万立方米）	Total Gas Supply(10 000 cu.m)	109052.1	105807.2	69.0	2.4	419.5	2754.0
# 家庭用量	Residential Households	20989.5	19242.6	69.0	2.3	175.6	1500.0
用气人口（万人）	Population with Access to Gas (10 000 persons)	344.5	333.1	0.4	0.3	4.5	6.1
二、液化石油气	**Liquefied Petroleum Gas**						
供气总量（吨）	Total Gas Supply (ton)	11469.2	8110.0	810.2	580.0	1600.0	369.0
# 家庭用量	Residential Households	7376.0	4430.0	521.0	550.0	1600.0	275.0
用气人口（万人）	Population with Access to Gas (10 000 persons)	31.2	7.0	5.9	5.0	6.9	6.4

8-13 市区及县供热（2010年）

Heating in Urban Area（2010）

指　　标	Item	西安 Xi'an	市区 City	蓝田县 Lantian	周至县 ZhouZhi	户县 Huxian	高陵县 GaoLing
供热能力	Heating Capacity						
蒸气（吨/小时）	Steam (ton/hour)	2235	2235				
热水（兆瓦）	Hot Water (1 billion kw)	3531	3251				280
供热总量	Volume Supplied						
蒸气（万吉焦）	Steam (10 000 gigajoules)	1674	1674				
热水（万吉焦）	Hot Water (10 000 gigajoules)	2570	1650				920
管道长度（公里）	Length of Pipelines (km)						
蒸气	Steam	180	180				
热水	Hot Water	361	343				18
供热面积（万平方米）	Heated Area (10 000sq.m)	6094	5994				100
#住宅	Residential Buildings	5009	4909				100

8-14 市区及县市政设施（2010年）

Municipal Facilities in Urban Area（2010）

指　　标	Item	西安 Xi'an	市区 City	蓝田县 Lantian	周至县 ZhouZhi	户县 Huxian	高陵县 GaoLing
一、道路长度（公里）	**Length of Roads （km)**	**2662.4**	**2428.0**	**64.6**	**33.0**	**56.3**	**80.5**
二、道路面积（万平方米）	**Area of Roads (10 000 sq.m)**	**5965.2**	**5342.0**	**106.5**	**70.8**	**186.7**	**259.2**
三、人行道面积（万平方米）	**Area of Sidewalks (10 000 sq.m)**	**1834.1**	**1602.0**	**48.0**	**23.0**	**73.9**	**87.2**
四、桥梁数（座）	**Number of Bridges (unit)**	**347**	**314**	**10**	**2**		**21**
#立交桥	Crossroads	71	71				
五、路灯盏数（万盏）	**Number of Street Lights (10000unit)**	**291754**	**277968**	**1550**	**2825**	**3616**	**5795**
六、排水管道长度（公里）	**Length of Drainage Pipelines (km)**	**3765**	**3388**	**66**	**38**	**91**	**182**
七、污水年排放量（万立方米）	**Annual Discharge Volume of Sewage (10 000 cu.m)**	**34706**	**33232**	**318**	**208**	**398**	**550**
八、污水处理厂日处理能力（万立方米/日）	**Daily Disposal Capacity of Sewage (10 000 cu.m/day)**	**106.5**	**100.0**	**2.5**		**3.0**	**1.0**
九、污水处理厂年处理量（万立方米）	**Yearly Disposal Capacity of Sewage Disposal Plant (10 000 cu.m)**	**25088**	**24667**	**12**		**300**	**109**
十、防洪堤长度（公里）	**Length of Flood Control Dikes (km)**	**168**	**119**	**20**	**22**		**7**

主要统计指标解释

标准运营车数 指不同类型的运营车辆按统一的标准当量折合成的运营车数。计算公式：

标准运营车数=∑（每类型车辆数×相应换算系数）

每万人拥有公共交通车辆 指按城市人口计算的每万人平均拥有的公共交通车辆标台数。计算公式：

每万人拥有公共交通车辆（标台）=全市公共交通运营车标台数/城市人口数（万人）

运营线路总长度 指全部运营线路长度之和。计算公式：

运营线路长度=∑各条运营线路长度

=∑[1/2（上行起点至终点里程+下行起点至终点里程+上下行终点掉头里程）]

单向行驶的环行线路长度等于起点至终点里程与终点下客站至起点里程之和的一半。不包括折返、试车、联络线等非运营线路。

运营线路网长度 指全部固定运营线路所经过的道路长度。计算公式：

运营线路网长度=运营线路总长度-∑重复线路长度

道路长度 指道路长度和道路相通的桥梁、隧道的长度，按车行道中心线计算。

道路面积 指道路面积和与道路相通的广场、桥梁、隧道的面积（统计时，将人行道面积单独统计）。

人行道面积按道路两侧面积相加计算。包括步行街和广场，含人车混行的道路。

人均拥有道路面积 指平均每个城市人口拥有的道路面积。计算公式：

人均拥有道路面积=道路面积/城市人口数

排水管道长度 指所有排水总管、干管、支管、检查井及连续井进出口等长度之和。计算时应按单管计算，即在同一条街道上如有两条或两条以上并排的排水管道时，应按每条排水管道的长度相加计算。

路灯盏数 指城市道路照明用灯盏数，一根电杆上有几盏即计算几盏。也可分别统计各类路灯盏数。

绿地面积 指报告期末用作园林和绿化的各种绿地面积。包括公园绿地、防护绿地、附属绿地和其他绿地的面积。

公园绿地面积 指城市中向公众开放的、以游憩为主要功能，有一定的游憩设施和服务设施，同时兼有健全生态、美化景观、防灾减灾等综合作用的绿化用地。

公园面积 指报告期末综合公园、专类公园和带状公园的全部占地总面积。即公园内的园路及铺装场地，管理建筑用地，游览、休憩、服务公用建筑用地，绿化用地及水域面积的总和。

生活垃圾无害化处理率 指报告期生活垃圾无害化处理量与生活垃圾产生量的比率。计算公式：

生活垃圾无害化处理率=生活垃圾无害化处理量/生活垃圾产生量×100%

在统计时，由于生活垃圾产生量不易取得，可用清运量代替。

Explanatory Notes on Main Statistical Indicators

Number of standard vehicles under operating refers to equivalent of number of vehicles under operating which was converted by number of different kinds of vehicles with related standard equivalent.

The formula is as following:

Number of standard vehicles = Σ (number of each kind of vehicle × related reduction coefficient)

Number of public transportation vehicles per 10,000 persons refers to number of public transportation vehicles per 10,000 persons based on urban population.

The formula is as following:

Number of public transportation vehicles per 10,000 persons = total number of public transportation vehicles / urban population (10,000 person)

Total length of lines under operating refers to sum of every line under operating.The formula is as following:

Total length of lines under operating = Σ length of every line under operating

Σ [1/2 (mileage from start to end in upline + mileage from start to end in downline + mileage of turning around between ends of upline and downline)

Length of unidirection loop line equals to half of sum of mileage from start to end and mileage from end-station to start, which excludes line without operating such as line of turning back, test-drive, communication and so on..

Length of line network under operating refers to length of paved roads which were passed by total fixed line under operating.

The formula is as following:

Length of line network under operating = total length of line under operating - Σ length of lines repeated

Length of paved road refers to length of paved surface including bridge and tunnel connecting with the paved road, it was measured by central line in carriageway.

Area of paved road refers to area of paved road and square or bridge or tunnel connecting to paved road. (area of pavement was accounted separately)

Area of sidewalks equals area of both side of road which includes road for man and car, including pedestrian street and square.

Per capita area of paved road refers to Per capita area of paved road of urban residents

The formula is as following:

Per capita area of paved road = area of paved road / urban population

Length of sewer pipelines refers to sum of length of header sewer pipelines, main sewer pipeline, branch sewer pipeline, inspection pit , entrance and exit of continuous well, etc. it was calculated on single pipeline, which was equal to sum of length of every pipe while two and more pipelines in same street

Number of street lights refers to number of lights for road lighting, it was calculated on the number of lights on electric poles or accounted by each kind of street lights respectively.

Greening land area refers to the various greenbelt area used as gardens and afforestation at the end of reference time, including green parks, green space protection, subsidiary green space and other area.

Park green area refers to the green space open to the public and take strolling and having a rest as main function , which have a certain recreational facilities and services facilities, have the comprehensive functions of perfect ecological, beautify landscapes and disaster prevention and reduction.

Park area refers to total park floor area of synthetical parks, ribbon categories parks and tape parks at the end of reference time ,including alley and paved ground in park, administrative building plot, public building plot used for visit, rest and service, sum of green space and water area.

Innocent treatment rate of household garbage refers to ratio of volume of household garbage under innocent treatment in reference time to volume of household garbage produced.The formula is as following:

Innocent treatment rate of household garbage = volume of household garbage under innocent treatment / volume of household garbage produced ×100%

In practical statistic, volume of household garbage produced is replaced by volume of household garbage transported, as it is difficult to estimate.

9 环境保护

ENVIRONMENT PROTECTION

资料整理：陈超毅　刘　婷
Data management:Chen Chaoyi Liu Ting

第九部分　环境保护

一、简要说明

本章资料反映环境保护、工业污染排放及处理利用情况、危险废物集中处置情况、生活及其他污染情况和工业污染治理项目建设情况，由西安市统计局社会科技处根据西安市环保局提供的数据资料整理。

二、主要指标

工业废水排放达标率（%）	95.88	比上年提高 2.4个百分点
工业用水重复利用率（%）	79.50	比上年提高 0.3个百分点
工业固体废物综合利用率（%）	98.05	比上年提高 0.2个百分点
污水处理厂处理能力（万吨/日）	111.10	比上年增长 38.9%
污水处理量（万吨）	23236.00	比上年增长 28.5%

9　ENVIRONMENT PROTECTION

Ⅰ.Brief Introduction

This chapter contain information that reflect environment protection, discharge and treatment of industrial pollutant, centralized treatment of dangerous wastes, domestic pollution and other pollution, construction of projects of industrial pollution treatment. Data in this chapter is compiled by Social & Science and Technology Division of the Xi'an Bureau of Statistics according to the reported data from Environment Protection Administration department of the municipal government.

Ⅱ.Major Indicators

		Increase over Preceding Year
Percentage of Industrial Waste Water up to the Standards for Discharge (%)	95.88	2.4 percentage points
Percentage of Industrial Water Recycled (%)	79.50	0.3 percentage points
Percentage of Industrial Solid Waste Utilized (%)	98.05	0.2 percentage points
Daily Disposal Capacity of Sewage(10 000 tons/day)	111.10	38.9%
Volume of Sewgae Disposal(10 000 tons)	23236.00	28.5%

9-1 城市环境保护（2010年）

Urban Environmental Protection（2010）

指　　标	Item	2010
一、饮用水环境	**Potable Water**	
1.水资源总量(万立方米)	Total Amount of Water Resources(10 000cu.m)	34735.0
#地表水资源量	Surface Water Resources	29001.2
地下水资源量	Groundwater Resources	5733.8
2.全市饮用水水质达标率(%)	Percentage of Urban Potable Water Quality up to the Standards(%)	100.0
二、大气环境	**Air**	
1.可吸入颗粒物浓度年平均值(毫克/立方米)	Annual Average Concentration of Particulate Matters(mg/cu.m)	0.13
二氧化硫浓度年平均值	Annual Average Concentration of Sulphur Dioxide	0.04
二氧化氮浓度年平均值	Annual Average Concentration of Nitrogen Dioxide	0.05
2.全年空气质量达到及好于二级天数(天)	Days of Air Quality up to the Standards(day)	304
空气质量达到及好于二级天数占全年比重(%)	Percentage of Air Quality up to the Standards(%)	83.3
三、声环境	**Voice**	
1.功能区噪声平均值(Db(A))	Average Noise Value of Functional Districts(Db(A))	
0类区	Class 0	53.3
1类区	Class 1	55.7
2类区	Class 2	59.1
3类区	Class 3	68.2
4类区	Class 4	74.1
2.道路交通噪声平均值(Db(A))	Average Noise Value of Road Traffic(Db(A))	68.0
3.区域噪声平均值(Db(A))	Average Noise Value of Region(Db(A))	55.2

9-2 主要年份工业"三废"排放及处理利用情况

Discharge and Treatrment of Waste Gas, Water & Solid Wastes in Repersentative Years

指标	Item	2000	2006
一、工业废水排放量（万吨）	**Volume of Waste Water Discharge (10 000 tons)**	**9145**	**16389**
工业废水排放达标量	Industrial Waste Wster Meeting Discharge Standards	6130	15267
工业废水排放达标率(%)	Percentage of Industrial Waste Wster Meeting Discharge Standards(%)	67.03	93.15
二、工业废气排放量 (万标立方米）	**Total Volume of Industrial Waste Gas Emission (10 000 cu.m)**	**2759719**	**6425076**
#燃料燃烧过程中排放量	Volume of Waste Gas in the Process of Fuel Burning	1942884	3885611
生产工艺过程中排放量	Volume of Waste Gas from the Process of Production	816835	2539465
废气治理设施数（套）	Number of Facilities for Treatment of Waste Gas(set)		466
三、工业固体废物产生量（万吨）	**Volume of Industrial Solid Wastes Produced (10 000 tons)**	**107**	**161**
工业固体废物处置量	Volume of Industrial Solid Wastes Treated	20	5
工业固体废物综合利用量	Volume of Industrial Solid Waste Utilized in a Comprehensive Way	63	143
工业固体废物综合利用率（%）	Percentage of Volume of Industrial Solid Waste Utilized in a Comprehensive Way(%)	58.88	89.07
四、工业锅炉（台/蒸吨）	**Industrial Boilers (unit/ton)**	**691/6258**	**447/5679**
#烟尘排放达标的	Volume of Soot Discharged Up to the Standards	662/6107	441/5655

9–2 续表 continued

指　标	Item	2007	2008	2009	2010
一、工业废水排放量（万吨）	**Volume of Waste Water Discharge (10 000 tons)**	**19069**	**18304**	**13168**	**13840**
工业废水排放达标量	Industrial Waste Wster Meeting Discharge Standards	18352	17862	12106	13269
工业废水排放达标率(%)	Percentage of Industrial Waste Wster Meeting Discharge Standards(%)	96	98	94	96
二、工业废气排放量（万标立方米）	**Total Volume of Industrial Waste Gas Emission (10 000 cu.m)**	**11494114**	**15191799**	**7372387**	**7915628**
#燃料燃烧过程中排放量	Volume of Waste Gas in the Process of Fuel Burning	3731610	8980681	4275975	4368727
生产工艺过程中排放量	Volume of Waste Gas from the Process of Production	7762504	6211118	3096412	3546901
废气治理设施数（套）	Number of Facilities for Treatment of Waste Gas(set)	846	920	852	816
三、工业固体废物产生量（万吨）	**Volume of Industrial Solid Wastes Produced (10 000 tons)**	**193**	**220**	**246**	**267**
工业固体废物处置量	Volume of Industrial Solid Wastes Treated	6	5	5	4
工业固体废物综合利用量	Volume of Industrial Solid Waste Utilized in a Comprehensive Way	171	215	241	262
工业固体废物综合利用率（%）	Percentage of Volume of Industrial Solid Waste Utilized in a Comprehensive Way(%)	88.48	97.78	97.83	98.05
四、工业锅炉（台/蒸吨）	**Industrial Boilers (unit/ton)**	**560/10198**	**617/11438**	**569/11987**	**526/11595**
#烟尘排放达标的	Volume of Soot Discharged Up to the Standards	538/9662	607/11274	561/11665	525/11593

9-3 工业污染排放及处理利用情况（2010年）

Discharge and Treatment of Industrial Pollution（2010）

指　　标	Item	2010
一、被调查企业基本情况	**Basic condition of Enterprises investigated**	
1.企业数（个）	Number of Enterprises (unit)	326
2.工业总产值（万元）	Gross Industry Output Value (10 000 yuan)	16321451.7
3.企业专职环保人员（人）	Number of professional staff of Environmental Protection(person)	1383
4."三废"综合利用产品产值（万元）	Output Value of Produsts Made from Waste Gas, Waste Water and Solid Wastes (10 000 yuan)	11068.9
5.工业锅炉数（台/蒸吨）	Number of Industrial Boilers (unit/ton)	526/11595
#烟尘排放达标的	Soot Emission up to the Discharge Standards	525/11593
二氧化硫排放达标的	Sulphur Dioxide Emission up to the Discharge Standards	509/11219
6.工业炉窑数（座）	Number of Industrial Grates (item)	149
#烟尘排放达标的	Soot Emission up to the Discharge Standards	144
二氧化硫排放达标的	Sulphur Dioxide Emission up to the Discharge Standards	142
二、工业废水	**Industrial Waste Water**	
1.工业用水总量（万吨）	Total Volume of Industrial Water (10 000 tons)	93679.83
#新鲜水量	Volume of Fresh Water	19202.54
重复用水量	Volume of Water Recycled	74477.52
2.工业用水重复利用率（%）	Percentage of Industrial Water Recycled (%)	79.5
3.废水治理设施数（套）	Number of Facilities for Treatment of Waste Water (set)	346
4.废水治理设施处理能力（万吨/日）	Disposal Capacity of Facilities for Treatment of Waste Water (10 000 tons/day)	44.23
5.废水治理设施运行费用（万元）	Operating Expense of Facilities for Treatment of Waste Water (10 000 yuan)	12907.1
6.工业废水排放量（万吨）	Volume of Industrial Waste Water Discharged (10 000 tons)	13839.52
7.工业废水排放达标量（万吨）	Volume of Industrial Waste Water up to the Standards for Discharge (10 000 tons)	13269.22
8.工业废水排放达标率（%）	Percentage of Industrial Waste Water up to the Standards for Discharge (%)	95.88
三、工业废气	**Industrial Waste Gas**	
1.煤炭消费总量（万吨）	Total Coal Consumption (10 000 tons)	789.18
2.燃料油消费量（万吨）	Fuel Oil Consumption (10 000 tons)	1.71
3.洁净燃气消费量（万标立方米）	Natural Gas Consumption (10 000 cu.m.)	7395
4.工业废气排放总量（万标立方米）	Total Volume of Industrial Waste Gas Emission (10 000 cu.m.)	7915628
5.废气治理设施数（套）	Number of Facilities for Treatment of Waste Gas (set)	816
6.废气治理设施处理能力（万标立方米/时）	Disposal Capacity of Facilities for Treatment of Waste Gas (10 000 cu.m./h)	2743.16
7.废气治理设施设备运行费用（万元）	Operating Expense of Facilities for Treatment of Waste gas(10 000 yuan)	17320.7
8.二氧化硫去除量（吨）	Volume of Sulphur Dioxide Removed (ton)	63563.02
9.二氧化硫排放量（吨）	Volume of Sulphur Dioxide Emission (ton)	81505.83
#燃料燃烧过程中排放量	Volume of Emission from the Burning Process of Fuels	80629.77
#排放达标量	Volume of Emission up to the Standards for Discharge	73767.01
生产工艺过程中排放量	Volume of Emission from the Process of Production	848.68
#排放达标量	Volume of Emission up to the Standards for Discharge	848.68
10.烟尘去除量（吨）	Volume of Soot Removed (ton)	1299579.70
11.烟尘排放量（吨）	Volume of Soot Emission (ton)	16674.78
#排放达标量	Volume of Emission up to the Standards for Discharge	16461.11
12.工业粉尘去除量（吨）	Volume of Industrial Dust Removed (ton)	137872.93
13.工业粉尘排放量（吨）	Volume of Industrial Dust Emission (ton)	3337.16
#排放达标量	Volume of Emission up to the Standards for Discharge	3062.61
四、工业固体废物	**Industrial Solid Waste**	
1.工业固体废物产生量（万吨）	Volume of Industrial Solid Waste Produced (10 000tons)	267.29
2.工业固体废物综合利用量（万吨）	Volume of Industrial Solid Waste Utilized (10 000tons)	262.09
3.工业固体废物综合利用率（%）	Percentage of Industrial Solid Waste Utilized (%)	98.05
4.工业固体废物贮存量（万吨）	Volume of Industrial Solid Waste Accumulated (10 000tons)	1.51
5.工业固体废物处置量（万吨）	Volume of Industrial Solid Waste Treated (10 000tons)	3.56
6.工业固体废物排放量（万吨）	Volume of Industrial Solid Waste Discharged (10 000tons)	0.20

9-4 城市污水处理情况（2010年）
Urban Sewage Disposal（2010）

指　　标	Item	2010
一、污水处理厂数（座）	**Number of Sewage Treatment Works(unit)**	**12**
污水处理厂处理能力（万吨/日）	Daily Disposal Capacity of Sewage(10 000 tons/day)	111
二、污水年处理量（万吨）	**Volume of Sewgae Disposal(10 000 tons)**	**23236.0**
#处理生活污水量	Volume of Domestic Sewgae Disposal	21597.9
处理工业废水量	Volume of Industrial Sewage Disposal	1638.1
三、污水再生利用量（万吨）	**Volume of Sewage Recycled(10 000 tons)**	**407**
四、化学需氧量去除量（吨）	**Volume of COD Removed (ton)**	**112494**
五、氨氮去除量（吨）	**Volume of Ammonia and Nitrogen Removed(ton)**	**8496**
六、总磷去除量（吨）	**Volume of Total Phosphorus Removed(ton)**	**1027.9**
七、污泥产生量（吨）	**Volume of Sludge Produced(ton)**	**140646**
八、污泥处置量（吨）	**Volume of Sludge Disposal(ton)**	**138123**
九、污泥利用量（吨）	**Volume of Sludge Utilized(ton)**	**2523**
十、污泥排放量（吨）	**Volume of Sludge Discharged(ton)**	
十一、本年运行费用（万元）	**Operating Expense(10 000 yuan)**	**6433.9**

注：污水处理厂数及污水处理能力为市建委部门统计数据。

Note:The number of sewage disposal plant and the disposal capacity of sewage were statistics from Municipal Construction Commission.

9-5 危险废物集中处置情况（2010年）

Condition of Collected Dangerous Wastes Treated（2010）

指　　标	Item	2010
一、危险废物集中处置厂数（座）	**Number of Colleted Dangerous Wastes Treated Plants(item)**	**3**
#当年新增	Newly Increased in Current year	
二、危险废物实际处置能力（吨/日）	**Actual Disposal Capacity of Dangerous Wastes (ton/day)**	**50.0**
#当年新增	Newly Increased in Current year	
三、危险废物处置量（吨）	**Volume of Dangerous Wastes Treated (ton)**	**11876.0**
四、危险废物综合利用量（吨）	**Volume of Dangerous Wastes Utilized in a Comprehensive Way (ton)**	**530.0**
五、焚烧残渣流向（吨）	**Flow Direction of Residuum after Burning (ton)**	
（1）焚烧残渣量	Volume of Residuum after Burning	586.0
（2）焚烧残渣利用量	Volume of Residuum after Burning Utilized	
（3）焚烧残渣填埋量	Volume of Residuum after Burning Landfilled	
六、当年运行费用（万元）	**Operating Expenses in Current year(10 000 yuan)**	**3048.0**

9-6 生活及其他污染情况（2010年）

Domestic Pollution and Other conditions（2010）

指　　标	Item	2010
一、基本情况	**Basic Condition**	
1.煤炭消费总量（万吨）	Total Coal Consumption (10 000 tons)	849.02
#工业煤炭消费量	Industrial Coal Consumption	789.18
生活及其他煤炭消费量	Domestic and Other Coal Consumption	59.84
2.生活及其他煤炭含硫量（%）	Percentage of Sulphur Content in Domestic and Other Coal (%)	0.77
3.生活及其他煤炭灰份（%）	Percentage of Ash Content in Domestic and Other Coal (%)	14.06
二、污染排放情况	**Discharge of Pollutant**	
1.城镇生活污水排放量（万吨）	Volume of Urban Domestic Sewage Discharged(10 000 tons)	29782.7
2.城镇生活污水中COD去除量（吨）	Volume of COD in Urban Domestic Sewage Removed (ton)	69403.7
3.城镇生活污水中氨氮产生量（吨）	Volume of Ammonia and Nitrogen in Urban Domestic Sewage Produced (ton)	13629.7
4.城镇生活污水中氨氮排放量（吨）	Volume of Ammonia and Nitrogen in Urban Domestic Sewage Discharged (ton)	8169.3
5.污水处理厂去除生活污水中氨氮量（吨）	Sewage Disposal Plant Removing the Amount of Ammonia Nitrogen in Wastewater.(ton)	5460.4
6.生活及其他二氧化硫排放量（吨）	Volume of Domestic and Other Sulphur Dioxide Emission (ton)	3494.0
7.生活及其他烟尘排放量（吨）	Volume of Domestic and Other Soot Emission (ton)	8591.0

9-7 工业污染治理项目建设情况（2010年）

Condition of Anti-Industrial-Pollution Projects（2010）

指　　标	Item	2010
一、工业企业数（个）	**Number of Industrial Enterprises (unit)**	**27**
二、本年施工项目总数（个）	**Total Number of Projects Under Construction (unit)**	**32**
#废水治理项目	Treatment of Waste Water	9
废气治理项目	Treatment of Waste Gas	17
固体废物治理项目	Treatment of Solid Wastes	2
三、施工项目本年完成投资额（万元）	**Investment Completed in Anti-pollution Projects**	**9678.4**
	Under Construction (10 000 yuan)	
#废水治理项目	Treatment of Waste Water	3026.5
废气治理项目	Treatment of Waste Gas	4279.6
固体废物治理项目	Treatment of Solid Wastes	65.0
四、施工项目本年投资来源合计（万元）	**Investment Sources of Projects Under Construction (10 000 yuan)**	**9678.4**
#排污费补助	Pollution Charges Subsidies	679.3
政府其他补助	Other Government Subsidies	2297.1
企业自筹	Self-raising Funds	6702.0
#银行贷款	Loans	507.0
五、本年竣工项目数（个）	**Number of Projects Completed(unit)**	24
#废水治理项目	Treatment of Waste Water	7
废气治理项目	Treatment of Waste Gas	13
噪声治理项目	Treatment of Noise Pollution	
六、本年竣工项目新增设计处理能力	**Newly Increased Disposal Capacity of Projects Completed**	
#治理废水（吨/日）	Treatment of Waste Water (ton/day)	5865
治理废气（万标立方米/时）	Treatment of Waste Gas (10 000 cu.m./h)	144.30
治理固体废物（吨/日）	Treatment of Solid Wastes (ton/day)	90

9-8 各区县环境保护基本情况（2010年）

区 县	Region	环境污染治理本年完成投资额（万元）Completed Investment on Environmental Pollution Treatment (10 000 yuan)	工业二氧化硫排放量（吨）Volume of Industrial Sulphur Dioxide Discharged (ton)	工业废水排放达标率（%）Percentage of Industrial Waste Water up to the Standards for Discharge (%)
全 市	**Total**	**9678.4**	**81504**	**95.9**
新城区	Xincheng	75.1	310	100
碑林区	Beilin		2136	75.5
莲湖区	Lianhu	258.7	1966	98.7
灞桥区	Baqiao	5184.5	16882	88.7
未央区	Weiyang	1931.1	28484	100
雁塔区	Yanta		1226	98.8
阎良区	Yanliang	550	1852	100
临潼区	Lintong	614	2236	73.7
长安区	Chang'an	465	5649	100
蓝田县	Lantian		617	98.8
周至县	Zhouzhi		86	44.5
户 县	Huxian		13798	99.4
高陵县	Gaoling		625	74.6

Condition of Environment Protection by Regions（2010）

工业烟尘排放量达标率（%）Percentage of Industrial Soot up to the Standards for Discharge (%)	工业化学需氧量排放量（吨）Volume of COD Removed (ton)	垃圾处理站数（座）Number of Rubbish Disposal Works (unit)	污水处理厂数（个）Number of Sewage Treatment Works (unit)
98.7	**38864**	**1**	**11**
100	521		
100	26		
100	1039		1
99.9	5344	1	1
100	6559		1
93.4	1544		1
100	736		1
100	6689		1
100	9052		1
98.3	30		1
85.1	779		1
93.6	4519		1
99.2	314		1

主要统计指标解释

工业废水排放量 指经过企业厂区所有排放口排到企业外部的工业废水量。包括生产废水、外排的直接冷却水、超标排放的矿井地下水和与工业废水混排的厂区生活污水，不包括外排的间接冷却水（清污不分流的间接冷却水应计算在内）。

工业废水排放达标量 指各项指标都达到国家或地方排放标准的外排工业废水量，包括未经处理外排达标和经过处理后外排达标两部分。

工业废水处理量 指报告期内各种水治理设施实际处理的工业废水量，包括处理后外排和处理后回用的工业废水量和虽经处理但未达到国家或地方排放标准的废水量。如车间和厂排放口均有治理设施，并对同一废水分级处理时，不应重复计算工业废水处理量。

工业废气排放量 指企业厂区内燃料燃烧和生产工艺过程中产生的各种排入空气的含有污染物的气体总量，按标准状态〔273K，101325Pa〕计算。

工业二氧化硫排放量 指企业在燃料燃烧和生产工艺过程中排入大气的二氧化硫数量。

烟尘排放量 指企业厂区内燃料燃烧产生的烟气中夹带的颗粒物数量。

工业粉尘排放量 指企业在生产工艺过程中排放的颗粒物重量，如钢铁企业的耐火材料粉尘、焦化企业的筛焦系统粉尘、烧结机的粉尘、石灰窑的粉尘、建材企业的水泥粉尘等。不包括电厂排入大气的烟尘。

工业固体废物产生量 指企业在生产过程中产生的固体状、半固体状和高浓度液体状废弃物的总量，包括危险废物、冶炼废渣、粉煤灰、炉渣、煤矸石、尾矿、放射性废物和其他废物等;不包括矿山开采的剥离废石和掘进废石（煤矸石和呈酸性或碱性的废石除外）。酸性或碱性废石指采掘的废石其流经水、雨淋水的pH值小于4或pH值大于10.5者。

工业固体废物处置量 指将固体废物焚烧或者最终置于符合环境保护规定要求的场所，并不再回取的工业固体废物量（包括当年处置往年的工业固体废物累计贮存量）。处置方法有填埋（其中危险废物应安全填埋）、焚烧、专业贮存场（库）封场处理、深层灌注、回填矿井等。

工业固体废物排放量 指将所产生的固体废物排到固体废物污染防治设施、场所以外的数量，不包括矿山开采的剥离废石和掘进废石（煤矸石和呈酸性或碱性的废石除外）。

Explanatory Notes on Main Statistical Indicators

Volume of Industrial Waste Water Discharged refers to the volume of industrial waste water discharged, through all outlets, to the outside of industrial enterprises, including waste water produced, direct-cooling water, underground water from mines that does not meet the standard of discharge, and the domestic sewage mixed up with industrial waste water when discharged, but excluding discharged indirect-cooling water.

Volume of Waste Water up to the Standard for Discharge refers to the volume of discharged industrial waste water that, with or without treatment, has come up to the national or local standards for discharge.

Volume of Treated Industrial Waste Water refers to the volume of industrial waste water after being treated and purified through various water treatment facilities in the reference period, including the volume discharged or recovered after being treated. The volume of waste water that fails to meet the national or local standards after treatment is also included. If there are treatment facilities both at the outlets of workshops and at the outlets of the factory, and the same volume of waste water has been treated twice, duplication should be avoided in the calculation of the volume of treated industrial waste water.

Volume of Waste Industrial Gas Emission refers to waste gas emitted from burning of fuels and from production process in the area of the factory, and is measured by 10000 standard cubic meters each year under normal condition.

Volume of Industrial Sulphur Dioxide Discharged refers to the volume of sulphur dioxide discharged to the air in the process of fuel burning or in the production process.

Volume of Industrial Soot Discharged refers to the volume of solid soot in the smoke discharged in the process of fuel burning in the area of the factory.

Industrial Dust Discharged refers to the total weight of solid dust discharged by industrial enterprises in the production process, such as dust of refractory materials from iron plants, dust from coke-screening system or from sintering machines of coking plants, dust from lime kilns, cement dust from building material enterprises, etc., but excluding smoke and dust discharged by power plants.

Volume of Industrial Solid Wastes Produced refers to the total volume of solid, semi-solid or high concentration liquid residue produced by industrial enterprises in their production process, including dangerous wastes, residues from melting, slag, powdered coal ash, gangue, chemical residues, tailings, radioactive residues and other residues, but excluding stripped or dug stones in mining (except gangue and acid or alkali stones which are stones washed or soaked by water with a pH value smaller than 4 or larger than 10.5)

Volume of Industrial Solid Wastes Treated refers to solid wastes disposed of in a non-recoverable place that meet the requirement of environmental protection, such as burying (The dangerous wastes should be buried safely), burning, piling in designated sites, pouring water into the deep strata, filling of old mines, etc. (including treatment of solid wastes piled up in the previous years).

Volume of Industrial Solid Wastes Discharged refers to the volume of industrial solid wastes produced and discharged at the places outside the special facilities or special sites for preventing against pollution, excluding stripped or dug stones in mining (except gangue and acid or alkali waste stones).

10 农 业

AGRICULTURE

资料整理：张喜兰　刘栋婷　薛　丰
Data management:Zhang Xilan　Liu Dongting　Xue Feng

第十部分　农业

一、简要说明

本章资料主要包括农村基本情况、农业生产条件与生产情况、耕地、农林牧渔及服务业产值、主要农产品产量以及各区县农业生产和农村经济效益主要指标，由西安市统计局农村处提供，其中除10-1、10-2、10-3、10-4、10-5、10-6、10-13、10-14、10-20、10-21、10-22表外，其余表2006年和2007年数据为第二次农业普查衔接数。

二、主要指标

年末耕地面积（万亩）	383.32	比上年减少	1.2%
农林牧渔及服务业总产值（亿元）	227.10	比上年增长	7.4%
农作物播种面积（万亩）	751.74	比上年减少	0.7%
粮食产量（万吨）	221.65	比上年增长	1.6 %

10 AGRICULTURE

Ⅰ.Brief Introduction

Data in this chapter reflects basic condition of agriculture production of Xi'an city. It is primarily consist of basic condition of rural area, condition of agriculture production, plow land, production value of farming, forestry, animal husbandry and fishery, gross yield of primary produce and primary Indicators of agriculture production and rural area economic performance. The data are provided and compiled by Rural Area Division of the Xi'an Bureau of Statistics.The data in this chapter in 2006 and 2007 is conformity with the second national agriculture census, except table of 10-1、10-2、10-3、10-4、10-5、10-6、10-13、10-14、10-20、10-21、10-22.

Ⅱ.Major Indicators

		Increase over Preceding Year
Cultivated Area Year-end(10 000 mu)	383.32	-1.2%
Gross Output Value of Farming, Forestry, Animal Husbandry,Fishery and Service(100 mil. yuan)	227.10	7.4%
Sown Area of Crops(10 000 mu)	751.74	-0.7%
Grain Output(10 000 tons)	221.65	1.6%

10-1 农村基层组织、乡村户数、人口及劳动力情况

Grass-root Organizations, Households, Population and Labor Resources in Rural Area

指　　标	Item	2000	2005	2006	2007	2008	2009	2010
一、农村基层组织情况	**Village Units**							
1.乡镇个数（个）	Number of Township and Towns(unit)	168	102	97	84	82	73	73
#镇个数	Number of Towns	52	50	45	37	35	31	31
2.村民委员会个数（个）	Number of Villagers' Committees(unit)	3165	3162	3161	3161	3145	3104	3063
3.村民小组个数（个）	Number of Village Groups(unit)	16294	16281	16275	16260	16272	16068	15981
二、乡村户数（万户）	**Number of Households (10 000 households)**	**98.77**	**101.50**	**102.35**	**100.85**	**101.02**	**101.00**	**101.43**
三、农村人口和从业人员情况	**Rural Population and Employment**							
1.乡村人口数（万人）	Rural Population(10 000 persons)	401.64	408.90	409.77	403.02	404.18	404.17	405.17
2.乡村劳动力资源总数（万人）	Total Number of Rural Labor Source (10 000 persons)	240.76	255.93	257.66	254.06	256.17	255.00	256.36
#劳动年龄内人口	Population at Labor Age	232.43	229.74	234.12	230.28	231.96	231.04	232.06
3.乡村从业人员数（万人）	Rural Laborers(10 000 persons)	212.65	223.30	225.99	222.09	223.85	223.13	225.04
#劳动年龄内人口	Population at Labor Age		205.97	208.36	201.29	202.51	201.79	202.89
#女性	Female	99.07	103.22	103.87	101.83	103.11	102.76	103.25
(1)农业	Laborers of Farming	146.07	137.69	135.64	131.96	126.46	121.78	116.58
(2)工业	Laborers of Industry	15.43	18.41	19.92	20.60	22.29	22.67	23.94
(3)建筑业	Laborers of Construction	16.45	21.73	22.37	23.28	25.27	26.24	29.20
(4)交通仓储邮电业	Laborers of Transportation,Postal and Telecommunications Services	7.64	8.74	9.26	9.22	10.45	10.92	11.91
(5)批零贸易、餐饮业	Laborers of Trade and Catering	8.14	12.70	14.14	14.18	16.61	18.09	18.91
(6)金融、保险业	Laborers of Banking and Insurance	0.45						
(7)其他	Laborers of Others	18.47	24.03	24.66	22.85	22.77	23.43	24.50
四、国有农林牧渔业从业人员数（万人）	**Number of staff and Workers in State-owned farms(10 000 persons)**	**0.29**	**0.11**	**0.11**	**0.08**	**0.07**	**0.07**	**0.06**
五、自来水受益村数（个）	**Number of Villages Benefited from the Tap Water System (unit)**	**1527**	**1756**	**1794**	**1881**	**1934**	**2058**	**2184**
六、通汽车村数（个）	**Number of Villages Accessible by motor Vehicles (unit)**	**2785**	**2952**	**2923**	**2973**	**2996**	**2989**	**2989**
七、通电话村数（个）	**Number of Villages Accessible by Telephone (unit)**	**2885**	**3101**	**3113**	**3129**	**3086**	**3071**	**3052**

注：农村基层组织数据来自民政报表，镇数不包括四县的中心镇和工矿镇。

Note:Figures of rural gross-roots organizations are from report of civil administration department. Number of townships exclude central townships and plant townships of the four counties.

10-2 各区县农村基层组织、乡村户数及人口（2010年）

Grass-root Organizations, Households and Population in Rural Area by Region（2010）

区 县	Region	乡镇个数（个）Number of Townships and Towns (unit)	镇个数 Number of Towns	村民委员会个数（个）Number of Villagers' Committees (unit)	村民小组个数（个）Number of Village Groups (unit)	乡村户数（万户）Number of Households (10000household)	乡村人数（万人）Number Rural Population (10000 person)
合 计	**Total**	**73**	**31**	**3063**	**15991**	**101.43**	**405.17**
新城区	Xincheng			1	2		
碑林区	Beilin						
莲湖区	Lianhu			5	8		
灞桥区	Baqiao			226	841	7.33	28.6
未央区	Weiyang			192	598	6.05	21.62
雁塔区	Yanta			103	415	4.56	16.1
阎良区	Yanliang	2	2	80	592	4.24	16.18
临潼区	Lintong	3		284	2081	13.41	55.59
长安区	Chang'an	5		671	3228	20.96	82.46
蓝田县	Lantian	21	9	519	2479	13.6	55.77
周至县	Zhouzhi	21	8	376	2535	13.91	59.59
户 县	Huxian	14	9	518	2472	11.91	47.75
高陵县	Gaoling	7	3	88	740	5.46	21.51

10-3 各区县从业人员数（2010年）

Number of Labours in Families by Region（2010）

单位：万人 (10 000 persons)

区 县	Region	乡村从业人员数合计 Rural Laborers Total	女性 Female	农林牧渔业 Farming,Forestry Animal Husbandry and Fishery	工业 Industry	建筑业 Laborers of Construction
合 计	**Total**	**225.04**	**103.25**	**116.58**	**23.94**	**29.20**
新城区	Xincheng					
碑林区	Beilin					
莲湖区	Lianhu					
灞桥区	Baqiao	15.84	6.83	6.88	1.77	1.77
未央区	Weiyang	12.05	5.30	2.66	2.91	1.07
雁塔区	Yanta	8.06	4.02	1.22	0.82	0.80
阎良区	Yanliang	8.87	3.75	5.25	0.61	1.37
临潼区	Lintong	29.64	14.48	19.50	1.69	3.81
长安区	Chang'an	43.55	18.60	18.40	5.40	8.40
蓝田县	Lantian	31.94	15.49	19.61	1.67	2.60
周至县	Zhouzhi	34.63	15.59	20.36	3.72	4.11
户 县	Huxian	28.30	13.26	17.08	4.27	2.91
高陵县	Gaoling	12.16	5.93	5.62	1.08	2.36

10-3 续表 continued

单位：万人 (10 000 persons)

区 县	Region	交通运输、仓储及邮政业 Transportation,Postal and Telecommunication Services	批零贸易餐饮业 Trade and Catering	金融、保险业 Banking and Insurance	其 他 Others
合 计	**Total**	**11.91**	**18.91**		**24.50**
新城区	Xincheng				
碑林区	Beilin				
莲湖区	Lianhu				
灞桥区	Baqiao	1.19	1.11		3.12
未央区	Weiyang	0.89	1.85		2.67
雁塔区	Yanta	0.79	1.76		2.67
阎良区	Yanliang	0.41	0.47		0.76
临潼区	Lintong	0.97	1.58		2.09
长安区	Chang'an	2.97	4.08		4.30
蓝田县	Lantian	1.30	3.04		3.72
周至县	Zhouzhi	1.59	2.54		2.31
户 县	Huxian	1.00	1.34		1.70
高陵县	Gaoling	0.80	1.14		1.16

10-4 主要年份耕地面积

Area of Cultivated Land in Representative Years

单位：万亩 (10 000 mu)

年 份 Year	年末实有耕地面积 Cultivated Area Year-end	#水 田 Paddy Field	水浇地 Irrigable Land
1970	554.09	18.20	297.05
1975	538.35	20.34	349.13
1978	530.96	16.70	370.46
1980	526.29	17.45	372.96
1985	508.88	17.63	328.10
1990	495.32	17.97	311.91
1991	492.09	17.03	309.17
1992	485.30	16.44	298.19
1993	479.04	14.36	304.49
1994	471.44	13.98	299.58
1995	463.97	17.04	278.01
1996	451.50	14.21	283.76
1997	456.62	11.90	290.49
1998	455.15	11.18	282.23
1999	450.74	11.31	281.96
2000	443.37	10.26	284.04
2001	431.69	9.00	274.73
2002	424.46	7.98	275.96
2003	413.84	6.65	263.75
2004	404.87	6.59	254.04
2005	400.17	5.55	254.04
2006	395.79	5.33	263.75
2007	391.77	4.80	255.95
2008	390.77	4.64	255.36
2009	387.89	4.39	260.71
2010	383.32	4.03	257.43

10-5 各区县耕地面积（2010年）

单位：亩

区 县	Region	年末实有耕地面积 Cultivated Area Year-end	水田 Paddy Field	旱地 Dry Land	水浇地 Irrigable Land	当年增加的耕地面积 Area of Newly Increased Cultivated Land	新开荒地面积 Area of Newly Reclamation of Wasteland
合 计	**Total**	**3833150**	**40260**	**3792890**	**2574270**	**8740**	**2144**
新城区	Xincheng						
碑林区	Beilin						
莲湖区	Lianhu						
灞桥区	Baqiao	170611	450	170161	94233		
未央区	Weiyang	52097	300	51797	51797		
雁塔区	Yanta	20199		20199	15863		
阎良区	Yanliang	237645		237645	230860		
临潼区	Lintong	739943	998	738945	566980	234	
长安区	Chang'an	693974	23503	670471	337812	4123	771
蓝田县	Lantian	610000	10000	600000	177000	2360	820
周至县	Zhouzhi	502884	3203	499681	367675	544	544
户 县	Huxian	574700	1806	572894	500953	475	
高陵县	Gaoling	231097		231097	231097	1004	9

Area of Cultivated Land by Region（2010）

(mu)

当年减少的耕地面积 Decrease in Cultivated Area in the Year	国家基建占地 Capital Construction	乡村集体基建占地 Village Collective Construction	农民个人建房占地 Peasant Housing Construction	退耕改果、茶、桑面积 Area for Change into Fruit, Tea and Mulberry	退耕造林面积 Area for Change into Woods
63721	**45367**	**2521**	**1897**	**8379**	**1168**
15546	10458	14	28	3046	
10172	10172				
5176	2995	46	6	300	
4311	2160	109	89	1675	
7678	3991	298	397	2542	168
9500	6000	1300	1000	200	1000
367	296	71			
1935	1500		15	420	
9036	7795	683	362	196	

10-6 主要年份农业机械拥有量（年末数）

Possession of Agricultural Machinery in Representative Years（Number of year-end）

指　标	Item	2004	2005	2006
农业机械总动力(千瓦)	**Total Power of Agricultural Machinery(kw)**	**2140737**	**2239001**	**2277584**
主要农业机械与设备	**Major Agricultural Machinery and Equipment**			
大中型拖拉机(台)	Large and Medium Tractors(unit)	7500	8415	8963
(千瓦)	(kw)	246978	290638	312325
小型拖拉机(台)	Mini-tractors(unit)	27225	26326	23437
(千瓦)	(kw)	307382	303831	263565
大中型拖拉机配套农具（部）	Number of Large and Medium Tractor Towing Farm Machinery(unit)	18446	19334	18724
小型拖拉机配套农具（部）	Mini-Tractor Towing Farm Machinery (unit)	47260	47883	30439
#柴 油 机(台)	Diesel Engines(unit)	2522	2219	3547
(千瓦)	(kw)	21865	22993	29112
电 动 机(台)	Motors(unit)	78542	79666	76614
(千瓦)	(kw)	343230	369843	360684
农用水泵（台）	Agricultural Water Pump(unit)	74701	77567	73039
节水灌溉类机械（套）	Equipment in Water-saving Irrigation(set)	1141	1290	2656
联合收割机（台）	Combine Harvesters(unit)	4053	4802	5026
(千瓦)	(kw)	150982	173183	183313
自走式机动割晒机（台）	Self-propelled Motorized Swather(unit)	3147	4226	1342
(千瓦)	(kw)	150982	173183	52740
机动脱粒机（台）	Motorized Huller (unit)	13060	13870	5806
农用运输车（辆）	Agricultucal Transporter(unit)	42247	47348	50395
#三轮运输车	Three-wheel Transporter	34736	36436	41907

10-6 续表 continued

指　标	Item	2007	2008	2009	2010
农业机械总动力(千瓦)	**Total Power of Agricultural Machinery(kw)**	**2348856**	**2712616**	**2616053**	**2677334**
主要农业机械与设备	**Major Agricultural Machinery and Equipment**				
大中型拖拉机(台)	Large and Medium Tractors(unit)	10431	11092	11479	14675
(千瓦)	(kw)	387962	421581	474115	568653
小型拖拉机(台)	Mini-tractors(unit)	21555	19036	18406	14194
(千瓦)	(kw)	237550	213806	204965	167724
大中型拖拉机配套农具（部）	Number of Large and Medium Tractor Towing Farm Machinery(unit)	23487	25125	26575	29215
小型拖拉机配套农具（部）	Mini-Tractor Towing Farm Machinery (unit)	28780	26984	29039	24393
#柴 油 机(台)	Diesel Engines(unit)	2709	2670	2691	3309
(千瓦)	(kw)	24445	23546	23008	31859
电 动 机(台)	Motors(unit)	84416	85349	83243	79462
(千瓦)	(kw)	387042	421435	400534	333107
农用水泵（台）	Agricultural Water Pump(unit)	80722	80462	80174	77367
节水灌溉类机械（套）	Equipment in Water-saving Irrigation(set)	1991	1728	1799	1710
联合收割机（台）	Combine Harvesters(unit)	5294	5390	6155	6718
(千瓦)	(kw)	211490	220185	252976	271577
自走式机动割晒机（台）	Self-propelled Motorized Swather(unit)	4918	2174	1220	208
(千瓦)	(kw)	211388	90899	52129	9877
机动脱粒机（台）	Motorized Huller (unit)	11585	23781	11960	13231
农用运输车（辆）	Agricultucal Transporter(unit)	49576	54860	50671	51665
#三轮运输车	Three-wheel Transporter	40373	44953	41899	42749

10-7 各区县农业机械拥有量（2010年）

指　　标	Item	西安市 Xi'an	灞桥区 Baqiao	未央区 Weiyang
农业机械总动力(千瓦)	Total Power of Agricultural Machinery(kw)	2677334	171810	76023
主要农业机械与设备	Major Agricultural Machinery and Equipment			
大中型拖拉机(台)	Large and Medium Tractors(unit)	14675	428	296
(千瓦)	(kw)	568653	20746	11175
小型拖拉机(台)	Mini-tractors(unit)	14194	250	17
(千瓦)	(kw)	167724	2832	234
大中型拖拉机配套农具（部）	Number of Large and Medium Tractor Towing Farm Machinery(unit)	29215	768	1080
小型拖拉机配套农具（部）	Mini-Tractor Towing Farm Machinery (unit)	24393	652	51
农用排灌柴油机(台)	Agricultural Diesel Engines(unit)	3309		
(千瓦)	(kw)	31859		
农用排灌电动机(台)	Agricultural Motors(unit)	79462	3098	1864
(千瓦)	(kw)	333107	22417	8280
农用水泵（台）	Agricultural Water Pump(unit)	77367	3098	1864
节水灌溉类机械	Equipment in Water-saving Irrigation	1710	2	214
联合收割机（台）	Combine Harvesters(unit)	6718	231	
(千瓦)	(kw)	271577	10084	
自走式机动割晒机	Self-propelled Motorized Swathers	208	208	
(千瓦)	(kw)	9877	9877	
机动脱粒机（台）	Motorized Huller (unit)	13231	231	
农用运输车（辆）	Agricultucal Transporters	51665	3681	852
#三轮运输车	Three-wheel Transporter	42749	2545	635

Possession of Agricultural Machinery by Region（2010）

雁塔区 Yanta	阎良区 Yanliang	临潼区 Lintong	长安区 Chang'an	蓝田县 Lantian	周至县 Zhouzhi	户 县 Huxian	高陵县 Gaoling
83960	152667	511906	442931	285112	352487	371667	228771
70	879	2149	3011	894	1302	4267	1379
2194	52610	79539	129789	32885	55430	129915	54370
20	1205	1342	593	3180	5087	2059	441
224	15560	15409	6409	35341	52568	33532	5615
38	2655	6147	5002	1765	2307	5143	4310
20	1860	4016	1020	4272	8380	3124	998
610		253	1476	625	289	56	
9060		2907	9227	7575	2522	568	
	5980	17303	15732	3293	15718	12804	3670
	23920	97817	16199	26247	58467	59942	19818
228	6110	16458	16506		17050	12383	3670
1	55	6	982	88	272	90	
38	498	1381	1117	212	381	2096	764
1582	23435	58240	43211	9798	16593	72072	36562
	950	4258	670	2211	2130	2271	510
725	2244	14207	7511	4373	8197	4050	5825
536	2110	13683	4410	3713	7318	3599	4200

10-8 主要年份农业机械、化肥、水利、水电情况

Agricultural Machinery,Chemical Fertilizers,Water Conservancy, Hydropower in Representative Years

指　　标	Item	2000	2005	2006
一、农业机械化情况(万亩)	**Statistics on Agricultural Machinery (10 000 mu)**			
当年实际机耕地面积	Area Ploughed by Tractors	366.81	360.68	354.05
当年实际机播面积	Seeded Area by Tractors	482.74	485.62	519.00
当年实际机械收获面积	Harvest Area by Tractors	272.83	271.77	280.88
二、农用化肥施用量(吨)	**Use of Agricultural Fertilizers and Insecticides(Ton)**			
1.按实物量计算	Practicality Consumption	697243	749802	759882
氮 肥	Nitrogenous Fertilizer	392366	411161	413514
磷 肥	Phosphate Fertilizer	155480	161444	164781
钾 肥	Potash Fertilizer	31841	34114	31414
复合肥	Compound Fertilizer	78620	115458	121124
2.按折纯量计算	Standard Consumption	196343	211790	216093
氮 肥	Nitrogenous Fertilizer	102982	107645	110137
磷 肥	Phosphate Fertilizer	18658	19368	19772
钾 肥	Potash Fertilizer	15921	17055	15709
复合肥	Compound Fertilizer	39313	57009	59731
三、农用塑料薄膜使用量（公斤）	**Plastic Sheet for Agricultural Use(kg)**	**1622198**	**1855383**	**1931527**
四、农用柴油（吨）	**Diesel Oil for Agricultural Use (ton)**	**52706**	**50832**	**49686**
五、农药使用量（公斤）	**Pesticide (kg)**	**1559333**	**1427879**	**1471672**
六、农村办沼气池（个）	**Number of Mash Gas Pond Managed by Village Government(unit)**	**10199**	**12445**	**16211**
七、农村水利化情况（万亩）	**Irrigation and Water Conservancy (10 000 mu)**			
有效灌溉面积	Effective Irrigation Area	335.97	280.10	276.58
旱涝保收面积	Stable-Harvesting Arable Land	294.06	255.37	253.66
机电排灌面积	Electrical Irrigation Area	249.11	223.74	214.03
八、农村电气化情况	**Rural electrization**			
乡村及村以下办水电站（个）	Hydropower Station in Rural Areas(unit)	67	79	79
装机容量（千瓦）	Installed Power Generation Capacity(kw)	7236	13775	14252
发 电 量（万千瓦小时）	Generating Capacity (10 000 kwh)	1138	2239	2253
已配套机电井（眼）	Electricity Powered Well(unit)	50289	46505	46112

10-8 续表 continued

指　　标	Item	2007	2008	2009	2010
一、农业机械化情况(万亩)	**Statistics on Agricultural Machinery (10 000 mu)**				
当年实际机耕地面积	Area Ploughed by Tractors	361.62	404.42	413.70	367.32
当年实际机播面积	Seeded Area by Tractors	521.36	539.81	544.86	548.28
当年实际机械收获面积	Harvest Area by Tractors	296.06	313.11	342.82	403.50
二、农用化肥施用量(吨)	**Use of Agricultural Fertilizers and Insecticides(Ton)**				
1.按实物量计算	Practicality Consumption	762401	767980	776319	781072
氮 肥	Nitrogenous Fertilizer	408847	413397	414481	397975
磷 肥	Phosphate Fertilizer	160932	157145	153825	152943
钾 肥	Potash Fertilizer	34284	34149	33069	37715
复合肥	Compound Fertilizer	124784	132481	142137	158062
2.按折纯量计算	Standard Consumption	220251	225949	230299	235532
氮 肥	Nitrogenous Fertilizer	109484	112000	112275	108868
磷 肥	Phosphate Fertilizer	19311	18855	18457	18315
钾 肥	Potash Fertilizer	17141	17077	16534	17997
复合肥	Compound Fertilizer	62398	66247	71042	78811
三、农用塑料薄膜使用量（公斤）	**Plastic Sheet for Agricultural Use(kg)**	**2096169**	**2122310**	**2141969**	**2450496**
四、农用柴油（吨）	**Diesel Oil for Agricultural Use (ton)**	**50137**	**51097**	**51346**	**61917**
五、农药使用量（公斤）	**Pesticide (kg)**	**1444867**	**1465819**	**1325459**	**1243105**
六、农村办沼气池（个）	**Number of Mash Gas Pond Managed by Village Government(unit)**	**26448**	**36540**	**46737**	**50710**
七、农村水利化情况（万亩）	**Irrigation and Water Conservancy (10 000 mu)**				
有效灌溉面积	Effective Irrigation Area	276.28	274.48	273.17	281.28
旱涝保收面积	Stable-Harvesting Arable Land	247.99	249.31	247.60	234.15
机电排灌面积	Electrical Irrigation Area	210.51	211.01	213.42	224.60
八、农村电气化情况	**Rural electrization**				
乡村及村以下办水电站（个）	Hydropower Station in Rural Areas(unit)	76	76	75	44
装机容量（千瓦）	Installed Power Generation Capacity(kw)	24827	24827	25047	22325
发 电 量（万千瓦小时）	Generating Capacity (10 000 kwh)	10085	10477	10678	7268
已配套机电井（眼）	Electricity Powered Well(unit)	45783	47032	46790	44310

10-9 各区县农业机械、化肥、水利、水电情况（2010年）

指　　标	Item	西安市 Xi'an	灞桥区 Baqiao	未央区 Weiyang
一、农业机械化情况(万亩)	**Statistics on Agricultural Machinery (10 000 mu)**			
当年实际机耕地面积	Area Ploughed by Tractors	367	19	6
当年实际机播面积	Seeded Area by Tractors	548	23	7
当年实际机械收获面积	Harvest Area by Tractors	404	15	4
二、农用化肥施用量(吨)	**Use of Agricultural Fertilizers and Insecticides(Ton)**			
1.按实物量计算	Practicality Consumption	781072	25137	4327
氮 肥	Nitrogenous Fertilizer	397975	14045	2380
磷 肥	Phosphate Fertilizer	152943	2281	363
钾 肥	Potash Fertilizer	37715	2348	49
复合肥	Compound Fertilizer	158062	6388	1121
2.按折纯量计算	Standard Consumption	235532	9425	1603
氮 肥	Nitrogenous Fertilizer	108868	4748	769
磷 肥	Phosphate Fertilizer	18315	273	43
钾 肥	Potash Fertilizer	17997	1174	24
复合肥	Compound Fertilizer	78811	3194	560
三、农用塑料薄膜使用量（公斤）	**Plastic Sheet for Agricultural Use(kg)**	2450496	166803	16007
四、农用柴油（吨）	**Diesel Oil for Agricultural Use (ton)**	61917	1778	945
五、农药使用量（公斤）	**Pesticide (kg)**	1243105	43656	13638
六、农村办沼气池（个）	**Number of Mash Gas Pond Managed by Village Government(unit)**	50710	720	8
七、农村水利化情况（万亩）	**Irrigation and Water Conservancy (10 000 mu)**			
有效灌溉面积	Effective Irrigation Area	281	12	3
旱涝保收面积	Stable-Harvesting Arable Land	234	11	3
机电排灌面积	Electrical Irrigation Area	225	12	5
八、农村电气化情况	**Rural electrization**			
乡村及村以下办水电站（个）	Hydropower Station in Rural Areas(unit)	44		
装机容量（千瓦）	Installed Power Generation Capacity(kw)	22325		
发 电 量（万千瓦小时）	Generating Capacity (10 000 kwh)	7268		
已配套机电井（眼）	Electricity Powered Well(unit)	44310	2017	1206

Agricultural Machinery,Chemical Fertilizers,Water Conservancy, Hydropower by Region（2010）

雁塔区 Yanta	阎良区 Yanliang	临潼区 Lintong	长安区 Chang'an	蓝田县 Lantian	周至县 Zhouzhi	户　县 Huxian	高陵县 Gaoling
	23	47	77	61	64	48	23
	30	96	112	66	81	91	44
	21	77	82	41	46	78	39
1264	53428	148235	129523	96125	138632	105398	79003
429	24166	75697	64789	52750	64698	66358	32663
88	10760	45872	23683	19368	15134	14089	21305
114	3671	2026	8197	6240	7595	2901	4574
244	12857	22686	25187	16322	38296	19256	15705
516	18517	38815	31140	36292	43039	30850	25335
133	7975	19985	7775	22735	15893	16929	11926
10	1291	5504	2840	2300	1816	1682	2556
57	1835	1013	4098	2496	3563	1450	2287
122	6429	11343	12593	8161	19038	9518	7853
268	823805	195703	189321	175800	93026	597094	192669
308	2492	6355	13202	10260	3292	10480	12805
73	174998	368699	129461	78250	160198	63423	210709
	4229	4738	4088	1730	18065	11681	5451
0	22	55	46	24	50	48	20
0	22	51	34	17	28	47	20
3	23	42	51	13	16	48	13
			7	5	26	6	
			5065	13600	1100	2560	
			1180	5440	410	238	
590	3774	7288	8619	1777	5931	10125	2983

10-10 主要年份农林牧渔及服务业总产值及指数

Gross Output Value of Farming,Forestry,Animal Husbandry,Fishery,Service and Related Indices in Representative Years

单位：万元　　　　(10 000yuan)

年 份 Year	农林牧渔及服务业总产值（现价） Gross Output Value (At current prices)	农业 Farming	林业 Forestry	牧业 Animal Husbandry	渔业 Fishery	农林牧渔服务业 Service of Farming, Forestry, Animal Husbandry and Fishery	指数（上年=100）（可比价） Indices(preceding year=100) (At constant prices)
1970	40617	35965	713	3896	43		111.2
1975	55322	47378	1509	6403	32		93.9
1978	65423	56519	1444	7427	33		104.7
1980	65322	54004	1177	10106	35		85.0
1985	134933	105888	2559	26186	300		106.4
1990	262073	191088	3134	65840	2011		102.5
1991	295620	208324	3362	81070	2864		108.6
1992	321155	219160	4225	94045	3725		108.6
1993	387068	261959	5031	115810	4268		112.8
1994	565056	359609	7819	192140	5488		102.4
1995	754597	513348	7185	228598	5466		106.8
1996	786003	552726	7573	219214	6490		102.1
1997	836201	585973	9226	233623	7379		110.3
1998	853279	625465	8146	212045	7623		107.5
1999	739905	530029	8883	194552	6441		100.7
2000	743712	514845	8482	212612	7773		104.3
2001	767511	527160	8427	223861	8063		102.8
2002	797444	539978	11378	238761	7327		103.0
2003	837857	551398	10550	269610	6299		101.5
2004	967946	580798	12773	314517	6728	53130	108.4
2005	1065437	657262	13086	329856	7340	57893	107.7
2006	1141484	686748	15188	346626	7017	85905	107.2
2007	1341450	798163	15845	410213	9051	108178	105.3
2008	1682725	956549	19031	564095	11084	131966	107.8
2009	1787032	1061756	22663	546191	11830	144592	106.5
2010	2270994	1438934	26787	629376	12830	163067	107.4

10-11 主要年份农林牧渔及服务业总产值指数

Related Indices of Gross Output Value of Farming,Forestry,Animal Husbandry,Fishery,Service and Related Indices in Representative Years

年 份 Year	农林牧渔及服务业总产值指数（上年=100）（可比价） Indices(preceding year=100) (At constant prices)	农业 Farming	林业 Forestry	牧业 Animal Husbandry	渔业 Fishery	农林牧渔服务业 Service of Farming, Forestry, Animal Husbandry and Fishery
2005	107.7	108.0	98.7	107.3	112.6	107.9
2006	107.2	106.0	102.5	109.3	104.5	109.4
2007	105.3	106.4	101.3	102.4	106.3	108.7
2008	107.8	107.9	112.2	106.0	100.5	113.7
2009	106.5	105.4	121.3	106.8	107.4	110.2
2010	107.4	108.7	115.2	104.3	92.7	108.9

10-12 各区县农林牧渔及服务业总产值（2010年）

Gross Output Value of Farming, Forestry, Animal Husbandry, Fishery and Service by Region（2010）

单位：万元 （10 000yuan)

区 县	Region	农林牧渔及服务业总产值 Gross Output Value	农业 Farming	林业 Forestry	牧业 Animal Husbandry	渔业 Fishery	农林牧渔服务业 Service of Farming, Forestry, Animal Husbandry and Fishery
全 市	**Total**	**2270994**	**1438934**	**26787**	**629376**	**12830**	**163067**
新城区	Xincheng						
碑林区	Beilin						
莲湖区	Lianhu						
灞桥区	Baqiao	178275	129383	700	34372	1820	12000
未央区	Weiyang	40781	21859	19	13558	1995	3350
雁塔区	Yanta	30143	19187	77	7879		3000
阎良区	Yanliang	214232	155854	546	41278	254	16300
临潼区	Lintong	411121	210315	6221	163914	1671	29000
长安区	Chang'an	382196	254489	2025	95537	2720	27425
蓝田县	Lantian	286829	179846	12213	72766	2050	19954
周至县	Zhouzhi	262734	185555	3438	57080	628	16033
户 县	Huxian	260295	174767	853	62876	824	20975
高陵县	Gaoling	204388	107679	695	80116	868	15030

10-13 各区县农林牧渔及服务业总产值指数及构成（2010年）

Gross Output Value and Its Composition of Farming, Forestry, Animal Husbandry,Fishery and Service at Current Price by Region（2010）

单位：%　　(%)

区　县	Region	农林牧渔及服务业总产值 Gross Output Value	农业 Farming	林业 Forestry	牧业 Animal Husbandry	渔业 Fishery	农林牧渔服务业 Service of Farming, Forestry, Animal Husbandry and Fishery
全市指数	**Total**	**107.4**	**108.7**	**115.2**	**104.3**	**92.7**	**108.9**
新城区	Xincheng						
碑林区	Beilin						
莲湖区	Lianhu						
灞桥区	Baqiao	107.5	104.3	183.3	117.4	90.7	113.4
未央区	Weiyang	96.4	101.9	115.2	90.1	85.2	98.2
雁塔区	Yanta	95.4	94.0	48.5	96.7	100.0	103.6
阎良区	Yanliang	107.9	107.6	104.3	106.4	96.1	115.4
临潼区	Lintong	107.2	106.4	326.5	106.3	84.2	103.9
长安区	Chang'an	107.3	108.1	106.8	103.9	114.3	112.4
蓝田县	Lantian	107.3	107.3	94.6	109.5	94.7	109.6
周至县	Zhouzhi	111.4	121.9	80.4	91.6	77.7	104.6
户　县	Huxian	107.4	108.4	93.1	104.8	82.9	109.9
高陵县	Gaoling	107.7	111.4	163.8	103.1	97.0	109.3
全市构成	**Total**	**100.0**	**63.4**	**1.2**	**27.7**	**0.6**	**7.2**
新城区	Xincheng						
碑林区	Beilin						
莲湖区	Lianhu						
灞桥区	Baqiao	100.0	72.6	0.4	19.3	1.0	6.7
未央区	Weiyang	100.0	53.6		33.2	4.9	8.2
雁塔区	Yanta	100.0	63.7	0.3	26.1		10.0
阎良区	Yanliang	100.0	72.8	0.3	19.3	0.1	7.6
临潼区	Lintong	100.0	51.2	1.5	39.9	0.4	7.1
长安区	Chang'an	100.0	66.6	0.5	25.0	0.7	7.2
蓝田县	Lantian	100.0	62.7	4.3	25.4	0.7	7.0
周至县	Zhouzhi	100.0	70.6	1.3	21.7	0.2	6.1
户　县	Huxian	100.0	67.1	0.3	24.2	0.3	8.1
高陵县	Gaoling	100.0	52.7	0.3	39.2	0.4	7.4

10-14 主要年份农林牧渔及服务业增加值

Value-Added of Farming, Forestry, Animal Husbandry, Fishery and Service in Representative Years

单位:万元 (10 000 yuan)

年 份 Year	农林牧渔及服务业增加值 Farming,Forestry, Animal Husbandry, Fishery and Service	农 业 Farming	林 业 Forestry	牧 业 Animal Husbandry	渔 业 Fishery	农林牧渔服务业 Service of Farming, Forestry, Animal Husbandry and Fishery
1995	413981	329662	4413	76746	3160	
2000	446481	336777	4323	101353	4028	
2001	458720	342427	4258	108096	3939	
2002	477691	351358	6419	116591	3323	
2003	458378	312849	5473	137236	2820	
2004	582009	393349	6811	164572	2919	14358
2005	660148	444320	6888	169701	3373	35866
2006	704427	465823	8556	177431	3227	49390
2007	825053	538794	8420	210930	4467	62442
2008	1034471	639071	10592	301305	5598	77905
2009	1103793	698043	11958	303594	5913	84285
2010	1400575	935489	14362	349204	6503	95017

10-15 主要年份农林牧渔及服务业增加值指数

Indices of Value-Added of Farming, Forestry, Animal Husbandry, Fishery and Service in Representative Years

年 份 Year	农林牧渔及服务业增加值指数（上年=100）（可比价）Farming,Forestry,Animal Husbandry,Fishery and Service	农 业 Farming	林 业 Forestry	牧 业 Animal Husbandry	渔 业 Fishery	农林牧渔服务业 Service of Farming, Forestry, Animal Husbandry and Fishery
2008	7.6	7.6	12.0	5.8		14.0
2009	6.3	3.6	14.6	11.2	6.3	8.8
2010	6.9	7.9	8.7	4.3	-6.0	8.9

10-16 各区县农林牧渔及服务业增加值（2010年）

Value-Added of Farming, Forestry, Animal Husbandry, Fishery and Service by Region（2010）

单位:万元 (10 000yuan)

区 县	Region	农林牧渔及服务业增加值 Farming,Forestry, Animal Husbandry, Fishery and Service	农 业 Farming	林 业 Forestry	牧 业 Animal Husbandry	渔 业 Fishery	农林牧渔服务业 Service of Farming, Forestry, Animal Husbandry and Fishery
全 市	**Total**	**1400575**	**935489**	**14362**	**349204**	**6503**	**95017**
新城区	Xincheng						
碑林区	Beilin						
莲湖区	Lianhu						
灞桥区	Baqiao	115005	86909	420	20348	728	6600
未央区	Weiyang	24767	13706	4	8082	798	2178
雁塔区	Yanta	21277	13623	54	5200	0	2400
阎良区	Yanliang	142573	104734	273	27450	124	9992
临潼区	Lintong	255840	137546	3422	95890	1003	17980
长安区	Chang'an	244961	188831	1013	37307	1904	15907
蓝田县	Lantian	166373	104311	6778	42932	923	11430
周至县	Zhouzhi	152735	113189	1547	29625	327	8049
户 县	Huxian	155856	106957	469	37506	437	10488
高陵县	Gaoling	121187	65684	382	44865	260	9995

10-17 各区县农林牧渔及服务业增加值指数（2010年）

Indices of Value-Added of Farming, Forestry, Animal Husbandry, Fishery and Service by Region （2010）

（上年=100）（可比价） (preceding year = 100)（At constant prices）

区　县	Region	农林牧渔及服务业增加值指数（上年=100）（可比价） Farming,Forestry,Animal Husbandry,Fishery and Service	农　业 Farming	林　业 Forestry	牧　业 Animal Husbandry	渔　业 Fishery	农林牧渔服务业 Service of Farming, Forestry, Animal Husbandry and Fishery
全　市	**Total**	**106.9**	**107.9**	**108.7**	**104.3**	**94.0**	**108.9**
新城区	Xincheng						
碑林区	Beilin						
莲湖区	Lianhu						
灞桥区	Baqiao	107.3	104.5	149.5	117.4	90.7	113.4
未央区	Weiyang	96.8	102.0	115.2	90.1	85.2	98.2
雁塔区	Yanta	95.4	94.0	48.5	96.7	100.0	103.6
阎良区	Yanliang	107.6	107.2	104.3	106.4	96.1	115.4
临潼区	Lintong	106.9	106.2	280.5	106.3	84.2	103.9
长安区	Chang'an	107.5	107.8	106.8	103.9	114.3	112.4
蓝田县	Lantian	106.8	107.3	92.7	107.8	94.7	109.6
周至县	Zhouzhi	108.0	115.2	66.5	91.6	77.7	104.6
户　县	Huxian	107.3	108.4	85.3	104.8	82.9	109.9
高陵县	Gaoling	107.7	111.5	142.8	102.5	97.0	109.3

10-18 主要年份农作物播种面积

Sown Areas of Farm Crops In Representative Years

单位：万亩 （10 000 mu)

年 份 Year	总播种面积 Total Sown Area	粮 食 Grain Crops	小 麦 Wheat	玉 米 Corn	棉 花 Cotton	油 料 Oil-bearing Crops	蔬 菜 Vegetables
1980	835.43	706.35	324.17	273.14	81.23	10.01	24.02
1985	795.41	704.36	378.20	271.14	21.02	8.01	45.03
1990	816.41	731.42	387.20	282.14	15.02	12.00	51.03
1991	820.41	731.37	389.19	283.14	19.01	13.01	47.03
1992	820.65	715.50	384.60	273.60	26.70	16.20	54.60
1993	821.63	713.49	380.40	273.69	17.66	14.84	63.90
1994	821.10	719.00	375.90	272.40	19.70	13.80	59.90
1995	784.74	690.63	370.41	259.55	11.07	18.57	57.59
1996	797.40	709.00	366.30	286.80	7.70	18.80	55.50
1997	755.78	670.83	367.71	248.79	4.50	15.53	59.36
1998	789.99	705.03	370.17	285.45	3.56	14.69	60.95
1999	793.08	709.95	371.94	294.00	2.85	12.74	60.68
2000	784.94	697.55	369.89	283.70	2.48	13.46	64.35
2001	763.16	678.05	359.19	278.57	2.91	11.87	61.77
2002	751.10	655.59	350.64	271.95	2.63	11.40	67.71
2003	737.06	632.55	336.05	261.89	3.38	11.04	69.44
2004	753.83	630.63	311.52	286.50	4.94	9.74	77.55
2005	757.91	642.75	325.10	287.87	5.40	9.51	83.33
2006	769.49	648.00	313.23	307.89	6.09	8.58	87.03
2007	762.38	637.05	306.98	304.13	6.93	7.41	91.07
2008	756.06	630.31	319.39	286.69	6.35	8.59	93.02
2009	757.11	628.69	318.36	285.20	6.45	8.59	94.83
2010	751.74	621.71	317.18	279.93	6.26	8.98	95.71

10–19 各区县主要农作物播种面积（2010年）

Sown Areas of Major Farm Crops by Region（2010）

单位：万亩 （10 000 mu）

区 县	Region	总播种面积 Total Sown Area	粮 食 Grain Crops	夏 粮 Summer Grain	小 麦 Wheat	秋 粮 Autumn Grain	稻 谷 Rice	玉 米 Corn
合 计	**Total**	**751.74**	**621.71**	**319.87**	**317.18**	**301.84**	**1.62**	**279.93**
新城区	Xincheng							
碑林区	Beilin							
莲湖区	Lianhu							
灞桥区	Baqiao	33.36	24.23	13.97	13.94	10.26		9.28
未央区	Weiyang	10.04	7.41	4.22	4.22	3.19		3.16
雁塔区	Yanta	1.62	0.19	0.14	0.14	0.05		0.05
阎良区	Yanliang	48.95	22.41	11.80	11.80	10.61		10.56
临潼区	Lintong	139.49	118.73	62.95	62.79	55.77	0.78	52.48
长安区	Chang'an	147.29	119.97	62.20	62.16	57.77	0.47	55.95
蓝田县	Lantian	119.10	104.16	51.90	50.87	52.26	0.37	38.70
周至县	Zhouzhi	97.55	87.73	43.34	42.58	44.39		42.92
户 县	Huxian	103.84	92.81	46.66	46.01	46.15		45.88
高陵县	Gaoling	50.50	44.07	22.69	22.69	21.38		20.95

10-20 主要年份农作物产品产量

Yield of Major Farm Crops in Representative Years

单位：万吨 (10 000 ton)

年 份 Year	粮食作物 Grain Crops	夏 粮 Summer Grain	小麦 Wheat	秋 粮 Autumn Grain	稻谷 Rice	玉米 Corn	棉 花 Cotton	油 料 Oil-bearing Crops	油菜籽 Rapeseeds	蔬 菜 Vegetables
1978	132.8	64.2	58.2	68.7	5.1	55.8	2.85	0.09	0.07	45.66
1979	145.7	81.8	74.2	63.9	4.5	53.4	2.63	0.33	0.29	49.11
1980	114.4	56.6	52.2	57.8	4.7	47.7	1.97	0.54	0.50	40.13
1981	116.1	78.7	74.3	37.4	3.4	31.5	1.36	0.76	0.75	34.06
1982	148.9	85.6	82.2	63.3	4.9	55.5	2.88	0.51	0.49	53.71
1983	148.1	81.8	79.6	66.3	4.8	58.5	0.85	0.36	0.34	46.99
1984	157.6	82.4	81.0	75.2	5.0	66.5	1.49	0.46	0.29	75.47
1985	150.1	76.1	74.8	74.0	5.1	65.1	0.49	0.75	0.39	86.44
1986	162.4	91.7	90.1	70.7	4.8	61.8	0.44	1.25	0.82	85.84
1987	171.2	87.0	85.2	84.2	5.0	74.3	0.47	1.57	1.22	95.16
1988	158.0	86.8	84.6	71.1	3.8	61.4	0.42	0.89	0.51	113.50
1989	173.6	93.5	91.2	80.2	4.7	70.4	0.55	1.33	0.94	129.32
1990	172.4	91.7	89.7	80.8	5.5	70.4	0.70	1.35	0.94	119.32
1991	178.8	91.1	89.2	87.7	5.0	77.5	0.97	1.20	0.74	117.41
1992	183.4	101.7	99.6	81.7	4.7	72.3	0.74	1.49	0.87	128.12
1993	190.0	101.1	99.0	88.9	4.9	78.6	0.75	1.40	1.00	145.80
1994	157.4	86.9	84.9	70.5	4.5	61.4	0.65	1.08	0.78	135.26
1995	175.3	99.8	97.4	75.5	3.4	67.8	0.29	2.17	1.90	133.60
1996	187.5	80.1	78.4	107.4	3.4	95.6	0.24	1.83	1.55	138.01
1997	190.5	114.3	112.3	76.3	3.5	69.4	0.17	1.86	1.65	142.11
1998	212.7	104.4	104.0	108.3	3.2	99.1	0.14	1.67	1.36	148.87
1999	204.4	95.5	94.4	108.9	2.9	99.7	0.15	1.30	1.00	153.24
2000	201.9	92.6	91.6	109.3	3.1	100.5	0.14	1.34	0.95	162.14
2001	197.1	98.1	97.2	98.9	2.7	91.3	0.17	1.23	0.90	152.80
2002	192.4	94.5	93.5	97.9	2.1	91.6	0.18	1.22	0.84	169.74
2003	176.3	98.2	96.7	78.2	1.6	72.3	0.22	1.13	0.70	169.67
2004	195.8	97.8	96.0	98.0	1.7	91.6	0.40	1.14	0.84	180.96
2005	205.5	100.0	99.1	105.5	1.6	99.3	0.45	1.16	0.89	195.70
2006	193.5	86.0	85.4	107.4	1.4	101.2	0.48	1.08	0.87	189.30
2007	189.1	77.3	76.7	111.8	1.5	105.6	0.59	0.96	0.77	204.30
2008	214.4	105.9	105.6	108.5	0.9	103.0	0.62	1.15	0.95	221.53
2009	218.2	103.0	102.1	115.2	0.9	109.5	0.63	1.12	0.93	242.41
2010	221.7	106.6	105.8	115.1	0.8	108.9	0.60	1.20	1.00	253.10

10-21 各区县主要农作物产品产量（2010年）

Yield of Major Farm Crops by Region（2010）

单位：万吨 (10 000 tons)

区 县	Region	粮食总产量 Total Yield of Grain Crops	夏 粮 Summer Grain	小 麦 Wheat	秋 粮 Autumn Grain	玉 米 Corn
合 计	**Total**	**221.65**	**106.60**	**105.83**	**115.05**	**108.89**
新城区	Xincheng					
碑林区	Beilin					
莲湖区	Lianhu					
灞桥区	Baqiao	7.28	3.91	3.91	3.37	3.14
未央区	Weiyang	2.68	1.43	1.43	1.25	1.23
雁塔区	Yanta	0.06	0.04	0.04	0.02	0.02
阎良区	Yanliang	9.60	5.00	5.00	4.60	4.58
临潼区	Lintong	40.10	19.87	19.83	20.23	19.04
长安区	Chang'an	41.49	20.21	20.20	21.28	20.61
蓝田县	Lantian	33.53	14.71	14.42	18.82	15.60
周至县	Zhouzhi	28.86	13.94	13.70	14.92	14.42
户 县	Huxian	37.15	17.59	17.40	19.56	19.49
高陵县	Gaoling	20.90	9.90	9.90	11.00	10.76

10-21 续表 continued

单位：万吨 (10 000 tons)

区 县	Region	棉 花 Cotton	油 料 Oil-bearing Crops	油菜籽 Rapeseeds	蔬 菜 Vegetables
合 计	**Total**	**0.59**	**1.17**	**0.95**	**253.1**
新城区	Xincheng				
碑林区	Beilin				
莲湖区	Lianhu				
灞桥区	Baqiao	0.01	0.07	0.06	27.82
未央区	Weiyang		0.01	0.01	5.55
雁塔区	Yanta				4.22
阎良区	Yanliang	0.43	0.01	0.01	52.53
临潼区	Lintong	0.12	0.24	0.16	36.82
长安区	Chang'an		0.26	0.25	51.25
蓝田县	Lantian	0.03	0.3	0.23	14.86
周至县	Zhouzhi		0.19	0.16	15.68
户 县	Huxian		0.09	0.07	25.88
高陵县	Gaoling				18.49

10-22 主要年份农作物单位面积产量

Yield of Farm Crops Per Hectare in Representative Years

单位：公斤/亩 (kg/mu)

年份 Year	粮食作物 Grain Crops	夏粮 Summer Grain	小麦 Wheat	秋粮 Autumn Grain	玉米 Corn	棉花 Cotton	油料 Oil-bearing Crops	油菜籽 Rapeseeds	蔬菜 Vegetables
1990	236	232	232	241	249	46	103	101	2349
1991	245	229	229	264	274	51	94	89	2332
1992	256	259	259	253	264	28	92	101	2344
1993	266	260	260	274	287	42	94	107	2282
1994	219	226	226	211	225	33	79	84	2260
1995	254	263	263	243	261	27	117	128	2320
1996	265	214	214	321	333	32	86	100	2489
1997	284	305	306	257	279	38	76	129	2395
1998	302	278	279	328	347	40	114	121	2443
1999	288	253	254	327	339	52	102	106	2526
2000	289	247	248	338	354	55	102	112	2520
2001	291	270	271	314	328	60	104	113	2474
2002	293	266	267	326	337	70	107	115	2507
2003	279	287	288	269	276	67	102	110	2444
2004	310	308	308	313	320	81	117	129	2333
2005	320	304	305	336	345	84	121	132	2349
2006	299	273	273	323	329	80	125	135	2175
2007	297	250	250	341	347	85	129	132	2245
2008	340	330	331	350	359	97	134	137	2382
2009	347	320	321	375	384	97	131	131	2556
2010	357	333	334	381	389	94	130	131	2644

10-23 各区县主要农作物单位面积产量（2010年）

The Output of Main Crops per Hectare by Region（2010）

单位：公斤/亩 (kg/mu)

区县	Region	粮食作物 Grain Crops	夏粮 Summer Grain	小麦 Wheat	秋粮 Autumn Grain	玉米 Corn
合 计	**Total**	**357**	**333**	**334**	**381**	**389**
新城区	Xincheng					
碑林区	Beilin					
莲湖区	Lianhu					
灞桥区	Baqiao	301	280	280	328	338
未央区	Weiyang	361	339	339	391	391
雁塔区	Yanta	294	275	275	346	346
阎良区	Yanliang	429	424	424	433	434
临潼区	Lintong	338	316	316	363	363
长安区	Chang'an	346	325	325	368	368
蓝田县	Lantian	322	284	283	360	403
周至县	Zhouzhi	329	322	322	336	336
户 县	Huxian	400	377	378	424	425
高陵县	Gaoling	474	436	436	514	513

10-23 续表 continued

单位：公斤/亩 (kg/mu)

区　县	Region	棉　花 Cotton	油　料 Oil-bearing Crops	油菜籽 Rapeseeds	蔬　菜 Vegetables
合　计	**Total**	**94**	**130**	**131**	**2644**
新城区	Xincheng				
碑林区	Beilin				
莲湖区	Lianhu				
灞桥区	Baqiao	55	245	125	3574
未央区	Weiyang		539	259	2505
雁塔区	Yanta				3000
阎良区	Yanliang	94	250	114	3361
临潼区	Lintong	97	194	96	2606
长安区	Chang'an	80	328	180	2200
蓝田县	Lantian	106	254	105	1833
周至县	Zhouzhi		365	157	1921
户　县	Huxian	95	341	182	2943
高陵县	Gaoling				2989

10-24 主要年份林业生产情况

Statistics on Forestry in Representative Years

指　　标	Item	2000	2005	2006	2007	2008	2009	2010
一、营林情况	**Afforestation**							
当年造林面积合计（万亩）	Build Forestry Areas(10 000 mu)	27.47	16.56	12.95	6.17	8.76	15.60	16.10
更新造林面积（万亩）	Reforestation Areas(10 000 mu)	1.08	0.62	0.63	0.65	0.45	0.48	
封山育林面积（万亩）	Hill-closeure for Afforestation Areas (10 000 mu)	18.78	18.65	20.71	23.97	30.19	37.40	55.10
零星四旁植树（万株）	Planting(10 000 plants)	731	1064	1096	1176	952	931	509.20
育苗面积（万亩）	Raise Seedlings Areas(10 000 mu)	2.05	5.99	5.34	6.03	4.72	3.41	11.95
#本年新育	New Seedling of Current Year	1.69	2.54	3.00	3.15	2.19	1.86	1.75
二、主要林产品产量（吨）	**Main Forestry Product(ton)**							
生漆	Lacquer	11	2	4	5	6	5	10
核桃	Walnuts	997	3351	3120	3349	4589	4306	7875
板栗	Chinese Chestnut	744	2076	1944	2153	2728	3122	7736
花椒	Pepper	140	525	507	575	842	689	1420
三、村及村以下采伐木材（万立方米）	**Timber Harvested at or below Village Level（10 000 cu.m)**	**1.62**	**1.87**	**1.41**	**0.96**	**1.23**	**0.97**	**3.30**

注：1.2009年迹地更新面积改为更新造林面积；
　　2.2010年起，根据统计制度要求，林业统计数据取自林业部门。

Note:1.Slash updating areas in 2009 were reforestation areas.
　　2.Since 2010, according to the requirement of statistical system, statistics on forestry were from forestry departments.

10-25 各区县林业生产情况（2010年）

Statistics On Forestry by Region（2010）

区 县	Region	当年造林面积（亩）Build Forestry Areas in The Year (mu)	零星植树（万株）Planting (10 000 plants)	育苗面积（亩）Raise Seedlings Areas (mu)	核桃产量（吨）Output of Walnuts (ton)	板栗产量（吨）Output of Chinese Chestnut (ton)	村及村以下木材采伐量（万立方米）Timber Harvesting at\under Vallage level (10 000 cu.m)
全 市	**Total**	**160980**	**509.20**	**119475**	**7875**	**7736**	**3.30**
新城区	Xincheng						
碑林区	Beilin						
莲湖区	Lianhu						
灞桥区	Baqiao	6390	40.00	1425	250	18	
未央区	Weiyang	465	56.10	2265			
雁塔区	Yanta	885	3.00	3480			
阎良区	Yanliang	4500	30.00	540			0.92
临潼区	Lintong	18900	72.00	975	340	340	
长安区	Chang'an	21075	118.00	7590	320	195	
蓝田县	Lantian	53745	1.10	37200	4500	4663	
周至县	Zhouzhi	32370	75.00	61005	2400	2500	2.12
户 县	Huxian	20655	84.00	4500	65	20	0.26
高陵县	Gaoling	1995	30.00	495			

10-26 主要年份果业生产情况

Statistics on Fruits in Representative Years

指 标	Item	2000	2005	2006	2007	2008	2009	2010
果园面积(万亩)	**Areas of Orchards (10 000 mu)**	**47.86**	**55.55**	**57.68**	**60.86**	**64.31**	**71.08**	**74.95**
苹果园	Apple Orchards	12.15	5.96	5.95	5.94	5.82	5.66	3.55
梨 园	Pears Orchards	5.79	3.01	2.76	2.90	2.82	2.66	2.27
葡萄园	Grapes Orchards	1.89	3.02	3.20	3.18	3.55	4.59	4.83
桃 园	Peach Orchards	3.47	8.66	9.01	8.87	8.75	8.48	7.68
猕猴桃园	Chinese Goosebeery Orchards	16.83	4.33	18.39	21.04	23.61	29.01	34.92
杏 园	Apricot Orchards	0.62	2.50	2.54	2.65	2.78	2.97	3.62
柿子园	Presimmons Orchards	1.96	2.69	2.73	2.97	3.28	3.26	3.16
石榴园	Pomegranate Orchards					3.94	3.61	3.43
水果产量（吨）	**Output of Fruits (ton)**	**343551**	**512869**	**553433**	**605075**	**716902**	**789587**	**847821**
苹 果	Apple	89416	53387	51809	52180	53194	53023	39130
梨	Pears	65459	57059	51517	52869	55945	57929	55122
葡 萄	Grapes	16647	30951	35504	43621	50185	56731	64885
桃	Peach	27010	89755	103142	124393	139058	146651	142051
猕猴桃	Chinese Goosebeery	96640	137853	153678	146301	210393	233296	296023
杏	Apricot					39690	55535	48544
柿 子	Persimmon					28540	34780	35287
石 榴	Pomegranate					43701	42122	40211

10-27 各区县果业生产情况（2010年）

Area and Output of Fruits by Region（2010）

区　县	Region	果园（万亩） Area of Orchards(10 000 mu)	水果产量（吨） Output of Fruits(ton)
全　市	**Total**	**74.95**	**847821**
新城区	Xincheng		
碑林区	Beilin		
莲湖区	Lianhu		
灞桥区	Baqiao	7.13	85565
未央区	Weiyang	0.99	15770
雁塔区	Yanta	0.8	11907
阎良区	Yanliang	2.5	53143
临潼区	Lintong	5.45	64090
长安区	Chang'an	5.53	65277
蓝田县	Lantian	9.45	118046
周至县	Zhouzhi	35.22	298363
户　县	Huxian	4.75	85650
高陵县	Gaoling	3.13	50010

10–28 主要年份畜牧业生产情况

Statistics on Livestock Husbandry in Representative Years

指　　标	Item	2000	2005	2006	2007	2008	2009	2010
一、大牲畜年末总头数(头)	**Large Animals In Stock at Year-end (head)**	**260742**	**322521**	**175435**	**181353**	**204723**	**208358**	**216043**
#能繁殖母畜	Female Animals of Reprductive Ability	137087	176682	105042	110451	132772	136276	144104
#役 畜	Draught Animals	98130	90717	44416	39968	36069	42670	42243
1.牛	Cattle	256073	320773	173834	180200	203596	207237	215072
#能繁殖母畜	Female Animals of Reprductive Ability	136626	176445	104391	109970	132657	136143	144012
当年生仔畜	Newborn Livestock in the Year	69015	72163	39836	43313	41457	39403	40052
肉 牛	Farm Cattle					60490	63804	65447
奶 牛	Dairy Cattle	48164	96498	78056	96400	108164	112071	118747
2.马（匹）	Horses	736	559	527	477	499	515	456
3.驴	Donkeys	476	175	97	108	83	87	67
4.骡	Mutes	3457	1014	977	568	545	519	448
二、猪年末头数（头）	**Hogs in Stock Year-end (head)**	**1284592**	**1472869**	**764579**	**774534**	**864083**	**918734**	**943183**
#能繁殖母猪	Female Hogs of Reprductive Ability	93775	123543	65313	71600	85419	96522	106610
三、羊年末只数（只）	**Sheeps and Goats in Stock at Year-end(head)**	**421103**	**532471**	**221809**	**234900**	**263164**	**279463**	**294539**
1.山 羊	Goats	397121	520354	213981	226810	258287	274359	288738
#奶山羊	Milch Goats	266525	358733	156429	177547	201007	229301	246442
2.绵 羊	Sheeps	23982	12117	7828	8090	4877	5104	5801
四、家禽年末存栏数（万只）	**Poultry in Stock at Year-end (10 000 heads)**	**1623.81**	**1372.56**	**831.25**	**849.12**	**919.91**	**980.83**	**1034.2**
五、年末养蜂箱数（箱）	**Honey (box)**	**20408**	**24287**	**18871**	**18371**	**22124**	**22779**	**22984**

10-29 各区县畜牧业生产情况（2010年）

Statistics On Livestock, Animal Husbandry by Region（2010）

区 县	Region	大牲畜年末头数（头）Large Animals In Stock at Year-end (head)	#能繁殖母畜 Female Animals of Reprductive Ability	役畜 Draught Animals	牛（头）Cattle (head)	奶牛 Dairy Cattle	马（匹）Horses (head)	驴（头）Donkeys (head)
全 市	**Total**	**216043**	**144104**	**42243**	**215072**	**118747**	**456**	**67**
新城区	Xincheng							
碑林区	Beilin							
莲湖区	Lianhu							
灞桥区	Baqiao	14240	8591	886	14224	12764	16	
未央区	Weiyang	6397	4791		6397	6097		
雁塔区	Yanta	345	230		345	267		
阎良区	Yanliang	15823	11375	110	15823	13408		
临潼区	Lintong	73359	57177	7720	73359	65639		
长安区	Chang'an	7683	3212	1105	7025	3685	304	
蓝田县	Lantian	44855	28318	20125	44750	2200	40	30
周至县	Zhouzhi	33923	17649	12102	33898	2909	5	
户 县	Huxian	11953	6957	30	11953	6627		
高陵县	Gaoling	7465	5804	165	7298	5151	91	37

10-29 续表 continued

区 县	Region	骡（头）Mutes (head)	猪（头）Hogs (head)	能繁殖母猪 Female Hogs of Reprductive Ability	羊（只）Sheep and Goats (head)	山羊 Goats	奶山羊 Milch Goats	家禽（万只）Poultry (10 000 head)	蜂（箱）Honey (box)
全 市	**Total**	**448**	**943183**	**106610**	**294539**	**288738**	**246442**	**1034.20**	**22984**
新城区	Xincheng								
碑林区	Beilin								
莲湖区	Lianhu								
灞桥区	Baqiao		50080	4392	12327	11976	10483	44.42	334
未央区	Weiyang		39991	3669	997	997	639	7.35	
雁塔区	Yanta				220	220	200	2.40	
阎良区	Yanliang		34536	4144	45203	45173	45173	49.35	578
临潼区	Lintong		248223	22501	120302	120302	120302	265.00	3700
长安区	Chang'an	354	95140	9895	14462	11698	4759	276.20	3457
蓝田县	Lantian	35	84156	11005	71465	71465	47890	80.00	3120
周至县	Zhouzhi	20	200101	27966	11555	11445	2257	84.34	7653
户 县	Huxian		146201	17220	6458	6458	6314	131.14	4100
高陵县	Gaoling	39	44755	5818	11550	9004	8425	94.00	42

10-30 主要年份畜产品和水产品产量

Output of Livestock Products and Aquatic Products in Representative Years

单位：吨 (ton)

年 份 Year	肉类总产量 Output of Meat	猪 肉 Pork	牛 肉 Beef	羊 肉 Mutton	禽 肉 Poultry
1990	63273	50646	4667	1931	5885
1991	72268	55086	5623	2162	9062
1992	88994	68134	6468	2460	11290
1993	93420	71274	7249	2220	12174
1994	106691	79433	8298	2350	15681
1995	127815	86513	11251	3731	23948
1996	91468	63750	5402	2578	19324
1997	106597	75381	6672	3468	20596
1998	134152	98974	8788	4710	21424
1999	130124	93859	9827	4147	21963
2000	147571	106137	12066	4766	23760
2001	157277	113353	11900	5153	20540
2002	161092	118634	11516	5394	20515
2003	165860	122759	13241	5180	19682
2004	171545	126404	13641	5874	18493
2005	182046	136503	14031	6106	18803
2006	108634	81199	8267	2841	13417
2007	102191	73254	8589	3111	14075
2008	115352	84654	9840	3335	16060
2009	126182	94490	10142	3677	17190
2010	136501	102296	10854	3875	18338

注：2010年起，根据统计制度要求，水产品产量及养殖面积统计数据取自水务部门

Note:Since 2010, according to the requirement of statistical system, statistics of aquatic product output and cultivating area were from water supply departments.

10-30 续表 continued

单位：吨 (ton)

年 份 Year	奶类总产量 Output of Milk	牛 奶 Cow Milk	禽蛋 Poultry Eggs	蜂蜜（公斤） Honey(kg)	水产品 Output of Aquatic Products	养殖面积（万亩） Water Raise Areas (10 000 mu)
1990	82017	50528	55938	1035392	4259	2.55
1991	91006	57700	90558	1022797	4949	2.63
1992	100080	63586	104970	739275	6015	2.80
1993	111070	73897	125244	662049	7132	2.97
1994	145412	99025	146503	547808	7900	3.10
1995	132909	85753	141227	535891	8517	3.21
1996	133372	86103	138044	613290	8910	3.51
1997	150964	98078	156066	713918	10054	3.46
1998	174099	119719	142519	537304	10480	3.40
1999	209144	145191	135981	541613	11061	3.38
2000	245913	176155	138305	460598	11384	3.35
2001	255437	179977	132303	479839	12480	3.17
2002	288009	202826	134336	497530	12017	3.31
2003	336296	245407	128833	537805	9967	2.48
2004	384319	289564	117597	449765	9721	2.46
2005	422229	327961	118115	421052	9370	2.38
2006	471438	374813	97816	414271	11937	1.60
2007	528037	428462	98140	401761	12402	1.38
2008	589697	475681	108515	503031	12487	1.40
2009	618186	498394	116685	528731	13044	1.52
2010	633663	509178	123793	436759	11850	2.24

10-31 各区县主要畜产品和水产品产量（2010年）

Output of Major Livestock Products and Aquatic Products by Region（2010）

单位：吨 (ton)

区 县	Region	肉类总产量 Output of Meat	猪肉 Pork	牛肉 Beef	羊肉 Mutton	禽肉 Poultry
全 市	**Total**	**136501**	**102296**	**10854**	**3875**	**18338**
新城区	Xincheng					
碑林区	Beilin					
莲湖区	Lianhu					
灞桥区	Baqiao	6850	5164	771	127	768
未央区	Weiyang	3617	3415	102	13	87
雁塔区	Yanta	3124	3077	7	3	37
阎良区	Yanliang	4980	3368	453	443	657
临潼区	Lintong	36768	27470	2839	1765	4451
长安区	Chang'an	17807	10808	473	233	5747
蓝田县	Lantian	15647	9833	3380	950	1350
周至县	Zhouzhi	24710	21323	1908	161	1298
户 县	Huxian	16875	13850	656	67	2285
高陵县	Gaoling	6123	3988	265	113	1658

10-31 续表 continued

单位：吨 (ton)

区 县	Region	奶类总产量 Output of Milk	牛奶 Cow Milk	禽蛋 Poultry Eggs	蜂 蜜（公斤） Honey(kg)	水产品 Output of Aquatic Products	养殖面积（亩） Water Raise Areas(mu)
全 市	**Total**	**633663**	**509178**	**123793**	**436759**	**11850**	**22365**
新城区	Xincheng						
碑林区	Beilin						
莲湖区	Lianhu						
灞桥区	Baqiao	63613	56799	5330	8350	1500	2850
未央区	Weiyang	24481	24284	541		2100	1560
雁塔区	Yanta	1250	1150	300			
阎良区	Yanliang	75329	53632	5922	15620	202	255
临潼区	Lintong	339102	283356	31201	110689	1830	4695
长安区	Chang'an	20206	17219	34532	62220	3140	5445
蓝田县	Lantian	36100	9300	9345	46800	900	3660
周至县	Zhouzhi	12926	11862	9412	72660	828	2310
户 县	Huxian	33726	30485	15594	120000	800	1065
高陵县	Gaoling	26930	21091	11616	420	550	525

10-32 主要年份农产品人均占有量

Per Capita Output of Major Farm Products in Representative Years

单位：公斤/人 (kg/person)

年份 Year	粮食 Grain	棉花 Cotton	油料 Oil-bearing Crops	猪牛羊肉 Pork Beef and Mutton	禽蛋 Poultry Eggs	奶类 Milk	水果 Fruits	蔬菜 Vegetables
1978	266.7	5.7	0.2	5.4	0.9	3.3	6.8	91.7
1979	288.6	5.2	0.6	6.7	1.0	4.0	5.1	97.3
1980	223.5	3.8	1.1	5.9	1.2	4.1	6.9	78.4
1981	222.9	2.6	1.5	6.6	1.7	4.7	5.8	65.4
1982	281.5	5.5	1.0	4.9	2.7	5.6	5.9	101.6
1983	276.6	1.6	0.7	4.9	3.2	6.5	5.0	87.8
1984	289.4	2.7	0.8	4.8	6.2	8.7	4.8	138.6
1985	271.4	0.9	1.4	6.8	5.7	10.2	7.6	156.3
1986	288.0	0.8	2.2	7.8	6.4	12.1	9.6	152.2
1987	298.0	0.8	2.7	7.3	6.8	13.8	10.6	165.6
1988	269.7	0.7	1.5	8.0	8.9	15.6	11.1	193.7
1989	290.7	0.9	2.2	8.4	7.6	13.1	10.2	216.5
1990	298.7	1.2	2.1	9.4	9.2	14.2	11.5	196.0
1991	290.6	1.6	2.0	10.2	14.7	14.8	11.7	190.8
1992	294.3	1.2	2.4	12.4	16.8	16.2	17.3	205.6
1993	301.2	1.2	2.2	12.8	19.9	17.6	25.9	231.1
1994	246.1	1.0	1.7	14.1	22.9	22.7	28.0	211.5
1995	270.4	0.5	3.4	15.7	21.8	20.5	37.5	206.1
1996	286.3	0.4	3.2	11.0	21.1	20.4	43.9	210.8
1997	287.8	0.3	2.8	12.9	23.6	22.8	43.3	214.7
1998	318.3	0.2	2.5	16.8	21.3	26.1	50.0	222.8
1999	303.0	0.2	1.9	16.0	20.2	31.0	52.7	227.2
2000	293.5	0.2	1.9	17.9	20.1	35.7	49.9	235.7
2001	283.7	0.2	1.8	18.8	19.0	36.8	48.8	219.9
2002	273.8	0.3	1.7	19.3	19.1	41.0	53.5	241.6
2003	246.0	0.3	1.6	19.7	18.0	46.9	53.6	236.8
2004	270.1	0.6	1.6	20.1	16.2	53.0	63.9	249.6
2005	277.1	0.6	1.6	21.1	15.9	56.9	69.1	263.8
2006	256.9	0.6	1.4	12.3	13.0	62.6	73.5	251.4
2007	247.4	0.8	1.3	11.1	12.8	69.1	79.2	267.3
2008	256.0	0.7	1.4	11.7	13.0	70.4	85.6	264.5
2009	258.7	0.7	1.3	12.8	13.8	73.3	93.6	287.4
2010	261.8	0.7	1.4	13.8	14.6	74.8	100.1	298.9

10-33 主要年份农村经济效益主要指标

Main Indicators of Rural Economic Benefit in Representative Years

年 份 Year	每一农业劳动力创造的 Average Labor Force Production 农林牧渔及服务业总产值（元） Gross Output Value of Farming,Forestry，Animal Husbandry, Fishery and Service (yuan)	粮食（公斤） Grain Crops(kg)	棉花（公斤） Cotton (kg)	油料（公斤） Oil-bearing Crops(kg)	每亩耕地种植业产值（元） Output of Each Unit of Area Planting(yuan)	每百元物耗生产的总产值（元） Output per 100-Yuan of Material Consumed(yuan)
1978	504.7	1024.6	22.0	0.7	104.3	
1979	549.0	1096.5	19.8	2.3	116.0	
1980	483.1	846.1	14.5	4.0	99.2	
1981	502.8	840.5	9.9	5.5	105.4	
1982	631.5	1058.9	20.5	3.6	139.3	
1983	606.5	1053.2	6.1	2.6	124.1	
1984	850.7	1154.2	10.9	3.4	163.6	
1985	1020.1	1134.6	3.7	5.6	183.1	
1986	1132.2	1236.4	3.4	9.5	204.6	
1987	1280.3	1277.2	3.5	11.7	231.5	
1988	1558.4	1148.0	3.0	6.5	273.2	
1989	1605.3	1231.9	3.9	9.5	295.0	
1990	1766.3	1279.1	5.2	10.0	343.4	233.3
1991	1958.8	1326.6	7.2	8.9	380.4	238.4
1992	2093.7	1360.7	5.5	11.1	451.6	241.8
1993	2528.9	1409.7	5.6	10.4	546.8	240.1
1994	3705.0	1167.8	4.8	8.0	762.8	227.6
1995	4953.0	1300.6	2.2	16.1	1106.5	225.9
1996	5154.8	1391.2	1.8	13.6	1224.2	234.5
1997	5493.0	1413.4	1.3	13.8	1283.3	239.2
1998	5615.9	1578.1	1.0	12.4	1374.3	247.0
1999	4826.5	1516.6	1.1	9.7	1175.9	251.7
2000	5091.5	1498.0	1.0	9.9	1161.1	250.2
2001	5328.5	1462.4	1.3	9.1	1221.1	248.6
2002	5617.4	1427.5	1.3	9.1	1272.0	265.9
2003	5761.2	1308.1	1.6	8.4	1332.4	254.3
2004	6885.4	1452.7	3.0	8.5	1434.6	261.7
2005	7737.9	1524.7	3.3	8.6	1642.3	262.9
2006	8415.5	1435.7	3.6	8.0	1756.9	263.1
2007	10165.6	1403.0	4.4	7.1	2037.3	259.8
2008	13306.4	1695.4	4.9	9.1	2447.9	259.6
2009	14674.3	1791.7	5.1	9.2	2737.9	261.6
2010	19480.7	1901.3	5.1	10.0	3753.4	260.9

主 要 统 计 指 标 解 释

农林牧渔及服务业产值 指以货币表现的农、林、牧、渔业全部产品和服务业收入的总量，它反映一定时期内农林牧渔及服务业生产总规模和总成果。农林牧渔及服务业总产值的计算方法通常是按农、林、牧、渔业产品产值加上服务业产值。

粮食产量 指全社会的产量。包括国有经济经营的、集体统一经营的和农民家庭经营的粮食产量，还包括工矿企业办的农场和其他生产单位的产量。粮食除包括稻谷、小麦、玉米、高粱、谷子及其他杂粮外，还包括薯类和豆类。其产量计算方法，豆类按去豆荚后的干豆计算;薯类（包括甘薯和马铃薯，不包括芋头和木薯）按5公斤鲜薯折1公斤粮食计算。城市郊区作为蔬菜的薯类（如马铃薯等）按鲜品计算，并且不作粮食统计。其他粮食一律按脱粒后的原粮计算。

棉花产量 指全社会的产量。包括春播棉和夏播棉。产量按皮棉计算。

油料产量 指全部油料作物的生产量。包括花生、油菜籽、芝麻、向日葵籽、胡麻籽（亚麻籽）和其他油料。不包括大豆、木本油料和野生油料。花生以带壳干花生计算。

水产品产量 指人工养殖的水产品和天然生长的水产品的捕捞量。包括海水的鱼类、虾蟹类、贝类和藻类以及内陆水域的鱼类、虾蟹类和贝类。

猪、牛、羊肉产量 指当年出栏并已屠宰、除去头蹄下水后带骨肉（即胴体重）的重量。

期初（末）畜禽存栏头（只）数 指报告期初（末）农村各种合作经济组织和国营农场、农民个人、机关、团体、学校、工矿企业、部队等单位以及城镇居民饲养的大牲畜、猪、羊、家禽等畜禽的存栏数。

常用耕地 是指耕地总资源中专门种植农作物并经常进行耕种、能够正常收获的土地。包括当年实际耕种的熟地;弃耕、休闲不满三年，随时可以复耕的地;开荒利用三年以上的地。不包括临时种植农作物的坡度在25度以上的陡坡地;在河套、湖畔、库区临时开发的成片或零星土地;也不包括已列为国家和省（区、市）退耕计划但临时耕种的土地。

农作物播种面积 指实际播种或种植有农作物的面积。凡是实际种植有农作物的面积，不论种植在耕地上还是种植在非耕地上，均包括在农作物播种面积中。在播种季节基本结束后，因遭灾而重新改种和补种的农作物面积，也包括在内。

有效灌溉面积 指具有一定的水源，地块比较平整，灌溉工程或设备已经配套，在一般年景下当年能够进行正常灌溉的耕地面积。在一般情况下，有效灌溉面积应等于灌溉工程或设备已经配备，能够进行正常灌溉的水田和水浇地面积之和。

农用化肥施用量 指本年内实际用于农业生产的化肥数量，包括氮肥、磷肥、钾肥和复合肥。化肥施用量要求按折纯量计算数量。折纯量是指把氮肥、磷肥、钾肥分别按含氮、含五氧化二磷、含氧化钾的百分之一百成份进行折算后的数量。复合肥按其所含主要成分折算。

农业机械总动力 指主要用于农、林、牧、渔业的各种动力机械的动力总和。包括耕作机械、排灌机械、收获机械、农用运输机械、植物保护机械、牧业机械、林业机械、渔业机械、农产品加工机械和其他农业机械〔内燃机按引擎马力折成瓦（特）计算、电动机按功率折成瓦（特）计算〕。不包括专门用于乡、镇、村、组办工业、基本建设、非农业运输、科学试验和教学等非农业生产方面用的动力机械与作业机械。

农林牧渔业劳动力 指全社会直接参加农林牧渔业生产活动的劳动力。

Explanatory Notes on Main Statistical Indicators

Gross Output Value of Farming, Forestry, Animal Husbandry, Fishery and Service refers to the total value of products of farming, forestry, animal husbandry, fishery and service, which reflects the total scale and result of agricultural production during a given period. The calculation method of gross output value of agriculture generally obtained value of product and its service of farming, forestry, animal husbandry and fishery.

Grain Output refers to the grain production in the whole country including grains produced by state farms, collective units, industrial enterprises and mines. Grain includes rice, wheat, corn, sorghum, millet and other miscellaneous grains as well as tubers and beans. Output of beans refers to dry beans without pods. The output of tubers (sweet potatoes and potatoes, not including taros and cassava) was converted into that of grain at the ratio 5:1. Tubers supplied as vegetables (such as potatoes) in cities and suburbs are calculated as fresh vegetables and their output is not included in the output of grain. Output of all other grains refers to husked grain.

Cotton Output refers to the cotton production in the whole country including cotton sown in spring and in autumn. Output is measured as the weight of ginned cotton.

Output of Oil-bearing Crops refers to the total production of oil bearing crops of various kinds, including peanuts, (dry, in shell) rapeseeds, sesame, sunflower seeds, flax seeds, and other oil bearing crops. Soybeans, oil-bearing woody plants, and wild oil-bearing crops are not included.

Output of Aquatic Products refers to catches of both artificially cultured and naturally grown aquatic products, including fish, shrimps, crabs and shellfish in sea and inland water as well as seaweed.

Output of Pork, Beef, and Mutton refers to the meat of slaughtered hogs, cattle, sheep and goats with head, feet, and offal taken away.

Number of Livestock or Poultry in Stock at Beginning (or End) refers to the total number of large animals, pigs, sheep, fowls, etc. raised by rural cooperative organizations, state farms, rural individuals, government agencies, schools, industrial and mining enterprises, army, and urban residents at the beginning (or end) of the reference period.

Regularly Cultivated Land refers to farmland among the total land resources which is exclusively used for farming and is under regular cultivation with harvest in normal years. Included are currently cultivated land, land that has been abandoned or put in idle for less than 3 years and could be re-used for cultivation at any time, and new-claimed land that has been put into cultivation for more than 3 years. Excluded under this category are steep slope land over 25 degrees under temporary cultivation, land (large or small plots) that is claimed along river bends, lake sides or banks of reservoirs, as well as land that has been designated under the "Green for Grain" programmes of the state and provincial governments but is still temporarily under cultivation.

Sown Area of Crops refers to area of land sown or transplanted with crops regardless of being in cultivated area or non cultivated area. Area of land re-sown due to natural disasters is also included.

Irrigated Area refers to areas that are effectively irrigated, i.e. level land which has water source and complete sets of irrigation facilities to lift and move adequate water for irrigation purpose under normal conditions. Under normal conditions, irrigated area is the sum of watered fields and irrigated fields where irrigation systems or equipment have been installed for regular irrigation purpose.

Consumption of Chemical Fertilizers in Agriculture refers to the quantity of chemical fertilizers applied in agriculture in the year, including nitrogenous fertilizer, phosphate fertilizer, potash fertilizer, and compound fertilizer. The consumption of chemical fertilizers is required in calculation to convert the gross weight into weight containing 100% effective component (e.g. 100% nitrogen content in nitrogenous fertilizer, 100% phosphorous pentoxide contents in phosphate fertilizer, 100% potassium oxide contents in potash fertilizer). Compound fertilizer is converted with its major component.

Total Power of Farm Machinery refers to total mechanical power of machinery used in farming, forestry, animal husbandry, and fishery, including ploughing,irrigation and drainage, harvesting, transport, plant protection, stock breeding, forestry and fishery. The power of internal combustion engines is required to convert horsepower into watts and the power of electric motors is required to be converted into watts. Machinery employed for non agricultural purposes, such as the machines used in township run and village-run industry, construction, non agricultural transport, scientific experiments and teaching, is excluded.

Labour Force Engaged in Farming, Forestry, Animal Husbandry and Fishery refers to the total laborers who are directly engaged in production of farming, forestry, animal husbandry and fishery.

11 工 业

INDUSTRY

资料整理：赵　晖　王风玲　赵　博　陈小兵　李　玫　王　玥
Data management:Zhao Hui Wang Fengling Zhao Bo Chen Xiaobing Li Mei Wang Yue

第十一部分　工业

一、简要说明

本章资料包括全部工业总产值，规模以上工业企业单位数、总产值、主要经济指标等，由西安市统计局工业处提供。

二、主要指标

规模以上工业企业单位数（个）	1126	比上年减少 5个
#大中型工业企业	203	比上年增加 13个
全部工业增加值（亿元）	1003.57	比上年增长 18.1 %
#规模以上工业增加值	862.28	比上年增长 19.7%

11 INDUSTRY

Ⅰ.Brief Introduction

Data in this chapter reflects Gross Industrial Output Value, number of industrial enterprises above designated size and gross product, primary economic. Data in this chapter are provided and compiled by Industry Division of the Xi'an Bureau of Statistics.

Ⅱ.Major Indicators

		Increase over Preceding Year
Number of Industrial Enterprises Above Designated Size(item)	1126	-5
Large-size and Medium-size Industrial Enterprises	203	13
Value Added of Industry(100 mil. yuan)	1003.57	18.1%
Value Added of Industry Above Designated Size	862.28	19.7%

11-1 主要年份全部工业总产值

Gross Output Value of Industry In Representative Years

单位：万元 （10 000 yuan）

年 份 Year	全部工业总产值 Gross Industrial Output Value	工业总产值指数 (上年=100) Index of Gross Industry Output Value (Preceding Year=100)	国有经济 State-owned Enterprises	集体经济 Collective-owned Enterprises	其他经济类型 Enterprises of Other Ownership
1952	23512	139.6	9917	464	13131
1962	120833	86.8	102103	17599	1131
1965	200416	132.1	183164	17252	
1970	333386	143.5	305303	28083	
1975	385509	106.1	332982	52527	
1978	483262	116.9	405376	77886	
1979	517483	106.6	438850	78633	
1980	531755	101.8	440139	91577	39
1981	524587	98.6	433740	90675	172
1982	549200	107.1	450308	98516	456
1983	603507	112.2	493773	108923	811
1984	674963	112.8	520593	153056	1314
1985	853196	120.4	632702	218893	1601
1986	976326	112.1	706380	267282	2664
1987	1142220	114.2	809186	328701	4341
1988	1429811	116.0	1012268	416217	1326
1989	1653472	106.1	1160877	486754	5814
1990	1771310	107.4	1196777	548605	25928
1991	2002727	110.0	1325242	604495	72990
1992	2300472	112.5	1488541	561369	250562
1993	3045988	121.7	1748145	1071122	226721
1994	3891584	120.6	1960533	1581321	349730
1995	4058952	108.7	2071755	1663536	323661
1996	5338510	133.4	2132140	2836176	370194
1997	5794532	121.8	1915536	2005610	1873386
1998	6738224	117.3	2593405	2077273	2067546
1999	7151528	117.1	2128243	2174220	2849065
2000	6394812	115.3	2749778	2094680	1550354
2001	7361510	116.4	3098431	2380910	1882169
2002	8379363	115.8	3472067	2312923	2594373
2003	9750800	115.1	4149015	1501372	4100413
2004	11853224	118.4	5414952	875412	5562860
2005	13085580	106.3	5916553	674900	6494127
2006	15573516	119.0	7527607	514810	7531099
2007	19798593	122.1	10179303	365329	9253961
2008	23881446	120.6	12479652	441987	10959807
2009	28270652	118.3	14440321	388777	13441554
2010	35628753	126.0	18353877	435206	16839669

11-1 续表 continued

单位：万元 （10 000 yuan）

年　份 Year	轻工业 Ligth Industry	重工业 Heavy Industry	大型工业 Large-size Industry Enterprises	中型工业 Medium-size Industry Enterprlses	小型工业 Small-size Industry Enterprises
1952	20800	2712			
1962	68221	52618			
1965	98631	101785			
1970	124467	208919			
1975	167285	218224	145262	130592	109655
1978	220480	262782	168397	121813	193052
1979	243043	274440	189877	133759	193847
1980	283475	248280	193092	130053	208610
1981	309199	215388	178130	140810	205639
1982	303249	246031	213015	128597	207668
1983	315785	287722	245053	127164	231290
1984	321678	353285	241842	143165	289956
1985	401748	451448	333820	147488	371888
1986	458270	518056	401037	150644	424609
1987	516776	625452	472958	171698	497572
1988	699593	730210	615946	210089	603776
1989	712743	940729	696368	258414	698690
1990	787857	983453	716421	279098	775791
1991	897676	1105051	888052	303151	811524
1992	967104	1333368			
1993	1121957	1924031	1258137	384255	1403596
1994	1578875	2312709	1479613	390233	2021738
1995	1636219	2432733	1575030	371156	2112766
1996	2347887	2990623	1693985	358913	3285612
1997	2700085	3094447	1675521	274888	3844123
1998	3232681	3505543	1821556	308424	4608244
1999	3488547	3662981	1744637	337795	5069096
2000	3121419	3273393	2320973	328494	3745345
2001	3518054	3843456	2656010	368497	4337003
2002	3935764	4443599	3038828	398834	4941701
2003	4028859	5721941	2662073	2027256	5061471
2004	4211592	7641632	3595150	3237701	5020373
2005	4078417	9007163	4640325	3228553	5216702
2006	4510970	11062546	5970535	3414468	6188513
2007	7331719	12466874	8351303	4171131	7276159
2008	6010865	17870581	10472686	5005676	8403084
2009	6636464	21634188	12309192	6186395	9775065
2010	7841869	27786884	15002737	8537140	12088876

11-2 各区县、开发区规模以上工业总产值（2010年）

Gross Output Value of Industrial Enterprises above Designated Size by Region（2010）

单位：亿元 （100 million yuan）

区县名称	Name of District and County	单位数（个） Name of Enterprises (unit)	工业总产值 Gross Industrial Output Value	国有经济 State-owned Enterprises	集体经济 Collective-owned Enterprises	其他经济类型 Enterprises of Other Ownership
新城区	Xingcheng	35	272.13	74.68	0.38	197.07
区属	Under District	27	148.18	71.70	0.38	76.10
碑林区	Beilin	38	108.14	86.80	3.85	17.49
区属	Under District	28	95.52	83.56	3.85	8.11
莲湖区	Lianhu	65	458.30	197.85	1.09	259.36
区属	Under District	57	437.30	192.15	1.09	244.06
灞桥区	Baqiao	148	242.15	21.13	10.90	210.12
区属	Under District	144	225.52	17.02	10.90	197.60
未央区	Weiyang	189	499.88	114.48	7.76	377.64
区属	Under District	87	198.77	111.84	7.76	79.17
雁塔区	Yanta	196	286.19	73.81	2.50	209.88
区属	Under District	62	47.39	6.72	2.50	38.17
阎良区	Yanliang	65	163.55	3.02	1.09	159.44
区属	Under District	55	42.53	1.95	1.09	39.49
临潼区	Lintong	44	222.01	59.92	0.10	161.99
区属	Under District	44	222.01	59.92	0.10	161.99
长安区	Chang'an	111	334.89	18.90	3.58	312.41
区属	Under District	63	34.52	0.65	3.58	30.29
蓝田县	Lantian	26	31.93	5.24	0.62	26.07
县属	Under County	24	27.02	0.33	0.62	26.07
周至县	Zhouzhi	27	11.11		0.72	10.39
县属	Under County	27	11.11		0.72	10.39
户县	Huxian	93	96.89	18.31	2.74	75.84
县属	Under County	92	78.66	18.31	2.74	57.61
高陵县	Gaoling	89	402.98	10.40		392.58
县属	Under County	63	55.37	0.66		54.71
在总计中:	Among of Total:					
高新区	GaoXin	185	511.00	51.44		459.56
经开区	JingKai	124	640.99	18.09		622.90
航空基地	Aviation Industry Base	8	3.37			3.37
航天基地	Aerospace Base	13	43.89	18.63		25.26

11-2 续表 continued

单位：亿元　　　　　　　　　　　　　　　　　　　　　　　　　　　　（100 million yuan）

区县名称	Name of District and County	轻工业 Ligth Industry	重工业 Heavy Industry	大型工业 Large-size Industry Enterprises	中型工业 Medium-size Industry Enterprises	小型工业 Small-size Industry Enterprises
新城区	Xingcheng	58.67	213.46	238.07	25.08	8.98
区属	Under District	57.20	90.98	118.91	20.63	8.64
碑林区	Beilin	14.13	94.01		92.95	15.19
区属	Under District	9.15	86.37		85.47	10.05
莲湖区	Lianhu	58.09	400.21	365.44	57.96	34.90
区属	Under District	58.10	379.20	369.03	34.86	33.41
灞桥区	Baqiao	40.57	201.58	16.55	34.81	190.79
区属	Under District	40.27	185.25	5.01	31.00	189.51
未央区	Weiyang	119.01	380.87	126.29	256.47	117.12
区属	Under District	24.28	174.49	27.33	140.47	30.97
雁塔区	Yanta	53.59	232.60	42.92	157.67	85.60
区属	Under District	9.52	37.87		13.31	34.08
阎良区	Yanliang	25.53	138.02	116.58	1.07	45.90
区属	Under District	25.22	17.31			42.53
临潼区	Lintong	86.97	135.04	66.82	79.37	75.82
区属	Under District	86.97	135.04	66.82	79.37	75.82
长安区	Chang'an	27.88	307.01	241.06	40.62	53.21
区属	Under District	17.55	16.97		4.23	30.29
蓝田县	Lantian	4.29	27.64		16.03	15.90
县属	Under County	4.29	22.73		11.76	15.26
周至县	Zhouzhi	6.94	4.17		0.88	10.23
县属	Under County	6.94	4.17		0.88	10.23
户县	Huxian	40.50	56.39	18.23	41.72	36.94
县属	Under County	40.51	38.15		41.72	36.94
高陵县	Gaoling	17.30	385.68	268.34	49.09	85.55
县属	Under County	17.03	38.34		20.90	34.47
在总计中：	Among of Total:					
高新 区	GaoXin	60.62	450.38	256.65	174.27	80.08
经开区	JingKai	95.00	545.99	369.97	135.60	135.42
航空基地	Aviation Industry Base	0.31	3.06			3.37
航天基地	Aerospace Base	0.54	43.35	15.45	23.98	4.46

11-3 规模以上工业企业主要产品产量

Output of Major Industrial Products Of Enterprises Above Designated Size

产品名称	Name of Products	2010	比上年增长（%）Increase over Preceding Year (%)
铁矿石成品矿（吨）	Iron Ore(ton)	20154	180.3
发电量（万千瓦小时）	Electricity Generation Volume(10 000 kw.h)	969356	17.1
#火电	Thermal Power	951705	16.9
水力发电	Hydroelectric Power	17651	32.3
自来水生产量（万吨）	Tap Water Production (10 000 tons)	31140.3	27.2
大米（吨）	Rice (ton)	66213	88.1
小麦粉（万吨）	Wheat Flour (10 000 tons)	112.3	29.1
精制食用植物油（吨）	Edible Vegetable Oil (ton)	282238	33.3
鲜、冷藏肉(吨)	Fresh/Frozen Meat(ton)	15233	37.3
配混合饲料（吨）	Mixed Feed(ton)	528769	24.4
糕点（吨）	Cake (ton)	5468	19.7
方便面 （吨）	Instant Noodle	88603	30.8
乳制品（吨）	Dairy Products (ton)	1020722	28.9
液体乳	Milk	953264	29.6
罐头（吨）	Canned Food (ton)	2529	15.2
饮料酒（千升）	Beverage Wine (kiloliter)	452353	11.0
白酒（折65度，商品量）	Liquor (as 65 degree, amount of goods)	502	22.4
啤酒	Beer	451851	11.0
软饮料（吨）	Soft Beverage (ton)	722293.00	-6.0
其中： 碳酸饮料 （汽水）	Carbonated Beverage	177574	62.8
果汁和蔬菜汁饮料	Juice and Fruit Beverage	190460	-20.5
包装饮用水类	Canned Drinking Water	92418.00	-47.2
纱（吨）	Yarn (ton)	43210	-7.1
1. 棉纱	Cotton Yarn	27185	7.0
2.棉混纺纱	Blend Fabric	6695.2	-9.6
3. 化学纤维纱	Pure Chemical-Fibre Yarn	9329.2	-31.8
布（万米）	Cloth (10 000 m)	23810.5	7.2
1.棉布	Cotton Cloth	12469.8	-0.6
2. 棉混纺布	Blend Fabric	7801	56.3
3.化学纤维布	Pure Chemical-Fibre Cloth	3540	-24.0
无纺布（无纺织物）（吨）	Non-textile fabrics(Non-extile stuff) (ton)	999	-23.1
服装（万件）	Garment (10 000 units)	1234.6	40.2
梭织服装	Shuttle-Woven Garment	1231.8	40.3
皮革鞋靴（万双）	Leather Shoes (10 000 pairs)	129.2	67.4

11-3 续表1 continued 1

产品名称	Name of Products	2010	比上年增长（%）Increase over Preceding Year (%)
人造板（立方米）	Artificial Board (cu.m)	368957	18.6
纤维板	Fibre Board	368957	18.6
家具（件）	Furniture (unit)	526078	26.6
木质家具	Wooden Furniture	410572	29.5
软体家具	Soft Furniture (inc.: Sofa ,Mattress etc.)	115506	17.3
机制纸及纸板（外购原纸加工除外）（吨）	Machine Made Paper(not including processing of procured base paper)(ton)	495966	4.1
涂布类印刷纸	Coated Printing Paper	2417	-11.8
卫生用纸原纸	Body Paper of Sanitary Paper	85003	-24.3
纸制品（吨）	Paper-Made Products (ton)	79313	25.2
其中：瓦楞纸箱	Corrugated Paper	79313	25.2
多色印刷品（万对开色令）	Colored Printed products(10000 reams)	518.9	-5.9
本册(万本）	book（10000 book)	71.9	-45.9
原油加工量（吨）	Crude Oil Processing (ton)	1741676	3.1
汽油	Petrol	203146	-9.7
柴油	Diesel	456105	1.4
燃料油	Fuel Oil	131293	5.1
石油沥青（吨）	Petroleum pitch (ton)	706493	18.0
液化石油气（吨）	Liquefied Petroleum Gas (ton)	48193	4.0
盐酸（含量31%以上）（吨）	Salt Acid (Content over 31%) (ton)	43862	-3.4
氢氧化钠（烧碱）（折100%）（吨）	Caustic Soda (100%)(ton)	63333	-1.1
碳化钙（电石）（折 300升/千克)（吨）	Calcium Carbide Lonverted into(ton)	56812	8.6
化学农药原料药(折有效成分100%)（吨）	Chemical Pesticide(100% effective content)(ton)	761	-47.2
涂料（吨）	Construction Paint(ton)	14022	19.9
初级形态的塑料（塑料树脂及共聚物）（吨）	Plastic,Resin and Copolymer (ton)	34130	4.6
聚氯乙烯树酯	PVC	34130	4.6
合成洗涤剂（吨）	Synthetic Detergents (ton)	83434	5.1
合成洗衣粉	Washing Power	22875	6.0
化学原料药（吨）	Chemical Medicine (ton)	528	-13.4
中成药（吨）	Traditional Chinese Medicine (ton)	2769	-89.0
塑料制品（吨）	Plastic Product (ton)	139733	15.1
1.塑料薄膜	Plastic Sheet	5086	48.2
农用薄膜	Agricultural Sheet	5086	48.2
2.塑料管及其附件	Plastic Pipe and Accessories	12238	38.3
3.塑料条、棒、型材	Plastic Wicker,Rod and Section Bar	56745	14.9
4.泡沫塑料	Plastic Foam	1964	15.0
5.塑料包装箱及容器	Plastic Package and Container	16184	-13.3

11-3 续表2 continued 2

产品名称	Name of Products	2010	比上年增长（%）Increase over Preceding Year (%)
水泥（万吨）	Cement (10 000 tons)	236.5	9.2
水泥熟料（万吨）	Cement Clinker (10 000 tons)	678.3	42.0
水泥混凝土电杆（根）	Cement Pole(unit)	38992	-38.2
商品混凝土（万立方米）	Ready-mixed Concrete（10 000 cu.m）	1441	28.5
沥青和改性沥青防水卷材（平方米）	Asphalt and Modified Bitumen Membrane(sq.m)	774	7.9
平板玻璃（重量箱）	Plate Glass (wt.cases)	595312	-28.5
钢化玻璃(平方米)	Toughened Glass(sq.m)	568001	-11.6
日用玻璃制品（吨）	Glassware(ton)	6634	61.8
生铁（吨）	Csat iron(ton)	70315	28.0
粗钢（吨）	Thick Steel (ton)	23728	157.0
钢材（吨）	Rolled-steel Final Products (ton)	1107663	0.2
中小型型钢	Rolled-steel Medium and Small	9395	6.9
钢筋	Corrugated Steel Bar	563671	-5.0
盘条(线材)	Wire Rod	516308	8.5
冷轧薄板	Non-hot-roll Thin Steel	3040	9.0
无缝钢管	Seamless Steel Pipe	9141	-41.0
焊接钢管	Welded Steel Pipes	6108	-33.8
铁合金（吨）	Ferroalloy	14830	18.4
铝材（吨）	Aluminum Material (ton)	42258	1.9
黄金（千克）	Gold (kilogramme)	330	-17.5
单晶硅（千克）	Monocrystalline Silicon	800506	114.9
工业锅炉（蒸发量吨）	Industrial Boiler steam(ton)	840	-15.0
发动机（万千瓦）	Engine (10000kw)	128.5	1113.6
汽车发动机（万千瓦）	Motor Engine (10000kw)	128.5	1113.6
金属切削机床（台）	Metal-cutting Machines (unit)	2691	171.0
泵（液体泵）（台）	Pump (Liquid pump)(unit)	2172	41.3
风机（台）	Fan(unit)	1656	132.3
气体压缩机（台）	Gas Compressor(unit)	539	169.7
阀门（吨）	Valves (ton)	819	-6.5
粉末冶金制品（吨）	Powder Melallurgy Products(ton)	242	-36.4
采矿专用设备（吨）	Mining Equipment (ton)	9270	15.3
粮食加工机械（台）	Food Processing Machine(unit)	123	12.8
炼油、化工专用设备（吨）	Oil Refining and Chemical Industry Machine(ton)	581716	80.8

11-3 续表3 continued 3

产品名称	Name of Products	2010	比上年增长（%）Increase over Preceding Year (%)
金属冶炼设备（吨）	Metal Smelting Equipments(ton)	2941	-16.6
金属轧制设备（吨）	Metal-rolling Machine(ton)	20725	-14.1
挖掘、铲土运输机械（台）	Earth-moving Machine(unit)	3193	10.4
铲土运输机械（台）	Earth-moving and Transport Machine(unit)	25	-84.3
混凝土机械（台）	Concrete Machinery(unit)	261	59.1
环境保护专用设备（台、套）	Special Equipment for Environment Protection	161	3.9
大气污染防治设备	Equipment for Preventing Atmospheric Pollution	143	7.5
铁路货车（辆）	Freight(unit)	3120	17.4
汽车（辆）	Motor Vehicle (unit)	652050	28.7
载货汽车	Trucks	123540	59.4
客车	Passenger Vehicles	7278	382.9
大型客车（车长>10)	Buses	3135	108.0
轻型客车（车长<7)	Large(40seats and above)	4143	0.0
其中：基本型乘用车（轿车）	Basic Passenger Vehicles (Cars)	521232	21.9
排气量1.0升及以下	1.0L and Below Gas Displacement	149096	46.1
排气量1.0-1.6升（含1.6升）	1.0L-1.6L Gas Displacement(1.6L included)	313846	14.7
排气量1.6-2.0升（含2.0升）	1.6L-2.0L Gas Displacement(2.0L included)	53205	7.9
排气量2.0-2.5升（含2.5升）	2.0L-2.5L Gas Displacement(2.5L included)	5008	77.5
改装汽车（辆）	Refit Trucks (unit)	3471	27.7
交流电动机（千瓦）	Alternating Current Motor (kw)	4575111	-9.4
变压器（千伏安）	Transformer (kwa)	114611312	3.6
高压开关板（面）	High-voltage Switch Panel(unit)	3363	-2.0
低压开关板（面）	Low-voltage Switch Panel(unit)	23527	55.8
电力电缆（千米）	Electric Power Cables(km)	6205	40.0
通讯及电子网络用电缆（对千米）	Communication Cables(pair km)	2356	-22.7
光缆（光纤通迅电缆）（芯千米）	Cable (Optical Communication Cable) (Core.km)	2053881	-6.9
绝缘制品（吨）	Insulating Products(ton)	5394	26.5
家用电冰箱（台）	Household refrigerator(unit)	107571	16.7
电子计算机整机（台）	Air-conditioner Compressor(unit)	45997	18.0
彩色显像管（只）	Color kinescope (unit)	7040816	-6.8
半导体分立器件（万只）	Semiconductor Discrete Device(10 000units)	24.8	-8.7
电子元件（万只）	Electronic Components(10 000units)	138933.1	217.3
工业自动化调节仪表与控制系统（台、套）	Automatization meter and system (unit)	49237	-29.1
电工仪器仪表（台）	Electronic Instruments and Meters(unit)	264931	-6.9

11-4 主要年份规模以上工业企业主要经济指标

Main Economic Indicators of all Industrial Enterprises above Designated Size In Representative Years

单位：亿元 （100 million yuan）

年　份 Year	企业单位数（个）Number of Enterprises (unit)	工业总产值(现价) Gross Industrial Output Value	工业增加值(现价) Value-added of Industry	从业人员年平均人数（万人）Annual Average Employed Persons (10 000 persons)
1998	793	350.38	99.20	51.71
1999	770	366.59	106.56	45.64
2000	816	417.97	130.18	43.25
2001	785	482.61	149.06	40.12
2002	771	544.78	170.39	38.48
2003	735	638.66	202.74	36.55
2004	1066	830.06	254.17	38.08
2005	902	981.02	314.01	37.92
2006	904	1187.74	370.11	37.94
2007	937	1577.05	499.96	38.55
2008	1032	2007.85	605.25	40.17
2009	1131	2468.27	700.13	43.42
2010	1126	3130.15	862.28	47.11

11-4 续表 continued

单位：亿元 （100 million yuan）

年　份 Year	资产合计 Total Assets	负债合计 Total Liabilities	所有者权益 Owners' Equities	主营业务收入 Revenue from Principal Business	利润总额 Total Profits	利税总额 Total Pre-tax Profits
1998	810.56	548.68	261.88	346.84	-1.26	14.82
1999	853.90	577.94	275.96	346.26	8.26	27.30
2000	958.05	622.46	323.72	420.42	16.11	36.29
2001	1054.36	657.88	384.65	451.62	17.97	40.84
2002	1065.76	643.78	412.27	541.64	25.43	51.31
2003	1195.69	733.04	460.97	645.53	33.82	64.99
2004	1333.91	869.30	464.60	812.46	38.57	74.23
2005	1503.85	977.42	508.82	980.97	28.72	67.25
2006	1651.67	1062.11	578.33	1183.51	61.46	110.23
2007	1940.52	1254.01	686.51	1561.25	106.22	168.54
2008	2426.13	1518.86	907.27	1928.05	84.89	168.63
2009	2913.56	1779.38	1130.76	2384.52	177.20	280.68
2010	3592.13	2069.29	1515.65	3011.09	245.37	373.56

11-5 各区县规模以上工业企业主要经济指标（2010年）

Main Economic Indicators of All Industrial Enterprises Above Designated Size by Region（2010）

单位：亿元

区县名称	Name of District and County	企业单位数（个）Number of Enterprises（unit）	工业总产值（现价）(亿元) Gross Industrial Output Value (At Current Prices) (100 mil.yuan)	从业人员年平均人数（万人）Annual Average Employers (10 000 persons)
新城区	Xingcheng	35	272.13	4.05
区属	Under District	27	148.18	1.36
碑林区	Beilin	38	108.14	0.97
区属	Under District	28	95.52	0.79
莲湖区	Lianhu	65	458.30	7.11
区属	Under District	57	437.30	5.96
灞桥区	Baqiao	148	242.10	4.22
区属	Under District	144	225.52	3.44
未央区	Weiyang	189	499.88	7.23
区属	Under District	87	198.77	2.84
雁塔区	Yanta	196	286.19	6.61
区属	Under District	62	47.39	1.23
阎良区	Yanliang	65	163.55	2.73
区属	Under District	55	42.53	0.51
临潼区	Lintong	44	222.01	1.88
区属	Under District	44	222.01	1.88
长安区	Chang'an	111	334.89	5.35
区属	Under District	63	34.52	1.02
蓝田县	Lantian	26	31.90	0.45
县属	Under County	24	27.02	0.29
周至县	Zhouzhi	27	11.11	0.30
县属	Under County	27	11.11	0.30
户县	Huxian	93	96.89	1.92
县属	Under County	92	78.66	1.44
高陵县	Gaoling	89	402.98	4.29
县属	Under County	63	55.37	0.94

11-5 续表1 continued 1

单位：亿元 （100 million yuan）

区县名称	Name of District and County	资产合计 Total Assets	负债合计 Total Liabilites	所有者权益合计 Total Owners' Equities
新城区	Xingcheng	318.93	221.79	97.07
区属	Under District	134.59	111.46	23.07
碑林区	Beilin	210.33	146.66	63.53
区属	Under District	182.46	132.31	50.01
莲湖区	Lianhu	616.41	272.61	343.66
区属	Under District	532.76	223.99	308.73
灞桥区	Baqiao	145.70	80.50	63.60
区属	Under District	113.46	67.81	43.94
未央区	Weiyang	542.30	302.77	239.41
区属	Under District	186.09	109.36	76.67
雁塔区	Yanta	512.45	257.64	252.93
区属	Under District	55.98	36.80	18.91
阎良区	Yanliang	335.11	224.21	110.04
区属	Under District	16.34	7.05	8.67
临潼区	Lintong	197.79	109.23	86.91
区属	Under District	197.79	109.23	86.91
长安区	Chang'an	225.67	116.98	108.34
区属	Under District	25.86	14.57	10.98
蓝田县	Lantian	38.80	18.00	20.70
县属	Under County	18.34	10.53	7.72
周至县	Zhouzhi	8.72	4.76	3.87
县属	Under County	8.72	4.76	3.87
户县	Huxian	103.38	66.69	36.66
县属	Under County	71.14	50.21	20.89
高陵县	Gaoling	336.51	247.44	88.99
县属	Under County	58.86	34.57	24.32

11-5 续表2 continued 2

单位：亿元 （100 million yuan）

区县名称	Name of District and County	主营业务收入 Revenue from Principal Business	利润总额 Total Profits	利税总额 Total Pre-tax Profits
新城区	Xingcheng	280.38	57.59	70.34
区属	Under District	161.21	52.27	62.09
碑林区	Beilin	107.04	6.46	8.80
区属	Under District	97.02	4.83	6.55
莲湖区	Lianhu	427.63	33.13	54.99
区属	Under District	396.54	32.24	53.83
灞桥区	Baqiao	236.90	24.90	34.90
区属	Under District	220.74	23.01	32.38
未央区	Weiyang	510.58	31.42	60.30
区属	Under District	218.28	11.35	30.04
雁塔区	Yanta	290.15	23.14	37.71
区属	Under District	46.14	3.72	6.00
阎良区	Yanliang	176.88	9.54	11.70
区属	Under District	39.57	1.91	2.64
临潼区	Lintong	183.64	11.01	17.54
区属	Under District	183.64	11.01	17.54
长安区	Chang'an	308.00	25.07	37.98
区属	Under District	31.60	0.61	1.53
蓝田县	Lantian	23.60	4.50	5.60
县属	Under County	19.29	4.05	5.09
周至县	Zhouzhi	9.81	0.42	0.64
县属	Under County	9.81	0.42	0.64
户县	Huxian	89.43	4.08	7.18
县属	Under County	71.60	3.37	5.82
高陵县	Gaoling	367.04	14.08	25.89
县属	Under County	59.96	3.03	6.56

11-6 主要年份规模以上工业企业经济效益指标（2010年）

Indicators of Economic Benefit of Industrial Enterprises Above Designated Size in Representative Years（2010）

年 份 Year	总资产贡献率（%） Ratio of Total Assets to Industrial Output Value (%)	资产负债率（%） Assets-Liability Ratio (%)	流动资产周转次数（次/年） Rate of Annual Turnover Working Capitals (times/year)	成本费用利润率（%） Ratio of Profits to cost (%)	全员劳动生产率（元/人.年） Overall Labor Productivity (yuan/person yea	产品销售率（%） Proportion of Industrial Products Sold (%)
1998		67.7	-266.1	0.9	19185	95.3
1999		67.7	2.5	0.9	22878	95.9
2000		65.0	4.2	1.0	29496	97.1
2001	5.8	62.4	4.1	0.9	38267	96.7
2002	6.2	60.4	5.1	1.1	46940	96.7
2003	7.0	61.3	5.7	1.1	58801	96.3
2004	6.9	65.2	5.0	1.2	66752	97.9
2005	8.4	65.0	3.1	1.3	82815	97.5
2006	7.8	64.3	5.5	1.4	97561	98.2
2007	10.2	64.6	7.3	1.6	129706	96.8
2008	8.6	62.6	4.6	1.5	150641	96.1
2009	11.3	61.1	8.1	1.7	161289	97.6
2010	12.2	57.6	8.8	1.6	188483	97.1

11-7 规模以上工业企业主要经济指标（2010年）

单位：万元

分　组	Item	企业单位数（个） Number of Enterprises (unit)	亏损企业 Loss Making Enterprises	工业总产值（当年价） Gross Industrial Output Value (At Current Prices)
总　计	**Total**	**1126**	**189**	**31301452.6**
#市　区	Urban Area	892	141	25495037.6
按隶属关系分	Grouped by Jurisdiction of Management			
中央企业	Central Enterprises	71	10	9229772.5
省属企业	Provincial Enterprises	87	19	6332658.8
市属企业	Municipal Enterprises	968	160	15739021.3
按登记注册类型分组	Grouped by Registion Status			
内资企业	Domestic Investment Enterprises	990	159	25060320.3
国有经济	State-owned Enterprises	89	23	6845136.0
集体经济	Collective-owned Enterprises	58	9	353441.6
股份合作	Share-holding Corperative	14	1	118878.8
联营企业	Joint Ownership Enterprises	3		72932.7
有限责任公司	Limited Liability Corporations	447	77	13345761.0
国有独资公司	State Sole Funded Enterprises	23	2	2910350.1
其他有限责任公司	Other Limited Liability Corporation	424	75	10435410.9
股份有限公司	Share-holding Corperation Ltd.	72	11	1731545.7
私营企业	Private Enterprises	305	37	2570360.0
其他内资企业	Other Domestic Funded Enterprises	2	1	22264.5
港、澳、台商投资企业	Enterprises with Funds from Hong Kong,Macao and Taiwan	32	8	234685.7
外商投资企业	Enterprises with Foreign Investment	104	22	6006446.6
在总计中:亏损企业	Deficit Enterprises	189	189	1623179.7
按轻重工业分	Grouped by Light Industry and Heavy Industry			
轻工业	Light Industry	333	70	5534662.1
重工业	Heavy Industry	793	119	25766790.5
按企业规模分	Grouped by Size of Enterprises			
大型工业	Large-size	31	1	15002736.9
中型工业	Medium-size	172	26	8537139.7
小型工业	Small-size	923	162	7761576.0
按经济组织类型分	Grouped by Economic Type of Orgnization			
独资企业	Appropratorship	230	41	8664372.9
合作、合伙企业	Partnership	30	3	271771.5
股份有限公司	Corporaton	99	14	2161825.3
有限责任公司	Limited Liability Company	767	131	20203482.9
按工业行业大类分	Grouped by Sector			
煤炭开采和洗选业	Mining and Washing of Coal			
石油和天然气开采业	Extraction of Petroleum and Natural Gas	3		183195.9
黑色金属矿采选业	Mining and Processing of Ferrous Metal Ores	1		200.5
有色金属矿采选业	Mining and Processing of Non-ferrous Metal Ores	1		30017.8
非金属矿采选业	Mining and Processing of Nonmetal Ores			
其他采矿业	Mining of other Ores			

Main Economic Indicators of All Industrial Enterprises Above Designated Size（2010）

（10 000 yuan）

工业销售产值（当年价）Value of Industry Products Sales (At Current Prices)	从业人员年平均人数（人）Annual Average Employers (person)	资产合计 Total Assets	流动资产小计 Total Working Capitals	固定资产小计 Total Fixed Assets	固定资产原价合计 Origing Value of Fixed Assets	累计折旧 Accumulative Total Depreciation
30390547.7	**471141**	**35921319.2**	**21288525.1**	**11448944.6**	**15092993.3**	**5591293.3**
24904474.4	399321	30937376.7	18369975.3	9760947.3	13011138.3	4990704.2
9041679.3	152856	15768415.6	8892061.9	5671650.3	7711777.8	2949614.1
5995558.7	70574	5302202.8	3571255.8	1332343.8	1638970.9	520622.0
15353309.7	247711	14850700.8	8825207.4	4444950.5	5742244.6	2121057.2
24296718.8	398707	31428203.5	18750526.2	9932726.5	13046088.3	4875148.9
6698123.4	91157	10886611.3	5957148.3	4241391.8	5487798.8	1885700.9
332013.6	9265	151757.4	104554.2	41309.9	55842.5	22072.5
126679.1	2310	111544.0	72777.5	17259.1	32543.5	16054.0
65978.7	1659	111151.3	95085.6	8645.6	12798.7	4425.7
12964990.9	215060	15488560.7	10007635.7	4103496.6	5868885.9	2364349.2
2748344.5	63035	4131499.7	2425669.3	1292524.0	1870733.3	772057.4
10216646.4	152025	11357061.0	7581966.4	2810972.6	3998152.6	1592291.8
1671433.4	33292	3054031.1	1522933.0	1041044.2	980752.6	416776.1
2417913.1	45237	1606418.3	981060.1	470781.8	595158.7	162260.4
19586.6	727	18129.4	9331.8	8797.5	12307.6	3510.1
224644.5	6128	357290.7	182528.6	77369.9	145405.9	73465.0
5869184.4	66306	4135825.0	2355470.3	1438848.2	1901499.1	642679.4
1507459.9	42485	2832661.1	1350653.7	1100644.8	1611227.9	555851.7
5517641.3	96866	4182912.0	2154946.1	1429938.3	2237545.4	935835.2
24872906.4	374275	31738407.2	19133579.0	10019006.3	12855447.9	4655458.1
14449650.0	227289	19155412.0	12114381.7	5587198.2	7305454.8	2895181.7
8430468.4	135638	11158710.0	5597337.7	4271636.5	5616443.2	1976533.4
7510429.3	108214	5607197.2	3576805.7	1590109.9	2171095.3	719578.2
8444638.7	119487	12076707.6	6599572.1	4683466.1	6154825.2	2138670.1
266811.9	5856	265707.5	194458.0	39360.3	64819.7	26673.6
2133836.1	38935	3657824.9	1891419.1	1236977.0	1235265.4	481996.6
19545261.0	306863	19921079.2	12603075.9	5489141.2	7638083.0	2943953.0
154535.6	6673	578521.0	370739.6	87118.8	156770.1	69651.4
138.2	120	2358.6	1521.6	669.0	1206.2	542.4
30517.8	525	26335.8	13268.7	7721.3	13410.1	6050.0

11-7 续表1

单位：万元

分组	Item	负债合计 Total Liabilites	流动负债小计 Total Working Liabilities	长期负债小计 Long-term Liabilities
总　　计	**Total**	**20692867.2**	**16283867.7**	**3744298.3**
#市　区	Urban Area	17147446.9	13435405.8	3239403.4
按隶属关系分	Grouped by Jurisdiction of Management			
中央企业	Central Enterprises	9514971.6	6922980.8	2325513.9
省属企业	Provincial Enterprises	3486957.4	2925320.9	355133.0
市属企业	Municipal Enterprises	7690938.2	6435566.0	1063651.4
按登记注册类型分组	Grouped by Registion Status			
内资企业	Domestic Investment Enterprises	18447023.9	14342853.0	3455491.3
国有经济	State-owned Enterprises	6697585.5	4678422.2	1797711.9
集体经济	Collective-owned Enterprises	115352.4	97881.6	5785.3
股份合作	Share-holding Corperative	77400.8	69851.3	7429.1
联营企业	Joint Ownership Enterprises	56228.2	55880.4	
有限责任公司	Limited Liability Corporations	9297285.6	7736491.2	1202627.6
国有独资公司	State Sole Funded Enterprises	1906899.4	1468197.5	257538.4
其他有限责任公司	Other Limited Liability Corporation	7390386.2	6268293.7	945089.2
股份有限公司	Share-holding Corperation Ltd.	1320282.9	951456.1	356071.3
私营企业	Private Enterprises	871984.1	742250.8	85581.1
其他内资企业	Other Domestic Funded Enterprises	10904.4	10619.4	285.0
港、澳、台商投资企业	Enterprises with Funds from Hong Kong,Macao and Taiwan	163980.9	150198.0	13782.7
外商投资企业	Enterprises with Foreign Investment	2081862.4	1790816.7	275024.3
在总计中:亏损企业	Deficit Enterprises	1914554.3	1301498.2	514976.6
按轻重工业分	Grouped by Ligth Industry and Heavy Industry			
轻工业	Light Industry	2156531.7	1814297.3	285771.4
重工业	Heavy Industry	18536335.5	14469570.4	3458526.9
按企业规模分	Grouped by Size of Enterprises			
大型工业	Large-size	10904330.1	8567298.6	1898945.5
中型工业	Medium-size	6684908.4	4906074.1	1625605.6
小型工业	Small-size	3103628.7	2810495.0	219747.2
按经济组织类型分	Grouped by Economic Type of Orgnization			
独资企业	Appropratorship	7262526.3	5155783.0	1868374.4
合作、合伙企业	Partnership	154769.5	145215.4	8994.9
股份有限公司	Corporaton	1670560.2	1187120.3	437443.2
有限责任公司	Limited company	11605011.2	9795749.0	1429485.8
按工业行业大类分	Grouped by Sector			
煤炭开采和洗选业	Mining and Washing of Coal			
石油和天然气开采业	Extraction of Petroleum and Natural Gas	255447.4	212754.8	42692.5
黑色金属矿采选业	Mining and Processing of Ferrous Metal Ores	2873.3	624.8	248.5
有色金属矿采选业	Mining and Processing of Non-ferrous Metal Ores	14368.3	14239.3	129.0
非金属矿采选业	Mining and Processing of Nonmetal Ores			
其他采矿业	Mining of other Ores			

continued 1

(10 000 yuan)

所有者权益合计 Total Owners' Equities	实收资本 Total Capital Hold	主营业务收入 Revenue from Principal Business	主营业务成本 Cost of Principal Business	主营业务税金及附加 Taxes and Other Charges on Principal Business
15156455.2	**5786946.3**	**30110914.0**	**24861921.0**	**274376.9**
13720862.6	4843110.5	24890362.2	20244382.9	261276.0
6252103.3	1838428.5	9470514.3	7643648.0	129549.7
1810143.5	668887.8	5899549.1	5026875.9	15324.3
7094208.4	3279630.0	14740850.6	12191397.1	129502.9
12919659.5	4643423.4	24345572.4	20251471.9	205928.7
4182478.1	1191036.0	6638371.5	5163408.2	129258.6
35071.0	20951.2	341261.1	303273.4	1937.2
34142.8	16188.6	114393.7	101243.3	310.9
54923.1	50290.8	74023.1	59366.0	267.3
6159959.5	2420898.2	13080012.2	11249965.2	49701.5
2224600.1	565389.2	2867819.5	2404348.0	11465.0
3935359.4	1855509.0	10212192.7	8845617.2	38236.5
1726552.1	548529.9	1719078.9	1362422.4	10667.2
719307.9	384491.4	2356290.0	1990881.9	13692.2
7225.0	11037.3	22141.9	20911.5	93.8
193036.1	159613.3	228977.3	164773.6	86.2
2043759.6	983909.6	5536364.3	4445675.5	68362.0
916861.4	927081.3	1596389.3	1486921.0	7199.2
1999718.7	1084496.8	5274829.9	4175992.6	26037.2
13156736.5	4702449.5	24836084.1	20685928.4	248339.7
8248427.5	2223552.3	14324408.9	11691710.1	113108.0
4460763.0	1966773.3	8370071.4	6896798.9	130618.7
2447264.7	1596620.7	7416433.7	6273412.0	30650.2
4803179.5	1586837.0	8391492.8	6540189.7	135426.5
110137.3	89617.4	264321.8	225437.8	979.9
1970622.6	619031.1	2137549.3	1734710.0	12064.1
8272515.8	3491460.8	19317550.1	16361583.5	125906.4
323073.6	191680.0	354020.8	341734.9	5365.1
-514.7	300.0	2357.6	1367.7	42.1
11967.5	5500.0	29617.7	26568.6	53.3

11-7 续表2

单位：万元

分　　组	Item	营业费用 Expenses for Operation	管理费用 Expenses for Management
总　　计	**Total**	**1227386.9**	**1675898.3**
#市　区	Urban Area	1059795.8	1470656.5
按隶属关系分	Grouped by Jurisdiction of Management		
中央企业	Central Enterprises	225993.5	637225.4
省属企业	Provincial Enterprises	361798.0	225938.7
市属企业	Municipal Enterprises	639595.4	812734.2
按登记注册类型分组	Grouped by Registion Status		
内资企业	Domestic Investment Enterprises	758617.9	1457789.1
国有经济	State-owned Enterprises	163110.4	464809.6
集体经济	Collective-owned Enterprises	8933.2	14544.0
股份合作	Share-holding Corperative	4374.9	6198.0
联营企业	Joint Ownership Enterprises	5329.2	6975.9
有限责任公司	Limited Liability Corporations	410609.5	741379.1
国有独资公司	State Sole Funded Corporations	77471.1	196321.7
其他有限责任公司	Other Limited Liability Corporations	333138.4	545057.4
股份有限公司	Share-holding Corperation Ltd.	82581.9	105192.5
私营企业	Private Enterprises	83397.0	117453.5
其他内资企业	Other Domestic Funded Enterprises	281.8	1236.5
港、澳、台商投资企业	Enterprises with Funds from Hong Kong,Macao and Taiwan	34314.8	20058.2
外商投资企业	Enterprises with Foreign Investment	434454.2	198051.0
在总计中:亏损企业	Deficit Enterprises	83546.6	120919.9
按轻重工业分	Grouped by Light Industry and Heavy Industry		
轻工业	Light Industry	530245.1	269693.3
重工业	Heavy Industry	697141.8	1406205.0
按企业规模分	Grouped by Size of Enterprises		
大型工业	Large-size	607604.3	788445.9
中型工业	Medium-size	393069.2	491259.2
小型工业	Small-size	226713.4	396193.2
按经济组织类型分	Grouped by Economic Type of Orgnization		
独资企业	Appropratorship	320593.3	558354.9
合作、合伙企业	Partnership	12113.0	17170.5
股份有限公司	Corporaton	99113.9	126178.0
有限责任公司	Limited company	795566.7	974194.9
按工业行业大类分	Grouped by Sector		
煤炭开采和洗选业	Mining and Washing of Coal		
石油和天然气开采业	Extraction of Petroleum and Natural Gas	1776.6	15225.4
黑色金属矿采选业	Mining and Processing of Ferrous Metal Ores	15.7	451.0
有色金属矿采选业	Mining and Processing of Non-ferrous Metal Ores	753.0	991.6
非金属矿采选业	Mining and Processing of Nonmetal Ores		
其他采矿业	Mining of other Ores		

continued 2

(10 000 yuan)

财务费用 Financial cost	营业利润 Operating Profit	利润总额 Total Profits	亏损企业亏损总额 Total Loss of Deficit Enterprises	利税总额 Total Pre-tax Profits	本年应交增值税 Value Added Tax Payable
250623.4	**2630754.6**	**2453712.7**	**107835.9**	**3735565.3**	**1007475.7**
209117.9	2361377.0	2219228.4	90535.7	3332066.2	851561.8
115901.5	982283.2	1027969.3	25128.5	1427412.5	269893.5
35215.8	273943.2	282657.9	7465.4	521574.7	223592.5
99506.1	1374528.2	1143085.5	75242.0	1786578.1	513989.7
214755.9	2071969.0	1965113.0	78454.5	2935661.1	764619.4
78426.3	814105.5	875757.2	27049.1	1276927.0	271911.2
1759.1	15981.8	13291.3	651.4	23210.4	7981.9
2210.7	2929.4	3107.1	31.3	5224.3	1806.3
-51.8	3587.8	2998.1		4931.7	1666.3
84352.5	816201.8	746268.8	43080.9	1142563.4	346593.1
14987.6	191296.9	218575.2	3347.1	335051.7	105011.5
69364.9	624904.9	527693.6	39733.8	807511.7	241581.6
24396.8	175673.4	184167.3	2489.2	263210.9	68376.4
23654.4	243877.1	139761.4	4909.0	218796.4	65342.8
7.9	-387.8	-238.2	243.6	797.0	941.4
1482.3	12889.2	13355.1	3464.3	24242.7	10801.4
34385.2	545896.4	475244.6	25917.1	775661.5	232054.9
34477.0	-43411.8	-107835.9	107835.9	-55138.8	45497.9
55185.4	508276.0	308864.0	31454.8	561074.3	226173.1
195438.0	2122478.6	2144848.7	76381.1	3174491.0	781302.6
87854.7	1188101.8	1286422.2	9785.4	1888414.7	488884.5
111014.9	801523.2	646958.2	60875.4	1047491.6	269914.7
51753.8	641129.6	520332.3	37175.1	799659.0	248676.5
83689.7	1003423.5	1015803.4	40663.1	1491794.8	340564.9
2587.9	9517.3	9617.1	293.8	16158.8	5561.8
33578.0	242346.3	199824.7	7830.8	288497.7	76608.9
130767.8	1375467.5	1228467.5	59048.2	1939114.0	584740.1
-2199.5	-10516.4	10050.1	1530.4	46157.3	30742.1
184.0	297.2	294.7		700.5	363.7
368.0	2480.9	1014.2		1651.3	583.8

11-7 续表3

单位：万元

分组	Item	企业单位数(个) Number of Enterprises (unit)	亏损企业 Loss Making Enterprises	工业总产值（当年价）Gross Industrial Output Value (At Current Prices)
农副食品加工业	Processing of Food from Agricultural Porducts	59	4	1251391.2
食品制造业	Manufacture of Foods	31	3	780917.8
饮料制造业	Manufacture of Beverages	18	6	605607.0
烟草加工业	Manufacture of Tobacco	1		3714.5
纺织业	Manufacture of Textile	20	5	221369.7
纺织服装、鞋、帽制造业	Manufacture of Textile Wearing Apparel,Footwear and Caps	9	1	103964.7
皮革、毛皮、羽毛(绒)及其制品业	Manufacture of Leather, Fur, Feather (eiderdown) and Related Products	1		15017.6
木材加工及竹、藤、棕、草制品业	Processing of Timber,Manufacture of Wood,Plam and Straw Products	12	3	95318.7
家具制造业	Manufacture of Furniture	7		34534.9
造纸及纸制品业	Manufacture of Paper and Paper Products	27	6	231271.2
印刷业、记录媒介的复制	Printing,Reproduction of Recording Media	26	8	398794.1
文教体育用品制造业	Manufacture of Articles For Cultural,Educational and Sports Activities	2		23722.3
石油加工、炼焦及核燃料加工业	Processing of Petroleum, Cokeing,Processing of Nuclear and Nuclear Fuel	6	1	1337336.1
化学原料及化学制品制造业	Manufacture of Raw Chemical Materials and Chemical Products	49	7	990331.6
医药制造业	Manufacture of Medicines	53	12	1004164.5
化学纤维制造业	Manufacture of Chemical Fibers	3		80430.1
橡胶制品业	Manufacture of Rubber	6		25041.9
塑料制品业	Manufacture of Plastics	36	8	376674.2
非金属矿物制品业	Manufacture of Non-metallic Mineral Products	102	21	1269175.7
黑色金属冶炼及压延加工业	Smelting and Pressing of Ferrous Metals	14	2	378230.2
有色金属冶炼及压延加工业	Smelting and Pressing of Non-ferrous Metals	29	4	545606.5
金属制品业	Manufacture of Metal Products	67	9	366036.6
通用设备制造业	Manufacture of General Purpose Machinery	105	10	1419330.2
专用设备制造业	Manufacture of Special Equipment	119	16	2225921.8
交通运输设备制造业	Manufacture of Transport Equipment	64	2	10188151.1
电气机械及器材制造业	Manufacture of Electric Equipment and Machinery	122	26	3314534.8
通信设备、计算机及其他电子设备制造业	Manufacture of Communication Equipment, Computers and other Electronic Equipment	50	10	1011886.2
仪器仪表及文化办公用	Manufacture of Measuring Instruments and Machinery for Cultural Activity and Office Work	46	7	661713.9
工艺品及其他制造业	Manufacture of Artwork and Other Manufacturing	11	5	77640.6
废弃资源和废旧材料回收加工业	Recycling and Disposal of Waste			
电力、热力的生产和供应业	Production and Supply of Electric Power and Heat Power	14	9	1808939.4
燃气生产和供应业	Gas Mining and Supplying Industry	4		170382.4
水的生产和供应业	Production and Supply of Water	8	4	70886.9

continued 3

(10 000 yuan)

工业销售产值（当年价） Value of Industry Products Sales (At Current Prices)	从业人员年平均人数（人） Annual Average Employers (person)	资产合计 Total Assets	流动资产小计 Total Working Capitals	固定资产小计 Total Fixed Assets	固定资产原价合计 Origing Value of Fixed Assets	累计折旧 Accumulative Total Depreciation
1228171.9	9490	579639.3	370035.8	153917.5	210649.9	66779.8
732223.7	10083	337136.9	167168.2	103672.5	164561.1	67284.3
759874.4	8361	800513.4	348453.4	332948.9	494882.5	163094.4
3713.1	194	9698.8	6641.9	2590.6	4758.0	2167.4
216905.7	15576	201997.9	101563.3	68520.3	108233.1	54169.7
102452.7	2443	76828.4	62524.6	12243.3	14386.6	5524.2
27503.0	979	37505.0	11124.1	26380.9	5045.8	1382.9
81329.6	1684	122633.6	51180.6	58079.7	74752.5	19761.6
32899.4	1739	13797.1	8589.7	3596.3	8323.6	4853.6
219364.5	8705	148313.3	53848.1	87530.7	102376.0	17569.5
391824.7	9049	499078.4	214934.7	179890.8	313219.3	159414.4
23373.1	226	4915.6	1444.0	3471.6	3502.8	175.2
1333324.6	1678	315178.2	182525.5	94196.2	149282.4	55990.0
968212.5	23109	1167916.4	550775.5	450133.4	613128.9	258148.7
961638.5	15212	846962.9	462000.0	208455.0	346452.3	149561.9
82400.4	295	48079.0	23971.4	24004.3	56973.5	33109.8
21870.8	700	13535.2	8257.1	4095.6	6379.5	2283.9
358286.3	6346	373634.9	216571.1	97200.6	135569.7	44009.3
1237238.3	14558	799172.0	417508.6	331205.0	454730.7	138527.0
370534.7	2130	146280.8	94573.5	49138.7	58661.4	10828.0
554003.7	7157	727930.6	403349.8	153414.5	202371.4	54901.9
354202.7	8314	322467.0	229099.0	66644.4	99326.8	36090.1
1332951.1	21915	2058174.7	1599918.3	263564.0	401435.6	154564.7
2102806.1	50030	3414158.9	2259315.6	914878.7	1475835.4	639455.1
9787954.7	135771	11020359.3	7332837.0	2727224.5	3277967.6	1198821.1
3216021.1	47495	4203122.3	3066330.1	1052428.1	1032909.5	383381.3
945158.8	24235	2207780.7	1131809.2	833515.2	732978.3	311989.3
635247.8	18042	1103774.9	703306.2	320728.1	471295.2	213476.2
75475.1	1463	38510.3	21682.8	12395.1	11947.9	5043.9
1808319.2	10651	3177800.2	618444.9	2437593.6	3463802.4	1091113.3
170167.9	2430	343573.1	133317.8	178600.0	202128.8	36342.2
69906.0	3763	153634.7	49893.4	101177.4	223738.4	135234.8

11-7 续表4

单位：万元

分　　组	Item	负债合计 Total Liabilites	流动负债小计 Total Working Liabilities	长期负债小计 Long-term Liabilities
农副食品加工业	Processing of Food from Agricultural Porducts	372426.6	319257.9	14522.7
食品制造业	Manufacture of Foods	166058.5	158708.2	6708.7
饮料制造业	Manufacture of Beverages	447509.6	351475.5	95834.0
烟草加工业	Manufacture of Tobacco	4679.7	4679.7	
纺织业	Manufacture of Textile	99707.0	86224.8	13482.1
纺织服装、鞋、帽制造业	Manufacture of Textile Wearing Apparel,Footwear and Caps	57480.9	49405.6	8070.3
皮革、毛皮、羽毛(绒)及其制品业	Manufacture of Leather, Fur, Feather (eiderdown) and Related Products	23628.0	16049.1	7578.9
木材加工及竹、藤、棕、草制品业	Processing of Timber,Manufacture of Wood,Plam and Straw Products	57009.4	39431.6	17577.8
家具制造业	Manufacture of Furniture	6122.5	6030.9	1.6
造纸及纸制品业	Manufacture of Paper and Paper Products	80453.5	54123.3	15457.1
印刷业、记录媒介的复制	Printing,Reproduction of Recording Media	162899.9	137738.9	25098.3
文教体育用品制造业	Manufacture of Articles For Cultural,Educational and Sports Activities	2464.3	2464.3	
石油加工、炼焦及核燃料加工业	Processing of Petroleum, Cokeing,Processing of Nuclcar and Nuclear Fuel	233193.0	233151.3	41.6
化学原料及化学制品制造业	Manufacture of Raw Chemical Materials and Chemical Products	614879.2	492768.0	75294.6
医药制造业	Manufacture of Medicines	406134.8	366324.9	37524.0
化学纤维制造业	Manufacture of Chemical Fibers	9056.4	9056.4	
橡胶制品业	Manufacture of Rubber	6604.0	6597.1	6.9
塑料制品业	Manufacture of Plastics	235984.1	195278.6	39259.4
非金属矿物制品业	Manufacture of Non-metallic Mineral Products	439959.5	404950.1	31231.2
黑色金属冶炼及压延加工业	Smelting and Pressing of Ferrous Metals	104990.8	102665.0	1200.0
有色金属冶炼及压延加工业	Smelting and Pressing of Non-ferrous Metals	426078.5	335741.9	82318.0
金属制品业	Manufacture of Metal Products	177085.5	148650.1	27981.7
通用设备制造业	Manufacture of General Purpose Machinery	1131437.0	1080878.7	48990.4
专用设备制造业	Manufacture of Special Equipment	1786234.9	1571973.5	204527.1
交通运输设备制造业	Manufacture of Transport Equipment	6737499.1	5619545.5	952492.9
电气机械及器材制造业	Manufacture of Electric Equipment and Machinery	1898578.5	1696618.6	48794.2
通信设备、计算机及其他电子设备制造业	Manufacture of Communication Equipment, Computers and other Electronic Equipment	1200024.1	747287.2	385588.7
仪器仪表及文化办公用	Manufacture of Measuring Instruments and Machinery for Cultural Activity and Office Work	533671.5	438486.3	39754.3
工艺品及其他制造业	Manufacture of Artwork and Other Manufacturing	26604.0	26508.9	34.1
废弃资源和废旧材料回收加工业	Recycling and Disposal of Waste			
电力、热力的生产和供应业	Production and Supply of Electric Power and Heat Power	2726999.1	1163597.2	1467713.1
燃气生产和供应业	Gas Mining and Supplying Industry	172216.0	142020.3	30195.7
水的生产和供应业	Production and Supply of Water	72508.3	48559.4	23948.9

continued 4

(10 000 yuan)

所有者权益合计 Total Owners' Equities	实收资本 Total Capital Hold	主营业务收入 Revenue from Principal Business	主营业务成本 Cost of Principal Business	主营业务税金及附加 Taxes and Other Charges on Principal Business
204260.5	105435.5	1173482.8	1076207.0	2298.7
170847.7	95174.6	688044.7	548253.6	794.1
342801.1	171915.6	697304.1	548107.0	10508.8
5019.1	1514.7	3885.8	2550.0	27.6
101693.6	29852.1	220216.3	193713.3	1313.1
17755.6	11534.1	118894.8	92965.2	2448.0
13877.0	6000.0	24101.0	22135.0	33.2
65624.2	25510.3	76301.2	65491.6	947.8
7199.7	5661.9	33631.1	26035.8	186.0
65499.9	32488.1	213150.3	196992.3	1072.5
336024.3	164470.0	387964.0	274861.3	3070.2
2117.0	1260.0	23346.1	16455.4	202.9
67307.4	51821.6	1244751.7	1044401.2	92967.4
550360.0	221402.6	989429.7	800463.2	3255.3
436827.7	238686.8	903066.1	491729.9	1975.4
39022.6	25400.0	82660.6	70230.9	57.1
6931.1	4566.0	19847.5	14637.7	26.0
135978.9	97249.2	347076.6	295184.3	1386.2
351525.0	182079.3	1207531.2	990777.3	7014.3
41216.4	25719.0	433318.5	384854.7	1043.9
300071.8	159183.2	554568.1	469164.7	2262.5
142355.3	74517.7	345306.3	291638.5	1962.7
921886.2	188033.5	1272382.7	990563.2	7205.5
1623154.1	701240.5	2130126.5	1733412.9	10413.6
4280255.1	1231579.8	9785773.8	8548292.4	82977.3
2303313.6	520413.0	2763715.9	2183798.4	20178.3
1007756.1	392219.1	1026332.5	854592.1	3280.4
566860.8	364916.1	648046.8	512513.5	4529.4
11492.7	10873.3	76868.3	66343.2	76.8
450411.0	275711.4	1992299.9	1474276.9	3630.4
171357.0	121680.0	171261.5	150038.8	1237.4
81126.3	51357.3	70231.5	61568.5	533.6

11-7 续表5

单位：万元

分　组	Item	营业费用 Expenses for Operation	管理费用 Expenses for Management
农副食品加工业	Processing of Food from Agricultural Porducts	34752.8	36845.9
食品制造业	Manufacture of Foods	84717.2	24212.5
饮料制造业	Manufacture of Beverages	86895.7	34273.4
烟草加工业	Manufacture of Tobacco	173.9	1055.0
纺织业	Manufacture of Textile	5137.1	12105.0
纺织服装、鞋、帽制造业	Manufacture of Textile Wearing Apparel,Footwear and Caps	7245.3	7627.2
皮革、毛皮、羽毛(绒)及其制品业	Manufacture of Leather, Fur, Feather (eiderdown) and Related Products	625.3	845.3
木材加工及竹、藤、棕、草制品业	Processing of Timber,Manufacture of Wood,Plam and Straw Products	3362.1	2782.0
家具制造业	Manufacture of Furniture	2180.2	1950.9
造纸及纸制品业	Manufacture of Paper and Paper Products	3113.0	5666.0
印刷业、记录媒介的复制	Printing,Reproduction of Recording Media	9957.9	41990.0
文教体育用品制造业	Manufacture of Articles For Cultural,Educational and Sports Activities	1017.2	1799.1
石油加工、炼焦及核燃料加工业	Processing of Petroleum, Cokeing,Processing of Nuclear and Nuclear Fuel	7783.6	16105.4
化学原料及化学制品制造业	Manufacture of Raw Chemical Materials and Chemical Products	36792.1	81742.4
医药制造业	Manufacture of Medicines	266087.9	57726.0
化学纤维制造业	Manufacture of Chemical Fibers	277.9	1899.2
橡胶制品业	Manufacture of Rubber	954.9	2214.2
塑料制品业	Manufacture of Plastics	15672.1	18475.8
非金属矿物制品业	Manufacture of Non-metallic Mineral Products	42342.7	47272.9
黑色金属冶炼及压延加工业	Smelting and Pressing of Ferrous Metals	4544.9	8912.0
有色金属冶炼及压延加工业	Smelting and Pressing of Non-ferrous Metals	8603.8	35749.8
金属制品业	Manufacture of Metal Products	11878.9	19319.5
通用设备制造业	Manufacture of General Purpose Machinery	47013.4	119273.2
专用设备制造业	Manufacture of Special Equipment	70715.3	193856.3
交通运输设备制造业	Manufacture of Transport Equipment	265460.2	421500.5
电气机械及器材制造业	Manufacture of Electric Equipment and Machinery	139942.5	210976.0
通信设备、计算机及其他电子设备制造业	Manufacture of Communication Equipment, Computers and other Electronic Equipment	33228.3	93892.6
仪器仪表及文化办公用	Manufacture of Measuring Instruments and Machinery for Cultural Activity and Office Work	20857.2	83457.1
工艺品及其他制造业	Manufacture of Artwork and Other Manufacturing	2493.9	2789.9
废弃资源和废旧材料回收加工业	Recycling and Disposal of Waste		
电力、热力的生产和供应业	Production and Supply of Electric Power and Heat Power	52.9	51896.4
燃气生产和供应业	Gas Mining and Supplying Industry	7940.2	12744.7
水的生产和供应业	Production and Supply of Water	3021.2	8274.1

continued 5

(10 000 yuan)

财务费用 Financial cost	营业利润 Operating Profit	利润总额 Total Profits	亏损企业亏损总额 Total Loss of Deficit Enterprises	利税总额 Total Pre-tax Profits	本年应交增值税 Value Added Tax Payable
8612.8	143384.4	33375.5	773.6	47124.4	11450.2
596.8	112581.7	23409.1	9154.1	48511.0	24307.8
7097.5	64778.2	63431.9	4094.8	100753.0	26812.3
10.0	191.6	191.6		470.1	250.9
960.0	8635.3	9123.9	2630.0	16861.6	6424.6
870.6	7953.5	6934.3	90.0	13128.0	3745.7
231.5	992.3	1112.8		1147.3	1.3
957.4	2714.0	7292.2	231.3	12904.2	4664.2
264.6	2541.4	2526.9		4304.1	1591.2
1728.1	7443.3	5713.4	1333.4	10829.3	4043.4
2297.7	65063.4	64133.3	3267.9	87632.0	20428.5
645.2	3310.2	3130.2		4262.7	929.6
3354.4	152280.5	84980.2	60.9	216780.6	38833.0
11438.0	68707.6	73731.5	13869.6	103296.7	26309.9
25389.4	63212.6	71660.0	2173.8	170801.0	97165.6
80.6	10117.3	10112.7		13587.7	3417.9
425.5	1469.2	1359.4		2269.4	884.0
4440.1	17156.0	16815.5	624.6	30082.7	11881.0
6837.3	139396.9	139681.5	3550.1	204292.1	57596.3
2337.7	32301.9	31017.8	951.1	47002.5	14940.8
10333.7	41374.7	39958.8	2002.9	57158.4	14937.1
2258.9	28526.2	21033.9	897.5	32574.3	9577.7
-1838.8	89880.2	119955.2	3133.0	174527.0	47366.3
17038.2	155486.3	161022.5	12794.4	233880.7	62444.6
42945.8	528725.3	570219.6	422.1	876186.4	222989.5
39952.3	241485.5	233574.7	6889.7	392084.1	138331.1
14831.3	88366.0	103301.3	6903.3	125362.7	18781.0
4055.4	30469.8	37894.8	2120.3	101892.0	59467.8
274.2	300.7	304.9	745.9	1516.1	1134.4
44493.5	512023.6	485299.1	26630.1	524113.1	35183.6
-1729.1	18038.6	18107.2		25024.6	5680.0
1080.3	-415.3	1948.0	961.1	6696.4	4214.8

11-8 规模以上国有及国有控股工业企业主要经济指标（2010年）

单位：万元

分 组	Item	企业单位数(个) Number of Enterprises (unit)	亏损企业 Loss Making Enterprises	工业总产值（当年价）Gross Industrial Output Value (At Current Prices)
总 计	**Total**	**219**	**50**	**18150497.5**
按隶属关系分	Grouped by Jurisdiction of Management			
中央企业	Central Enterprises	69	10	9190216.7
省属企业	Provincial Enterprises	39	10	5103017.9
市属企业	Municipal Enterprises	111	30	3857262.9
在总计中:亏损企业	Deficit Enterprises	50	50	603162.4
按轻重工业分	Grouped by Light Industry and Heavy Industry			
轻工业	Light Industry	45	13	970378.7
重工业	Heavy Industry	174	37	17180118.8
按企业规模分	Grouped by Size of Enterprises			
大型工业	Large-size	27	1	12042451.7
中型工业	Medium-size	82	16	4398294.1
小型工业	Small-size	110	33	1709751.7
按工业行业大类分	Grouped by Sector			
煤炭开采和洗选业	Mining and Washing of Coal			
石油和天然气开采业	Extraction of Petroleum and Natural Gas	1		75788.7
黑色金属矿采选业	Mining and Processing of Ferrous Metal Ores			
有色金属矿采选业	Mining and Processing of Non-ferrous Metal Ores			
非金属矿采选业	Mining and Processing of Nonmetal Ores			
其他采矿业	Mining of Other Ores			
农副食品加工业	Processing of Food from Agricultural Porducts	3		42759.0
食品制造业	Manufacture of Foods	3		153759.8
饮料制造业	Manufacture of Beverages	2	1	88906.5
烟草加工业	Manufacture of Tobacco	1		3714.5
纺织业	Manufacture of Textile	7	3	117029.9
纺织服装、鞋、帽制造业	Manufacture of Textile Wearing Apparel, Footwear and Caps	1	1	1410.5
皮革、毛皮、羽毛(绒)及其制品业	Manufacture of Leather, Fur, Feather (eiderdown) and Related Products	1		15017.6
木材加工及竹、藤、棕、草制品业	Processing of Timber,Manufacture of Wood,Plam and Straw Products	1	1	478.3

Economic Indicators of all State-owned and State-holding Share Industrial Enterprises above Designated Size（2010）

（10 000 yuan）

工业销售产值（当年价）Value of Industry Products Sales (At Current Prices)	从业人员年平均人数（人）Annual Average Employers (person)	资产合计 Total Assets	流动资产小计 Total Working Capitals	固定资产小计 Total Fixed Assets	固定资产原价合计 Origing Value of Fixed Assets	累计折旧 Accumulative Total Depreciation
17630620.7	**275716**	**26437028.3**	**15655568.2**	**8607326.9**	**11309602.4**	**4325760.9**
9002663.6	151809	15723640.0	8859641.5	5661491.4	7696036.2	2941256.3
4797567.5	55422	4536638.2	3018165.4	1186382.6	1385062.3	403666.9
3830389.6	68485	6176750.1	3777761.3	1759452.9	2228503.9	980837.7
591866.8	21971	1837549.4	815832.8	789814.1	1166048.5	397366.9
1085641.0	30302	944751.2	454170.8	396397.8	757405.8	422061.8
16544979.7	245414	25492277.1	15201397.4	8210929.1	10552196.6	3903699.1
11554260.1	190300	17789665.4	11338796.2	5096746.2	6774202.1	2708706.4
4392267.4	68839	7275344.8	3416170.6	3113189.2	4020158.3	1459312.6
1684093.2	16577	1372018.1	900601.4	397391.5	515242.0	157741.9
74197.6	4114	437391.1	260593.6	71003.2	121240.3	50237.2
42423.3	761	44472.0	18435.1	25753.1	32162.2	6570.5
151288.0	1421	30775.2	16474.6	12437.8	24692.7	12254.9
203002.8	1487	123657.4	73162.3	22888.0	53349.3	31214.5
3713.1	194	9698.8	6641.9	2590.6	4758.0	2167.4
117289.4	12992	138533.3	71019.1	35693.6	75129.8	46175.7
1151.1	105	1356.0	1163.6	192.4	393.6	201.2
27503.0	979	37505.0	11124.1	26380.9	5045.8	1382.9
575.5	86	4879.4	765.4	4114.0	4917.9	852.8

11-8 续表1

单位：万元

分组	Item	负债合计 Total Liabilites	流动负债小计 Total Working Liabilities	长期负债小计 Long-term Liabilities
总计	**Total**	**15798313.9**	**11994723.4**	**3235611.3**
按隶属关系分	Grouped by Jurisdiction of Management			
中央企业	Central Enterprises	9487959.2	6898539.5	2325513.9
省属企业	Provincial Enterprises	2989364.0	2447048.4	337065.2
市属企业	Municipal Enterprises	3320990.7	2649135.5	573032.2
在总计中:亏损企业	Deficit Enterprises	1283898.2	743864.0	447275.8
按轻重工业分	Grouped by Light Industry and Heavy Industry			
轻工业	Light Industry	396714.0	340618.1	55762.3
重工业	Heavy Industry	15401599.9	11654105.3	3179849.0
按企业规模分	Grouped by Size of Enterprises			
大型工业	Large-size	10260748.3	7977608.7	1845253.7
中型工业	Medium-size	4585683.7	3133752.1	1353732.3
小型工业	Small size	951881.9	883362.6	36625.3
按工业行业大类分	Grouped by Sector			
煤炭开采和洗选业	Mining and Washing of Coal			
石油和天然气开采业	Extraction of Petroleum and Natural Gas	167513.3	124820.7	42692.5
黑色金属矿采选业	Mining and Processing of Ferrous Metal Ores			
有色金属矿采选业	Mining and Processing of Non-ferrous Metal Ores			
非金属矿采选业	Mining and Processing of Nonmetal Ores			
其他采矿业	Mining of Other Ores			
农副食品加工业	Processing of Food from Agricultural Porducts	19588.8	15531.8	4057.0
食品制造业	Manufacture of Foods	16731.0	16731.0	
饮料制造业	Manufacture of Beverages	51585.5	51444.5	141.0
烟草加工业	Manufacture of Tobacco	4679.7	4679.7	
纺织业	Manufacture of Textile	63925.6	50960.8	12964.8
纺织服装、鞋、帽制造业	Manufacture of Textile Wearing Apparel, Footwear and Caps	1084.3	1084.3	
皮革、毛皮、羽毛(绒)及其制品业	Manufacture of Leather, Fur, Feather (eiderdown) and Related Products	23628.0	16049.1	7578.9
木材加工及竹、藤、棕、草制品业	Processing of Timber,Manufacture of Wood,Plam and Straw Products	4147.1	2739.3	1407.8

continued 1

(10 000 yuan)

所有者权益合计 Total Owners' Equities	实收资本 Total Capital Hold	主营业务收入 Revenue from Principal Business	主营业务成本 Cost of Principal Business	主营业务税金及附加 Taxes and Other Charges on Principal Business
10607744.9	**3476134.6**	**17698854.2**	**14676396.9**	**169114.5**
6234340.2	1831792.1	9432597.1	7610836.1	129537.8
1544177.5	501590.6	4567328.5	4003964.9	12565.2
2829227.2	1142751.9	3698928.6	3061595.9	27011.5
553250.1	503210.6	725571.0	728332.3	5657.2
543839.6	303529.2	1058371.9	819212.1	12665.1
10063905.3	3172605.4	16640482.3	13857184.8	156449.4
7526262.7	2024049.3	11647301.6	9553953.3	50500.6
2686277.2	1174891.8	4432033.6	3708078.4	115066.7
395205.0	277193.5	1619519.0	1414365.2	3547.2
269877.9	175771.4	192192.2	199681.6	2966.9
24883.2	12152.7	42008.2	35463.2	102.2
14044.2	14835.1	135836.6	107546.3	88.6
72071.9	31481.5	204347.1	161286.6	8155.0
5019.1	1514.7	3885.8	2550.0	27.6
74410.2	12041.1	121464.0	105513.5	714.1
271.7	581.9	892.6	641.6	5.7
13877.0	6000.0	24101.0	22135.0	33.2
732.3	867.0	575.5	454.1	5.6

11-8 续表2

单位：万元

分　组	Item	营业费用 Expenses for Operation	管理费用 Expenses for Management
总　计	**Total**	**531275.0**	**1113412.2**
按隶属关系分	Grouped by Jurisdiction of Management		
中央企业	Central Enterprises	225587.4	635405.5
省属企业	Provincial Enterprises	157849.4	180223.4
市属企业	Municipal Enterprises	147838.2	297783.3
在总计中:亏损企业	Deficit Enterprises	12747.5	62671.2
按轻重工业分	Grouped by Light Industry and Heavy Industry		
轻工业	Light Industry	56711.6	71311.7
重工业	Heavy Industry	474563.4	1042100.5
按企业规模分	Grouped by Size of Enterprises		
大型工业	Large-size	372603.7	731463.8
中型工业	Medium-size	120735.3	302391.4
小型工业	Small-size	37936.0	79557.0
按工业行业大类分	Grouped by Sector		
煤炭开采和洗选业	Mining and Washing of Coal		
石油和天然气开采业	Extraction of Petroleum and Natural Gas	334.8	9300.2
黑色金属矿采选业	Mining and Processing of Ferrous Metal Ores		
有色金属矿采选业	Mining and Processing of Non-ferrous Metal Ores		
非金属矿采选业	Mining and Processing of Nonmetal Ores		
其他采矿业	Mining of Other Ores		
农副食品加工业	Processing of Food from Agricultural Porducts	1873.7	1937.1
食品制造业	Manufacture of Foods	21200.2	5847.5
饮料制造业	Manufacture of Beverages	11990.3	4689.8
烟草加工业	Manufacture of Tobacco	173.9	1055.0
纺织业	Manufacture of Textile	2086.7	7773.9
纺织服装、鞋、帽制造业	Manufacture of Textile Wearing Apparel, Footwear and Caps	32.5	374.9
皮革、毛皮、羽毛(绒)及其制品业	Manufacture of Leather, Fur, Feather (eiderdown) and Related Products	625.3	845.3
木材加工及竹、藤、棕、草制品业	Processing of Timber,Manufacture of Wood,Plam and Straw Products	52.8	158.6

continued 2

(10 000 yuan)

财务费用 Financial cost	营业利润 Operating Profit	利润总额 Total Profits	亏损企业亏损总额 Total Loss of Deficit Enterprises	利税总额 Total Pre-tax Profits	本年应交增值税 Value Added Tax Payable
151520.4	**1512429.9**	**1515280.1**	**62748.4**	**2242445.2**	**558050.6**
115715.9	979536.8	1025524.0	25128.5	1423889.4	268827.6
18692.9	215112.6	225638.0	3369.5	357259.8	119056.6
17111.6	317780.5	264118.1	34250.4	461296.0	170166.4
25297.0	-55914.8	-62748.4	62748.4	-34378.4	22712.8
4985.9	115531.8	97868.3	8258.9	154930.4	44397.0
146534.5	1396898.1	1417411.8	54489.5	2087514.8	513653.6
67952.3	999346.9	1095886.6	9785.4	1513231.0	366843.8
71219.7	329022.8	302556.1	40452.5	541451.4	123828.6
12348.4	184060.2	116837.4	12510.5	187762.8	67378.2
-2276.7	-20675.5	-625.6	1530.4	14641.6	12300.3
1039.0	1645.1	1649.8		2691.6	939.6
24.6	21319.0	1035.3		4518.9	3395.0
273.3	20958.4	21162.1	175.2	37798.3	8481.2
10.0	191.6	191.6		470.1	250.9
345.3	5716.0	6518.3	1888.2	10635.8	3403.4
0.1	-90.0	-90.0	90.0	-27.5	56.8
231.5	992.3	1112.8		1147.3	1.3
-0.3	-95.3	-95.3	95.3	-37.1	52.6

11-8 续表3

单位：万元

分　组	Item	企业单位数（个）Number of Enterprises (unit)	亏损企业 Loss Making Enterprises	工业总产值（当年价）Gross Industrial Output Value (At Current Prices)
家具制造业	Manufacture of Furniture			
造纸及纸制品业	Manufacture of Paper and Paper Products			
印刷业、记录媒介的复制	Printing,Reproduction of Recording Media	6	1	264643.3
文教体育用品制造业	Manufacture of Articles For Cultural,Educational and Sports Activities			
石油加工、炼焦及核燃料加工业	Processing of Petroleum, Cokeing,Processing of Nuclear and Nuclear Fuel	2		1300650.0
化学原料及化学制品制造业	Manufacture of Raw Chemical Materials and Chemical Products	13	4	466973.9
医药制造业	Manufacture of Medicines	5		79752.1
化学纤维制造业	Manufacture of Chemical Fibers	1		77970.9
橡胶制品业	Manufacture of Rubber			
塑料制品业	Manufacture of Plastics	3		143436.5
非金属矿物制品业	Manufacture of Non-metallic Mineral Products	14	3	79416.0
黑色金属冶炼及压延加工业	Smelting and Pressing of Ferrous Metals	3	1	105727.8
有色金属冶炼及压延加工业	Smelting and Pressing of Non-ferrous Metals	9	1	241008.2
金属制品业	Manufacture of Metal Products	10	3	80806.8
通用设备制造业	Manufacture of General Purpose Machinery	9	2	774557.2
专用设备制造业	Manufacture of Special Equipment	34	5	1542955.6
交通运输设备制造业	Manufacture of Transport Equipment	27	1	7312004.9
电气机械及器材制造业	Manufacture of Electric Equipment and Machinery	16	5	2056163.6
通信设备、计算机及其他电子设备制造业	Manufacture of Communication Equipment, Computers and other Electronic Equipment	18	4	657756.1
仪器仪表及文化办公用	Manufacture of Measuring Instruments and Machinery for Cultural Activity and Office Work	12	3	467901.4
工艺品及其他制造业	Manufacture of Artwork and Other Manufacturing	1		2966.9
废弃资源和废旧材料回收加工业	Recycling and Disposal of Waste			
电力、热力的生产和供应业	Production and Supply of Electric Power and Heat Power	10	8	1789202.0
燃气生产和供应业	Gas Mining and Supplying Industry	1		141371.5
水的生产和供应业	Production and Supply of Water	5	3	66368.0

continued 3

(10 000 yuan)

工业销售产值（当年价） Value of Industry Products Sales (At Current Prices)	从业人员年平均人数（人） Annual Average Employers (person)	资产合计 Total Assets	流动资产小计 Total Working Capitals	固定资产小计 Total Fixed Assets	固定资产原价合计 Origing Value of Fixed Assets	累计折旧 Accumulative Total Depreciation
260601.0	4637	273434.5	137071.1	112733.9	210759.4	114611.5
1296523.0	1491	281690.5	157407.9	87493.5	139986.9	53393.4
451726.5	16556	788082.0	311629.8	378445.0	510628.5	223147.4
76887.0	1687	44635.5	24669.4	15354.7	25869.5	10514.8
79920.2	230	46233.3	22721.8	23408.3	56379.9	32971.6
143485.4	2854	239008.8	133808.6	56576.2	77840.7	22949.5
75943.4	2657	104944.4	67684.6	27797.1	41056.8	13815.2
106061.9	953	49137.5	38304.6	10707.8	11578.0	1776.4
231025.9	3615	433309.0	189546.7	100578.9	114239.9	19180.4
78688.3	1685	85418.5	56952.9	20328.5	25457.8	6088.6
712185.8	9090	1629026.2	1316058.7	152154.6	237050.6	92387.0
1441951.5	35412	2672143.5	1729528.2	768185.5	1251436.2	554022.0
6942692.2	96866	9578824.8	6466990.4	2253642.8	2837632.5	1071960.0
2041981.3	31437	3219244.1	2350679.8	861400.4	757294.4	282314.2
618937.7	15591	1732875.1	887580.2	624242.6	469542.4	234308.1
452115.7	13628	875835.5	535522.5	278255.7	419413.1	196927.4
3004.0	23	2128.0	1957.0	23.0	40.0	17.0
1789202.0	9701	3149496.1	608019.4	2424198.4	3445757.8	1086463.9
141157.0	2007	276488.3	119742.1	126081.1	152433.0	26351.9
65387.1	3457	126804.5	40312.8	84665.3	203515.4	131503.5

11-8 续表4

单位：万元

分　组	Item	负债合计 Total Liabilites	流动负债小计 Total Working Liabilities	长期负债小计 Long-term Liabilities
家具制造业	Manufacture of Furniture			
造纸及纸制品业	Manufacture of Paper and Paper Products			
印刷业、记录媒介的复制	Printing,Reproduction of Recording Media	65703.5	58200.7	7440.3
文教体育用品制造业	Manufacture of Articles For Cultural,Educational and Sports Activities			
石油加工、炼焦及核燃料加工业	Processing of Petroleum, Cokeing,Processing of Nuclear and Nuclear Fuel	212933.7	212892.0	41.6
化学原料及化学制品制造业	Manufacture of Raw Chemical Materials and Chemical Products	411780.6	329563.5	43514.8
医药制造业	Manufacture of Medicines	25480.5	25109.5	161.0
化学纤维制造业	Manufacture of Chemical Fibers	7886.3	7886.3	
橡胶制品业	Manufacture of Rubber			
塑料制品业	Manufacture of Plastics	170005.1	139245.6	29703.5
非金属矿物制品业	Manufacture of Non-metallic Mineral Products	80955.0	74480.9	4004.8
黑色金属冶炼及压延加工业	Smelting and Pressing of Ferrous Metals	38287.0	38287.0	
有色金属冶炼及压延加工业	Smelting and Pressing of Non-ferrous Metals	260441.9	191080.1	69361.7
金属制品业	Manufacture of Metal Products	55391.4	42945.7	12445.7
通用设备制造业	Manufacture of General Purpose Machinery	923074.5	884355.5	38719.0
专用设备制造业	Manufacture of Special Equipment	1427413.7	1245805.1	178243.8
交通运输设备制造业	Manufacture of Transport Equipment	6028085.4	4967229.5	897600.1
电气机械及器材制造业	Manufacture of Electric Equipment and Machinery	1387108.0	1216509.5	22436.8
通信设备、计算机及其他电子设备制造业	Manufacture of Communication Equipment, Computers and other Electronic Equipment	987977.2	595261.9	329728.6
仪器仪表及文化办公用	Manufacture of Measuring Instruments and Machinery for Cultural Activity and Office Work	444941.0	355415.0	34224.4
工艺品及其他制造业	Manufacture of Artwork and Other Manufacturing	571.0	510.0	
废弃资源和废旧材料回收加工业	Recycling and Disposal of Waste			
电力、热力的生产和供应业	Production and Supply of Electric Power and Heat Power	2700585.2	1153290.9	1454947.1
燃气生产和供应业	Gas Mining and Supplying Industry	155518.2	128771.0	26747.2
水的生产和供应业	Production and Supply of Water	61291.4	43842.5	17448.9

continued 4

(10 000 yuan)

所有者权益合计 Total Owners' Equities	实收资本 Total Capital Hold	主营业务收入 Revenue from Principal Business	主营业务成本 Cost of Principal Business	主营业务税金及附加 Taxes and Other Charges on Principal Business
207731.0	87411.5	259228.6	171645.4	2603.9
54079.3	39981.0	1206330.9	1010039.6	92910.4
376301.1	147095.8	472746.4	380999.3	1905.1
15154.9	21393.7	64948.8	40587.6	158.5
38347.0	24800.0	79920.2	67791.0	51.6
69003.5	41941.0	137406.3	116363.1	719.1
23526.2	23710.5	73007.8	63021.0	718.6
10850.5	11000.0	134695.3	118447.2	173.4
171867.0	68755.9	206784.8	167551.9	443.8
28261.9	25503.7	66304.4	57961.8	274.9
705951.3	58486.3	647927.8	478360.2	3839.2
1240449.6	509788.3	1459240.5	1204708.6	7238.0
3549199.2	1018043.8	7145021.5	6270801.4	19208.4
1832136.0	236842.7	1685845.6	1299899.6	15794.3
744897.7	220168.1	695701.1	575651.9	2409.2
428240.2	282726.7	455759.4	376812.6	3331.1
1557.0	1000.0	2633.0	2352.0	7.0
448520.8	256882.9	1973179.2	1456444.0	3577.6
120970.1	100000.0	141157.0	123673.6	1155.8
65513.1	45357.3	65712.6	58013.2	495.7

11-8 续表5

单位：万元

分　　组	Item	营业费用 Expenses for Operation	管理费用 Expenses for Management
家具制造业	Manufacture of Furniture		
造纸及纸制品业	Manufacture of Paper and Paper Products		
印刷业、记录媒介的复制	Printing,Reproduction of Recording Media	6928.8	29063.2
文教体育用品制造业	Manufacture of Articles For Cultural,Educational and Sports Activities		
石油加工、炼焦及核燃料加工业	Processing of Petroleum, Cokeing,Processing of Nuclear and Nuclear Fuel	7212.6	13043.6
化学原料及化学制品制造业	Manufacture of Raw Chemical Materials and Chemical Products	15869.9	60282.5
医药制造业	Manufacture of Medicines	5895.7	3389.6
化学纤维制造业	Manufacture of Chemical Fibers	151.0	1752.3
橡胶制品业	Manufacture of Rubber		
塑料制品业	Manufacture of Plastics	8350.2	7183.4
非金属矿物制品业	Manufacture of Non-metallic Mineral Products	3237.7	4691.1
黑色金属冶炼及压延加工业	Smelting and Pressing of Ferrous Metals	2368.0	4852.5
有色金属冶炼及压延加工业	Smelting and Pressing of Non-ferrous Metals	2151.4	20232.1
金属制品业	Manufacture of Metal Products	1961.3	4220.8
通用设备制造业	Manufacture of General Purpose Machinery	21213.2	86393.3
专用设备制造业	Manufacture of Special Equipment	41382.0	145736.7
交通运输设备制造业	Manufacture of Transport Equipment	226897.4	356761.2
电气机械及器材制造业	Manufacture of Electric Equipment and Machinery	106701.6	139197.9
通信设备、计算机及其他电子设备制造业	Manufacture of Communication Equipment, Computers and other Electronic Equipment	23848.5	71297.2
仪器仪表及文化办公用	Manufacture of Measuring Instruments and Machinery for Cultural Activity and Office Work	8619.8	62237.6
工艺品及其他制造业	Manufacture of Artwork and Other Manufacturing	101.0	101.0
废弃资源和废旧材料回收加工业	Recycling and Disposal of Waste		
电力、热力的生产和供应业	Production and Supply of Electric Power and Heat Power	23.3	51439.5
燃气生产和供应业	Gas Mining and Supplying Industry	7361.8	11804.7
水的生产和供应业	Production and Supply of Water	2629.6	7749.7

continued 5

(10 000 yuan)

财务费用 Financial cost	营业利润 Operating Profit	利润总额 Total Profits	亏损企业亏损总额 Total Loss of Deficit Enterprises	利税总额 Total Pre-tax Profits	本年应交增值税 Value Added Tax Payable
391.9	51999.2	51585.2	102.6	69559.2	15370.1
3218.6	152102.2	84789.8		215146.7	37446.5
5876.1	14894.6	20269.8	13780.0	40139.4	17964.5
743.9	7100.8	6284.4		8941.8	2498.9
80.6	10095.8	10057.2		13475.8	3367.0
2290.4	7684.4	8172.9		13678.8	4786.8
476.7	1546.5	2074.4	340.7	5698.5	2905.5
546.9	11259.4	11248.4	929.4	21137.0	9715.2
5443.6	26395.8	25337.3	637.2	32369.7	6588.6
478.5	7489.3	3302.9	543.9	4568.8	991.0
-6317.5	41796.2	79004.1	1622.3	112004.4	29161.1
12796.8	95266.7	102221.8	10364.1	150150.6	40690.8
36819.4	314659.0	355673.9	366.6	527703.3	152821.0
30723.4	137759.3	137803.1	1349.5	249446.7	95849.3
12276.6	69361.6	71673.8	916.9	87013.1	12930.1
3085.5	7979.1	14010.7	567.1	69926.9	52585.1
	148.0	148.0		221.3	66.3
44362.7	510220.8	483443.6	26523.6	521385.3	34364.1
-2118.8	16106.2	16353.2		22617.7	5108.7
698.3	-1396.6	966.6	925.4	5421.2	3958.9

11-9 规模以上股份制工业企业主要经济指标（2010年）

单位：万元

分组	Item	企业单位数（个）Number of Enterprises (unit)	亏损企业 Loss Making Enterprises	工业总产值（当年价）Gross Industrial Output Value (At Current Prices)
总　　计	**Total**	**866**	**145**	**22365308.2**
#市　区	Urban Area	688	103	17068472.2
按隶属关系分	Grouped by Jurisdiction of Management			
中央企业	Central Enterprises	34	4	3818830.1
省属企业	Provincial Enterprises	59	9	5985308.7
市属企业	Municipal Enterprises	773	132	12561169.4
在总计中:亏损企业	Deficit Enterprises	145	145	804356.9
按轻重工业分	Grouped by Light Industry and Heavy Industry			
轻工业	Light Industry	259	51	4379504.9
重工业	Heavy Industry	607	94	17985803.3
按企业规模分	Grouped by Size of Enterprises			
大型工业	Large-size	24	1	11122769.0
中型工业	Medium-size	119	15	4754065.2
小型工业	Small-size	723	129	6488474.0
按工业行业大类分	Grouped by Sector			
煤炭开采和洗选业	Mining and Washing of Coal			
石油和天然气开采业	Extraction of Petroleum and Natural Gas	3		114453.0
黑色金属矿采选业	Mining and Processing of Ferrous Metal Ores	1		200.5
有色金属矿采选业	Mining and Processing of Non-ferrous Metal Ores	1		30017.8
非金属矿采选业	Mining and Processing of Nonmetal Ores			
其他采矿业	Mining of Other Ores			
农副食品加工业	Processing of Food from Agricultural Porducts	50	4	1131497.9
食品制造业	Manufacture of Foods	25	2	308376.9
饮料制造业	Manufacture of Beverages	11	2	497490.0
烟草加工业	Manufacture of Tobacco			
纺织业	Manufacture of Textile	13	2	148353.0
纺织服装、鞋、帽制造业	Manufacture of Textile Wearing Apparel, Footwearand Caps	5		81085.1
皮革、毛皮、羽毛(绒)及其制品业	Manufacture of Leather, Fur, Feather (eiderdown) and Related Products			
木材加工及竹、藤、棕、草制品业	Processing of Timber,Manufacture of Wood,Plam and Straw Products	9	2	91382.1

Main Indicators of Share-holding Corporation Industrial Enterprises Above Designated Size（2010）

（10 000 yuan）

工业销售产值（当年价）Value of Industry Products Sales (At Current Prices)	从业人员年平均人数（人）Annual Average Employers (person)	资产合计 Total Assets	流动资产小计 Total Working Capitals	固定资产小计 Total Fixed Assets	固定资产原价合计 Origing Value of Fixed Assets	累计折旧 Accumulative Total Depreciation
21679097.1	**345798**	**23578904.1**	**14494495.0**	**6726118.2**	**8873348.4**	**3425949.6**
16686116.3	281488	19080321.1	11740089.0	5331801.1	7200009.7	2944765.3
3673211.9	90866	7765443.3	4885977.0	2018114.5	3046740.6	1373440.7
5660221.7	58842	4763185.4	3279995.2	1203750.8	1481239.0	467324.8
12345663.5	196090	11050275.4	6328522.8	3504252.9	4345368.8	1585184.1
739180.3	25177	1530466.7	827411.6	495062.4	747422.9	279916.5
4388200.0	75768	3404151.9	1743060.9	1165936.2	1841818.5	762164.3
17290897.1	270030	20174752.2	12751434.1	5560182.0	7031529.9	2663785.3
10649437.0	169308	12512844.4	7934583.7	3547687.0	4742959.1	1835741.4
4736019.5	92711	6339186.7	3507008.8	1859484.4	2346162.5	1008175.6
6293640.6	83779	4726873.0	3052902.5	1318946.8	1784226.8	582032.6
85810.7	2703	145891.2	113318.5	17468.8	37347.9	19879.1
138.2	120	2358.6	1521.6	669.0	1206.2	542.4
30517.8	525	26335.8	13268.7	7721.3	13410.1	6050.0
1098480.4	8231	495528.7	312661.4	141617.9	191873.9	59865.5
304140.4	5788	162383.4	52502.6	56650.7	78874.5	25440.0
646884.5	5893	661907.8	299845.5	268321.6	389451.3	122119.9
146995.1	13368	162555.1	84411.8	56839.1	89179.0	46796.7
80857.9	1955	71399.9	58587.0	10764.2	12198.6	4815.3
77296.0	1480	115997.5	48922.0	53702.2	69318.9	18656.6

11-9 续表1

单位：万元

分组	Item	负债合计 Total Liabilites	流动负债小计 Total Working Liabilities	长期负债小计 Long-term Liabilities
总计	**Total**	**13275571.4**	**10982869.3**	**1866929.0**
#市区	Urban Area	10077595.9	8300401.6	1543484.5
按隶属关系分	Grouped by Jurisdiction of Management			
中央企业	Central Enterprises	4539278.3	3695464.2	744457.1
省属企业	Provincial Enterprises	3081175.8	2624520.9	301456.5
市属企业	Municipal Enterprises	5655117.3	4662884.2	821015.4
在总计中:亏损企业	Deficit Enterprises	1017752.1	804737.0	118414.0
按轻重工业分	Grouped by Light Industry and Heavy Industry			
轻工业	Light Industry	1761804.4	1482411.5	233949.4
重工业	Heavy Industry	11513767.0	9500457.8	1632979.6
按企业规模分	Grouped by Size of Enterprises			
大型工业	Large-size	7306240.2	6041928.9	1024296.8
中型工业	Medium-size	3396840.7	2611313.7	663491.2
小型工业	Small-size	2572490.5	2329626.7	179141.0
按工业行业大类分	Grouped by Sector			
煤炭开采和洗选业	Mining and Washing of Coal			
石油和天然气开采业	Extraction of Petroleum and Natural Gas	89979.5	89979.5	
黑色金属矿采选业	Mining and Processing of Ferrous Metal Ores	2873.3	624.8	248.5
有色金属矿采选业	Mining and Processing of Non-ferrous Metal Ores	14368.3	14239.3	129.0
非金属矿采选业	Mining and Processing of Nonmetal Ores			
其他采矿业	Mining of Other Ores			
农副食品加工业	Processing of Food from Agricultural Porducts	313273.4	260632.4	14273.3
食品制造业	Manufacture of Foods	80777.2	74460.7	5795.3
饮料制造业	Manufacture of Beverages	389079.5	315186.8	73692.7
烟草加工业	Manufacture of Tobacco			
纺织业	Manufacture of Textile	74516.8	66212.2	8304.5
纺织服装、鞋、帽制造业	Manufacture of Textile Wearing Apparel, Footwearand Caps	55124.5	47207.1	7917.4
皮革、毛皮、羽毛(绒)及其制品业	Manufacture of Leather, Fur, Feather (eiderdown) and Related Products			
木材加工及竹、藤、棕、草制品业	Processing of Timber,Manufacture of Wood,Plam and Straw Products	51102.3	35085.0	16017.3

continued 1

（10 000 yuan）

所有者权益合计 Total Owners' Equities	实收资本 Total Capital Hold	主营业务收入 Revenue from Principal Business	主营业务成本 Cost of Principal Business	主营业务税金及附加 Taxes and Other Charges on Principal Business
10243138.4	**4110491.9**	**21455099.4**	**18096293.5**	**137970.5**
8944401.2	3286182.1	16729335.9	13891136.0	126216.8
3226164.4	1040606.8	4133690.2	3482883.9	13255.2
1678607.8	586488.8	5539922.1	4728051.1	13365.4
5338366.2	2483396.3	11781487.1	9885358.5	111349.9
512172.1	556424.0	732660.3	683913.7	3060.6
1617344.9	860583.7	4163219.9	3317052.7	21044.0
8625793.5	3249908.2	17291879.5	14779240.8	116926.5
5206604.2	1589947.1	10609992.3	9063012.3	86024.1
2932028.2	1212738.9	4691352.1	3827298.6	26364.8
2104506.0	1307805.9	6153755.0	5205982.6	25581.6
55911.6	17708.6	167301.4	145366.9	2445.3
-514.7	300.0	2357.6	1367.7	42.1
11967.5	5500.0	29617.7	26568.6	53.3
179303.1	95773.9	1054551.9	970388.2	1880.2
81606.1	60921.4	279818.5	233267.0	751.9
262625.7	95584.3	576550.5	463779.3	8620.1
87685.7	14783.6	148867.0	129615.3	864.4
14683.5	9929.2	96194.2	75997.7	2245.5
64895.2	24049.1	72267.4	61713.4	934.7

11-9 续表2

单位：万元

分 组	Item	营业费用 Expenses for Operation	管理费用 Expenses for Management
总 计	**Total**	**894680.6**	**1100372.9**
#市 区	Urban Area	746331.2	909259.2
按隶属关系分	Grouped by Jurisdiction of Management		
中央企业	Central Enterprises	103138.2	347646.0
省属企业	Provincial Enterprises	350915.4	181806.6
市属企业	Municipal Enterprises	440627.0	570920.3
在总计中:亏损企业	Deficit Enterprises	36201.9	76950.4
按轻重工业分	Grouped by Light Industry and Heavy Industry		
轻工业	Light Industry	400968.2	208953.2
重工业	Heavy Industry	493712.4	891419.7
按企业规模分	Grouped by Size of Enterprises		
大型工业	Large-size	446363.6	511228.4
中型工业	Medium-size	265420.0	279919.1
小型工业	Small-size	182897.0	309225.4
按工业行业大类分	Grouped by Sector		
煤炭开采和洗选业	Mining and Washing of Coal		
石油和天然气开采业	Extraction of Petroleum and Natural Gas	1776.6	6852.7
黑色金属矿采选业	Mining and Processing of Ferrous Metal Ores	15.7	451.0
有色金属矿采选业	Mining and Processing of Non-ferrous Metal Ores	753.0	991.6
非金属矿采选业	Mining and Processing of Nonmetal Ores		
其他采矿业	Mining of Other Ores		
农副食品加工业	Processing of Food from Agricultural Porducts	31431.0	32586.0
食品制造业	Manufacture of Foods	27485.7	14888.7
饮料制造业	Manufacture of Beverages	62193.6	22844.8
烟草加工业	Manufacture of Tobacco		
纺织业	Manufacture of Textile	2619.8	8053.0
纺织服装、鞋、帽制造业	Manufacture of Textile Wearing Apparel, Footwearand Caps	5288.4	5223.7
皮革、毛皮、羽毛(绒)及其制品业	Manufacture of Leather, Fur, Feather (eiderdown) and Related Products		
木材加工及竹、藤、棕、草制品业	Processing of Timber,Manufacture of Wood,Plam and Straw Products	3278.4	2577.9

continued 2

(10 000 yuan)

财务费用 Financial cost	营业利润 Operating Profit	利润总额 Total Profits	亏损企业亏损总额 Total Loss of Deficit Enterprises	利税总额 Total Pre-tax Profits	本年应交增值税 Value Added Tax Payable
164345.8	**1617813.8**	**1428292.2**	**66879.0**	**2227611.7**	**661349.0**
134032.9	1407308.8	1256929.9	50225.5	1916313.1	533166.4
40314.9	240125.4	275007.1	8741.7	367846.9	79584.6
30016.1	260924.9	260658.6	5212.9	487448.5	213424.5
94014.8	1116763.5	892626.5	52924.4	1372316.3	368339.9
16652.6	-66142.6	-66879.0	66879.0	-46277.6	17540.8
49373.2	398097.8	259803.2	17656.0	466849.5	186002.3
114972.6	1219716.0	1168489.0	49223.0	1760762.2	475346.7
62962.6	572979.7	607304.5	8255.0	990593.6	297265.0
58677.7	474494.0	369326.9	29804.9	556403.6	160711.9
42705.5	570340.1	451660.8	28819.1	680614.5	203372.1
148.6	11072.7	11580.5		33051.1	19025.3
184.0	297.2	294.7		700.5	363.7
368.0	2480.9	1014.2		1651.3	583.8
6479.8	139376.8	29256.8	773.6	41500.1	10363.1
1258.3	38620.7	8458.1	357.8	16653.0	7443.0
6714.7	59649.2	59403.5	2635.4	88768.9	20745.3
423.5	8585.4	9208.0	560.3	14741.8	4669.4
704.1	7410.3	6418.6		11588.6	2924.5
944.6	2766.9	7345.1	136.0	12841.7	4561.9

11-9 续表3

单位：万元

分组	Item	企业单位数（个）Number of Enterprises (unit)	亏损企业 Loss Making Enterprises	工业总产值（当年价）Gross Industrial Output Value (At Current Prices)
家具制造业	Manufacture of Furniture	5		28658.3
造纸及纸制品业	Manufacture of Paper and Paper Products	21	6	166689.8
印刷业、记录媒介的复制	Printing,Reproduction of Recording Media	21	5	363663.5
文教体育用品制造业	Manufacture of Articles For Cultural, Educational and Sports Activities	1		18807.8
石油加工、炼焦及核燃料加工业	Processing of Petroleum, Cokeing,Processing of Nuclear and Nuclear Fuel	4		538028.7
化学原料及化学制品制造业	Manufacture of Raw Chemical Materials and Chemical Products	39	5	912249.6
医药制造业	Manufacture of Medicines	48	12	887224.9
化学纤维制造业	Manufacture of Chemical Fibers	2		78789.4
橡胶制品业	Manufacture of Rubber	5		13435.6
塑料制品业	Manufacture of Plastics	25	7	203211.2
非金属矿物制品业	Manufacture of Non-metallic Mineral Products	80	19	1047840.9
黑色金属冶炼及压延加工业	Smelting and Pressing of Ferrous Metals	10	2	265672.0
有色金属冶炼及压延加工业	Smelting and Pressing of Non-ferrous Metals	25	3	482966.0
金属制品业	Manufacture of Metal Products	49	8	272238.5
通用设备制造业	Manufacture of General Purpose Machinery	75	8	645996.3
专用设备制造业	Manufacture of Special Equipment	97	12	1514433.1
交通运输设备制造业	Manufacture of Transport Equipment	47	2	9744566.4
电气机械及器材制造业	Manufacture of Electric Equipment and Machinery	99	23	1291894.8
通信设备、计算机及其他电子设备制造业	Manufacture of Communication Equipment, Computers and other Electronic Equipment	39	9	781566.0
仪器仪表及文化办公用	Manufacture of Measuring Instruments and Machinery for Cultural Activity and Office Work	36	5	423230.2
工艺品及其他制造业	Manufacture of Artwork and Other Manufacturing	6	2	21604.7
废弃资源和废旧材料回收加工业	Recycling and Disposal of Waste			
电力、热力的生产和供应业	Production and Supply of Electric Power and Heat Power	5	3	25290.7
燃气生产和供应业	Gas Mining and Supplying Industry	4		170382.4
水的生产和供应业	Production and Supply of Water	5	2	64011.1

continued 3

(10 000 yuan)

工业销售产值（当年价）Value of Industry Products Sales (At Current Prices)	从业人员年平均人数（人）Annual Average Employers (person)	资产合计 Total Assets	流动资产小计 Total Working Capitals	固定资产小计 Total Fixed Assets	固定资产原价合计 Origing Value of Fixed Assets	累计折旧 Accumulative Total Depreciation
27923.6	1444	10438.5	7070.1	2996.0	7498.2	4506.9
159387.7	6789	117581.7	40603.3	70590.2	82895.6	14736.1
356963.6	7574	436923.6	184172.3	165292.8	273528.0	133781.5
18431.6	180	3099.6	1009.0	2090.6	2018.6	72.0
538017.3	444	109841.5	81457.7	16594.8	18336.7	2645.7
892732.4	20454	1059862.9	479536.4	418606.7	582580.3	243462.3
841061.1	12317	732782.0	398627.6	172850.1	282262.8	117732.2
80732.6	253	47041.5	23227.4	23710.9	56607.5	33021.2
10496.7	590	12135.2	7867.1	3285.6	5496.5	2210.9
183578.6	2933	133285.8	80102.5	40632.0	57787.1	19718.5
1024954.4	10769	631858.2	353832.8	246794.7	345262.5	111216.7
258309.1	1652	102029.2	60417.2	39343.4	48512.7	9568.4
492759.2	6704	703819.8	383897.2	149544.1	190718.7	47119.6
265634.4	6108	248449.0	178823.7	50071.0	77039.5	29896.0
638449.0	12354	632710.4	448342.7	136744.8	199191.8	73090.7
1432433.3	38933	2329436.2	1430364.7	719012.2	1202019.7	543051.8
9379162.0	124770	10249058.0	6889903.7	2459703.4	2971018.8	1078411.9
1202957.6	16463	1023733.3	762191.1	190568.4	271489.9	97057.1
721083.5	17137	1728891.1	907151.5	693652.1	544123.3	251903.0
402579.1	10713	643281.9	413650.9	168394.9	251586.1	107978.2
20859.6	808	16340.8	9345.5	6124.8	8447.9	3119.8
25290.7	806	281042.2	190986.5	65260.5	95641.1	30380.6
170167.9	2430	343573.1	133317.8	178600.0	202128.8	36342.2
64011.1	3110	137330.6	43557.2	91899.4	214295.9	130760.8

11-9 续表4

单位：万元

分组	Item	负债合计 Total Liabilites	流动负债小计 Total Working Liabilities	长期负债小计 Long-term Liabilities
家具制造业	Manufacture of Furniture	5100.3	5100.3	
造纸及纸制品业	Manufacture of Paper and Paper Products	59838.2	44525.1	14842.0
印刷业、记录媒介的复制	Printing,Reproduction of Recording Media	134054.4	118270.5	15783.7
文教体育用品制造业	Manufacture of Articles For Cultural, Educational and Sports Activities	2005.3	2005.3	
石油加工、炼焦及核燃料加工业	Processing of Petroleum, Cokeing,Processing of Nuclear and Nuclear Fuel	68265.2	68265.2	
化学原料及化学制品制造业	Manufacture of Raw Chemical Materials and Chemical Products	534606.6	424970.0	64125.0
医药制造业	Manufacture of Medicines	370468.1	331926.6	36255.7
化学纤维制造业	Manufacture of Chemical Fibers	8416.8	8416.8	
橡胶制品业	Manufacture of Rubber	6014.0	6007.1	6.9
塑料制品业	Manufacture of Plastics	66680.8	56598.8	8635.9
非金属矿物制品业	Manufacture of Non-metallic Mineral Products	341744.2	314997.0	23179.2
黑色金属冶炼及压延加工业	Smelting and Pressing of Ferrous Metals	72624.6	71498.8	1000.0
有色金属冶炼及压延加工业	Smelting and Pressing of Non-ferrous Metals	402601.9	316369.7	78213.7
金属制品业	Manufacture of Metal Products	132486.4	110222.0	21859.4
通用设备制造业	Manufacture of General Purpose Machinery	298414.4	266239.1	30607.4
专用设备制造业	Manufacture of Special Equipment	1125604.3	989362.9	127267.3
交通运输设备制造业	Manufacture of Transport Equipment	6302633.5	5254244.0	901148.9
电气机械及器材制造业	Manufacture of Electric Equipment and Machinery	545739.8	520786.2	24682.8
通信设备、计算机及其他电子设备制造业	Manufacture of Communication Equipment, Computers and other Electronic Equipment	921332.6	580583.1	323956.2
仪器仪表及文化办公用	Manufacture of Measuring Instruments and Machinery for Cultural Activity and Office Work	340949.7	282699.3	2840.6
工艺品及其他制造业	Manufacture of Artwork and Other Manufacturing	8099.0	8097.4	1.6
废弃资源和废旧材料回收加工业	Recycling and Disposal of Waste			
电力、热力的生产和供应业	Production and Supply of Electric Power and Heat Power	220894.1	115532.6	12766.0
燃气生产和供应业	Gas Mining and Supplying Industry	172216.0	142020.3	30195.7
水的生产和供应业	Production and Supply of Water	63686.4	40503.4	23183.0

continued 4

（10 000 yuan）

所有者权益合计 Total Owners' Equities	实收资本 Total Capital Hold	主营业务收入 Revenue from Principal Business	主营业务成本 Cost of Principal Business	主营业务税金及附加 Taxes and Other Charges on Principal Business
4863.4	4111.9	28767.6	21997.3	157.5
55460.9	26812.8	148008.2	137125.9	650.9
302715.1	147342.7	352880.3	253659.8	1981.9
760.0	760.0	18431.6	12614.5	106.8
26898.6	8500.0	454350.3	419843.4	27.6
522579.4	201882.0	907404.2	736454.3	3014.0
358313.5	207217.3	781958.2	427931.8	1874.2
38624.7	25100.0	80992.8	68754.4	53.7
6121.1	3756.0	8473.4	6629.0	26.0
66562.9	50779.9	180820.4	152250.4	523.2
283061.9	152529.4	1001576.5	840849.5	5505.3
29331.9	15471.0	292459.5	262731.2	823.9
299437.6	152635.7	493196.8	414025.8	1905.4
112936.4	50327.1	257399.7	211925.2	1611.9
330931.5	147978.2	619446.3	511331.4	3069.0
1200844.4	496395.0	1463408.6	1197128.4	6100.0
3946055.4	1160146.4	9348808.1	8186161.6	81447.4
476783.3	281550.3	1094828.2	879007.2	4800.2
807558.0	289815.3	798902.0	669375.5	2171.3
302157.4	162522.2	413361.6	316867.5	1761.4
7828.2	6312.3	20726.6	17079.4	43.3
60148.0	25276.3	26099.7	37670.9	750.7
171357.0	121680.0	171261.5	150038.8	1237.4
73644.1	47040.0	64011.1	56776.2	490.0

11-9 续表5

单位：万元

分组	Item	营业费用 Expenses for Operation	管理费用 Expenses for Management
家具制造业	Manufacture of Furniture	2080.4	1642.0
造纸及纸制品业	Manufacture of Paper and Paper Products	1843.0	3325.9
印刷业、记录媒介的复制	Printing,Reproduction of Recording Media	7135.7	35642.0
文教体育用品制造业	Manufacture of Articles For Cultural, Educational and Sports Activities	946.2	1694.1
石油加工、炼焦及核燃料加工业	Processing of Petroleum, Cokeing,Processing of Nuclear and Nuclear Fuel	6190.4	1176.8
化学原料及化学制品制造业	Manufacture of Raw Chemical Materials and Chemical Products	34088.8	69565.6
医药制造业	Manufacture of Medicines	234349.2	47183.7
化学纤维制造业	Manufacture of Chemical Fibers	185.9	1833.6
橡胶制品业	Manufacture of Rubber	406.8	1117.9
塑料制品业	Manufacture of Plastics	7611.7	9490.6
非金属矿物制品业	Manufacture of Non-metallic Mineral Products	27145.0	38099.0
黑色金属冶炼及压延加工业	Smelting and Pressing of Ferrous Metals	1692.3	4455.1
有色金属冶炼及压延加工业	Smelting and Pressing of Non-ferrous Metals	5328.4	31696.6
金属制品业	Manufacture of Metal Products	10075.7	14615.7
通用设备制造业	Manufacture of General Purpose Machinery	24293.1	36581.6
专用设备制造业	Manufacture of Special Equipment	52910.5	130208.1
交通运输设备制造业	Manufacture of Transport Equipment	257727.9	373422.3
电气机械及器材制造业	Manufacture of Electric Equipment and Machinery	32147.2	68180.2
通信设备、计算机及其他电子设备制造业	Manufacture of Communication Equipment, Computers and other Electronic Equipment	25720.6	60341.4
仪器仪表及文化办公用	Manufacture of Measuring Instruments and Machinery for Cultural Activity and Office Work	15922.1	51091.2
工艺品及其他制造业	Manufacture of Artwork and Other Manufacturing	1180.9	963.7
废弃资源和废旧材料回收加工业	Recycling and Disposal of Waste		
电力、热力的生产和供应业	Production and Supply of Electric Power and Heat Power	46.7	4153.7
燃气生产和供应业	Gas Mining and Supplying Industry	7940.2	12744.7
水的生产和供应业	Production and Supply of Water	2869.7	6678.0

continued 5

(10 000 yuan)

财务费用 Financial cost	营业利润 Operating Profit	利润总额 Total Profits	亏损企业亏损总额 Total Loss of Deficit Enterprises	利税总额 Total Pre-tax Profits	本年应交增值税 Value Added Tax Payable
187.7	2300.3	2285.4		3867.1	1424.2
1579.1	4150.1	2600.3	1333.4	5942.0	2690.8
1971.8	61035.8	60118.6	3130.9	82082.6	19982.1
565.7	2588.2	2408.2		3420.1	905.1
278.7	99282.7	31928.4		47732.7	15776.7
10692.9	63539.2	65169.6	13348.6	92378.8	24195.2
23412.0	49112.8	58482.4	2173.8	148798.7	88442.1
80.6	10086.7	10082.1		13510.8	3375.0
98.0	78.9	82.8		432.8	324.0
1775.0	7837.7	7263.3	605.7	13661.9	5875.4
5183.5	98843.6	94161.5	3005.7	143707.0	44040.2
1597.4	19384.4	18190.5	951.1	24292.3	5277.9
9642.7	40337.3	39235.0	1691.4	54909.7	13769.3
2141.6	22264.5	14885.4	856.2	24317.7	7820.4
4632.6	39727.7	36126.3	3052.1	55104.4	15909.1
14647.8	102553.1	101551.3	10937.3	146880.1	39228.8
40360.5	509053.6	532722.2	422.1	819776.8	205607.2
11533.9	130981.6	125303.2	4921.8	175653.9	45550.5
11937.9	45986.3	46079.3	6846.9	63812.6	15562.0
3616.8	27281.3	31774.6	1557.9	57972.7	24436.7
242.0	782.0	783.9	92.2	1602.7	775.5
1775.6	-7219.5	-6116.7	7006.2	-5173.4	192.6
-1729.1	18038.6	18107.2		25024.6	5680.0
895.5	-473.2	2087.9	482.6	6406.1	3828.2

11-10 规模以上外商及港澳台商工业企业主要经济指标（2010年）

单位：万元

分组	Item	企业单位数（个） Number of Enterprises (unit)	亏损企业 Loss Making Enterprises	工业总产值（当年价） Gross Industrial Output Value (At Current Prices)
总　计	**Total**	**136**	**30**	**6241132.3**
按隶属关系分	Grouped by Jurisdiction of Management			
中央企业	Central Enterprises	3		111212.9
省属企业	Provincial Enterprises	9	1	687462.3
市属企业	Municipal Enterprises	124	29	5442457.1
按登记注册类型分组	Grouped by Registion Status			
港、澳、台商投资企业	Enterprises with Funds from Hong Kong, Macao and Taiwan	32	8	234685.7
与港、澳、台商合资经营	Co-investment with businessman from Hong Kong,Macao and Taiwan	24	7	140139.8
与港、澳、台商合作经营	Partnership with businessman from Hong Kong,Macao and Taiwan			
港澳台商独资	Wholly Funded from Hong Kong, Macao and Taiwan	7	1	89713.9
港澳台商投资股份有限公司	Share-holding Corporation with Funds from Hong Kong,Macao and Taiwan	1		4832.0
外商投资企业	Enterprises with Foreign Investment	104	22	6006446.6
中外合资经营企业	Joint Ownership Operation With Overseas	67	14	4817624.4
中外合作经营企业	Co-operation With Overseas	2		5952.1
外资企业	Foreign Funded Enterprises	30	6	1088298.3
外商投资股份有限公司	Foreign funded Share-holding Corporations	5	2	94571.8
在总计中:亏损企业	Deficit Enterprises	30	30	518354.2
按轻重工业分	Grouped by Ligtht Industry and Heavy Industry			
轻工业	Light Industry	51	16	2342075.3
重工业	Heavy Industry	85	14	3899057.0
按企业规模分	Grouped by Size of Enterprises			
大型工业	Large-size	4		2973878.1
中型工业	Medium-sized	29	4	2045506.2
小型工业	Small-size	103	26	1221748.0
按工业行业大类分	Grouped by Sector			
煤炭开采和洗选业	Mining and Washing of Coal			
石油和天然气开采业	Extraction of Petroleum and Natural Gas			
黑色金属矿采选业	Mining and Processing of Ferrous Metal Ores			
有色金属矿采选业	Mining and Processing of Non-ferrous Metal Ores			
非金属矿采选业	Mining and Processing of Nonmetal Ores			
其他采矿业	Mining of Other Ores			
农副食品加工业	Processing of Food from Agricultural Porducts	5	1	146234.0
食品制造业	Manufacture of Foods	5	2	611987.7
饮料制造业	Manufacture of Beverages	11	4	501240.8

Economic Indicators of Foreign Fund Industrial Enterprises Above Designated Size（2010）

（10 000 yuan）

工业销售产值（当年价） Value of Industry Products Sales (At Current Prices)	从业人员年平均人数（人） Annual Average Employers (person)	资产合计 Total Assets	流动资产小计 Total Working Capitals	固定资产小计 Total Fixed Assets	固定资产原价合计 Origing Value of Fixed Assets	累计折旧 Accumulative Total Depreciation
6093828.9	**72434**	**4493115.7**	**2537998.9**	**1516218.1**	**2046905.0**	**716144.4**
112741.9	1295	90846.5	53740.8	34245.4	73391.0	41920.7
676024.9	6240	349476.7	261973.7	48317.3	110973.6	62665.5
5305062.1	64899	4052792.5	2222284.4	1433655.4	1862540.4	611558.2
224644.5	6128	357290.7	182528.6	77369.9	145405.9	73465.0
126542.9	3985	261702.6	137768.0	43286.3	84925.2	44650.5
93708.1	1923	90391.6	41863.4	32177.6	58707.8	28150.9
4393.5	220	5196.5	2897.2	1906.0	1772.9	663.6
5869184.4	66306	4135825.0	2355470.3	1438848.2	1901499.1	642679.4
4681754.1	51519	2886820.8	1697768.9	939612.3	1176059.9	397769.6
5952.1	282	14000.8	10944.3	1563.9	1938.2	374.3
1046140.8	12070	853580.6	449171.1	329805.7	506317.8	194349.4
135337.4	2435	381422.8	197586.0	167866.3	217183.2	50186.1
462313.9	6257	424680.4	208206.9	114871.1	197547.8	87746.9
2301267.8	22959	1596196.5	855476.5	518964.3	854471.1	347559.0
3792561.1	49475	2896919.2	1682522.4	997253.8	1192433.9	368585.4
2911384.3	36552	1533556.9	826763.7	584630.3	632804.2	193348.6
1981816.8	23802	1777163.8	935047.1	650800.4	932099.4	309812.9
1200627.8	12080	1182395.0	776188.1	280787.4	482001.4	212982.9
146202.8	882	68993.8	56344.1	11384.9	21659.0	12782.9
567677.0	5053	248460.6	126130.1	60573.3	113162.0	55768.2
542315.0	6440	653701.3	260695.1	303533.2	431858.8	128409.4

11-10 续表1

单位：万元

分组	Item	负债合计 Total Liabilites	流动负债 小计 Total Working Liabilities	长期负债 小计 Long-term Liabilities
总　计	**Total**	**2245843.3**	**1941014.7**	**288807.0**
按隶属关系分	Grouped by Jurisdiction of Management			
中央企业	Central Enterprises	33126.5	30555.4	
省属企业	Provincial Enterprises	199736.3	188115.3	11421.0
市属企业	Municipal Enterprises	2012980.5	1722344.0	277386.0
按登记注册类型分组	Grouped by Registion Status			
港、澳、台商投资企业	Enterprises with Funds from Hong Kong, Macao and Taiwan	163980.9	150198.0	13782.7
与港、澳、台商合资经营	Co-investment with businessman from Hong Kong,Macao and Taiwan	130559.1	117994.5	12564.4
与港、澳、台商合作经营	Partnership with businessman from Hong Kong,Macao and Taiwan			
港澳台商独资	Wholly Funded from Hong Kong, Macao and Taiwan	30775.2	29556.9	1218.3
港澳台商投资股份有限公司	Share-holding Corporation with Funds from Hong Kong,Macao and Taiwan	2646.6	2646.6	
外商投资企业	Enterprises with Foreign Investment	2081862.4	1790816.7	275024.3
中外合资经营企业	Joint Ownership Operation With Overseas	1455251.4	1306459.6	137593.3
中外合作经营企业	Co-operation With Overseas	3902.7	3085.7	817.0
外资企业	Foreign Funded Enterprises	373381.1	308852.4	59705.9
外商投资股份有限公司	Foreign funded Share-holding Corporations	249327.2	172419.0	76908.1
在总计中:亏损企业	Deficit Enterprises	240502.5	217801.0	19494.1
按轻重工业分	Grouped by Light Industry and Heavy Industry			
轻工业	Light Industry	832418.7	707180.2	121831.1
重工业	Heavy Industry	1413424.6	1233834.5	166975.9
按企业规模分	Grouped by Size of Enterprises			
大型工业	Large-size	731568.7	654556.2	76812.5
中型工业	Medium-sized	960399.8	775234.0	182594.5
小型工业	Small-size	553874.8	511224.5	29400.0
按工业行业大类分	Grouped by Sector			
煤炭开采和洗选业	Mining and Washing of Coal			
石油和天然气开采业	Extraction of Petroleum and Natural Gas			
黑色金属矿采选业	Mining and Processing of Ferrous Metal Ores			
有色金属矿采选业	Mining and Processing of Non-ferrous Metal Ores			
非金属矿采选业	Mining and Processing of Nonmetal Ores			
其他采矿业	Mining of Other Ores			
农副食品加工业	Processing of Food from Agricultural Porducts	34119.1	34005.8	113.3
食品制造业	Manufacture of Foods	122280.8	121834.8	446.0
饮料制造业	Manufacture of Beverages	385790.9	291334.2	94456.6

continued 1

(10 000 yuan)

所有者权益合计 Total Owners' Equities	实收资本 Total Capital Hold	主营业务收入 Revenue from Principal Business	主营业务成本 Cost of Principal Business	主营业务税金及附加 Taxes and Other Charges on Principal Business
2236795.7	**1143522.9**	**5765341.6**	**4610449.1**	**68448.2**
57719.8	34194.0	114129.8	97711.4	64.9
149740.3	82013.1	687617.8	432431.2	55.4
2029335.6	1027315.8	4963594.0	4080306.5	68327.9
193036.1	159613.3	228977.3	164773.6	86.2
130968.5	118110.7	122299.3	89600.7	65.5
59517.7	39702.6	102010.8	71851.4	20.7
2549.9	1800.0	4667.2	3321.5	
2043759.6	983909.6	5536364.3	4445675.5	68362.0
1431568.3	650745.0	4362807.2	3537063.4	65677.1
9416.3	4712.6	5943.1	4051.7	8.1
479968.6	299803.5	1030561.6	771939.3	2635.2
122806.4	28648.5	137052.4	132621.1	41.6
183947.0	216221.0	432963.7	348972.9	138.4
753575.8	415131.2	2177932.1	1599265.6	2354.1
1483219.9	728391.7	3587409.5	3011183.5	66094.1
801988.2	281431.7	2716789.0	2175658.8	63476.5
807243.7	409178.5	1819484.1	1436615.1	2496.6
627563.8	452912.7	1229068.5	998175.2	2475.1
34874.7	26376.8	172554.4	159307.9	26.5
125949.2	71651.3	533034.2	416669.3	7.2
258621.0	130285.6	477807.4	377092.1	1857.7

11-10 续表2

单位：万元

分　　组	Item	营业费用 Expenses for Operation	管理费用 Expenses for Management
总　　计	**Total**	**468769.0**	**218109.2**
按隶属关系分	Grouped by Jurisdiction of Management		
中央企业	Central Enterprises	482.4	2888.4
省属企业	Provincial Enterprises	193593.5	23076.4
市属企业	Municipal Enterprises	274693.1	192144.4
按登记注册类型分组	Grouped by Registion Status		
港、澳、台商投资企业	Enterprises with Funds from Hong Kong, Macao and Taiwan	34314.8	20058.2
与港、澳、台商合资经营	Co-investment with businessman from Hong Kong,Macao and Taiwan	13167.8	11454.9
与港、澳、台商合作经营	Partnership with businessman from Hong Kong,Macao and Taiwan		
港澳台商独资	Wholly Funded from Hong Kong, Macao and Taiwan	20957.0	8307.5
港澳台商投资股份有限公司	Share-holding Corporation with Funds from Hong Kong,Macao and Taiwan	190.0	295.8
外商投资企业	Enterprises with Foreign Investment	434454.2	198051.0
中外合资经营企业	Joint Ownership Operation With Overseas	309003.1	132807.0
中外合作经营企业	Co-operation With Overseas	199.9	981.1
外资企业	Foreign Funded Enterprises	118687.6	54077.0
外商投资股份有限公司	Foreign funded Share-holding Corporations	6563.6	10185.9
在总计中:亏损企业	Deficit Enterprises	57900.6	29034.0
按轻重工业分	Grouped by Light Industry and Heavy Industry		
轻工业	Light Industry	383731.1	86457.5
重工业	Heavy Industry	85037.9	131651.7
按企业规模分	Grouped by Size of Enterprises		
大型工业	Large-size	237371.6	57432.7
中型工业	Medium-sized	186489.9	93338.6
小型工业	Small-size	44907.5	67337.9
按工业行业大类分	Grouped by Sector		
煤炭开采和洗选业	Mining and Washing of Coal		
石油和天然气开采业	Extraction of Petroleum and Natural Gas		
黑色金属矿采选业	Mining and Processing of Ferrous Metal Ores		
有色金属矿采选业	Mining and Processing of Non-ferrous Metal Ores		
非金属矿采选业	Mining and Processing of Nonmetal Ores		
其他采矿业	Mining of Other Ores		
农副食品加工业	Processing of Food from Agricultural Porducts	4794.3	3469.6
食品制造业	Manufacture of Foods	76148.4	13355.5
饮料制造业	Manufacture of Beverages	74104.0	27219.1

continued 2

（10 000 yuan）

财务费用 Financial cost	营业利润 Operating Profit	利润总额 Total Profits	亏损企业亏损总额 Total Loss of Deficit Enterprises	利税总额 Total Pre-tax Profits	本年应交增值税 Value Added Tax Payable
35867.5	**558785.6**	**488599.7**	**29381.4**	**799904.2**	**242856.3**
243.3	12465.2	12111.1		16835.1	4659.1
13425.1	35101.5	33539.3	2798.6	108003.4	74408.7
22199.1	511218.9	442949.3	26582.8	675065.7	163788.5
1482.3	12889.2	13355.1	3464.3	24242.7	10801.4
1370.6	6727.7	8023.4	3319.5	13803.7	5714.8
107.3	5791.6	4961.8	144.8	9788.0	4805.5
4.4	369.9	369.9		651.0	281.1
34385.2	545896.4	475244.6	25917.1	775661.5	232054.9
27240.7	402056.5	372922.0	8281.6	623223.0	184623.9
28.5	422.8	1069.3		1160.5	83.1
-386.4	147756.8	103334.9	12327.6	152700.8	46730.7
7502.4	-4339.7	-2081.6	5307.9	-1422.8	617.2
3742.6	28374.6	-29381.4	29381.4	-16571.9	12671.1
21927.2	213838.6	128959.3	17007.9	269462.5	138149.1
13940.3	344947.0	359640.4	12373.5	530441.7	104707.2
16310.3	201105.9	204411.0		391423.4	123535.9
11680.6	237257.7	165285.5	18608.8	238132.5	70350.4
7876.6	120422.0	118903.2	10772.6	170348.3	48970.0
-243.9	5737.8	5678.8	336.8	9473.9	3768.6
-669.7	94832.0	15532.2	9124.2	34635.0	19095.6
6246.4	42606.8	42080.9	3632.2	61975.4	18036.8

11-10 续表3

单位：万元

分 组	Item	企业单位数(个) Number of Enterprises (unit)	亏损企业 Loss Making Enterprises	工业总产值（当年价）Gross Industrial Output Value (At Current Prices)
烟草加工业	Manufacture of Tobacco			
纺织业	Manufacture of Textile	1	1	2180.5
纺织服装、鞋、帽制造业	Manufacture of Textile Wearing Apparel, Footwearand Caps			
皮革、毛皮、羽毛(绒)及其制品业	Manufacture of Leather, Fur, Feather (eiderdown) and Related Products			
木材加工及竹、藤、棕、草制品业	Processing of Timber,Manufacture of Wood,Plam and Straw Products	1	1	1075.7
家具制造业	Manufacture of Furniture			
造纸及纸制品业	Manufacture of Paper and Paper Products	2		28052.7
印刷业、记录媒介的复制	Printing,Reproduction of Recording Media	2	1	29265.0
文教体育用品制造业	Manufacture of Articles For Cultural, Educational and Sports Activities			
石油加工、炼焦及核燃料加工业	Processing of Petroleum, Cokeing,Processing of Nuclear and Nuclear Fuel	1	1	28997.4
化学原料及化学制品制造业	Manufacture of Raw Chemical Materials and Chemical Products	7	2	43856.5
医药制造业	Manufacture of Medicines	10	2	615573.4
化学纤维制造业	Manufacture of Chemical Fibers	1		77970.9
橡胶制品业	Manufacture of Rubber	1		5450.0
塑料制品业	Manufacture of Plastics	5		20361.3
非金属矿物制品业	Manufacture of Non-metallic Mineral Products	7		306482.6
黑色金属冶炼及压延加工业	Smelting and Pressing of Ferrous Metals	1		28476.5
有色金属冶炼及压延加工业	Smelting and Pressing of Non-ferrous Metals	4	1	116333.8
金属制品业	Manufacture of Metal Products	4	1	12008.3
通用设备制造业	Manufacture of General Purpose Machinery	9		134386.6
专用设备制造业	Manufacture of Special Equipment	13	1	224700.1
交通运输设备制造业	Manufacture of Transport Equipment	8		2491648.5
电气机械及器材制造业	Manufacture of Electric Equipment and Machinery	18	6	396711.0
通信设备、计算机及其他电子设备制造业	Manufacture of Communication Equipment, Computers and other Electronic Equipment	8	1	183475.6
仪器仪表及文化办公用	Manufacture of Measuring Instruments and Machinery for Cultural Activity and Office Work	8	3	80097.4
工艺品及其他制造业	Manufacture of Artwork and Other Manufacturing	3	2	13194.5
废弃资源和废旧材料回收加工业	Recycling and Disposal of Waste			
电力、热力的生产和供应业	Production and Supply of Electric Power and Heat Power			
燃气生产和供应业	Gas Mining and Supplying Industry	1		141371.5
水的生产和供应业	Production and Supply of Water			

continued 3

(10 000 yuan)

工业销售产值（当年价）Value of Industry Products Sales (At Current Prices)	从业人员年平均人数（人）Annual Average Employers (person)	资产合计 Total Assets	流动资产小计 Total Working Capitals	固定资产小计 Total Fixed Assets	固定资产原价合计 Origing Value of Fixed Assets	累计折旧 Accumulative Total Depreciation
2475.6	228	5288.3	4157.9	1130.4	6914.6	5849.2
1032.3	26	557.2	357.4	199.8	332.8	133.0
25462.2	348	23817.6	15700.1	4848.3	7285.4	2439.1
28373.1	912	68206.2	30269.6	13948.3	24383.5	10909.0
29124.3	42	9327.2	5971.3	2822.9	4331.2	1508.3
40089.5	425	28732.4	19399.4	6195.1	11634.3	5508.0
608852.2	6623	354629.3	243807.6	75726.1	155939.7	83764.4
79920.2	230	46233.3	22721.8	23408.3	56379.9	32971.6
3713.0	157	4089.9	2535.2	1077.0	1814.4	737.4
20502.9	533	37605.5	25656.1	11444.6	18309.6	8256.8
290394.6	1160	204321.6	72311.3	119384.1	146642.3	28826.7
26105.9	97	8225.4	3335.6	3386.8	4889.7	1502.9
105209.3	1102	189002.1	107780.7	53382.7	66144.0	16761.9
11603.4	494	15173.5	9579.1	4568.7	13067.6	8513.7
130227.4	1838	110549.8	82257.2	24089.4	52710.9	28677.1
227036.7	3378	260652.1	191077.2	48495.1	96621.6	50963.3
2428136.7	32212	1146064.9	649302.5	421099.1	385913.8	107496.8
373829.4	3199	277761.0	204462.9	49745.1	88726.8	39515.1
173310.8	3507	341803.9	199620.9	130053.3	161418.3	49664.0
78485.7	1133	105558.9	81108.7	17129.5	21795.9	8012.1
12591.9	408	7871.6	3675.0	2511.0	2535.9	821.6
141157.0	2007	276488.3	119742.1	126081.1	152433.0	26351.9

11-10 续表4

单位：万元

分组	Item	负债合计 Total Liabilites	流动负债小计 Total Working Liabilities	长期负债小计 Long-term Liabilities
烟草加工业	Manufacture of Tobacco			
纺织业	Manufacture of Textile	1422.6	1422.6	
纺织服装、鞋、帽制造业	Manufacture of Textile Wearing Apparel, Footwearand Caps			
皮革、毛皮、羽毛(绒)及其制品业	Manufacture of Leather, Fur, Feather (eiderdown) and Related Products			
木材加工及竹、藤、棕、草制品业	Processing of Timber,Manufacture of Wood,Plam and Straw Products	550.0	550.0	
家具制造业	Manufacture of Furniture			
造纸及纸制品业	Manufacture of Paper and Paper Products	11510.3	11510.3	
印刷业、记录媒介的复制	Printing,Reproduction of Recording Media	47374.2	36504.4	10869.8
文教体育用品制造业	Manufacture of Articles For Cultural, Educational and Sports Activities			
石油加工、炼焦及核燃料加工业	Processing of Petroleum, Cokeing,Processing of Nuclear and Nuclear Fuel	1763.1	1763.1	
化学原料及化学制品制造业	Manufacture of Raw Chemical Materials and Chemical Products	13276.5	8835.5	1233.8
医药制造业	Manufacture of Medicines	151149.4	147034.9	3914.5
化学纤维制造业	Manufacture of Chemical Fibers	7886.3	7886.3	
橡胶制品业	Manufacture of Rubber	2169.6	2166.0	3.6
塑料制品业	Manufacture of Plastics	16400.0	12174.5	4225.5
非金属矿物制品业	Manufacture of Non-metallic Mineral Products	80481.1	75322.4	5158.5
黑色金属冶炼及压延加工业	Smelting and Pressing of Ferrous Metals	5097.3	5097.3	
有色金属冶炼及压延加工业	Smelting and Pressing of Non-ferrous Metals	117438.4	75710.5	36507.8
金属制品业	Manufacture of Metal Products	5243.5	4711.1	532.4
通用设备制造业	Manufacture of General Purpose Machinery	35363.2	34950.3	412.9
专用设备制造业	Manufacture of Special Equipment	115662.4	107394.3	5697.0
交通运输设备制造业	Manufacture of Transport Equipment	574074.9	523891.1	50183.8
电气机械及器材制造业	Manufacture of Electric Equipment and Machinery	149886.8	133873.0	11191.0
通信设备、计算机及其他电子设备制造业	Manufacture of Communication Equipment, Computers and other Electronic Equipment	170555.0	136638.5	33916.4
仪器仪表及文化办公用	Manufacture of Measuring Instruments and Machinery for Cultural Activity and Office Work	37006.5	33809.6	3196.9
工艺品及其他制造业	Manufacture of Artwork and Other Manufacturing	3823.2	3823.2	
废弃资源和废旧材料回收加工业	Recycling and Disposal of Waste			
电力、热力的生产和供应业	Production and Supply of Electric Power and Heat Power			
燃气生产和供应业	Gas Mining and Supplying Industry	155518.2	128771.0	26747.2
水的生产和供应业	Production and Supply of Water			

continued 4

（10 000 yuan）

所有者权益合计 Total Owners' Equities	实收资本 Total Capital Hold	主营业务收入 Revenue from Principal Business	主营业务成本 Cost of Principal Business	主营业务税金及附加 Taxes and Other Charges on Principal Business
3865.7	3768.7	2512.7	1749.7	2.4
7.2	100.0	1032.3	984.1	
12307.3	2738.2	26336.6	22485.7	
20832.0	24437.9	24990.0	19621.2	14.9
7564.0	6840.6	28730.0	25838.8	39.6
15455.9	12216.9	42663.1	37446.7	213.7
203479.7	91305.2	592094.4	294412.8	94.8
38347.0	24800.0	79920.2	67791.0	51.6
1920.3	1030.0	2433.0	1856.7	
20425.0	18642.4	20005.3	15311.1	6.8
123840.3	37209.2	289241.2	211928.4	1889.6
3128.1	150.0	28575.8	20519.9	250.0
71563.7	47725.3	101999.3	80508.7	27.3
9930.0	8402.5	11603.4	8620.9	10.1
75186.3	39321.3	133793.5	112554.4	20.9
144989.5	70354.0	224793.5	181169.4	62.8
571989.7	159855.4	2229964.5	1935398.0	62355.5
127874.0	100597.7	332989.1	288824.2	197.1
171248.9	113499.8	176163.7	148919.4	110.6
68377.7	48163.7	79071.1	52718.1	51.3
4048.4	4050.4	11875.9	5047.0	2.0
120970.1	100000.0	141157.0	123673.6	1155.8

11-10 续表5

单位：万元

分　组	Item	营业费用 Expenses for Operation	管理费用 Expenses for Management
烟草加工业	Manufacture of Tobacco		
纺织业	Manufacture of Textile	357.2	410.1
纺织服装、鞋、帽制造业	Manufacture of Textile Wearing Apparel, Footwearand Caps		
皮革、毛皮、羽毛(绒)及其制品业	Manufacture of Leather, Fur, Feather (eiderdown) and Related Products		
木材加工及竹、藤、棕、草制品业	Processing of Timber,Manufacture of Wood,Plam and Straw Products	45.5	37.3
家具制造业	Manufacture of Furniture		
造纸及纸制品业	Manufacture of Paper and Paper Products	710.7	1783.5
印刷业、记录媒介的复制	Printing,Reproduction of Recording Media	1676.8	2561.2
文教体育用品制造业	Manufacture of Articles For Cultural, Educational and Sports Activities		
石油加工、炼焦及核燃料加工业	Processing of Petroleum, Cokeing,Processing of Nuclear and Nuclear Fuel	167.3	2590.7
化学原料及化学制品制造业	Manufacture of Raw Chemical Materials and Chemical Products	2111.5	2425.1
医药制造业	Manufacture of Medicines	221997.3	25728.8
化学纤维制造业	Manufacture of Chemical Fibers	151.0	1752.3
橡胶制品业	Manufacture of Rubber	140.6	283.8
塑料制品业	Manufacture of Plastics	581.6	2002.7
非金属矿物制品业	Manufacture of Non-metallic Mineral Products	14675.9	3442.6
黑色金属冶炼及压延加工业	Smelting and Pressing of Ferrous Metals	359.7	1128.6
有色金属冶炼及压延加工业	Smelting and Pressing of Non-ferrous Metals	4074.9	15002.1
金属制品业	Manufacture of Metal Products	310.3	1327.1
通用设备制造业	Manufacture of General Purpose Machinery	4994.2	5980.0
专用设备制造业	Manufacture of Special Equipment	6091.2	17691.4
交通运输设备制造业	Manufacture of Transport Equipment	26780.2	38617.8
电气机械及器材制造业	Manufacture of Electric Equipment and Machinery	10754.6	19235.4
通信设备、计算机及其他电子设备制造业	Manufacture of Communication Equipment, Computers and other Electronic Equipment	3484.0	10760.0
仪器仪表及文化办公用	Manufacture of Measuring Instruments and Machinery for Cultural Activity and Office Work	6703.5	8841.0
工艺品及其他制造业	Manufacture of Artwork and Other Manufacturing	192.5	658.8
废弃资源和废旧材料回收加工业	Recycling and Disposal of Waste		
电力、热力的生产和供应业	Production and Supply of Electric Power and Heat Power		
燃气生产和供应业	Gas Mining and Supplying Industry	7361.8	11804.7
水的生产和供应业	Production and Supply of Water		

continued 5

(10 000 yuan)

财务费用 Financial cost	营业利润 Operating Profit	利润总额 Total Profits	亏损企业亏损总额 Total Loss of Deficit Enterprises	利税总额 Total Pre-tax Profits	本年应交增值税 Value Added Tax Payable
0.2	-58.9	-62.1	62.1	170.6	230.3
8.8	-48.7	-43.4	43.4	-23.8	19.6
-37.1	3022.1	2802.1		4617.2	1815.1
1089.6	196.3	359.2	2798.6	2030.6	1656.5
46.3	-73.3	-60.9	60.9	1097.4	1118.7
129.2	1252.1	1014.5	56.0	2257.0	1028.8
14812.8	42539.4	43864.3	193.2	122765.9	78806.8
80.6	10095.8	10057.2		13475.8	3367.0
28.1	6.5	7.5		79.7	72.2
321.3	2340.8	2260.4		2878.9	611.7
526.8	67359.7	70227.1		89096.6	16979.9
74.5	3281.1	3039.9		4432.4	1142.5
2785.7	9719.8	9340.3	646.4	10980.6	1613.0
52.1	1155.5	1291.9	76.5	2011.2	709.2
326.1	10308.0	10368.2		13451.1	3062.0
784.7	21378.0	21170.7	1459.6	28677.5	7444.0
4021.2	178384.2	179525.7		296433.1	54551.9
3641.2	21449.3	14782.0	4168.0	30229.5	15250.4
3572.8	16161.7	27691.3	4665.9	32212.5	4410.6
377.4	11198.1	11471.1	1535.3	14171.7	2649.3
11.2	-164.7	-152.4	522.3	156.7	307.1
-2118.8	16106.2	16353.2		22617.7	5108.7

11-11 规模以上大中型工业企业主要经济指标（2010年）

单位：万元

分组	Item	企业单位数（个）Number of Enterprises (unit)	亏损企业 Loss Making Enterprises	工业总产值（当年价）Gross Industrial Output Value (At Current Prices)
总　计	**Total**	**203**	**27**	**23539876.6**
按隶属关系分	Grouped by Jurisdiction of Management			
中央企业	Central Enterprises	47	6	8914390.9
省属企业	Provincial Enterprises	27	4	5776108.7
市属企业	Municipal Enterprises	129	17	8849377.0
按登记注册类型分组	Grouped by Registion Status			
内资企业	Domestic Investment Enterprises	170	23	18520492.3
国有经济	State-owned Enterprises	43	8	6540836.1
集体经济	Collective-owned Enterprises	3	1	39915.3
股份合作	Share-holding Corperative	1		68243.7
联营企业	Joint Ownership Enterprises	1		61009.1
有限责任公司	Limited Liability Corporations	73	11	9685743.5
国有独资公司	State Sole Funded Corporations	21	2	2902919.3
其他有限责任公司	Other Limited Liability Corporations	52	9	6782824.2
股份有限公司	Share-holding Corperation Ltd.	33	1	1435205.7
私营企业	Private Enterprises	15	1	667860.4
其他内资企业	Other Domestic Funded Enterprises	1	1	21678.5
港、澳、台商投资企业	Enterprises with Funds from Hong Kong,Macao and Taiwan	5	1	131511.1
外商投资企业	Enterprises with Foreign Investment	28	3	4887873.2
在总计中:亏损企业	Deficit Enterprises	27	27	1001018.7
按轻重工业分	Grouped by Light Industry and Heavy Industry			
轻工业	Light Industry	58	10	3596455.7
重工业	Heavy Industry	145	17	19943420.9
按工业行业大类分	Grouped by Sector			
煤炭开采和洗选业	Mining and Washing of Coal			
石油和天然气开采业	Extraction of Petroleum and Natural Gas	2		176150.1
黑色金属矿采选业	Mining and Processing of Ferrous Metal Ores			
有色金属矿采选业	Mining and Processing of Non-ferrous Metal Ores	1		30017.8
非金属矿采选业	Mining and Processing of Nonmetal Ores			
其他采矿业	Mining of Other Ores			
农副食品加工业	Processing of Food from Agricultural Porducts	7		532525.1
食品制造业	Manufacture of Foods	7	1	676683.0
饮料制造业	Manufacture of Beverages	6	1	563780.4

Economic Indicators of Large and Medium-sized Industrial Enterprises Above Designated Size（2010）

（10 000 yuan）

工业销售产值（当年价）Value of Industry Products Sales (At Current Prices)	从业人员年平均人数（人）Annual Average Employers (person)	资产合计 Total Assets	流动资产小计 Total Working Capitals	固定资产小计 Total Fixed Assets	固定资产原价合计 Origing Value of Fixed Assets	累计折旧 Accumulative Total Depreciation
22880118.4	**362927**	**30314122.0**	**17711719.4**	**9858834.7**	**12921898.0**	**4871715.1**
8734228.3	149119	15535663.3	8739967.5	5603176.3	7596346.5	2900902.8
5450256.4	62751	4883288.4	3289167.2	1220725.4	1470648.6	456858.7
8695633.7	151057	9895170.3	5682584.7	3034933.0	3854902.9	1513953.6
17986917.3	302573	27003401.3	15949908.6	8623404.0	11356994.4	4368553.6
6408087.3	83729	10549339.6	5763353.5	4126128.5	5339177.8	1844357.2
38327.2	3455	23512.6	11719.7	11333.7	13270.7	2178.4
78806.2	618	67132.8	48992.6	5562.9	11720.0	6180.7
54533.6	1463	107266.0	92088.3	7791.7	11328.7	3537.0
9400068.9	174034	13101153.4	8407966.1	3456138.0	5005501.9	2105740.9
2740610.7	62785	4122716.1	2417555.3	1291898.4	1870018.5	771968.2
6659458.2	111249	8978437.3	5990410.8	2164239.6	3135483.4	1333772.7
1365994.8	28316	2658978.4	1329624.9	867011.3	789230.0	362885.4
622145.6	10286	479174.2	288056.5	140700.6	174667.3	40313.3
18953.7	672	16844.3	8107.0	8737.3	12098.0	3360.7
123887.3	3404	136448.9	72215.7	36714.2	71723.4	35557.0
4769313.8	56950	3174271.8	1689595.1	1198716.5	1493180.2	467604.5
927265.8	24865	1764908.4	776890.5	754817.8	1122790.9	389518.0
3657462.5	62572	2941667.3	1515376.7	994538.6	1603196.9	690501.7
19222655.9	300355	27372454.7	16196342.7	8864296.1	11318701.1	4181213.4
149062.9	6529	573759.7	367567.1	85765.6	154952.0	69186.5
30517.8	525	26335.8	13268.7	7721.3	13410.1	6050.0
522127.2	4107	365329.0	240550.6	85791.1	114377.2	35034.0
632105.7	6937	236079.7	142923.9	77135.7	131900.0	57695.1
719050.6	6981	716064.7	311070.1	305922.6	441473.9	136291.7

11-11 续表1

单位：万元

分　　组	Item	负债合计 Total Liabilites	流动负债 小计 Total Working Liabilities	长期负债 小计 Long-term Liabilities
总　　计	**Total**	**17589238.5**	**13473372.7**	**3524551.1**
按隶属关系分	Grouped by Jurisdiction of Management			
中央企业	Central Enterprises	9392132.3	6810484.4	2319866.2
省属企业	Provincial Enterprises	3186780.3	2643621.5	341751.2
市属企业	Municipal Enterprises	5010325.9	4019266.8	862933.7
按登记注册类型分组	Grouped by Registion Status			
内资企业	Domestic Investment Enterprises	15897270.0	12043582.5	3265144.1
国有经济	State-owned Enterprises	6455728.3	4450913.8	1786300.0
集体经济	Collective-owned Enterprises	23473.0	12561.0	510.0
股份合作	Share-holding Corperative	53920.1	53920.1	
联营企业	Joint Ownership Enterprises	53471.2	53123.4	
有限责任公司	Limited Liability Corporations	7844273.1	6425030.6	1105641.5
国有独资公司	State Sole Funded Corporations	1900293.1	1461591.2	257538.4
其他有限责任公司	Other Limited Liability Corporations	5943980.0	4963439.4	848103.1
股份有限公司	Share-holding Corperation Ltd.	1178769.1	821356.3	344846.3
私营企业	Private Enterprises	277829.0	216871.1	27846.3
其他内资企业	Other Domestic Funded Enterprises	9806.2	9806.2	
港、澳、台商投资企业	Enterprises with Funds from Hong Kong,Macao and Taiwan	81933.1	71063.3	10869.8
外商投资企业	Enterprises with Foreign Investment	1610035.4	1358726.9	248537.2
在总计中:亏损企业	Deficit Enterprises	1189269.9	667997.5	451721.2
按轻重工业分	Grouped by Light Industry and Heavy Industry			
轻工业	Light Industry	1534442.3	1267502.3	221320.3
重工业	Heavy Industry	16054796.2	12205870.4	3303230.8
按工业行业大类分	Grouped by Sector			
煤炭开采和洗选业	Mining and Washing of Coal			
石油和天然气开采业	Extraction of Petroleum and Natural Gas	253402.0	210709.4	42692.5
黑色金属矿采选业	Mining and Processing of Ferrous Metal Ores			
有色金属矿采选业	Mining and Processing of Non-ferrous Metal Ores	14368.3	14239.3	129.0
非金属矿采选业	Mining and Processing of Nonmetal Ores			
其他采矿业	Mining of Other Ores			
农副食品加工业	Processing of Food from Agricultural Porducts	271989.9	233291.5	5586.8
食品制造业	Manufacture of Foods	110443.5	106447.5	3996.0
饮料制造业	Manufacture of Beverages	424966.7	331063.4	93903.2

continued 1

(10 000 yuan)

所有者权益合计 Total Owners' Equities	实收资本 Total Capital Hold	主营业务收入 Revenue from Principal Business	主营业务成本 Cost of Principal Business	主营业务税金及附加 Taxes and Other Charges on Principal Business
12709190.5	**4190325.6**	**22694480.3**	**18588509.0**	**243726.7**
6142530.9	1764018.8	9130529.5	7352036.3	128539.1
1695407.4	553060.8	5275549.6	4454144.3	14084.1
4871252.2	1873246.0	8288401.2	6782328.4	101103.5
11099958.6	3499715.4	18158207.2	14976235.1	177753.6
4088466.8	1111196.3	6321623.1	4890178.0	127867.6
39.6	3982.4	41977.0	40911.5	701.3
13212.7	3964.7	68774.7	64992.5	1.0
53794.8	49000.0	62759.7	48924.2	251.0
5256244.7	1815130.5	9632295.2	8286246.3	37051.2
2222422.9	563350.1	2860175.1	2396942.9	11359.0
3033821.8	1251780.4	6772120.1	5889303.4	25692.2
1479817.0	420954.2	1409378.0	1106366.3	9289.6
201344.9	84487.3	599890.5	518257.4	2499.2
7038.1	11000.0	21509.0	20358.9	92.7
54515.8	43208.2	127167.7	89764.8	14.9
1554716.1	647402.0	4409105.4	3522509.1	65958.2
575018.1	501604.7	1033226.7	968666.9	4985.7
1397651.3	610061.2	3415929.0	2573411.4	19819.6
11311539.2	3580264.4	19278551.3	16015097.6	223907.1
320357.7	189880.0	348548.0	338421.3	5318.0
11967.5	5500.0	29617.7	26568.6	53.3
93339.1	42054.5	461865.6	419285.6	1088.5
125405.6	58984.7	593336.6	467629.3	320.2
281808.7	110529.2	654980.1	515778.3	9962.1

11-11 续表2

单位：万元

分组	Item	营业费用 Expenses for Operation	管理费用 Expenses for Management
总 计	**Total**	**1000673.5**	**1279705.1**
按隶属关系分	Grouped by Jurisdiction of Management		
中央企业	Central Enterprises	218782.1	620291.8
省属企业	Provincial Enterprises	348881.6	202046.4
市属企业	Municipal Enterprises	433009.8	457366.9
按登记注册类型分组	Grouped by Registion Status		
内资企业	Domestic Investment Enterprises	576812.0	1128933.8
国有经济	State-owned Enterprises	154326.8	437962.3
集体经济	Collective-owned Enterprises	571.0	1433.5
股份合作	Share-holding Corperative	2490.5	1777.4
联营企业	Joint Ownership Enterprises	5167.8	6751.6
有限责任公司	Limited Liability Corporations	316345.0	575798.7
国有独资公司	State Sole Funded Corporations	77353.0	196041.3
其他有限责任公司	Other Limited Liability Corporations	238992.0	379757.4
股份有限公司	Share-holding Corperation Ltd.	71831.0	85818.5
私营企业	Private Enterprises	25825.1	18194.7
其他内资企业	Other Domestic Funded Enterprises	254.8	1197.1
港、澳、台商投资企业	Enterprises with Funds from Hong Kong,Macao and Taiwan	22906.8	11946.4
外商投资企业	Enterprises with Foreign Investment	400954.7	138824.9
在总计中:亏损企业	Deficit Enterprises	62703.8	60068.0
按轻重工业分	Grouped by Light Industry and Heavy Industry		
轻工业	Light Industry	461863.6	166118.4
重工业	Heavy Industry	538809.9	1113586.7
按工业行业大类分	Grouped by Sector		
煤炭开采和洗选业	Mining and Washing of Coal		
石油和天然气开采业	Extraction of Petroleum and Natural Gas	1441.8	14297.9
黑色金属矿采选业	Mining and Processing of Ferrous Metal Ores		
有色金属矿采选业	Mining and Processing of Non-ferrous Metal Ores	753.0	991.6
非金属矿采选业	Mining and Processing of Nonmetal Ores		
其他采矿业	Mining of Other Ores		
农副食品加工业	Processing of Food from Agricultural Porducts	19363.5	10094.1
食品制造业	Manufacture of Foods	79394.9	18594.8
饮料制造业	Manufacture of Beverages	84875.2	28900.5

continued 2

(10 000 yuan)

财务费用 Financial cost	营业利润 Operating Profit	利润总额 Total Profits	亏损企业亏损总额 Total Loss of Deficit Enterprises	利税总额 Total Pre-tax Profits	本年应交增值税 Value Added Tax Payable
198869.6	**1989625.0**	**1933380.4**	**70660.8**	**2935906.3**	**758799.2**
114876.3	953446.8	997941.8	24181.5	1379921.6	253440.7
32465.9	261860.6	269650.7	4517.9	493572.3	209837.5
51527.4	774317.6	665787.9	41961.4	1062412.4	295521.0
170878.7	1551261.4	1563683.9	52052.0	2306350.4	564912.9
76120.6	796302.9	855664.9	23454.5	1239548.6	256016.1
171.6	435.3	441.5	106.5	2178.4	1035.6
1456.9	463.2	433.1		442.8	8.7
-80.2	3196.6	2606.9		4426.8	1568.9
63501.3	490084.1	519332.1	27261.0	795073.5	238690.2
14991.5	190949.9	218228.3	3347.1	334469.7	104882.4
48509.8	299134.2	301103.8	23913.9	460603.8	133807.8
22926.9	145334.1	153137.7	886.9	218359.1	55931.8
6781.1	115838.4	32311.3	99.5	45544.8	10734.3
0.5	-393.2	-243.6	243.6	776.4	927.3
1188.1	6553.6	6238.0	2798.6	12711.1	6458.2
26802.8	431810.0	363458.5	15810.2	616844.8	187428.1
26175.6	-4812.4	-70660.8	70660.8	-32914.9	32760.2
40808.0	396476.4	231070.5	21322.9	432300.8	181410.7
158061.6	1593148.6	1702309.9	49337.9	2503605.5	577388.5
			60875.4	1047491.6	269914.7
-2270.9	-11430.0	9145.3	1530.4	44621.9	30158.6
368.0	2480.9	1014.2		1651.3	583.8
6506.0	92061.6	8904.5		14042.2	4049.2
-61.0	105746.9	19927.4	8796.3	42016.8	21769.2
5709.7	63228.7	62741.2	2348.0	97490.7	24787.4

11-11 续表3

单位：万元

分 组	Item	企业单位数(个) Number of Enterprises (unit)	亏损企业 Loss Making Enterprises	工业总产值（当年价） Gross Industrial Output Value (At Current Prices)
烟草加工业	Manufacture of Tobacco			
纺织业	Manufacture of Textile	5	2	131652.9
纺织服装、鞋、帽制造业	Manufacture of Textile Wearing Apparel, Footwearand Caps	1		28490.2
皮革、毛皮、羽毛(绒)及其制品业	Manufacture of Leather, Fur, Feather (eiderdown) and Related Products	1		15017.6
木材加工及竹、藤、棕、草制品业	Processing of Timber,Manufacture of Wood,Plam and Straw Products	2		75889.2
家具制造业	Manufacture of Furniture			
造纸及纸制品业	Manufacture of Paper and Paper Products	3	1	73275.1
印刷业、记录媒介的复制	Printing,Reproduction of Recording Media	10	3	344507.7
文教体育用品制造业	Manufacture of Articles For Cultural, Educational and Sports Activities			
石油加工、炼焦及核燃料加工业	Processing of Petroleum, Cokeing,Processing of Nuclear and Nuclear Fuel	1		770310.0
化学原料及化学制品制造业	Manufacture of Raw Chemical Materials and Chemical Products	12	2	729214.5
医药制造业	Manufacture of Medicines	11		777584.6
化学纤维制造业	Manufacture of Chemical Fibers			
橡胶制品业	Manufacture of Rubber			
塑料制品业	Manufacture of Plastics	3	1	161429.1
非金属矿物制品业	Manufacture of Non-metallic Mineral Products	5		190879.0
黑色金属冶炼及压延加工业	Smelting and Pressing of Ferrous Metals	1	1	7838.9
有色金属冶炼及压延加工业	Smelting and Pressing of Non-ferrous Metals	5		164452.1
金属制品业	Manufacture of Metal Products	4		51234.8
通用设备制造业	Manufacture of General Purpose Machinery	7	1	833067.6
专用设备制造业	Manufacture of Special Equipment	31	3	1754595.7
交通运输设备制造业	Manufacture of Transport Equipment	28		9703891.3
电气机械及器材制造业	Manufacture of Electric Equipment and Machinery	12	2	2511691.4
通信设备、计算机及其他电子设备制造业	Manufacture of Communication Equipment, Computers and other Electronic Equipment	19	2	742257.1
仪器仪表及文化办公用	Manufacture of Measuring Instruments and Machinery for Cultural Activity and Office Work	9	1	517072.9
工艺品及其他制造业	Manufacture of Artwork and Other Manufacturing			
废弃资源和废旧材料回收加工业	Recycling and Disposal of Waste			
电力、热力的生产和供应业	Production and Supply of Electric Power and Heat Power	8	6	1776634.4
燃气生产和供应业	Gas Mining and Supplying Industry	1		141371.5
水的生产和供应业	Production and Supply of Water	1		58362.6

continued 3

(10 000 yuan)

工业销售产值（当年价）Value of Industry Products Sales (At Current Prices)	从业人员年平均人数（人）Annual Average Employers (person)	资产合计 Total Assets	流动资产小计 Total Working Capitals	固定资产小计 Total Fixed Assets	固定资产原价合计 Origing Value of Fixed Assets	累计折旧 Accumulative Total Depreciation
129779.3	13060	145517.1	71896.0	41803.3	76732.0	41603.1
33986.6	1367	61795.2	53864.4	6747.0	6262.8	2745.8
27503.0	979	37505.0	11124.1	26380.9	5045.8	1382.9
63869.4	796	101680.2	41757.2	51120.7	63106.2	15014.6
72719.5	4792	63826.9	10586.2	52777.4	54544.8	3535.1
338119.8	7177	452620.0	190910.4	163223.2	282435.2	144529.5
766183.0	1192	196009.5	95096.5	74778.5	126614.5	51836.0
714998.1	19368	966346.6	437548.3	370016.1	521395.7	224337.1
762696.9	10008	571203.4	314467.6	120731.0	219313.2	102213.6
155291.6	3132	265006.5	153153.8	61982.0	82033.1	22945.2
186185.8	2502	162309.5	63617.5	76936.3	95820.6	21373.7
7838.9	630	6612.5	5484.3	1109.2	1491.0	381.8
180955.7	4058	457503.6	224820.1	73279.4	95281.1	26175.2
54354.5	1782	62272.6	46374.1	15075.7	18820.2	4703.8
770301.7	11168	1679550.0	1350863.2	166101.7	270908.5	114051.2
1641764.8	39077	2870442.1	1884787.1	780727.1	1296250.5	586741.1
9301377.4	131323	10606772.7	6987139.7	2681899.6	3221058.8	1179193.6
2462441.0	36683	3512171.0	2538871.4	937856.7	850492.8	309771.7
683535.1	19716	1889917.7	888589.9	771120.8	656829.4	287246.4
497198.1	14342	910541.8	568354.1	281650.0	428607.3	202868.5
1776634.4	9964	2998732.6	544138.5	2347210.0	3355741.5	1073436.0
141157.0	2007	276488.3	119742.1	126081.1	152433.0	26351.9
58362.6	2725	101728.3	33152.5	67890.7	184566.8	125020.0

11-11 续表4

单位：万元

分组	Item	负债合计 Total Liabilites	流动负债 小计 Total Working Liabilities	长期负债 小计 Long-term Liabilities
烟草加工业	Manufacture of Tobacco			
纺织业	Manufacture of Textile	71118.8	58154.0	12964.8
纺织服装、鞋、帽制造业	Manufacture of Textile Wearing Apparel, Footwearand Caps	52079.7	44579.7	7500.0
皮革、毛皮、羽毛(绒)及其制品业	Manufacture of Leather, Fur, Feather (eiderdown) and Related Products	23628.0	16049.1	7578.9
木材加工及竹、藤、棕、草制品业	Processing of Timber,Manufacture of Wood,Plam and Straw Products	44739.8	29439.8	15300.0
家具制造业	Manufacture of Furniture			
造纸及纸制品业	Manufacture of Paper and Paper Products	33430.0	10902.1	12125.9
印刷业、记录媒介的复制	Printing,Reproduction of Recording Media	138144.4	116921.6	21160.1
文教体育用品制造业	Manufacture of Articles For Cultural, Educational and Sports Activities			
石油加工、炼焦及核燃料加工业	Processing of Petroleum, Cokeing,Processing of Nuclear and Nuclear Fuel	163164.7	163123.0	41.6
化学原料及化学制品制造业	Manufacture of Raw Chemical Materials and Chemical Products	501730.3	397113.0	61295.6
医药制造业	Manufacture of Medicines	251179.9	230630.2	18506.4
化学纤维制造业	Manufacture of Chemical Fibers			
橡胶制品业	Manufacture of Rubber			
塑料制品业	Manufacture of Plastics	191015.4	160255.9	29703.5
非金属矿物制品业	Manufacture of Non-metallic Mineral Products	86824.7	83899.9	2924.8
黑色金属冶炼及压延加工业	Smelting and Pressing of Ferrous Metals	6824.4	6824.4	
有色金属冶炼及压延加工业	Smelting and Pressing of Non-ferrous Metals	243094.6	176676.8	66417.8
金属制品业	Manufacture of Metal Products	49644.6	38448.5	11196.1
通用设备制造业	Manufacture of General Purpose Machinery	928577.6	889952.8	38624.8
专用设备制造业	Manufacture of Special Equipment	1490961.6	1297705.7	187320.1
交通运输设备制造业	Manufacture of Transport Equipment	6489193.7	5378776.2	944957.1
电气机械及器材制造业	Manufacture of Electric Equipment and Machinery	1545171.4	1361040.2	35789.4
通信设备、计算机及其他电子设备制造业	Manufacture of Communication Equipment, Computers and other Electronic Equipment	1015004.6	584166.2	373576.0
仪器仪表及文化办公用	Manufacture of Measuring Instruments and Machinery for Cultural Activity and Office Work	444143.2	356431.4	32883.4
工艺品及其他制造业	Manufacture of Artwork and Other Manufacturing			
废弃资源和废旧材料回收加工业	Recycling and Disposal of Waste			
电力、热力的生产和供应业	Production and Supply of Electric Power and Heat Power	2548091.8	1023656.4	1454947.1
燃气生产和供应业	Gas Mining and Supplying Industry	155518.2	128771.0	26747.2
水的生产和供应业	Production and Supply of Water	40786.7	24103.7	16683.0

continued 4

(10 000 yuan)

所有者权益合计 Total Owners' Equities	实收资本 Total Capital Hold	主营业务收入 Revenue from Principal Business	主营业务成本 Cost of Principal Business	主营业务税金及附加 Taxes and Other Charges on Principal Business
74398.3	18254.2	134188.2	118874.6	787.0
9715.5	7500.0	44190.5	33261.0	1950.4
13877.0	6000.0	24101.0	22135.0	33.2
56940.4	17501.1	59051.4	50462.8	519.0
30396.9	12526.3	67106.6	62455.4	433.2
314421.8	144101.2	336152.1	232140.8	2882.2
32844.8	36481.0	761671.4	598719.0	92900.2
464616.0	175113.2	728791.1	576688.7	1882.6
320023.5	115285.5	700729.3	347924.7	1227.9
73990.9	50589.0	154420.2	133959.2	718.2
75484.7	24000.0	171647.1	118550.3	897.4
-211.9	1000.0	7838.9	7706.8	48.4
214331.5	91255.9	204602.3	175649.5	1369.5
12072.7	8000.0	42825.1	33529.3	252.4
750972.0	83026.6	704315.3	523068.0	4144.4
1378242.1	558984.9	1685014.4	1378885.5	8250.7
4116378.4	1177577.8	9284894.3	8139777.2	81508.4
1966997.6	272082.5	2056227.4	1605908.1	16309.6
874912.9	308707.0	767278.5	642747.2	2452.0
463744.3	292607.6	509906.3	408492.2	3766.2
450250.8	243783.4	1961661.3	1433749.5	3058.9
120970.1	100000.0	141157.0	123673.6	1155.8
60941.6	39000.0	58362.6	52467.5	437.0

11-11 续表5

单位：万元

分组	Item	营业费用 Expenses for Operation	管理费用 Expenses for Management
烟草加工业	Manufacture of Tobacco		
纺织业	Manufacture of Textile	1676.8	8310.2
纺织服装、鞋、帽制造业	Manufacture of Textile Wearing Apparel, Footwearand Caps	3667.9	3826.7
皮革、毛皮、羽毛(绒)及其制品业	Manufacture of Leather, Fur, Feather (eiderdown) and Related Products	625.3	845.3
木材加工及竹、藤、棕、草制品业	Processing of Timber,Manufacture of Wood,Plam and Straw Products	2714.6	1874.4
家具制造业	Manufacture of Furniture		
造纸及纸制品业	Manufacture of Paper and Paper Products	942.5	1329.7
印刷业、记录媒介的复制	Printing,Reproduction of Recording Media	8555.0	36412.5
文教体育用品制造业	Manufacture of Articles For Cultural, Educational and Sports Activities		
石油加工、炼焦及核燃料加工业	Processing of Petroleum, Cokeing,Processing of Nuclear and Nuclear Fuel	1425.9	12337.9
化学原料及化学制品制造业	Manufacture of Raw Chemical Materials and Chemical Products	26953.7	63941.0
医药制造业	Manufacture of Medicines	245979.7	36657.3
化学纤维制造业	Manufacture of Chemical Fibers		
橡胶制品业	Manufacture of Rubber		
塑料制品业	Manufacture of Plastics	9848.8	7190.8
非金属矿物制品业	Manufacture of Non-metallic Mineral Products	19086.2	5339.8
黑色金属冶炼及压延加工业	Smelting and Pressing of Ferrous Metals		1076.7
有色金属冶炼及压延加工业	Smelting and Pressing of Non-ferrous Metals	1347.1	15799.0
金属制品业	Manufacture of Metal Products	3012.0	3099.1
通用设备制造业	Manufacture of General Purpose Machinery	26049.1	88515.4
专用设备制造业	Manufacture of Special Equipment	53391.9	156914.8
交通运输设备制造业	Manufacture of Transport Equipment	247054.5	390423.6
电气机械及器材制造业	Manufacture of Electric Equipment and Machinery	115361.3	165330.0
通信设备、计算机及其他电子设备制造业	Manufacture of Communication Equipment, Computers and other Electronic Equipment	24444.1	73880.6
仪器仪表及文化办公用	Manufacture of Measuring Instruments and Machinery for Cultural Activity and Office Work	12851.7	67687.4
工艺品及其他制造业	Manufacture of Artwork and Other Manufacturing		
废弃资源和废旧材料回收加工业	Recycling and Disposal of Waste		
电力、热力的生产和供应业	Production and Supply of Electric Power and Heat Power	17.1	48513.8
燃气生产和供应业	Gas Mining and Supplying Industry	7361.8	11804.7
水的生产和供应业	Production and Supply of Water	2478.1	5715.5

continued 5

(10 000 yuan)

财务费用 Financial cost	营业利润 Operating Profit	利润总额 Total Profits	亏损企业亏损总额 Total Loss of Deficit Enterprises	利税总额 Total Pre-tax Profits	本年应交增值税 Value Added Tax Payable
340.5	5425.7	6172.8	2000.4	10876.2	3916.4
405.6	1088.9	1014.4		4197.9	1233.1
231.5	992.3	1112.8		1147.3	1.3
900.3	2666.1	7145.3		11623.8	3959.5
1097.9	2244.3	1447.2	501.3	2685.3	804.9
1776.8	63241.0	62410.1	2967.9	83402.4	18110.1
3029.4	53071.1	53112.7		167950.5	21937.6
10801.7	52570.0	59009.4	13164.9	79895.4	19003.4
21767.4	53707.4	61699.8		151848.3	88920.6
2494.6	5828.0	6202.6	99.5	12567.4	5646.6
641.0	39330.2	44696.0		57982.5	12389.1
109.0	-918.9	-929.4	929.4	-396.8	484.2
5771.9	16844.6	16402.1		22130.6	4359.0
659.0	5203.1	980.7		2477.3	1244.2
-6201.9	45022.2	82399.0	1024.8	116600.0	30056.6
13387.7	120608.5	127573.0	9789.9	183617.4	47793.7
41687.0	484094.2	525375.4		805398.6	198514.8
32988.8	172630.0	166196.6	1683.4	294113.2	111607.0
12026.2	62843.9	77118.9	4861.3	89666.5	10095.6
3106.1	19420.5	25593.2	4.7	83414.5	54055.1
43696.0	516641.3	489008.6	20958.6	526775.2	34707.7
-2118.8	16106.2	16353.2		22617.7	5108.7
20.1	-1123.7	1553.4		5492.2	3501.8

11-12 规模以上工业高技术产业企业主要经济指标（2010年）

单位：万元

分组	Item	企业单位数（个）Number of Enterprises (unit)	亏损企业 Loss Making Enterprises	工业总产值（当年价）Gross Industrial Output Value (At Current Prices)
总　计	**Total**	**172**	**32**	**5223875.0**
按高技术产业行业分	**Classification by High-tech Industrial Sector**			
一、信息化学品制造	**Information Chemical Products**	**2**		**207074.2**
二、医药制造业	**Medicines Manufacturing**	**53**	**12**	**1004164.5**
#化学药品原药制造业	Chemical Medicine Manufacturing	21	5	724525.1
中成药制造业	Traditional Chinese Midicine	20	4	171193.4
生物、生化制品的制造业	Biology,Biochemistry Products	8	2	84947.0
三、航空航天器制造业	**Aviation and Aircrafts Manufacturing**	**15**	**1**	**2326027.0**
1.飞机制造及修理业	Manufacture and Repairing of Aircrafts	11	1	2095157.5
2.航天器制造业	Aircrafts Manufacturing	4		230869.5
四、电子及通讯设备制造业	**Electronic and Communication Equipment**	**48**	**10**	**991559.4**
1.通信设备制造业	Communication Equipment Manufacturing	14	3	128553.9
#通信传输设备制造业	Communication Transmitting Equipment	5		62288.8
通信交换设备制造业	Communication Exchanging Equipment	2		8899.2
通信终端设备制造业	Communication Terminal Equipment			
移动通信及终端设备制造业	Mobile Communication and Terminal Equipment	1	1	5500.0
2.雷达及配套设备制造业	Rader Equipments	1		143026.4
3.广播电视设备制造业	Broadcast and Television Equipments	3	1	16028.0
4.电子器件制造业	Electronic Appliances Manufacturing	16	4	451103.4
电子真空器件制造业	Electronic Vacuum Appliances	3		142703.5
半导体分立器件制造	Semiconductor Discreting Appliances	9	3	254443.6
集成电路制造	Integrate Circuit	2	1	42301.5
光电子器件及其他电子器件制造	Photoelectron Appliances and Other Electronic Appliances	2		11654.8
5.电子元件制造	Electronic Components Manufacturing	12	2	224414.6
6.家用视听设备制造	Household Audiovisual			
7.其他电子设备制造	Other Electronic Equipment	2		28433.1
五、电子计算机及办公设备制造业	**Computers and Office Equipment Manufacturing**	**2**		**20326.8**
1.电子计算机整机制造	Entired Computer Manufacturing	1		18276.5
2.计算机网络设备制造	Computer Network Equipment			
3.电子计算机外部设备制造	Computer Peripheral Equipment	1		2050.3
4.办公设备维修	Repairing of Office Equipment			
六、医疗设备及仪器仪表	**Medical Equipments and Meters**	**52**	**9**	**674723.1**
1.医疗仪器设备及器械制造	Medical Equipments and Instruments	6	2	13009.2
2.仪器仪表制造业	Instruments and Meters	46	7	661713.9
七、公共软件服务	**Public software Service**			
八、其他	**Others**			

Economic Indicators of High Technology Industry

Industrial Enterprises Above Designated Size（2010）

（10 000 yuan）

工业销售产值（当年价）Value of Industry Products Sales (At Current Prices)	从业人员年平均人数（人）Annual Average Employers (person)	资产合计 Total Assets	流动资产小计 Total Working Capitals	固定资产小计 Total Fixed Assets	固定资产原价合计 Origing Value of Fixed Assets	累计折旧 Accumulative Total Depreciation
5002893.4	**113034**	**10140217.1**	**6280568.1**	**2660645.4**	**3278689.0**	**1429747.5**
207215.8	**1733**	**176926.6**	**83602.8**	**35064.8**	**33934.7**	**9740.9**
961638.5	15212	846962.9	462000.0	208455.0	346452.3	149561.9
709177.1	9919	461615.6	310488.3	112751.6	200525.4	93157.9
147127.8	3453	188434.7	100684.6	49603.0	74168.7	27122.0
80347.6	1329	180958.4	38041.0	42993.6	67902.9	28348.7
2239353.6	52900	5773655.2	3884264.2	1249668.3	1678460.6	740298.5
2019788.9	46255	5211793.4	3592921.5	1013071.2	1426882.3	644794.0
219564.7	6645	561861.8	291342.7	236597.1	251578.3	95504.5
925043.7	23957	2191647.7	1125802.4	823622.8	718744.1	307647.5
123539.1	3778	273357.4	215907.3	47692.1	69530.8	32121.9
59395.5	1515	78562.0	58720.1	16110.4	17190.2	8643.7
8679.3	353	54261.9	48798.0	5463.9	17450.6	11986.7
3689.6	400	27126.8	11148.7	11217.6	15591.9	5243.5
124472.4	3595	347515.6	249467.4	61075.8	89510.0	28434.2
16026.0	440	25368.8	19205.3	4245.4	3738.2	1420.1
429763.9	7006	1218751.5	486091.9	649935.9	454099.6	202491.4
132763.1	2733	801239.7	260473.7	470497.9	250426.7	150721.5
243044.5	2639	246388.0	155756.9	83603.5	84018.9	19050.1
42301.5	909	162899.1	65881.0	92237.7	115284.8	31728.6
11654.8	725	8224.7	3980.3	3596.8	4369.2	991.2
202062.7	8808	316669.0	147416.8	58402.0	99392.1	42770.8
29179.6	330	9985.4	7713.7	2271.6	2473.4	409.1
20115.1	278	16133.0	6006.8	9892.4	14234.2	4341.8
17120.5	168	11566.0	2726.6	8839.4	12899.5	4060.1
2994.6	110	4567.0	3280.2	1053.0	1334.7	281.7
649526.7	18954	1134891.7	718891.9	333942.1	486863.1	218156.9
14278.9	912	31116.8	15585.7	13214.0	15567.9	4680.7
635247.8	18042	1103774.9	703306.2	320728.1	471295.2	213476.2

11-12 续表1

单位：万元

分　组	Item	负债合计 Total Liabilites	流动负债小计 Total Working Liabilities	长期负债小计 Long-term Liabilities
总　计	**Total**	**5835545.7**	**4557205.5**	**1130538.5**
按高技术产业行业分	**Classification by High-tech Industrial Sector**			
一、信息化学品制造	**Information Chemical Products**	107102.9	81786.5	20600.0
二、医药制造业	**Medicines Manufacturing**	406134.8	366324.9	37524.0
#化学药品原药制造业	Chemical Medicine Manufacturing	209555.7	195921.6	13434.1
中成药制造业	Traditional Chinese Midicine	109681.6	88464.5	21217.0
生物、生化制品的制造业	Biology,Biochemistry Products	81302.8	76610.7	2606.3
三、航空航天器制造业	**Aviation and Aircrafts Manufacturing**	3573924.2	2911408.0	644296.0
1.飞机制造及修理业	Manufacture and Repairing of Aircrafts	3273899.6	2678411.9	595487.6
2.航天器制造业	Aircrafts Manufacturing	300024.6	232996.1	48808.4
四、电子及通讯设备制造业	**Electronic and Communication Equipment**	1194158.4	744421.5	385588.7
1.通信设备制造业	Communication Equipment Manufacturing	139778.5	118209.8	13572.9
#通信传输设备制造业	Communication Transmitting Equipment	41874.5	38347.3	2000.0
通信交换设备制造业	Communication Exchanging Equipment	37420.9	31063.7	4060.0
通信终端设备制造业	Communication Terminal Equipment			
移动通信及终端设备制造业	Mobile Communication and Terminal Equipment	16512.5	11931.2	4581.2
2.雷达及配套设备制造业	Rader Equipments	257352.5	218724.9	38627.7
3.广播电视设备制造业	Broadcast and Television Equipments	18055.4	16704.2	341.7
4.电子器件制造业	Electronic Appliances Manufacturing	543202.8	245756.7	292432.7
电子真空器件制造业	Electronic Vacuum Appliances	314345.1	78720.3	235624.8
半导体分立器件制造	Semiconductor Discreting Appliances	153917.6	118637.0	30289.7
集成电路制造	Integrate Circuit	70732.2	44214.0	26518.2
光电子器件及其他电子器件制造	Photoelectron Appliances and Other Electronic Appliances	4207.9	4185.4	
5.电子元件制造	Electronic Components Manufacturing	235006.3	144263.0	40613.7
6.家用视听设备制造	Household Audiovisual			
7.其他电子设备制造	Other Electronic Equipment	762.9	762.9	
五、电子计算机及办公设备制造业	**Computers and Office Equipment Manufacturing**	5865.7	2865.7	
1.电子计算机整机制造	Entired Computer Manufacturing	3843.2	843.2	
2.计算机网络设备制造	Computer Network Equipment			
3.电子计算机外部设备制造	Computer Peripheral Equipment	2022.5	2022.5	
4.办公设备维修	Repairing of Office Equipment			
六、医疗设备及仪器仪表	**Medical Equipments and Meters**	548359.7	450398.9	42529.8
1.医疗仪器设备及器械制造	Medical Equipments and Instruments	14688.2	11912.6	2775.5
2.仪器仪表制造业	Instruments and Meters	533671.5	438486.3	39754.3
七、公共软件服务	**Public software Service**			
八、其他	**Others**			

continued 1

（10 000 yuan）

所有者权益合计 Total Owners' Equities	实收资本 Total Capital Hold	主营业务收入 Revenue from Principal Business	主营业务成本 Cost of Principal Business	主营业务税金及附加 Taxes and Other Charges on Principal Business
4296427.7	**1621083.4**	**5510140.4**	**4382480.0**	**17675.1**
69823.6	26268.0	207324.5	159899.2	49.7
436827.7	238686.8	903066.1	491729.9	1975.4
252059.7	113429.7	678605.4	349299.3	981.0
78753.0	70420.3	147911.2	90210.7	539.1
95655.5	50436.8	50038.1	28051.0	377.8
2198730.9	580978.7	2710853.0	2352218.1	7755.0
1936893.7	560755.3	2474504.3	2163620.1	6959.4
261837.2	20223.4	236348.7	188598.0	795.6
997488.8	385719.1	1006291.1	841122.5	3247.8
133578.9	103103.5	169696.0	138071.1	818.6
36687.6	31242.7	61105.1	51594.3	238.1
16841.0	49672.8	52808.3	42432.9	177.6
10614.3	6470.5	3689.6	3314.3	30.3
90163.1	18130.0	151289.8	131185.8	249.7
7313.3	2620.0	16626.4	13922.5	57.7
675548.5	206129.6	439063.3	377837.6	870.7
486894.6	77905.7	139947.8	116070.4	598.7
92470.2	54765.2	243557.1	212304.7	217.7
92166.9	71308.7	44051.1	39917.3	9.1
4016.8	2150.0	11507.3	9545.2	45.2
81662.5	54236.0	200436.0	157895.1	1044.7
9222.5	1500.0	29179.6	22210.4	206.4
10267.3	6500.0	20041.4	13469.6	32.6
7722.8	5000.0	16973.1	11788.7	7.2
2544.5	1500.0	3068.3	1680.9	25.4
583289.4	382930.8	662564.3	524040.7	4614.6
16428.6	18014.7	14517.5	11527.2	85.2
566860.8	364916.1	648046.8	512513.5	4529.4

11-12 续表2

单位：万元

分　组	Item	营业费用 Expenses for Operation	管理费用 Expenses for Management
总　计	**Total**	**396852.2**	**454041.6**
按高技术产业行业分	**Classification by High-tech Industrial Sector**		
一、信息化学品制造	**Information Chemical Products**	2010.4	4473.4
二、医药制造业	**Medicines Manufacturing**	266087.9	57726.0
#化学药品原药制造业	Chemical Medicine Manufacturing	229783.2	35778.9
中成药制造业	Traditional Chinese Midicine	27631.9	13414.8
生物、生化制品的制造业	Biology,Biochemistry Products	7708.9	6785.3
三、航空航天器制造业	**Aviation and Aircrafts Manufacturing**	73781.1	211886.9
1.飞机制造及修理业	Manufacture and Repairing of Aircrafts	71307.3	184242.9
2.航天器制造业	Aircrafts Manufacturing	2473.8	27644.0
四、电子及通讯设备制造业	**Electronic and Communication Equipment**	31094.0	92255.4
1.通信设备制造业	Communication Equipment Manufacturing	9765.9	23287.4
#通信传输设备制造业	Communication Transmitting Equipment	2728.3	5332.8
通信交换设备制造业	Communication Exchanging Equipment	3119.7	3082.6
通信终端设备制造业	Communication Terminal Equipment		
移动通信及终端设备制造业	Mobile Communication and Terminal Equipment	1165.6	2710.4
2.雷达及配套设备制造业	Rader Equipments	1475.8	13107.9
3.广播电视设备制造业	Broadcast and Television Equipments	949.7	1549.4
4.电子器件制造业	Electronic Appliances Manufacturing	10237.9	25365.5
电子真空器件制造业	Electronic Vacuum Appliances	7121.5	9880.5
半导体分立器件制造	Semiconductor Discreting Appliances	2851.8	13527.9
集成电路制造	Integrate Circuit		1552.7
光电子器件及其他电子器件制造	Photoelectron Appliances and Other Electronic Appliances	264.6	404.4
5.电子元件制造	Electronic Components Manufacturing	8285.9	26976.7
6.家用视听设备制造	Household Audiovisual		
7.其他电子设备制造	Other Electronic Equipment	378.8	1968.5
五、电子计算机及办公设备制造业	**Computers and Office Equipment Manufacturing**	2134.3	1637.2
1.电子计算机整机制造	Entired Computer Manufacturing	1974.1	845.2
2.计算机网络设备制造	Computer Network Equipment		
3.电子计算机外部设备制造	Computer Peripheral Equipment	160.2	792.0
4.办公设备维修	Repairing of Office Equipment		
六、医疗设备及仪器仪表	**Medical Equipments and Meters**	21744.5	86062.7
1.医疗仪器设备及器械制造	Medical Equipments and Instruments	887.3	2605.6
2.仪器仪表制造业	Instruments and Meters	20857.2	83457.1
七、公共软件服务	**Public software Service**		
八、其他	**Others**		

continued 2

（10 000 yuan）

财务费用 Financial Cost	营业利润 Operating Profit	利润总额 Total Profits	亏损企业亏损总额 Total Loss of Deficit Enterprises	利税总额 Total Pre-tax Profits	本年应交增值税 Value Added Tax Payable
72693.0	**323119.7**	**398060.0**	**12037.5**	**616886.0**	**201150.9**
2250.9	39140.6	40088.4		40635.4	497.3
25389.4	63212.6	71660.0	2173.8	170801.0	97165.6
15994.5	55496.1	56445.7	552.2	142280.9	84854.2
2983.2	6583.4	7362.8	742.9	15655.1	7753.2
6318.5	-428.8	7395.3	865.3	12018.3	4245.2
25669.9	102474.8	145053.0	366.6	177335.9	24527.9
23657.1	87580.4	123084.9	366.6	152959.2	22914.9
2012.8	14894.4	21968.1		24376.7	1613.0
14715.2	85513.0	100404.2	6903.3	122108.9	18456.9
1365.3	35317.2	36309.0	4837.7	41819.5	4691.9
161.5	2768.8	3482.5		5896.9	2176.3
599.1	2613.9	2659.1		3680.1	843.4
858.2	-4826.9	-4665.9	4665.9	-4287.0	348.6
2278.3	7400.7	7508.6		8245.0	486.7
411.9	298.4	823.7	45.0	881.4	
7169.3	29013.6	40543.8	1864.2	48592.7	7178.2
3669.7	5244.5	5835.0		9816.1	3382.4
3476.9	20670.4	20820.6	768.4	24619.9	3581.6
-35.8	2640.1	13306.3	1095.8	13407.3	91.9
58.5	458.6	581.9		749.4	122.3
3534.9	8762.3	11334.8	156.4	17326.5	4947.0
-44.5	4720.8	3884.3		5243.8	1153.1
116.1	2853.0	2897.1		3253.8	324.1
38.8	2466.5	2466.5		2545.6	71.9
77.3	386.5	430.6		708.2	252.2
4551.5	29925.7	37957.3	2593.8	102751.0	60179.1
496.1	-544.1	62.5	473.5	859.0	711.3
4055.4	30469.8	37894.8	2120.3	101892.0	59467.8

11-13 规模以上工业企业主要经济效益指标（2010年）

分　　组	Item	总资产贡献率（%） Ratio of Total Assets to Industrial Output Value (%)	资产负债率（%） Assets-Liability Ratio (%)
总　　计	**Total**	**12.19**	**57.61**
按工业行业大类分	Grouped by Sector		
煤炭开采和洗选业	Mining and Washing of Coal		
石油和天然气开采业	Extraction of Petroleum and Natural Gas	12.87	44.16
黑色金属矿采选业	Mining and Processing of Ferrous Metal Ores	36.94	121.82
有色金属矿采选业	Mining and Processing of Non-ferrous Metal Ores	7.96	54.56
非金属矿采选业	Mining and Processing of Nonmetal Ores		
其他采矿业	Mining of other Ores		
农副食品加工业	Processing of Food from Agricultural Porducts	10.82	64.25
食品制造业	Manufacture of Foods	16.69	49.26
饮料制造业	Manufacture of Beverages	14.66	55.90
烟草加工业	Manufacture of Tobacco	6.20	48.25
纺织业	Manufacture of Textile	8.97	49.36
纺织服装、鞋、帽制造业	Manufacture of Textile Wearing Apparel,Footwear and Caps	19.26	74.82
皮革、毛皮、羽毛(绒)及其制品业	Manufacture of Leather, Fur, Feather (eiderdown) and Related Products	3.13	63.00
木材加工及竹、藤、棕、草制品业	Processing of Timber,Manufacture of Wood,Plam and Straw Products	12.73	46.49
家具制造业	Manufacture of Furniture	36.11	44.38
造纸及纸制品业	Manufacture of Paper and Paper Products	8.97	54.25
印刷业、记录媒介的复制	Printing,Reproduction of Recording Media	18.56	32.64
文教体育用品制造业	Manufacture of Articles For Cultural,Educational and Sports Activities	102.33	50.13

Main Indicators of Economic Benefit of Industrial Enterprises Above Designated Size (2010)

流动资产周转率（次）Rate of Annual Turnover Working Capitals (times)	成本费用利润率（%）Ratio of Profits to Cost (%)	工业产品销售率（%）Proportion of Industrial Products Sold (%)	产值利税率（%）Ratio of Output Value to Profits and Tax (%)	每百元固定资产实现利税（元）Profit and Tax per 100 yuan of Fixed Assets (yuan)	每百元销售收入实现利税（元）Profit and Tax per 100 yuan of Sales Revenue (yuan)
1.57	**8.76**	**97.09**	**11.93**	**24.75**	**12.41**
1.59	2.82	84.36	25.20	29.44	13.04
1.55	14.60	68.93	349.38	58.07	29.71
2.67	3.54	101.67	5.50	12.31	5.58
3.66	2.89	98.14	3.77	22.37	4.02
4.65	3.56	93.76	6.21	29.48	7.05
2.26	9.38	125.47	16.64	20.36	14.45
0.82	5.06	99.96	12.66	9.88	12.10
2.26	4.31	97.98	7.62	15.58	7.66
2.00	6.38	98.55	12.63	91.25	11.04
2.08	4.67	183.14	7.64	22.74	4.76
1.46	10.05	85.32	13.54	17.26	16.91
4.13	8.30	95.26	12.46	51.71	12.80
4.30	2.75	94.85	4.68	10.58	5.08
1.88	19.49	98.25	21.97	27.98	22.59
10.57	15.72	98.53	17.97	121.69	18.26

11-13 续表

分　　组	Item	总资产贡献率（%） Ratio of Total Assets to Industrial Output Value (%)	资产负债率（%） Assets-Liability Ratio (%)
石油加工、炼焦及核燃料加工业	Processing of Petroleum, Cokeing,Processing of Nuclear and Nuclear Fuel	70.51	73.99
化学原料及化学制品制造业	Manufacture of Raw Chemical Materials and Chemical Products	10.86	52.65
医药制造业	Manufacture of Medicines	21.42	47.95
化学纤维制造业	Manufacture of Chemical Fibers	27.46	18.84
橡胶制品业	Manufacture of Rubber	20.63	48.79
塑料制品业	Manufacture of Plastics	9.83	63.16
非金属矿物制品业	Manufacture of Non-metallic Mineral Products	27.89	55.05
黑色金属冶炼及压延加工业	Smelting and Pressing of Ferrous Metals	36.52	71.77
有色金属冶炼及压延加工业	Smelting and Pressing of Non-ferrous Metals	9.77	58.53
金属制品业	Manufacture of Metal Products	12.26	54.92
通用设备制造业	Manufacture of General Purpose Machinery	9.43	54.97
专用设备制造业	Manufacture of Special Equipment	7.91	52.32
交通运输设备制造业	Manufacture of Transport Equipment	9.25	61.14
电气机械及器材制造业	Manufacture of Electric Equipment and Machinery	11.31	45.17
通信设备、计算机及其他电子设备制造业	Manufacture of Communication Equipment, Computers and other Electronic Equipment	7.65	54.35
仪器仪表及文化办公用	Manufacture of Measuring Instruments and Machinery for Cultural Activity and Office Work	9.80	48.35
工艺品及其他制造业	Manufacture of Artwork and Other Manufacturing	5.08	69.08
废弃资源和废旧材料回收加工业	Recycling and Disposal of Waste		
电力、热力的生产和供应业	Production and Supply of Electric Power and Heat Power	19.07	85.81
燃气生产和供应业	Gas Mining and Supplying Industry	7.89	50.12
水的生产和供应业	Production and Supply of Water	5.33	47.20

continued

流动资产周转率（次）Rate of Annual Turnover Working Capitals (times)	成本费用利润率（%）Ratio of Profits to Cost (%)	工业产品销售率（%）Proportion of Industrial Products Sold (%)	产值利税率（%）Ratio of Output Value to Profits and Tax (%)	每百元固定资产实现利税（元）Profit and Tax per 100 yuan of Fixed Assets (yuan)	每百元销售收入实现利税（元）Profit and Tax per 100 yuan of Sales Revenue (yuan)
6.71	7.93	99.70	16.21	145.22	17.42
2.08	7.92	97.77	10.43	16.85	10.44
2.01	8.52	95.77	17.01	49.30	18.91
3.36	13.95	102.45	16.89	23.85	16.44
2.44	7.46	87.34	9.06	35.57	11.43
1.70	5.04	95.12	7.99	22.19	8.67
3.03	12.85	97.48	16.10	44.93	16.92
5.14	7.74	97.97	12.43	80.13	10.85
1.49	7.63	101.54	10.48	28.24	10.31
1.72	6.47	96.77	8.90	32.80	9.43
0.90	10.39	93.91	12.30	43.48	13.72
1.03	7.99	94.47	10.51	15.85	10.98
1.45	6.15	96.07	8.60	26.73	8.95
1.01	9.07	97.03	11.83	37.96	14.19
1.03	10.37	93.41	12.39	17.10	12.21
0.98	6.10	96.00	15.40	21.62	15.72
4.47	0.42	97.21	1.95	12.69	1.97
3.99	30.90	99.97	28.97	15.13	26.31
1.40	10.71	99.87	14.69	12.38	14.61
1.75	2.63	98.62	9.45	2.99	9.53

主要统计指标解释

工业 指从事自然资源的开采，对采掘品和农产品进行加工和再加工的物质生产部门。具体包括:（1）对自然资源的开采，如采矿、晒盐等（但不包括禽兽捕猎和水产捕捞）;（2）对农副产品的加工、再加工，如粮油加工、食品加工、轧花、缫丝、纺织、制革等;（3）对采掘品的加工、再加工，如炼铁、炼钢、化工生产、石油加工、机器制造、木材加工等，以及电力、自来水、煤气的生产和供应等;（4）对工业品的修理、翻新，如机器设备的修理、交通运输工具（包括小卧车）的修理等。

工业统计调查单位 工业统计调查单位分为两类:独立核算法人工业企业和工业活动单位。

（1）独立核算法人工业企业 是指从事工业生产经营活动的单位。独立核算法人工业企业应同时具备以下条件:①依法成立，有自己的名称、组织机构和场所，能够承担民事责任;②独立拥有和使用资产，承担负债，有权与其他单位签订合同;③独立核算盈亏，并能够编制资产负债表。

（2）工业活动单位 是指在一个场所从事一种或主要从事一种工业生产活动的经济单位。它包括独立核算工业企业按主营业务活动（即工业生产活动）划分的主营业务活动单位和非工业企业所属的工业生产活动单位（即原非独立核算工业生产单位）。工业活动单位，一般应同时具备以下三个条件:①具有一个场所，从事一种或主要从事一种工业活动;②单独组织工业生产、经营或业务活动;③单独核算收入和支出。

本年鉴中涉及的企业登记注册类型:

（1）国有及国有控股企业 指国有企业加上国有控股企业。国有企业（即过去的全民所有制工业或国营工业）是指企业全部资产归国家所有，并按《中华人民共和国企业法人登记管理条例》规定登记注册的非公司制的经济组织。包括国有企业、国有独资公司和国有联营企业。1957年以前的公私合营和私营工业，后均改造为国营工业，这部分工业的资料不单独分列时，均包括在国有企业内。

（2）集体企业 指企业资产归集体所有，并按《中华人民共和国企业法人登记管理条例》规定登记注册的经济组织。是社会主义公有制经济的组成部分。包括城乡所有使用集体投资举办的企业，以及部分个人通过集资自愿放弃所有权并依法经工商行政管理机关认定为集体所有制的企业。

（3）股份合作企业 指以合作制为基础，由企业职工共同出资入股，吸收一定比例的社会资产投资组建，实行自主经营，自负盈亏，共同劳动，民主管理，按劳分配与按股分红相结合的一种集体经济组织。

（4）联营企业 指两个及两个以上相同或不同所有制性质的企业法人或事业单位法人，按自愿、平等、互利的原则，共同投资组成的经济组织。联营企业包括:

国有联营企业指国有企业与国有企业间的联营;

集体联营企业指集体企业与集体企业间的联营;

国有与集体联营企业指国有企业与集体企业间的联营。

（5）有限责任公司 指根据《中华人民共和国公司登记管理条例》规定登记注册，由两个以上，五十个以下的股东共同出资，每个股东以其所认缴的出资额对公司承担有限责任，公司以其全部资产对其债务承担责任的经济组织。

有限责任公司包括国有独资公司以及其他有限责任公司。

（6）股份有限公司 指根据《中华人民共和国企业法人登记管理条例》规定登记注册，其全部注册资本由等额股份构成并通过发行股票筹集资本，股东以其认购的股份对公司承担有限责任，公司以其全部资产对其债务承担责任的经济组织。

（7）私营企业 指由自然人投资设立或由自然人控股，以雇佣劳动为基础的营利性经济组织。包括按照《公司法》、《合伙企业法》、《私营企业暂行条例》规定登记注册的私营有限责任公司、私营股份有限公司、私营合伙企业和私营独资企业。

（8）港、澳、台商投资企业 指企业注册登记类型中的港、澳、台资合资、合作、独资经营企业和股份有限公司之和。

（9）外商投资企业 指企业注册登记类型中的中外合资、合作经营企业、外资企业和外商投资股份有限公司之和。

轻工业 指主要提供生活消费品和制作手工工具的工业。按其所使用的原料不同，可分为两大类:（1）以农产品为原料的轻工业，是指直接或间接以农产品为基本原料的轻工业。主要包括食品制造、饮料制造、烟草加工、纺织、缝纫、皮革和毛皮制作、造纸以及印刷等工业;（2）以非农产品为原料的轻工业，是指以工业品为原料的轻工业。主要包括文教体育用品、化学药品制造、合成纤维制造、日用化学制品、日用玻璃制品、日用金属制品、手工工具制造、医疗器械制造、文化和办公用机械制造等工业。

重工业 是指为国民经济各部门提供物质技术基础的主要生产资料的工业。按其生产性质和产品用途，可以分为下列三类:（1）采掘（伐）工业，是指对自然资源的开采，包括石油开采、煤炭开采、金属矿开采、非金属矿开采和木材采伐等工业;（2）原材料工业，指向国民经济各部门提供基本材料、动力和燃料的工业。包括金属冶炼及加工、炼焦及焦炭、化学、化工原料、水泥、人造板以及电力、石油和煤炭加工等工业;（3）加工工业，是指对工业原材料进行再加工制造的工业。包括装备国民经济各部门的机械设备制造工业、金属结构、水泥制品等工业，以及为农业提供的生产资料如化肥、农药等工业。

根据上述划分原则，修理业中以重工业产品为修理作业对象的划为重工业，反之划为轻工业。

工业总产值 是以货币表现的工业企业在一定时期内生产的已出售或可供出售工业产品总量，它反映一定时间内工业生产的总规模和总水平。它包括: 在本企业内不再进行加工，经检验、包装入库（规定不需包装的产品除外）的成品价值，对外加工费收入，自制半成品、在产品期末初差额价值。工业总产值采用“工厂法”计算，即以工业企业作为一个整体，按企业工业生产活动的最终成果来计算，企业内部不允许重复计算，不能把企业内部各个车间（分厂）生产的成果相加。但在企业之间、行业之间、地区之间存在着重复计算。

轻重工业总产值的划分是按“工厂法”计算的，即一个工业企业生产的主要产品性质属于轻工业，则该企业的全部总产值作为轻工业总产值; 如它的主要产品性质属于重工业，则该企业的全部总产值作为重工业总产值。

工业增加值 指工业行业在报告期内以货币表现的工业生产活动的最终成果。

实收资本 指企业实际收到的投资人投入的资本。按投资主体可分为国家资本、集体资本、法人资本、个人资本、港澳台资本和外商资本等。

资产合计 指企业拥有或控制的能以货币计量的经济资源。包括各种财产、债权和其他权利。资产按其流动性划分为流动资产、长期投资、固定资产、无形及递延资产和其他资产。

（1）流动资产 指企业可以在一年内或者超过一年的一个生产周期内变现或耗用的资产合计。包括现金及各种存款、短期投资、应收及预付款项、存货等。

（2）固定资产 指企业固定资产净值、固定资产清理、在建工程、待处理固定资产损失所占用的资金合计。

（3）无形资产 指企业长期使用而没有实物形态的资产。包括专利权、非专利技术、商标权、著作权、土地使用权、商誉等。

负债合计 指企业承担的能以货币计量，将以资产或劳务偿付的债务。负债一般按偿还期长短分为流动负债和长期负债、递延税项等。

（1）流动负债 指企业在一年内或者超过一年的一个营业周期内需要偿还的债务合计，其中包括短期借款、应付及预收款项、应付工资、应交税金和应交利润等。

（2）长期负债 指企业在一年以上或者超过一年的一个营业周期以上需要偿还的债务合计，其中包括长期借款、应付债务、长期应付款项等。

所有者权益 指企业投资人对企业净资产的所有权。企业净资产等于企业全部资产减去全部负债后的余额，其中包括投资者对企业的最初投入，以及资本公积金、盈余公积金和未分配利润，对股份制企业即为股东权益。

固定资产原价 指企业在建造、购置、安装、改建、扩建、技术改造某项固定资产时所支出的全部货币总额。它一般包括买价、包装费、运杂费和安装费等。

固定资产净值 是指固定资产原价减去历年已提折旧额后的净额。

流动资产 是指可以在一年或者超过一年的一个营业周期内变现或者耗用的资产，包括现金及各种存款、短期投资、应收及预付货款、存货等。

主营业务收入 根据会计“利润表”中对应指标的本年累计数填列。未执行2001年《企业会计制度》的企业，用“产品销售收入”的本期累计数代替。

主营业务成本 根据会计“利润表”中对应指标的本年累计数填列。未执行2001年《企业会计制度》的企业，用“产品销售成本”的本期累计数代替。

营业费用 根据会计“利润表”中对应指标的本年累计数填列。未执行2001年《企业会计制度》的企业，用“产品销售费用”的本期累计数代替。

主营业务税金及附加 根据会计“利润表”中对应指标的本年累计数填列。未执行2001年《企业会计制度》的企业，用“产品销售税金及附加”的本期累计数代替。

利润总额 指企业实现的利润。

应交增值税 指企业在报告期内应交纳的增值税额。

总资产贡献率 反映企业全部资产的获利能力，是企业经营业绩和管理水平的集中体现，是评价和考核企业盈利能力的核心指标。计算公式为:

总资产贡献率=(利润总额+税金总额+利息支出)/平均资产总额*100%

资本保值增值率 该指标反映企业净资产的变动状况，是企业发展能力的集中体现。计算公式为：

资本保值增值率（%）=报告期期末所有者权益/上年同期期末所有者权益*100%

资产负债率 该指标既反映企业经营风险的大小，也反映企业利用债权人提供的资金从事经营活动的能力。计算公式为:

资产负债率=负债总额/资产总额*100%

工业成本费用利润率 指在一定时期内实现的利润与成本费用之比，是反映工业生产成本及费用投入的经济效益指标，同时也是反映降低成本的经济效益的指标。计算公式为:

工业成本费用利润率(%)=利润总额/成本及费用总额*100%

工业增加值率 指在一定时期内工业增加值占同期工业总产值的比重，反映降低中间消耗的经济效益。计算公式为:

工业增加值率(%)=工业增加值(现价)/工业总产值*100%

流动资产周转次数 指在一定时期内流动资产完成的周转次数，反映流动资产的周转速度。计算公式为:

流动资产周转次数=产品销售收入/全部流动资产平均余额

产品销售率 指报告期工业销售产值与同期全部工业总产值之比，是反映工业产品已实现销售的程度，分析工业产销衔接情况，研究工业产品满足社会需求程度的指标。计算公式为:

产品销售率(%)=工业销售产值/工业总产值(现价)*100%

全员劳动生产率 指根据产品的价值量指标计算的平均每一个就业人员在单位时间内的产品生产量。是考核企业经济活动的重要指标，是企业生产技术水平、经营管理水平、职工技术熟练程度和劳动积极性的综合表现。目前我国的全员劳动生产率是将工业企业的工业增加值除以同一时期全部就业人员的平均人数来计算的。计算公式为:

全员劳动生产率(%)=工业增加值/全部就业人员平均人数*100%

Explanatory Notes on Main Statistical Indicators

Industry refers to the material production sector which is engaged in extraction of natural resources and processing and reprocessing of minerals and agricultural products, including (1) extraction of natural resources, such as mining, salt production, (but not including hunting and fishing); (2) processing and reprocessing of farm and sideline produces, such as rice husking, flour milling, wine making, oil pressing, cotton ginning, silk reeling, spinning and weaving, and leather making; (3) manufacture of industrial products, such as steel making, iron smelting, chemicals manufacturing, petroleum processing, machine building, timber processing; water and gas production and electricity generation and supply; (4)repairing of industrial products such as the repairing of machinery and means of transport (including cars).

Units of Industrial Statistics and Inquiry: They are classified into two categories (1) corporate industrial enterprises with independent accounting system (2) industrial establishments.

(1) Corporate industrial enterprises with independent accounting system refer to enterprises engaging in industrial production activities, which meet the following requirements: ① They are established legally, having their own names, organizations, location, able to take civil liability; ②They possess and use their assets independently, assume liabilities, and are entitled to sign contracts with other units; ③They are financially independent and compile their own balance sheets.

(2)Industrial establishments refer to economic units which located in one single place and engaged entirely or primarily in one kind of industrial activity, including financially independent industrial enterprises and units engaged in industrial activities under the non industrial enterprises (or financially dependent). Industrial establishments generally meet the following requirements: ① They have each one location and are engaged in one kind of industrial activity each; ② They operate and manage their industrial production activities separately;③ They have accounts of income and expenditures separately.

(1) State-owned Enterprises refer to industrial enterprises where the means of production or income are owned by the state. Joint state-private industries and private industries, which existed before 1957, have been transformed into state industries. Statistics on these enterprises has been included in the state-owned industries since 1957 when separation of data was no longer necessary.

(2) Collective-owned Enterprises refer to industrial enterprises where the means of production are owned collectively, including urban and rural enterprises invested by collectives and some enterprises which were formerly owned privately but have been registered in industrial and commercial administration agency as collective units through raising fund from the public.

(3) Share-holding Cooperative Enterprises refer to economic units set up on cooperative basis, with funding partly from members of the enterprise and partly from outside investment, where the operation and management is decided by the members who also participate in the production, and the distribution of income is based both on work (labour input) and on shares (capital input).

(4) Joint-operation enterprises refer to economic units that are established by joint investment by two or more corporate enterprises or institutions of the same or different types of ownership on voluntary, equal and mutual-beneficial basis. They include:

a) state-owned joint-operation enterprises (joint operation between state-owned enterprises);

b) collective joint-operation enterprises (joint operation between collective enterprises; and

c) state-collective joint-operation enterprises (joint operation between state and collective enterprises).

(5) Limited Liability Corporations refer to economic units registered in accordance with the Regulation of the People's Republic of China on the Management of Registration of Corporations, with capitals from 2 to 49 investors, each investor bears limited liability to the corporation depending on his/her holding of shares, and the corporation bears liability to its debt to the maximum of its total assets.

(6) Share-holding Corporations Ltd. refer to economic units registered in accordance with the Regulation of the People's Republic of China on the Management of Registration of Corporate Enterprises,with total registered capitals divided into equal shares and raised through issuing stocks. Each investor bears limited liability to the corporation depending on the holding of shares, and the corporation bears liability to its debt to the maximum of its total assets.

(7) Private Enterprises refer to economic unitsinvested or controlled (by holding the majority of the shares) by natural persons who hire labours for profit-making activities. Included in this category are private limited liability corporations, private share-holding corporations Ltd., private partnership enterprises and private sole investment enterprises registered in accordance with the Corporation Law, Partnership Enterprise Law and Tentative Regulation on Private Enterprises.

(8) Enterprises with Funds form Hong Kong, Macao and Taiwan refers to all industrial enterprises registered as the joint-venture, cooperative, sole (exclusive) investment industrial enterprises and limited liability corporations with funds from Hong Kong, Macao and Taiwan.

(9) Foreign Funded Enterprises refers to all industrial enterprises registered as the joint-venture, cooperative, sole (exclusive) investment industrial enterprises and limited liability corporations with foreign funds.

Light Industry refers to the industry that produces consumer goods and hand tools. It consists of two categories, depending on the materials used:

(1)Industries using farm products as raw materials. These are branches of light industry which directly or indirectly use farm products as basic raw materials, including the manufacture of food and beverages, tobacco processing, textile, clothing, fur and leather manufacturing, paper making, printing, etc.

(2)Industries using non farm products as raw materials. These are branches of light industry which use manufactured goods as raw materials, including the manufacture of cultural, educational articles and sports goods, chemicals, synthetic fiber, chemical products for daily use, glass products for daily use, metal products for daily use, hand tools, medical apparatus and instruments, and the manufacture of cultural and clerical machinery.

Heavy Industry refers to the industry which produces capital goods, and provides various sectors of the national economy with necessary material and technical basis. It consists of the following three branches according to the purpose of production or the use of products:

(1)Mining, quarrying and logging industry refers to the industry that extracts natural resources, including extraction of petroleum, coal, metal and non-metal ores and logging.

(2)Raw materials industry refers to the industry that provides various sectors of the national economy with raw materials, fuels and power. It includes smelting and processing of metals, coking and coke chemistry, chemical materials and building materials such as cement, plywood, and power, petroleum refining and coal dressing.

(3)Manufacturing industry refers to the industry that processes raw materials. It includes machine building industry which equips sectors of the national economy, industries of metal structure and cement products, industries producing means of agricultural production, such as chemical fertilizers and pesticides. According to the above principle of classification, the repairing trades which are engaged primarily in repairing products of heavy industry are classified into heavy industry while these engaged in repairing products of light industry are classified into light industry.

Gross Industrial Output Value is the total volume of industrial products sold or available for sale in value terms which reflects the total achievements and overall scale of industrial production during a given period. It includes the value of the finished products, which are not to be further processed in the enterprises and have been inspected, packed and put in storage, the value of industrial services rendered to other units, and the changes in the value of the semi-finished products and products in process between the beginning and closing of the period. The gross industrial output value is calculated with "factory method". No double calculations are to be made within the same enterprise. However, double counting does occur among different enterprises.

Output value of light and heavy industries is based on the "factory" method. If the major products of an industrial enterprise are classified as light industry products, the entire gross output value of that enterprise is classified into the light industry; the same principle applies to heavy industry.

Value-added of Industry refers to the final results of industrial production of the industrial trade in money terms during the reference period.

Capital Obtained refers to capital actually received by the enterprise from investors. It can be further classified by investors as state capital, collective capital, corporate capital, individual capital, capital from Hong Kong, Macau and Taiwan and foreign capital.

Total Assets refer to all economic resources, owned

or controlled by enterprises, that could be measured in monetary terms, including properties, creditors equity and other economic rights of all forms. Classified by the degree of equitability, total assets include circulating assets, long term investment, fixed assets, intangible assets anddeferred assets, and other assets.

(1)Circulating assets (working capital) refer to assets which can be cashed in or spent or consumed in anoperating cycle of one year or over one year, including cash, all kinds of deposits, short term investment, receivables, advance payment, stock, etc.

(2)Fixed assets refer to the net value of fixed assets, clearance of fixed assets, project under construction, fixed assets losses in suspense. These are corporations fund holdings.

(3)Intangible assets refer to the assets without material form used by enterprises over a long time, such as patents, non-patent technologies, trade marks, copyright, land use right, business reputation, etc.

Total Liabilities refer to the debts, measured in monetary terms, that enterprises are responsible for repayment in the form of cash, assets or labour. Classified by terms of repayment, liability include liquid liabilities and long-term liabilities.

(1)Liquid liabilities (also called quick liabilities or immediate liabilities) refer to enterprises' total debt payable within an operating cycle of one year or over one year, including short term loans, payable and advance payments, wages payable, taxes payable and profit payable, etc.

(2)Long term liabilities refers to total debt payable within an operating cycle of one year or over one year, including long-term loans, payable liabilities, long-term payable, etc.

Creditors' Equity refers to investors ownership of net assets of the enterprise. It is equal to the total assets of the enterprise minus its total liabilities, including the primary input from investors, capital accumulation fund, surplus accumulation fund and undistributed profit. It is the shareholder's equity in share-holding companies.

Original Value of Fixed Assets refers to the original value of all fixed assets owned by industrial enterprises, calculated at the cost paid at the time of purchase, installation, reconstruction, expansion, and technical innovation and transformation of the said assets, which includes expenses on purchase, package, transportation, and installation, etc.

Net Value of Fixed Assets is obtained by deducting depreciation over years from the original value of fixed assets.

Working Capital (Circulating Assets) refers to assets which can be cashed in or spent or consumed in an operating cycle of one year or over one year, which includes cash, various deposits, short term investment, and receivable payments, and advance payments, stock, etc.

Income from Main Operation Filled by cumulative number of related index in 'profit table' in current year. it is replaced by cumulative number of 'sales revenue' in current period, as to the enterprises not operating by 'Enterprise Accounting System' of 2001.

Cost of Main Operation Filled by cumulative number of related index in 'profit table' in current year. it is replaced by cumulative number of 'cost of sales' in current period, as to the enterprises not operating by 'Enterprise Accounting System' of 2001.

Expenses for Operation Filled by cumulative number of related index in 'profit table' in current year. it is replaced by cumulative number of 'sales of expense' in current period, as to the enterprises not operating by 'Enterprise Accounting System' of 2001.

Main Operation Tax and Extra Charges Filled by cumulative number of related index in 'profit table' in current year. it is replaced by cumulative number of 'sales tax and extra charges' in current period, as to the enterprises not operating by 'Enterprise Accounting System' of 2001.

Total Profits refer to the profits gained by the enterprises.

Value-added Tax Payable refers to the amount of the value added tax which should be paid by the enterprises in the reporting period.

Ratio of Profits, Taxes and Interests to Average Assets reflects the profit-making capability of all assets of the enterprise and is a key indicator manifesting the performance and management and evaluating the profit-making potential of the enterprise. It is calculated as follows:

Ratio of profits, taxes and interests to average assets (%) = [(Total profits+total Taxes+interest payment) / average assets]×100%

The Rate of Value-Sustained and Value-Added Assets reflects the indicator of net assets changes ofenterprises and the embodiment of the enterprise development.

The rate of value-sustained and value-added

assets=owner's equity at the end of current period/ owner's equity at the same period of last year*100%

Ratio of Debts to Assets reflect both the operation risk and the capability of the enterprise in making use ofthe capital from the creditors. It is calculated as follows:

Ratio of debts to assets (%) = (Total debts / total assets)×100%

Ratio of Profits to Total Industrial Costs refers to the ratio of profits realized in a given period to the total costs in the same period, which reflects the economic efficiency of input cost and is calculated as follows:

Ratio of Profits to Total Industrial Cost(%)=(Total Profits/ Total Costs)×100%

Value-added Rate of Industry refers to the ratio of value added of industry in a given period to the gross output value in the same period, which reflects the economic efficiency of cutting down the intermediate input and is calculated as follows:

Value-added Rate of Industry(%)=[Value-added of Industry (at current prices)] / [Gross Output Value (at Current Prices)]×100%

Turnover of Working Capital refers to the number of times of turnover of working capital in a given period of time, which reflects the speed of the turnover of working capital and is calculated as follows:

Turnover of Working Capital(%)=(Sales Revenue ofProducts) / (Average Balance of Total Working Capital)×100%

Ratio of Sales to Gross Output Value refers to the sales of industrial products to the gross industrial output value during the reference period, and is important in reflecting the linkage between production and sales and the extent of the needs of the society that has been met by the supply of industrial products. It is calculated as follows:

Ratio of Sales to Gross Output Value=[Industrial sales / Gross industrial output value (at current prices)] × 100%

Overall Labour Productivity of Industrial Enterprises refers to the average output per employed person in industrial enterprises in value terms. At present, the value added and the average number of staff and workers of an industrial enterprises in a given period are used to calculate the overall labour productivity. The formula used is:

Overall Labour Productivity=(Value Added of Industry) / (Average Number of Staff and Workers)*100%

12 能　源

ENERGY

资料整理：雷稳强　于元英
Data management:Lei Wenqiang Yu Yuanying

第十二部分　能源

一、简要说明

本章资料包括规模以上工业能源购销存情况、全市单位GDP能耗、单位GDP电耗、规模以上工业单位增加值能耗、规模以上工业企业用水情况等，由西安市统计局能源处提供。

二、主要指标

规模以上工业综合能源消费量（吨标准煤）	5126530	比上年增加	266579吨标准煤
单位GDP能耗（吨标准煤/万元）	0.803	比上年下降	2.06%
单位GDP电耗（千瓦时/万元）	761.98	比上年下降	0.998%
规模以上工业单位增加值能耗（吨标准煤/万元）	0.703	比上年下降	12.18%

12　ENERGY

Ⅰ.Brief Introduction

Data in this chapter reflects Energy Purchases Consumption and Inventory of Industrial Enterprises Above Designated size,Energy Consumption per Unit of GDP in Whole City,Electricity Consumption per Unit of GDP,Energy Consumption per Unit of Industrial Value-added above Designated Size and Statistics on Water Use of Industrial Enterprises above Designated Size. Data in this chapter are provided and compiled by Transportation Division of the Xi'an Bureau of Statistics.

Ⅱ.Major Indicators

		Increase over Preceding Year
Comprehensive Energy Consumption Above Designated Size(Tons of Standard Coal)	5126530	266579
Energy Consumption of GDP per Unit (Tons of Standard Coal /10,000yuan)	0.803	-2.06%
Power Consumption of GDP per Unit (kilowatt-hour/10,000yuan)	761.98	-0.998%
Energy Consumption of value added per Unit of Industrial Enterprises Above Designated Size (Tons of Standard Coal /10,000yuan)	0.703	-12.18%

12-1 规模以上工业企业能源购进、消费及库存（2010年）

Energy Purchases Consumption and Inventory of Industrial Enterprises Above Designated size（2010）

能源名称	Name(unit)	年初库存 Stock (year-beginning)	购进量 实物量 Quantity
原煤(吨)	Raw Coal（ton）	638860	7679685
洗精煤(吨)	Washed Coal(ton)		1667
其他洗煤(吨)	Other Washed Coals(ton)		17
煤制品(吨)	Briquettes(ton)	1373	20293
焦炭(吨)	Coke(ton)	2447	60489
其他焦化产品(吨)	Other Coking Products(ton)	413	6000
焦炉煤气(万立方米)	Other Gases(10 000cu.m)		23
天然气（气态）(万立方米)	Natural Gas(10 000cu.m)		10620
液化天然气（液态）(吨)	Liquefied Natural Gas (Liquid)(ton)		15
原油(吨)	Crude Oil(ton)	33486	1756745
汽油(吨)	Gasoline(ton)	249	30067
煤油(吨)	Kerosene(ton)	587	14558
柴油(吨)	Diesel Oil(ton)	1333	55037
燃料油(吨)	Fuel Oil(ton)	230	1282
液化石油气(吨)	LPG(ton)		1130
其他石油制品(吨)	Other Petroleum Products(ton)	67	5815
热力(百万千焦)	Heat (1 million kilo-joule)		8460446
电力(万千瓦时)	Electricity(10 000kwh)		747327
其他燃料(吨标准煤)	Other Fuels(ton of SCE)	81	4689
能源合计(吨标准煤)	Total Energy(ton of SCE)		

12-1 续表

能源名称	Name(unit)	购进量Purchases 金额（万元） Sum (10 000 yuan)
原煤(吨)	Raw Coal（ton）	429218
洗精煤(吨)	Washed Coal(ton)	98
其他洗煤(吨)	Other Washed Coals(ton)	1
煤制品(吨)	Briquettes(ton)	1103
焦炭(吨)	Coke(ton)	10241
其他焦化产品(吨)	Other Coking Products(ton)	900
焦炉煤气(万立方米)	Other Gases(10 000cu.m)	23
天然气（气态）(万立方米)	Natural Gas(10 000cu.m)	19425
液化天然气（液态）(吨)	Liquefied Natural Gas (Liquid)(ton)	9
原油(吨)	Crude Oil(ton)	761549
汽油(吨)	Gasoline(ton)	21418
煤油(吨)	Kerosene(ton)	9396
柴油(吨)	Diesel Oil(ton)	36198
燃料油(吨)	Fuel Oil(ton)	498
液化石油气(吨)	LPG(ton)	696
其他石油制品(吨)	Other Petroleum Products(ton)	7224
热力(百万千焦)	Heat (1 million kilo-joule)	38541
电力(万千瓦时)	Electricity(10 000kwh)	413619
其他燃料(吨标准煤)	Other Fuels(ton of SCE)	2022
能源合计(吨标准煤)	Total Energy(ton of SCE)	

continued

消费量 Consumption				年末库存
合　计 Total	工业生产消费 Industrial Production Consume	用于原材料 as Raw Material	非工业生产消费 Non-industrial Production Consume	Stock year-end
7774450	7648196	87148	126254	539198
1571	1571			96
17	17			
20564	18717		1847	1072
58630	58629	286	1	4078
4486	4486			1927
23	23			
10619	10133	262	486	
15	12		3	
1741676	1741676			48555
30004	23891	1381	6113	457
14276	14274	7	2	868
55290	54237	673	1053	1154
1237	1237			276
1130	1123		7	
5834	5834	652		47
12692357	11381084		1311273	
831956	813358		18598	
4709	4279		430	60
9645447	9469201		176246	

12-2 规模以上工业分行业主要能源品种消费量（2010年）

行　业	Sector	原煤（吨） Raw Coal (ton)
总　计	**Total**	**7774450**
按工业行业大类分列	Grouped by Sector	
煤炭开采和洗选业	Coal Mining and Dressing	
石油和天然气开采业	Petroleum and Natural Gas Extraction	
黑色金属矿采选业	Ferrous Metals Mining and Dressing	
有色金属矿采选业	Nonferrous Metals Mining and Dressing	
非金属矿采选业	Nonmetal Minerals Mining and Dressing	
其他采矿业	Other Mining Industry	
农副食品加工业	Agricultural Products and Non-stable Food Processing Industry	279648
食品制造业	Food Production	53399
饮料制造业	Beverage Production	114775
烟草制品业	Tobacco Processing	7
纺织业	Textile Industry	16416
纺织服装、鞋、帽制造业	Textile Clothing, Footwear and Headgear Industry	
皮革、毛皮、羽毛(绒)及其制品业	Leather, Fur, Feather (eiderdown) and Their Products Industry	
木材加工及木、竹、藤、棕、草制品制造	Timber Processing,Bamboo,Cane,Palm Fiber and Straw Products	6379
家具制造业	Furniture Manufacturing	
造纸及纸制品业	Papermaking and Paper products	407665
印刷业和记录媒介的复制	Printing,Record Medium Reproduction	754
文教体育用品制造业	Cultural,Educational and Sports Goods	215
石油加工、炼焦及核燃料加工业	Petroleum Refining, Ccoke Making and Nuclear Fuel Processing Industry	25201
化学原料及化学制品制造业	Raw Chemical Materials and Chemical Products	94168
医药制造业	Medical and Pharmaceutical Products	41285
化学纤维制造业	Chemical Fiber	974
橡胶制品业	Rubber Products	41
塑料制品业	Plastic Products	5075
非金属矿物制品业	Nonmetal Mineral Products	419157
黑色金属冶炼及压延加工业	Smelting and Pressing of Ferrous Metals	77697
有色金属冶炼及压延加工业	Smelting and Pressing of Nonferrou Metals	1737
金属制品业	Metal Products	15502
通用设备制造	General Equipment Manufacturing Industry	29729
专用设备制造业	Special Purpose Equipment	81722
交通运输设备制造业	Transport Equipment	349524
电气机械及器材制造业	Electric Equipment and Machinery	29274
通信设备、计算机及其他电子设备制造业	Communication Equipment, Computer and Other Electronic Equipment Manufacturing Industry	4193
仪器仪表及文化办公用机械制造业	Instruments,Meters,Cultural and Office	2443
工艺品及其他制造业	Handicraft and Other Stuff Manufacturing Industry	4660
废弃资源和废旧材料回收加工业	Discarded Resources and Waste Materials Salvaging and Processing Industry	
电力、热力的生产和供应业	Electric Power, Heating Power Generating and Supplying Industry	5712806
燃气生产和供应业	Gas Mining and Supplying Industry	
水的生产和供应业	Water Processing and Supplying Industry	3

Major Energy Consumption Above Designated Size by Sector（2010）

天然气(万立方米) Natural Gas(10 000cu.m)	原油(吨) Crude Oil (ton)	汽油（吨） Gasoline (ton)	柴油（吨） Diesel Oil (ton)	热力（百万千焦） Heat (million kilo-joule)	电力（万千瓦时） Electricity (10 000kwh)
10619	**1741676**	**30004**	**55290**	**12692357**	**831956**
188		147	892		574
					84
249				10259	2435
		988	1336	2101350	24842
41		3002	400	348795	9440
166		1615	397	480325	19954
		16		6486	102
		93	22	447621	30955
1		110			1287
		64		18064	141
		78	15		5992
		157	107		864
		1132	269	791192	28177
158		558	132	70967	7278
		31			266
156	1741676	7	221		34048
313		784	1124	1580856	62549
398		1158	141	309296	10676
		18	19	690756	2845
		72	23		1087
12		276	1655	8616	14233
254		1666	22549	80176	50359
		71	28	66614	19480
377		1155	555	151032	20099
136		907	189	5531	5386
122		1232	493	10176	17145
678		2942	1803	1201149	37846
3558		6660	14959	1218514	132810
2249		2239	1079	893292	35555
1004		626	76	614765	24240
116		1153	3533	390826	6829
		64	5		803
1		215	3088	1195700	211372
180		393	158		3206
263		374	22		8998

12-3 规模以上工业分行业综合能源消费量（2010年）

Comprehensive Energy Consumption by Sector Above Designated Size（2010）

单位：吨标准煤 (ton of SCE)

指　标	Item	2010	比上年增长（%）Increase over Preceding Year (%)
合　计	**Total**	**5126530**	**5.2**
煤炭开采和洗选业	Coal Mining and Dressing		
石油和天然气开采业	Petroleum and Natural Gas Extraction	6417	184.6
黑色金属矿采选业	Ferrous Metals Mining and Dressing	103	77.4
有色金属矿采选业	Nonferrous Metals Mining and Dressing	6081	16.0
非金属矿采选业	Nonmetal Minerals Mining and Dressing		
其他采矿业	Other Mining Industry		
农副食品加工业	Agricultural Products and Non-stable Food Processing Industry	226805	15.2
食品制造业	Food Production	71572	5.5
饮料制造业	Beverage Production	126728	-9.3
烟草制品业	Tobacco Processing	375	9.3
纺织业	Textile Industry	59215	-5.6
纺织服装、鞋、帽制造业	Textile Clothing, Footwear and Headgear Industry	1708	22.3
皮革、毛皮、羽毛(绒)及其制品业	Leather, Fur, Feather (eiderdown) and Their Products Industry	444	0.7
木材加工及木、竹、藤、棕、草制品制造	Timber Processing,Bamboo,Cane,Palm Fiber and Straw Products	11648	-5.8
家具制造业	Furniture Manufacturing	1434	28.7
造纸及纸制品业	Papermaking and Paper products	307772	-17.4
印刷业和记录媒介的复制	Printing,Record Medium Reproduction	14671	9.6
文教体育用品制造业	Cultural,Educational and Sports Goods	473	36.6
石油加工、炼焦及核燃料加工业	Petroleum Refining, Ccoke Making and Nuclear Fuel Processing Industry	321708	7.8
化学原料及化学制品制造业	Raw Chemical Materials and Chemical Products	228605	-12.5
医药制造业	Medical and Pharmaceutical Products	60787	-8.5
化学纤维制造业	Chemical Fiber	27795	-3.1
橡胶制品业	Rubber Products	2936	10.5
塑料制品业	Plastic Products	24109	5.3
非金属矿物制品业	Nonmetal Mineral Products	401926	10.7
黑色金属冶炼及压延加工业	Smelting and Pressing of Ferrous Metals	92144	-9.3
有色金属冶炼及压延加工业	Smelting and Pressing of Nonferrou Metals	39448	45.0
金属制品业	Metal Products	20186	25.0
通用设备制造	General Equipment Manufacturing Industry	53737	3.4
专用设备制造业	Special Purpose Equipment	139621	5.9
交通运输设备制造业	Transport Equipment	461957	19.2
电气机械及器材制造业	Electric Equipment and Machinery	119465	-2.3
通信设备、计算机及其他电子设备制造业	Communication Equipment, Computer and Other Electronic Equipment Manufacturing Industry	54777	-1.4
仪器仪表及文化办公用机械制造业	Instruments,Meters,Cultural and Office	22877	-10.1
工艺品及其他制造业	Handicraft and Other Stuff Manufacturing Industry	5357	-18.1
废弃资源和废旧材料回收加工业	Discarded Resources and Waste Materials Salvaging and Processing Industry		
电力、热力的生产和供应业	Electric Power, Heating Power Generating and Supplying Industry	2193601	9.1
燃气生产和供应业	Gas Mining and Supplying Industry	7009	-1.3
水的生产和供应业	Water Processing and Supplying Industry	13039	22.4

12-4 主要年份单位GDP能耗

Energy Consumption per Unit of GDP in Representative Years

单位：吨标准煤/万元 (ton of SCE/10 000 yuan)

年 份 Year	单位GDP能耗 Energy Consumption per Unit of GDP	比上年增长（%） Increase Over Preceding Year (%)
2005	1.030	
2006	0.987	-4.15
2007	0.930	-5.75
2008	0.869	-6.65
2009	0.820	-5.56
2010	0.803	-2.06

12-5 各区县单位GDP能耗

Energy Consumption per Unit of GDP by Region

单位：吨标准煤/万元 (ton of SCE/10 000 yuan)

区 县	Region	2005	2006	2007	2008	2009
新城区	Xincheng	0.828	0.794	0.749	0.705	0.664
碑林区	Beilin	0.801	0.768	0.726	0.685	0.644
莲湖区	Lianhu	0.942	0.904	0.862	0.794	0.749
灞桥区	Baqiao	1.803	1.757	1.648	1.545	1.456
未央区	Weiyang	1.026	0.985	0.932	0.870	0.817
雁塔区	Yanta	0.929	0.885	0.835	0.787	0.739
阎良区	Yanliang	0.831	0.783	0.745	0.700	0.661
临潼区	Lintong	1.035	1.004	0.946	0.869	0.829
长安区	Chang'an	1.339	1.257	1.187	1.125	1.063
蓝田县	Lantian	1.698	1.645	1.579	1.492	1.420
周至县	Zhouzhi	1.831	1.786	1.689	1.596	1.508
户 县	Huxian	2.532	2.454	2.311	2.133	2.015
高陵县	Gaoling	0.953	0.907	0.845	0.798	0.753

12-5 续表 continued

区 县	Region	比上年增长（%）Increase over Preceding Year(%)			
		2006	2007	2008	2009
新城区	Xincheng	-4.15	-5.67	-5.79	-5.80
碑林区	Beilin	-4.18	-5.44	-5.65	-5.95
莲湖区	Lianhu	-4.07	-4.60	-7.93	-5.65
灞桥区	Baqiao	-2.54	-6.20	-6.24	-5.80
未央区	Weiyang	-3.97	-5.44	-6.63	-6.05
雁塔区	Yanta	-4.71	-5.64	-5.80	-6.08
阎良区	Yanliang	-5.77	-4.80	-6.08	-5.62
临潼区	Lintong	-3.03	-5.73	-8.16	-4.58
长安区	Chang'an	-6.15	-5.53	-5.22	-5.50
蓝田县	Lantian	-3.13	-4.01	-5.50	-4.84
周至县	Zhouzhi	-2.46	-5.43	-5.51	-5.50
户 县	Huxian	-3.07	-5.85	-7.70	-5.50
高陵县	Gaoling	-4.85	-6.85	-5.50	-5.70

12-6 主要年份规模以上工业单位增加值能耗

Energy Consumption per Unit of Industrial Value-added above Designated Size in Representative Years

单位：千瓦时/万元 (kwh/10 000 yuan)

年 份 Year	单位工业增加值能耗 Energy Consumption per Unit of Industrial Value-added	比上年增长（%） Increase Over Preceding Year (%)
2005	1.220	
2006	1.100	-3.04
2007	1.092	-12.56
2008	0.915	-13.43
2009	0.800	-10.48
2010	0.703	-12.18

12-7 各区县规模以上工业单位增加值能耗

Energy Consumption per Unit of Industrial Value-added above Designated Size by Region

单位：吨标准煤/万元 (ton of SCE/10 000 yuan)

区 县	Region	2005	2006	2007	2008	2009
新城区	Xincheng	0.822	0.798	0.716	0.663	0.420
碑林区	Beilin	0.876	0.846	0.782	0.763	0.293
莲湖区	Lianhu	0.861	0.832	0.775	0.639	0.269
灞桥区	Baqiao	3.029	2.871	2.446	2.078	2.072
未央区	Weiyang	1.030	1.000	0.876	0.770	1.008
雁塔区	Yanta	1.358	1.308	1.123	1.000	0.578
阎良区	Yanliang	0.876	0.849	0.761	0.625	0.354
临潼区	Lintong	1.031	0.992	0.882	0.715	0.644
长安区	Chang'an	1.370	1.300	1.208	1.087	0.725
蓝田县	Lantian	2.579	2.515	2.133	2.084	3.670
周至县	Zhouzhi	1.946	1.900	1.891	1.842	0.364
户 县	Huxian	7.467	7.168	5.857	4.910	4.514
高陵县	Gaoling	0.966	0.905	0.719	0.693	0.239

12-7 续表 continued

区 县	Region	比上年增长（%）Increase over Preceding Year（%）			
		2006	2007	2008	2009
新城区	Xincheng	-2.92	-10.26	-7.38	-2.68
碑林区	Beilin	-3.42	-7.59	-2.45	-0.44
莲湖区	Lianhu	-3.47	-6.91	-17.61	0.89
灞桥区	Baqiao	-5.22	-14.79	-15.04	0.29
未央区	Weiyang	-2.91	-10.63	-12.15	-15.20
雁塔区	Yanta	-3.68	-14.14	-10.98	-13.98
阎良区	Yanliang	-3.05	-10.42	-17.83	-18.36
临潼区	Lintong	-3.82	-11.06	-18.99	3.05
长安区	Chang'an	-5.11	-4.06	-10.05	-18.68
蓝田县	Lantian	-2.48	-15.18	-2.29	-3.39
周至县	Zhouzhi	-2.38	-0.48	-2.62	-12.27
户 县	Huxian	-4.01	-18.29	-16.17	-18.48
高陵县	Gaoling	-6.32	-20.52	-3.56	-18.90

12-8 主要年份单位GDP电耗

Electricity Consumption per Unit of GDP

单位：千瓦时/万元 (kwh/10 000 yuan)

年 份 Year	单位GDP电耗 Electricity Consumption per Unit of GDP	比上年增长（%） Increase Over Preceding Year (%)
2005	963.34	
2006	920.19	-4.48
2007	856.29	-6.94
2008	796.92	-6.93
2009	754.45	-5.33
2010	761.98	1.00

12-9 各区县单位GDP电耗

Electricity Consumption per Unit of GDP by Region

单位：千瓦小时/万元 (kw.h/10 000 yuan)

区 县	Region	2005	2006	2007	2008	2009
新城区	Xincheng	1201.50	1161.10	1013.50	954.20	878.66
碑林区	Beilin	825.40	800.50	772.50	746.90	685.32
莲湖区	Lianhu	1213.30	1160.80	1137.00	1068.60	992.04
灞桥区	Baqiao	990.90	950.30	927.50	872.20	811.26
未央区	Weiyang	1104.20	1055.40	1011.60	945.70	950.76
雁塔区	Yanta	989.70	946.90	827.10	773.40	735.33
阎良区	Yanliang	742.00	715.50	650.20	595.80	570.37
临潼区	Lintong	869.20	839.30	790.00	724.10	658.19
长安区	Chang'an	764.10	733.50	687.90	645.70	592.61
蓝田县	Lantian	722.60	701.50	689.90	640.20	629.32
周至县	Zhouzhi	675.90	657.20	633.30	601.00	596.15
户 县	Huxian	1018.90	971.00	933.30	879.50	843.19
高陵县	Gaoling	1141.00	1067.50	923.90	824.90	725.76

注:表中数据为当年公报数。

Note: The data are taken from Communique in this year.

12-9 续表 continued

区 县	Region	比上年增长（%）Increase over Preceding Year（%）			
		2006	2007	2008	2009
新城区	Xincheng	-3.36	-12.71	-5.85	-7.92
碑林区	Beilin	-3.02	-3.49	-3.31	-8.25
莲湖区	Lianhu	-4.32	-2.05	-6.02	-7.16
灞桥区	Baqiao	-4.11	-2.40	-5.96	-6.99
未央区	Weiyang	-4.42	-4.15	-6.51	0.53
雁塔区	Yanta	-4.32	-12.65	-6.49	-4.92
阎良区	Yanliang	-3.57	-9.12	-8.37	-4.27
临潼区	Lintong	-3.44	-5.87	-8.34	-9.10
长安区	Chang'an	-4.00	-6.21	-6.14	-8.22
蓝田县	Lantian	-2.91	-1.66	-7.20	-1.70
周至县	Zhouzhi	-2.77	-3.63	-5.10	-0.81
户 县	Huxian	-4.71	-3.88	-5.76	-4.13
高陵县	Gaoling	-6.45	-13.45	-10.72	-12.02

12-10 规模以上工业企业用水情况

Statistics on Water Use of Industrial Enterprises above Designated Size

指 标	Item	取水量（立方米） Water Use (Cubic meter)	支付费用的取水量（立方米） Paid Water Use (Cubic meter)	取水支付金额（千元） Money Paid for Water Use (1 000yuan)	外供水量（立方米） Outward Water Supply (Cubic meter)
合 计	Total	528111804	407066040	473187	402188857
1.陆地地表水	Surface Water	330803677	305189271	235281	758898
2.地下水	Ground-water	104893072	33181806	27614	15738303
3.自来水	Tap Water	80932100	57456581	196409	385691656
4.其他水	Other Water	11482955	11238382	13884	
#雨水收集利用	Rain Water Collected	200			
再生水（中水）	Reclaimed Water	5601691	5582154	6592	

12-11 规模以上工业企业分行业用水量（2010年）

行　业	Sector	取水量（立方米）Water Use (Cubic meter)
总　计	**Total**	528111804
按工业行业大类分列	Grouped by Sector	
煤炭开采和洗选业	Coal Mining and Dressing	
石油和天然气开采业	Petroleum and Natural Gas Extraction	256682
黑色金属矿采选业	Ferrous Metals Mining and Dressing	116305
有色金属矿采选业	Nonferrous Metals Mining and Dressing	70820
非金属矿采选业	Nonmetal Minerals Mining and Dressing	
其他采矿业	Other mining industry	
农副食品加工业	Agricultural products and non-stable food processing industry	2133276.00
食品制造业	Food Production	2756130.00
饮料制造业	Beverage Production	9605945.00
烟草制品业	Tobacco Processing	5572
纺织业	Textile Industry	2071078
纺织服装、鞋、帽制造业	Textile clothing, footwear and headgear industry	186635
皮革、毛皮、羽毛(绒)及其制品业	Leather, fur, feather (eiderdown) and their products industry	22917
木材加工及木、竹、藤、棕、草制品制造	Timber Processing,Bamboo,Cane,Palm Fiber and Straw Products	44115
家具制造业	Furniture Manufacturing	32479
造纸及纸制品业	Papermaking and Paper products	13990002
印刷业和记录媒介的复制	Printing,Record Medium Reproduction	614387
文教体育用品制造业	Cultural,Educational and Sports Goods	3550
石油加工、炼焦及核燃料加工业	Petroleum refining, coke making and nuclear fuel processing industry	839106
化学原料及化学制品制造业	Raw Chemical Materials and Chemical Products	12908855
医药制造业	Medical and Pharmaceutical Products	3320829
化学纤维制造业	Chemical Fiber	477275
橡胶制品业	Rubber Products	41016
塑料制品业	Plastic Products	1440544
非金属矿物制品业	Nonmetal Mineral Products	2418764
黑色金属冶炼及压延加工业	Smelting and Pressing of Ferrous Metals	508339
有色金属冶炼及压延加工业	Smelting and Pressing of Nonferrou Metals	1155767
金属制品业	Metal Products	372665
通用设备制造	General equipment manufacturing industry	917926
专用设备制造业	Special Purpose Equipment	6899944
交通运输设备制造业	Transport Equipment	15959526
电气机械及器材制造业	Electric Equipment and Machinery	4887754
通信设备、计算机及其他电子设备制造业	Communication equipment, computer and other electronic equipment manufacturing industry	3469842
仪器仪表及文化办公用机械制造业	Instruments,Meters,Cultural and Office	1727859
工艺品及其他制造业	Handicraft and other stuff manufacturing industry	51883
废弃资源和废旧材料回收加工业	Discarded resources and waste materials salvaging and processing industry	
电力、热力的生产和供应业	Electric power, heating power generating and supplying industry	32027377
燃气生产和供应业	Gas mining and supplying industry	154581
水的生产和供应业	Water processing and supplying industry	406622059

Volume of Water Use of Industrial Enterprises above Designated Size by Sector（2010）

支付费用的取水量（立方米）Paid Water Use (Cubic meter)	取水支付金额（千元）Money Paid for Water Use (1000yuan)	外供水量（立方米）Outward Water Supply (Cubic meter)
407066040	473187	402188857
256682	1595	
115000	14	
70820	278	
1863229	2069	
2679825	5178	
7514488	24795	1859109
5572	21	
2028016	6175	
186635	672	
22917	82	
42075	130	
32479	80	
13164496	10151	
614187	2209	
2500	3	
538544	1957	
11121546	20586	1764879
3244006	9326	
476825	646	
35696	102	
1436207	2818	
1342548	2890	
453220	886	
1150394	2160	
344684	1067	
848024	2651	
5100477	17107	710910
15956634	48671	
4850188	17084	
3469032	11495	
1706506	5193	
51463	161	
31649289	52318	
154581	510	
294537255	222109	397853959

主 要 统 计 指 标 解 释

能源消费量 指能源使用单位在报告期内实际消费的一次能源或二次能源的数量。具体包括原煤和原油及其制品、天然气、电力等。

工业生产能源消费 指工业企业为进行工业生产活动所消费的能源。

非工业生产能源消费 指在工业企业能源消费中，除“工业生产能源消费”以外的能源消费，即非工业生产用能和工业企业附属的不从事工业生产活动的非独立核算单位用能。

交通运输工具用能 指在厂区内、外进行交通运输活动的交通运输工具所消费的能源。

能源加工转换投入 能源的加工转换是指为了特定的用途，将一种能源（一般为一次能源），经过一定的工艺，加工或转换成另外一种能源（一般为二次能源）。能源加工转换的投入即能源加工、转换消费。

一次能源 是指自然界中以现成形式存在，不经任何改变或转换的天然能源资源，即从自然界直接取得并不改变其形态和品位的能源。如原煤、原油、天然气、核燃料、植物燃料、风能、水能、太阳能、地热能、海洋能、潮汐能等。

二次能源 是指为了满足生产工艺和生活的特定需要以合理利用能源，将一次能源直接或间接加工转换产生的其它种类和形式的人工能源。如原煤加工产出的洗煤；由煤炭加工转换产出的焦炭，煤气；由原油加工产出的汽油、煤油、柴油、燃料油、液化石油气、炼厂干气等；由煤炭、石油、天然气转换产出的电力。

综合能源消费量 报告期内工业企业在工业生产活动中实际消费的各种能源的总和净值。计算综合能源消费量时，需要先将使用的各种能源折算成标准燃料后再进行计算。

Explanatory Notes on Main Statistical Indicators

Energy Consumption refers to the volume of primary or secondary energy actually consumed by energy utilization units in the reference period. Including raw coal, crude oil with its products , natural gas, electric power etc.

Industry Consumption Energy refers to the volume of energy consumed by Industrial enterprises for industrial production activities.

Non-industry Consumption Energy refers to the energy consumed by industrial enterprises except for industrial production activities , means that energy consumed by non-industry production and not independent accounting units which was not engaged in industrial production activities affiliated to industrial enterprises.

Vehicle Energy refers to the energy consumed by vehicles which carried out transport activities in and out of factories.

Energy Processing Conversion Devoted energy processing conversion refers to for specialized application , a source of energy (normally primary energy), after a certain technology , processed or converted to another kind of energy (normally secondary energy). The input of energy conversion processing that is energy processing, and conversion consumption.

Primary Energy Source refers to natural energy resources as found naturally in the form of ready-made , without any change or conversion , as energy obtained directly from natural and not change its shape and grade, such as raw coal, crude oil, natural gas, nuclear fuel, plant fuel, wind energy, water energy, solar energy, geothermal energy, oceanic energy, tidal energy and so on .

Secondary Energy refers to other types and forms of artificial energy which was processed and conversed from primary energy sources directly or indirectly , in order to meet the specific needs in production process and life to use energy more effectively. Such as washing coal processed from raw coal; coke and coal gas processed and transformed from raw coal; gasoline, kerosene, diesel oil, fuel oil, liquefied petroleum gas, dry gas refinery processed from crude oil; electric power conversed from coal, oil and natural gas.

Comprehensive energy consumption refers to the total and net energy actually consumed in industrial production activities by industrial enterprises in the reference period. When calculated the volume of consumption of comprehensive energy , should converted sorts of energy which was used into standards fuel firstly.

13 建筑业

CONSTRUCTION

资料整理：陈海生

Data management:Chen Haisheng

第十三部分　建筑业

一、简要说明

本章资料主要包括建筑业基本情况，建筑业施工企业生产情况和财务状况，由西安市统计局固定资产投资处提供。

二、主要指标

企业个数（个）	324	比上年减少 4个
建筑业总产值（亿元）	1820.34	比上年增长 40.3%
#国有及国有控股企业	1520.39	比上年增长 42.5%
房屋建筑竣工面积（万平方米）	1391.91	比上年增长 15.1%
房屋建筑面积竣工率（%）	30.3	比上年提高 0.3个百分点

13 CONSTRUCTION

Ⅰ.Brief Introduction

This chapter consists of primarily the data basic situation of the construction industry, production situation and financial situation of the construction enterprises, provided by Fixed Asset Investment Division of the Xi'an Bureau of Statistics.

Ⅱ.Major Indicators

		Increase over Preceding Year
Number of Enterprises(item)	324	-4
Total Output Value of Construction(100 mil. yuan)	1820.34	40.3%
State-owned Or State Holding Majority Shares	1520.39	42.5%
Floor Space of Buildings Completed(10 000 sq.m)	1391.91	15.1%
Rate of Floor Space of Buildings Completed(%)	30.3	0.3 percentage points

13-1 主要年份建筑业总产值

Total Output Value of Construction in Representative Year

单位:万元 （10 000 yuan）

年份 Year	建筑业总产值 Total Output Value of Construction	国有及国有控股企业 State-owned Or State Holding Majority Shares	集体企业 Collective-owned Enterprises
2000	1059250	788704	148709
2001	1148091	918169	154749
2002	1334713	850278	153482
2003	1771126	1199911	134010
2004	2444242	2016792	165922
2005	3266535	2766785	196111
2006	4164782	3482016	236493
2007	6047524	4326279	326658
2008	9151199	6761190	4601423
2009	12965787	10672178	471533
2010	18203449	15203874	583928

注：1.1996年以后建筑业年报统计范围由往年的县及县以上（含县级建制镇）各种经济类型的建筑企业，改为具有建筑业资质等级四级及四级以上的各种经济类型的建筑施工企业；2002年改为具有建筑业资质等级的各种经济类型的建筑施工企业。

2.本表资料含劳务分包企业。

Note:1.Since 1996, the boundary of annual report of construstion had change from enterprises of all economic types of county and above (including towns of county level) to enterprises at fourth or higher quality grades. Since 2002, it has changed to enterprises of all economic types with qualification grades.

2.Data in this table includes labor subcontracting enterprises.

13-2 全市建筑施工企业基本情况（2010年）

Main Indicators on Construction Enterprise of Xi'an（2010）

指标	Item	合计 Total	国有及国有控股 State-owned Or State Holding Majority Shares
企业个数(个)（施工总承包）	Number of Enterprises (unit) (Overall Contractor For Construction)	208	65
#二级以上企业	First and Second Class Enterprise	147	58
计算劳动生产率的平均人数（人）（施工总承包）	Average Number of Employed Persons in Calculation of Labor Productivity (person) (Overall Contractor For Construction)	537732	401180
#二级以上企业	First and Second Class Enterprise	510544	399229
建筑业总产值（千元）（施工总承包）	Total Output Value of Construction(1 000 yuan) (Overall Contractor For Construction)	172795133	149030907
#二级以上企业	First and Second Class Enterprise		
全员劳动生产率(元/人)	Overall Labor Productivity (yuan/person)		
按总产值计算	Calculated by Total Output Value	321340	1472929

13-3 施工总承包和专业承包建筑业企业生产情况（2010年）

分　组	Item	签定的合同额（万元）Contract Value (1 0000 yuan)
总　计	**Total**	**42231113**
#国有及国有控股	State-Owned and State Holding Majority Shares	38047019
一、按登记注册类型分	**Grouped by Registion Status**	
内资	Domestic Investment Enterprises	42230412
国有企业	State-owned Enterprises	19682936
集体企业	Collective-owned Enterprises	1228015
股份合作企业	Share-holding Corperative Enterprises	1737
联营企业	Joint Ownership Enterprises	4648
有限责任公司	Limited Liability Corporations	20270963
股份有限公司	Share-holding Corperation Ltd.	478949
私营企业	Private Enterprises	563164
其他企业	Others	
港澳台商投资企业	Enterprises with Funds from Hong Kong,Macao and Taiwan	701
外商投资企业	Enterprises with Foreign Investment	
二、按国民经济行业分	**Grouped by Sector**	
房屋和土木工程建筑业	Building Engineering and Civil Engineering Construction	40591537
房屋工程建筑	Building Engineering Construction	7773304
土木工程建筑	Civil Engineering Construction	32818234
建筑安装业	Installation of Construction	1153382
建筑装饰业	Fitting and Decoration	167723
其他建筑业	Others	318471
三、按隶属关系分	**Grouped by Administrative Relationship**	
中　央	Central	31919951
地　方	Region	10311162
四、按企业资质等级分	**Grouped by Class of Enterprises**	
1.施工总承包	Overall Contractor for Construction	41045518
#特级	Special Class	19159707
一级	First Class	17822487
二级	Second Class	3650500
2.专业承包	Special Contractor	1185595
#一级以上	First Class	683378

Main Indicators on Overall Constructing Contractors and Professional Contractors by Registration Status（2010）

建筑业总产值（万元）Total Output Value of Constrution (1 0000 yuan)	建筑工程产值 Output Value of Constrution	安装工程产值 Output Value of Installation	其他产值 Others	计算劳动生产率的平均人数（人）Average Number of Employed Persons in Calculation of Labour Productivity(person)	期末从业人数（人）Number of Employment at Year-end (person)	工程技术人员 Technical Personnel	企业总产值（万元）Total Output Value of Enterprises (1 0000 yuan)
18203450	**16414108**	**1262046**	**527296**	**578257**	**539000**	**56915**	**18500089**
15434593	14194058	775712	464824	413443	396029	39246	15718439
18202796	16413458	1262042	527296	578199	538950	56903	18499436
9032523	8299210	444686	288628	228275	181932	22647	9237139
583928	528405	47228	8295	44071	45282	4814	584497
1505	1505			88	71	35	1505
4205	4065	140		195	182	37	4205
7853697	6996737	665561	191399	276115	287993	25506	7935340
315869	278991	2849	34030	5486	4129	1282	316222
411070	304545	101579	4945	23969	19361	2582	420529
653	650	3		58	50	12	653
16974164	15751089	772255	450820	529462	504878	51276	17256985
4484329	3941626	449734	92968	244078	198168	21383	4536273
12489836	11809463	322521	357851	285384	306710	29893	12720712
797187	381666	390820	24702	29366	25849	3813	802831
149621	44906	52949	51766	8858	3691	715	150317
282477	236447	46021	9	10571	4582	1111	289956
11994079	11263810	346299	383969	269993	276953	27629	12260434
6209371	5150297	915747	143327	308264	262047	29286	6239655
17279513	15940620	881270	457624	537732	512362	52531	17566480
6413996	5907081	150040	356875	118344	158283	12655	6549336
8733489	8182802	517144	33543	329809	273505	28212	8845580
1777364	1544793	180864	51707	62391	57674	9273	1815982
923936	473488	380776	69673	40525	26638	4384	933609
471777	205012	204346	62419	16233	11140	2249	472651

13-3 续表

分组	Item	房屋建筑施工面积（平方米） Number of Projects under Constrution (sq.m)	本年新开工 Beginning Projects in this year
总　计	**Total**	**45925710**	**19940025**
#国有及国有控股	State-Owned and State Holding Majority Shares	27910956	10887339
一、按登记注册类型分	**Grouped by Registion Status**		
内资	Domestic Investment Enterprises	45925710	19940025
国有企业	State-owned Enterprises	22645521	8770584
集体企业	Collective-owned Enterprises	6409868	3557110
股份合作企业	Share-holding Corperative Enterprises		
联营企业	Joint Ownership Enterprises	28680	15899
有限责任公司	Limited Liability Corporations	14036945	6466017
股份有限公司	Share-holding Corperation Ltd	330867	186845
私营企业	Private Enterprises	2473829	943570
其他企业	Others		
港澳台商投资企业	Enterprises with Funds from Hong Kong,Macao and Taiwan		
外商投资企业	Enterprises with Foreign Investment		
二、按国民经济行业分	**Grouped by Sector**		
房屋和土木工程建筑业	Building Engineering and Civil Engineering Construction	44367103	19189102
房屋工程建筑	Building Engineering Construction	39438640	16570880
土木工程建筑	Civil Engineering Construction	4928463	2618222
建筑安装业	Installation of Construction	1014775	567305
建筑装饰业	Fitting and Decoration	45707	37020
其他建筑业	Others	498125	146598
三、按隶属关系分	**Grouped by Administrative Relationship**		
中　央	Central	9030314	2252192
地　方	Region	36895396	17687833
四、按企业资质等级分	**Grouped by Class of Enterprises**		
1.施工总承包	Overall Contractor for Construction	43971387	18550958
#特级	Special Class	3753207	1204772
一级	First Class	32369666	13472104
二级	Second Class	6086748	2790595
2.专业承包	Special Contractor	1954323	1389067
#一级以上	First Class	270941	184894

continued

房屋建筑 竣工面积 (平方米) Floor Space of Buildings Completed (sq.m)	自有机械设备 年末净值 (万元) Net Value of Mechanical Equipment owned by Constructions Enterprises at Year-end(1 0000yuan)	自有机械设备 年末总台数 (台) Number of Mechanical Equipment Owned By Construction Enterprises at Year-end(unit)	自有机械设备 年末总功率 (千瓦) Total Power of Mechanical Equipment Owned by Construction Enterprises at Year-end(kw)
13919136	**547070**	**79180**	**3370604**
6999400	449353	46436	2199031
13919136	547015	79156	3370204
5516077	257611	32998	1158909
2597545	21083	14346	265295
	9	7	528
	341	41	390
4815193	243377	27231	1837223
162899	3834	993	20041
827422	20761	3540	87818
	56	24	400
13718742	523685	70872	2714581
13116995	97319	32747	774601
601747	426367	38125	1939980
181394	14003	6138	275558
19000	5387	828	339359
	3996	1342	41106
2246011	383442	31815	1869151
11673125	163628	47365	1501453
13510071	513659	70488	2703790
740807	236997	18909	1117836
9300291	209536	29042	1049951
2499456	54865	14361	375162
409065	33411	8692	666814
117813	24425	4437	178853

13-4 施工总承包和专业承包建筑业企业财务状况（2010年）

单位: 万元

指 标	Item	总 计 Total
流动资产小计	Circulating Assets	9890753
#存货	Stocks	2761319
长期投资	Long-term Investment	350894
固定资产合计	Fixed Assets	1409716
固定资产原价	Original Value of Fixed Assets	2056208
#生产经营用	Using for Production and Management	1768441
累计折旧	Accumulative Total Depreciation	841460
#本年折旧	Depreciation Within the Year	263910
在建工程	Projects Under Construction	97167
无形及递延资产合计	Intangible and Deferred Assets	133610
#无形资产	Intangible Assets	133610
资产合计	Total Assets	12655850
流动负债小计	Liquid Liabilities	9801153
长期负债小计	Long-term Liabilities	320861
负债合计	Total Liabilities	10122014
所有者权益合计	Owner Rights and Interests	2533836
#实收资本	Actual Capital Hold	1893527
1.国家资本	State Capital	266795
2.集体资本	Collective Capital	105228
3.法人资本	Corporation Capital	1275898
4.个人资本	Individual Capital	245437
5.港澳台资本	Capital from HongKong,Macao and Taiwan	169
6.外商资本	Foreign Capital	
工程结算收入	Revenue of Project Settlement Accounts	19424443
工程结算成本	Costs of Project Settlement Accounts	17800743
工程结算税金及附加	Taxs and Extra Charges on Project Settlement Accounts	593425
工程结算利润	Profits of Projet Settlement Accounts	983413
其他业务收入	Other Income from Business	78005
其他业务利润	Other Profits from Business	8413
经营费用	Running Expenses	46862
管理费用	Management Expenses	522602
#税金	Tax Revenue	14362
财产保险费	Expense of Property and Insurance	4212
财务费用	Financial Expenditures	86153
营业利润	Operating Surplus	387639
利润总额	Total Profits	211878
# 应交所得税	Income taxes Payable	52513
应付利润	Profits Payable	159365
劳动、待业保险费	Expense of Insurance for Laboring, Employment	30701
本年应付工资总额	Total Wages Payable this Year	2168937
本年应付福利费总额	Total Welfare Expense Payable in this Year	75339
应收工程款	Accounts Receivable From Project Construction	4660239

Financial Status of Overall Constructing Contractors and Professional Contractors（2010）

(1 0000yuan)

国有及国有控股 State-Owned and State Holding Majority Shares Enterprises	中央企业 Enterprises Central	省属企业 Province Enterprises	市属企业 Municipal Enterprises
8804408	6912137	1304014	642021
2532300	2265673	241313	45647
318397	210108	99061	8826
1047322	808459	171192	62992
1707108	1436331	170391	88547
1490479	1309434	129176	74782
734049	655478	43317	29577
244932	228078	11043	5967
45208	7397	41308	3075
106514	75164	21939	25340
106514	75164	21939	25340
11122067	8810918	1633770	752752
9071761	7364232	1173246	591632
253848	202099	33918	24626
9325608	7566331	1207163	616258
1796459	1244587	426606	136494
1290651	907119	301886	91071
263348	73549	144022	28076
	1770	18976	30066
1022526	830163	126593	19698
4776	1636	12295	13062
			169
16914273	13779003	2043790	1020215
15590821	12721790	1871021	949997
515495	417873	63028	33547
784871	626668	106737	35046
73477	43649	11961	20359
5981	6187	-4339	5870
23086	12672	3004	1626
438416	348115	59613	29939
8720	6233	1226	1395
3346	2653	496	109
72728	62962	315	1532
284266	230960	37524	9444
194479	180237	8640	4966
44139	36084	6088	1837
150340	144153	2551	3129
24920	22732	997	1980
1801072	1199432	388565	217239
37532	23307	4186	10357
4107680	3372443	444173	204909

13-5 劳务分包建筑业企业基本情况（2010年）

Basic Statistic on Enterprises of Work Subcontractors（2010）

单位: 万元 (1 0000yuan)

指 标	Item	2010
一、生产情况	**Main Indicators**	
1.企业个数（个）	Number of Enterprises（unit）	1
2.建筑业总产值	Total Output Value of Constrution	15
3.从业人员情况	Employed persons	
计算建筑业劳动生产率的平均人数（人）	Average Number of Employed Persons in Calculation of Labour Productivity (person)	12
年末从业人数（人）	Number of Employment at Year-end (person)	10
#工程技术人员	Technical Personnel	2
二、财务状况	**Finacial Status**	
1.资产负债	Funds and Liabilities	
固定资产原值	Original Value of Fixed Assets	
本年折旧	Depreciation In The Year	
资产总计	Total Assets	70
负债总计	Total Liabilities	50
实收资本	Paid in Capital	18
国家资本	State Capital	
集体资本	Collective Capital	
法人资本	Corporation Capital	
个人资本	Individual Capital	38
港澳台资本	Capital from HongKong,Macao and Taiwan	
外商资本	Foreign Capital	
2.损益及分配	Profits,Loss and Allocation	
营业收入	Income from Operation	15
#主营业务收入	Income from Main Operation	15
主营业务成本	Cost of Main Operation	12
主营业务税金及附加	Sales Tax and Extra Charges	1
费用合计	Total of Expenses	8
营业利润	Business Profits	-6
利润总额	Total Profit	
3.从业人员劳动报酬	Earnings of Employed persons	8
4.劳动失业保险费	Expenses of Insurance for laboring and Unemployment	

13-6 各区县建筑业主要经济指标（2010年）

Main Indicators of Construction Enterprises by Region（2010）

区 县 名 称	Name of District and County	企业个数（个）Number of Enterprises (unit)	总产值（万元）Total Output Value (1 0000 yuan)	计算劳动生产率的平均人数（人）Average Number of Employed Persons in Calculation of Labor Productivity(person)	全员劳动生产率（万元/人）Overall Labor Productivity (10 000 yuan/person)	利税总额（万元）Total Pre-tax Profits (1 0000yuan)
新城区	Xincheng	28	20729090	68757	30.15	597403
碑林区	Beilin	33	29710194	125829	23.61	1345978
莲湖区	Lianhu	30	14910443	71866	20.75	445299
灞桥区	Baqiao	25	1953470	9370	20.85	62391
未央区	Weiyang	50	45016654	135777	33.15	1361125
雁塔区	Yanta	88	58922091	91554	64.36	1878159
阎良区	Yanliang	15	1616848	9804	16.49	45816
临潼区	Lintong	10	781298	5173	15.10	52944
长安区	Chang'an	17	2340053	11683	20.03	74457
蓝田县	Lantian	9	945585	8865	10.67	45258
周至县	Zhouzhi	5	374300	10817	3.46	11945
户 县	Huxian	7	987371	10318	9.57	31756
高陵县	Gaoling	6	3747098	18444	20.32	125339

13-7 各区县建筑业房屋施工及竣工面积（2010年）

Floor Space of Buildings under Construction & Completed by Region（2010）

区 县	Region	房屋建筑施工面积（万平方米）Floor Space under Construction	本年新开工面积 Newly Started This Year	房屋建筑竣工面积（万平方米）Floor Space of Buildings Completed	竣工房屋价值（亿元）Value of Buildings Completed
新城区	Xincheng	664.29	266.27	151.72	19.72
碑林区	Beilin	1644.51	742.75	490.12	83.62
莲湖区	Lianhu	828.95	224.08	166.26	23.63
灞桥区	Baqiao	56.67	24.01	28.26	3.66
未央区	Weiyang	386.65	204.75	77.07	10.24
雁塔区	Yanta	277.7	105.24	224.93	39.12
阎良区	Yanliang	80.12	47.25	32.02	2.35
临潼区	Lintong	93.31	30.18	63.73	4.97
长安区	Chang'an	183.82	57.61	58.47	6.97
蓝田县	Lantian	65.21	49.09	47.55	6.18
周至县	Zhouzhi	18.22	10.41	10.95	1.49
户 县	Huxian	120.38	69.6	53.37	5.93
高陵县	Gaoling	172.75	162.75	163.47	21.64

13-8 分区县建筑业企业主要经济效益指标（2010年）

Main Economic Benefit Indicators on Construction Enterprises by Region（2010）

区 县	Region	人均利润总额（元/人）Per Profit (yuan/person)	人均利税（元/人）Per Pre-tax Profits (yuan/person)	人均竣工产值（元/人）Per Output Value of Buildings Completed (yuan/person)	人均施工面积（平方米/人）Per Floor Space of Buildings Under Construcyion (sq.m/person)	人均竣工面积（平方米/人）Per Floor Space of Buildings Completed (sq.m/person)
全 市	**Total**	3664	10511	124987	79	27
新城区	Xincheng	2235	8689	178938	97	22
碑林区	Beilin	2940	10697	95830	131	39
莲湖区	Lianhu	1417	6196	71484	115	23
灞桥区	Baqiao	1416	6659	128027	61	30
未央区	Weiyang	4028	10025	30505	29	6
雁塔区	Yanta	8794	20514	340074	30	25
阎良区	Yanliang	835	4673	103400	82	33
临潼区	Lintong	3007	10235	117717	180	123
长安区	Chang'an	1421	6373	75931	157	50
蓝田县	Lantian	322	5105	74873	74	54
周至县	Zhouzhi	677	1104	21982	17	10
户 县	Huxian	1974	3078	61446	117	52
高陵县	Gaoling	3104	6796	122208	94	89

13-8 续表 continued

区 县	Region	产值利润率（%）Ratio of Profits to Output Value (%)	产值利税率（%）Ratio of Pre-tax Profits to Output Value (%)	资本利润率（%）Ratio of Profits to Assets (%)	资本利税率（%）Ratio of Pre-tax Profits to Assets (%)	资产负债率（%）Ratio of Debts to Assets (%)
全 市	**Total**	1.2	3.3	1.7	4.8	80.0
新城区	Xincheng	0.7	2.9	1.4	5.3	88.6
碑林区	Beilin	1.2	4.5	1.4	5.2	79.5
莲湖区	Lianhu	0.7	3.0	0.7	3.3	78.1
灞桥区	Baqiao	0.7	3.2	1.2	5.6	64.6
未央区	Weiyang	1.2	3.0	1.7	4.2	84.4
雁塔区	Yanta	1.4	3.2	2.1	5.0	78.6
阎良区	Yanliang	0.5	2.8	0.5	2.8	67.0
临潼区	Lintong	2.0	6.8	6.4	21.9	28.8
长安区	Chang'an	0.7	3.2	1.3	6.0	62.9
蓝田县	Lantian	0.3	4.8	1.4	22.1	23.8
周至县	Zhouzhi	2.0	3.2	4.4	7.2	49.9
户 县	Huxian	2.1	3.2	8.6	13.3	32.5
高陵县	Gaoling	1.5	3.3	7.7	16.8	14.6

主要统计指标解释

建筑业统计单位 指从事房屋、构筑物建造和设备安装活动的法人企业。建筑业法人企业应同时具备的条件是：①依法成立，有自己的名称、组织机构和场所，能够承担民事责任；②独立拥有和使用资产，承担负债，有权与其他单位签订合同；③独立核算盈亏，能够编制资产负债表。

建筑业总产值（即自行完成施工产值） 是以货币表现的建筑安装企业在一定时期内生产的建筑业产品的总和。建筑业总产值包括：

（1）建筑工程产值：指列入建筑工程预算内的各种工程价值。

（2）设备安装工程产值：指设备安装工程价值，不包括被安装设备本身价值。

（3）房屋、构筑物修理产值：指房屋、构筑物修理所完成的价值，但不包括被修理房屋、构筑物本身的价值和生产设备的修理价值。

（4）非标准设备制造产值：指加工制造没有定型的、非标准的生产设备的加工费和原材料价值，以及附属加工厂为本企业承建工程制作的非标准设备的价值。

建筑业增加值 指建筑业企业在报告期内以货币表现的建筑业生产经营活动的最终成果。目前建筑业增加值采用分配法（收入法）计算，即从收入的角度出发，根据生产要素在生产过程中应得的收入份额计算。具体计算公式为：

建筑业增加值＝本年提取的固定资产折旧+主营业务应付工资+主营业务应付福利费+管理费用中的劳动待业保险金、税金+工程结算税金及附加+营业利润

房屋建筑施工面积 指在报告期内施工的全部房屋建筑面积，包括本期新开工的房屋面积、上期施工跨入本期继续施工的房屋面积、上期停缓建在本期恢复施工的房屋面积、本期竣工的房屋面积及本期施工后又停缓建的房屋面积。

房屋建筑竣工面积 指在报告期内房屋建筑按照设计要求全部完工，达到了住人和使用条件，经验收鉴定合格，正式移交使用单位的房屋建筑面积。

自有机械设备年末总台数 指归本企业所有，属于本企业固定资产的生产性机械设备年末总台数。包括施工机械、生产设备、运输设备以及其他设备。

自有机械设备年末总功率 指本企业自有施工机械、生产设备、运输设备以及其他设备等列为在册固定资产的生产性机械设备年末总功率，按设定能力或查定能力计算。包括机械本身的动力和为该机械服务的单独动力设备，如电动机等。计算单位用千瓦，动力换算可按1马力＝0.735千瓦折合成千瓦数。电焊机、变压器、锅炉不计算动力。

工程结算收入 指企业承包工程实现的工程价款结算收入，以及向发包单位收取的除工程价款以外的按规定列作营业收入的各种款项，如临时设施费、劳动保险费、施工机械调迁费等以及向发包单位收取的各种索赔款。

工程结算利润 指已结算工程实现的利润，如亏损以“－”号表示。计算公式为：

工程结算利润＝工程结算收入－工程结算成本－工程结算税金及附加

企业总收入 指与企业生产经营直接有关的各项收入，包括工程结算收入和其他业务收入。计算公式为：

企业总收入＝工程结算收入＋其他业务收入

Explanatory Notes on Main Statistical Indicators

Statistical Unit in Construction refers to corporate enterprise engaged in the construction of buildings and structures and in the installation of equipment. A corporate construction enterprise should meet the following 3 requirements:① being set up in line with relevant legal basis, having its full name, organization and location, and capable of taking civil liabilities;② independently possessing and using its assets and assuming its liabilities, and entitled to sign contracts with other institutions; and ③ making independent accounts of its profits and losses, and capable of compiling its own balance sheet.

Gross Output Value of Construction (Output Value of Projects Under Construction) refers to total of construction products, expressed in money terms, completed by construction and installation enterprises during a given period of time. It includes:

(1)Output value of construction projects, that is the value of projects covered by the project budgets;

(2)Output value of installation projects, that is the value of the installation of equipment, (excluding the value of the equipment to be installed);

(3)Output value of repair of buildings and structures, that is the value created through the repairs of buildings or structures, but does not include the value of buildings or structures being repaired and the value of the repair of production equipment;

(4)Output value of manufactured non-standard equipment, that is the value of non-standard production equipment (including raw materials and manufacturing cost) made for the construction project, and the equipment manufactured by subsidiary workshops.

Value-added of Construction refers to the final result of the activities of production and management of construction in monetary terms in the reference period. At present, the value-added of construction is calculated with the income approach. In other words, it is the sum of income of various production factors in the production process. The formula is as follows:

Value-added of construction=depreciation of fixed assets in the year+wages payable+welfare expensespayable+insurance premium and tax for waiting for employment in the administrative expenses +taxes and surcharges on project settlement+profit gained from project settlement.

Floor Space of Buildings Under Construction refers to floor space of buildings under construction during the reference period, including newly started buildings, buildings started earlier and continued during the reference period, and buildings suspended earlier but restarted during the reference period, buildings completed during the reference period, and buildings under construction and then suspended during the reference period.

Floor Space of Buildings Completed refers to the floor space of buildings that are completed in the reference period in accordance with the requirements of the design, up to the standard for putting them into use, and have been checked and accepted by concerned departments as qualified ones.

Total Number of Machinery and Equipment Owned by the End of Year refers to the number of machines and equipment owned by the enterprises, and listed as the fixed assets of the enterprises by the end of the year, including machinery and equipment for construction, production and transportation.

Total Power of Machinery and Equipment Owned by the End of Year refers to the total power of machinery and equipment owned by the enterprises, and listed as the fixed assets of the enterprises by the end of the year, including machinery and equipment for construction, production and transportation. The power of the machinery is calculated on basis of the designed or verified capacity, covering the power of the machinery/equipment and the separate power equipment serving the machinery/ equipment (such as electric motors), but excluding welders, transformers and boilers. The unit used for the calculation of power is kilowatt, with horsepower converted to kilowatt by 1 horsepower=0.735 kilowatt.

Income from Settlement of Projects refers to the income received by the construction enterprise from the contracted project through settlement procedures, and other charges to the contractoree as operational costs in addition to the value of the project, such as temporary facility fee, labour insurance premium, moving cost of construction equipment, as well as various types of claimsto the contractee.

Profit from Settlement of Projects refers to profit realized through settled projects. It is calculated with the following formula:

Profit from Settlement of Projects=Income from Settlement of Projects-Settled Cost-Settled Taxes and Other Cost

Total Revenue of Enterprises refers to the sum of income from production and operation of enterprises, including income from settlement of projects and other operational income, namely:

Total Revenue of Enterprises=Income from Settlement of Projects+Other Operational Income

14 运输和邮电

TRANSPORT, POSTAL AND TELECOMMUNICATION SERVICE

资料整理：曾文元
Data management:Zeng Wenyuan

第十四部分　运输和邮电

一、简要说明

本章资料包括交通运输业和邮电通信业的基本情况，主要是交通运输工具、货物和旅客运输量、邮电业务、邮政局所及服务点等基本情况。资料由西安市统计局社会科技处根据有关部门提供资料整理。

二、主要指标

旅客周转量（亿人公里）	294.30	比上年增长 14.0%
货物周转量（亿吨公里）	430.17	比上年增长 14.2%
邮电业务总量（亿元）	323.11	比上年增长 8.1%
全社会车辆数（万辆）	125.35	比上年增长 23.7%
#民用小轿车	49.20	比上年增长 31.3%

14 TRANSPORT,POSTAL AND TELECOMMUNICATION SERVICES

Ⅰ.Brief Introduction

Data in this chapter consists of primarily basic data of communication, transportation and postal service industry, transportation facility, amount of goods and passenger transportation, basic data of postal service, post offices and service establishments of Xi'an City. Data in this chapter is compiled by Social & Science and Technology Division of the Xi'an Bureau of Statistics according to the data provided by department concerned of the municipal government.

Ⅱ.Major Indicators

		Increase over Preceding Year
Passenger-Km (100 mil. person-km)	294.30	14.0%
Freight Ton-Km (100 mil. ton-km)	430.17	14.2%
Amount of Postal and Telecommunication Service(100 mil. yuan)	323.11	8.1%
Civil Motor Vehicles(10 000 units)	125.35	23.7%
Small Saloon Car	49.20	31.3%

14-1 主要年份各种交通线路和桥梁

Transportation Routes and Number of Bridges in Representative Years

年 份 Year	铁路营业 里程（公里） Length of Railways in Operation (km)	公路里程 （公里） Length of Highways (km)	桥 梁 （座） Bridges (seat)
1978	555		
1979	555		
1980	555		
1981	569		
1982	569		
1983	569		
1984	569		
1985	697		
1986	697		
1987	1333		
1988	1339		
1989	1339	2563	
1990	1339	2586	
1991	1357	2785	
1992	1357	2786	
1993	1356	2801	
1994	1357	2830	
1995	1357	2852	
1996	1358	2877	
1997	1489	3026	
1998	1492	3047	
1999	1478	2789	
2000	1540	3010	
2001	1536	3298	
2002	1543	7862	629
2003	1522	8360	629
2004	1608	8360	629
2005	202	8500	634
2006	269	9530	634
2007	269	9672	1319
2008	269	11895	1710
2009	269	12378	1856
2010	269	12378	1856

注：2005年开始，铁路统计执行新的统计口径。

Note: Since 2005, Railway statistics has followed the renewed data.

14-1 续表 continued

年 份 Year	桥梁长度 （米） Length of Bridge (m)	永久式桥梁 （座） Permanent Bridges (seat)	永久式桥梁长度 （米） Length of Permanent Bridges (m)	民航通航里程（公里） （重复航线） Length of Total Civil Aviation Routes(km)
1978				
1979				
1980				
1981				
1982				
1983				
1984				
1985				
1986				
1987				
1988				
1989				
1990				
1991				
1992				65007
1993				83215
1994				100800
1995				119753
1996				126433
1997				173010
1998				180000
1999				141284
2000				139764
2001				154614
2002	29799	629	29799	211000
2003	29799	629	29799	381800
2004	29799	629	29799	386953
2005	46973	632	46915	485749
2006	46973	632	46915	418852
2007	91412	1275	90716	553355
2008	151996	1657	150980	515524
2009	154866	1803	153850	587904
2010	154866	1803	153850	742375

14-2 各种交通线路里程和桥梁数

Length of Transportation Routes and Number of Bridges

指　　标	Item	2009	2010
铁路营业里程（公里）	**Length of Railways in Operation (km)**	**269**	**269**
电气化营业里程	Length of Electrified Railways in Operation	205	205
复线里程	Double-Tracking Length	133	133
公路里程(公里)	**Length of Highways (km)**	**12378**	**12378**
等级公路	Expressways and Class Ⅰ to Ⅳ Highways	11839	11839
高速	Expressway	377	377
一级	First Class	317	317
二级	Second Class	952	952
三级	Third Class	1186	1186
四级	Forth Class	9007	9007
等外公路	Highways below Class Ⅳ	539	539
桥梁	**Bridges**		
座(座)	Seat (seat)	1856	1856
长度(米)	Length (m)	154866	154866
永久式桥梁	Permanent		
座(座)	Seat (seat)	1803	1803
长度(米)	Length (m)	153850	153850
半永久式桥梁	Semi Permanent		
座(座)	Seat (seat)	12	12
长度(米)	Length (m)	291	291
民航通航里程(公里)（重复航线）	**Length of Total Civil Aviation Routes(km)**	**587904**	**742375**

14-3 主要年份全社会车辆数

Possession of Civil Vehicles in Representative Years

单位：辆、台 (unit)

年份 Year	合计 Total	汽车 Motor	载客汽车 Passenget Vehicles	载货汽车 Ordinary Trucks	摩托车 Motorcycles	拖拉机 Tractors
1999	279335	133192	63772	44348		38023
2000	310252	138318	89783	44974		37177
2001	369988	172436	110744	55453		31355
2002	454998	206653	134527	64623	176960	36083
2003	516719	242599	163872	70781	191834	34733
2004	512802	276012	195524	74557	156709	34755
2005	544586	377628	240923	82463	131440	34741
2006	608155	393778	296078	89772	131449	33236
2007	840376	522616	360081	97614	284594	32028
2008	875005	595735	430472	89093	247079	30176
2009	1012937	754803	567326	113430	224121	31347
2010	1253461	961283	739038	145740	259239	29151

14-4 全社会车辆数

Possession of Civil Vehicles

指 标	Item	2007	2008	2009	2010
合 计	**Total**	**840376**	**875005**	**1012937**	**1253461**
民用汽车 (辆)	Motor(unit)	522616	595735	754803	961283
载客汽车	Passenget Vehicles	360081	430472	567326	739038
#大 型	Large	9624	10007	11352	12610
轿 车	Car	229805	281726	374827	492049
普通载货汽车	Ordinary Trucks	97614	89093	113430	145740
#重、中型	Heavy and Medium	38585	37752	48783	60178
其他汽车	Others	64921	76170	74047	76505
#三 轮	Three Wheelers	40454	41309	38739	38866
拖拉机 (台)	Tractors(unit)	32028	30176	31347	29151
#大中型	Large and Medium	10499	11016	11890	12330
小 型	Small-sized	17663	16332	15905	16764
摩托车 (辆)	Motorcycle (unit)	284594	247079	224121	259239
普通摩托车	Bicycle Motor	235833	212581	201302	243335
挂车 (辆)	Articulated Trailers (unit)	966	1850	2552	3709
其他类型车 (辆)	Others (unit)	172	165	114	79

14-5 主要年份交通运输量及周转量

Passenger Traffic and Kilometers and Freight Traffic and Ton-kilometers in Representative Years

年 份 Year	客运量 （万人次） Passenger Traffic (10 000 person-times)	旅客周转量 （万人公里） Passenger-Km (10 000 person-Km)	货运量 （万吨） Freight Traffic (10 000 tons)	货物周转量 （万吨公里） Freight Ton-Km (10 000 ton-Km)
1978	1334		3723	
1979	1420		3919	
1980	1508		3655	
1981	1839		3379	
1982	2340		4067	
1983	3054		4225	
1984	2899		4966	
1985	2404		5681	
1986	2186		5409	
1987	3781		6294	
1988	5721		6968	
1989	6092		8742	
1990	5748		6980	
1991	4193		3389	
1992	4368		8233	
1993	8036		8406	
1994	8321		8754	
1995	9069		9590	
1996	9854		10577	
1997	8922		9358	
1998	9223		9429	
1999	10311	2130383	9766	3452383
2000	8068	2507896	6999	3691963
2001	9078	2658037	7728	4229430
2002	12527	2524444	9484	4544040
2003	11413	2596402	9392	5037684
2004	10832	3112374	14845	5850029
2005	10479	1607568	12051	1249525
2006	11245	1721217	11832	1354318
2007	12466	1753464	15124	1473182
2008	26501	2529007	27560	3490707
2009	28693	2582025	30606	3766806
2010	30294	2942957	34323	4301680

14-6 交通运输量及运输周转量

Passenger Traffic and Kilometers and Freight Traffic and Ton-kilometers

指　标	Item	2009	2010	2010年比2009年增长(%) Increase Rate in 2010 over 2009(%)
一、客运量（万人次）	**Passenger Traffic(10 000 person-times)**	**28693**	**30294**	**5.6**
铁路	Railway	2585	2781	7.6
公路	Highway	25271	26536	5.0
航空	Civil Aviation	837	977	16.7
二、旅客周转量（万人公里）	**Passenger-Km (10 000 person-Km)**	**2582025**	**2942957**	**14.0**
铁路	Railway	512686	552498	7.8
公路	Highway	1229172	1346104	9.5
民用航空	Civil Aviation	840167	1044355	24.3
三、货运量（万吨）	**Freight Traffic(10 000 tons)**	**30606**	**34323**	**12.1**
铁路	Railway	614	706	15.0
公路	Highway	29986	33610	12.1
航空	Civil Aviation	6	7	16.7
四、货物周转量（万吨公里）	**Freight Ton-Km (10 000 ton-Km)**	**3766806**	**4301680**	**14.2**
铁路	Railway	1650050	1800074	9.1
公路	Highway	2107236	2487692	18.1
航空	Civil Aviation	9520	13914	46.2

14-7 主要年份邮政电信情况

年 份 Year	邮电业务总量（万元） Business Volume of Postal and Telecommunication Services(10 000 yuan)	电信业务总量 Business Volume of Telecommunication Services	邮政业务总量 Business Volume of Postal Services
1978	1420		
1979	1616		
1980	1640		
1981	1713		
1982	2154		
1983	2250		
1984	2484		
1985	2972		
1986	3244		
1987	3911		
1988	5327		
1989	5973		
1990	7843		
1991	5700		
1992	6610		
1993	36581		
1994	54034		
1995	76450		
1996	104566		
1997	124601		
1998	204927		
1999	306457		
2000	461628		
2001	367620		
2002	515259	470492	44767
2003	820943	770673	50270
2004	1027415	975045	52370
2005	1320447	1261033	59414
2006	1867560	1796533	71027
2007	2267633	2191250	76383
2008	2646662	2564524	82138
2009	2989246	2900836	88410
2010	3231059	3167750	63309

注：2002年及以后，邮政电信机构分离。

Basic Statistic on Postal and Telecommunication Service

固定电话年末户数（户） Number of Immobile Telephone at Year-end (subscriber)	#农村电话年末户数 Number of Telephone in Rural Areas at Year-end	移动电话用户年末数（户） Number of Mobile Phone at Year-end (subscriber)	互联网年末宽带用户（户） Number of Broad Band Net User (subscriber)
12828	1062		
13487	1052		
14024	1086		
14497	1125		
15357	1129		
16922	1156		
18611	1203		
21624	1239		
26373	1235		
30200	1290		
34265	1357		
39506	1498		
45267	1668		
49516	2479		
60727	2613		
101327	2671		
197398	5067		
299485	8386		
430270	13654		
573244	21202		
736998	37863		
874586	74761		
1242637	170199		
1711500	259374	1277400	17183
2095230	358803	1964200	35230
2538393	415593	2412392	160900
2934424	480276	3500900	243448
3214806	500847	4199570	339280
3159639	467526	5510720	508775
3145819	419446	6645863	586213
3068807	383869	7377575	813987
2891009	358238	11200566	1167916
2617691	335048	14230800	1461804

Note: Since 2002, the postal service and telecommunication service have been seperated.

14-8 邮政业务及服务网点

Postal service and branch post office

指 标	Item	2009	2010
一、邮政业务总量（万元）	**Business Volume of Postal Services(10 000 yuan)**	**88410**	**63309**
二、邮政业务总收入（万元）	**Gross Income of Post Services (10 000 yuan)**	**79460**	**58831**
三、函件（万件）	**Number of Letters (10 000 pcs)**	**6128**	**8176**
四、包件（万件）	**Parcels (10 000 pcs)**	**81**	**59**
五、汇票（万张）	**Money Order (10 000 pcs)**	**208**	**123**
六、报纸订销累计份数（万份）	**Accumulated Newspaper Prescribing and Sales Volume (10 000 pcs)**	**11187**	**11724**
七、杂志订销累计份数（万份）	**Accumulated Magazine Prescribing and Sales Volume (10 000 pcs)**	**561**	**550**
八、特快专递类业务（万件）	**Express Mail Service Volume (10 000 pcs)**	**497**	**582**
九、集邮业务量（万枚）	**Stamps For Collection (10 000 pcs)**	**1494**	**860**
十、邮政储蓄余额（万元）	**Postal savings deposit balance (10 000 yuan)**	**1287892**	
十一、邮政营销网点（处）	**Number of Post Office Branch Establishments (unit)**	**300**	**305**
#设在农村的局所	In it: number of post offices in rural area	92	50
十二、邮政信筒信箱（个）	**Number of Mailboxes(unit)**	**998**	**1108**

注：2010年邮政储蓄业务归入金融业。

Note: Since 2010, post saving service has been included in finance.

14-9 电信业务情况

Telecommunication service

指 标	Item	2009	2010
一、电信业务总量（万元）	**Business Volume of Telecommunication Services (10 000 yuan)**	**2900836**	**3167750**
二、电信业务总收入（万元）	**Gross Income of Telecommunication Services (10 000 yuan)**	**951343**	**1038865**
三、固定电话年末户数（户）	**Number of Immobile Telephone at Year-end (subscriber)**	**2891009**	**2617691**
#农村电话年末户数	Number of Telephone in Rural Areas at Year-end	358238	335048
四、长途电话通话总数（万次）	**Number of Long-distance Telephone Call (10 000 times)**	**30633**	**101935**
五、电话交换机容量（门）	**Capacity (number) of Telephone Switchboard (line)**	**4411059**	**4490470**
六、移动电话用户年末数（户）	**Number of Mobile Phone at Year-end(subscriber)**	**11200566**	**14230800**
七、互联网年末宽带用户（户）	**Number of Broad Band Net User (subscriber)**	**1167916**	**1461804**

主要统计指标解释

铁路营业里程　又称营业长度（包括正式营业和临时营业里程），指办理客货运输业务的铁路正线总长度。凡是全线或部分建成双线及以上的线路，以第一线的实际长度计算;复线、站线、段管线、岔线和特殊用途线以及不计算运费的联络线都不计算营业里程。铁路营业里程是反映铁路运输业基础设施发展水平的重要指标，也是计算客货周转量、运输密度和机车车辆运用效率等指标的基础资料。

公路里程　指在一定时期内实际达到《公路工程技术标准JTJ01-88》规定的等级公路，并经公路主管部门正式验收交付使用的公路里程数。包括大中城市的郊区公路以及通过小城镇街道部分的公路里程和桥梁、隧道渡口的长度，不包括大中城市的街道、厂矿、林区生产用道和农业生产用道的里程。两条或多条公路共同经由同一路段，只计算一次，不得重复计算里程长度。它是反映公路建设发展规模的重要指标，也是计算运输网密度等指标的基础资料。

民用航空航线里程　指民航运输定期班机飞行的航线长度的总和。航线长度按机场之间的距离计算，通常有两种计算方法：一是将每条航线长度相加称为重复计算航线里程；一是将两线或两条以上航线经过同一区段里程，只计算一次航线长度称为不重复计算航线里程。一般常用的是后者，它能确切反映民航运输网的规模，是表明民航事业为国民经济服务和方便人民生活程度的主要指标。

货（客）运量　指在一定时期内，各种运输工具实际运送的货物（旅客）数量。它是反映运输业为国民经济和人民生活服务的数量指标，也是制定和检查运输生产计划、研究运输发展规模和速度的重要指标。货运按吨计算，客运按人计算。货物不论运输距离长短、货物类别，均按实际重量统计。旅客不论行程远近或票价多少，均按一人一次客运量统计;半价票、小孩票也按一人统计。

货物（旅客）周转量　指在一定时期内，由各种运输工具运送的货物（旅客）数量与其相应运输距离的乘积之总和。它是反映运输业生产总成果的重要指标，也是编制和检查运输生产计划，计算运输效率、劳动生产率以及核算运输单位成本的主要基础资料。计算货物周转量通常按发出站与到达站之间的最短距离，也就是计费距离计算。计算公式为:

货物（旅客）周转量 = ∑货物（旅客）运输量 × 运输距离

民用汽车拥有量　指报告期末，在公安交通管理部门按照《机动车注册登记工作规范》，已注册登记领有民用车辆牌照的全部汽车数量。汽车拥有量统计的主要分类：根据汽车结构分为载客汽车、载货汽车及其他汽车；根据汽车所有者不同分为个人(私人)汽车、单位汽车；根据汽车的使用性质分为营运汽车、非营运汽车；根据汽车大小规格不同载客汽车分为大型、中型、小型和微型，载货汽车分为重型、中型、轻型和微型。

邮电业务总量　指以价值量形式表现的邮电通信企业为社会提供各类邮电通信服务的总数量。邮电业务量按专业分类包括函件、包件、汇票、报刊发行、邮政快件、特快专递、邮政储蓄、集邮、公众电报、用户电报、传真、长途电话、出租电路、无线寻呼、移动电话、分组交换数据通信、出租代维等。计算方法为各类产品乘以相应的平均单价（不变价）之和，再加上出租电路和设备、代用户维护电话交换机和线路等的服务收入。它综合反映了一定时期邮电业务发展的总成果，是研究邮电业务量构成和发展趋势的重要指标。计算公式为:

邮电业务总量 = ∑（各类邮电业务量 × 不变单价）+ 出租代维及其他业务收入

移动电话用户　是指通过移动电话交换机进入移动电话网、占用移动电话号码的电话用户。用户数量以报告期末在移动电话营业部门实际办理登记手续进入移动电话网的户数进行计算，一部移动电话统计为一户。

电话用户　指接入国家公众固定电话网，并按固定电话业务进行经营管理的电话用户。1997年以前，电话用户分为市内电话用户和农村电话用户。“市内电话用户”是指接入县城及县以上城市的电话网上的电话用户;“农村电话用户”是指接入县邮电局农话台及县以下农村电话交换点，以县城为中心（除市话用户外）联通县、乡（镇）、行政村、村民小组的用户。从1997年起，电话用户数分组调整为以用户所在区域划分为“城市电话用户”和“乡村电话用户”，与过去的按市内电话和农村电话划分方法不同。而电话用户总数、电话机总部数统计范围不变。

城市电话用户　指直辖市、省辖市、地级市、县级市的市区、市郊区及县城（包括县人民政府所在地的县城关区或行政建制相当于县人民政府所在地的镇）范围内接入局用交换机的电话用户数，包括分布在农村地区的独立工矿区、林区、驻军等接入局用交换机的电话用户数。

乡村电话用户 指县城关区以下的集镇和农村接入局用交换机的电话用户数。

住宅电话用户 是指安装在居民住宅或农民家里并按照住宅电话用户登记注册和收费的电话用户。包括私人付费、单位付费和按规定免费安装的住宅电话用户。

局用交换机容量 是指安装在本地电信运营商内用于接续本地固定电话的电话交换机容量，有倍增设备按倍增后的数量计数。包括现用和备用的人工或自动交换机的全部容量。

互联网宽带接入端口 指用于接入互联网用户的各类实际安装运行的接入端口的数量，包括xDSL用户接入端口、LAN接入端口以及其他类型接入端口等，不包括窄带拨号接入端口。

Explanatory Notes on Main Statistical Indicators

Length of Railways in Operation refers to the total length of the trunk line under passenger and freight transportation (including both full operation and temporary operation). The calculation is based on the actual length of the first line even if this line has a full or partial double track or more tracks, excluding double tracks, station sidings, tracks under the charge of stations, branch lines, special-purpose lines and the non-payable connecting lines. The length of railways in operation is an important indicator to show the development of the infrastructure for the railway transport, and also the essential data to calculate volume of passenger freight transport, traffic density and utilization efficiency of the locomotives and carriages.

Length of Highways refers to the length of highways which are built in conformity with the grades specified by the highway engineering standard formulated by the Ministry of Communications, and have been formally checked and accepted by the departments of highways and put into use. The length of highways includes that of the suburb highways at large and medium-sized cities, highways passing through streets at small cities and towns, and also the length of bridges、 tunnel and ferries. It does not include the length of streets in big and medium-sized cities and highways built for the production purpose at factories, mines, forest areas and agricultural areas. If two or more highways go the same section of the way, the length of the section is only calculated for once and no duplication is allowed. The length of highways is an important indicator to show the development of the highway construction and to provide essential information to calculate the transport network density.

Length of Civil Aviation Routes refers to the length of all routes for regular civil aviation flights. There are usually two ways to calculate the distance between airports connected by the route length: one is to put the length of all air routes together, called duplicated calculation of the length of the routes; the other is not to allow the duplication in calculation when two or more routes passing the same section of aviation routes. The latter is usually used, as it can precisely show the size of the civil aviation network and indicate the extent of civil aviation serving the national economy and the people.

Freight (Passenger) Traffic refers to the volume of freight (passenger) transported with various means. Freight transport is calculated in tons and passenger traffic is calculated in the number of persons. Despite the type of freight and travelling distance, the freight transport is calculated in the actual weight of the goods: and despite the travelling distance and ticket price, the passenger traffic is calculated by the principle that one person can be counted only once in one travel. The passenger who travel with a half price ticket or a child ticket is also calculated as one person. The freight (passenger) traffic provides a quantitative measure to show how the transport industry serves the national economy and people, and is also an important indicator for planning the transport industry and for studying the development scale and speed of the transport industry.

Freight Ton-kilometers (Passenger-kilometers) refer to the sum of the products of the volume of transported cargo (passengers) multiplying by the transport distance, usually using ton-kilometer and passenger-kilometer as units for measurement. Normally, the shortest distance between the departure station and the destination station (i.e., the payable distance) is the basis to calculate the freight ton-kilometers. This is an important indicator to show the total results of the transport industry, to prepare and examine the transport plan and to measure the efficiency, the labour productivity and the unit cost of transport.

The formula is as follows:

Freight Ton-kilometers (Passenger-kilometers) =Σ {Freight (Passenger) Traffic x Distance of Transportation}

Measuring unit: ton-kilometer (person-kilometer)

Possession of Civil Motor Vehicles refer to the total numbers of vehicles that are registered and received vehicles license tags according to the Work Standard for Motor Vehicles Registration formulated by the Transport Management Office under the department of public security at the end of the reference period. They are divided into categories. According to the structure of motor vehicles, they are divided into passenger vehicles, trucks and others; according to ownership into private vehicles and vehicles for the unit' s use; according to kind of usage into working vehicles and non-working vehicles; and according to size of vehicles into large passenger vehicles, medium-sized passenger vehicles, small passenger vehicles and mini passenger vehicles,heavy trucks, light-heavy trucks, light trucks and mini-trucks.

Business Volume of Post and Telecommunications refers to the total amount of post and telecommunications services, expressed in value terms, provided by the post and telecommunications departments for the society. Post and telecommunication services can be classified asletters, parcels, remittance, issue of newspapers and magazines, fast mail service, express mail service, savings deposits, stamps for collection, public and individual telegraph service, facsimiles, long-distance telephone service,leasing of telephone lines, urban paging service, mobile telephone service, data transfer and transmission, etc. The accounting approach is to multiply the service products of all types with their average unit price (constant price) to get sum of business value, plus income from other services such as leasing of telephone lines and equipment, maintenance of telephone switchboards and lines on behalf of customers. This indicator reflects the overall results of post and telecommunications service during a given period, and is important to study the composition of business service and the development of post and telecommunications service.

The formula is as follows:

Business Volume of Post and Telecommunications=Σ (Transaction of Post and Telecommunication Service x Constant Price) + Income from Leasing, Maintenance and other Services

Mobile Telephone Subscribers refer to the persons who own mobile telephone numbers and are connected with the mobile telephone communication network through the mobile telephone switchboards. The number of subscribers is calculated by the subscribers who have completed registration at mobile communication business centers and entered into the mobile telephone network. One mobile telephone is taken as a subscriber.

Telephone Subscribers refer to subscribers that are connected to the public line telephone network provided with telephone services. Before 1997, telephone subscribers were classified as city subscribers and village subscribers. City subscribers referred to those connected to city telephone networks in county towns and cities, while village subscribers referred to those connected to village telephone stations at and below counties. Since 1997, the classification of telephone subscribers was modified on the basis of physical location of the subscribers as Urban telephone subscribers and rural telephone subscribers , which is different from the previous classification of categorizing local telephones and rural telephones , while the definition of total subscribers and total number of telephones remain unchanged.

Urban Telephone Subscribers refer to subscribers telephone subscribers, located at municipalities, cities under the jurisdiction of province, cities at prefectural level, downtown and suburb of city at county level town and county towns (including country towns where county government located, and towns of county level according to the administrative organizational system), that are connected to the public line telephone network, including rural mineral area, forest area, military area.

Rural Telephone Subscribers refer to telephone subscribers, located at towns under county town and country, that are connected to the public line telephone network.

Household Telephone Subscribers refer to telephone sets installed in the dwelling units of urban or rural residents, and registered as residence subscribers for payment, including 3 types of payment for the service: private payment, public payment and free service.

Capacity of Office Telephone Exchanges refers to the capacity (measured in gate) of telephone exchanges installed in the offices of local telecommunication service providers for communication between fixed telephones. It includes the capacity of both manual and automatic exchanges in use and for stand-by purpose. Equipment with expansion function is to be counted by the expanded capacity.

Broadband Connection Terminals refer to the connection terminals to internet users actually installed and put into operation, including connection terminals for xDSL, connection terminals for LAN, and other connection terminals for xDSL. N-ISDN connection terminals are not included.

15 国内贸易

DOMESTIC TRADE

资料整理：马晓庆　杨　骏　左　宇　赵琳瑛　胡树建
Data management: Ma Xiaoqing　Yang Jun　Zuo Yu　Zhao Linying　Hu Shujian

第十五部分　国内贸易

一、简要说明

本章资料主要包括社会消费品零售总额，批发零售贸易业商品购、销等情况，限额以上批发零售贸易业主要商品销售情况，限额以上批发零售贸易和住宿餐饮企业财务状况、经济效益，以及交易市场情况，由西安市统计局贸易外经处提供。

二、主要指标

批发零售贸易业网点（万个）	20.11	比上年增长	4.6%
餐饮业网点（万个）	4.13	比上年增长	4.6%
社会消费品零售总额（亿元）	1637.04	比上年增长	18.5%
#批发零售贸易业零售额	1431.23	比上年增长	17.0%

15 DOMESTIC TRADE

Ⅰ.Brief Introduction

Content of this chapter consists of total retail sales of consumer goods, sails data on commodity purchasing and sails of wholesale and retail trade, sales data on primary goods exceeds quotation, financial, economic performance and market data on wholesale and retail trade and food services industry exceeds quotation. Data in this chapter is compiled and provided by Trade and Foreign Economy Division of the Xi'an Bureau of Statistics.

Ⅱ.Major Indicators

		Increase over Preceding Year
Establishments Engaged in Whole-sale and Retail Trade(10 000 unit)	20.11	4.6%
Establishments Engaged in Trade(10 000 unit)	4.13	4.6%
Establishments Engaged in Catering Trade(10 000 unit)	1637.04	18.5%
Total Retail Sales of Consumer Goods (100 mil. yuan)	1431.23	17.0%
Retail Sales of Wholesale and Retail Enterprises		

15-1 主要年份社会消费品零售总额

Total Retail Sales of Consumer Goods in Representative Years

单位:亿元 (100 million yuan)

年份 Year	社会消费品零售总额 Total Retail Sales of Consumer Goods	城镇 Urban	乡村 Village	批发零售贸易业 Wholesale Trades and Retail Trades	住宿餐饮业 Accommodation and Catering Trade	其他行业 Others
1978	12.70	8.82	3.88	11.01	0.53	0.21
1979	13.94	9.88	4.06	11.88	0.60	0.21
1980	15.88	11.53	4.35	13.05	0.80	0.20
1981	17.41	12.85	4.56	14.31	0.80	0.19
1982	18.54	13.79	4.75	15.25	0.88	0.27
1983	20.82	15.14	5.68	16.95	1.03	0.32
1984	24.87	19.13	5.74	19.47	1.29	0.46
1985	32.92	26.09	6.83	25.04	1.69	0.48
1986	37.50	29.25	8.25	28.88	1.97	0.64
1987	43.86	34.62	9.24	33.32	2.50	0.49
1988	59.65	47.74	11.91	44.84	2.97	0.78
1989	68.05	54.60	13.45	54.41	2.98	0.76
1990	72.77	59.42	13.35	57.46	3.79	0.90
1991	81.04	66.93	14.11	60.35	4.43	1.26
1992	100.84	89.17	11.67	71.86	6.13	2.30
1993	115.38	104.41	10.97	75.99	7.49	2.71
1994	144.64	131.56	13.08	89.79	9.12	3.43
1995	186.60	165.98	20.62	115.46	11.97	3.73
1996	222.94	198.19	24.75	145.05	15.83	4.02
1997	264.47	238.17	26.30	169.08	22.12	4.17
1998	291.45	257.39	34.06	183.43	30.97	4.27
1999	323.37	283.32	40.05	207.96	34.78	4.85
2000	360.42	317.12	43.30	232.89	41.42	5.43
2001	406.21	358.97	47.24	265.25	48.87	5.86
2002	459.76	409.86	49.90	309.36	51.42	6.45
2003	502.65	449.62	53.03	440.28	53.30	9.07
2004	578.60	520.94	57.66	509.60	56.87	12.13
2005	670.56	604.63	65.93	592.77	63.59	14.20
2006	784.95	708.31	76.64	694.03	74.77	16.15
2007	936.21	845.59	90.62	828.63	89.32	18.26
2008	1176.58	1063.93	112.65	1033.00	122.90	20.68
2009	1381.12	1249.79	131.33	1222.98	134.54	23.60
2010	1637.04	1570.16	66.88	1431.23	179.82	25.99

注：1.依据2008年第二次经济普查数据，对2005-2007年数据进行调整。

2. 2009年以前按经营单位所在地分为市和县及县以下。

3. 2002年以前按行业分组中不包括制造业零售额和农业对非农业居民零售额。

Note:1.According to the Secong Economic Census statistics,datas from 2005 to 2007 were adjusted.

2.Before 2009, the sales was categorized into city and county and below by location of operation units.

3.Before 2002,the categories by sector did not include the retailing sales of manufacture and agricultural over non-agricultural residents.

15-2 社会消费品零售总额（2010年）

Total Retail Sales of Consumer Goods（2010）

单位:亿元 (100 million yuan)

分　　类	Classify	金　额 Sum
社会消费品零售总额	**Total Retail Sales of Consumer Goods**	**1637.04**
（一）按销售单位所在地分:	Grouped by Region	
（1）城镇	Urban	1570.16
其中：城区	District	1177.30
（2）乡村	Village	66.88
（二）按行业分:	Grouped by Sector	
（1）批发业	Wholesale Enterprises	194.88
限额以上企业	Enterprises Above Designated Size	90.58
限额以下企业和个体户	Enterprises Below Designated Size and Self-employed Laborers	104.30
#个体户	Self-employed Laborers	23.09
（2）零售业	Retail Enterprises	1236.35
限额以上企业	Enterprises Above Designated Size	860.03
限额以下企业和个体户	Enterprises Below Designated Size and Self-employed Laborers	376.32
#个体户	Self-employed Laborers	202.61
（3）住宿和餐饮业	Accommodation and Catering Trade	179.82
限额以上企业	Enterprises Above Designated Size	68.72
限额以下企业和个体户	Enterprises Below Designated Size and Self-employed Laborers	111.10
#个体户	Self-employed Laborers	88.44
（4）其他行业	Others	25.99

15-3 各区县社会消费品零售总额（2010年）

Total Retail Sales of Consumer Goods by Region（2010）

单位：亿元 (100 million yuan)

区县名称	Name of District and County	社会消费品零售总额 Total Retail Sales of Consumer Goods	批发零售贸易业 Wholesale and Retail Trade of Retail Sales	住宿餐饮业 Accommodation and Catering Trade of Retail Sales
新城区	Xincheng	285.04	262.76	17.38
碑林区	Beilin	285.18	246.30	36.05
莲湖区	Lianhu	234.58	208.39	24.91
灞桥区	Baqiao	38.30	32.68	5.32
未央区	Weiyang	232.17	216.85	14.93
雁塔区	Yanta	316.17	265.05	39.85
阎良区	Yanliang	19.28	15.61	3.45
临潼区	Lintong	40.30	34.60	4.83
长安区	Chang'an	91.07	69.00	20.24
蓝田县	Lantian	29.60	25.40	3.80
周至县	Zhouzhi	19.79	17.48	1.87
户　县	Huxian	32.34	26.97	4.99
高陵县	Gaoling	13.22	10.11	2.20

15-3 续表 continued

单位：亿元 (100 million yuan)

区县名称	Name of District and County	社会消费品零售总额 Total Retail Sales of Consumer Goods	
		城镇 Urban	乡村 Village
新城区	Xincheng	285.04	
碑林区	Beilin	285.18	
莲湖区	Lianhu	234.58	
灞桥区	Baqiao	38.30	
未央区	Weiyang	232.17	
雁塔区	Yanta	316.17	
阎良区	Yanliang	16.75	2.53
临潼区	Lintong	26.65	13.65
长安区	Chang'an	61.93	29.14
蓝田县	Lantian	21.95	7.65
周至县	Zhouzhi	16.28	3.51
户　县	Huxian	24.39	7.95
高陵县	Gaoling	10.76	2.46

15-4 主要年份批发零售贸易业、餐饮业网点和人员

Wholesale and Retail Trade, Catering Outlets and Staff in Representative Years

单位:个、人 (unit,person)

年份 Year	批发业 Wholesale Trade		零售业 Retail Trade		餐饮业 Catering Services	
	网点 Branch Shop	人员 Personnel	网点 Branch Shop	人员 Personnel	网点 Branch Shop	人员 Personnel
1978	586	22136	5862	51462	442	9043
1979	462	14002	5387	49252	815	10349
1980	1505	28320	6312	51927	1893	16297
1981	597	17780	8800	74095	3397	25626
1982	881	25023	9811	68734	6422	25879
1983	1642	32597	17130	77863	6387	28054
1984	1875	34906	27043	136852	8484	25977
1985	1247	43311	35860	223076	11907	41025
1986	1706	42270	37503	241052	11977	48335
1987	3351	44475	42484	260450	13673	51361
1988	1829	40324	44330	282911	9576	47131
1989	1638	80078	46613	229705	10228	46420
1990	1558	37077	43244	219413	9800	34561
1991	1918	45583	48171	236235	10369	36813
1992	1864	36012	48422	258491	9916	38935
1993	5177	54255	43289	226572	11804	38318
1994	6338	58154	60292	318287	14296	56502
1995	6564	63337	69623	364430	15485	68782
1996	8008	67840	76828	437655	15668	78313
1997	8414	71178	80379	468811	20259	82917
1998	10780	85420	95056	515723	22500	100862
1999	10865	86630	96516	516163	24977	118442
2000	10393	81519	93928	492083	27531	124988
2001	10534	78285	95414	497448	28219	128738
2002	12220	107352	96815	465320	29219	140623
2003	13274	117740	99764	490169	32899	150883
2004	19696	102779	106477	281221	27905	132855
2005	20392	106138	112541	298285	30156	142176
2006	21243	110595	117168	312426	31694	148317
2007	21835	114497	122810	330583	34249	161517
2008	26813	148403	164642	470886	38134	201978
2009	26403	154777	165921	507706	39515	205364
2010	27887	166735	173218	544487	41289	219793

15-5 批发贸易业机构、网点、人员（2010年）

单位:个、人

分类	Classify	合计 Total 法人单位 Constitutional Unit	活动单位 Movemental Unit	网点 Branch Shop	人员 Personnel
总计	**Total**	**8321**	**8606**	**27887**	**166735**
一、按登记注册类型分组	**Grouped by Registered Kind**				
内资企业	Civil Funded Enterprises	8278	8555	10715	107541
国有企业	State-owned Enterprises	328	393	618	16164
集体企业	Collective-owned Enterprises	266	272	527	4014
股份合作企业	Cooperative Enterprises	24	27	28	577
联营企业	Joint Ownership Enterprises	17	19	19	468
有限责任公司	Limited Liability Corporations	2046	2088	2286	28250
股份有限公司	Share-holding Corporations Ltd.	110	115	160	6978
私营企业	Private Enterprises	5307	5458	6679	48908
其他企业	Other Enterprises	180	183	398	2182
港澳台商投资企业	Enterprises with Funds from Hong Kong，Macao &Taiwan	18	24	24	987
外商投资企业	Foreign Funded Enterprises	25	27	27	534
个体经济	Individuals			17121	57673
二、按国民经济行业分组	**Grouped by Sector**				
农畜产品批发	Wholesale of Farm Produce and Livestock Products	159	173	1031	4424
食品、饮料及烟草制品批发	Wholesale of Food, Beverages and Tobaccos	335	377	4024	21526
纺织、服装及日用品批发	Wholesale of Textiles, Garments and Daily Articles	530	549	3404	23509
文化、体育用品及器材批发	Wholesale of Culture , Sports Articles and Equipments	371	401	2725	11425
医药及医疗器材批发	Wholesale of Medicines and Medical Appliances	448	508	1102	8925
矿产品、建材及化工产品批发	Wholesale of Mineral Products, Building Materials and Chemical Products	2225	2265	5095	30691
机械设备、五金交电及电子产品批发	Wholesale of Machinery, Hardwares, Transport Means and Electronic Equipment	3491	3548	7549	49252
贸易经纪与代理	Trade Broker and Agency	76	78	118	677
其他批发	Other Wholesales	686	707	2839	16306

Organizations, Establishments and Persons Engaged in Whole-sale Trade（2010）

（unit,person）

城镇 Urban				城区 County				乡村 Village			
法人单位 Constitutional Unit	活动单位 Movemental Unit	网 点 Branch Shop	人 员 Personnel	法人单位 Constitutional Unit	活动单位 Movemental Unit	网 点 Branch Shop	人 员 Personnel	法人单位 Constitutional Unit	活动单位 Movemental Unit	网 点 Branch Shop	人 员 Personnel
8156	**8422**	**26246**	**160933**	**7974**	**8191**	**24600**	**155034**	**165**	**184**	**1641**	**5802**
8113	8371	10531	104759	7932	8141	10220	101892	165	184	184	2782
286	339	564	14645	247	274	454	13432	42	54	54	1519
220	225	480	3367	185	190	410	2846	46	47	47	647
24	26	27	543	21	23	23	490		1	1	34
17	19	19	468	17	19	19	468				
2040	2082	2280	28034	2029	2070	2268	27827	6	6	6	216
110	115	160	6978	104	109	154	6953				
5242	5389	6610	48573	5157	5282	6503	47740	65	69	69	335
174	176	391	2151	172	174	389	2136	6	7	7	31
18	24	24	987	17	23	23	971				
25	27	27	534	25	27	27	534				
		15664	54653			14330	51637			1457	3020
117	126	837	3704	73	74	620	2948	42	47	194	720
308	344	3839	20044	282	314	3419	18408	27	33	185	1482
524	542	3319	23100	510	526	2918	21997	6	7	85	409
371	401	2685	11335	368	395	2649	11267			40	90
448	506	1080	8870	443	485	1042	8262		2	22	55
2183	2223	4675	29730	2141	2169	4386	28840	42	42	420	961
3490	3547	7380	48924	3475	3532	7227	48503	1	1	169	328
73	75	95	637	72	74	94	631	3	3	23	40
642	658	2336	14589	610	622	2245	14178	44	49	503	1717

15-6 零售贸易业机构、网点、人员（2010年）

单位：个、人

分　类	Classify	合计 法人单位 Constitutional Unit	Total 活动单位 Movemental Unit	网点 Branch Shop	人员 Personnel
总计	**Total**	**6373**	**7253**	**173218**	**544487**
一、按登记注册类型分组	**Grouped by Registered Kind**				
内资企业	Civil Funded Enterprises	6329	7173	7640	135350
国有企业	State-owned Enterprises	220	283	368	17831
集体企业	Collective-owned Enterprises	338	403	512	4247
股份合作企业	Cooperative Enterprises	52	70	70	6726
联营企业	Joint Ownership Enterprises	28	39	39	317
有限责任公司	Limited Liability Corporations	1351	1771	1972	45774
股份有限公司	Share-holding Corporations Ltd.	91	114	144	4424
私营企业	Private Enterprises	4088	4323	4365	53891
其他企业	Other Enterprises	161	170	170	2140
港澳台商投资企业	Enterprises with Funds from Hong Kong，Macao & Taiwan	17	35	35	4605
外商投资企业	Foreign Funded Enterprises	27	45	51	5910
个体经济	Individuals			165492	398622
二、按国民经济行业分组	**Grouped by Sector**				
综合零售	Intergrated Retail	760	948	33759	110593
食品、饮料及烟草制品专门零售	Retail of Food,Beverages and Tobaccos	440	536	34424	90499
纺织、服装及日用品专门零售	Special Retail of Textiles,Garments and Daily Consumer Articles	807	876	37479	128500
文化、体育用品及器材专门零售	Retail of Culture, Sports Appliances and Equipments	498	548	8349	29312
医药及医疗器材专门零售	Retail of Medicines and Medical Appliances	586	890	7218	22526
汽车、摩托车、燃料及零售配件专门零售	Retail of Motor Vehicles, Motorcycles, Fuel and Parts	637	686	13682	61391
家用电器及电子产品专门零售	Special Retail of Household Electric Appliances and Electronic Products	1164	1221	12349	39064
五金、家具及室内装修材料专门零售	Special Retail of Hardware, Furniture and Decoration Materials	986	1031	16598	36319
无店铺及其他零售	Non-shop and Other Retail	495	517	9360	26283

Organizations, Establishments and Persons Engaged in Retail Trade（2010）

（unit,person）

城镇 Urban				城区 County				乡村 Village			
法人单位 Constitutional Unit	活动单位 Movemental Unit	网点 Branch Shop	人员 Personnel	法人单位 Constitutional Unit	活动单位 Movemental Unit	网点 Branch Shop	人员 Personnel	法人单位 Constitutional Unit	活动单位 Movemental Unit	网点 Branch Shop	人员 Personnel
6175	**7031**	**140826**	**475743**	**5806**	**6579**	**121141**	**433404**	**198**	**222**	**32392**	**68744**
6131	6951	7333	132457	5762	6499	6821	127260	198	222	307	2893
210	269	341	17297	188	227	256	16798	10	14	27	534
303	368	411	3794	270	287	312	3270	35	35	101	453
52	70	70	6726	46	64	64	6535				
25	36	36	277	24	35	35	271	3	3	3	40
1340	1759	1960	45676	1314	1733	1934	45445	11	12	12	98
91	114	144	4424	89	99	129	4156				
3958	4174	4210	52294	3686	3900	3937	48847	130	149	155	1597
152	161	161	1969	145	154	154	1938	9	9	9	171
17	35	35	4605	17	35	35	4605				
27	45	51	5910	27	45	51	5910				
		133407	332771			114234	295629			32085	65851
702	887	20626	84264	581	761	16289	72371	58	61	13133	26329
419	509	28212	79179	394	478	23388	69739	21	27	6212	11320
791	854	34137	123059	733	794	26520	109193	16	22	3342	5441
494	544	7435	27538	478	528	7088	26834	4	4	914	1774
574	873	6425	20920	538	800	5798	19550	12	17	793	1606
589	638	10106	50324	546	569	9187	47962	48	48	3576	11067
1145	1198	10257	32851	1117	1170	9802	31578	19	23	2092	6213
979	1024	16187	35505	950	988	15739	34534	7	7	411	814
482	504	7441	22103	469	491	7330	21643	13	13	1919	4180

15-7 餐饮业机构、网点、人员（2010年）

单位:个、人

分　类	Classify	合　计 法人单位 Constitutional Unit	活动单位 Movemental Unit	网 点 Branch Shop	Total 人 员 Personnel
总计	**Total**	**1680**	**1923**	**41289**	**219793**
一、按登记注册类型分组	**Grouped by Type of Registration**				
内资企业	Domestic Funded Enterprises	1643	1795	1949	75173
国有企业	State-owned Enterprises	55	67	68	4447
集体企业	Collective-owned Enterprises	24	26	26	679
股份合作企业	Share-holding Cooperative Enterprises	5	5	5	196
联营企业	Joint Ownership Enterprises	21	21	21	698
有限责任公司	Limited Liability Corporations	313	365	416	22603
股份有限公司	Share-holding Corporations Ltd.	24	40	41	4346
私营企业	Private Enterprises	1162	1227	1309	40592
其他企业	Other Enterprises	39	44	63	1612
港、澳、台商投资企业	Enterprises with Funds from Hong Kong，Macao & Taiwan	14	89	89	5719
外商投资企业	Foreign Funded Enterprises	23	39	39	2151
个体经济	Individuals			39212	136750
二、按餐饮业行业分组	**Grouped by Sector of Catering Trade**				
正餐服务	Restaurant	1362	1471	21873	144606
快餐服务	Fast Food	83	176	4045	13704
饮料及冷料服务	Beverages and Cold Drinks	114	130	1669	5414
其他餐饮服务	Others	121	146	13702	56069

Organizations Staff and Branch Shopes of Catering Trade（2010）

(unit,person)

城镇 Urban				城区 County				乡村 Village			
法人单位 Constitutional Unit	活动单位 Movemental Unit	网点 Branch Shop	人员 Personnel	法人单位 Constitutional Unit	活动单位 Movemental Unit	网点 Branch Shop	人员 Personnel	法人单位 Constitutional Unit	活动单位 Movemental Unit	网点 Branch Shop	人员 Personnel
1594	**1830**	**36150**	**201982**	**1441**	**1671**	**31730**	**184382**	**86**	**93**	**5139**	**17811**
1558	1703	1857	73560	1405	1544	1694	70427	85	92	92	1613
54	66	67	4333	51	63	63	4115	1	1	1	114
24	26	26	679	24	26	26	679				
5	5	5	196	4	4	4	186				
19	19	19	629	16	16	16	533	2	2	2	69
312	364	415	22436	305	352	404	21832	1	1	1	167
24	40	41	4346	22	38	38	4290				
1085	1143	1225	39389	950	1007	1086	37262	77	84	84	1203
35	40	59	1552	33	38	57	1530	4	4	4	60
13	88	88	5633	13	88	88	5633	1	1	1	86
23	39	39	2151	23	39	39	2151				
		34166	120638			29909	106171			5046	16112
1280	1382	20202	135031	1141	1236	18829	127835	82	89	1671	9575
79	172	3362	12424	77	171	2536	11011	4	4	683	1280
114	130	1669	5414	114	130	1669	5414				
121	146	10917	49113	109	134	8696	40122			2785	6956

15-8 各区县批发、零售、餐饮业机构、网点、人员（2010年）

Organizations, Branch Shops and Staff of Wholesale,Retail and Catering Trade by Region（2010）

单位：个、人 (unit,person)

分 类	Classify	合 计 Total			
		法人单位 Constitutional Unit	活动单位 Movemental Unit	网 点 Branch Shop	人 员 Personnel
一、批发业	**Wholesale Trade**	**8321**	**8606**	**27887**	**166735**
新城区	Xincheng	1207	1237	9300	46527
碑林区	Beilin	1336	1378	2755	26930
莲湖区	Lianhu	1501	1521	5082	25473
灞桥区	Baqiao	227	235	351	3618
未央区	Weiyang	2321	2420	3527	24695
雁塔区	Yanta	1293	1302	2833	24151
阎良区	Yanliang	56	58	388	1371
临潼区	Lintong	83	100	595	3606
长安区	Chang'an	55	60	686	2758
蓝田县	Lantian	61	68	908	2454
周至县	Zhouzhi	49	69	755	1804
户 县	Huxian	100	116	485	2300
高陵县	Gaoling	32	42	222	1048
二、零售业	**Retail Trade**	**6373**	**7253**	**173218**	**544487**
新城区	Xincheng	1143	1230	23540	109734
碑林区	Beilin	1385	1797	21851	72748
莲湖区	Lianhu	860	868	17105	52639
灞桥区	Baqiao	409	463	6556	19296
未央区	Weiyang	664	694	19031	57672
雁塔区	Yanta	1184	1351	21270	92364
阎良区	Yanliang	73	78	5085	9006
临潼区	Lintong	93	113	7645	12586
长安区	Chang'an	150	155	21119	60781
蓝田县	Lantian	78	78	8010	14321
周至县	Zhouzhi	72	72	10219	13856
户 县	Huxian	194	273	8891	23043
高陵县	Gaoling	68	81	2896	6441

15-8 续表 continued

单位：个、人　(unit,person)

分　类	Classify	合　计 Total 法人单位 Constitutional Unit	活动单位 Movemental Unit	网点 Branch Shop	人员 Personnel
三、餐饮业	**Catering Trade**	**1680**	**1923**	**41289**	**219793**
新城区	Xincheng	141	159	2514	16787
碑林区	Beilin	353	453	5356	39606
莲湖区	Lianhu	189	189	4219	24738
灞桥区	Baqiao	162	174	2193	9458
未央区	Weiyang	127	158	4430	24828
雁塔区	Yanta	380	441	7797	49875
阎良区	Yanliang	30	32	1238	5046
临潼区	Lintong	26	32	1765	5760
长安区	Chang'an	96	103	6398	24921
蓝田县	Lantian	84	84	1601	4876
周至县	Zhouzhi	10	10	1474	3071
户　县	Huxian	47	51	1692	8546
高陵县	Gaoling	35	37	612	2281

15-9 限额以上批发零售贸易企业财务状况（2010年）

单位：万元

分类	Classify	单位数（个）Number (unit)	流动资产 小计 Circulating Funds	存货 Inventories	固定资产原价 Original Value of Fixed Assets
总　计	**Total**	**453**	**5892801.5**	**1038775.0**	**1486360.1**
一、批发企业	**Wholesale Enterprises**	**178**	**3427191.7**	**431223.4**	**485094.3**
#国有控股	State-holding Majority Shares	41	1336761.8	189346.5	237949.9
1.按登记注册类型分组	Grouped by Category of Commodities				
内资企业	Domestic Funded Enterprises	174	2932421.7	419490.9	477863.0
国有企业	State-owned Enterprises	30	1050259.5	130110.3	177490.4
集体企业	Collective-owned Enterprises	3	34807.3	3298.9	7924.7
股份合作企业	Corperative Enterprises				
联营企业	Joint Ownership Enterprises	1	227.3	193.0	
国有联营企业	State Joint Ownership Enterprises				
集体联营企业	Collective Joint Ownership Enterprises	1	227.3	193.0	
国有与集体联营企业	Joint State-collective Enterprises				
其他联营企业	Others Joint Ownership Enterprises				
有限责任公司	Limited Liability Corporrations	104	1368119.9	199555.6	189458.7
国有独资	State Funded Corporations	1	13561.6	4193.6	707.6
其他有限责任公司	Other Limited Liability Corporrations	103	1354558.3	195362.0	188751.1
股份有限公司	Share-holding Corporations Ltd.	3	65483.9	23476.9	49910.0
私营企业	Private Enterprises	32	413488.0	62850.4	52956.6
私营独资企业	Private-funded Enterprises	1	5949.2	4.9	1380.7
私营有限责任公司	Private Limited Liability Corporations	31	407538.8	62845.5	51575.9
私营股份有限公司	Private Share-holding Corporations Ltd.				
其他企业	Other Enterprises	1	35.8	5.8	122.6
港、澳、台商投资企业	Enterprises with Funds from Hong Kong，Macao &Taiwan	2	27039.2		513.5
与港澳台商合资经营	Joint-venture Enterprises	1	18541.2		179.6
港澳台商独资	Enterprises with Sole Investment	1	8498.0		333.9
外商投资企业	Foreign Funded Enterprises	2	467730.8	11732.5	6717.8
中外合资经营	Joint-venture Enterprises	2	467730.8	11732.5	6717.8
外资企业	Foreign Owned Enterprises				
2.按国民经济行业分组	Grouped by Sector				
农畜产品批发业	Wholesale of Farm produce and Livestock Products	2	35310.1	3434.2	7973.9
食品、饮料及烟草制品批发	Wholesale of Beverages and Tobaccos	8	193563.5	25942.9	77349.4
烟草制品批发业	Wholesale of Tobaccos	1	151666.9	16335.5	67039.2
纺织、服装及日用品批发业	Wholesale of Textiles, Garments and Daily Consumer Articles	10	39183.9	19255.4	72402.7
文化、体育用品及器材批发	Wholesale of Culture, Sports Applionces and Equipments	5	50480.0	13001.1	7406.7

Financial Status of Enterprises Above Designated Size in Wholesale and Retail（2010）

(10 000 yuan)

累计折旧 Accumulated Depreciation	本年折旧 In The Year	资产合计 Total Assets	负债合计 Total Liabilities	实收资本 Paid in Capital	营业收入 Total Revenue	主营业务收入 Revenue from Principal Business	主营业务成本 Cost of Principal Business
420464.4	**96997.4**	**8078862.1**	**6283575.7**	**1303465.6**	**19720723.4**	**19547438.8**	**17438056.4**
138884.0	**37010.9**	**4291429.3**	**3418413.0**	**714856.1**	**11374869.3**	**11337228.5**	**10637999.3**
75508.1	19015.5	1728090.2	1349692.8	210976.5	5953006.7	5938795.4	5541462.6
137771.1	36330.9	3627841.1	2931824.3	572022.4	10051237.3	10014993.9	9331007.3
49081.3	10637.4	1356903.5	1037229.6	160330.6	3844210.9	3833201.2	3540199.1
3050.6	403.6	66814.4	68305.9	5698.0	33841.6	33220.3	32490.6
		292.3		292.3	5787.4	5787.4	5310.8
		292.3		292.3	5787.4	5787.4	5310.8
44174.9	14208.8	1599215.2	1303290.8	319819.6	3934340.9	3919096.9	3651358.6
490.4	34.0	14286.3	9580.2	7847.1	75373.6	75306.9	73772.1
43684.5	14174.8	1584928.9	1293710.6	311972.5	3858967.3	3843790.0	3577586.5
21800.2	6794.5	129429.6	111706.2	17698.8	923435.6	920753.1	843158.8
19647.8	4278.5	475044.0	411257.8	68168.0	1307498.5	1300812.6	1256503.2
778.8	167.5	19626.2	12925.1	5800.0	93536.0	93536.0	91587.3
18869.0	4111.0	455417.8	398332.7	62368.0	1213962.5	1207276.6	1164915.9
16.3	8.1	142.1	34.0	15.1	2122.4	2122.4	1986.2
353.6	266.3	27263.9	27058.2	1973.7	281455.0	281455.0	270227.3
130.9	43.6	18619.3	18618.6	1000.0	230413.4	230413.4	222427.8
222.7	222.7	8644.6	8439.6	973.7	51041.6	51041.6	47799.5
759.3	413.7	636324.3	459530.5	140860.0	1042177.0	1040779.6	1036764.7
759.3	413.7	636324.3	459530.5	140860.0	1042177.0	1040779.6	1036764.7
2992.8	392.7	67372.3	65849.3	8869.6	19027.1	18400.2	17948.1
20914.3	4303.2	276256.6	88578.6	10202.0	651188.5	650178.6	482148.8
16879.9	3321.7	208178.8	56429.3	2283.1	556785.7	556086.2	412593.6
20484.8	3396.0	95630.3	81072.8	126761.4	290431.4	289419.6	237216.7
2883.3	419.1	101295.0	45761.1	31000.0	106426.5	106366.2	98269.0

15-9 续表1

单位：万元

分　　类	Classify	主营业务税金及附加 Taxs and Other Changes on Principal Business	主营业务利润 Profits from Prinapal Business	营业费用 Expenses for Operation
总　　计	**Total**	**133660.5**	**1975721.9**	**709431.0**
一、批发企业	**Wholesale Enterprises**	**54313.3**	**644915.9**	**241511.2**
#国有控股	State-holding Majority Shares	41851.1	355481.7	121238.3
1.按登记注册类型分组	Grouped by Category of Commodities			
内资企业	Domestic Funded Enterprises	54266.1	629720.5	232112.1
国有企业	State-owned Enterprises	40661.1	252341.0	84357.2
集体企业	Collective-owned Enterprises	29.3	700.4	385.5
股份合作企业	Corperative Enterprises			
联营企业	Joint Ownership Enterprises	176.2	300.4	19.2
国有联营企业	State Joint Ownership Enterprises			
集体联营企业	Collective Joint Ownership Enterprises	176.2	300.4	19.2
国有与集体联营企业	Joint State-collective Enterprises			
其他联营企业	Others Joint Ownership Enterprises			
有限责任公司	Limited Liability Corporations	11998.3	255740.0	108313.9
国有独资	State Funded Corporations	11.8	1523.0	764.8
其他有限责任公司	Other Limited Liability Corporations	11986.5	254217.0	107549.1
股份有限公司	Share-holding Corporations Ltd.	801.0	76793.3	21280.8
私营企业	Private Enterprises	600.2	43709.2	17723.1
私营独资企业	Private-funded Enterprises	28.8	1919.9	1208.2
私营有限责任公司	Private Limited Liability Corporations	571.4	41789.3	16514.9
私营股份有限公司	Private Share-holding Corporations Ltd.			
其他企业	Other Enterprises		136.2	32.4
港、澳、台商投资企业	Enterprises with Funds from Hong Kong，Macao &Taiwan	47.2	11180.5	8094.0
与港澳台商合资经营	Joint-venture Enterprises	13.7	7971.9	5625.7
港澳台商独资	Enterprises with Sole Investment	33.5	3208.6	2468.3
外商投资企业	Foreign Funded Enterprises		4014.9	1305.1
中外合资经营	Joint-venture Enterprises		4014.9	1305.1
外资企业	Foreign Owned Enterprises			
2.按国民经济行业分组	Grouped by Sector			
农畜产品批发业	Wholesale of Farm Produce and Livestock Products	21.5	430.6	174.3
食品、饮料及烟草制品批发	Wholesale of Beverages and Tobaccos	33185.3	134844.5	24406.2
烟草制品批发业	Wholesale of Tobaccos	32824.1	110668.5	13349.0
纺织、服装及日用品批发业	Wholesale of Textiles, Garments and Daily Consumer Articles	5241.8	46961.1	5457.5
文化、体育用品及器材批发	Wholesale of Culture, Sports Appliances and Equipments	29.0	8068.2	3149.1

continued 1

(10 000 yuan)

管理费用 Management Expenses	财务费用 Financial Expenses	利息支出 Interest Expenditure	营业利润 Business Profits	利润总额 Total Profits	应交所得税 Income Tax Payable	应付工资 Salary Payable	应付福利费 Welfare Funds	全部从业人员年平均人数（人） Average Number of Employed Persons(person)
446907.4	**102307.7**	**34780.9**	**868515.0**	**766332.3**	**117118.6**	**289103.0**	**29263.2**	**98182**
143511.1	**25124.3**	**17294.8**	**257638.7**	**243129.0**	**39674.7**	**119003.7**	**10754.6**	**32930**
66988.2	9266.9	7561.2	164676.2	150066.6	30767.4	44804.4	3561.5	10886
141052.1	23270.8	15443.8	255421.6	240822.2	37909.9	115635.8	10390.1	32538
60820.2	7035.8	6129.1	106100.2	92500.6	24942.6	31689.6	2412.0	7106
1061.4	27.1	26.3	-152.3	26.1	14.4	386.4	39.1	220
22.7	5.9	5.9	252.6	252.6		11.3		5
22.7	5.9	5.9	252.6	252.6		11.3		5
63749.6	10750.3	5129.5	85136.8	82543.6	7424.4	60361.9	5257.7	17756
230.5	146.7	146.7	427.2	430.8	119.8	222.0	30.6	74
63519.1	10603.6	4982.8	84709.6	82112.8	7304.6	60139.9	5227.1	17682
2404.2	848.6	446.0	52573.3	51383.8	4282.8	9316.4	1001.8	3025
12955.4	4598.3	3702.8	11450.6	14055.1	1245.7	13772.0	1679.5	4401
175.6	1.5		534.6	323.1	80.8	38.8		25
12779.8	4596.8	3702.8	10916.0	13732.0	1164.9	13733.2	1679.5	4376
38.6	4.8	4.2	60.4	60.4		98.2		25
491.2	-18.8	-21.3	2614.1	2670.9	853.0	2957.4	307.7	326
367.0	-20.2	-20.2	1999.4	2058.4	853.0	2060.7		146
124.2	1.4	-1.1	614.7	612.5		896.7	307.7	180
1967.8	1872.3	1872.3	-397.0	-364.1	911.8	410.5	56.8	66
1967.8	1872.3	1872.3	-397.0	-364.1	911.8	410.5	56.8	66
906.2	113.6	62.7	-136.6	153.9	13.2	309.5	26.3	302
28757.2	-0.5	-441.4	82688.7	83175.3	21367.7	39122.7	4495.5	9187
19358.0	-404.6	-404.6	79065.6	79121.0	20293.3	13755.8	1090.2	1673
14666.5	135.0	72.9	27486.9	27669.9	577.4	25316.2	2025.9	7918
4188.3	18.9	17.5	757.0	581.9	346.9	1617.8	45.9	340

15-9 续表2

单位：万元

分　　类	Classify	单位数（个）Number (unit)	流动资产 小　计 Circulating Funds	存 货 Inventories	固定资产原价 Original Value of Fixed Assets
医药及医疗器材批发	Wholesale of Medicines and Medical Appliances	24	209842.7	41525.5	9901.5
矿产品、建材及化工产品批发	Wholesale of Mineral Products, Building Materials and Chemical Products	85	2310396.2	260875.9	288359.8
煤炭及制品批发	Wholesale of Coal and Related Products	6	371541.1	29000.7	16286.5
石油及制品批发业	Wholesale of Petrolem and Related Products	22	612177.9	113694.8	179946.5
金属及金属矿批发业	Wholesale of Metals and Metals Minerals	41	1092708.4	79661.6	27014.5
建材批发业	Wholesale of Building Materials	9	167754.9	14139.4	63040.9
化肥批发业	Wholesale of Chemicel Fertilizer	4	45734.5	23823.5	917.9
其他化工产品批发	Wholesale of Other Chemical Products	2	1031.9	503.7	1122.9
机械设备、五金交电及电子产品批发业	Wholesale of Machinery, Hardware, and Electronic Equipment	42	575016.3	63600.7	21492.7
汽车、摩托车及零配件批发业	Wholesale of Motor Vehicles, Motocycles and Parts	7	267695.5	19162.9	9779.6
家用电器批发业	Wholesale of Household Electrical Appliances	5	150752.5	14628.5	1910.6
计算机、软件及辅助设备批发业	Wholesale of Computers,Software and Assisant Appliances	5	39109.7	779.2	675.2
贸易经纪与代理	Trade Borker and Agency	2	13399.0	3587.7	207.6
其他批发业	Other wholesale not Classified Elsewhere				
二、零售企业	**Retail Trade**	**275**	**2465609.8**	**607551.6**	**1001265.8**
#国有控股	State-holding Majority Shares	18	154571.7	54132.4	32052.8
1.按登记注册类型分组	Grouped by Category of Commodities				
内资企业	Domestic Funded Enterprises	252	2031876.6	452926.6	888024.8
国有企业	State-owned Enterprises	14	108090.8	37616.0	10845.3
集体企业	Collective-owned Enterprises	18	4661.5	2582.8	3429.7
股份合作企业	Share-holding Cooperative Enterprises	1	37.8	5.3	244.5
有限责任公司	Limited Liability Corporations	126	951442.3	240490.1	546543.8
国有独资	State Funded Corporations	2	22934.8	7487.7	19925.9
其他有限责任公司	Other Limited Liability Corporations	124	928507.5	233002.4	526617.9
股份有限公司	Share-holding Corporations Ltd.	4	395840.3	79182.8	162105.2
私营企业	Private Enterprises	87	571348.0	92688.1	164388.0
私营独资企业	Private-funded Enterprises	13	7326.1	3613.9	1410.2
私营合伙企业	Private Partnership Enterprises	5	10335.7	2793.7	2167.9
私营有限责任公司	Private Limited Liability Corporations	65	528336.2	83284.7	158745.4
私营股份有限公司	Private Share-holding Corporations Ltd.	4	25350.0	2995.8	2064.5
其他企业	Other Enterprises	1	302.5	276.4	300.0

continued 2

(10 000 yuan)

累计折旧 Accumulated Depreciation	本年折旧 In The Year	资产合计 Total Assets	负债合计 Total Liabilities	实收资本 Paid in Capital	营业收入 Total Revenue	主营业务收入 Revenue from Principal Business	主营业务成本 Cost of Principal Business
4518.1	828.1	228168.6	202290.1	25171.9	528859.6	527662.0	486724.5
78800.7	25508.4	2897821.2	2341958.1	479744.6	8388230.7	8356972.7	8001996.7
4156.9	2374.4	393837.5	348572.1	14600.0	499404.7	486515.9	424972.3
58841.3	15418.5	896903.3	748144.3	182644.8	4961934.9	4949997.3	4765026.8
9464.2	3301.6	1291311.0	1045162.0	223244.5	2256299.5	2250026.8	2175150.4
4954.0	4126.0	244059.0	137340.5	51013.0	588431.7	588365.7	555752.7
295.0	95.5	50508.9	42647.7	7592.3	41641.6	41633.2	43573.9
1078.7	189.7	1734.0	524.1	600.0	8314.5	8314.5	8207.2
8245.2	2149.5	610981.1	579965.7	32167.7	1356921.2	1354765.6	1283734.3
3091.2	743.3	281488.8	272995.8	10306.0	555060.7	554758.6	519376.9
477.9	184.0	152254.1	152414.3	2180.0	220090.6	219963.8	211697.1
478.4	287.0	46310.0	44920.7	5773.7	322634.8	322633.9	310166.7
44.8	13.9	13904.2	12937.3	938.9	33784.3	33463.6	29961.2
281580.4	**59986.5**	**3787432.8**	**2865162.7**	**588609.5**	**8345854.1**	**8210210.3**	**6800057.1**
12290.6	1321.8	182890.7	145907.4	10671.8	384559.3	380363.5	326846.3
247314.9	50902.4	3120176.5	2413459.0	461496.6	7017997.2	6917537.9	5708143.1
5503.2	782.2	117374.4	88162.4	6385.4	249118.0	245629.8	208561.6
797.5	62.7	7885.9	7765.9	2136.0	54733.3	54611.5	51063.9
244.4	2.7	292.4	270.3	10.6	3745.0	3745.0	3259.6
140438.6	33398.0	1512333.9	1127642.9	280363.8	4413536.1	4346565.9	3518796.5
6525.9	393.7	37411.9	27404.6	2786.4	37508.6	37363.0	28404.7
133912.7	33004.3	1474922.0	1100238.3	277577.4	4376027.5	4309202.9	3490391.8
56613.3	8370.6	605640.9	429684.1	53892.2	496960.1	476347.4	409295.5
43449.6	8196.4	875901.6	759289.3	118358.6	1793383.1	1784116.7	1511931.2
379.9	96.2	9121.2	4411.9	7821.5	29117.5	29018.7	23433.9
802.4	178.3	11748.1	9047.1	1635.0	41028.8	41024.8	28782.5
41596.4	7782.2	827777.8	719904.8	107682.1	1681521.8	1672477.9	1429948.4
670.9	139.7	27254.5	25925.5	1220.0	41715.0	41595.3	29766.4
194.0	75.0	500.0	526.0	300.0	3295.8	3295.8	2307.0

15-9 续表3

单位：万元

分类	Classify	主营业务税金及附加 Taxs and Other Changes on Principal Business	主营业务利润 Profits from Prinapal Business	营业费用 Expenses for Operation
医药及医疗器材批发	Wholesale of Medicines and Medical Appliances	2248.1	38689.4	13655.1
矿产品、建材及化工产品批发	Wholesale of Mineral Products, Building Materials and Chemical Products	12691.2	342284.8	148586.5
煤炭及制品批发	Wholesale of Coal and Related Products	1451.5	60092.1	32013.3
石油及制品批发业	Wholesale of Petrolem and Related Products	2204.2	182766.3	73941.7
金属及金属矿批发业	Wholesale of Metals and Metals Minerals	7884.4	66992.0	27523.9
建材批发业	Wholesale of Building Materials	966.4	31646.6	11406.3
化肥批发业	Wholesale of Chemicel Fertilizer	176.2	-2116.9	907.2
其他化工产品批发	Wholesale of Other Chemical Products	5.1	102.2	51.2
机械设备、五金交电及电子产品批发业	Wholesale of Machinery, Hardware, and Electronic Equipment	894.7	70136.6	42864.8
汽车、摩托车及零配件批发业	Wholesale of Motor Vehicles, Motocycles and Parts	455.5	34926.2	19384.1
家用电器批发业	Wholesale of Household Electrical Appliances	87.8	8178.9	7557.5
计算机、软件及辅助设备批发业	Wholesale of Computers,Software and Peripherals	51.4	12415.8	9254.8
贸易经纪与代理	Trade Borker and Agency	1.7	3500.7	3217.7
其他批发业	Other wholesale not Classified Elsewhere			
二、零售企业	**Retail Trade**	**79347.2**	**1330806.0**	**467919.8**
#国有控股	State-owned ding Majority Shares	1497.1	52020.1	20940.5
1.按登记注册类型分组	Grouped by Category of Commodities			
内资企业	Domestic Funded Enterprises	74923.7	1134471.1	366863.6
国有企业	State-owned Enterprises	1172.3	35895.9	12040.1
集体企业	Collective-owned Enterprises	798.8	2748.8	1049.9
股份合作企业	Share-Holding Cooperative Enterprises	112.3	373.1	161.0
有限责任公司	Limited Liability Corporrations	61048.3	766721.1	261714.6
国有独资	State Funded Corporations	139.8	8818.5	4509.8
其他有限责任公司	Other Limited Liability Corporrations	60908.5	757902.6	257204.8
股份有限公司	Share-holding Corporations Ltd.	2044.6	65007.3	27265.9
私营企业	Private Enterprises	9711.3	262474.2	64141.9
私营独资企业	Private-funded Enterprises	445.0	5139.8	742.3
私营合伙企业	Private Partnership Enterprises	26.3	12216.0	555.5
私营有限责任公司	Private Limited Liability Corporations	9203.5	233326.0	62378.4
私营股份有限公司	Private Share-holding Corporations Ltd.	36.5	11792.4	465.7
其他企业	Other Enterprises	33	956.1	262.0

continued 3

(10 000 yuan)

管理费用 Management Expenses	财务费用 Financial Expenses	利息支出 Interest Expenditure	营业利润 Business Profits	利润总额 Total Profits	应交所得税 Income Tax Payable	应付工资 Salary Payable	应付福利费 Welfare Funds	全部从业人员年平均人数（人） Average Number of Employed Persons(person)
15129.9	1675.4	1177.8	9311.4	9390.6	1031.2	6646.0	401.7	2091
63354.0	22328.8	16450.2	126610.5	111080.0	14126.1	30004.2	2886.7	9048
12371.1	3081.5	977.5	23125.8	14557.4	2660.0	5067.6	601.5	632
31477.9	11673.2	9981.2	70139.2	68525.7	6696.7	16948.8	1678.7	6419
13950.1	6129.7	5044.4	22984.5	11573.7	3635.2	6117.7	421.0	1385
4737.4	1313.2	318.6	14135.5	16109.0	1106.7	1556.1	164.1	440
576.7	128.7	126.2	-3726.3	365.8	14.8	181.9	17.1	115
111.4	8.3	8.1	-68.7	-72.1	6.5	67.5	4.3	32
16176.9	874.0	-23.4	10855.2	11009.6	2210.3	15792.7	872.6	3993
7074.6	727.7	611.4	8026.4	6416.0	399.1	5256.1	248.1	1337
2357.4	-699.5	-699.5	-994.1	-1016.3	367.2	2475.6	108.5	620
609.5	93.1	-15.5	2459.0	2513.7	944.7	3519.9	307.7	434
332.1	-20.9	-21.5	65.6	67.8	1.9	194.6		51
303396.3	**77183.4**	**17486.1**	**610876.3**	**523203.3**	**77443.9**	**170099.3**	**18508.6**	**65252**
29991.8	1195.6	799.9	3525.3	3166.1	1282.9	18179.9	1757.1	4836
263245.9	74367.1	15985.7	524415.5	443302.3	66638.9	133033.8	14412.2	51841
19202.4	599.9	246.1	6982.6	6595.5	711.6	12495.5	1122.8	2980
1202.9	60.7	49.0	556.9	438.0	158.6	2768.2	777.5	916
83.9	0.9	0.8	127.3	127.3	32.0	51.0	1.2	26
183909.8	59024.0	10658.5	327429.6	268801.9	34025.6	70645.2	5751.2	28964
4169.3	-64.3	-66.2	349.3	358.7	4.6	3118.7	449.6	1122
179740.5	59088.3	10724.7	327080.3	268443.2	34021.0	67526.5	5301.6	27842
25603.5	6463.8	1320.0	24143.3	26833.2	3403.2	10907.3	426.6	5899
32950.8	8185.9	3709.4	164739.8	140070.6	28285.6	36125.9	6326.7	13036
1106.0	122.4	6.9	3265.8	3324.4	273.6	707.9	162.1	585
1327.6	235.9	205.5	10101.0	10100.7	1032.2	894.5	35.5	407
30100.4	7720.0	3390.3	140541.3	115813.8	26645.3	34083.2	6105.4	11817
416.8	107.6	106.7	10831.7	10831.7	334.5	440.3	23.7	227
232.0	32.0	2.0	430.1	430.1	22.3	26.3	6.2	12

15-9 续表4

单位：万元

分类	Classify	单位数（个）Number (unit)	流动资产 小计 Circulating Funds	存货 Inventories	固定资产原价 Original Value of Fixed Assets
港、澳、台商投资企业	Enterprises with Funds from Hong Kong，Macao &Taiwan	11	309044.9	110927.9	60957.1
与港澳台商合资经营企业	Joint-venture Enterprises	1	21495.5	12224.5	4363.0
港澳抬商独资	Wholly Funded from Hong Kong, Macao and Taiwan	9	160106.2	70568.8	40730.0
外商投资股份有限公司	Share-holding Corporations Ltd.	1	127443.2	28134.6	15864.1
外商投资企业	Foreign Funded Enterprises	12	124688.3	43697.1	52283.9
中外合资经营企业	Joint-venture Enterprises	4	39002.7	11319.0	39005.4
外资企业	Enterprises with Sole Fund	7	76762.2	31442.4	10998.7
外商投资股份有限公司	Share-holding Corporations Ltd.	1	8923.4	935.7	2279.8
2.按国民经济行业分组	Grouped by Sector				
综合零售	Integrated Retail	71	834694.7	206895.0	416463.5
百货零售	Retail of General Merchandise	34	534768.3	88508.1	272013.1
超级市场零售	Retail of Supermarkets	27	298173.1	117682.6	142328.3
其他综合零售	Other Integrated Retail	10	1753.3	704.3	2122.1
食品、饮料及烟草制品专门零售	Food, Beverages and Tobaccos Special Retail Trade	9	124961.3	51129.8	95288.6
纺织、服装及日用品专门零售	Textiles, Garments and Daily Consumer Articles Special Retail Trade	21	251048.9	40181.5	245081.1
#服装零售	Retail of Garments	13	215575.9	14027.8	239147.9
文化、体育用品及器材专门零售	Culture,Sports Appliances and Equipments Special Retail Trade	15	86735.3	30162.6	21824.3
#图书零售	Retail of Book	4	36085.9	17415.2	20651.5
医药及医疗器材专门零售	Medinces and Medical Appliances Special Retail Trade	10	57427.0	19330.0	5786.9
#药品零售	Retail of Medinces	10	57427.0	19330.0	5786.9
汽车、摩托车、燃料及零配件专门零售	Motor Vehicles, Motorcycle,Fuel and Parts Special Retail Trade	114	751162.3	190530.5	124745.7
#汽车零售业	Retail of Motorcar Vehicles	89	708980.8	181336.1	107047.4
家用电器及电子产品专门零售	Household Appliances and Electronic products Special retail trade	19	257666.2	56568.8	44808.8
#家用电器零售	Retail of Household Electric Appliances	11	229796.7	49824.3	43192.6
计算机、软件及辅助设备零售	Retail of Computer, Software and Peripherals	6	19065.6	1787.1	939.3
通讯设备零售	Retail of Communication Equipment	2	8803.9	4957.4	676.9
五金、家具及室内装修材料专门零售	Ironware, Furniture and Room fitting stuff Special Retail Trade	13	88854.5	8265.6	45147.8
无店铺及其他零售	Retail of No Stores and Others	3	13059.6	4487.8	2119.1

continued 4

(10 000 yuan)

累计折旧 Accumulated Depreciation	本年折旧 In The Year	资产合计 Total Assets	负债合计 Total Liabilities	实收资本 Paid in Capital	营业收入 Total Revenue	主营业务收入 Revenue from Principal Business	主营业务成本 Cost of Principal Business
20017.5	3948.2	450401.9	321884.2	54788.5	830825.9	804720.6	675706.8
1028.0	286.3	25858.5	17271.4	1900.0	121479.4	120892.2	106990.6
15598.3	3238.0	282936.8	189021.4	29338.5	585295.0	562364.4	469750.4
3391.2	423.9	141606.6	115591.4	23550.0	124051.5	121464.0	98965.8
14248.0	5135.9	216854.4	129819.5	72324.4	497031.0	487951.8	416207.2
8119.2	3731.8	119944.1	55000.8	56045.0	233641.8	230285.3	208830.6
5246.4	1335.5	86588.0	67224.3	14779.4	217494.5	213419.9	171100.7
882.4	68.6	10322.3	7594.4	1500.0	45894.7	44246.6	36275.9
171625.3	34421.3	1383836.8	1021822.2	251868.7	2116548.1	2020897.7	1702634.7
87918.7	13140.4	908037.9	628211.6	202886.0	1037863.4	1011367.2	831086.2
83062.9	21224.9	472139.5	390751.8	48276.7	1052176.1	983022.1	848751.4
643.7	56.0	3659.4	2858.8	706.0	26508.6	26508.4	22797.1
21198.7	5399.9	209059.3	157533.0	14011.0	113657.4	113622.4	92909.1
20935.2	3869.0	605833.5	550709.0	39033.7	659239.6	652136.5	444209.8
19498.4	3357.7	563278.0	524472.5	34651.6	533084.2	531557.1	357750.0
7628.6	574.7	106269.2	67631.8	25415.0	170906.3	170183.7	134386.9
6902.5	426.5	51392.0	37836.8	5570.0	43604.5	42911.6	31323.9
2651.3	189.7	63059.1	59008.9	16551.3	101867.1	100900.6	85596.0
2651.3	189.7	63059.1	59008.9	16551.3	101867.1	100900.6	85596.0
35388.9	10710.7	947921.9	734146.1	170226.0	3637530.2	3632483.8	3033567.7
31430.9	9118.0	849299.4	681577.1	120654.8	3419519.9	3414638.6	2831889.6
4930.9	1375.4	300960.3	167865.8	37156.8	958955.6	934804.0	823482.7
4215.4	1246.9	271061.1	148216.8	30367.8	847753.7	824785.6	723698.1
287.8	116.2	20608.9	14658.2	5710.0	69645.5	69393.0	64668.6
427.7	12.3	9290.3	4990.8	1079.0	41556.4	40625.4	35116.0
16274.1	3146.8	155626.8	96635.9	31147.0	554438.0	554042.1	459852.7
947.4	299.0	14865.9	9810.0	3200.0	32711.8	31139.5	23417.5

15-9 续表5

单位：万元

分 类	Classify	主营业务税金及附加 Taxs and Other Changes on Principal Business	主营业务利润 Profits from Principal Business	营业费用 Expenses for Operation
港、澳、台商投资企业	Enterprises with Funds from Hong Kong，Macao &Taiwan	2764.3	126249.5	65063.7
与港澳台商合资经营企业	Joint-venture Enterprises		13901.6	5537.8
港澳台商独资	Wholly Funded from Hong Kong, Macao and Taiwan	1973.8	90640.2	49797.7
港澳台商投资股份有限公司	Share-holding Corporations Ltd.	790.5	21707.7	9728.2
外商投资企业	Foreign Funded Enterprises	1659.2	70085.4	35992.5
中外合资经营企业	Joint-venture Enterprises	455.9	20998.8	10102.0
外资企业	Enterprises with Sole Fund	918.9	41400.3	25890.5
外商投资股份有限公司	Share-holding Corporations Ltd.	284.4	7686.3	
2.按国民经济行业分组	Grouped by Sector			
综合零售	Integrated Retail	16221.2	302041.8	184781.2
百货零售	Retail of General Merchandise	9154.7	171126.3	58611.9
超级市场零售	Retail of Supermarkets	6283.1	127987.6	124851.7
其他综合零售	Other Integrated Retail	783.4	2927.9	1317.6
食品、饮料及烟草制品专门零售	Food, Beverages and Tobaccos Special Retail Trade	528.3	20185.0	7661.0
纺织、服装及日用品专门零售	Textiles, Garments and Daily Consumer Articles Special Retail Trade	8044.4	199882.3	48262.0
#服装零售	Retail of Garments	7953.4	165853.7	34403.9
文化、体育用品及器材专门零售	Culture,Sports Appliances and Equipments Special Retail Trade	755.3	35041.5	8146.0
#图书零售	Retail of Book	272.9	11314.8	4085.1
医药及医疗器材专门零售	Medinces and Medical Appliances Special Retail Trade	237.6	15067.0	10587.4
#药品零售	Retail of Medinces	237.6	15067.0	10587.4
汽车、摩托车、燃料及零配件专门零售	Motor Vehicles, Motorcycle,Fuel and Parts Special Retail Trade	43627.8	555288.3	135870.8
#汽车零售业	Retail of Motorcar Vehicles	43289.4	539459.6	125826.8
家用电器及电子产品专门零售	Household Appliances and Electronic products Special retail trade	2309.2	109012.1	56515.4
#家用电器零售	Retail of Household Electric Appliances	1938.1	99149.4	49047.0
计算机、软件及辅助设备零售	Retail of Computer, Software and Peripherals	191.7	4532.7	2664.4
通讯设备零售	Retail of Communication Equipment	179.4	5330.0	4804.0
五金、家具及室内装修材料专门零售	Ironware, Furniture and Room fitting stuff Special Retail Trade	7282.4	86907.0	12946.7
无店铺及其他零售	Retail of No Stores and Others	341.0	7381.0	3149.3

continued 5

(10 000 yuan)

管理费用 Managenment Expenses	财务费用 Financial Expenses	利息支出 Interest Expenditure	营业利润 Business Profits	利润总额 Total Profits	应交所得税 Income Tax Payable	应付工资 Salary Payable	应付福利费 Welfare Funds	全部从业人员年平均人数（人） Average Number of Employed Persons(person)
23506.7	1946.3	1546.2	61361.6	54993.2	6159.9	27579.2	3047.9	10217
1851.1	46.6		7023.1	7036.5	1781.6	1306.9	868.9	150
17593.7	1377.5	1206.8	44827.0	38527.2	2871.7	24382.6	1914.5	9641
4061.9	522.2	339.4	9511.5	9429.5	1506.6	1889.7	264.5	426
16643.7	870.0	-45.8	25099.2	24907.8	4645.1	9486.3	1048.5	3194
6164.6	788.1	231.4	7128.6	7180.3	1652.7	4547.5	736.9	1181
6775.8	185.4	-173.7	12338.3	12091.4	2140.2	4891.9	306.8	1872
3703.3	-103.5	-103.5	5632.3	5636.1	852.2	46.9	4.8	141
101529.8	6823.9	5279.0	102780.1	95221.0	17997.3	70089.3	6549.2	29934
83474.1	7768.6	6710.7	46043.6	45875.4	11052.6	35449.0	4116.6	11200
17248.1	-972.9	-1448.3	55961.8	48677.4	6798.6	33796.3	2379.2	18279
807.6	28.2	16.6	774.7	668.2	146.1	844.0	53.4	455
4364.5	5210.8	13.2	3765.3	3318.4	77.2	4054.8	464.6	2038
53321.1	2765.6	108.1	100936.6	95502.0	19850.7	30362.3	4990.8	10516
47182.7	2341.1	72.1	83102.6	79209.0	16898.6	19604.9	3586.0	6535
8962.1	1056.2	737.2	17560.1	10611.3	663.2	5425.1	563.2	1876
6525.9	93.9	-5.0	1295.8	1205.2	1.1	3969.1	477.6	1302
3548.7	170.1	110.8	1172.0	2346.8	386.5	4463.0	545.2	3099
3548.7	170.1	110.8	1172.0	2346.8	386.5	4463.0	545.2	3099
93559.5	57523.8	8541.6	271753.7	217548.4	18853.7	35545.8	3832.6	10349
87723.0	57079.3	8312.5	272093.1	218180.0	18516.2	31618.9	3148.0	9135
23851.4	736.9	113.9	49996.8	49035.0	10139.4	11891.4	659.6	4916
22601.8	493.0	98.3	47912.7	48755.5	9731.6	8969.7	572.2	4228
677.4	212.2	11.1	1231.0	-544.5	166.8	1047.6	85.8	316
572.2	31.7	4.5	853.1	824.0	241.0	1874.1	1.6	372
10421.0	2907.0	2595.2	60935.0	47687.2	9227.6	5208.9	466.8	1827
3838.2	-10.9	-12.9	1976.7	1933.2	248.3	3058.7	436.6	697

15-10 限额以上住宿和餐饮业企业主要财务状况（2010年）

单位：万元

分　　类	Classify	单位数（个）Number (unit)	流动资产 合计 Circulating Funds	存货 Inventories	固定资产原价 Original Value of Fixed Assets
总　计	**Total**	**441**	**493651.1**	**37415.7**	**1163712.4**
一、住宿业	**Hotel Services**	**177**	**299954.0**	**17269.2**	**942090.1**
#国有控股	State-holding Majority Shares	54	77565.3	4857.2	339697.2
1.按登记注册类型分组	Grouped by Type of Registration				
内资企业	Domestic Funded Enterprises	163	252134.3	14710.4	675404.8
国有企业	State-owned Enterprises	43	63711.9	3802.2	285728.0
集体企业	Collective-owned Enterprises	3	349.0	40.6	4337.9
股份合作企业	Cooperative Enterprises	1	434.5	52.8	133.2
联营企业	Joint Ownership Enterprises				
国有联营企业	State Joint Ownership Enterprises				
集体联营企业	Collective Joint Ownership Enterprises				
国有与集体联营企业	Joint State-collective Enterprises				
其他联营企业	Others Joint Ownership Enterprises				
有限责任公司	Limited Liability Corporations	69	148650.7	6187.3	246779.6
国有独资企业	State Sole Funded Corporations				
其他有限责任公司	Other Limited Liability Corporations	69	148650.7	6187.3	246779.6
股份有限公司	Share-holding Corporations Ltd.	5	1999.6	92.3	13808.6
私营企业	Private Enterprises	36	34164.9	4300.7	121526.8
私营独资企业	Private-funded Enterprises	5	1773.8	302.6	2493.7
私营合伙企业	Private Partnership Enterprises				
私营有限责任公司	Private Limited Liability Corporations	28	27249.2	3486.8	113176.9
私营股份有限公司	Private Share-holding Corporations Ltd.	3	5141.9	511.3	5856.2
其他企业	Other Enterprises	6	2823.7	234.5	3090.7
港、澳、台商投资企业	Enterprises with Funds from Hong Kong, Macao &Taiwan	8	25629.7	1256.1	113747.6
合资经营企业（港或澳、台资）	Joint-venture Enterprises	3	12083.4	620.6	23608.2
合作经营企业（港或澳、台资）	Cooperative Enterprises	2	6524.7	409.4	60508.7
港澳台商独资	Enterprise with Sole Fund	3	7021.6	226.1	29630.7
港澳台商独资股份有限公司	Share-holding Corporations Ltd. With their Investment				
外商投资企业	Foreign Funded Enterprises	6	22190.0	1302.7	152937.7
中外合资经营企业	Joint-venture Enterprises	2	6332.8	317.7	59756.7
中外合作经营企业	Cooperation Enterprises	2	2912.6	210.1	20675.0
外资企业	Foreign Funded Enterprises	2	12944.6	774.9	72506.0
外商投资股份有限公司	Share-holding Corporations Ltd. With Foreign Funds				
2.按住宿行业小类分组	Grouped by Major Group of Hotel Services				
旅游饭店	Tourist Hotel	143	281248.9	15450.9	901886.4
一般旅馆	Normal Hotel	31	15673.5	1652.2	32730.4
其他住宿服务	Others	3	3031.6	166.1	7473.3

Finacial Status of Catering Enterprises Above Designated Size（2010）

(10 000 yuan)

累计折旧 Accumulated Depreciation	本年折旧 In The Year	资产合计 Total Assets	负债合计 Total Liabilities	实收资本 Paid in Capital	营业收入 Total Revenue	主营业务收入 Revenue from Principal Business	主营业务成本 Cost of Principal Business
434091.2	**69040.1**	**1579682.7**	**1180722.6**	**813981.5**	**952694.6**	**938619.9**	**365365.5**
336681.5	**52456.9**	**1112492.8**	**913451.6**	**557814.5**	**415809.6**	**407326.3**	**125160.6**
137097.0	**17734.6**	**360049.8**	**296584.2**	**167860.9**	**139556.6**	**138883.3**	**43974.5**
209016.6	36523.6	904273.2	661747.9	362654.1	333065.4	326576.5	102841.8
110042.9	15170.4	309619.1	222474.9	148861.4	101761.0	101341.6	32550.8
1785.4	211.9	4095.7	4202.0	594.6	1088.7	1068.7	592.3
41.7	14.6	627.6	393.8	467.6	2190.8	2190.8	1111.9
62801.1	10347.3	413374.1	297696.0	109901.1	154456.0	150253.2	47505.2
62801.1	10347.3	413374.1	297696.0	109901.1	154456.0	150253.2	47505.2
3864.6	607.1	14718.3	11829.2	3657.4	5957.1	5957.1	992.2
29445.3	9942.2	156725.4	121948.1	96438.4	57653.8	56738.3	18198.6
1002.3	645.9	3434.3	3349.1	1843.8	4101.7	3367.1	1623.7
27789.8	9076.4	142914.9	109684.9	41222.6	44974.9	44794.0	12347.9
653.2	219.9	10376.2	8914.1	53372.0	8577.2	8577.2	4227.0
1035.6	230.1	5113.0	3203.9	2733.6	9958.0	9026.8	1890.8
63603.3	6844.9	91868.7	111838.8	48051.0	31793.1	31080.2	7531.8
16187.2	1704.6	28542.0	13847.3	14274.0	12558.3	12556.2	2935.8
41898.5	1422.9	26360.1	67913.0	10836.0	12786.1	12348.0	3472.9
5517.6	3717.4	36966.6	30078.5	22941.0	6448.7	6176.0	1123.1
64061.6	9088.4	116350.9	139864.9	147109.4	50951.1	49669.6	14787.0
31947.4	1698.9	35114.4	69290.5	90420.7	16129.6	16129.6	6357.5
14743.9	897.2	8845.6	30370.8	7767.4	3759.0	3759.0	432.4
17370.3	6492.3	72390.9	40203.6	48921.3	31062.5	29781.0	7997.1
324471.7	49604.8	1028085.0	864937.4	518399.7	373499.1	365808.6	112482.0
10191.6	2258.0	48421.6	33470.6	25014.8	34159.0	33366.2	10421.9
2018.2	594.1	35986.2	15043.6	14400.0	8151.5	8151.5	2256.7

15-10 续表1

单位：万元

分　类	Classify	主营业务税金及附加 Taxs and Other Changes on Principal Business	主营业务利润 Profits from Principal Business	营业费用 Expenses for Operation
总　计	**Total**	**54668.2**	**518586.2**	**297990.6**
一、住宿业	**Hotel Services**	**23328.0**	**258837.7**	**121851.8**
#国有控股	State-holding Majority Shares	7339.1	87569.7	44681.6
1.按登记注册类型分组	Grouped by Type of Registration			
内资企业	Domestic Funded Enterprises	17733.9	206000.8	104810.3
国有企业	State-owned Enterprises	5294.7	63496.1	35180.4
集体企业	Collective-owned Enterprises	43.7	432.7	151.3
股份合作企业	Cooperative Enterprises	120.5	958.4	463.5
联营企业	Joint Ownership Enterprises			
国有联营企业	State Joint Ownership Enterprises			
集体联营企业	Collective Joint Ownership Enterprises			
国有与集体联营企业	Joint State-collective Enterprises			
其他联营企业	Others Joint Ownership Enterprises			
有限责任公司	Limited Liability Corporations	8375.1	94372.9	49231.3
国有独资企业	State Sole Funded Corporations			
其他有限责任公司	Other Limited Liability Corporations	8375.1	94372.9	49231.3
股份有限公司	Share-holding Corporations Ltd.	335.7	4629.2	2720.5
私营企业	Private Enterprises	3136.3	35403.4	14736.5
私营独资企业	Private-funded Enterprises	175.5	1567.9	1049.5
私营合伙企业	Private Partnership Enterprises			
私营有限责任公司	Private Limited Liability Corporations	2484.2	29961.9	12328.1
私营股份有限公司	Private Share-holding Corporations Ltd.	476.6	3873.6	1358.9
其他企业	Other Enterprises	427.9	6708.1	2326.8
港、澳、台商投资企业	Enterprises with Funds from Hong Kong, Macao &Taiwan	3067.8	20480.6	8455.3
合资经营企业（港或澳、台资）	Joint-venture Enterprises	602.1	9018.3	4224.4
合作经营企业（港或澳、台资）	Cooperative Enterprises	2153.3	6721.8	2477.1
港澳台商独资	Enterprise with Sole Fund	312.4	4740.5	1753.8
港澳台商独资股份有限公司	Share-holding Corporations Ltd. With their Investment			
外商投资企业	Foreign Funded Enterprises	2526.3	32356.3	8586.2
中外合资经营企业	Joint-venture Enterprises	813.2	8958.9	1935.3
中外合作经营企业	Cooperation Enterprises	197.5	3129.1	1393.7
外资企业	Foreign Funded Enterprises	1515.6	20268.3	5257.2
外商投资股份有限公司	Share-holding Corporations Ltd. With Foreign Funds			
2.按住宿行业小类分组	Grouped by Major Group of Hotel Services			
旅游饭店	Tourist Hotel	21050.4	232276.2	110928.1
一般旅馆	Normal Hotel	1839.9	21104.4	8918.0
其他住宿服务	Others	438	5457.1	2005.7

continued 1

(10 000 yuan)

管理费用 Managenment Expenses	财务费用 Financial Expenses	利息支出 Interest Expenditure	营业利润 Business Profits	利润总额 Total Profits	应交所得税 Income Tax Payable	应付工资 Salary Payable	应付福利费 Welfare Funds	全部从业人员年平均人数（人） Average Number of Employed Persons(person)
173215.5	**17254.8**	**7251.7**	**35623.8**	**36048.2**	**8480.3**	**159511.7**	**16585.6**	**7776**
121485.5	**12188.5**	**4526.1**	**5621.0**	**1738.6**	**2297.7**	**74788.5**	**10544.7**	**3416**
41735.1	4670.8	2952.0	-2956.9	-3577.7	440.8	29628.7	2622.8	1364
92302.8	10437.1	4236.9	-398.6	-2614.0	1076.0	62566.4	7576.9	2994
29659.0	4214.7	2655.1	-5183.5	-6187.5	217.0	22304.5	1716.4	1063
227.0	3.0		54.0	-1.1		215.5	14.8	9
492.9	1.6		0.4	4.4	1.1	504.7		19
41481.5	3821.1	942.7	560.9	2238.4	758.8	27011.2	4545.6	1267
41481.5	3821.1	942.7	560.9	2238.4	758.8	27011.2	4545.6	1267
489.6	8.0	4.3	1411.1	1406.4	72.0	1211.0	115.1	66
16523.3	2377.8	640.3	1817.6	-729.7	14.2	9781.2	892.7	498
431.0	91.6	57.2	-4.2	-92.7	0.2	369.0	18.6	33
14038.0	2197.9	496.1	1449.7	-1009.1	14.0	8260.1	546.7	411
2054.3	88.3	87.0	372.1	372.1		1152.1	327.4	53
3429.5	10.9	-5.5	940.9	655.1	12.9	1538.3	292.3	73
11742.4	1881.3	1295.6	-1333.9	-2807.0	1.0	5135.8	1458.5	191
5498.1	57.3		-760.3	-806.1	1.0	1822.3	157.0	70
4035.8	427.4	181.9	44.8	84.6		2393.0	1285.9	87
2208.5	1396.6	1113.7	-618.4	-2085.5		920.5	15.6	34
17440.3	-129.9	-1006.4	7353.5	7159.6	1220.7	7086.3	1509.3	232
6946.2	-462.2	-552.0	539.6	559.0	60.9	2457.9	430.4	91
1737.8	83.1	76.9	-85.5	-160.4		799.3	251.5	46
8756.3	249.2	-531.3	6899.4	6761.0	1159.8	3829.1	827.4	94
107871.7	10643.7	3753.8	4843.1	558.8	2114.3	66057.9	9743.7	3007
10496.1	950.1	772.3	1038.9	1199.4	183.4	7119.4	691.6	354
3117.7	594.7		-261.0	-19.6		1611.2	109.4	56

15-10 续表2

单位：万元

分 类	Classify	单位数（个）Number (unit)	流动资产合计 Circulating Funds	存货 Inventories	固定资产原价 Original Value of Fixed Assets
二、餐饮业	**Catering Trade**	**264**	**193697.1**	**20146.5**	**221622.3**
#国有及国有控股	State-owned and State-holding Majority Shares	7	9190.8	1296.3	17195.7
1.按登记注册类型分组	Grouped by Type of Registration				
内资企业	Domestic Funded Enterprises	245	149258.9	14991.7	160851.7
国有企业	State-owned Enterprises	3	1238.6	162.9	2019.7
集体企业	Collective-owned Enterprises	3	198.7	64.5	664.2
股份合作企业	Share-Holding Cooperative Enterprises	1	386.6	15.5	121.9
有限责任公司	Limited Liability Corporations	106	76985.0	7141.3	52338.4
其他有限责任公司	Others Limited Liability Corporations	106	76985.0	7141.3	52338.4
股份有限公司	Corporations Ltd.	7	15829.8	2461.0	45103.1
私营企业	Private Enterprises	120	53722.4	4888.2	58225.3
私营独资企业	Private-funded Enterprises	20	2050.8	436.5	2580.3
私营合伙企业	Private Partnership Enterprises	8	1944.5	103.5	724.3
私营有限责任公司	Private Limited Liability Corporations	86	48240.5	4278.6	54511.1
私营股份有限公司	Private Share-holding Corporations Ltd.	6	1486.6	69.6	409.6
其他企业	Other Enterprises	5	897.8	258.3	2379.1
港、澳、台商投资企业	Enterprises with Funds from Hong Kong，Macao &Taiwan	8	25868.7	3048.2	32043.9
合资经营企业（港或澳、台资）	Joint-venture Enterprises	4	9406.8	1349.4	18338.4
合作经营企业（港或澳、台资）	Cooperative Enterprises				
独资经营企业	Enterprise with Sole Fund	4	16461.9	1698.8	13705.5
外商投资企业	Foreign Funded Enterprises	11	18569.5	2106.6	28726.7
中外合资经营企业	Joint-venture Enterprises	3	1471.3	204.7	253.9
中外合作经营企业	Cooperation Enterprises	1	94.8	6.4	69.1
外资企业	Foreign Funded Enterprises	7	17003.4	1895.5	28403.7
2.按国民经济行业分组	Grouped by Sector				
正餐服务业	Dinner	253	167849.0	17567.7	198246.9
快餐服务业	Fast Food	10	25810.8	2575.1	23315.4
其他餐饮服务业	Other Catering Services	1	37.3	3.7	60.0

continued 2

(10 000 yuan)

累计折旧 Accumulated Depreciation	本年折旧 In The Year	资产合计 Total Assets	负债合计 Total Liabilities	实收资本 Paid in Capital	营业收入 Total Revenue	主营业务收入 Revenue from Principal Business	主营业务成本 Cost of Principal Business
97409.7	**16583.2**	**467189.9**	**267271.0**	**256167.0**	**536885.0**	**531293.6**	**240204.9**
8804.7	1242.8	19693.3	12856.8	8046.3	24572.7	24529.5	12039.2
67642.4	13094.5	352942.8	222684.1	199740.4	405914.0	404367.0	194337.8
753.1	214.0	4366.0	3868.1	2890.1	4847.6	4829.8	3088.0
364.2	16.4	506.2	465.6	285.0	2451.0	2451.0	1619.2
59.3	49.8	504.6	498.1	200.0	1474.0	1474.0	757.2
25847.1	5135.7	143369.7	101682.2	116165.3	191707.2	191458.3	87027.0
25847.1	5135.7	143369.7	101682.2	116165.3	191707.2	191458.3	87027.0
19470.5	2661.1	76758.2	29571.2	27846.5	50370.0	50370.0	21332.5
20261.5	4748.5	122497.2	82960.1	50565.2	147255.9	145975.6	76873.2
1207.5	230.2	5258.6	3011.3	2764.3	19141.1	18442.3	11346.7
312.5	130.1	3982.6	3202.8	896.8	7242.2	7242.2	4691.9
18500.8	4265.5	110980.5	75116.1	45694.1	117442.7	116892.6	59003.7
240.7	122.7	2275.5	1629.9	1210.0	3429.9	3398.5	1830.9
886.7	269.0	4940.9	3638.8	1788.3	7808.3	7808.3	3640.7
17999.8	1473.4	58075.4	21320.8	32038.2	56246.8	56090.5	21965.2
9216.8	1137.7	19633.3	11605.9	8691.2	19293.0	19293.0	8423.1
8783.0	335.7	38442.1	9714.9	23347.0	36953.8	36797.5	13542.1
11767.5	2015.3	56171.7	23266.1	24388.4	74724.2	70836.1	23901.9
192.0	31.1	1581.2	883.1	1690.0	1551.8	1551.8	747.2
59.2	9.5	158.0	116.0	100.0	461.2	461.2	214.8
11516.3	1974.7	54432.5	22267.0	22598.4	72711.2	68823.1	22939.9
85448.0	15301.7	409787.2	244574.9	232681.9	472063.9	470517.1	215327.0
11923.0	1269.5	57332.7	22656.1	23455.1	64521.9	60477.5	24668.9
38.7	12.0	70.0	40.0	30.0	299.2	299.0	209.0

15-10 续表3

单位：万元

分　类	Classify	主营业务税金及附加 Taxs and Other Changes on Principal Business	主营业务利润 Profits from Principal Business	营业费用 Expenses for Operation
二、餐饮业	**Catering Trade**	31340.2	259748.5	176138.8
#国有及国有控股	State-owned and State-holding Majority Shares	1132.5	11357.8	6884.1
1.按登记注册类型分组	Grouped by Type of Registration			
内资企业	Domestic Funded Enterprises	24972.3	185056.9	125538.4
国有企业	State-owned Enterprises	227.7	1514.1	664.8
集体企业	Collective-owned Enterprises	136.6	695.2	433.0
股份合作企业	Share-Holding Cooperative Enterprises	84.8	632.0	249.8
有限责任公司	Limited Liability Corporations	11403.8	93027.5	62035.9
其他有限责任公司	Others Limited Liability Corporations	11403.8	93027.5	62035.9
股份有限公司	Corporations Ltd.	2554.7	26482.8	20398.3
私营企业	Private Enterprises	10071.0	59031.4	39264.5
私营独资企业	Private-funded Enterprises	964.9	6130.7	4204.5
私营合伙企业	Private Partnership Enterprises	282.9	2267.4	1952.2
私营有限责任公司	Private Limited Liability Corporations	8666.9	49222.0	32066.6
私营股份有限公司	Private Share-holding Corporations Ltd.	156.3	1411.3	1041.2
其他企业	Other Enterprises	493.7	3673.9	2492.1
港、澳、台商投资企业	Enterprises with Funds from Hong Kong，Macao &Taiwan	2743.6	31381.7	21797.1
合资经营企业（港或澳、台资）	Joint-venture Enterprises	885.6	9984.3	6548.8
合作经营企业（港或澳、台资）	Cooperative Enterprises			
独资经营企业	Enterprise with Sole Fund	1858.0	21397.4	15248.3
外商投资企业	Foreign Funded Enterprises	3624.3	43309.9	28803.3
中外合资经营企业	Joint-venture Enterprises	81.6	723.0	639.3
中外合作经营企业	Cooperation Enterprises	23.3	223.1	67.6
外资企业	Foreign Funded Enterprises	3519.4	42363.8	28096.4
2.按国民经济行业分组	Grouped by Sector			
正餐服务业	Dinner	28225.3	226964.8	150473.8
快餐服务业	Fast Food	3098.4	32710.2	25604.8
其他餐饮服务业	Other Catering Services	16.5	73.5	60.2

continued 3

(10 000 yuan)

管理费用 Management Expenses	财务费用 Financial Expenses	利息支出 Interest Expenditure	营业利润 Business Profits	利润总额 Total Profits	应交所得税 Income Tax Payable	应付工资 Salary Payable	应付福利费 Welfare Funds	全部从业人员年平均人数（人） Average Number of Employed Persons(person)
51730.0	5066.3	2725.6	30002.8	34309.6	6182.6	84723.2	6040.9	4359
2702.1	379.7	240.6	1417.1	1148.3	208.2	4085.7	185.8	205
38636.6	4515.7	2421.1	16749.0	20807.2	2938.6	65033.7	4116.3	3364
514.0	5.8	-0.1	329.5	60.7	1.0	1133.1		38
369.9	7.6		-115.3	-5.5		346.8	12.9	22
370.1	13.0		-0.9	-0.9		312.0	43.6	11
17402.9	1868.9	419.1	11937.3	10554.5	1104.1	31772.5	1936.7	1646
17402.9	1868.9	419.1	11937.3	10554.5	1104.1	31772.5	1936.7	1646
4384.3	728.9	1203.4	987.8	4469.3	1170.3	7893.4	695.5	431
15331.6	1809.1	797.7	2775.0	4922.1	616.9	22685.4	1323.2	1171
1161.5	32.2		746.5	1397.4	241.5	2678.5	135.6	137
310.8	42.3		-37.9	393.0	11.9	870.2	42.8	52
13435.3	1706.8	792.7	2148.1	3222.1	354.1	18658.2	1134.9	955
424.0	27.8	5.0	-81.7	-90.4	9.4	478.5	9.9	26
263.8	82.4	1.0	835.6	807.0	46.3	890.5	104.4	45
5123.3	576.5	391.5	4033.8	4240.5	945.6	7383.0	274.5	431
2226.4	421.1	287.9	788.0	1001.7	190.2	2911.4	193.7	166
2896.9	155.4	103.6	3245.8	3238.8	755.4	4471.6	80.8	266
7970.1	-25.9	-87.0	9220.0	9261.9	2298.4	12306.5	1650.1	565
231.0	10.8		-158.1	-158.6	0.8	510.5	12.0	20
92.5			63.0	63.0		104.3	7.9	6
7646.6	-36.7	-87.0	9315.1	9357.5	2297.6	11691.7	1630.2	538
47109.4	4935.6	2621.9	24556.0	28747.0	4836.9	76774.6	5541.2	3954
4600.6	130.7	103.7	5453.5	5569.7	1345.7	7910.0	499.7	403
20.0			-6.7	-7.1		38.6		2

15-11 限额以上批发和零售业商品购进、销售和库存总额（2010年）

Total Sales of Enterprises Above Designated Size in Wholesale and Retail Trades Grouped by Category of Commodities（2010）

单位：个、万元 (unit,10 000 yuan)

分　类	Classify	单位数 Number of Enterprises	销售合计 Total	批发额 Wholesale Trade	零售额 Retail Trade
总　计	**Total**	**564**	**21703789.3**	**11728596.6**	**9975192.7**
一、批发企业	**Wholesale Enterprises**	**191**	**12419428.0**	**11039682.8**	**1379745.2**
#国有控股	State-holding Enterprises	41	6492943.7	5577754.8	915188.9
1.按登记注册类型分组	Grouped by Registration Status				
内资企业	Domestic Funded Enterprises	175	10976524.8	9688864.4	1287660.4
国有企业	State-owned Enterprises	30	4068547.8	3643827.6	424720.2
集体企业	Collective-owned Enterprises	3	40930.6	40257.3	673.3
股份合作企业	Cooperative Enterprises				
联营企业	Joint Ownership Enterprises	1	5787.4	5765.0	22.4
国有联营企业	State Joint Ownership Enterprises				
集体联营企业	Collective Joint Ownership Enterprises	1	5787.4	5765.0	22.4
国有与集体联营企业	Joint State-collective Ownership Enterprises				
其他联营企业	Other Joint Ownership Enterprises				
有限责任公司	Limited Liability Corporations	104	4331539.5	3928788.3	402751.2
国有独资公司	State-funded Corporations	1	88109.1	88109.1	
其他有限责任公司	Other Limited Liability Corporations	103	4243430.4	3840679.2	402751.2
股份有限公司	Stock Limited Corporation	4	1089221.3	667452.9	421768.4
私营企业	Private Enterprises	32	1438375.8	1400650.9	37724.9
私营独资企业	Private-funded Enterprises	1	93823.6	93823.6	
私营合伙	Private Partnership Enterprises				
私营有限责任公司	Private Limited Liability Corporations	31	1344552.2	1306827.3	37724.9
私营股份有限公司	Private Share Holding Corporations				
其他	Others	1	2122.4	2122.4	
港、澳、台商投资企业	Enterprises Funded by Hong Kong, Macao and Taiwan	3	338307.9	264624.5	73683.4
与港澳台商合资经营	Joint-venture with Funds from Hong Kong, Macao and Taiwan	1	269583.6	195900.2	73683.4
与港澳台商合作经营	Cooperative Enterprises with Funds from Hong Kong Macau and Taiwan				
港澳台商独资	Enterprises with Sole Investment from Hong Kong Macau and Taiwan	2	68724.3	68724.3	
港澳台商投资股份有限公司	Share Holding Enterprises Funded by Overseas Chinese from Hong Kong, Macao & Taiwan				
外商投资企业	Foreign Funded Enterprises	2	1040779.6	1040779.6	
中外合资企业	Sino-foreign Joint Ventures	2	1040779.6	1040779.6	
中外合作企业	Sino-Foreign Cooperative Operation Enterprises				
外资企业	Foreign Owned Enterprises				
外商投资股份有限公司	Limited Company Funded by Foreign Investment				
个体工商户	Individually-owned Business	11	63815.7	45414.3	18401.4

15-11 续表1 continued 1

单位：个、万元 (unit、10 000 yuan)

分　类	Classify	单位数 Number of Enterprises	销售合计 Total	批发额 Wholesale Trade	零售额 Retail Trade
2.按国民经济行业分组	Grouped by Economic Sector				
农畜产品批发业	Wholesale of Agricultural and Livestock Products	2	24911.2	24911.2	
#谷物、豆及薯类批发	Wholesale of Cereal, Bean and Tuber	1	4281.5	4281.5	
食品、饮料及烟草制品批发	Wholesale of Food, Beverages and Tobacco Products	9	765232.4	744198.4	21034.0
#烟草制品批发业	Wholesale of Tobacco and Tobacco Products	1	650621.0	650621.0	
纺织、服装及日用品批发业	Wholesale of Textiles, Garments and Daily Articles	11	336325.7	242214.0	94111.7
文化、体育用品及器材批发	Wholesale of Culture, Sports Articles and Equipments	5	116729.8	115474.5	1255.3
医药及医疗器材批发	Wholesale of Medicines and Medical Appliances	24	625977.6	528670.6	97307.0
矿产品、建材及化工产品批发	Wholesale of Mineral Products, Building Materials and Chemical Products	89	8986564.4	8047928.0	938636.4
#煤炭及制品批发	Wholesale of Coal and Related Products	6	517444.5	375610.2	141834.3
石油及制品批发业	Wholesale of Petroleum and Related Products	25	5399972.6	4640480.8	759491.8
金属及金属矿批发业	Wholesale of Metals and Metal Minerals	41	2340503.7	2336098.8	4404.9
建材批发业	Wholesale of Building Materials	10	637374.1	604491.1	32883.0
其他化工产品批发	Wholesale of Other Chemical Products	2	9728.0	9728.0	
机械设备、五金交电及电子产品批发业	Wholesale of Machinery, Hardwares, Transport Means and Electronic Products	42	1512590.8	1285348.0	227242.8
#汽车、摩托车及零配件批发业	Wholesale of Motor Vehicles, Motorcycles and Parts	7	613603.3	462433.2	151170.1
家用电器批发	Wholesale of Electronic Household Equipments	5	256182.8	254259.0	1923.8
计算机、软件及辅助设备批发业	Wholesale of Computers,Softwares and Peripherals	5	367030.6	292912.4	74118.2
贸易经纪与代理	Trade Manage and Agent	8	50154.4	49996.4	158.0
其他批发	Other Wholesales	1	941.7	941.7	
3.经营形式分组	Grouped by Means of Operation				
独立门店	Independent Shop	131	6907784.6	5688272.2	1219512.4
连锁总店	Headquarter of Chain Store	1	650621.0	650621.0	
连锁门店	Chain Store				
其他	Other	59	4861022.4	4700789.6	160232.8
二、零售企业	**Retail Trade**	**373**	**9284361.3**	**688913.8**	**8595447.5**
#国有控股	State-holding Enterprises	18	425773.9	179.3	425594.6
1.按登记注册类型分组	Grouped by Registration Status				
内资企业	Domestic Funded Enterprises	255	7732875.3	665858.9	7067016.4
国有企业	State-owned Enterprises	17	294753.5	142.8	294610.7
集体企业	Collective-owned Enterprises	18	61180.2	39.3	61140.9
股份合作企业	Cooperative Enterprises	1	3910.0		3910.0

15-11 续表2 continued 2

单位：个、万元 (unit,10 000 yuan)

分　类	Classify	单位数 Number of Enterprises	销售合计 Total	批发额 Wholesale Trade	零售额 Retail Trade
联营企业	Joint Ownership Enterprises	1	3225.8		3225.8
国有联营企业	State Joint Ownership Enterprises				
集体联营企业	Collective Joint Ownership Enterprises	1	3225.8		3225.8
国有与集体联营企业	Joint State-collective Ownership Enterprises				
其他联营企业	Other Joint Ownership Enterprises				
有限责任公司	Limited Liability Corporations	126	4855345.6	435262.0	4420083.6
国有独资公司	State-funded Corporations	2	44026.4	36.5	43989.9
其他有限责任公司	Other Limited Liability Corporations	124	4811319.2	435225.5	4376093.7
股份有限公司	Stock Limited Corporation	4	535269.2	158263.6	377005.6
私营企业	Private Enterprises	87	1975895.2	72151.2	1903744.0
私营独资企业	Private-funded Enterprises	13	32872.8	1523.5	31349.3
私营合伙企业	Private Partnership Enterprises	5	47883.3		47883.3
私营有限责任公司	Private Limited Liability Corporations	65	1846584.7	70397.6	1776187.1
私营股份有限公司	Private Share Holding Corporations	4	48554.4	230.1	48324.3
其他企业	Others	1	3295.8		3295.8
港、澳、台商投资企业	Enterprises Funded by Hong Kong, Macao and Taiwan	11	856256.4	4481.8	851774.6
与港澳台商合资经营	Joint-venture with Funds from Hong Kong, Macao and Taiwan	1	126065.6		126065.6
与港澳台商合作经营	Cooperative Enterprises with Funds from Hong Kong Macau and Taiwan				
港澳台商独资	Enterprises with Sole Investment from Hong Kong Macau and Taiwan	9	588077.9	4481.8	583596.1
港澳台商投资股份有限公司	Share Holding Enterprises Funded by Overseas Chinese from Hong Kong, Macao & Taiwan	1	142112.9		142112.9
外商投资企业	Foreign Funded Enterprises	13	536104.1		536104.1
中外合资营企业	Sino-foreign Joint Ventures	4	263254.6		263254.6
中外合作企业	Sino-Foreign Cooperative Operation Enterprises				
外资企业	Foreign Owned Enterprises	8	228602.9		228602.9
外商投资股份有限公司	Limited Company Funded by Foreign Investment	1	44246.6		44246.6
个体工商户	Individually-owned Business	94	159125.5	18573.1	140552.4
2.按国民经济行业分组	Grouped by Registered Kind				
综合零售	General Retail Sales Trade	94	2336996.0	21981.2	2315014.8
#百货零售	Retail of Daily Goods	40	1211111.9	94.3	1211017.6
超级市场零售	Retail of Supermarkets	41	1071993.0	21886.9	1050106.1
食品、饮料及烟草制品专门零售	Retail of Food，Beverage and Tobaccos	23	132772.2	92154.9	40617.3
纺织、服装及日用品专门零售	Retail of Textiles，Garments and Daily Articles	51	762623.5	78924.0	683699.5
#服装零售	Retail of Garments	36	605554.5	68030.7	537523.8

15-11 续表3 continued 3

单位：个、万元 (unit,10 000 yuan)

分 类	Classify	单位数 Number of Enterprises	销售合计 Total	批发额 Wholesale Trade	零售额 Retail Trade
文化、体育用品及器材专门零售	Retail of Culture , Sports Articles and Equipments	25	200382.8	16117.0	184265.8
#图书零售	Retail of Books and Mangzines	4	50636.2		50636.2
医药及医疗器材专门零售	Retail of Medicines and Medical Appliances	10	116951.6	17517.7	99433.9
#药品零售	Retail of Medicines	10	116951.6	17517.7	99433.9
汽车、摩托车、燃料及零配件专门零售	Retail of Motor Vehicles，Motorcycles, Feuls and Parts	117	3978301.4	352803.9	3625497.5
#汽车零售业	Retailof Motor Vehicles	89	3744134.0	348321.3	3395812.7
家用电器及电子产品专门零售	Retail of Household Electronic Equipments and Products	27	1050192.8	109246.1	940946.7
#家用电器零售	Retail of Household Electronic Equipments	17	922930.2	90301.1	832629.1
计算机、软件及辅助设备零售	Retail of Computer , Software and Auxiliary Equipments	6	84297.2	18945.0	65352.2
通讯设备零售	Retail of Communications	4	42965.4		42965.4
五金、家具及室内装修材料专门零售	Retail of Hardwares , Furniture and Room Decorative Building	19	661553.5	160.0	661393.5
无店铺及其他零售	No Fixed Stores and Other Retails	7	44587.5	9.0	44578.5
3.按经营形式分	Grouped by Means of Operation				
独立门店	Independent Shop	323	7077372.0	585658.4	6491713.6
连锁总店	Headquarter of Chain Store	13	640539.1	15996.2	624542.9
连锁门店	Chain Store	9	735375.5	59819.6	675555.9
其他	Other	28	831074.7	27439.6	803635.1
4.按零售业态分	Grouped by Retail Size				
有店铺零售	Retail of Shop	371	9251359.0	688913.8	8562445.2
食杂店	Grocery Store				
便利店	Convenience Store	5	11343.7		11343.7
折扣店	Dime Store				
超市	Supermarket	31	112541.0	2361.8	110179.2
大型超市	Larget Supermarket	11	738445.2	6484.3	731960.9
仓储会员店	Warehouse Club				
百货店	Department Store	46	1393180.8	60474.2	1332706.6
专业店	Special Store	154	2812904.6	537948.7	2274955.9
专卖店	Monopoly Store	98	2632866.9	42841.4	2590025.5
家居建材商店	Home-building Material Store	11	691123.8		691123.8
购物中心	Shopping Center	10	757093.0	38803.4	718289.6
厂家直销中心	Factory Outlet Center	5	101860.0		101860.0
无店铺零售	Retail of No-shop	2	33002.3		33002.3
电视购物	TV Shopping	2	33002.3		33002.3
邮购	Mail Order				
网上商店	Online Stores				
自动售货亭	Vending Machine				
电话购物	Tele Shopping				

15-12 限额以上住宿和餐饮业经营情况（2010年）

Statistic on Hotel Services and Catering Services above Designed Size（2010）

单位：个、万元 (unit、10 000 yuan)

分　　类	Classify	单位数 Number of Enterprises	营业额 Business Revenue	客房收入 From Hotel Room	餐费收入 From Meals	商品销售收入 From Commodities
总　　计	**Total**	**557**	**1018597.7**	**235785.1**	**672636.4**	**50170.6**
一、住宿业	**Lodging Services**	**187**	**432203.9**	**213242.8**	**173067.7**	**7964.5**
#国有控股	State-holding Enterprises	54	137004.7	63270.1	59390.1	3270.6
（一）按登记注册类型分组	Grouped by Registration Status					
内资企业	Domestic Funded Enterprises	172	348819.1	167203.2	141914.1	7294.3
国有企业	State-owned Enterprises	49	110248.2	49496.6	48066.6	3455.0
集体企业	Collective-owned Enterprises	3	1077.6	723.5	147.4	
股份合作企业	Cooperative Enterprises	1	2190.8	424.0	1126.0	32.8
有限责任公司	Limited Liability Corporations	72	161459.7	82650.4	60039.8	2607.7
国有独资企业	State-funded Corporations					
其他有限责任公司	Other Limited Liability Corporations	72	161459.7	82650.4	60039.8	2607.7
股份有限公司	Stock Limited Corporation	5	6083.0	3241.2	747.4	370.4
私营企业	Private Enterprises	36	58687.3	25857.8	27963.0	719.1
私营独资企业	Private-funded Enterprises	5	3367.1	1003.9	2006.3	68.3
私营有限责任公司	Private Limited Liability Corporations	28	46743.0	20244.9	22032.2	650.8
私营股份有限公司	Private Share Holding Corporations	3	8577.2	4609.0	3924.5	
其他企业	Others	6	9072.5	4809.7	3823.9	109.3
港、澳、台商投资企业	Enterprises Funded by Hong Kong, Macao and Taiwan	8	32037.7	17048.5	11106.7	148.1
合资经营企业(港或澳、台资)	Joint-venture with Funds from Hong Kong, Macao and Taiwan	3	12556.2	5335.5	4391.3	146.4
合作经营企业(港或澳、台资)	Cooperative Enterprises with Funds from Hong Kong Macau and Taiwan	2	12786.1	6862.4	5308.6	1.7
外商投资企业	Foreign Funded Enterprises	6	51167.1	28901.1	19956.9	522.1
中外合资经营企业	Sino-foreign Joint Ventures	2	16154.6	9299.7	6025.3	93.3
中外合作经营企业	Sino-Foreign Cooperative Operation Enterprises	2	3950.0	2056.5	1828.9	
个体工商户	Individually-owned Business	1	180.0	90.0	90.0	
（二）按住宿行业小类分组	Grouped in Classes According to Lodging Industry					
旅游饭店	Tour Restaurant	150	388867.4	193081.3	154140.2	7367.1
一般旅馆	Common Hotel	34	35219.0	17422.6	15898.8	597.4

15-12 续表 continued

单位：个、万元 (unit、10 000 yuan)

分 类	Classify	单位数 Number of Enterprises	营业额 Business Revenue	客房收入 From Hotel Room	餐费收入 From Meals	商品销售收入 From Commodities
二、餐饮业	**Catering Trade**	**370**	**586393.8**	**22542.3**	**499568.7**	**42206.1**
#国有控股	State-holding Enterprises	7	24529.4	1195.9	16683.4	4622.5
1.按登记注册类型分组	Grouped by Registration Status					
内资企业	Domestic Funded Enterprises	250	421422.1	20481.2	348585.5	35667.5
国有企业	State-owned Enterprises	4	8816.5	818.0	2659.4	3912.1
集体企业	Collective-owned Enterprises	3	2451.0		2451.0	
股份合作企业	Cooperative Enterprises	1	1474.0		1474.0	
联营企业	Joint Ownership Enterprises					
集体联营企业	Collective Joint Ownership Enterprises					
有限责任公司	Limited Liability Corporations	109	203433.0	13390.6	161801.9	22049.0
国有独资公司	State-funded Corporations					
其他有限责任公司	Other Limited Liability Corporations	109	203433.0	13390.6	161801.9	22049.0
股份有限公司	Stock Limited Corporation	7	50407.6	4470.8	32373.2	7779.7
私营企业	Private Enterprises	120	146480.3	1601.4	139915.2	1678.2
私营独资企业	Private-funded Enterprises	20	19207.4	70.0	17599.2	362.1
私营合伙企业	Private Partnership Enterprises	8	7348.3	10.0	7284.3	9.0
私营有限责任公司	Private Limited Liability Corporations	86	116526.1	1409.0	111778.0	1304.7
私营股份有限公司	Private Share Holding Corporations	6	3398.5	112.4	3253.7	2.4
其他企业	Others	6	8359.7	200.4	7910.8	248.5
港、澳、台商投资企业	Enterprises Funded by Hong Kong, Macao and Taiwan	8	56190.1	1088.3	50716.4	3604.3
合资经营企业（港或澳、台资）	Joint-venture with Funds from Hong Kong, Macao and Taiwan	4	19237.3	515.5	14537.1	3558.9
合作经营企业（港或澳、台资）	Cooperative Enterprises with Funds from Hong Kong Macau and Taiwan					
独资经营企业	Enterprises with Sole Investment	4	36952.8	572.8	36179.3	45.4
外商投资企业	Foreign Funded Enterprises	11	74580.0	170.5	69621.3	857.6
中外合资经营企业	Sino-foreign Joint Ventures	3	1551.8		1489.5	62.3
中外合作经营企业	Sino-Foreign Cooperative Operation Enterprises	1	461.2		461.2	
外资企业	Foreign Owned Enterprises	7	72567.0	170.5	67670.6	795.3
个体工商户	Individually-owned Business	101	34201.6	802.3	30645.5	2076.7
2.按餐饮行业小类分组	Grouped by Catering Middle Sector					
正餐服务	Dinner Services	347	517590.9	21959.5	435642.9	42155.1
快餐服务	Fast Food Services	16	67189.1	572.8	62573.0	
饮料及冷饮服务	Beverage and Cold Beverage Services					
其他餐饮服务	Other Catering Services	7	1613.8	10.0	1352.8	51.0

15-13 限额以上批发和零售业主要商品分类销售额（2010年）

Sale Values of Enterprises above Designated Size of Wholesale and Retail Trades by Category of Main Commodities（2010）

单位：万元 (10 000 yuan)

分　类	Classify	销售合计 Total Sales Value	批发 Wholesale Value	零售 Retail Value
粮油、食品、饮料、烟酒类	Grain and Oil, Food and Beverages, Alcoholic Drinks and Tobacco	1633583.3	787083.4	846499.9
粮油、食品类	Cereals, Oils and Foodstuffs	599628.7	68640.0	530988.7
#粮油类	Grain and Oil	235026.9	29542.3	205484.6
肉禽蛋类	Meat, Poultry and Eggs	139205.3	11.2	139194.1
水产品类	Aquatic Products	16691.4		16691.4
蔬菜类	Vegetables	45595.1	15521.7	30073.4
干鲜瓜果类	Fresh and Dried Fruit Category	33673.0	2264.7	31408.3
饮料类	Beverages	190185.1	28197.0	161988.1
烟酒类	Tobacco and Liquor	843769.5	690246.4	153523.1
服装、鞋帽、针纺织品类	Clothing, Shoes, Hats and Textiles	1602582.4	163825.9	1438756.5
服装类	Clothing	1191853.8	99703.2	1092150.6
鞋帽类	Shoes and Hats	254533.1	12727.3	241805.8
针纺织品类	Knitwear and Textiles	156195.5	51395.4	104800.1
化妆品类	Cosmetics	199589.9	28749.2	170840.7
金银珠宝类	Gold,Silver and Jewelry	281823.2	13869.1	267954.1
日用品类	Articles for Daily Use	410425.0	61803.7	348621.3
#洗涤用品类	Bathing and Washing	130183.4	42914.4	87269.0
儿童玩具类	Children's Toys	54960.8	9233.4	45727.4
五金、电料类	Hardwear and Electrical Materials	160645.4	83155.6	77489.8
体育、娱乐用品类	Sports and Recreation Articles	125136.9	8377.7	116759.2
书报杂志类	Newspapers and Magazines	142909.3	82340.3	60569.0
电子出版物及音像制品类	E-journal and Video Products	3066.0		3066.0
家用电器和音像器材类	Household Appliances and Video Products	865856.0	287900.7	577955.3
中西药品类	Traditional Chinese and Western Medicine	748422.2	551843.1	196579.1
#西药类	Western Medicine	530764.5	361029.8	169734.7
中草药及中成药类	Chinese Herbal Medicine and Traditional Chinese Medicine	60812.3	50415.1	10397.2
文化办公用品类	Cultural and Official Goods	514073.4	258889.9	255183.5
家具类	Furniture	413019.7		413019.7
通讯器材类	Communication Appliances	177530.1	42797.3	134732.8
煤炭及制品类	Coal and Related Products	323922.4	314870.5	9051.9
木材及制品类	Wood and Wooden Products	3.6	3.6	
石油及制品类	Petroleum and Related Products	4715409.8	3921496.1	793913.7
化工材料及制品类	Raw Chemical Materials	41479.2	41479.2	
#化肥类	Chemical Fertilizers	31932.8	31932.8	
金属材料类	Metal Materials	2727902.2	2727902.2	
建筑及装潢材料类	Buildings and Decoration Materials	452615.1	129185.8	323429.3
机电产品及设备类	Mechanical and Electrical Products	395460.6	393044.4	2416.2
#农机类	Agricultural Machinery			
汽车类	Automobile	4189555.3	783138.8	3406416.5
种子饲料类	Seeds and Feedstuff	14.1	14.1	
棉麻类	Cotton,Hemp	15868.8	15868.8	
其他类	Others	68037.0	5226.0	62811.0

15-14 亿元以上商品交易市场成交情况（2010年）

Basic Statistics on Commodity Exchange Markets of Transaction Value over 100 Million Yuan（2010）

分 类	Classify	年末出租摊位数（个）Number of Rental Booths at Year-end (unit)	成交额（万元）Turnover (10 000 yuan)
粮油、食品、饮料、烟酒类	Grain and Oil, Food and Beverages, Alcoholic Drinks and Tobacco	3382	578448
粮油、食品类	Cereals, Oils and Foodstuffs	2187	535945
#粮油类	Grain and Oil	269	216762
肉禽蛋类	Meat, Poultry and Eggs	247	65823
水产品类	Aquatic Products	47	3567
蔬菜类	Vegetables	1044	189782
干鲜果品类	Fresh and Dried Fruit Category	550	54179
饮料类	Beverages	1098	39775
烟酒类	Tobacco and Liquor	97	2728
服装、鞋帽、针纺织品类	Clothing, Shoes, Hats and Textiles	6558	380475
服装类	Clothing	4542	159850
鞋帽类	Shoes and Hats	898	150000
针纺织品类	Knitwear and Textiles	1118	70625
化妆品类	Cosmetics	23	989
金银珠宝类	Gold,Silver and Jewelry		
日用品类	Articles for Daily Use	102	2465
#洗涤用品类	Bathing and Washing	90	1440
儿童玩具类	Children's Toys		
五金、电料类	Hardwear and Electrical Materials	195	11126
体育、娱乐用品类	Sports and Recreation Articles	32	1350
书报杂志类	Newspapers and Magazines	4	95
电子出版物及音像制品类	E-journal and Video Products	187	4620
家用电器和音像器材类	Household Appliances and Video Products	165	27693
中西药品类	Traditional Chinese and Western Medicine	373	30000
#西药类	Western Medicine		
中草药及中成药类	Chinese Herbal Medicine and Traditional Chinese Medicine	373	30000
文化办公用品类	Cultural and Official Goods	2068	131081
家具类	Furniture		
通讯器材类	Communication Appliances	2	80
煤炭及制品类	Coal and Related Products		
木材及制品类	Wood and Wooden Products		
石油及制品类	Petroleum and Related Products		
化工材料及制品类	Raw Chemical Materials		
#化肥类	Chemical Fertilizers		
金属材料类	Metal Materials		
建筑及装潢材料类	Buildings and Decoration Materials	706	33200
机电产品及设备类	Mechanical and Electrical Products		
#农机类	Agricultural Machinery		
汽车类	Automobile	640	178050
种子饲料类	Seeds and Feedstuff		
棉麻类	Cotton,Hemp		
其他类	Others	58	852

15-15 批发和零售业连锁经营情况（2010年）

Basic Statistics on Chain Business of Wholesale and Retail Trades（2010）

指　标	Item	本年合计 Total	上年合计 Total Last Year	本年直营店 Ragular Chain
一、门店总数（个）	**Number of Stores(unit)**	**453**	**413**	**389**
二、年末从业人员数（人）	**Employees at Year-end(person)**	**11921**	**11207**	**11072**
三、年末零售营业面积（平方米）	**Operating Area of Retail at Year-end(sq.m)**	**409983**	**442265**	**315983**
四、连锁门店商品购进额（万元）	**Purchases Value of Chain Stores(1 0000 yuan)**	**978607**	**857495.4**	**940076.4**
#统一配送商品购进额	Centralized Purchases and Delivery	535127.7	477354.7	535127.7
#自有配送中心配送商品购进额	Self Centralized Purchases and Delivery	489021.8	430797.9	489021.8
非自有配送中心配送商品购进额	Non-self Centralized Purchases and Delivery	29553.5	34468.6	29553.5
五、连锁门店商品销售额（万元）	**Sales Value of Chain Store(1 0000 yuan)**	**1278805.7**	**1076906.4**	**1220729.8**
#零售额	Retail Value	628184.7	540780.4	570108.8

15-15 续表 continued

指　标	Item	上年直营店 Ragular Chain Last Year	本年加盟店 Franchise	上年加盟店 Franchise Last Year
一、门店总数（个）	**Number of Stores(unit)**	**360**	**64**	**53**
二、年末从业人员数（人）	**Employees at Year-end(person)**	**10374**	**849**	**833**
三、年末零售营业面积（平方米）	**Operating Area of Retail at Year-end(sq.m)**	**349605**	**94000**	**92660**
四、连锁门店商品购进额（万元）	**Purchases Value of Chain Stores(1 0000 yuan)**	**837809**	**38530.6**	**19686.4**
#统一配送商品购进额	Centralized Purchases and Delivery	477354.7		
#自有配送中心配送商品购进额	Self Centralized Purchases and Delivery	430797.9		
非自有配送中心配送商品购进额	Non-self Centralized Purchases and Delivery	34468.6		
五、连锁门店商品销售额（万元）	**Sales Value of Chain Store(1 0000 yuan)**	**1055500.4**	**58075.9**	**21406**
#零售额	Retail Value	519374.4	58075.9	21406

15-16　住宿和餐饮业连锁经营情况（2010年）

Basic Statistics on Chain Business of Hotels and Catering Services（2010）

指　　标	Item	本年合计 Total	上年合计 Total Last Year
一、门店总数（个）	**Number of Stores(unit)**	**77**	**65**
二、年末从业人员数（人）	**Employees at Year-end(person)**	**6814**	**5647**
三、年末餐饮营业面积（平方米）	**Operating Area of Retail at Year-end(sq.m)**	**31850**	**28399**
四、客房总数（间）	**Guest Rooms(room)**		
五、床位数（张）	**Guest Beds(bed)**		
六、餐位数（位）	**Dining Seats(set)**	**10848**	**8312**
七、连锁门店商品购进额（万元）	**Operating Area of Catering Services at Year end(room)(1 0000 yuan)**	**39391.1**	**31749.3**
#统一配送商品购进额	Centralized Purchases and Delivery	34313.4	26414.4
#自有配送中心配送商品购进额	Self Centralized Purchases and Delivery	10984	10022.7
非自有配送中心配送商品购进额	Non-self Centralized Purchases and Delivery		
八、连锁门店商品营业额（万元）	**Sales Value of Chain Store(1 0000 yuan)**	**75028.2**	**56692.1**
#餐费收入	Catering Revenues	74667.2	56461.7
商品销售额	Sales Value	361	200.4

15-16　续表 continued

指　　标	Item	本年直营店 Ragular Chain	上年直营店 Ragular Chain Last Year
一、门店总数（个）	**Number of Stores(unit)**	**77**	**65**
二、年末从业人员数（人）	**Employees at Year-end(person)**	**6814**	**5647**
三、年末餐饮营业面积（平方米）	**Operating Area of Retail at Year-end(sq.m)**	**31850**	**28399**
四、客房总数（间）	**Guest Rooms(room)**		
五、床位数（张）	**Guest Beds(bed)**		
六、餐位数（位）	**Dining Seats(set)**	**10848**	8312
七、连锁门店商品购进额（万元）	**Operating Area of Catering Services at Year end(room)(1 0000 yuan)**	**39391.1**	**31749.3**
#统一配送商品购进额	Centralized Purchases and Delivery	34313.4	26414.4
#自有配送中心配送商品购进额	Self Centralized Purchases and Delivery	10984	10022.7
非自有配送中心配送商品购进额	Non-self Centralized Purchases and Delivery		
八、连锁门店商品营业额（万元）	**Sales Value of Chain Store(1 0000 yuan)**	**75028.2**	**56692.1**
#餐费收入	Catering Revenues	74667.2	56461.7
商品销售额	Sales Value	361	200.4

15-17 成品油批发企业（单位）能源购进、销售与库存（2010年）

Purchases,Sales and Stock of Refined Oil Wholesale Enterprises（2010）

指　标	Item	年初库存量 Stock at Beginning of the Year	本年购进量 Purchases This Year	购自省（区、市）外 From Other Provinces（Regions,Cities）	本年销售量 Sales This Year	销往省(区、市)外 For Other Provinces（Regions,Cities）	售予批发和零售业 For Wholesale and Retail Trades	年末库存量 Stock at End of the Year
汽油(吨)	Gasoline(ton)	62874	2428169	197478	2432068	778638	1421955	45506
#93″	#93″	12026	1568395	99022	1565451	549974	822569	26512
柴油(吨)	Diesel Oil(ton)	58078	4046451	785954	4195186	1159451	2518503	60828
#0″	#0″	40271	3449234	618332	3537401	974905	2072941	29036
煤油(吨)	Kerosene(ton)	18577	550851	186691	551377	185071	366305	174790
燃料油(吨)	Fuel Oil(ton)		62927	58927	62927	53288	9639	
润滑油(吨)	Lube(ton)	2036	18926	17408	19120	9309	8651	1146

15-18 成品油零售企业（单位）能源商品销售与库存（2010年）

Purchases,Sales and Stock of Refined Oil Retail Enterprises（2010）

指　标	Item	年初库存量 Stock at Beginning of the Year	本年销售量 Sales This Year	年末库存量 Stock at End of the Year
汽油(吨)	Gasoline(ton)	13469	499055	13283
#93″	#93″	7524	361188	7954
柴油(吨)	Diesel Oil(ton)	12087	581331	11367
#0″	#0″	8589	524426	7912
煤油(吨)	Kerosene(ton)			
燃料油(吨)	Fuel Oil(ton)			
润滑油(吨)	Lube(ton)	27	1282	60

主要统计指标解释

社会消费品零售额 指各种经济类型的批发零售贸易业、餐饮业和其他行业对城乡居民和社会集团的消费品零售额总和。这个指标反映通过各种商品流通渠道向居民和社会集团供应的生活消费品来满足他们生活需要，是研究人民生活、社会消费品购买力，货币流通等问题的重要指标。对居民的消费品零售额：指售给城乡居民用于生活消费的商品。对社会集团的消费品零售额：指售给机关、团体、部队、学校、企业、事业单位和城市街道居民委员会，农村村民委员会用公款购买的用作非生产、非经营使用的消费品。

社会消费品零售额包括：

售给社会集团的办公用品、纸张、账册、文印用品和纺织品、针织品；学校用的教学用具；文体用品；非专用的劳动保护用品，如工作服、套袖、围群、手套、毛巾、肥皂等；日用百货和杂品，包括职工食堂用的餐具、炊具、设备和清洁卫生工具等；家具、设备、日用电器、电讯设备、电影器材和照相器材等；取暖用的设备和燃料，防署、降温的饮料；非生产经营用的交通工具如小轿车、面包车、工具车、卡车和油料；零星修理用的各种零配件、材料、工具、建筑材料等；举办各种招待会、茶话会、宴会用的烟酒茶和各种食品及馈赠的礼品；从公费医疗经费中开支的中、西药品、中药材和医疗器材以及其他非生产性设备和用品。

商品销售总额 指对本企业（单位）以外的单位和个人出售（包括对境外直接出口）的商品总额。它反映批发零售贸易业在国内市场上销售商品以及出口商品的总量。商品销售总额包括:（1）售给城乡居民和社会集团消费用的商品;（2）售给工业、农业、建筑业、运输邮电业、批发零售贸易业、餐饮业、服务业等作为生产、经营使用的商品;（3）售给批发零售贸易业作为转卖或加工后转卖的商品;（4）对国（境）外直接出口的商品。不包括出售本企业（单位）自用的废旧包装用品;未通过买卖行为付出的商品;经本单位介绍，由买卖双方直接结算，本单位只收取手续费的业务;购货退出的商品以及商品损耗和损失等。

住宿和餐饮业营业额 指住宿和餐饮业法人企业、产业活动单位在经营活动中的因提供服务或销售商品等取得的收入。包括：客房收入、餐费收入、商品销售收入和其它收入。

客房收入 指住宿和餐饮业法人企业、产业活动单位在经营活动中因提供住宿服务取得的客房收入。

餐费收入 指住宿和餐饮业法人企业、产业活动因为顾客提供就餐服务取得的收入。包括：经烹饪、调制加工之后出售的各种食品，如主食、炒菜、凉拌菜等的收入。

商品销售收入 指住宿和餐饮业法人企业、产业活动单位伴随服务而出售商品所取得的收入。

其他收入 指营业收入中除客房收入、餐费收入、商品销售收入以外的其它收入。包括：娱乐、健身和商业服务等。

Explanatory Notes on Main Statistical Indicators

Total Retail Sales of Consumer Goods it refers to sum of retail amount of consumer goods sold by wholesale and retail trade in all kinds of economic type, accommodation trade and other industry sold to urban and countryside citizens and social groups. This indicator reflects all living consumer goods supplied by all kinds of commodity channel to residents and social group to meet the needs of their life, and it is an important indicator to study people's life, social consumer goods purchasing power and circulation of currency and so on. Volume of retail sales of consumer goods to residents: it refers to commodities sold to residents of urban and rural area used for daily consuming. Volume of retail sales of consumer goods to social groups: it refers to the amount of consumer goods bought by government functionary office, groups, army, schools, enterprises, institutions, residents committees in urban area and villagers committees in rural area using public money, used for non-productive, non-operational purposes.

Volume of retail sales of social consumer goods consists of items sold to social groups such as stationery, papers, account books, printing articles, computing instruments, books, newspapers, magazines and awards; public facilities, dry goods and hosiery; teaching instruments for schools; recreation and sports facilities; non-special labor safety articles, such as work clothes, over sleeves, apron, gloves, towels, soaps etc.; articles for everyday use, commodities and sundry goods, include table wares, cooking utensils, equipment and cleaning and sanitary facilities for staff eateries; furniture, equipment, electrical appliances of daily use, telecommunication equipment, film equipment, photo equipment etc.; equipment and fuel for heating, drinks for sunstroke prevention and lowering the temperature; non-productive and operational vehicles such as sedans, vans, tool cars, trucks and fuels; various parts, fittings, materials, tools, building materials for fragmentary repairing; cigarettes, alcoholic drinks and tea leafs for various receptions, tea parties and banquets and all kinds of foods and gifts for present; Chinese traditional medicine, Western medicine, Chinese traditional medicinal materials, medical treatment equipment paid by public health service outlays and other non-productive equipment and facilities.

Total Sales of Commodities refer to value of commodities sold by the establishments to other establishments and individuals (including direct export). This indicator is used to show the total value of sales of commodities at domestic markets and export. The total sales include: (1) commodities sold to urban and rural residents and social groups for their consumption; (2) commodities sold to establishments in industry, agriculture, construction, transportation, post and telecommunications, wholesale and retail trades, catering trade and public utility for their production and operation; (3) commodities sold to wholesale and retail establishments for re selling, with or without further processing; and (4)commodities for direct export to other countries. Excluded are selling of waste packaging materials used by the establishments (units) themselves, commodities transferred without buying or selling procedures, commission income from brokerage in transactions whose settlement is directly handled by buyers and sellers, rejected commodities in the purchase, loss in commodities, etc.

Turnover of Hotel and Catering refers to revenue from providing services or selling products by Hotel and Catering corporate enterprises and economic active units. It includes revenue of guest room, revenue of meal cost, revenue of products sale and other revenue.

Revenue of guest room refers to revenue from providing hotel services by Hotel and Catering corporate enterprises and economic active units.

Revenue of meal cost refers to revenue from providing catering services by Hotel and Catering corporate enterprises and economic active units. It includes revenue from selling sorts of food after cooking and processing, for example: staple food, cooking dish, cold and dressed dish, etc.

Revenue of product sale refers to revenue from product sale by Hotel and Catering corporate enterprises and economic active units.

Other revenue refers to other revenue from deducting revenue of guest room, revenue of meal cost and revenue of product sale from total operating revenue.

16 对外经济贸易和旅游

FOREIGN TRADE AND ECONOMIC COOPERATION TOURISM

资料整理：马晓庆　赵琳瑛
Data management:Ma Xiaoqing　Zhao Linying

第十六部分　对外经济贸易和旅游

一、简要说明

本章资料包括对外经济贸易、利用外资以及与国外友好城市交流和旅游等方面资料，由西安市统计局贸易外经处根据西安市商务局、海关、政府对外办公室和旅游局提供资料整理。

二、主要指标

进出口总额（亿美元）	103.93	比上年增长	43.4%
#出　口	53.17	比上年增长	59.6%
实际利用外商直接投资额（亿美元）	15.67	比上年增长	28.5%
国际旅游人数（万人次）	84.18	比上年增长	25.1%
国际旅游收入（亿美元）	5.30	比上年增长	35.8%

16 FOREIGN TRADE AND ECONOMIC COOPERATION,TOURISM

Ⅰ.Brief Introduction

Data in this chapter consists of data on foreign trade, using of foreign capital and fund and tourism. Data on foreign economy and trade, intercommunion to foreign cities of friendship and tourism are compiled and provided by Foreign Economy Division of the Xi'an Bureau of Statistics according to the data from Xi'an Bureau of Commerce, Xi'an Custom Office, Foreign Affairs Office of the Xi'an Municipal Government and Xi'an Bureau of Tourism.

Ⅱ.Major Indicators

		Increase over Preceding Year
Total Imports and Exports (USD 100 mil.)	103.93	43.4%
Toal Exports	53.17	59.6%
Total Amount of Foreign Capital Actually Used(USD 100 mil.)	15.67	28.5%
Total Number of International Tourists (10 000 persons)	84.18	25.1%
Total Foreign Exchange Earnings (100 mil. Yuan)	5.30	35.8%

16-1 主要年份外资、外贸和国际旅游基本情况

Main Indicators on Foreign Investments,International Trading and International Tourism In Representative Years

指 标	Item	1990	1995	2000	2004	2005
一、利用外资签订协议项目(个)	**Number of Projects of Foreign Capital Used through the Signed Agreements and Contracts (unit)**	**11**	**184**	**135**	**159**	**157**
利用外资签订协议金额(万美元)	Value of Foreign Capital Used through the Signed Agreements and Contracts(USD 10 000)	415	28956	54123	78312	121499
外商实际直接投资额(万美元)	Value of Foreign Direct Investment (USD 10 000)	1154	18653	15633	27595	57113
二、进出口总额(万美元)	**Total Imports and Exports (USD 10 000)**	**38229**	**137510**	**173696**	**309295**	**390146**
#进口总额	Total Imports	9939	27347	67634	105756	126705
出口总额	Total Exports	28290	110163	106062	203539	263441
进出口差额	Balance of Imports and Exports	18351	82816	38428	97783	136736
三、国际旅游人数总计(万人次)	**Total Number of International Tourists (10 000 person-times)**	**25.88**	**41.35**	**65.03**	**65.03**	**77.56**
#外国人	Foreigners	15.40	37.11	54.65	52.75	65.86
港澳台同胞	Chinese Compatriot From Hong Kong, Macao and Taiwan	10.07	4.16	10.38	12.28	11.70
四、国际旅游者人天数总计(万人天)	**Total Number of Days of International Tourists (10 000 person/day)**	**55.03**	**84.44**	**162.69**	**186.80**	**224.93**
#外国人	Foreigners	33.48	75.71	131.44	151.11	190.99
港澳台同胞	Chinese Compatriot From Hong Kong, Macao and Taiwan	21.55	8.56	31.15	35.69	33.94
五、国际旅游收入(亿元)	**Earning of International Tourism (100 millon yuan)**	**1.96**	**10.38**	**22.41**	**27.39**	**33.54**
#商品收入	Income from Mercantile	0.44	2.57	7.71	10.44	11.25
劳务收入	Income from Labour Service	1.52	7.81	14.70	16.95	22.29
六、旅游者在西安人均停留天数(天)	**Number of Days of Average Tourists Staying in Xi'an (day)**	**2.1**	**2.0**	**2.5**	**2.9**	**2.9**
七、旅游者在西安人均消费(元)	**Consumption of Average Tourists in Xi'an (yuan)**	**759**	**2511**	**3445**	**4212**	**4324**

注：1990年和1995年国际旅游者中含华侨。

Note:The international tourists included overseas Chinese in 1990 and 1995.

16-1 续表 continued

指　　标	Item	2006	2007	2008	2009	2010
一、利用外资签订协议项目(个)	**Number of Projects of Foreign Capital Used through the Signed Agreements and Contracts (unit)**	**190**	**135**	**100**	**65**	**82**
利用外资签订协议金额(万美元)	Value of Foreign Capital Used through the Signed Agreements and Contracts(USD 10 000)	182525	143978	118230	60027	119689
外商实际直接投资额(万美元)	Value of Foreign Direct Investment (USD 10 000)	82463	111567	114738	121872	156653
二、进出口总额(万美元)	**Total Imports and Exports (USD 10 000)**	**415403**	**536162**	**704029**	**724618**	**1039273**
#进口总额	Total Imports	142541	189029	256916	391504	507544
出口总额	Total Exports	272862	347133	447113	333114	531729
进出口差额	Balance of Imports and Exports	130321	158104	190197	-58391	24185
三、国际旅游人数总计(万人次)	**Total Number of International Tourists (10 000 person-times)**	**86.73**	**100.01**	**63.20**	**67.29**	**84.18**
#外国人	Foreigners	73.40	85.09	53.58	59.09	73.21
港澳台同胞	Chinese Compatriot From Hong Kong, Macao and Taiwan	13.33	14.92	9.62	8.20	10.97
四、国际旅游者人天数总计(万人天)	**Total Number of Days of International Tourists (10 000 person/day)**	**253.17**	**290.02**	**162.93**	**195.14**	**241.67**
#外国人	Foreigners	214.10	246.76	138.72	171.36	211.48
港澳台同胞	Chinese Compatriot From Hong Kong, Macao and Taiwan	39.07	43.26	24.21	23.78	30.19
五、国际旅游收入(亿元)	**Earning of International Tourism (100 millon yuan)**	**37.83**	**42.43**	**28.72**	**31.05**	**42.40**
#商品收入	Income from Mercantile	15.93	15.19	9.74	8.94	11.87
劳务收入	Income from Labour Service	21.90	27.24	18.98	22.11	30.53
六、旅游者在西安人均停留天数(天)	**Number of Days of Average Tourists Staying in Xi'an (day)**	**2.9**	**2.9**	**2.6**	**2.9**	**2.9**
七、旅游者在西安人均消费(元)	**Consumption of Average Tourists in Xi'an (yuan)**	**4353**	**4242**	**4544**	**4614**	**5037**

16-2 主要年份利用外资情况

Utilization of Foreign Capital In Representative Years

单位：万美元 (USD 10 000)

年 份 Year	利用外资签定协议金额 Value of Foreign Capital Used through the Signed Agreements and Contracts	外商实际直接投资额 Direct Foreign Investment
1983	3500	800
1984	8	
1985	8361	1106
1986	19919	4010
1987	3218	5552
1988	2423	6758
1989	1645	11632
1990	415	1154
1991	591	1094
1992	24165	5200
1993	57289	8996
1994	20321	15240
1995	28956	18653
1996	35978	20510
1997	27214	22057
1998	40034	22286
1999	40390	13801
2000	54123	15633
2001	60736	17687
2002	70692	20281
2003	96380	25557
2004	78312	27595
2005	121499	57113
2006	182525	82463
2007	143978	111567
2008	118230	114738
2009	60027	121872
2010	119689	156653

16-3 外国和港澳台地区在西安直接投资（2010年）

Direct Investments from Foreign Countries and Hong Kong, Macao and Taiwan in Xi'an（2010）

分类	Classity	新签协议情况 New-signed Agreement Circumstances		外商实际直接投资额（万美元） Value of Foreign Direct Investment (USD10 000)
		合同数(个) Number of Constracts (unit)	利用外资签订协议金额(万美元) Value of Foreign Captial Used through the Signed (USD10 000)	
合计	Total	82	119689.3	156653.3
一、按投资方式分	Grouped by Investment Mode			
1.中外合资经营企业	Joint-venture Enterprises	34	27708.8	32219.6
2.中外合作经营企业	Cooperation Enterprises	3	5936.6	13969.0
3.外资企业	Wholly Foreign-owned Enterprises	45	86043.9	108464.7
4.外资企业再投资	Re-investment from Foreign-funded Enterprises			
二、按国民经济行业分组	Grouped by Sector			
1.农林牧渔水利业	Agriculture,Forestry,Animal,Husbandy and Fishery	4	5300.3	160.0
2.制造业	Manufacturing	37	63316.4	63854.5
3.电力、煤气及水的生产和供应业	Production and Distribution of Electricity,Gas and Water			12569.2
4.建筑业	Construction			
5.交通运输、仓储及邮电通信业	Transporation,Storage,Postal and Telecommunications			320.0
6.批发和零售贸易、餐饮业	Wholesale, Retail Trads and Catering Services	3	42.1	4011.2
7.房地产业	Real Estate	9	41186.1	54536.5
8.社会服务业	Social Services	18	9283.7	18000.8
9.其他行业	Others	11	560.7	3201.1
三、按投资国别、地区分组	Grouped by Different Countries and Regions			
香港	Hong Kong	37	83428.8	92743.5
澳门	Macao			
台湾	Taiwan	5	90.7	89.7
日本	Japan	2	-363.3	2154.3
泰国	Tailand			
马来西亚	Malaysia	2	5.8	183.0
新加坡	Singapore	2	5554.2	10039.1
韩国	Korea			6.0
德国	Germany	3	560.1	32.5
意大利	Italy	1	0.4	24.7
法国	France	2	10.0	
英国	England	2	4399.7	3100.0
捷克	Czechoslovakia			
加拿大	Canada	1	540.0	5225.0
美国	America	6	6892.4	16288.6
澳大利亚	Australia	1	-393.6	39.5
维尔京群岛	Virgin Islands	6	11085.9	10055.1
其它	Others	12	7877.2	16672.3

16-4 各区县、开发区外商实际直接投资（2010年）

Direct Investment by Foreign Entrepreneurs by Region and Economic Zone（2010）

单位：万美元 （USD 10 000）

区县及开发区名称	Name of Region and Economic Zone	2009	2010
区县合计	**Sum of Region**	**29766**	**38855**
新城区	Xincheng	3740	4900
碑林区	Beilin	4780	5150
莲湖区	Lianhu	3953	5471
灞桥区	Baqiao	4300	5215
未央区	Weiyang	3902	5023
雁塔区	Yanta	4087	5488
阎良区	Yanliang	675	1208
临潼区	Lintong	970	1200
长安区	Chang'an	1219	1680
蓝田县	Lantian	605	950
周至县	Zhouzhi	315	550
户　县	Huxian	560	970
高陵县	Gaoling	660	1050
开发区合计	**Sum of Development Zones**	**92107**	**117798**
高新区	GaoXin	40613	51130
经开区	JingKai	33661	42608
曲江新区	Qujiang	12589	17187
浐灞生态区	Chanba Eco-District	2400	3070
航空基地	Aviation Industry Base	1016	1239
航天基地	Aerospace Base	1208	1554
国际港务区	International Trade&Logistic Park	620	1010

16-5 主要年份进出口总额

Total Imports and Exports In Representative Years

单位：万美元 (USD 10 000)

年份 Year	进出口总额 Total Imports and Exports	出口总额 Total Exports	进口总额 Total Imports
1987	13596	7540	6056
1988	36750	24632	12118
1989	32715	21564	11151
1990	38229	28290	9939
1991	55356	41511	13845
1992	70467	53060	17407
1993	93330	62393	30937
1994	104752	76897	27855
1995	137510	110163	27347
1996	143187	91745	51442
1997	150668	107753	42915
1998	180589	100492	80097
1999	172919	94495	78424
2000	173696	106062	67634
2001	169914	87948	81966
2002	186966	112479	74487
2003	230932	140327	90605
2004	309295	203539	105756
2005	390146	263441	126705
2006	415403	272862	142541
2007	536162	347133	189029
2008	704029	447113	256916
2009	724618	333114	391504
2010	1039273	531729	507544

16-6 外贸商品进出口总额分国别和地区（2010年）

Total Value of Imports and Exports by Country and Region（2010）

单位：万美元 (USD10 000)

国别和地区	Country and Region	进出口总额 Total Imports and Exports	出口 Exports
亚洲	**Asia**	**431531**	**221323**
#香港	Hong kong	50799	47271
台湾	Taiwan	51949	6506
日本	Japan	76704	38410
菲律宾	Phiilippines	6333	5126
马来西亚	Malaysia	8112	4998
韩国	Korea	35277	14063
非洲	**Africa**	**62686**	**57513**
#埃及	Egypt	3992	3992
突尼斯	Tunisia	300	298
埃塞俄比亚	Ethiopia	1482	1167
博茨瓦那	Botswana	26	26
南非	South Africa	6860	5315
欧洲	**Europe**	**254299**	**135684**
#德国	Germany	68062	29707
法国	France	17783	10779
意大利	Italy	15429	8404
荷兰	Netherland	21294	17373
英国	England	19093	13804
瑞士	Switzerland	6584	215
西班牙	Spain	8822	7788
俄罗斯联邦	Russia	8939	7746
拉丁美洲	**Latin America**	**63836**	**24200**
#哥伦比亚	Colombia	794	794
巴西	Brazil	12516	4176
阿根廷	Argentina	1264	1206
北美洲	**North America**	**202042**	**87774**
#加拿大	Canada	14517	4914
美国	America	187525	82860
大洋洲及太平洋岛屿	**Oceanic and Pacific Islands**	**24847**	**5223**
#澳大利亚	Australia	23920	4359
新西兰	New Zealand	469	436

16-7 主要商品分大类出口金额

Export Value of Major Merchandise by Type

单位：万美元 (USD 10 000)

商品分类	HS Section and Division	2000	2001	2002	2003
食用蔬菜、根及块茎	Edible Vegetables, Certain,Roots amd Tubers	1095	1957	1275	1379
蔬菜、水果、坚果或植物其它部分的制品	Vegetables, Fruits, Nuts, or Products Made of Other Parts of Plants	2076	2684	3470	4490
矿砂、矿渣及矿灰	Ores,Slags and Ash	4083	4649	8714	11224
无机化学品；贵金属、稀土金属、放射性元素及其同位素的有机及无机化合物	Inorganic Chemicals,Organic or Inorganic Compounds of Precious Metals,of Rare Earth Metals,of Radioactive Elements or of Isotopes	3714	4141	4141	5814
有机化学品	Organic Chemicals	2367	3279	4883	4757
羊毛、动物细毛或粗毛、马毛纱线及其机织物	Wool ,Fine or Coarse Animal Hair; Horsehair Yarn and Woven Fabric	810	829	1313	1600
棉花	Cotton	3197	2734	3826	3984
化学纤维短纤	Short Staple Chemical Fibers	5061	3612	2512	2120
针织或钩编的服装及衣着附件	Articles of Apparel and Clothing Accessories, Knitted or Crocheted	6753	1632	2660	341
非针织或非钩编的服装及衣着附件	Articles of Apparel and Clothing Accessories, not Knitted or Crocheted	7269	3319	3629	4981
其它纺织制成品；成套物品；旧衣着及旧纺织品	Other Made Up Textile Articles;Sets;Worn Clothing and Worn Textile Articles;Rags Articles	1649	1002	1432	2203
鞋靴、护腿和类似品及其零件	Footwear,Gaiters and The Like;Parts of Such Articles Headgear and Parts Thereof	1347	279	296	585
玻璃及其制品	Glass and Glassware	3376	3838	5542	6667
钢铁	Iron and Steel	3534	1197	2167	2779
钢铁制品	Articles of Iron or Steel	5535	6401	7414	8474
铅及制品	Lead Areticles Thereof	1371	1363	444	232
锌及制品	Zinc Areticles Thereof	4031	1945	1895	2200
其它贱金属、金属陶瓷及其制品	Other Base Metals,Germets;Areticles Thereof	1066	1704	1546	3150
贱金属工具、器具、利口器、餐匙、餐叉及其零件	Tools,Implements,Cutlery,Spons and Forks, of Base Metal;Parts Thereof of Base Metal	2933	2669	2613	3232
核反应堆、锅炉、机器、机械器具及其零件	Nuclear Reactors ,Boilers, Machinery and Mechanical Appliances; and Parts Thereof	10915	11979	16140	21281
电机、电气设备及其零件；录音机及放声机、电视图像、声音的录制和重放设备及其零件、附件	Electrical Machinery and Equipment and Parts Thereof;Sound Recorders and Repreducers, Television Image and Sound Recordes and Repreducers,and Parts and Accessories of Such Articles	8339	8696	8962	15106
光学、照相、电影、计量、检验、医疗或外科用仪器及设备、精密仪器及设备；上述物品的零件、附件	Optical,Photographic,Cinematographic,Measuring, Checking,Precision Medical or Surgical Instruments and Apparatus;Parts and Accessories Thereof	2020	2818	5395	3339
家具、寝具、褥垫、弹簧床垫、软床垫及类似的填充制品；未列名灯具及照明装置；发光标志、发光名牌及类似品；活动房屋	Mattresses,Mattress Supports,Cushions and Similar Stuffed Furnishings;Lamps and Lighting Fittings, not Elsewhere Spcified or Included;Illumihated Signs,Illuminated	2587	2150	2715	3994

16-7 续表1 continued 1

单位：万美元 (USD 10 000)

商品分类	HS Section and Division	2004	2005	2006	2007
食用蔬菜、根及块茎	Edible Vegetables, Certain,Roots amd Tubers	1386	1190	1136	1232
蔬菜、水果、坚果或植物其它部分的制品	Vegetables, Fruits, Nuts, or Products Made of Other Parts of Plants	7786	10531	15374	37426
矿砂、矿渣及矿灰	Ores,Slags and Ash	30590	63247	52046	47378
无机化学品；贵金属、稀土金属、放射性元素及其同位素的有机及无机化合物	Inorganic Chemicals,Organic or Inorganic Compounds of Precious Metals,of Rare Earth Metals,of Radioactive Elements or of Isotopes	5806	10997	10916	16508
有机化学品	Organic Chemicals	4837	8569	11923	11182
羊毛、动物细毛或粗毛、马毛纱线及其机织物	Wool ,Fine or Coarse Animal Hair; Horsehair Yarn and Woven Fabric	1640	903	1400	1065
棉花	Cotton	3133	3240	3808	3255
化学纤维短纤	Short Staple Chemical Fibers	1987	1471	1556	1767
针织或钩编的服装及衣着附件	Articles of Apparel and Clothing Accessories, Knitted or Crocheted	7465	5736	5332	5345
非针织或非钩编的服装及衣着附件	Articles of Apparel and Clothing Accessories, not Knitted or Crocheted	5543	5068	4078	3875
其它纺织制成品；成套物品；旧衣着及旧纺织品	Other Made Up Textile Articles;Sets;Worn Clothing and Worn Textile Articles;Rags Articles	2667	3000	3342	3090
鞋靴、护腿和类似品及其零件	Footwear,Gaiters and The Like;Parts of Such Articles Headgear and Parts Thereof	2687	1368	216	348
玻璃及其制品	Glass and Glassware	8083	8576	8272	6246
钢铁	Iron and Steel	5244	5314	4900	11366
钢铁制品	Articles of Iron or Steel	10398	13959	16903	17329
铅及制品	Lead Areticles Thereof	43	12	158	1650
锌及制品	Zinc Areticles Thereof	522	135	4119	2470
其它贱金属、金属陶瓷及其制品	Other Base Metals,Germets;Areticles Thereof	6419	11233	17695	23414
贱金属工具、器具、利口器、餐匙、餐叉及其零件	Tools,Implements,Cutlery,Spons and Forks, of Base Metal;Parts Thereof of Base Metal	3406	3052	3607	3917
核反应堆、锅炉、机器、机械器具及其零件	Nuclear Reactors ,Boilers, Machinery and Mechanical Appliances; and Parts Thereof	24696	30832	36174	47381
电机、电气设备及其零件；录音机及放声机、电视图像、声音的录制和重放设备及其零件、附件	Electrical Machinery and Equipment and Parts Thereof;Sound Recorders and Repreducers, Television Image and Sound Recordes and Repreducers,and Parts and Accessories of Such Articles	19812	23605	22801	33393
光学、照相、电影、计量、检验、医疗或外科用仪器及设备、精密仪器及设备；上述物品的零件、附件	Optical,Photographic,Cinematographic,Measuring, Checking,Precision Medical or Surgical Instruments and Apparatus;Parts and Accessories Thereof	1847	2341	3521	4230
家具、寝具、褥垫、弹簧床垫、软床垫及类似的填充制品；未列名灯具及照明装置；发光标志、发光名牌及类似品；活动房屋	Mattresses,Mattress Supports,Cushions and Similar Stuffed Furnishings;Lamps and Lighting Fittings, not Elsewhere Spcified or Included;Illumihated Signs,Illuminated	4955	4773	5086	8301

16-7 续表2 continued 2

单位：万美元 (USD 10 000)

商品分类	HS Section and Division	2008	2009	2010
食用蔬菜、根及块茎	Edible Vegetables, Certain,Roots amd Tubers	1374	803	4740
蔬菜、水果、坚果或植物其它部分的制品	Vegetables, Fruits, Nuts, or products made of other parts of plants	29270	21920	41289
矿砂、矿渣及矿灰	Ores,Slags and Ash	40502	6141	325
无机化学品；贵金属、稀土金属、放射性元素及其同位素的有机及无机化合物	Inorganic Chemicals,Organic or Inorganic Compounds of Precious Metals,of Rare Earth Metals,of Radioactive Elements or of Isotopes	15882	9774	24875
有机化学品	Organic Chemicals	13954	16294	982
羊毛、动物细毛或粗毛、马毛纱线及其机织物	Wool ,Fine or Coarse Animal Hair; Horsehair Yarn and Woven Fabric	720	460	10133
棉花	Cotton	3213	2346	98
化学纤维短纤	Short staple chemical fibers	1181	2217	479
针织或钩编的服装及衣着附件	Articles of Apparel and Clothing Accessories, Knitted or Crocheted	4371	3617	3209
非针织或非钩编的服装及衣着附件	Articles of Apparel and Clothing Accessories, not Knitted or Crocheted	3623	2919	3394
其它纺织制成品；成套物品；旧衣着及旧纺织品	Other Made Up Textile Articles;Sets;Worn Clothing and Worn Textile Articles;Rags Articles	3187	2813	544
鞋靴、护腿和类似品及其零件	Footwear,Gaiters and The Like;Parts of Such Articles Headgear and Parts Thereof	380	367	150
玻璃及其制品	Glass and Glassware	6538	5574	928
钢铁	Iron and Steel	11966	4254	18549
钢铁制品	Articles of Iron or Steel	26568	11943	5998
铅及制品	Lead Areticles Thereof	2	1	10
锌及制品	Zinc Areticles Thereof	46	78	28545
其它贱金属、金属陶瓷及其制品	Other Base Metals,Germets;Areticles Thereof	27576	11276	3556
贱金属工具、器具、利口器、餐匙、餐叉及其零件	Tools,Implements,Cutlery,Spons and Forks, of Base Metal;Parts Thereof of Base Metal	4083	2777	2893
核反应堆、锅炉、机器、机械器具及其零件	Nuclear Reactors ,Boilers, Machinery and Mechanical Appliances; and Parts Thereof	75911	52372	130296
电机、电气设备及其零件；录音机及放声机、电视图像、声音的录制和重放设备及其零件、附件	Electrical Machinery and Equipment and Parts Thereof;Sound Recorders and Repreducers, Television Image and Sound Recordes and Repreducers,and Parts and Accessories of Such Articles	56758	53355	136
光学、照相、电影、计量、检验、医疗或外科用仪器及设备、精密仪器及设备；上述物品的零件、附件	Optical,Photographic,Cinematographic,Measuring, Checking,Precision Medical or Surgical Instruments and Apparatus;Parts and Accessories Thereof	6348	5255	196
家具、寝具、褥垫、弹簧床垫、软床垫及类似的填充制品；未列名灯具及照明装置；发光标志、发光名牌及类似品；活动房屋	Mattresses,Mattress Supports,Cushions and Similar Stuffed Furnishings;Lamps and Lighting Fittings, not Elsewhere Spcified or Included;Illumihated Signs,Illuminated	8296	4769	5328

16-8 主要商品分大类进口金额

Import Value of Major Merchandise by Type

单位:万美元 (USD 10 000)

商品分类	HS Section and Division	2000	2003	2004	2005
无机化学品；贵金属、稀土金属、放射性元素及其同位素的有机及无机化合物	Inorganic Chemicals,Organic or Inorganic Compounds of Precious Metals,of Rare Earth Metals,of Radioactive Elements or of Isotopes	1467	4082	89	317
有机化学品	Organic Chemicals	7257	11852	14829	15237
塑料及其制品	Plastic and Articles Thereof	2559	2358	2560	4317
钢铁	Iron and Steel	2467	2086	1205	752
铜及制品	Copper and Articles Thereof	2367	1487	842	689
铝及制品	Aluminium and Articles Thereof	2652	1194	1634	3627
核反应堆、锅炉、机器、机械器具及其零件	Nuclear Reactors ,Boilers, Machinery and Mechanical Appliances; and Parts Thereof	12990	31100	37185	38050
电机、电气设备及其零件；录音机及放声机、电视图像、声音的录制和重放设备及其零件、附件	Electrical Machinery and Equipment and Parts Thereof;Sound Recorders and Repreducers, Television Image and Sound Recordes and Repreducers,and Parts and Accessories of Such Articles	5911	12200	16102	23337
车辆及其零件、附件，铁道及电车道车辆除外	Vehicles Other Than Railway or Tramway Rolling-Stock, and Rarts and Accessories Thereof	1530	2759	3291	1387
航空器、航天器及其零件	Aircraft,Spacecraft and Parts Thereof	10443	768	814	8800
光学、照相、电影、计量、检验、医疗或外科用仪器及设备、精密仪器及设备	Optical,Photographic,Cinematographic,Measuring, Checking,Precision Medical or Surgical	3673	8111	10358	10424

16-8 续表 continued

单位:万美元 (USD 10 000)

商品分类	HS Section and Division	2006	2007	2008	2009	2010
无机化学品；贵金属、稀土金属、放射性元素及其同位素的有机及无机化合物	Inorganic Chemicals,Organic or Inorganic Compounds of Precious Metals,of Rare Earth Metals,of Radioactive Elements or of Isotopes	709	1039	6001	5040	7513
有机化学品	Organic Chemicals	13521	14536	15692	14186	13949
塑料及其制品	Plastic and Articles Thereof	2889	5149	2553	3134	4091
钢铁	Iron and Steel	1014	1270	3888	2537	10949
铜及制品	Copper and Articles Thereof	8035	22683	11097	41195	43343
铝及制品	Aluminium and Articles Thereof	3172	3223	4767	6505	3116
核反应堆、锅炉、机器、机械器具及其零件	Nuclear Reactors ,Boilers, Machinery and Mechanical Appliances; and Parts Thereof	33065	55243	68504	87493	134753
电机、电气设备及其零件；录音机及放声机、电视图像、声音的录制和重放设备及其零件、附件	Electrical Machinery and Equipment and Parts Thereof;Sound Recorders and Repreducers, Television Image and Sound Recordes and Repreducers,and Parts and Accessories of Such Articles	21279	25164	48008	113034	207937
车辆及其零件、附件，铁道及电车道车辆除外	Vehicles Other Than Railway or Tramway Rolling-Stock, and Rarts and Accessories Thereof	1228	1529	3789	1798	3109
航空器、航天器及其零件	Aircraft,Spacecraft and Parts Thereof	17879	2463	26148	13057	3620
光学、照相、电影、计量、检验、医疗或外科用仪器及设备、精密仪器及设备	Optical,Photographic,Cinematographic,Measuring, Checking,Precision Medical or Surgical	12152	17026	17737	24210	37414

16-9 主要年份旅游人数及收入

Number of Tourists and Tourism Earnings In Representative Years

年 份 Year	接待旅游人数（万人次） Number of Tourists (10 000 person-times)	#国际人数旅游 Number of International Tourists	旅游总收入（万元） Total Tourism Earnings (10 000 yuan)	#国际旅游收入 Earning of International Tourists	国际旅游者在西安人均停留天数（天） Number of Days of Average International Tourists Staying in Xi'an(day)	国际旅游者在西安人均消费（元/人） Consumption of Average International Tourists in Xi'an (yuan/person)
1980	4.00	4.00	1757	1757	3.8	438.7
1981	6.71	6.71	2314	2314	3.4	345.2
1982	9.09	9.09	3172	3172	2.8	348.3
1983	12.38	12.38	3720	3720	2.5	300.6
1984	15.13	15.13	4579	4579	2.3	302.6
1985	21.15	21.15	7029	7029	2.2	332.3
1986	25.78	25.78	10886	10886	2.2	422.2
1987	30.15	30.15	16588	16588	2.1	550.3
1988	36.58	36.58	21152	21152	2.0	578.3
1989	21.20	21.20	14125	14125	1.9	666.2
1990	25.88	25.88	19628	19628	2.1	758.5
1991	31.00	31.00	29051	29051	2.3	936.9
1992	40.16	40.16	40966	40966	2.2	1020.2
1993	43.50	43.50	48951	48951	1.9	1125.2
1994	41.49	41.49	82000	82000	2.2	1975.9
1995	791.35	41.35	440000	103818	2.0	2510.8
1996	925.39	45.39	470000	149400	2.6	3291.8
1997	1010.53	48.53	510000	166359	2.6	3428.2
1998	1105.80	47.98	560000	160244	2.6	3393.8
1999	1260.40	55.41	830000	186282	2.5	3362.0
2000	1567.00	65.03	1050000	224100	2.5	3445.0
2001	1752.20	67.20	1130000	240700	2.4	3582.0
2002	1984.13	74.13	1310000	260000	2.2	3507.3
2003	1647.67	33.66	1064200	121200	2.5	3584.0
2004	2149.03	65.03	1544000	273900	2.9	4212.0
2005	2423.60	77.56	1785000	335380	2.9	4324.0
2006	2738.70	86.73	2043000	378270	2.9	4353.0
2007	3118.01	100.01	2372000	424263	2.9	4242.0
2008	3232.20	63.20	2435200	287200	2.6	4544.3
2009	3929.29	67.29	2974000	310500	2.9	4614.4
2010	5285.18	84.18	4051800	424000	2.9	5036.8

16-10 主要年份国际旅游收入

Earning of International Tourism In Representative Years

单位:万美元 (USD10 000)

项　目	Item	2000	2001	2002	2003	2004	2005	2006	2007	2008	2009	2010
合　计	**Total**	**27000**	**29002**	**32000**	**14600**	**33000**	**40900**	**46700**	**54323**	**35900**	**39000**	**53000**
一、长途交通费	**Long Distance Transportation**	**7047**	**7946**	**6816**	**3109**	**8415**	**12311**	**11442**	**14286**	**10016**	**12597**	**19292**
1.飞机	Airplane	6011	7395	5536	2526	7524	9407	9527	10918	7467	9438	15264
2.火车	Train	273	203	288	131	264	858	561	2009	1436	2262	2968
3.汽车	Highway	763	348	992	452	627	2046	1354	1359	1113	897	1060
二、游览	**Sightseeing**	**1296**	**1276**	**1120**	**511**	**1155**	**2045**	**2335**	**2335**	**1831**	**2262**	**3445**
三、住宿	**Accommodation**	**3051**	**3684**	**4480**	**2044**	**4752**	**4621**	**5977**	**6573**	**4523**	**5343**	**6572**
四、餐饮	**Food and Beverage**	**2673**	**3074**	**3264**	**1489**	**2673**	**3823**	**2195**	**3804**	**2908**	**3471**	**4929**
五、娱乐	**Entertainment**	**1512**	**1074**	**896**	**409**	**990**	**1779**	**747**	**1847**	**2046**	**1833**	**2120**
六、购物	**Shopping**	**6615**	**7047**	**9600**	**4380**	**9900**	**9897**	**17466**	**15645**	**9262**	**7761**	**9911**
七、邮电通讯	**Post and Communication Services**	**1350**	**899**	**1120**	**512**	**957**	**2454**	**1261**	**1794**	**1652**	**1131**	**1272**
八、市内交通	**Local Transportation**	**1566**	**899**	**768**	**350**	**726**	**858**	**841**	**1249**	**1041**	**975**	**2120**
九、其他	**Others**	**1890**	**3103**	**3936**	**1796**	**3432**	**3112**	**4436**	**6790**	**2621**	**3627**	**3339**

16-11 主要年份涉外星级宾馆接待海外旅游者情况

Mainly Concerning Oversea Tourists Reception in Star-rated

单位：人次 (person-time)

项　目	Item	2004	2005	2006	2007	2008	2009	2010
海外旅游者人数合计	**International Tourists**	**650325**	**775620**	**867273**	**1000063**	**632036**	**672909**	**841819**
外国人	Foreigners	527480	658578	733963	850905	535837	590870	732065
#日本	Japan	99614	75639	85708	93135	43017	60192	70368
菲律宾	Philippines	876	2165	1910	2162	1466	1708	2213
新加坡	Singapore	3990	6148	6395	7309	6335	7570	10158
美国	America	89499	116913	121788	146089	104742	100445	106042
加拿大	Canada	13132	16807	20075	29193	19047	21901	28409
英国	England	36279	45956	50046	56560	40299	43068	41023
法国	France	30837	49414	49113	58216	37415	39350	42337
德国	Germany	29051	37527	41446	50882	32892	36371	40166
意大利	Italy	7693	16909	16493	21444	9445	15316	15868
瑞士	Switzerland	2390	3748	4080	5047	3763	4479	5528
澳大利亚	Australia	19231	28645	30146	36581	24784	26349	30507
新西兰	New Zealand	2451	4522	3296	4978	4027	4238	5005
港澳和台湾同胞	Chinese Compatriots from Hong Kong,Macao and Taiwan	122845	117042	133310	149158	96199	82039	109754
#台湾同胞	Taiwan	64209	57958	66601	74962	44552	37464	54119

16-12 主要年份旅行社及A级景点

Statistics of Travel Agencies and Level-A Scenic Spots

项　目	Item	2005	2006	2007	2008	2009	2010
旅行社数（个）	Number of Travel Agencies (unit)	221	240	262	271	303	334
旅行社营业收入（万元）	Revenue of Travel Agencies (10000yuan)	178171	199843	264800	178500	213417	312229
旅游A级景点数（个）	Number of Level-A Scenic Spots(unit)	18	23	23	23	24	34
旅游A级景点年接待客人数（万人次）	Number of Tourists Received at Level-A Scenic Spots (10 000 person times)	9300	13140	14100	14200	15040	27262

主 要 统 计 指 标 解 释

进出口总额 海关进出口总额指实际进出我国国境的货物总金额。包括对外贸易实际进出口货物，来料加工装配进出口货物，国家间、联合国及国际组织无偿援助物资和赠送品，华侨、港澳台同胞和外籍华人捐赠品，租赁期满归承租人所有的租赁货物，进料加工进出口货物，边境地方贸易及边境地区小额贸易进出口货物（边民互市贸易除外），中外合资企业、中外合作经营企业、外商独资经营企业进出口货物和公用物品，到、离岸价格在规定限额以上的进出口货样和广告品（无商业价值、无使用价值和免费提供出口的除外），从保税仓库提取在中国境内销售的进口货物，以及其他进出口货物。进出口总额用以观察一个国家在对外贸易方面的总规模。我国规定出口货物按离岸价格统计，进口货物按到岸价格统计。

利用外资 指我国各级政府、部门、企业和其他经济组织通过对外借款、吸收外商直接投资以及用其他方式筹措的境外现汇、设备、技术等。

外商直接投资 指外国企业和经济组织或个人（包括华侨、港澳台胞以及我国在境外注册的企业）按我国有关政策、法规，用现汇、实物、技术等在我国境内开办外商独资企业、与我国境内的企业或经济组织共同举办中外合资经营企业、合作经营企业或合作开发资源的投资（包括外商投资收益的再投资），以及经政府有关部门批准的项目投资总额内企业从境外借入的资金。

旅游者人数

（1）入境国际旅游者人数：指来中国参观、访问、旅行、探亲、访友、休养、考察、参加会议和从事经济、科技、文化、教育、宗教等活动的外国人、华侨、港澳同胞和台湾同胞的人数。不包括外国在我国的常驻机构，如使领馆、通讯社、企业办事处的工作人员；来我国常住的外国专家、留学生以及在岸逗留不过夜人员。

（2）出境居民人数：指大陆居民因公务活动或私人事务短期出境的人数。公务活动出境居民人数包括在国际交通工具上的中国服务员工，因私出境居民人数不包括在国际交通工具上的中国服务员工。

（3）国内旅游者人数：指我国大陆居民和在我国常住1年以上的外国人、华侨、港澳台同胞离开常住地在境内其他地方的旅游设施内至少停留一夜，最长不超过6个月的人数。

国际旅游（外汇）收入 指入境旅游的外国人、华侨、港澳同胞和台湾同胞在中国大陆旅游过程中发生的一切旅游支出，对于国家来说就是国际旅游（外汇）收入。

国际旅行社 指经营对外招徕并接待外国人、华侨、港澳同胞和台湾同胞来中国、归国或回内地旅游业务的旅行社。

国内旅行社 指负责经营招徕、组团、接待国内旅客的旅游业务，以及不对外招徕，负责经营接待国际旅行社或其它涉外部门组织的外国人、华侨、港澳同胞和台湾同胞来中国、归国或回内地的旅游业务的旅行社。

Explanatory Notes on Main Statistical Indicators

Total Imports and Exports at Customs refer to the value of commodities imported into and exported from the boundary of China. They include the actual imports and exports through foreign trade, imported and exported goods under the processing and assembling trades and materials, supplies and gifts as aid given gratis between governments and by the United Nations and other international organizations, and contributions donated by overseas Chinese, compatriots in Hong Kong and Macao and Chinese with foreign citizenship, leasing commodities owned by tenant at the expiration of leasing period, the imported and exported commodities processed with imported materials, commodities trading in border areas (excluding mutual exchange goods), the imported and exported commodities and articles for public use of the Sino-foreign joint ventures, cooperative enterprises and ventures exclusively with foreign own investment. Also included are import or export of samples and advertising goods for whose CIF or FOB value are beyond the permitted ceiling (excluding goods of no trading or use value and free commodities for export), imported goods sold in China from bonded warehouses and other imported or exported goods. The indicator of the total imports and exports at customs can be used to observe the total size of external trade in a country. In accordance with the stipulation of the Chinese government, imports are calculated at CIF, while exports are calculated at FOB

Utilization of Foreign Capital refers to remittance, equipment and technology financed from abroad, by loans, foreign direct investment and other forms undertaken by the Chinese governments at all levels, by various departments, enterprises and other economic units.

Direct Investment by Foreign Entrepreneurs refers to the investments inside China by foreign enterprises and economic organizations or individuals (including overseas Chinese, compatriots from Hong Kong and Macao, and Chinese enterprises registered abroad), following the relevant policies and laws of China, for the establishment of ventures exclusively with foreign own investment, Sino-foreign joint ventures and cooperative enterprises or for co-operative exploration of resources with enterprises or economic organizations in China. It includes the re investment of the foreign entrepreneurs with the profits gained from the investment and the funds that enterprises borrow from abroad in the total investment of projects which are approved by the relevant department of the government.

Number of Tourists

(1) International tourists refer to foreigners, overseas Chinese, Chinese compatriots from Hong Kong, Macao and Taiwan coming to China for sight-seeing, visits, tours, family reunions, vacations, study tours, conferences and other activities of a business, scientific and technological, cultural, educational and religious nature. It does not include representatives and employees of resident institutions of foreign countries in China such as embassies, consulates, news agencies and offices of foreign companies and organizations, nor does it include long-term foreign experts or students residing in China, or persons in transition without spending a night in China.

(2) Chinese residents going abroad refer to Chinese residents going abroad for short terms for either public business or private purposes. Chinese employees working on international transport carriers are included in those going abroad for public business purpose, not in those for private purpose.

(3) Domestic tourists refer to residents of the mainland of China who stay for one night at least but no more than 6 months at tourist facilities in other places than their permanent residence within the territory of the mainland China, including foreigners, overseas Chinese and Chinese compatriots from Hong Kong, Macao and Taiwan who have resided in China for over one year.

Foreign Exchange Earnings from International Tourism refer to the total expenditures of foreigners, overseas Chinese, Chinese compatriots from Hong Kong, Macao and Taiwan during their stay in the mainland of China, which are earnings of foreign exchange from international tourism from the point of view from China.

International Travel Agencies refer to travel

agencies engaged in the promotion, solicitation, organization and reception of tours to the mainland of China by foreigners, overseas Chinese, Chinese compatriots from Hong Kong, Macao and Taiwan.

Domestic Travel Agencies refer to travel agencies engaged in the promotion, solicitation, organization and reception of domestic tourists, and in the reception of foreigners, overseas Chinese, Chinese compatriots from Hong Kong, Macao and Taiwan organized by international travel agencies or other departments concerned, without their own promotion and solicitation programmes.

17

金融业

FINANCIAL INTERMEDIATION

资料整理：刘 婷 张小文
Data management: Liu Ting Zhang Xiaowen

第十七部分 金融业

一、简要说明

本章资料包括金融、证券和保险业情况，由西安市统计局综合处根据省银监局、人民银行西安分行营业管理部、省证监局和省保监局提供资料整理。

二、主要指标

金融机构人民币（含外资）存款余额（亿元）	8933.23	比年初增加	1263.03亿元
金融机构人民币（含外资）贷款余额（亿元）	6482.28	比年初增加	1001.94亿元
金融机构现金收入（亿元）	10880.23	比上年增长	19.3%
金融机构现金支出（亿元）	10610.75	比上年增长	20.0%
保费收入（亿元）	162.27	比上年增长	32.9%

17 FINANCIAL INTERMEDIATION

Ⅰ.Brief Introduction

This chapter includes information of the financial, securities and insurance, compiled by Integration Division of the Xi'an Bureau of Statistics, according to data from Xi'an Branch Management Department of the People's Bank of China, Provincial Banking Bureau, Securities Supervisory Authority and Insurance Supervisory Authority.

Ⅱ.Major Indicators

		Increase over Preceding Year
Deposit in Financial Institution(100 mil. yuan)	8933.23	1263.03
Loans in Financial Institutions(100 mil. yuan)	6482.28	1001.94
Cash Income of Financial Institutions(100 mil. yuan)	10880.23	19.3%
Cash Expenditure of Financial Institutions(100 mil. yuan)	10610.75	20.0%
Premiums(100 mil. yuan)	162.27	32.9%

17-1 西安银行系统机构、人员数

Number of Institution and Employed Person in Finance System in Xi'an

机构名称	Name of Institution	2009		2010	
		机构数（个）Number of Institution (unit)	年末人数（人）Number of Staff and Workers (person)	机构数（个）Number of Institution (unit)	年末人数（人）Number of Staff and Workers (person)
合　计	**Total**	**935**	**22253**	**941**	**23413**
人民银行西安分行营业管理部	Management Department of the People's Bank of China Xi'an Branch	1	400	**1**	**401**
国家开发银行陕西省分行	National Development Bank Shaanxi Branch	1	159	1	162
进出口银行陕西省分行	Export Import Bank of Shaanxi Branch	1	57	1	58
农业发展银行陕西省分行	Agricultural Development Bank of China Shaanxi Branch	12	257	10	258
工商银行陕西省分行	Industrial and Commercial Bank of China Shaanxi Branch	194	4212	193	4974
农业银行陕西省分行	Agricultural Bank of China Shaanxi Branch	166	3055	165	3033
中国银行陕西省分行	Bank of China Shaanxi Branch	122	3106	120	3073
建设银行陕西省分行	Construction Bank of China Shaanxi Branch	174	3898	175	3694
中国光大银行西安分行	China Everbright Bank Xi'an Branch	14	431	16	499
华夏银行西安分行	China Huaxia Bank Xi'an Branch	8	243	9	290
招商银行西安分行	China Merchants Bank Xi'an Branch	22	957	23	981
浦发银行西安分行	Pufa Bank Xi'an Branch	9	350	11	480
民生银行西安分行	China Minsheng Banking Corp., Ltd Xi'an Branch	13	612	14	698
福建兴业银行西安分行	Fujian Industrial Bank Xi'an Branch	10	299	13	378
西安市商业银行	Xi'an City Commercial Bank	114	2286	114	2284
东亚银行西安分行	Dongya Bank Xi'an Branch	5	201	5	218
汇丰银行西安分行	Huifeng Bank Xi'an Branch	3	61	3	63
交通银行西安分行	Bank of Communication Xi'an Branch	50	1063	48	1066
中信实业银行西安分行	CITIC Industrial Bank Xi'an Branch	15	508	17	639
浙商银行西安分行	China Zheshang Bank Xi'an Branch	1	98	2	164

17-2 金融机构（含外资）本外币存贷款年末余额（2010年）

Financial institution Including Foreign-funded Balance of Bisic Currency and Foreign Currency at Year-end（2010）

单位：亿元 (100 million yuan)

指　　标	Item	2010	比年初增减数 Increase or decrease compared with the beginning of the Year
存款余额合计（汇率：6.6227）	**Total Deposit （Exchange Rate：6.6227）**	**9044.15**	**1270.52**
一、企事业单位存款	**Enterprise and Institution Deposit**	**3617.79**	**602.52**
1.活期存款	Demand Deposits	2660.13	369.50
2.定期存款	Time Deposits	957.65	233.02
二、储蓄存款	**Savings Deposits**	**3677.77**	**551.60**
1.活期储蓄	Current Saving	1453.60	337.00
2.定期储蓄	Time Saving	2224.17	214.60
三、信托存款	**Trusted Deposits**		
四、委托存款	**Consignment Deposits**	**74.00**	**-200.57**
五、其他存款	**Other Deposits**	**1674.59**	**316.97**
贷款余额合计（汇率：6.6227）	**Total Loans（Exchange Rate：6.6227）**	**6591.73**	**1030.93**
一、短期贷款	**Short-term Loans**	**1128.88**	**-165.22**
二、中长期贷款	**Medium-term and Long-term loans**	**5124.63**	**1310.28**
三、信托贷款	**Trusted Loans**		
四、委托贷款	**Consignment Loans**	**24.23**	**-40.76**
五、其他贷款	**Other Loans**	**32.82**	**4.89**
六、票据融资	**Bill Financing**	**280.59**	**-78.09**
七、各项垫款	**Various Advance Funds**	**0.57**	**-0.17**

17-3 金融机构（不含外资）本外币存贷款年末余额（2010年）

Domestic Funded Financial institution balance of Bisic Currency and Foreign Currency at Year-end（2010）

单位：亿元 (100 million yuan)

指　　标	Item	2010	比年初增减数 Increase or decrease compared with the beginning of the Year
存款余额合计（汇率：6.6227）	**Total Deposit（Exchange Rate：6.6227）**	**8971.10**	**1265.84**
一、企事业单位存款	**Enterprise and Institution Deposit**	**3562.82**	**601.89**
1.活期存款	Demand Deposits	2634.92	368.34
2.定期存款	Time Deposits	927.90	233.55
二、储蓄存款	**Savings Deposits**	**3660.76**	**547.50**
1.活期储蓄	Current Saving	1448.60	335.72
2.定期储蓄	Time Saving	2212.15	211.78
三、信托存款	**Trusted Deposits**		
四、委托存款	**Consignment Deposits**	**74.00**	**-200.57**
五、其他存款	**Other Deposits**	**1673.52**	**317.02**
贷款余额合计（汇率：6.6227）	**Total Loans（Exchange Rate：6.6227）**	**6526.66**	**1018.43**
一、短期贷款	**Short-term Loans**	**1117.10**	**-168.88**
二、中长期贷款	**Medium-term and Long-term loans**	**5072.11**	**1302.19**
三、信托贷款	**Trusted Loans**		
四、委托贷款	**Consignment Loans**	**24.23**	**-40.76**
五、其他贷款	**Other Loans**	**32.67**	**4.75**
六、票据融资	**Bill Financing**	**279.98**	**-78.70**
七、各项垫款	**Various Advance Funds**	**0.57**	**-0.17**

17-4 主要年份金融机构（含外资）人民币存款年末余额

Year-end Balance of Deposit in Financial Institutions Including Foreign-funded in Representative Years

单位：亿元 (100 million yuan)

年 份 Year	合 计 Total	其 中：Among 企业存款 Deposits of Enterprises	 储蓄存款 Savings Deposits
1978	12.82		3.72
1980	20.99		5.48
1985	40.68		16.70
1990	112.37	31.10	62.23
1995	359.51	114.54	230.63
1996	619.98	199.85	394.02
1997	602.50	227.61	358.78
1998	799.54	245.44	499.68
1999	1014.27	347.49	586.40
2000	1335.63	540.19	675.83
2001	1629.72	674.49	800.86
2002	2191.47	884.69	988.04
2003	2665.87	1041.43	1210.56
2004	3061.66	1159.98	1432.86
2005	3599.70	1237.37	1716.76
2006	4066.16	1374.91	1950.53
2007	4582.71	1702.12	2002.38
2008	5749.35	2213.67	2513.70
2009	7522.08	3077.99	3084.20
2010	8933.23	3556.78	3641.09

17-5 主要年份金融机构（含外资）人民币贷款年末余额

Year-end Balance of Loans in Financial Institutions Including Foreign-funded in Representative Years

单位：亿元 (100 million yuan)

年 份 Year	合 计 Total	其 中：Among	
		短期贷款 Short-term Loans	中长期贷款 Medium-term&Long-term Loans
1978	23.56		
1980	26.40		
1985	48.60		
1990	131.67	101.13	23.78
1995	334.50	252.30	73.32
1996	477.97	333.88	90.12
1997	443.76	342.79	87.27
1998	597.34	448.74	118.42
1999	786.20	589.52	150.64
2000	972.51	652.00	241.27
2001	1185.97	666.41	387.82
2002	1598.42	780.69	502.03
2003	1954.18	946.61	743.72
2004	2052.33	950.50	850.01
2005	2158.10	830.68	1013.32
2006	2344.77	812.33	1310.57
2007	2683.77	883.32	1593.37
2008	3275.12	1031.62	1905.08
2009	4482.63	1155.83	2908.75
2010	6482.28	1097.60	5075.98

17-6 金融机构（含外资）人民币存贷款年末余额（2010年）

Year-end Balance of Deposit and Loans in Financial Institutions Including Foreign-funded（2010）

单位：亿元 (100 million yuan)

指标	Item	2010	比年初增减数 Increase or decrease compared with the beginning of the Year
存款余额合计	**Total Deposit**	**8933.23**	**1263.03**
一、企业存款	**Deposits by Enterprses**	**3556.78**	**588.98**
1 .活期存款	Demand Deposits	2620.42	363.91
2 .定期存款	Time Deposits	936.36	225.07
二、财政存款	**Fiscal Deposits**	**52.49**	**-27.62**
三、机关团体存款	**Deposits of Government Departments and Organizations**	**934.29**	**166.59**
四、储蓄存款	**Savings Deposits**	**3641.09**	**555.99**
#定期储蓄	Time Savings	2198.37	218.82
五、农业存款	**Agricultural Deposits**	**196.88**	**65.75**
六、信托存款	**Credit Deposits**		
七、委托存款	**Trusted Deposits**	**73.76**	**-200.48**
八、其他存款	**Other Deposits**	**477.94**	**113.82**
贷款余额合计	**Total Loans**	**6482.28**	**1001.94**
一、短期贷款	**Short-term Loans**	**1097.62**	**-180.67**
1.个人贷款及透支	Individual Loans and Overdrafts	76.96	32.64
2.单位贷款及透支	Unit Loans and Overdrafts	973.70	-226.55
3.普通并购贷款	Ordinary Merging Loans		
4.银团贷款	Syndicated Loans	11.02	-2.58
5.贸易融资	Trade Finance	35.94	15.83
二、中长期贷款	**Medium-term&Long-term Loans**	5075.98	1301.40
1.个人贷款	Individual Loans and Overdrafts	1006.74	358.35
2.单位贷款	Unit Loans and Overdrafts	3500.93	740.41
3.普通并购贷款	Ordinary Merging Loans	5.60	
4.银团贷款	Syndicated Loans	**561.90**	**202.85**
5.贸易融资	Trade Finance	**0.81**	**-0.21**
三、信托贷款	**Credit Loans**		
四、融资租赁	**Financial Leasing**	**3.28**	**-1.45**
五、委托贷款	**Trusted Loans**	**24.23**	**-40.76**
六、票据融资	**Bill Financing**	280.60	-76.41
七、各项垫款	**Various Advance Funds**	0.57	-0.17

17-7 金融机构（不含外资）人民币存贷款年末余额（2010年）

Year-end Balance of Deposit and Loans in Financial Institutions Not Including Foreign-funded（2010）

单位：亿元 (100 million yuan)

指　　标	Item	2010	比年初增减数 Increase or decrease compared with the beginning of the Year
存款余额合计	**Total Deposit**	**8863.36**	**1257.53**
一、企业存款	**Deposits by Enterprses**	**3503.24**	**587.89**
1 .活期存款	Demand Deposits	2596.57	362.26
2 .定期存款	Time Deposits	906.67	225.63
二、财政存款	**Fiscal Deposits**	**52.50**	**-27.61**
三、机关团体存款	**Deposits of Government Departments and Organizations**	**934.29**	**166.59**
四、储蓄存款	**Savings Deposits**	**3625.12**	**551.80**
#定期储蓄	Time Savings	2187.02	215.90
五、农业存款	**Agricultural Deposits**	**196.88**	**65.75**
六、信托存款	**Credit Deposits**		
七、委托存款	**Trusted Deposits**	**73.76**	**-200.48**
八、其他存款	**Other Deposits**	**477.57**	**113.59**
贷款余额合计	**Total Loans**	**6420.72**	**986.51**
一、短期贷款	**Short-term Loans**	**1087.25**	**-186.93**
1.个人贷款及透支	Individual Loans and Overdrafts	76.48	32.41
2.单位贷款及透支	Unit Loans and Overdrafts	963.81	-232.58
3.普通并购贷款	Ordinary Merging Loans		
4.银团贷款	Syndicated Loans	11.02	-2.58
5.贸易融资	Trade Finance	35.94	15.83
二、中长期贷款	**Medium-term&Long-term Loans**	5025.41	1292.84
1.个人贷款	Individual Loans and Overdrafts	1000.84	355.82
2.单位贷款	Unit Loans and Overdrafts	3456.26	734.38
3.普通并购贷款	Ordinary Merging Loans	5.60	
4.银团贷款	Syndicated Loans	561.90	202.85
5.贸易融资	Trade Finance	**0.81**	**-0.21**
三、信托贷款	**Credit Loans**		
四、融资租赁	**Financial Leasing**	3.28	-1.45
五、委托贷款	**Trusted Loans**	24.23	-40.76
六、票据融资	**Bill Financing**	279.98	-77.02
七、各项垫款	**Various Advance Funds**	**0.57**	**-0.17**

17-8 金融机构现金收入、支出（2010年）

Cash Income and Expenditure of Domestic Funded Financial Institutions（2010）

单位：亿元 (100 million yuan)

指　标	Item	2010	比去年增减（%） Increase or down over Preceding Year (%)
现金收入合计	**Total Cash Income**	**10880.23**	**19.3**
一、商品销售收入	**Income from Commodity Sales**	**944.00**	**20.0**
二、服务业收入	**Income from Service Trade**	**321.01**	**9.4**
三、行政税费收入	**The Tax and Fee Income**	**70.96**	**8.6**
四、城乡个体经营收入	**Income from Urban and Rural Individual Business**	**296.54**	**40.1**
五、储蓄存款收入	**Income from Savings Deposits**	**8175.88**	**19.0**
六、其他金融性公司收入	**Income from Other Financial Institutions**	**36.42**	**12.6**
七、居民归还贷款收入	**Income from Repayment of Loans by Residents**	**60.15**	**24.2**
八、汇兑收入	**Income from Remittances**	**75.25**	**-0.5**
九、有价证券及其他投资性收入	**Income from Securities and Other Investment**	**6.72**	**-14.2**
十、其他收入	**Other Income**	**893.30**	**22.8**
现金支出合计	**Total Cash Expenditure**	**10610.75**	**20.0**
一、工资性及个人其他支出	**Wages and Other Personal Expenses**	**373.91**	**7.5**
二、农副产品采购支出	**Purchases of Agricultural and Sideline Products**	**105.89**	**4.7**
三、工矿及其他产品采购支出	**Expenditure for Purchases of Individual Business**	**82.41**	**14.7**
四、行政企业管理与经营费支出	**Expenditure for Administration Overhead and Management**	**606.81**	**24.7**
五、城乡个体经营支出	**Expenditure for Individual Business**	**407.17**	**36.7**
六、储蓄存款支出	**Expenditure for Savings Deposits**	**8239.04**	**20.1**
七、其他金融性公司支出	**Expenditure for Other Financial Companies**	**11.96**	**21.3**
八、居民提取贷款支出	**Expenditure for Loans by Residents**	**28.77**	**8.5**
九、汇兑支出	**Expenditure for Remittances**	**52.09**	**3.7**
十、有价证券支出	**Expenditure for Securities**	**8.75**	**-21.5**
十一、其他支出	**Other Expenditure**	**693.95**	**19.3**
投放（+）回笼（-）	**Currency Issue(+)cash withdrawn(-)**	**-269.48**	**-3.3**

17-9 保险业务情况

Indicators of Insurance Business

指　　标	Item	2009	2010
保险金额（亿元）	**Amount Insured(100 million yuan)**	**18999.6**	**30066.8**
保费收入（万元）	**Premiums(10 000 yuan)**	**1221132.7**	**1622663.2**
一、财产险	**Property Insurance**	**258976.3**	**380865.3**
（一）财产保险	Property Insurance	249582.3	367459.6
1.机动车辆及第三者责任	Motor Vehicle and Outside Person Liability	211182.1	318477.1
2.企业财产险	Enterprise Property Insurance	18826.6	29529.7
3.货物运输保险	Freight Transport Insurance	3443.2	3979.6
4.家庭财产保险	Family Property Insurance	448.4	183.7
5.建工及安工保险及其责任险	Construction and Installation Projects Insurance and Related Libility Insurance	13330.8	13832.3
6.其他	Others	2351.2	1457.2
（二）责任保险	Liability Insurance	4313.4	7051.1
（三）信用保险	Export Credit Insurance	3896.1	3528.5
（四）保证保险	Guarantee Insurance	-444.9	2274.5
（五）农业保险	Agriculture Insurance	1629.3	551.6
二、人身险	**Personnel Insurance**	**962156.5**	**1241797.9**
（一）人寿保险	Life Insurance	852259.0	1128004.2
1.普通寿险	Ordinary Life Insurance	89159.3	89818.5
2.分红保险	Dividend Insurance	624794.8	829050.2
3.投资连接保险	Insurance Connection Insurance	7252.6	6408.1
4.万能保险	Universal Insurance	131052.4	202727.5
（二）意外伤害保险	Unforeseen Injury Insurance	23189.7	29263.5
（三）健康保险	Health Insurance	86707.7	84530.1
赔款支出和各项给付（万元）	**Indemnity and Other Expenditure(10 000 yuan)**	**251562.6**	**288003.4**
一、财产险	**Property Insurance**	**126091.3**	**153215.7**
（一）财产保险	Property Insurance	120205.7	147530.1
1.机动车辆及第三者责任	Motor Vehicle and Outside Person Liability	99329.9	126677.7
2.企业财产险	Enterprise Property Insurance	15177.0	15157.4
3.家庭财产保险	Freight Transport Insurance	78.3	121.1
4.货物运输保险	Family Property Insurance	1548.8	987.6
5.建工及安工保险及其责任险	Construction and Installation Projects Insurance and Related Libility Insurance	2869.1	4367.1
6.其他	Others	1202.7	219.1
（二）责任保险	Liability Insurance	1247.7	2338.5
（三）信用保险	Export Credit Insurance	868.7	1159.9
（四）保证保险	Guarantee Insurance	2053.0	196.6
（五）农业保险	Agriculture Insurance	1716.1	1990.6
二、人身险	**Personnel Insurance**	**125471.3**	**134787.7**
（一）人寿保险	Life Insurance	101989.5	102038.3
1.普通寿险	Ordinary Life Insurance	28996.4	34054.2
2.分红保险	Dividend Insurance	59740.4	65941.4
3.投资连接保险	Insurance Connection Insurance	51.7	345.7
4.万能保险	Universal Insurance	13200.9	1697.0
（二）意外伤害保险	Unforeseen Injury Insurance	5531.8	7570.1
（三）健康保险	Health Insurance	17950.0	25179.4
退保金（万元）	**Withdrawal(10 000 yuan)**	**129091.2**	**127115.1**
#人寿保险	Life Insurance	120209.0	115558.6
1.普通寿险	Ordinary Life Insurance	7310.9	4296.7
2.分红保险	Dividend Insurance	72283.0	62175.5
3.投资连接保险	Insurance Connection Insurance	26520.0	14501.3
4.万能保险	Universal Insurance	14095.1	34585.1

17-10 西安证券期货系统机构、人员数（2010年）

Number of Institution and Employed Person in Securities and Futures System in Xi'an（2010）

机 构 名 称	Name of Institution	机构数（个）Number of Institution (unit)	年末人数（人）Number of Staff and Workers (person)
证券经营机构	**Securities Company and the Sales Department**		
一、证券公司及营业部	**Securities Company**	**23**	**924**
西部证券股份有限公司及营业部	Western Securities Company Ltd.	17	770
陕西开源证券经纪有限责任公司及营业部	Shaanxi KaiYuan Securities Company Ltd.	3	79
西安华弘证券经纪有限责任公司及营业部	Xi□An HuaHong Securities Company Ltd.	3	75
二、证券营业部	**Sales Department**	**65**	**2806**
期货经纪机构	**Futures Company**	**3**	**247**
迈科期货经纪有限公司	Maike Futures Company Ltd.	1	108
陕西长安期货经纪有限公司	Shaanxi ChangAn Futures Company Ltd.	1	47
西部期货经纪有限公司	Western Futures Brokerage Co., Ltd.	1	92

注：1.证券公司及营业部包括三家证券公司在西安和外地的营业部。
2.证券营业部包含外地证券公司在西安的营业部。

Note:1.Securities companies and departments include departments in and out of Xi'an of the three securities companies.
2.Securities departments include Xi'an departments of nonlocal companies.

17-11 证券期货市场基本情况（2010年）

Basic Facts on Securities and Futures Markets（2010）

指 标	Item	2010
一、上市证券公司情况	**Listed Securities Companies**	
拥有上市股份公司（个）	Number of Listed Share-holding Companies(unit)	27
占全国比重（%）	Percentage to National Total(%)	1.32
上市股份公司总股本（亿股）	Total Capital of Listed Share-holding Companies (100 millon shares)	180.12
#流通股（亿股）	Negotiable Shares(100 million shares)	85.95
总市值（亿元）	Total Market Capitalization(100 million yuan)	2668.13
累计证券市场筹措资金（亿元）	Accumulated Capital Raised by Securities Markets(100 millon yuan)	503.51
二、证券经营机构情况	**Securities Trading Organizations**	
拥有证券公司（个）	Number of Securities Companies(unit)	3
证券营业部(含外地公司在西安营业部）（个）	Number of Securities Business Departments(unit)	65
投资者开户数（万户）	Number of Investors Who have Opened an Account(10 000 accounts)	152.25
证券交易总额（亿元）	Total Turnover(100 million yuan)	12105.51
三、期货市场情况	**Futures Market**	
拥有期货经纪公司（个）	Number of Futures Business Management Companies(unit)	3
期货营业部（个）	Number of Futures Business Departments(unit)	13
期货代理交易额（亿元）	Total Transaction Value in Futures Commissioning (100 million yuan)	46114.55
每个经纪公司平均拥有注册资金（万元）	Average Registered Capital of Each Business Management Company(10 000 yuan)	7666.7

主要统计指标解释

信贷资金 指金融机构以信用方式积聚和分配的货币资金。金融机构信贷资金的来源有各项存款、对国际金融机构负债、流通中货币、银行自有资金及当年结益等;信贷资金的运用有各项贷款、黄金占款、外汇占款、财政借款及在国际金融机构中的资产等。

存款 指企业、机关、团体或居民根据资金必须收回的原则，把货币资金存入银行或其他信用机构保管并取得一定利息的一种信用活动形式。根据存款对象的不同可划分为企业存款、财政存款、机关团体存款、基本建设存款、城镇储蓄存款、农村存款等科目。它是银行信贷资金的主要来源。

贷款 指银行或其他信用机构根据资金必须归还的原则，按一定利率，为企业、个人等提供资金的一种信用活动形式。我国银行贷款分为流动资金贷款、固定资产贷款、城乡个体工商户贷款以及农业贷款等科目。

保险金额 指保险人承担赔偿或者给付保险金责任的最高限额。

保费 指投保人为取得保险人在约定范围内所承担赔偿责任而支付给保险人的费用。

赔款 指保险人根据保险合同的规定，向被保险人支付的赔偿保险责任损失的金额。

给付 包括死伤医疗给付和满期给付。死伤医疗给付是指保险人根据人寿保险及长期健康保险合同的规定，因被保险人在保险期内发生保险责任范围内的保险事故支付给被保险人（或受益人）的金额。满期给付是指被保险人生存期满，保险人按人寿保险合同规定支付给被保险人的满期保险金额。

Explanatory Notes on Main Statistical Indicators

Credit Funds refer to the funds issued as loans by banking institutions. The sources of credit funds of the banking institutions included deposits, liabilities to international financial institutions, currency in circulation, self-owned funds and current retained profits, etc. The credit funds can be used in forms of loans, gold, foreign exchange, government debt and assets in the international financial institutions.

Deposit is a form of credit by which enterprises, institutions, organizations or households can put money into banks and other credit institutions for safekeeping and interest earning under the principle of free withdrawal. According to different depositors, deposits are divided into enterprise deposits, treasury deposits, deposits of government agencies and organizations, capital construction deposits, urban savings deposits, rural deposits and other deposits. Deposits are major sources of the credit funds of banks.

Loan is a form of credit by which banks and other credit institutions provide funds at certain interest rate to enterprises and individuals in the light of the principle of unconditional repayment. Loans from Chinese banks include circulating capital loans, fixed assets loans, loans to urban and rural individuals engaged in industrial and commercial business and agricultural loans.

Amount Insured refers to the maximum that the insurant will get for the claim of the case insured.

Premium is the fee paid by the insurant to the insurer to obtain the obligation of compensation from the insurance within the agreed terms.

Settled Claim is the compensation paid by the insurer to the insurant in accordance with the insurance contract.

Payment includes payment for death, injury or medical treatment and mature payment. Payment for death, injury or medical treatment refers to the money paid to the insurant (or the beneficiary) in accordance with the life orhealth insurance contract when the insurant encounters accidents within the insured period covered in the contract. Mature payment refers to the mature payment to the insurant in accordance with the life insurance contract at the end of the insured period.

18 教育和科技

EDUCATION,SCIENCE AND TECHNOLOGY

资料整理：陈超毅　蔺秀玲

Data management:Chen Chaoyi Lin Xiuling

第十八部分　教育和科技

一、简要说明

本章资料包括教育事业、科技事业基本情况，由西安市统计局社会科技处根据西安市教委等有关部门提供资料整理。

二、主要指标

普通高等学校数（所）	50	比上年增加　1所
普通高等学校（本专科）在校学生（万人）	65.74	比上年增长　4.0%
研究生人数（万人）	7.70	比上年增长　6.4%

18　EDUCATION,SCIENCE AND TECHNOLOGY

Ⅰ.Brief Introduction

Data in this chapter consists of primarily data of educational undertakings, science and technology Activities of Xi'an city, compiled by Social & Science and Technology Division of the Xi'an Bureau of Statistics according to data from Xi'an Municipal Government Departments concerned.

Ⅱ.Major Indicators

		Increase over Preceding Year
Number of Schools Regular Institutions of Higher Education(unit)	50	1
Student Enrollment of Regular Institutions of Higher Education(10 000 persons)	65.74	4.0%
Postgraduates(10 000 persons)	7.70	6.4%

18-1 主要年份各类普通教育基本情况

Basic Statistics on Regular Eduction in Representative Years

指　　标	Item	2000	2005	2006	2007	2008	2009	2010
学校数(所)	**Number of Schools (unit)**							
普通高等教育	Regular Institutions of Higher Education	25	44	47	48	48	49	50
中等学校	Secondary Schools	671	648	660	648	637	678	660
#专业学校	Specialized Secondary Schools	47	32	31	30	29	28	28
普通中学	Regular Secondary Schools	466	460	457	453	442	439	436
小学	Primary Schools	2323	1980	1929	1872	1781	1666	1531
幼儿园	Kindergartens	367	737	863	830	905	896	1004
毕业生数(万人)	**Graduates (10 000 persons)**							
普通高等教育	Regular Institutions of Higher Education	3.03	11.12	13.01	15.84	17.55	16.90	18.25
中等学校	Secondary Schools	15.09	23.26	23.00	23.70	24.67	25.67	25.30
#专业学校	Specialized Secondary Schools	1.63	1.44	1.84	2.03	2.58	2.70	2.50
普通中学	Regular Secondary Schools	12.01	18.82	18.04	18.37	17.99	17.80	17.00
小学	Primary Schools	13.83	11.92	11.53	11.38	10.58	9.96	9.60
招生数(万人)	**New Enrollment (10 000 persons)**							
普通高等教育	Regular Institutions of Higher Education	7.49	16.54	17.06	18.98	21.46	21.28	21.70
中等学校	Secondary Schools	21.58	25.87	26.83	27.93	27.75	28.33	26.30
#专业学校	Specialized Secondary Schools	1.90	2.26	2.61	2.91	2.55	2.15	2.10
普通中学	Regular Secondary Schools	17.88	18.53	18.61	17.96	17.16	16.57	16.20
小学	Primary Schools	11.51	8.47	9.16	8.67	8.33	7.84	8.60
幼儿园	Kindergartens	8.71	6.57	6.87	6.67	7.68	7.20	8.40
在校学生(万人)	**Total Enrollment (10 000 persons)**							
普通高等教育	Regular Institutions of Higher Education	19.41	53.06	57.10	62.31	66.68	70.31	73.30
中等学校	Secondary Schools	58.75	72.81	76.70	77.20	78.39	80.66	77.90
#专业学校	Specialized Secondary Schools	6.02	6.16	7.30	7.97	8.06	7.44	6.80
普通中学	Regular Secondary Schools	48.31	55.74	56.11	54.68	52.83	50.63	48.90
小学	Primary Schools	77.81	60.47	59.33	56.83	54.66	52.52	51.60
幼儿园	Kindergartens	12.85	12.75	13.38	14.11	15.46	16.30	18.40
教职工（人）	**Staff and Teachers (person)**							
普通高等教育	Regular Institutions of Higher Education	38067	57285	61414	65624	69048	70818	72247
中等学校	Secondary Schools	48194	52674	53722	53462	56059	57477	57773
#专业学校	Specialized Secondary Schools	6964	3924	3621	3548	3417	2965	3249
普通中学	Regular Secondary Schools	34385	39456	39341	39171	39088	39002	39207
小学	Primary Schools	35336	33907	34460	34901	34653	34389	34118
幼儿园	Kindergartens	6346	10528	12335	13468	14932	15928	18710
专任教师(人)	**Number of Full-time Teachers (person)**							
普通高等教育	Regular Institutions of Higher Education	15679	29498	32891	36717	38926	40605	42098
中等学校	Secondary Schools	32923	39416	37399	38613	41321	44137	43822
#专业学校	Specialized Secondary Schools	3172	2130	2014	2011	1904	1720	1845
普通中学	Regular Secondary Schools	26230	31094	31203	31373	31425	31415	31506
小学	Primary Schools	30215	29674	30018	30533	30382	30334	29944
幼儿园	Kindergartens	2995	5959	7106	7951	8704	9240	10638

注：幼儿园中包括学前班；普通高等教育含高校研究生。

Note:'Kindergartens' here including units providing pre-school education;Regular institution of higher education includes postgraduates .

18-2 各级普通教育基本情况（2010年）

Basic Facts on Regular Education by School Type（2010）

指　标	Item	学校数（所） Number of Schools (unit)	毕业生数(人) Number of Graduates (person)	招生数(人) New Enrollment (person)
一、研究生	**Postgraduates**	**(46)**	**19526**	**25971**
1.普通高校	Regular Institutions of Higher Education	(20)	19129	25477
2.科研机构	Scientific Research Institution	(26)	397	494
二、普通高等学校	**Regular Institutions of Higher Education**	**50**	**163332**	**191558**
三、普通中等学校	**Regular Institutions of Secondary Schools**	**660**	**253390**	**263395**
1.中等专业学校	Specialized Secondary Schools	28	24453	20813
2.普通中学	Regular Secondary Schools	436	170135	161510
3.技工学校	Technical Schools	111	40677	51007
4.职业高中	Vocational Middle Schools	84	18100	30042
5.工读学校	Reformatory Schools	1	25	23
四、小学	**Primary Schools**	**1531**	**96077**	**86393**
五、特殊教育学校	**Special Education Schools**	**8**	**214**	**402**
六、幼儿园及学前班	**Kindergartens**	**1004**	**53860**	**83947**

注：（）为含研究生教育的普通高等学校和科研机构数。

Note:Institutions of regular higher education and scientific research which contain post-graduate education.

18-2 **续表** continued

指　标	Item	在校学生数(人) Total Enrollment (person)	教职工数(人) Number of Staff and Teachers(person)	专任教师 Full-time Teachers
一、研究生	**Postgraduates**	**76993**		
1.普通高校	Regular Institutions of Higher Education	75483		
2.科研机构	Scientific Research Institution	1510		
二、普通高等学校	**Regular Institutions of Higher Education**	**657357**	**72247**	**42098**
三、普通中等学校	**Regular Institutions of Secondary Schools**	**778946**	**57773**	**43822**
1.中等专业学校	Specialized Secondary Schools	67525	3249	1845
2.普通中学	Regular Secondary Schools	488925	39207	31506
3.技工学校	Technical Schools	144166	10051	7266
4.职业高中	Vocational Middle Schools	78244	5222	3178
5.工读学校	Reformatory Schools	86	44	27
四、小学	**Primary Schools**	**515628**	**34118**	**29944**
五、特殊教育学校	**Special Education Schools**	**1529**	**340**	**235**
六、幼儿园及学前班	**Kindergartens**	**183621**	**18710**	**10638**

18-3 主要年份普通高等教育基本情况

Basic Statistics on Regular Institutions in Representative Years

年 份 Year	学校数(所) Number of Schools (unit)	毕业生数(万人) Number of Graduates (10 000 persons)	招生数(万人) New Enrollment (10 000 persons)	在校学生数(万人) Total Enrollment (10 000 persons)	教职工数(万人) Number of Staff and Teachers (10 000 persons)	专任教师 Full-time Teachers
1978	21			2.88		0.87
1980	25			4.17		0.97
1985	28			6.49		1.28
1990	31	2.17	2.15	8.02	4.15	1.56
1995	32	3.04	3.40	10.87	4.21	1.59
1998	29	2.84	3.69	12.66	3.91	1.50
1999	29	3.13	5.62	15.09	3.95	1.52
2000	25	3.03	7.49	19.41	3.80	1.57
2001	32	3.69	9.24	25.49	4.30	1.75
2002	35	4.23	11.88	33.00	4.67	2.06
2003	37	6.49	13.65	40.12	4.92	2.21
2004	41	7.66	13.17	40.29	5.45	2.69
2005	44	10.08	14.68	47.79	5.73	2.95
2006	47	11.75	15.15	51.40	6.14	3.29
2007	48	14.33	16.96	56.03	6.56	3.67
2008	48	15.82	19.31	60.10	6.90	3.89
2009	49	15.04	18.84	63.22	7.08	4.06
2010	50	16.33	19.16	65.74	7.22	4.21

注：本表不含研究生。

Note:Graduate students educatedare not included.

18-4 主要年份研究生情况

Basic Situation of the major Year on Post-graduates in Representative Years

单位：人 (person)

年 份 Year	毕业生数 Graduates	高等学校 Institution of Higher Education	招生数 New Enrollment	高等学校 Institution of Higher Education	在校人数 Total Enrollment	高等学校 Institution of Higher Education
1978						
1980					651	651
1985					4799	4799
1990	2051	2051	1662	1662	5275	5275
1995	1769	1769	2712	2712	7974	7974
1998	2316	2316	3888	3888	10833	10833
1999	2903	2903	5020	5020	12986	12986
2000	3236	3236	6924	6924	16620	16620
2001	3881	3770	9274	8966	22564	21855
2002	4103	3952	11282	10882	28446	27471
2003	5971	5765	14322	13882	36936	35790
2004	8384	8127	17310	16871	45402	44169
2005	10416	10127	18583	18106	52699	51310
2006	12914	12552	19581	19105	58433	56951
2007	15506	15124	20570	20167	64137	62801
2008	17234	16788	21892	21443	67296	65834
2009	19025	18574	24879	24400	72366	70908
2010	19526	19129	25971	25477	76993	75483

注：2000年以前不含科研机构研究生。

Note:Graduate students educated in scientific research institutions are not included in the data before 2000.

18-5 普通高等学校分学校研究生（2010年）

Post-graduates in Regular Institutions of Higher Education（2010）

单位：人 （person）

校 名	毕业生 Graduates	招 生 New Enrollment	在校学生 Total Enrollment	博 士 Doctor	硕 士 Master	毕业班学生数 Number of Students in Graduate-class
西安交通大学	3292	4195	12829	3675	9154	4556
陕西师范大学	1647	2515	7252	798	6454	2598
西北工业大学	2574	2903	9503	3003	6500	3904
西安理工大学	1379	1644	4587	435	4152	1359
西安电子科技大学	2363	3332	9823	1702	8121	3543
西安工业大学	433	520	1838		1838	600
西安建筑科技大学	1354	1770	5465	825	4640	2013
西安科技大学	647	788	2235	193	2042	736
西安石油大学	281	465	1185		1185	327
长安大学	1508	1983	5972	896	5076	2125
西安工程大学	289	556	1442	11	1431	381
西北政法大学	659	781	2366		2366	801
西安体育学院	117	221	563		563	140
西北大学	1646	2029	6027	782	5245	2005
西安外国语大学	291	503	1253		1253	348
西安音乐学院	62	96	244		244	69
西安美术学院	93	128	341	45	296	107
西安邮电学院	63	305	578		578	105
陕西科技大学	396	530	1617	95	1522	581
西安财经学院	35	213	363		363	57

18-6 全市普通高等学校分学校情况（2010年）

Basic Facts on Regular Higher Education by Unit（2010）

单位：人 （person）

校　　名 Name of Schools	在校学生数 Total Enrollment 合计 Total	本科 Regular College	专科 Junior College	教职工 Staff and Teachers 合计 Total	#专任教师 Full-time Teachers
合　计	**657357**	**418347**	**239010**	**72247**	**42098**
一、国家部委直属院校	**92453**	**91975**	**478**	**18166**	**9578**
西安交通大学	15973	15973		5505	2502
西北工业大学	14125	14125		3369	1955
西安电子科技大学	21152	21152		3172	1870
长安大学	23979	23979		3518	1791
陕西师范大学	17224	16746	478	2602	1460
二、陕西省属院校	**453218**	**245812**	**207406**	**45730**	**27340**
西北大学	19448	12690	6758	2391	1266
西安理工大学	18185	15820	2365	2381	1309
西安工业大学	16178	15332	846	1404	1006
西安建筑科技大学	9592	9592		2399	1523
西安科技大学	18679	17385	1294	1850	1061
西安石油大学	18920	16619	2301	1618	1021
陕西科技大学	18278	16770	1508	1968	1178
西安工程大学	20404	18337	2067	1701	1125
西安外国语大学	17835	14497	3338	1506	970
西北政法大学	13202	11935	1267	1318	846
西安体育学院	7505	7505		812	567
西安音乐学院	3391	3391		491	291
西安美术学院	6009	5412	597	897	681
西安培华学院	19349	15051	4298	1597	905
西安财经学院	15506	14621	885	1468	1062
西安邮电学院	9851		9851	1265	972
西安医学院	14578	7795	6783	1958	1106
西安欧亚学院	18654	6759	11895	1433	793
西安外事学院	19814	7797	12017	2100	1182
西安翻译学院	17559	6989	10570	2090	1222
西京学院	22058	7993	14065	1836	1102
西安航空技术高等专科学校	21184	11186	9998	749	486
西安电力高等专科学校	4178		4178	1109	237
陕西电子信息职业技术学院	2075		2075	225	106
陕西国防工业职业技术学院	8865		8865	581	514
西安航空职业技术学院	8428		8428	612	476
陕西省交通职业技术学院	7036		7036	408	261
陕西职业技术学院	8584		8584	656	448
西安思源职业学院	13362	2336	11026	1226	712
西安高新科技职业学院	5539		5539	495	279
西安三资职业学院	4419		4419	402	163
西安科技商贸职业学院	7283		7283	667	372
西安海棠职业学院	7298		7298	787	285
西安汽车科技职业学院	6552		6552	737	367

注:军校只包括地方招生计划招收的部分。其他院校属成人学校，只统计按普通高校招生计划招收的部分。

Note: Military school includes only that recruited under local recruiting plan. Other schools mean adult schools, only that recruited under ordinary colleges and universities` recruiting plan are taken into account.

18-6 续表 continued

单位：人 (person)

校 名 Name of Schools	在校学生数 Total Enrollment 合计 Total	本科 Regular College	专科 Junior College	教职工 Staff and Teachers 合计 Total	#专任教师 Full-time Teachers
西安东方亚太职业技术学院	274		274	121	89
陕西警官职业学院	4172		4172	348	201
陕西经济管理职业技术学院	3654		3654	433	171
陕西青年职业学院	5809		5809	296	203
陕西工商职业学院	602		602	231	140
陕西电子科技职业学院	5462		5462	644	268
陕西旅游烹饪职业学院	1077		1077	130	88
西安医科高等专科学校	2370		2370	390	286
三、西安市直属院校	**22854**	**9825**	**13029**	**2340**	**1296**
西安文理学院	11204	9825	1379	1176	697
西安铁路职业技术学院	6224		6224	648	313
西安职业技术学院	5426		5426	516	286
西安师范学院大专班					
四、其他院校	**73425**	**70735**	**2690**	**6011**	**3884**
武警工程学院					
空军工程大学					
西安通信学院					
第四军医大学					
第二炮兵工程学院					
西安陆军学院					
西安交通大学城市学院	8749	8749		555	366
西北大学现代学院	6776	6776		461	385
西安建筑科技大学华清学院	10647	10647		941	630
西安财经学院行知学院	5905	5905		495	290
西安工业学院北方信息工程学院	7888	7888		677	500
延安大学西安创新学院	7633	7633		708	429
西安电子科技大学长安学院	3138	3138		323	224
西北工业大学明德学院	8505	8505		610	383
长安大学兴华学院	1721	1721		115	80
西安理工大学高科学院	3414	3414		336	207
西安科技大学高新学院	9049	6359	2690	790	390
五、成人高校举办的普专班	**15407**		**15407**		
陕西航天职工大学	1132		1132		
西安航空职工大学	1785		1785		
西安飞机工业公司职工学院	990		990		
陕西兵器工业职工大学					
西安铁路工程职工大学	1652		1652		
西安电力机械制造公司机电学院	1103		1103		
陕西省建筑工程总公司职工大学	1667		1667		
西安市职工大学					
西安外贸职工大学	281		281		
陕西工运学院	877		877		
陕西教育学院	5920		5920		
陕西省广播电视大学					
西安市广播电视大学					

注：军队院校2010年无数据。

Note:There is no data of Military schools in 2010.

18-7 主要年份博士后、博士、硕士流动站情况

Mobile research centers for post-doctors, Doctors and Masters in Representative Years

指　　标 Item	2005	2006	2007	2008	2009	2010
博士后流动站（个） Mobile Postdoctoral Centers(unit)	66	62	87	88	94	90
博士点（个） Ph.D Programs(unit)	355	436	494	505	516	469
硕士点（个） Master Programs(unit)	832	1097	1201	1208	1234	1196
本科专业（个） Undergraduate Specialties(unit)	981	1077	1215	1176	1197	1232
重点学科（个） Important Fields of Study(unit)	409	401	459	419	491	564
院士（人事关系在学校）（人） Academicians (organizational affiliation with educational institutions)(person)	22	25	25	22	20	23

18-8 主要年份普通中等专业学校基本情况

Basic Statistics on Specialized Secondary Schools In Representative Years

年 份 Year	学校数(所) Number of Schools (unit)	毕业生数(万人) Number of Graduates (10 000 persons)	招生数(万人) New Enrollment (10 000 persons)	在校学生数(万人) Total Enrollment (10 000 persons)	教职工数(人) Number of Staff and Teachers (person)	专任教师 Full-time Teachers
1978	19			0.87		1110
1980	33			1.50		1474
1985	37			1.70		2363
1990	44	0.56	0.68	2.09	7136	2891
1995	46	0.97	1.37	3.74	5903	2533
1996	47	1.15	1.61	4.18	5940	2573
1997	47	1.20	1.65	4.63	6124	2731
1998	47	1.26	1.62	5.08	6181	2840
1999	46	1.42	2.11	5.75	6385	2865
2000	47	1.63	1.90	6.02	6964	3172
2001	47	1.70	1.58	5.63	5252	2467
2002	46	1.60	1.69	5.57	5170	2508
2003	34	1.62	1.80	5.28	4562	2302
2004	35	1.40	2.09	5.71	4676	2388
2005	32	1.44	2.26	6.16	3924	2130
2006	31	1.84	2.61	7.30	3621	2014
2007	30	2.03	2.91	7.97	3548	2011
2008	29	2.58	2.55	8.06	3278	1814
2009	28	2.70	2.15	7.44	2965	1720
2010	28	2.45	2.08	6.75	3249	1845

18-9 中等技术（中等专业）学校分学校基本情况（2010年）

Situation of Every Secondary Technical and Specialized Secondary school（2010）

单位：人 （person）

校名 Name of Schools	毕业生数 Number of graduates	招生数 New Enrollment	在校学生数 Total Enrollment	教职工数 Number of Staff and Teachers	专任教师 Full-time Teachers
总 计	**24453**	20813	67525	3249	1845
一、中央部门属学校	1227	1268	3628	350	181
1.西安军需工业学校	150	140	490	77	56
2.西安交大医学院附设卫生学校	386	697	1733	43	15
3.西安航天工业学校	691	431	1405	230	110
二、陕西省属学校	**19602**	15599	50193	2528	1455
4.西安体育学院附属竞技体校	33	54	171		
5.西安体育学院附属体校					
6.西安电力工业学校	493	74	227	281	111
7.陕西省城市经济学校	536	135	424	91	55
8.陕西省城乡建设学校	300	376	1042	75	44
9.陕西省对外贸易学校	316	903	3535		
10.陕西省体育运动学校	114	178	532	81	48
11.陕西省电影电视学校	63	47	134	54	27
12.陕西省旅游学校	511	440	1552	82	55
13.陕西省电子信息学校	3705	1743	6325	243	163
14.西安环境信息工程学校					
15.陕西省理工学校	1674	1405	5112	243	120
16.西安音乐学院附属中专	62	110	342	26	17
17.西安美术学院附属中专	105	116	490	37	28
18.陕西省石油化工学校	2612	566	2593	228	112
19.陕西省经贸学校	1463	966	3306	158	114
20.陕西银行学校	897	950	2806	127	89
21.陕西省商贸学校	392	209	983	95	61
22.陕西省建筑材料工业学校	2891	1245	4259	96	77
23.陕西医科学校	817	2634	6678	291	150
24.陕西科技卫生学校	2247	3071	8318	194	106
25.陕西省艺术学校	371	377	1364	126	78
三、西安市属学校	**2265**	1718	6712	371	209
26.西安市体育运动学校	18	32	79	115	43
27.西安市艺术学校	147	130	583	102	72
28.西安市卫生学校	1732	883	3652	154	94
西安文理学院		189	606		
西安职业技术学院	368	484	1792		
西安铁路职业技术学院					
四、其他机构	**1359**	2228	6992		
西安外国语大学高职部		556	1752		
陕西职业技术学院		140	291		
陕西交通职业技术学院					
西安医学院	681	649	2730		
陕西工运学院					
西安航空职业技术学院					
陕西国防工业职业技术学院	326	392	1025		
西安外事学院	183	232	441		
西安三资职业学院	74	61	207		
西安科技商贸职业学院	95	198	546		

18-10 主要年份普通中学基本情况

Baisc Statistics on Regular Secondary Schools in Representative Years

年 份 Year	学校数(所) Number of Schools (unit)	毕业生数(万人) Number of Graduates (10 000 person)	招生数(万人) New Enrollment (10 000 person)	在校学生数(万人) Total Enrollment (10 000 person)	教职工数(人) Number of Staff and Teachers(person)	专任教师 Full-time Teachers
1978	962			44.16		20660
1980	1002	12.33	14.03	44.08	29867	22530
1985	563	10.72	13.05	38.24	30063	22050
1990	518	9.11	10.49	30.03	30739	22386
1995	485	8.13	12.40	32.32	30423	21984
1996	462	8.67	13.03	35.25	30902	22478
1997	466	9.96	13.83	37.16	31682	23129
1998	467	10.64	15.00	39.79	32371	23884
1999	469	11.21	16.58	43.49	33387	25114
2000	466	12.01	17.88	48.31	34385	26230
2001	470	13.85	18.98	52.50	35442	27190
2002	467	15.76	19.68	55.36	36706	28335
2003	467	16.76	18.78	56.44	38252	29887
2004	461	18.01	18.85	56.54	39121	30600
2005	460	18.82	18.83	55.74	39456	31094
2006	457	18.04	18.61	56.11	39341	31203
2007	453	18.37	17.96	54.68	39171	31373
2008	442	17.99	17.16	52.83	39088	31425
2009	439	17.80	16.57	50.63	39002	31415
2010	436	17.01	16.15	48.89	39207	31506

18-11 各区县普通中学基本情况（2010年）

Baisc Statistics on Regular Secondary Schools by Region （2010）

单位：所、人 （unit,person）

区 县	Region	学校数 Number of Schools	毕业生数 Number of Graduates	高中 Senior	招生数 New Enrollment	高中 Senior	在校学生数 Total Enrollment	高中 Senior	教职工数 Number of Staff and Teachers	专任教师 Full-time Teachers
合 计	**Total**	**436**	**170135**	**58691**	**161510**	**63053**	**488925**	**183118**	**39207**	**31506**
新城区	Xincheng	25	12488	4415	13164	4431	37658	12820	2601	1982
碑林区	Beilin	37	16167	7272	16569	7088	50226	20965	3996	2916
莲湖区	Lianhu	21	11725	4212	12045	4364	35703	12812	2732	2133
灞桥区	Baqiao	31	8413	2805	7998	2873	24139	8522	2154	1691
未央区	Weiyang	35	10564	4220	11968	4603	33518	12816	2995	2265
雁塔区	Yanta	51	14695	5332	16668	5726	48097	17178	3926	3017
阎良区	Yanliang	12	5577	2067	4555	1839	14713	6188	1272	1005
临潼区	Lintong	33	15575	4472	14208	5137	43878	14668	3300	2902
长安区	Chang'an	55	21268	6913	18252	7929	56307	22967	4881	4125
蓝田县	Lantian	46	13883	4029	14015	4888	42650	13747	3227	2525
周至县	Zhouzhi	36	19420	5852	14720	6422	48078	17763	3601	2926
户 县	Huxian	39	15219	5594	12919	5803	39730	16981	3271	2915
高陵县	Gaoling	15	5141	1508	4429	1950	14228	5691	1251	1104

18-12 主要年份职业中学基本情况

Basic Statistics on Vocational Secondary Schools in Representative Years

年 份 Year	学校数(所) Number of Schools (unit)	毕业生数（人）Number of Graduates (person)	招生数（人）New Enrollment (person)	在校学生数（人）Total Enrollment (person)	教职工数（人）Number of Teachers and Staff (person)	专任教师 Full-time Teachers
1985	40	1661	8346	17621	1375	868
1990	58	5936	8095	20151	2674	1574
1995	71	8976	12490	32673	2394	1877
1996	67	9235	10563	25955	3098	1735
1997	73	8756	13390	29068	2993	1709
1998	89	7753	13949	31264	3152	1823
1999	91	8480	13062	31973	3217	1908
2000	95	9949	13903	32188	3311	1997
2001	85	10300	15591	34336	3517	2113
2002	78	8659	17231	39428	3461	2192
2003	87	10755	17310	44033	4036	2458
2004	83	12177	17865	46358	4101	2515
2005	91	15092	20603	51766	4750	2892
2006	96	14887	21158	53828	5193	3126
2007	86	14881	24434	56012	4899	3064
2008	84	15813	30201	62963	4878	3008
2009	84	14691	31042	72388	5129	3179
2010	84	18100	30042	78244	5222	3178

18-13 各区县职业中学基本情况（2010年）

Baisc Statistics on Vocational Secondary Schools by Region （2010）

区县	Region	学校数（所）Number of Schools (unit)	毕业生数（人）Number of Graduates (person)	招生数（人）New Enrollment (person)	在校学生数（人）Total Enrollment (person)	教职工数（人）Number of Teachers and Staff (person)	专任教师 Full-time Teachers
合计	**Total**	**84**	**18100**	**30042**	**78244**	**5222**	**3178**
新城区	Xincheng	10	2956	4017	12009	820	512
碑林区	Beilin	8	2131	3334	8342	677	340
莲湖区	Lianhu	6	1612	2820	7532	457	253
灞桥区	Baqiao	10	977	2016	5153	561	267
未央区	Weiyang	7	1690	2522	7348	389	249
雁塔区	Yanta	18	1638	2820	9962	679	340
阎良区	Yanliang	1	428	1231	2016	113	100
临潼区	Lintong	5	1631	2465	4904	298	213
长安区	Chang'an	7	1507	3268	8336	723	489
蓝田县	Lantian	1	724	528	1729	17	13
周至县	Zhouzhi	5	1043	2261	4104	178	143
户县	Huxian	5	798	1730	3914	245	208
高陵县	Gaoling	1	965	1030	2895	65	51

18-14 主要年份小学基本情况

Basic Statistics on Primary Schools in Representative Years

年份 Year	学校数(所) Number of Schools (unit)	毕业生数（万人）Number of Graduates (10 000 person)	招生数（万人）New Enrollment (10 000 person)	在校学生数（万人）Total Enrollment (10 000 person)	教职工数（人）Number of Teachers and Staff (person)	专任教师 Full-time Teachers
1978	2667			74.03	29744	26428
1980	2337	11.91	12.57	73.36	31770	28360
1985	2337	11.21	9.57	62.16	31075	26430
1990	2343	8.67	10.85	61.87	37788	29090
1995	2360	9.93	14.09	79.36	35568	30270
1996	2362	10.48	13.63	81.81	35821	30267
1997	2368	10.98	12.48	82.67	35767	30117
1998	2361	12.18	11.88	82.03	35576	30089
1999	2354	13.65	11.61	79.81	35639	30196
2000	2323	13.83	11.51	77.81	35336	30215
2001	2277	14.20	11.07	74.51	34257	29281
2002	2137	13.89	10.13	70.78	34143	29428
2003	2084	12.97	9.28	66.78	34080	29531
2004	2016	12.37	9.12	63.75	33794	29367
2005	1980	11.92	8.47	60.47	33907	29674
2006	1929	11.53	9.16	59.33	34460	30018
2007	1872	11.38	8.67	56.83	34901	30533
2008	1781	10.58	8.33	54.66	34653	30382
2009	1666	9.96	7.84	52.52	34389	30334
2010	1531	9.61	8.64	51.56	34118	29944

18-15 各区县小学基本情况（2010年）

Basic Statistics on Primary Schools by Region （2010）

单位：所、人 (unit、person)

区 县	Region	学校数 Number of Schools	毕业生数 Number of Graduates	招生数 New Enrollment	在校学生数 Total Enrollment	教职工数 Number of Teachers and Staff	专任教师 Full-time Teachers
合 计	**Total**	**1531**	**96077**	**86393**	**515628**	**34118**	**29944**
新城区	Xincheng	35	7288	6206	39653	2073	1784
碑林区	Beilin	44	6900	6307	38469	2145	1771
莲湖区	Lianhu	49	7965	7357	43743	2540	2152
灞桥区	Baqiao	78	5577	5663	32268	2114	1732
未央区	Weiyang	73	8247	9668	53362	2954	2533
雁塔区	Yanta	67	11022	11651	66433	3456	2954
阎良区	Yanliang	39	2739	2247	13774	1155	1026
临潼区	Lintong	208	9311	6744	43329	3553	3212
长安区	Chang'an	212	10353	9352	52926	4300	3623
蓝田县	Lantian	307	9005	6872	43697	3116	2958
周至县	Zhouzhi	181	8075	6541	39446	2777	2509
户 县	Huxian	152	7058	5437	34785	2450	2329
高陵县	Gaoling	86	2537	2348	13743	1485	1361

18-16 主要年份幼儿园基本情况

Basic Statistics on Kindergartens in Representative Years

年 份 Year	园 数(所) Number of Kindergartens (unit)	班 数(个) Number of Class (unit)	在园幼儿数(万人) Student Enrollment (10000 person)	教职工数(人) Number of Staff and Teachers (person)	专任教师 Full-time Teachers
1978	363		4	3568	1315
1980	186		10	5525	2657
1985	310	3135	10	6887	2770
1990	256	3816	14	6123	2058
1995	257	4464	16	6173	2659
1996	244	4313	15	5918	2661
1997	228	4243	15	6065	2748
1998	235	4195	13	6272	2910
1999	234	4222	13	6329	2982
2000	367	4142	13	6346	2995
2001	366	4306	12	6224	3069
2002	378	4186	12	6541	3397
2003	610	4470	12	8959	4853
2004	660	4507	12	9870	5577
2005	737	4712	13	10528	5959
2006	863	5037	13	12335	7106
2007	830	5081	14	13468	7951
2008	905	5506	15	14932	8704
2009	896	5710	16	15928	9240
2010	1004	6420	18	18710	10638

注:幼儿园中包括学前班。

Note:"Kindergartens" here including units providing pre-school education.

18-17 主要年份特殊教育学校基本情况

Basic Statistics on Special Education Schools in Representative Years

单位：所、人 (unit,person)

年 份 Year	学校数 Number of Schools	毕业生数 Number of Graduates	招生数 New Enrollment	在校学生数 Total Enrollment	教职工数 Number of Teachers and Staff	专任教师 Full-time Teachers
1978						
1980	1	48	64	315	66	43
1985	2	14	36	318	94	59
1990	5	35	111	451	142	96
1995	5	27	147	1363	204	141
1996	5	60	164	1520	210	150
1997	5	153	164	1655	210	148
1998	5	266	140	2145	232	157
1999	5	349	115	1912	235	160
2000	5	269	145	1880	230	156
2001	5	237	209	1915	238	162
2002	5	216	148	1661	232	157
2003	5	156	161	1380	237	166
2004	5	137	142	1290	236	167
2005	5	184	182	1445	240	169
2006	6	171	143	1425	254	178
2007	6	169	114	1342	259	190
2008	6	83	96	1286	259	190
2009	7	311	202	1523	335	234
2010	8	214	402	1529	340	235

注:包括盲、聋、哑、弱智儿童教育在内。

Note:Including schools providing education for blind, deaf and dumb children and children with weak intelligence .

18-18 主要年份小学、初中升学率

Rate of Graduates from Junior Schools and Primary Schools Entering Higher Level Schools in Representative Years

年 份 Year	小 学 Primary Schools 小学毕结业生数（万人） Graduates of Primary Schools (10 000 person)	升学人数（万人） Number of Graduates from Primary Schools (10 000 persons)	升学率 (%) Percentage of Graduates from Primary Schools Entering Junior Secondary Schools (%)
1978			
1980	11.91	10.43	87.60
1985	11.21	9.56	85.30
1990	8.68	8.09	91.50
1995	10.02	9.50	94.85
1997	11.04	10.56	95.65
1998	12.25	11.76	96.02
1999	13.77	13.23	96.04
2000	13.83	13.44	97.21
2001	14.22	13.83	97.25
2002	13.92	13.54	97.25
2003	12.97	12.61	97.26
2004	12.37	11.98	96.79
2005	11.92	11.84	99.31
2006	11.53	12.22	104.23
2007	11.38	11.69	102.70
2008	10.58	10.98	103.81
2009	9.96	10.14	101.76
2010	9.61	9.85	102.48

18-18 续表 continued

年 份 Year	初 中 JunionSchools 初中毕结业生数(万人) Graduates from Junior Secondary Schools (10 000 persons)	升学人数（万人） Number of Graduates from Junior Secondary (10 000persons)	升学率 (%) Percentage of Graduates from Junior Secondary Schools Entering Senior Secondary Schools (%)
1978			
1980			60.71
1985	8.36	4.63	55.30
1990	6.86	2.39	52.70
1995	6.35	4.60	72.35
1997	7.98	6.14	76.93
1998	8.53	6.56	76.90
1999	9.19	7.08	77.00
2000	9.35	7.53	80.50
2001	10.88	8.77	80.56
2002	12.31	10.19	82.80
2003	12.66	10.16	80.26
2004	12.90	10.53	81.60
2005	12.93	10.52	81.39
2006	12.17	10.52	86.06
2007	12.04	10.68	88.70
2008	11.88	10.69	90.03
2009	11.67	10.52	90.09
2010	11.23	10.18	90.67

注：小学升学率的分子项含外地转学生，故升学率大于100，本数据为市教育局部门统计数据。

Note:As the molecular item of percentage of graduates from primary schools entering junior secondary schools includes outland transfer students, the percentage is bigger than 100.The number comes from the City Board of Education.

18-19 主要年份小学学龄儿童入学率

Percentage of School-Age Children Enrolled in Representative Years

年 份 Year	学龄儿童总数 (万人) Total School-Age Children (10 000 persons)	农 村 Rural Areas	入学儿童总数 (万人) Total School-Age Children (10 000 persons)	农 村 Rural Areas	入学率（%） Enrollment Rate (%)	农 村 Rural Areas
1978						
1980					98.42	
1985	63.02	32.57	62.16	31.95	98.62	98.10
1990	62.42	34.35	61.87	33.88	99.11	98.66
1995	77.86	29.12	77.62	28.98	99.69	99.49
1996	81.40	27.69	81.19	27.58	99.75	99.61
1997	82.45	24.30	82.24	24.21	99.74	99.65
1998	81.69	22.52	81.54	22.44	99.82	99.66
1999	79.66	21.67	79.55	21.61	99.86	99.75
2000	77.68	20.44	77.56	20.37	99.85	99.68
2001	69.69	41.31	69.58	41.22	99.84	99.77
2002	65.76	36.59	65.66	36.50	99.85	99.75
2003	62.44	33.78	62.37	33.72	99.88	99.81
2004	59.95	35.49	59.87	35.43	99.87	99.83
2005	57.00	31.53	56.95	31.49	99.90	99.85
2006	56.05	31.50	56.01	31.46	99.92	99.88
2007	53.71	28.97	53.68	28.95	99.94	99.90
2008	52.00	27.03	51.97	27.01	99.95	99.91
2009	50.26	25.19	50.24	25.17	99.96	99.92
2010	49.62	24.33	49.60	24.35	99.96	99.94

18-20 主要年份平均每万人口在校学生数和大中小学生构成

Student Enrollment Per 10000 Populations and Composition of Students Enrolled in Representative Years

年 份 Year	占全市人口(%) Percentage of Population of Whole City (%)	平均每万人口中 Students Per 10 000 Population		
		大学生（人） University and College Students(person)	中学生（人） Secondary School Students(person)	小学生（人） Primary School Students(person)
1978	25.37	58	886	1486
1980	25.92	84	906	1434
1985	22.24	117	692	1124
1990	19.84	123	493	1016
1995	22.86	168	639	1224
1996	23.37	177	672	1249
1997	23.54	180	701	1249
1998	23.62	189	740	1228
1999	24.06	224	798	1183
2000	24.56	282	854	1131
2001	25.17	366	903	1072
2002	25.84	470	940	1007
2003	27.84	560	939	932
2004	27.83	618	980	879
2005	27.10	715	981	815
2006	27.46	760	1018	788
2007	27.57	817	1009	744
2008	27.88	863	1015	708
2009	28.16	901	1032	672
2010	26.15	867	919	609

注：2010年数据按年底常住人口计算，往年按户籍人口计算。

Note:Statistics of 2010 was calculated by permanent population at year end, and that of former years by registered household population.

18-20 续表 continued

年 份 Year	大中小学生各占学生总数比重(%) Students of Different Level as Percentage of Total Students (%) 大学生 University and College Students	中学生 Secondary School Students	小学生 Primary School Students
1978	2.28	34.94	58.57
1980	3.14	33.21	55.27
1985	5.32	31.34	50.93
1990	6.71	25.10	51.71
1995	7.33	27.96	53.55
1996	7.57	28.78	53.46
1997	7.63	29.77	53.05
1998	8.01	31.34	52.01
1999	9.30	33.18	49.18
2000	11.48	34.77	46.04
2001	14.57	35.88	42.59
2002	18.17	36.40	38.99
2003	20.11	33.75	33.47
2004	22.22	35.23	31.59
2005	26.39	36.22	30.08
2006	27.68	37.09	28.69
2007	29.30	36.32	26.67
2008	30.77	36.09	25.17
2009	31.84	36.46	23.74
2010	33.00	35.00	23.17

18-21 成人教育情况（2010年）

Adult Education （2010）

分 类	Classify	学校数（所）Number of Schools (unit)	毕业生数（人）Graduates (person)	招生数（人）New Enrollment (person)
合 计	**Total**	**2278**	**471273**	**63374**
一、成人高等学校	**Adult Higher Education Institution**	**16**	**7499**	**8348**
1.广播电视大学	Radio and TV Universities	2	2759	2853
2.职工高等学校	Schools of Higher Education for Staff and Workers	11	4137	4531
3.管理干部学院	Colleges for Management Cadres	2	144	238
4.教育学院	Pedagogical Colleges	1	459	726
二、普通高校成教学院	**Adult Education Units in Regular Institutions**		**32264**	**47869**
1.函授部	Correspondence Divisions	(21)	23609	31097
2.夜大学	Evening Schools	(26)	4081	16772
3.成人脱产班	Short-cycle Courses for Adults	(20)	4574	
三、成人中等学校	**Adult middle school**	**2218**	**430525**	**7157**
1.成人中等专业学校	Specialized Secondary Schools for Adults	11	3223	7157
（1）广播电视中专	Radio and TV Specialized Secondary School	4	2643	6584
（2）职工、干部、函授中专	Schools for Workers, Cadres and Correspondence Secondary	7	580	573
2.成人中学	Adult Middle School			
3.成人技术培训学校	Adult Technology Training School	2207	427302	
#教师进校	Teacher Training Schools	13	24033	
四、成人初等学校	**Adult Elementary School**	**44**	**985**	

注:1.本表是西安市行政辖区内各级各类成人学校的全口径数据；2.( )内数因与普通高校重复,不加入总计数。

Note:1.First,The table Shows the Data of All the Adult Education Schools in Xi'an Administrative Region (Party Schools not included).

2. Number in brackets overlapped over that of Regular Schools for higher education, so it is not excluded from the total.

18-21 续表 continued

分　类	Classify	在校学生数（人）Total Enrollment (person)	教职工数（人）Teachers and Staff (person)	专任教师 Full-time Teachers
合　计	**Total**	**646675**	**16488**	**8165**
一、成人高等学校	**Adult Higher Education Institution**	**21720**	**3548**	**2055**
1.广播电视大学	Radio and TV Universities	6853	375	186
2.职工高等学校	Schools of Higher Education for Staff and Workers	12796	2310	1334
3.管理干部学院	Colleges for Management Cadres	506	175	137
4.教育学院	Pedagogical Colleges	1565	688	398
二、普通高校成教学院	**Adult Education Units in Regular Institutions**	**133695**		
1.函授部	Correspondence Divisions	89289		
2.夜大学	Evening Schools	41657		
3.成人脱产班	Short-cycle Courses for Adults	2749		
三、成人中等学校	**Adult Middle School**	**490269**	**12873**	**6066**
1.成人中等专业学校	Specialized Secondary Schools for Adults	13645	1576	858
（1）广播电视中专	Radio and TV Specialized Secondary School	11884	1177	664
（2）职工、干部、函授中专	Schools for Workers, Cadres and Correspondence Secondary	1761	399	194
2.成人中学	Adult Middle School			
3.成人技术培训学校	Adult Technology Training School	476624	11297	5208
#教师进校	Teacher Training Schools	23998	532	331
四、成人初等学校	**Adult Elementary School**	**991**	**67**	**44**

18-22 研究与试验发展（R&D）情况

Research and Experiment Development Facts

指标名称	Item	2009	2010
一、单位数（个）	**Number of Units(unit)**	**304**	**358**
科研单位	Units of Scientific Research	68	100
高等院校	Institutions of Higher Education	49	50
大中型工业企业	Large-scale and Medium-scale Industrial Enterprises	187	208
#有R&D活动单位数	Number of Units with R&D Activities	**155**	**163**
科研单位	Units of Scientific Research	41	52
高等院校	Institutions of Higher Education	29	26
大中型工业企业	Large-scale and Medium-scale Industrial Enterprises	85	85
二、科技活动人员（人）	**Personnel Eagaged in Scientific and Technical Activities (person)**	**110363**	**128559**
科研单位	Units of Scientific Research	33680	40482
高等院校	Institutions of Higher Education	36095	36380
大中型工业企业	Large-scale and Medium-scale Industrial Enterprises	40588	51697
三、R&D经费内部支出（万元）	**Interier Expenditures for R&D(10 000 yuan)**	**1521086**	**1672712**
科研单位	Units of Scientific Research	979727	1010424
高等院校	Institutions of Higher Education	180522	213382
大中型工业企业	Large-scale and Medium-scale Industrial Enterprises	360837	448906
四，R&D项目（课题）（个）	**Number of Projects of R&D(item)**	**19056**	**26814**
科研单位	Units of Scientific Research	1374	1601
高等院校	Institutions of Higher Education	15613	23393
大中型工业企业	Large-scale and Medium-scale Industrial Enterprises	2069	1820

注：2009年为西安市第二次R&D资源清查数据。

Note:Statistics of 2009 was statistics of the second R&D resources investigation in Xi'an.

18-23 科研院所研究与试验发展（R&D）情况

Research and Experiment Development Facts in Scientific Research Institutions

指标名称	Item	2009	2010
一、基本情况	**Basic Facts**		
单位数（个）	Number of Unit(unit)	68	100
#有（R&D）活动的单位数	Number of Units with Scientific and Technical Activities	41	52
科技活动人员（人）	Number of Personnel Engaged in Scientific Research (person)	33680	40482
#（R&D）人员	R&D Personnel	25537	27333
其中：女性	Female	8200	8742
其中：博士毕业	Doctor	573	765
硕士毕业	Master	4844	6177
本科毕业	Undergraduate	10958	11578
二、R&D人员折合全时当量（人/年）	**Full Time Equivalent of R&D Personnel (person/year)**	**23599**	**25596**
其中：研究人员	Personnel Engaged in Research	14368	15610
其中：基础研究	Basic Research	911	367
应用研究生	Applied Research	7859	8970
试验发展	Experiment Development	14829	16259
三、R&D经费内部支出（万元）	**Raising and Use of Funds for Scientific and(10 000 yuan) Technical Activities**	**979727**	**1010424**
在支出中：1.基础研究	Expenditure on: Basic Research	23889	21750
2.应用研究	Applied Research	204067	210624
3.试验发展	Experiment Development	751771	778050
在支出中：1.日常支出	Expenditure on: Daily Expenditure	704805	752936
#人员劳务费	Service Fees of Personnel	124400	149753
2.资产性支出	Assets Expenditure	273712	257488
#仪器和设备	Instruments and Equipment	116584	177899
在支出中：1.政府资金	Expenditure on: Government Funds	891630	930234
2.企业资金	Enterpreises Funds	43999	13810
3.境外资金	Overseas Funds		
4.其他资金	Others	44099	66380
四、R&D产出	**Achievements of R&D**		
专利申请数（件）	Number of Patent Applications (item)	684	1240
#发明专利	Number of Invention Patents	522	867
专利授权数（件）	Number of Patents Awarded (item)	221	655
#发明专利	Number of Invention Patents	117	292
有效发明专利数（件）	Number of Effective Invention Patents	346	775
发表科技论文（篇）	Scientific and Technical Thesis (piece)	3548	5155
出版科技著作（种）	Scientific and Technical Works Published (book)	73	78

18-24 大专院校研究与试验（R&D）情况

Research and Experiment Development Facts in Universities

指标名称	Item	2009	2010
一、基本情况	**Basic Facts**		
单位数（个）	Number of Unit(unit)	49	50
#有（R&D）活动的单位数	Number of Units with Scientific and Technical Activities	29	26
从事科技活动人员（人）	Number of Personnel Engaged in Scientific Research (person)	36095	36380
#（R&D）人员	R&D Personnel	14440	15431
其中：女性	Female	4173	4861
其中：博士毕业	Doctor	3811	4119
硕士毕业	Master	5110	5611
本科毕业	Undergraduate	3695	4434
二、R&D人员折合全时当量（人/年）	**Full Time Equivalent of R&D Personnel (person/year)**	**7888**	**7747**
其中：研究人员	Personnel Engaged in Research	6913	6891
其中：基础研究	Basic Research	2716	3168
应用研究生	Applied Research	4236	3236
试验发展	Experiment Development	936	1343
三、R&D经费内部支出（万元）	**Raising and Use of Funds for Scientific and Technical Activities(10 000 yuan)**	**180522**	**213382**
在支出中：1.基础研究	Expenditure on: Basic Research	49411	60974
2.应用研究	Applied Research	88231	98367
3.试验发展	Experiment Development	42880	54041
在支出中：1.日常支出	Expenditure on: Daily Expenditure	157585	179886
#人员劳务费	Service Fees of Personnel	26417	32250
2.资产性支出	Assets Expenditure	22936	33496
#仪器和设备	Instruments and Equipment	18645	29788
在支出中：1.政府资金	Expenditure on: Government Funds	97867	127480
2.企业资金	Enterpreises Funds	76169	76701
3.境外资金	Overseas Funds	1422	1029
4.其他资金	Others	5064	8172
四、R&D产出	**Achievements of R&D**		
专利申请数（件）	Number of Patent Applications (item)	2894	3741
#发明专利	Number of Invention Patents	1829	2185
专利授权数（件）	Number of Patents Awarded (item)	1177	1954
#发明专利	Number of Invention Patents	644	865
有效发明专利数（件）	Number of Effective Invention Patents	5708	6200
发表科技论文（篇）	Scientific and Technical Thesis (piece)	36452	37116
出版科技著作（种）	Scientific and Technical Works Published (book)	984	984

18-25 大中型企业研究与试验发展（R&D）情况

Research and Experiment Development Facts in Large-size and Medium-size Industrial Enterprises

指标名称	Item	2009	2010
一、基本情况	**Basic Facts**		
单位数（个）	Number of Unit(unit)	187	208
#有（R&D）活动的单位数	Number of Units with Scientific and Technical Activities	85	85
从事科技活动人员（人）	Number of Personnel Engaged in Scientific Research (person)	40588	51697
#（R&D）人员	R&D Personnel	20571	23571
其中：女性	Female	5908	6775
二、R&D人员折合全时当量（人/年）	**Full Time Equivalent of R&D Personnel (person/year)**	**13071**	**17416**
其中：研究人员	Personnel Engaged in Research	6408	10348
其中：基础研究	Basic Research		35
应用研究生	Applied Research	184	226
试验发展	Experiment Development	12887	17155
三、R&D经费内部支出（万元）	**Raising and Use of Funds for Scientific and Technical Activities(10 000 yuan)**	**360837**	**448906**
在支出中：1.基础研究	Expenditure on: Basic Research		912
2.应用研究	Applied Research	8240	8824
3.试验发展	Experiment Development	352597	439170
在支出中：1.日常支出	Expenditure on: Daily Expenditure	313809	371893
#人员劳务费	Service Fees of Personnel	57719	62356
2.资产性支出	Assets Expenditure	47028	77013
#仪器和设备	Instruments and Equipment	45223	74701
在支出中：1.政府资金	Expenditure on: Government Funds	63024	79730
2.企业资金	Enterpreises Funds	289194	361121
3.境外资金	Overseas Funds		
4.其他资金	Others	8619	8055
四、R&D产出	**Achievements of R&D**		
专利申请数（件）	Number of Patent Applications (item)	1200	1612
#发明专利	Number of Invention Patents	404	610
专利授权数（件）	Number of Patents Awarded (item)		
#发明专利	Number of Invention Patents		
有效发明专利数（件）	Number of Effective Invention Patents	748	670
发表科技论文（篇）	Scientific and Technical Thesis (piece)	851	1372
出版科技著作（种）	Scientific and Technical Works Published (book)		

18-26 主要年份企事业单位知识产权情况

Intellectual Property Right of Enterprises and Institutions in Representative Years

指标名称	Name of Item	2005	2006	2007	2008	2009	2010
一、科技活动情况	**Science and technology activities**						
1.科技活动人员（人）	People involved into activities(person)	82789	86978	87095	91994	137934	128559
2.科技活动机构数（个）	Units involved into activities(unit)	358	365	380	411	569	490
二、知识产权拥有量情况	**Number of IPR**						
1.专利情况（件）	Patents(item)						
（1）累计申请专利	Accumulated patent applications	21912	26084	32852	42436	55208	74694
当年申请专利	Patent applictions in this year	2950	4172	6768	9584	12772	19486
#发明专利	Invention patents	1268	1325	1886	3049	5014	7176
（2）累计授权专利	Accumulated patents awarded	11670	13442	15971	19256	23962	31999
当年授权专利	Patents awarded in this year	1280	1772	2529	3285	4706	8037
#发明专利	Invention patents	331	461	595	749	1121	1651
2.商标情况（件）	Trade marks(item)						
（1）当年注册商标申请	Trade mark registration claimed in this year	3682	7132	5559	7613	8972	21562
（2）累计注册商标	Accumulated trade mark registrations	18461	20808	22860	26386	23078	52387
#当年注册商标	Trade mark registrations in this year	2330	2347	2052	3526	5278	18107
三、民事知识产权维权情况（件）	**IPR controversy(item)**	**106**	**108**	**131**	**212**	**427**	**241**
1.专利纠纷	Patent controversies	27	30	44	47	37	69
2.商标纠纷	Trade mark controversies	19	24	32	51	42	29
3.著作权纠纷	Copyright controversies	53	49	36	91	319	110
4.技术合同纠纷	Technological contract controversies	1	1	3	3	9	6
5.发现权与发明权纠纷	Discover and invention controversies	1					
6.其他知识产权纠纷	Others IPR controvers	5	4	16	20	20	27

注：本表数据由市科技局、陕西省工商局、陕西省新闻出版局、西安市中级人民法院等提供。

Note:Figures in this table are provided by Xi'an Bureau of Science and Technology, Industrial and Commercial Bureau of Shaanxi Province, Press and Publication Bureau of Shaanxi Province, Xi'an Intermediate People's Court and other department concerned.

18–27 主要年份高新技术产业开发区情况

Basic Statistics of Hi-Tech Development Zone in Representative Years

指　　标	Item	2005	2006	2007	2008	2009	2010
1.高新技术企业数	Number of High-tech Enterprises	1029	1062	1311	1324	592	672
2.年末从业人员(人)	Number of Persons Employed at year-end (person)	296401	346000	368757	388644	275141	287140
从事技术开发人数	Number of Persons Engaged in Technology Development	28792	34600	39248	48355	64212	67708
3.技术开发经费筹集额（万元）	Funds for Technology Development (10 000 yuan)	259950	583018	759112	832144	903467	
4.技术开发经费支出总额（万元）	Expenditures on Technology Development (10 000 yuan)	254161	565166	705066	777516	756767	1031223
研究与发展支出	Expenditures on Research and Development	115026	414537	533924	581716	585449	669083
5.利润总额（万元）	Total Profits (10 000 yuan)	388404	654258	1087311	1231146	1308432	1707925
6.上缴税费总额（万元）	Sum of tax (10 000yuan)	356599	464700	1394194	1576472	1486556	1964820
7.出口创汇总额（千美元）	Foreign Exchange Earnings of Exports (USD 1 000)	527014	1460251	1927114	2188721	1177000	4951265

注：2010年统计制度变化，取消技术开发经费筹集额指标。

Note:The statistics system has changed since 2010, thus indicator of funding for technology development was abolished.

18-28 高新技术产业开发区发展规模（2010年）

Development Status of Hi-Tech Development Zone（2010）

指 标	Item	合计 Total	新建区 Newlyconstructed Zone
累计已开发面积（平方公里）	Accumulated Areas Developed (sq.km)	35	35
高新区工商注册（个）	Registered Enterprises in Hi-tech Zones (unit)	13070	13070
#工业型技术开发技术服务型企业数	Number of industrial technology developing enterprises	7698	7698
#三资企业数	Enterprises of Joiut Venture,Cooperation and Foreign-funded	1031	1031
已认定的高新技术企业数	Hi-tech Enterprises Designated	672	672

注：此表数据来源于西安市高新技术开发区。

Note:Date on this bable is from Hi-Tech Development Zone of Xi'an.

18-29 主要年份高新技术产业开发区建设与集资情况

Capital Construction and Funds-Raising of Hi-Tech Development Zone in Representative Years

指 标	Item	2005	2006	2007	2008	2009	2010
一、基建投资（亿元）	**Investment on Capital Construction (100 million yuan)**						
本年基建投资	Investment on Capital Construction of this year	91.26	114.59	132.17	159.78	196.90	255.57
1.生产业务用房	Building for Production	31.81	50.76	59.69	60.53	69.23	94.74
2. 住宅	Residential Buildings	41.35	40.61	47.75	77.05	79.00	97.30
3.公用设施	Public Installations	6.36	10.15	11.94	6.72	4.91	7.35
4.基础设施	Fundamental Facilities	8.63	8.53	7.50	9.60	24.66	32.98
5.征地拆迁	Resettlement	3.11	4.54	5.29	5.88	17.00	13.59
二、开发面积	**Area Developed**						
新建区累计开发土地面积（平方公里）	Accumulated Area Developed in Newly Constructed Zone (sq.km)	22.35	35.00	35.00	35.00	35.00	35.00
#当年新开发土地面积	Area Developed in this year		1.27				
累计竣工建筑面积（万平方米）	Accumulated Floor Space Completed (10 000 sq.m)	1104.72	1325.98	1558.70	1782.43	2085.66	2419.87
#当年竣工建筑面积	Floor Space Completed in this year	188.60	221.30	232.70	223.76	303.23	334.20
三、当年内资金筹集情况（亿元）	**Funds Raised in this year(100 million yuan)**						
当年内资金筹集总额	Total Funds Raised in this year	160.20	155.58	152.85	179.57	202.58	300.30
#政府拨款	Allocations from the Government	5.50	6.50	11.66	21.41	25.98	33.07
贷款	Loans	108.20	108.34	100.00	106.18	125.47	165.68
四、吸引外资（亿美元）	**Foreign Investment(100 million USD)**						
年末累计境外客商协议投资额	Contracted Foreign Investment Accumulated at Year-end	21.92	28.14	32.35	36.26	43.76	52.76
年末累计境外客商实际投资额	Actual Foreign Investment Accumulated at Year-end	9.26	12.18	16.08	20.29	24.63	29.75
#当年实际投资额	Actual Investmen in this year	1.98	2.92	3.90	4.21	4.34	5.11

注：此表数据来源于西安市高新技术开发区。

Note:Date on this bable is from Hi-Tech Development Zone of Xi'an.

主要统计指标解释

普通高等学校 指按照国家规定的设置标准和审批程序批准举办，通过国家统一招生考试，招收高中毕业生为主要培养对象，实施高等教育的全日制大学、独立设置的学院和高等专科学校、短期职业大学。

成人高等学校 指按照国家有关规定审批，招收通过全国成人高教统一招生考试的具有高中毕业或同等学历的在职从业人员，利用脱产、半脱产、业余或函授等多种形式对其实施高等学历教育，培养高等教育专科或本科毕业水平的专门人才，修业年限、课程设置和总学时数均按高等学历教育要求付诸实施的学校。包括广播电视大学、职工高等学校、农民高等学校、管理干部学院、教育学院、独立设置的函授学院等。

小学学龄儿童入学率 指调查范围内已入小学学习的学龄儿童占校内外学龄儿童总数（包括弱智儿童，不包括盲聋哑儿童）的比重。计算公式为:

小学学龄儿童入学率＝已入学的小学学龄儿童数/校内外小学学龄儿童总数*100%

科技活动 指在自然科学、农业科学、医药科学、工程与技术科学、人文与社会科学领域（简称科学技术领域）中，与科技知识的产生、发展、传播和应用密切相关的有组织的活动。可分为研究与试验发展（R&D）、研究与试验发展成果应用及相关的科技服务三类活动。

科技活动人员 指直接从事科技活动、以及专门从事科技活动管理和为科技活动提供直接服务的人员。累计从事科技活动的实际工作时间占全年制度工作时间10%及以上的人员。（1）直接从事科技活动的人员包括:在独立核算的科学研究与技术开发机构、高等学校、各类企业及其他事业单位内设的研究室、实验室、技术开发中心及中试车间（基地）等机构中从事科技活动的研究人员、工程技术人员、技术工人及其它人员;虽不在上述机构工作，但编入科技活动项目（课题）组的人员;科技信息与文献机构中的专业技术人员;从事论文设计的研究生等。（2）专门从事科技活动管理和为科技活动提供直接服务的人员包括:独立核算的科学研究与技术开发机构、科技信息与文献机构、高等学校、各类企业及其他事业单位主管科技工作的负责人，专门从事科技活动的计划、行政、人事、财务、物资供应、设备维护、图书资料管理等工作的各类人员，但不包括保卫、医疗保健人员、司机、食堂人员、茶炉工、水暖工、清洁工等为科技活动提供间接服务的人员。

研究与试验发展（R&D） 指在科学技术领域，为增加知识总量、以及运用这些知识去创造新的应用而进行的系统的创造性的活动，包括基础研究、应用研究、试验发展三类活动。

基础研究 指为了获得关于现象和可观察事实的基本原理的新知识（揭示客观事物的本质、运动规律，获得新发现、新学说）而进行的实验性或理论性研究，它不以任何专门或特定的应用或使用为目的。其成果以科学论文和科学著作为主要形式。

应用研究 指为获得新知识而进行的创造性研究，主要针对某一特定的目的或目标。应用研究是为了确定基础研究成果可能的用途，或是为达到预定的目标探索应采取的新方法（原理性）或新途径。其成果形式以科学论文、专著、原理性模型或发明专利为主。

试验发展 指利用从基础研究、应用研究和实际经验所获得的现有知识，为产生新的产品、材料和装置，建立新的工艺、系统和服务，以及对已产生和建立的上述各项作实质性的改进而进行的系统性工作。其成果形式主要是专利、专有技术、具有新产品基本特征的产品原型或具有新装置基本特征的原始样机等。在社会科学领域，试验发展是指把通过基础研究、应用研究获得的知识转变成可以实施的计划（包括为进行检验和评估实施示范项目）的过程。人文科学领域没有对应的试验发展活动。

研究与试验发展人员 指参与研究与试验发展项目研究、管理和辅助工作的人员，包括项目（课题）组人员，企业科技行政管理人员和直接为项目（课题）活动提供服务的辅助人员。

研究与试验发展人员全时当量 指全时人员数加非全时人员按工作量折算为全时人员数的总和。例如:有两个全时人员和三个非全时人员（工作时间分别为20%、30%和70%），则全时当量为2+0.2+0.3+0.7=3.2人年。

专业技术人员 指从事专业技术工作和专业技术管理工作的人员，即企事业单位中已经聘任专业技术职务从事专业技术工作和专业技术管理工作的人员，以及未聘任专业技术职务，现在专业技术岗位上工作的人员。包括工程技术人员、农业技术人员、科学研究人员、卫生技术人员、教学人员、经济人员、会计人员、统计人员、翻译人员、图书资料、档案、文博人员、新闻出版人员、律师、公证人员、广播电视播音人员、工艺美术人员、体育人员、艺术人员及企业政治思想工作人员，共十七个专业技术职务类别。

政府资金 指从各级政府部门获得的计划用于科技活动的经费，包括科学事业费、科技三项费、科研基建费、科学基金、教育等部门事业费中计划用于科技活动的经费以及政府部门预算外资金中计划用于科技活动的经费等。

企业资金 指从自有资金中提取或接受其他企业委托的、科研院所和高校等事业单位接受企业委托获得的，计划用于科研和技术开发的经费。不包括来自政府、金融机构及国外的计划用于科技活动的资金。

科技活动经费内部支出 指报告年内用于科技活动的实际支出包括劳务费、科研业务费、科研管理费，非基建投资购建的固定资产、科研基建支出以及其他用于科技活动的支出。不包括生产性活动支出、归还贷款支出及转拨外单位支出。

劳务费 指以货币或实物形式直接或间接支付给从事科技活动人员的劳动报酬及各种费用。包括各种形式的工资、津贴、奖金、奖金、福利、离退休人员费用、人民助学金等。

固定资产购建费 指报告年内使用非基建投资购建的固定资产和用于科研基建投资的实际支出额，即固定资产实际支出和科研基建投资实际完成额之和。固定资产是指长期使用而不改变原有实物形态的主要物资设备、图书资料、实验材料和标本以及其他设备和家具、房屋、建筑物。

新产品 指采用新技术原理、新设计构思研制、生产的全新产品，或在结构、材质、工艺等某一方面比原有产品有明显改进，从而显著提高了产品性能或扩大了使用功能的产品。既包括政府有关部门认定并在有效期内的新产品，也包括企业自行研制开发，未经政府有关部门认定，从投产之日起一年之内的新产品。

专利 是专利权的简称，是对发明人的发明创造经审查合格后，由专利局依据专利法授予发明人和设计人对该项发明创造享有的专有权。包括发明、实用新型和外观设计。

发明 指对产品、方法或者其改进所提出的新的技术方案。

实用新型 指对产品的形状、构造或者其结合所提出的适于实用的新的技术方案。

外观设计 指对产品的形状、图案、色彩或者其结合所作出的富有美感并适于工业上应用的新设计。

Explanatory Notes on Main Statistical Indicators

Regular Institutions of Higher Learning refer to educational establishments set up according to the government evaluation and approval procedures, enrolling graduates from senior secondary schools and providing higher education courses and training for senior professionals. They include full-time universities, colleges, high professional schools and short-term professional universities.

Institutions of Higher Learning for Adults refer to educational establishments, set up in line with relevant rules approved by the government, enrolling staff and workers with senior secondary school or equivalent education ,and providing higher education courses in many forms of full time, part time, spare time, or correspondence for adults. Professionals thus trained receive a qualification equivalent to graduates studying regular courses at regular universities, colleges and professional colleges. Institutions of higher learning for adults include Radio and TV universities, schools of high education for staff and workers and peasants, colleges for management cadres, pedagogical colleges, independent correspondence colleges.

Enrollment Rate of Primary School Age Children refers to the proportion of school age children enrolled at schools to the total number of school age children both in and outside schools (including retarded children ,but excluding blind, deaf and mute children). The formula is:

Enrollment Rate of Primary School-age Children = (Total Primary School-age Children at Schools) (Total Primary School age Children Both at and Outside Schools) 100%

Scientific and Technological Activities (S&T Activities) refer to organized activities which are closely related with the creation, development, dissemination and application of the scientific and technical knowledge in the fields of natural sciences, agricultural science, medical science, engineering and technological science, humanities and social sciences (referred to as scientific and technological fields). S&T activities can be classified in to 3 categories: research and development (R&D) activities, application of R&D results, and related S&T services.

Personnel Engaged in S&T Activities refer to personnel directly engaged in S&T activities, in the management of S&T activities, and in providing direct service to S&T activities, who spend over 10% of the total working hours in a year in S&T activities. (1) Personnel directly engaged in S&T activities include researchers, engineers, technicians and other related personnel engaged in S&T activities in independent-accounting R&D institutions, institutions of higher learning, and in research institutes, laboratories, technology development centers and central experiment workshops under enterprises and institutions. Also included are people working in S&T research project teams, professional and technical personnel working in S&T information archiving institutes, and graduate students working on the design of their thesis. (2) Personnel engaged in the management of S&T activities and in providing direct service to S&T activities include senior management people responsible for S&T activities in independent-accounting R&D institutions, S&T information archiving institutes, institutions of higher learning, and in enterprises and institutions where S&T activities are undertaken. Also included are people responsible for the planning, administration, personnel management, financial management, logistics supply, equipment maintenance, information and library management that are related with S&T activities. People providing indirect services are excluded, such as security, medical service, drivers, plumbers, cleaners and those providing catering and related service.

Research and Development (R&D) refers to systematic and creative activities in the field of science and technology aiming at increasing the knowledge and using the knowledge for new application. R&D includes 3 categories of activities: basic research, applied research and experiments and development.

Basic Research refers to empirical or theoretical research aiming at obtaining new knowledge on the fundamental principles of phenomena of observable facts reveal the nature and law of movement of objects and to acquire new discoveries or new theories. basic research takes no specific or designated application as the aim of the research. Results of basic research are mainly releasedor disseminated in the form of scientific papers or monographs.

Applied research refers to creative research aimingat obtaining new knowledge on a specific objective or target. Purpose of the applied research is to identify the

Possible use of results from basic research, or to explore new (fundamental) methods or new approaches. Results of applied research are expressed in the form of scientific papers, monographs, fundamental models or invention patents.

Experiments and Development refer to systematic activities aiming at using the knowledge from basic and applied researches or from practical experience to develop new products, materials and equipment, to establish new production process, systems and services, or to make substantial improvement on the existing products, process or services. Results of experiment and development activities are embodied in patents, exclusive technology, monotype of new products or equipment. In social sciences, experiment and development activities refer to the process of converting the knowledge from basic or applied researches into feasible programmes (including conduct of demonstration projects for assessment and evaluation). There is no experiment and development activities in the science of humanities.

R&D Personnel refer to persons engaged in research, management and supporting activities of R&D, including persons in the project teams, persons engaged in the management of S&T activities of enterprises and supporting staff providing direct service to the research projects.

Full-time Equivalent of R&D Personnel refers to the sum of the full-time persons and the full-time equivalent of part-time persons converted by workload. For instance, if there are 2 full-time persons and 3 part-time workers (20%, 30% and 70% of working hours respectively on R&D activities), the full-time equivalent is 2+0.2+0.3+0.7=3.2person-years.

Professional and Technical Personnel refer to person engaged in professional and technical work or in the management of professional and technical activities, i.e., people with professional or technical positions who are engaged in professional and technical work or in the management of professional and technical activities, and people without professional or technical positions but are working on professional or technical posts. They include professionals and technicians working in 17 categories of technical occupations including engineering, agriculture, scientific researches, medical service, teaching, economic research and application, accounting, statistics, translation, libraries, archives, cultural and museum service, journalism and publication, lawyers, notarization service, radio and television broadcasting, handicraft and fine arts, sports, performing art, and political workers in enterprises.

Government Funds refer to funds obtained from government agencies at all levels to be used for S&T activities, including fund for scientific undertakings, 3 kinds of fund for S&T activities, fund for capital construction for scientific researches, science fund, funds from education expenditures by education departments for S&T activities, and extra-budget fund from government agencies for S&T activities.

Self-raised Funds by Enterprises refers to self-raised funds by enterprises from their own expenditure or from other enterprises and funds received by universities or research institutions from enterprises for scientific research or technical development projects. Excluded in this category are funds from government agencies, financial institutions or from foreign institutions.

Internal Expenditures on S&T activities refer to the actual expenditures on S&T activities during the reference year, including service fees, expenditure on research activities, expenditure on research management, purchase or construction of fixed assets not included in the activities, expenditure on research management, purchase or construction of fixed assets not included in the investment for capital construction, expenditure on capital construction for scientific researches, and other expenditures on S&T activities. Not included are expenditure on production activities, repayment of loans and transfer expenditure.

Service Fees refer to direct or indirect payment, in cash or in kind, made to personnel engaged in S&T activities as remuneration and other fees. They include, in various forms, salaries, subsidies, bonus, benefits, retirement pension, stipend, etc.

Purchase or Construction of Fixed Assets refers to the fixed assets purchased or constructed using funds other than the investment in capital construction, and the actual expenditure on capital construction for scientific researches. In other words, it is the sum of the actual expenditure on fixed assets and the accomplished investment in capital construction for scientific researches. Fixed assets refer to main materials and equipment, literatures and documents in libraries, Materials for experiments, specimen, instruments, furniture, buildingsand constructions that can be used for a long time without changing the form and shape of those articles or constructions.

New Products refer to new products produced with

new technology and new design, or products that representnoticeable improvement in terms of structure,material, or production process so as to improve significantly the character or function of the older versions. They include new products certified by relevant government agencies within the period of certification, as well as new products designed and produced by enterprises within a year without certification by government agencies.

Patent is an abbreviation for the patent right and refers to the exclusive right of ownership by the inventors or designers for the creation or inventions, given from the patent offices after due process of assessment and approval in accordance with the Patent Law. Patents are granted for inventions, utility models and designs.

Inventions refer to the new technical proposals to the products or methods or their modifications.

Utility Models refer to the practical and new technical proposals on the shape and structure of the product or the combination of both.

Designs refer to the aesthetics and industrially applicable new designs for the shape, pattern and color of the product, or their combinations.

19 文化、体育、卫生、社会福利和其他

CULTURE,SPORTS,PUBLIC HEALTH,SOCIAL WELFARE INSTITUTIONS AND OTHER SOCIAL ACTIVITIES

资料整理：陈超毅

Data management:Chen Chaoyi

第十九部分　文化、体育、卫生、社会福利和其他

一、简要说明

本章资料主要包括文化、卫生、民政、体育、计划生育、共青团、妇联以及公检法等方面的内容，由西安市统计局社会科技处根据西安市文广新局、卫生局、民政局、体育局、妇联、共青团市委、计划生育委员会以及公安局、检察院、法院等部门提供资料整理。

二、主要指标

图书馆总藏量（千册件）	4465	比上年增加　141千册件
医院数（所）	258	比上年减少　3所
医院床位数（万张）	3.43	比上年增加　1900张

19　CULTURE,SPORTS,PUBLIC HEALTH,SOCIAL WELFARE INSTITUTIONS AND OTHER SOCIAL ACTIVITIES

Ⅰ.Brief IntroductionData in this chapter primarily consists of data of culture, sanitation, civil administration, physical education, family planning, Communist Youth League, the Women's Federation, public security organs, procuratorial organs and people's court, compiled by Social Science & Technology Division of Xi'an Bureau of Statistics according to data from Xi'an Bureau of Cuture, Bureau of Sanitation, Bureau of Civial Adnimistration, Bureau of PE, the Women's Federation, Municipal Committee of Communist Youth League, Committee of Family Planning, Bureau of Public Security, Procuratorate, People's Court and other department concerned.

Ⅱ.Major Indicators

		Increase over Preceding Year
Number of Collections in Libraries (1 000 volumes)	4465	141
Number of Hospitals(unit)	258	-3
Number of Beds(10 000 units)	3.43	1900 units

19-1 文化事业机构和人数（2010年）

Number of Institutions and Personnel in Culture and Art（2010）

项　　目	Item	机构数（个）Number of Institutions (unit)	人员数（人）Number of Personnel (person)
一、电影事业	**Career of Film**		
制片厂	Studio	1	
发行放映管理机构	Number of Film Projection and Publication Administrating Institutions	2	
电影放映单位	Unit of Film shows		
#电影院	Cinema	19	
影剧院	Theaters	12	
放映队	Film Projection Team	123	
二、艺术事业	**Art**		
表演团体	Performance Troupes	18	2039
表演场所	Art Centers	18	280
三、图书馆事业	**Libraries**	**15**	**476**
四、群众文化事业	**Mass Culture**	**197**	**933**
#文化馆	Cultural Centers	15	355
文化站	Culture Stations	182	579
五、教育事业	**Educations**		

注：2010年电影事业的数据口径发生变化，与往年不可比。

Note:Aperture of data of film career has changed since 2010, not comparable with former years.

19-2 文化事业发展情况

Basic Statistics on Culture Development

指 标	Item	2005	2006	2007	2008	2009	2010
电影放映场数 (千场)	Number of Film Shows (1 000 shows)	33	32	29	25	44	196
观众人数(千人次)	Number of Spectators (1 000 person-times)	3186	2568	1890	1295	1299	5960
艺术表演团体演出场次(国内)(千场)	Number of Art Performance Troupes Performers (1 000 shows)	4	4	4	4	5	5
观众人数(千人次)	Number of Spectators (1 000 person-times)	6138	22765	4416	3972	5573	12316
图书馆总藏量(千册件)	Number of Collections in Libraries (1000 volumes)	3671	3807	3893	4040	4324	4465
书刊文献外借人次(千人次)	Books, Journals and Documents Borrowing (1 000 person-times)	384	416	432	478	435	682
书刊文献外借册次(千册)	Books, Journals and Documents Borrowing (1 000 Volume-time)	656	884	813	917	727	1368

19-3 群众艺术馆、文化馆（站）活动情况

Basic Statistics on Activities of Mass Art Centers and Cultural Centers

指 标	Item	2005	2006	2007	2008	2009	2010
机构数(个)	Number of Insititutions (unit)	192	193	197	197	197	197
举办展览个数(个)	Number of Exhibitions (unit)	458	667	511	520	716	705
组织文艺活动次数(次)	Art Performances and Story-telling Sessions (time)	1439	2251	2884	2378	3158	3729
举办训练班班次(个)	Number of Training Courses (unit)	1137	1327	1625	1109	1467	3018
培训人次(千人次)	Number of Trained Persons (1 000 person-times)	37	43	67	87	96	133
藏 书(千册)	Collections (1 000 volumes)	322	336	227	270	299	331
本年收入(千元)	Income of this year (1 000 yuan)	11257	12981	21111	22571	40891	42937
本年支出(千元)	Expenditure of this year (1 000 yuan)	10924	12706	21007	22458	42826	45160

19-4 文物保护业基本情况（2010年）

Basic Statistics on Cultural Relics Protection（2010）

指　　标	Item	机构（个）Insititution (unit)	人员（人）Personnel (person)	文物藏品实际数量（件）Factual Number of Collections(piece)	一级品 Grade One	参观人员（千人次）Number of Visitors (1000 person-times)
总　计	**Total**	**57**	**3163**	**591885**	**4819**	**9179**
文物保护管理机构	Protection and Management Agencies	27	459	14010	32	1834
其他文物机构	Other Agencies	8	222			
博物馆	Museums	19	2235	550471	4579	7345
文物商店	Cultural Relics Agencies					
文物科研机构	Scientific Research of Historical Relics Preservation	3	247	27404	208	

注：文物科研机构文物藏品数2009年统计口径发生变化，与往年不可比。

Note:As statistical caliber of scientific research of historical relics preservation and number of relics has changed since 2009,so they couldn't be compared with those of former years.

19-5 广播电台及节目制作情况

Basic Statistics of Broadcasting Stations and Program Production

指　　标	Item	2005	2006	2007	2008	2009	2010
省、地广播电台(座)	Broadcasting Stations at the Province and District Level(set)	2	2	2	2	2	2
县级广播电视台(座)	Number of Wire Broadcasting Stations and TV Relaying Stations(set)	6	6	6	6	6	6
中短波、调频发射台及转播台(座)	Medium/Short Ware and FM Broadcast Transmission Stations and Relaying Stations(set)	280	290	40	46	51	55
节目(套)	Number of Programs(set)	14	15	17	17	18	18
平均每日播出时间(时)	Broadcasting Hours per Day(hour:minute)	244	248	297	311	337	340
广播人口覆盖率(%)	Listener Rating(%)	99.35	99.36	99.37	99.37	99.37	99.4
制作广播节目(时)	Productions of Broadcasting(hour)	81840	84083	97013	103328	110455	110639
#新闻资讯类	News Programs	12189	11013	12274	9139	10586	13786
专题服务类	Special Subject Programs	23196	31662	33182	17539	29764	24451
综艺类	Variety Programs						37720
广播剧类	Literature Programs	29837	32698	32270	48014	46859	2406
广告类	Advertisements						28339
其他类	Service Programs	12056	8710	19287	28636	23246	3937

注：2009年以前制作广播节目分类为新闻节目、专题节目、文艺节目和服务节目。

Note: Before 2009, the prodution of broadcasting programs was sorted into news programs, special subject programs, literature programs and service programs.

19-6　电视台及节目制作情况

Basic Statistics of TV Stations and Production of TV Program

指　　标	Item	2005	2006	2007	2008	2009	2010
电视台(座)	Number of Television Stations（set）	2	2	2	2	2	2
发射台及转播台(座)	Number of Television Transmission Stations and Relaying Stations（set）	297	297	8	8	10	10
无线电视节目(套)	Program Productions of Non-cable television Stations（set）	6	5	5	5	7	6
有线电视节目(套)	Program Productions of cable television Stations（set）	9	10	16	17	15	16
平均每周播出时间(时)	Average Broadcasting Hours per Week（hour）	2294	2289	2504	2704	2661	2728
电视人口覆盖率(%)	Viewer Rating（%）	97.67	97.85	98.33	98.35	98.41	98.57
卫星电视地面站(座)	Earth Stations of Satellite TV（set）	1319	1251		32638	26167	41163
制作电视节目 (时)	Productions of TV Programs(hour)	27377	36337	25883	26897	27131	29626
#新闻资讯类	News and Information Programs						8930
专题服务类	Special Subject Programs	9031	9918	6596	6726	6520	7762
综艺类	Variety Programs	7378	10593	9646	10819	9652	3942
影视剧类	Literature Programs						1729
广告类	Advertisement						3313
其他类	Service Programs	5136	10526	3880	4774	5805	3950
有线电视用户(万户)	Users of Cable television Stations（10 000 households）	102.21	115.16	125.28	138.79	146.84	164.64

注：1.2007年中短波、调频发射台及转播台功率50瓦以下不计算在内，故数据与往年不可比。

2.卫星电视地面站（座）2007年无数据。

3.2009年以前制作广播节目分类为新闻节目、专题节目、文艺节目和服务节目。

Notes:1.2007 years,MW and SW,FM transmitters and relay stations,power of 50 watts is not taken into account,so the data are not comparable with previous years.

2.Satellite TV stations (Block) 2007 no data.

3.Before 2009, the prodution of broadcasting programs was sorted into news programs, special subject programs, literature programs and service programs.

19-7　体育事业基本情况（市属）（2010年）

The Basic Situations of Sports (Under Municipality)（2010）

单位：人、枚　(person、unit)

指　　标	Item	2010
一、体育系统职工人数	**Number of Staffs and Workers in Physical Education System**	**987**
#运动员	Athletes	665
教练员	Coaches	98
二、等级裁判员发展人数	**Number of the Development of Grade Referees**	**157**
三、等级运动员发展人数	**Number of the Development of Grade Athletes**	**164**
四、全年获得奖牌数	**Number of Full-year Medals**	**739**
#国家级金牌	National Gold	32
国家级银牌	National Silver	18
省级金牌	Provincial Gold	349
省级银牌	Provincial Silver	149

19-8 少年儿童分项业余体校情况（市属）（2010年）

Basic Statistics of Youth Part-time Physical Training School（2010）

单位：人 （person）

指　　标	Items	2010
一、在读学生数	**Total Enrollment**	
总　计	**Total**	**2072**
田　径	Track and Field	277
游　泳	Swimming	80
体　操	Gymnastics	30
举　重	Weightlifting	469
国际式摔跤	Wrestling	73
柔　道	Judo	102
射　击	Shooting	120
射　箭	Archery	55
足　球	Football	83
蓝　球	Basketball	198
排　球	Volleyball	30
乒乓球	Table Tennis	105
拳　击	Boxing	30
武　术	Wu Shu	94
跆拳道	Kickboxing	260
跳　水	Diving	15
棒　球	Baseball	51
二、职工数	**Number of Staff and Workers**	**235**

19-9 卫生机构、床位及人员数（2010年）

卫生机构	Health Care Institutions	机构数(个) Number of Institutions (unit)	床位数(张) Number of Beds (unit)
总 计	**Total**	**2385**	**39407**
一、医院	**Hospitals**	**258**	**34274**
综合医院	General Hospitals	197	27406
中医医院	Hospitals Specialized in Traditional Chinese Medicine	34	2802
中西医结合医院	Hospitals Integrating Traditional Chinese Medicine with Western Therapeutics in Practice	1	20
民族医院	Nationalities Hospitals		
专科医院	Specialized Hospitals	26	4046
口腔医院	Dental Hospitals	3	76
眼科医院	Eye Hospitals	3	151
耳鼻喉科医院	ENT Hospitals		
肿瘤医院	Cancer Hospitals	1	610
心血管病医院	Cardiovascular Hospitals		
胸科医院	Chest Hospitals		
血液病医院	Blood Disease Hospitals		
妇产（科）医院	Obstetrics and Gynecologist Hospitals	2	68
儿童医院	Children's Hospitals	1	790
精神病医院	Psychiatric Hospitals	4	910
传染病医院	Hospitals for Infectious Diseases	1	200
皮肤病医院	Skin Hospitals		
结核病医院	Tuberculosis Hospitals	1	600
麻风病医院	Leprosy Hospitals		
职业病医院	Occupational Diseases Hospitals		
骨科医院	Orthopedic Hospitals	2	101
康复医院	Rehabilitation Hospitals	3	28

Number of Health Care Institutions, Beds and Employed Persons in Health Care Institutions（2010）

人员合计(人) Total Number of Employed Persons (person)	卫生技术人员 Medical Technical Personnel	其他技术人员 Other Technical Personnel	管理人员 Administrative Personnel	工勤人员 Logistics Technical Workers
71230	**56579**	**1156**	**6416**	**7079**
51672	**40379**	**761**	**5032**	**5500**
43017	34002	595	3903	4517
3549	2687	121	398	343
43	34		4	5
5063	3656	45	727	635
360	275		64	21
211	158	4	39	10
787	583	9	100	95
146	127	5	12	2
1269	1018	2	155	94
781	454	9	116	202
397	237	3	84	73
421	303	3	74	41
110	101	3	6	
96	55		9	32

19-9 续表

卫生机构	Health Care Institutions	机构数(个) Number of Institutions (unit)	床位数(张) Number of Beds (unit)
整形外科医院	Plastic Surgery Hospitals		
美容医院	Beauty Hospitals		
其他专科医院	Other Specialized Hospitals	5	512
护理院	Nursing Centets		
二、疗养院	**Sanitary**	**3**	**468**
三、社区卫生服务中心	**Commuting health care service centre**	**148**	**914**
社区卫生服务中心	Community Health Care Center	73	886
社区卫生服务站	Community Health Care Station	75	28
四、卫生院	**Small hospital**	**154**	**2522**
街道卫生院	Urban Township Health Centers	27	515
乡镇卫生院	Rural Township Heatth Centers	127	2007
五、门诊部	**Policlinic**	**162**	**27**
六、急救中心（站）	**Emergency centre (station)**	**1**	
七、采供血机构	**Blood collect and supply institution**	**1**	
八、妇幼保健院（所、站）	**Health center for women and children (institute, station)**	**15**	**802**
九、专科疾病防治院（所、站）	**Special disease prevention and cure hospital (institute, station)**	**1**	**400**
十、疾病预防控制中心（防疫站）	**Disease prevention and control centre (epidemic prevention station)**	**17**	
十一、卫生监督所	**Hygiene supervision centre**	**15**	
十二、医学科学研究机构	**Medicine science research institution**	**4**	
十三、医学在职培训机构	**Medicine incumbency training institution**	**5**	
十四、健康教育所（站、中心）	**Health education centre**	**2**	
十五、诊所、卫生所、医务室	**Clinic**	**1590**	
诊所	Clinic	1268	
卫生所、医务室	Clinic	322	
十六、其他卫生机构	**Other hygiene institution**	**9**	

continued

人员合计(人) Total Number of Employed Persons (person)	卫生技术人员 Medical Technical Personnel	其他技术人员 Other Technical Personnel	管理人员 Administrative Personnel	工勤人员 Logistics Technical Workers
485	345	7	68	65
197	**106**	**7**	**34**	**50**
3447	**2855**	**72**	**244**	**276**
2829	2311	63	206	249
618	544	9	38	27
4254	**3489**	**69**	**277**	**419**
567	474	8	31	54
3687	3015	61	246	365
2254	**1944**	**46**	**141**	**123**
103	**37**	**10**	**27**	**29**
144	**88**	**11**	**34**	**11**
1946	**1575**	**22**	**185**	**164**
290	**230**	**6**	**15**	**39**
1012	**707**	**39**	**144**	**122**
550	**303**	**13**	**159**	**75**
176	**95**	**22**	**28**	**31**
204	**77**	**59**	**48**	**20**
64	**20**	**14**	**26**	**4**
4795	**4595**			**200**
3514	3399			115
1281	1196			85
122	**79**	**5**	**22**	**16**

19-10 各区县卫生机构、床位及人员数（2010年）

Number of Health Care Institutions, Beds and Employed Persons in Health Care Institutions By Region（2010）

区　县	Region	机构数(个) Number of Health Care Institutions (unit)	床位数合计(张) Number of Beds (unit)	人员合计(人) Total Number of Employed Persons （person）	卫生技术人员 Total Number of Medical Technical Personnel
全　市	**Total**	**2385**	**39407**	**71230**	**56579**
新城区	Xincheng	300	6422	13389	10393
碑林区	Beilin	327	5846	11307	8575
莲湖区	Lianhu	337	4740	8878	7192
灞桥区	Baqiao	304	2373	3804	3239
未央区	Weiyang	142	2585	4560	3793
雁塔区	Yanta	375	7490	13103	10146
阎良区	Yanliang	70	1323	1891	1511
临潼区	Lintong	92	1439	2316	1877
长安区	Chang'an	157	2413	4128	3491
蓝田县	Lantian	72	1179	1518	1247
周至县	Zhouzhi	67	779	2069	1611
户　县	Huxian	83	1962	2984	2436
高陵县	Gaoling	59	856	1283	1068

19-11 卫生机构各类人员数

Number of Employed Persons in Health Care Institutions

单位：人 (person)

指　标	Item	2000	2005	2006	2007	2008	2009	2010
人员总数	**Total**	**53111**	**52821**	**54912**	**55551**	**59934**	**65003**	**71230**
卫生技术人员	Medical Technical Personnel	41836	42255	43862	43707	47433	51641	56579
执业（助理）医师	Licensed（Assistant） Doctors	18750	17730	18007	17266	18066	19284	18763
#执业医师	Chartered Doctors	16146	15533	15778	15142	15975	17286	16613
注册护士	Registered Nurses	14344	14004	15538	15337	17186	20167	22640
药师（士）	Junior Paramedics	3475	3084	2987	2707	2721	2814	3030
技　师（士）	Technicians	2179	2252	2242	3046	3168	3350	4589
#检验师	Laboratory Technicians	2179	2252	2242	2150	2204	2290	2439
其　他	Other	3088	5185	5088	5351	6292	6026	7557
其他技术人员	Other Technical Personnel	855	1425	1601	1399	1051	1325	1156
管理人员	Administrative Personnel	5647	5199	5309	5532	6007	6067	6416
工勤人员	Logistics Technical Workers	4773	3942	4140	4913	5443	5970	7079

19–12 医院、卫生院诊疗人次及诊疗情况（2010年）

卫生机构	Health Care Institutions	诊疗人次数总计	
		总计 Total	合计（人） Count(person)
总 计	**Total**	**31887382**	**31330565**
在总计中：	**Among the Total:**		
一、医院	**Hospitals**	**19546147**	**19269844**
综合医院	General Hospitals	16362833	16119012
中医医院	Hospitals Specialized in Traditional Chinese Medicine	1554635	1530190
中西医结合医院	Hospitals Integrating Traditional Chinese Medicine with Western Therapeutics in Practice	8410	8410
民族医院	Nationalities Hospitals		
专科医院	Specialized Hospitals	1620269	1612232
口腔医院	Dental Hospitals	206707	202058
眼科医院	Eye Hospitals	87660	87660
耳鼻喉科医院	ENT Hospitals		
肿瘤医院	Cancer Hospitals	19623	19623
心血管病医院	Cardiovascular Hospitals		
胸科医院	Chest Hospitals		
血液病医院	Blood Disease Hospitals		
妇产（科）医院	Obstetrics and Gynecologist Hospitals	56711	56711
儿童医院	Children□s Hospitals	942005	940317
精神病医院	Psychiatric Hospitals	83549	83219
传染病医院	Hospitals for Infectious Diseases	22770	22770
皮肤病医院	Skin Hospitals		
结核病医院	Tuberculosis Hospitals	57007	57007
麻风病医院	Leprosy Hospitals		
职业病医院	Occupational Diseases Hospitals		
骨科医院	Orthopedic Hospitals	39705	38664
康复医院	Rehabilitation Hospitals	21160	21160
整形外科医院	Plastic Surgery Hospitals		
美容医院	Beauty Hospitals		
其他专科医院	Other Specialty Hospitals	83372	83043
护理院	Nursing Centers		
二、卫生院	**Health Centers**	**1697624**	**1690664**
街道卫生院	Urban Health Centers	383956	383330
乡镇卫生院	Rural Health Centers	1313668	1307334
中心卫生院	Town Health Centers	682570	679983
乡村卫生院	Village Health Centers	631098	627351

Number of Visits and Inpatients in Medical Institutions（2010）

Total Number of Clinics			观察室	Observation Room
其中:门、急诊人次数	Number of Outpatient and Emergency		收容病人数 （人）	死亡人数 (人)
门诊人次数	急诊人次数	Number of Emergency		
Number of Outpatients	小计 Subtotal	死亡人数 Number of Deaths	Number of Patients Receiving(person)	Number of Deaths (person)
29458462	**1872103**	**1859**	**137199**	**226**
17612268	**1657576**	**1850**	**16605**	**226**
14739937	1379075	1819	16231	220
1486532	43658	6	322	6
8298	112			
1377501	234731	25	52	
199489	2569			
86586	1074			
19620	3			
40758	15953		5	
732379	207938	23		
82349	870			
17837	4933			
56531	476			
38304	360			
20810	350		29	
82838	205	2	18	
1610132	**80532**	**2**	**32560**	
350025	33305		5454	
1260107	47227	2	27106	
651074	28909	2	13974	
609033	18318		13132	

19–13 医院、卫生院床位及病人治疗情况（2010年）

Beds and Patients Treated Conditions in Health Care Institutions（2010）

卫生机构	Health Care Institutions	实有病床数（张）Number Hospital Beds (unit)	平均开放病床数（张）Average Daily Number of Open Beds (unit)	治愈率(%) Curative Ratio (%)	好转率(%) Improvement Rate (%)	死亡率(%) Mortality Rate (%)
总计	**Total**	**39407**	**38116**	**60.77**	**36.95**	**0.80**
在总计中:	**Among the Total:**					
一、医院	**Hospitals**	**34274**	**33177**	**58.26**	**39.37**	**0.88**
综合医院	General Hospitals	27406	26744	58.79	38.88	0.95
中医医院	Hospitals Specialized in Traditional Chinese Medicine	2802	2695	44.73	52.85	0.56
中西医结合医院	Hospitals Integrating Traditional Chinese Medicine with Western Therapeutics in Practice	20	20	28.57	71.43	
民族医院	Nationalities Hospitals					
专科医院	Specialized Hospitals	4046	3718	63.01	34.29	0.45
口腔医院	Dental Hospitals	76	76	90.35	9.48	
眼科医院	Eye Hospitals	151	151	90.03	9.75	
耳鼻喉科医院	ENT Hospitals					
肿瘤医院	Cancer Hospitals	610	610	67.16	28.65	1.08
心血管病医院	Cardiovascular Hospitals					
胸科医院	Chest Hospitals					
血液病医院	Blood Disease Hospitals					
妇产（科）医院	Obstetrics and Gynecologist Hospitals	68	68	96.03	2.95	0.16
儿童医院	Children's Hospitals	790	733	78.87	19.73	0.28

19-13 续表 continued

卫生机构	Health Care Institutions	实有病床数（张）Number Hospital Beds (unit)	平均开放病床数（张）Average Daily Number of Open Beds (unit)	治愈率(%) Curative Ratio (%)	好转率(%) Improvement Rate (%)	死亡率(%) Mortality Rate (%)
精神病医院	Psychiatric Hospitals	910	720	33.36	63.96	0.07
传染病医院	Hospitals for Infectious Diseases	200	200	53.34	41.95	0.89
皮肤病医院	Skin Hospitals					
结核病医院	Tuberculosis Hospitals	600	545	3.77	90.76	0.60
麻风病医院	Leprosy Hospitals					
职业病医院	Occupational Diseases Hospitals					
骨科医院	Orthopedic Hospitals	101	101	42.38	51.68	
康复医院	Rehabilitation Hospitals	28	27	61.92	28.15	
整形外科医院	Plastic Surgery Hospitals					
美容医院	Beauty Hospitals					
其他专科医院	Other Specialty Hospitals	512	487	35.28	62.78	0.09
护理院	Nursing Centers					
二、卫生院	**Health Centers**	**2522**	**2464**	**81.96**	**17.03**	
街道卫生院	Urban Health Centers	515	494	79.79	19.06	
乡镇卫生院	Rural Health Centers	2007	1970	82.52	16.52	
中心卫生院	Town Health Centers	1281	1254	83.07	15.73	
乡村卫生院	Village Health Centers	726	716	81.40	18.09	

19-14 县（区）村卫生室基本情况（2010年）

单位：个、人、次

指 标	Item	总计 Total	村办 Run by Village
机构数	Number of Health Care Institutions	3247	2355
执业（助理）医师	Licensed (Assistant) Doctors	965	745
注册护士	Registered Nurses	212	139
乡村医生和卫生员	Village Doctors and Medics	4576	3209
乡村医生数	Number of Village Doctors	4084	2909
#大专及以上学历	College Education or Above	481	339
中专学历及中专水平	Vocational Education and Secondary School Level	3138	2192
在职培训合格者	Qualified Job Training	436	352
卫生员	Number of Medics	492	300
诊疗人次数	Number of Treatments	9607364	6577602

Basic Statistics on Clinics in Counties and Villages（2010）

(unit、person、time)

按设置/主办单位分 Grouped by Setering/Owner				按行医方式分 Grouped by Medical Mode		
乡卫生院设点 Division of Township Health Center	联合办 Collectively	私人办 Privately	其他 Others	西医为主 Mainly Western Medicine	中医为主 Mainly Chinese Medicine	中西医结合 Integrating Chinese Medicine with Western Medicine
21	242	584	45	50	2442	755
0	58	133	29	14	725	226
0	29	34	10	3	152	57
19	387	882	79	65	3328	1183
15	342	745	73	58	3058	968
3	39	86	14	9	345	127
11	277	601	57	39	2372	727
1	26	55	2	10	326	100
4	45	137	6	7	270	215
52838	828976	2039611	108337	113389	7049744	2444231

19-15 社会福利事业单位基本情况（2010年）

Basic Statistics on Social Welfare Insititutions（2010）

单位：个、人 （unit,person）

指　　标	Item	福利院数 Number of Homes	工作人员 Number of Staff	床位数 Number of Beds	年末在院人数 Number of Persons Housed at the Year-end
一、社会福利院情况	**Statistics on Social Welfare**	**59**	**1542**	**10081**	**7113**
1.社会福利院	Social Welfare Homes	4	89	1245	903
2.儿童福利院	Baby Welfare Homes	1	78	900	828
3.社会福利医院	Social Welfare Hospitals	1	149	500	474
4.收养性老年福利机构	Welfare Units Adopting the Elderly	53	1226	7436	4908
城镇	Urban	31	1016	5220	3694
农村	Rural	22	210	2216	1214

19-16 社会福利事业单位机构、人员数

Number of Social Welfare Institutions and Employed Persons

单位：个、人 （unit,person）

项　　目	Item	2000	2005	2006	2007	2008	2009	2010
一、机构	**Insititutions**							
烈士纪念建筑物管理单位	Institutions Managing Memorial Buildings of Martyrs	2	2	2	2	2	2	2
救助类单位	Units Providing Assistance	8	8	8	8	8	8	8
殡仪服务单位	Funeral Service Units	18	20	22	21	20	20	22
殡仪馆	Funeral Homes	4	4	4	5	4	4	4
公墓	Cemeteries	12	13	14	13	12	12	14
殡葬管理单位	Funeral Management Units	2	3	4	3	4	4	4
二、人员	**Staff**							
烈士纪念建筑物管理单位	Institutions Managing Memorial Buildings of Martyrs	43	43	40	37	39	39	37
救助类单位	Units Providing Assistance	99	112	116	113	110	118	116
殡仪服务单位	Funeral Service Units	613	756	765	902	1015	1046	1371
殡仪馆	Funeral Homes	164	204	177	239	220	218	375
公墓	Cemeteries	425	516	533	624	745	776	939
殡葬管理单位	Funeral Management Units	24	36	55	39	50	52	57

19-17　各区县优抚对象人员情况（2010年）

Statistics on Persons Enjoying Favoured Treatment by Region（2010）

单位：人　　(person)

指　标	Item	全市 Total	新城区 Xincheng	碑林区 Beilin	莲湖区 Lianhu
合　计	**Total**	**27248**	**909**	**927**	**1029**
1.革命伤残人员	Number of Disabled Veterans	4926	659	559	690
2.烈军属人员	Number of Family Members of Martyrs and Soldiers	382	27	15	26
3.在乡红军老战士	Old Red Army Men in Hometown	5		2	1
4.在乡复原军人	Demobilized Soldiers in Hometown	7346	19	15	36
5.在乡退伍军人	Veterans in Hometown	1988	170		205

19-17　续表1 continued 1

单位：人　　(person)

指　标	Item	灞桥区 Baqiao	未央区 Weiyang	雁塔区 Yanta	阎良区 Yanliang	临潼区 Lintong
合　计	**Total**	**2024**	**1021**	**1732**	**1077**	**3131**
1.革命伤残人员	Number of Disabled Veterans	266	244	614	87	328
2.烈军属人员	Number of Family Members of Martyrs and Soldiers	32	13	11	22	63
3.在乡红军老战士	Old Red Army Men in Hometown					
4.在乡复原军人	Demobilized Soldiers in Hometown	613	241	140	299	1286
5.在乡退伍军人	Veterans in Hometown		184		219	89

19-17　续表2 continued 2

单位：人　　(person)

指　标	Item	长安区 Chang'an	蓝田县 Lantian	周至县 Zhouzhi	户县 Huxian	高陵县 Gaoling
合　计	**Total**	**4849**	**2222**	**3819**	**2664**	**1757**
1.革命伤残人员	Number of Disabled Veterans	403	225	349	287	128
2.烈军属人员	Number of Family Members of Martyrs and Soldiers	38	47	44	20	24
3.在乡红军老战士	Old Red Army Men in Hometown			1		1
4.在乡复原军人	Demobilized Soldiers in Hometown	1203	795	1105	935	659
5.在乡退伍军人	Veterans in Hometown	309	46	227	387	152

19-18 计划生育和婚姻情况（2010年）

Conditions of Birth Control and Marriage Registration（2010）

区 县	Region	晚婚率(%) Late Marriage Rate	计划生育率(%) Family Planning Rate	综合节育率(%) Contraceptive Rate
全 市	**Total**	**68.5**	**98.8**	**91.7**
新城区	Xingcheng	99.2	99.9	88.4
碑林区	Beilin	99.1	99.8	90.3
莲湖区	Lianhu	70.2	99.8	90.5
灞桥区	Baqiao	70.6	99.5	92.0
未央区	Weiyang	65.1	99.8	89.9
雁塔区	Yanta	57.5	99.9	87.9
阎良区	Yanliang	61.0	99.2	93.2
临潼区	Lintong	74.6	97.7	93.9
长安区	Chang'an	56.0	98.2	93.9
蓝田县	Lantian	68.9	97.6	91.4
周至县	Zhouzhi	67.5	97.3	92.7
户 县	Huxian	43.0	99.0	93.9
高陵县	Gaoling	64.3	98.9	90.6

19-18 续表 continued

区 县	Region	独生子女领证率(%) Only-child Certificate Rate	结婚对数（对） Marriages (couple)	再婚数（人） Remarriages	离婚对数（对） Divorced Couple (couple)
全 市	**Total**	**48.7**	**83645**	**22797**	**19060**
新城区	Xingcheng	55.9	4985	1877	1560
碑林区	Beilin	61.1	9484	2279	2116
莲湖区	Lianhu	66.6	6467	2300	1875
灞桥区	Baqiao	52.1	6188	1621	1183
未央区	Weiyang	64.3	6987	2014	1854
雁塔区	Yanta	58.8	9541	3457	3708
阎良区	Yanliang	45.5	2693	890	622
临潼区	Lintong	32.8	7372	1559	1143
长安区	Chang'an	35.4	11292	3157	2179
蓝田县	Lantian	22.2	5426	1045	787
周至县	Zhouzhi	12.8	5087	717	653
户 县	Huxian	35.4	4576	974	773
高陵县	Gaoling	26.4	3547	907	607

19-19 律师、公证及调解基本情况

Basic Statistics on Lawyer, Notaries and Mediation

指标	Item	2000	2005	2006	2007	2008	2009	2010
一、律师工作	**Lawyers**							
律师事务所（个）	Number of Law Offices (unit)	46	65	70	71	73	79	95
律师（人）	Lawyers(person)	534	866	902	864	940	1058	1202
#专职	Full-time	469	825	851	808	865	1001	1139
兼职	Part-time	65	41	51	56	66	55	63
二、公证工作	**Notarization**							
公证处（个）	Number of Notary Offices (unit)	14	14	14	14	14	14	14
公证人员（人）	Notarial Personnel (person)	158	192	205	243	189	194	202
#公证员	Notaries	96	93	102	156	100	102	112
办理公证件数（件）	Number of Notarized Documents Issued (case)	79199	68110	70777	70863	74440	88637	106491
国内	Domestic	62060	46427	45717	42996	43640	57190	72670
民事	Civil	24576	11737	13258	15466	15782	22337	24813
经济	Economics	37484	34690	32459	27530	27858	34853	47857
涉外	Foreign-related	16990	21451	24857	27616	30481	31082	33410
涉港、澳、台	Hong Kong、Macco and Taiwan related	149	232	203	251	319	365	411
三、人民调解工作	**Number of People Mediations**							
已建调委会数（个）	Number of Mediation Committees (unit)	4379	3904	3952	3952	3961	3961	3911
调解人员数（人）	Number of Mediators (person)	13059	16156	15930	15525	15424	17198	15717
调解纠纷数（件）	Number of Civil Disputes Mediated (case)	34212	17770	17608	14986	12223	23185	22247
#调解成功数	Number of Cases Successfully Mediated	31574	14084	14597	13756	11201	21373	22164

19-20 共青团组织情况

Basic Facts on Communist Youth League

单位：个、人 (unit,person)

指 标	Item	2000	2005	2006	2007	2008	2009	2010
一、基层团组织	**Grass-root Youth League Organisations**	**10323**	**7726**	**9560**	**9329**	**10985**	**9054**	**7076**
二、共青团员	**Youth League Members**	**278165**	**344035**	**329669**	**327332**	**348141**	**324785**	**250743**
#女团员	Female Youth League Members	134289	153493	142431	141271	145777	144027	128713
三、专职团干部	**Full-time Youth League Cadre**	**845**	**537**	**524**	**576**	**601**	**387**	**723**

19-21 妇联组织状况

Women's Organizations Status

单位：个 (unit)

项 目	Item	2010
一、妇联组织	**Women's Organizations**	
市级妇联	Municipal Women's Federation	1
街道妇联	Street Women's Federation	264
社区妇联	Community Women's Federation	1121
县（区）妇联	County (district) Women's Federation	13
乡（镇)妇联	Township (town) Women's Federation	93
村妇代会	Village Women's Representative Conference	3022
二、非公有制经济组织中妇女组织	**Women's Organizations in Non-public Economic Organizations**	
个体劳动者协会中的妇女组织	Women's Organizations in Association of Individual Workers	10
专业市场中的妇女组织	Women's Organizations in the Professional Market	
私营企业中的妇女组织	Women's Organizations in the Private Sector	70
三资企业中的妇女组织	Foreign-funded Enterprises in the Women's Organizations	
三、机关事业单位妇女组织	**Women's Organizations in Government Departments and Institutions**	
直属机关妇委会（妇工委）	Women's Committee of Direct-affiliated Departments	21
部门机关妇委会（妇工委）	Women's Committee of Affiliated Departments	333
事业单位妇委会（妇工委）	Women's Committee of Government Institutions	79
四、民主党派妇女组织	**Women's Organizations of Democratic Parties**	
民主党派妇委会	Women's Committee of Democratic Parties	7
五、团体会员	**Members of Organisation**	
工会女职工委员会	Women Staff Committee of Labor Unions	3398
民政部门登记注册的妇女社团	Women's Communities Registered at Civil Administration Departments	10

19–22 妇联工作情况

Basic Facts on Women's Federation

单位：人、个 （person,unit）

项　目	Item	2010
一、双学双比活动	**Double Learning and Double Competition Activities**	
(一)科技培训	Scientific and Technical Training	
接受技术培训人数	Number of People Receiving Technical Training	127661
获绿色证书人数	Number of People Gaining Green Certificates	171
妇代会主任中农民技术员数	Number of Farmer in Women's Head Technicians	90
(二)巾帼扶贫	Women Aid-the-poor Project	
脱贫户数	Households out of Poverty	6
扶贫项目数	Number of Poverty Alleviation Projects	1
二、巾帼建功活动	**Women Make Achievements**	
(一)巾帼建功	Women Make Achievements	
评选巾帼建功标兵数	Number of Pacemakes	142
巾帼建功先进工作者数	Number of Advanced Workers	113
巾帼建功先进协调单位数	Number of Advanced Supporting Units	
巾帼文明示范岗数	Number of Model Workers	151
(二)下岗失业妇女再就业	Re-employment of Laid-off and Unemployed Women	
妇女就业服务机构数	Number of Institutions for Women's Employment Services	
妇联主办的劳务市场	Labor Markets Sponsored by Women's Federation	10
三、三八红旗手	**Models of Women**	**43**
四、三八红旗集体	**Models of Women Group**	**24**
五、实施春蕾计划	**Carrying out of CHUNLEI Project**	
资助女童入学或返校数	Helping Women Children Enter School or Back School	100
社会捐资总额(万元)	Amount of Money That Social Attributes（10 000yuan）	10
六、来信来访情况	**Conditions of Letters and Visits**	
女职工劳动保护信访案件	Cases about Labor Protection of Employed Women through Letters and Visits	41
侵犯妇女财产权利信访案件	Cases about Encroachment of Women's Property through Letters and Visits	286

19-23 交通事故情况

Statistics on Traffic Accidents

指标	Item	2000	2005	2006	2007	2008	2009	2010
次 数(起)	Number of Traffic Accidents（case）	4099	4903	3709	3643	2576	2702	2323
死亡人数（人）	Number of Deaths（person）	589	617	617	597	551	531	531
受伤人数 （人）	Number of Injuries（person）	2884	3081	3075	3002	2464	2247	2520
直接财产损失（万元）	Direct Property Loss（10000yuan）	1116.1	2024.4	1328.3	1038.0	522.8	851.7	736.6

注：2006年及以前道路交通数据不含高速公路数据,故年度数据不可比。

Note:As road data of traffic didn't include expressways, annual data were not comparable.

19-24 火灾情况

Statistics on Fires

指标	Item	2000	2005	2006	2007	2008	2009	2010
次 数（起）	Number of Traffic Accidents（case）	1040	2664	2310	2009	1537	1485	1825
死亡人数（人）	Number of Deaths（person）	17	13	9	13	11	17	13
受伤人数（人）	Number of Injuries（person）	12	15	9	11	4	3	7
直接财产损失(万元）	Direct Property Loss（10000yuan）	472.4	1565.5	1376.0	773.9	1907.7	1850.6	2224.2

19–25 安全生产情况

Dato on Sasfety in Production

指　　标	Item	2006	2007	2008	2009	2010
全市合计	**Sum of Entire City**					
起数（起）	Number of Cases（case）	6065	5685	4138	4225	4173
死亡人数（人）	Number of Deaths（person）	676	648	591	586	568
受伤人数（人）	Number of Injuries（person）	3090	3013	2472	2264	2529
损失（万元）	Economic Loss（10 000yuan）	3004.1	2308.4	2802.0	3128.9	3666.8
道路交通事故	**Road Accidents**					
起数（起）	Number of Cases（case）	3709	3643	2576	2702	2323
死亡人数（人）	Number of Deaths（person）	617	597	551	531	531
受伤人数（人）	Number of Injuries（person）	3075	3002	2464	2247	2520
损失（万元）	Economic Loss（10 000yuan）	1328.3	1038.0	522.8	851.7	736.6
火灾事故	**Fire Accidents**					
起数（起）	Number of Cases（case）	2310	2009	1537	1485	1825
死亡人数（人）	Number of Deaths（person）	9	13	11	17	13
受伤人数（人）	Number of Injuries（person）	9	11	4	3	7
损失（万元）	Economic Loss（10 000yuan）	1376.0	773.9	1907.7	1850.6	2224.2
农机事故	**Farm Machinery Accidents**					
起数（起）	Number of Cases（case）	2	3	2	11	5
死亡人数（人）	Number of Deaths（person）	1	3	1		
受伤人数（人）	Number of Injuries（person）	1		1	2	2
损失（万元）	Economic Loss（10 000yuan）				1.1	3.1
工矿商贸事故	**Accidents in Industry,Mine, Business and Trade**					
起数（起）	Number of Cases（case）	42	30	22	27	20
死亡人数（人）	Number of Deaths（person）	47	35	27	38	24
受伤人数（人）	Number of Injuries（person）	5		3	12	
损失（万元）	Economic Loss（10 000yuan）	293.0	496.5	366.5	425.5	703.0
特种设备	**Special Accidents**					
起数（起）	Number of Cases（case）	2		1		
死亡人数（人）	Number of Deaths（person）	2		1		
受伤人数（人）	Number of Injuries（person）					
损失（万元）	Economic Loss（10 000yuan）	7		5		

注：1.2006年及以前道路交通数据不含高速公路数据,故年度数据不可比.

2.2007年、2009年工矿商贸事故数据含特种设备数据.

Note: 1.As statistics of roads did not include that of highway before 2006, the indexes were not comparable with those in corresponding period.

2.Data of accidents in industry , mine, business and trade include special equipment in 2007 and 2009.

19-26 刑事案件情况

Data on Criminal Cases

指　　标	Item	2005	2006	2007	2008	2009	2010
一、案件数情况	**Data on Number of Cases**						
立案数（起）	Number of Registered Cases(caes)	23537	43856	43583	41811	42321	48566
破案数（起）	Number of Cleared up Cases(caes)	13145	13952	17241	19284	21921	18906
破案率（%）	Percent of Cleared up Cases(%)	56	32	40	46	52	39
抓获作案人员（人）	Number of Criminals Caught(person)	10690	11068	12717	12364	11870	13104
二、查获犯罪集团情况	**Data on Hunted down and Seized Criminal Gangs**						
查获犯罪集团个数（个）	Number of Hunted down and Seized Criminal Gangs（person）	221	203	230	211	154	186
查获犯罪集团人数（人）	Number of Members of Hunted down and Seized Criminal Gangs（person）	985	938	1061	916	663	939
涉及案件（起）	Number of Cases Involved(case)	1102	847	1225	1328	622	1172
三、涉枪案件情况	**Data on Cases with Guns Involved**						
立案数（起）	Number of Registered Cases(caes)	34	37	10	11	25	16
破案数（起）	Number of Cleared up Cases(caes)	32	35	8	9	24	11
破案率（%）	Percent of Cleared up Cases(%)	94.1	94.6	80.0	81.8	96.0	68.8

19-27 治安案件情况

Data on Public Order Cases

指　　标	Item	2005	2006	2007	2008	2009	2010
案件数情况	**Data on Number of Cases**						
受理数（起）	Number of Accepted Cases	45484	40550	41213	45226	45925	58968
查处数（起）	Number of Investigated and Prosecuted Cases	40743	35598	38737	44202	45871	57151
查处率（%）	Percent of Investigated and Prosecuted Cases(%)	89.6	87.8	94.0	97.7	99.9	96.9
查处违法犯罪人数（人）	Number of Investigated and Prosecuted Law-breakers and Crime Committer(person)	48949	37109	36739	38606	39214	45856

19-28 分区县刑事、治安案件情况（2010年）

Data on Criminal Cases and Public Order Cases Grouped by District and County（2010）

单位：件 (case)

区县	Region	刑事案件 Criminal cases			治安案件 Public order cases		
		立案数 Number of Registered Cases	破案数 Number of Cleared up Cases	破案率 (%) Percent of Ceared up Cases (%)	受理数 Number of Accepted Cases	查处数 Number of Investigated and Prosecuted Cases	查处率 (%) Percent of Investigated and Prosecuted Cases(%)
新城区	Xincheng	5950	1938	32.6	7044	7044	100.0
碑林区	Beilin	5272	3428	65.0	10714	10699	99.9
莲湖区	Lianhu	5511	2342	42.5	3340	3203	95.9
灞桥区	Baqiao	2939	1157	39.4	5703	5703	100.0
未央区	Weiyang	4227	2173	51.4	7356	6079	82.6
雁塔区	Yanta	7962	2122	26.7	11880	11868	99.9
阎良区	Yanliang	1165	339	29.1	491	430	87.6
临潼区	Lintong	2402	933	38.8	1900	1831	96.4
长安区	Chang'an	3073	999	32.5	2664	2664	100.0
蓝田县	Lantian	1073	428	39.9	1689	1643	97.3
周至县	Zhouzhi	891	377	42.3	442	442	100.0
户　县	Huxian	894	387	43.3	886	851	96.0
高陵县	Gaoling	1208	320	26.5	796	796	100.0

19-29 西安市人民检察院案件受理情况

Data on Acceptance of Cases of Xi'an People's Procuratorate

指　标	Item	受案 Acceptance of Cases				
		2006	2007	2008	2009	2010
总　计	**Toatl**	**7354**	**7972**	**8924**	**8462**	**8044**
一、贪污贿赂案件（件）	**Cases about Corporation and Bribery（case）**	**425**	**383**	**431**	**316**	**327**
二、渎职、侵权案件（件）	**Cases about Misprision and Tortious（case）**	**99**	**83**	**115**	**89**	**89**
三、审查逮捕（件）	**Examination and Arresting（case)**	**3175**	**3497**	**3835**	**3656**	**3476**
决定逮捕贪污贿赂犯罪嫌疑人（人）	Suspects of Corporation and Bribery to be Arrested（person）	101	73	104	97	51
决定逮捕渎职、侵权犯罪嫌疑人（人）	Suspects of Misprision and Tortious to be Arrested（person）	16	4	11	11	2
批准逮捕刑事犯罪嫌疑人（人）	Suspects of Criminal to be Arrested（person）	4480	4935	5702	5321	6130
四、刑事立案监督、侦查活动监督（件）	**Supervision of Acceptance of Criminal Cases and Investigation（case）**	**163**	**204**	**218**	**159**	**343**
五、审查起诉（件）	**EXamination and Prosecution（case)**	**3492**	**3805**	**4325**	**4242**	**3809**
起诉贪污贿赂犯罪被告人（人）	Prosecution of Corporation and Bribery to be Defendants（person）	169	126	158	159	163
起诉渎职、侵权犯罪被告人（人）	Prosecution of Misprision and Tortious to be Defendants（person）	16	23	15	11	22
起诉刑事犯罪被告人（人）	Prosecution of Criminal to be Defendants（person）	4524	4947	5435	5444	5761

19-30 西安市中级人民法院案件基本情况（2010年）

Xi'an Intermediate People's Court Basic Data of the Law Cases（2010）

单位：件 (case)

指标	Item	陪审员参加 Number of Jurors Partcipating	回避 Withdrawn	诉讼财产保全 Preserving of Property of Lawsuit	先予执行 Execute in Advance
合 计	**Total**	**3919**		**41**	
一、刑 事	**Criminal**	**2105**			
二、婚姻家庭、继承	**Marriage，Family and Inheritance**	**403**		**4**	
三、合 同	**Contract**	**777**		**31**	
四、权属、侵权及其他民事案件	**Tort and Other Civil Cases**	**531**		**6**	
五、行 政	**Administration**	**103**			
六、申诉、申请再审	**Appeals，Apply for Retrial**				
七、司法赔偿	**Judicial Indemnification**				
八、执 行	**Execution**				
合计中	Collegiating	3919		41	
海事海商	Maritime Affairs & Business				
知识产权	Intellectual Property	5			
一 审	First Instance	3919		41	
二 审	Second Instance				
审判监督	Trial Supervision				

19-30 续表

指　　标	Item	审委会讨论（件）Under Discussing of Judicial Board (case)	法律援助（件）Legal Aids (case)	结案合计（件）Wound up Cases （case）	诉讼标的总总额合计（万元）Amount of Lawsuit object (10 000 yuan)
合　计	**Total**	**495**	**11**	**65620**	**1104008.4**
一、刑　事	**Criminal**	**194**	**6**	**4320**	**7185.2**
二、婚姻家庭、继承	**Marriage，Family and Inheritance**	**18**	**1**	**11761**	**27555.6**
三、合　同	**Contract**	**119**	**1**	**20910**	**516336.2**
四、权属、侵权及其他民事案件	**Tort and Other Civil Cases**	**90**	**3**	**12336**	**163093.4**
五、行　政	**Administration**	**17**		**683**	
六、申诉、申请再审	**Appeals，Apply for Retrial**	**7**		**382**	
七、司法赔偿	**Judicial Indemnification**			**2**	
八、执　行	**Execution**	**50**		**15226**	**389838.0**
合计中	Collegiating	495	11	65620	1104008.4
海事海商	Maritime Affairs & Business				
知识产权	Intellectual Property			297	4107.3
一　审	First Instance	345	11	43904	596421.2
二　审	Second Instance			5895	113769.4
审判监督	Trial Supervision	93		211	3979.7

continued

中级人民法院结案（件） Intermediate People's Court closed（case）	中级人民法院诉讼标的总金额（万元） Total Amount of Intermediate People's Court Subject Matter of Litigation (10 000 yuan)	基层人民法院结案（件） Primary People's Courts Closed（case）	基层人民法院诉讼标的总金额（万元） Total Amount of Primary People's Court Subject Matter of Litigation (10 000 yuan)	其中人民法庭结案（件） Courtroom Closed（case）	其中人民法庭诉讼标的总金额（万元） Total Amount of Courtroom Subject Matter of Litigation (10 000 yuan)
8117	**560347.0**	**57503**	**543661.3**	**12848**	**40332.5**
857	**2047.1**	**3463**	**5138.1**		
512	**9372.5**	**11249**	**18183.1**	**5173**	**8421.3**
3881	**249877.1**	**17029**	**266459.1**	**3310**	**18163.4**
1561	**109049.0**	**10775**	**54044.3**	**4235**	**13533.7**
214		**469**			
374		**8**			
1		**1**			
717	**190001.3**	**14509**	**199836.7**	**130**	**214.1**
8117	560347.0	57503	543661.3	12848	40332.5
283	4107.3	14			
1007	253172.5	42897	343248.7	12718	40118.3
5895	113769.4				
123	3403.9	88	575.9		

主要统计指标解释

文化事业机构 指从事专业文化工作和为专业文化工作服务的独立建制的单位。不包括这些单位另外举办独立核算的其他机构和各部门的业余文化组织。

艺术表演团体 指从事戏曲、音乐、舞蹈、杂技等专业艺术表演，有独立帐户的单位，不包括半工半艺、半农半艺和民间职业剧团。

电影放映单位 指具有放映机器设备、固定或不固定的放映场所与专职或兼职的放映技术人员，经有关部门登记批准，经常为一定的观众对象放映电影的机构。包括经批准对外开放进行营业，并与电影发行放映管理机构分帐的专用放映单位和军委系统租片单位。

艺术表演观众人数（人次） 指售票、包场演出或民族地区免费演出的艺术表演观众人次数，不包括彩排审查和内部观摩演出的观看人次数。

等级运动员人数 指经考核正式批准授予等级运动员称号的人数。运动员等级分为国际级运动健将、运动健将、一级运动员、二级运动员、三级运动员、少年级运动员。

等级裁判员人数 指经考核正式批准授予等级裁判员称号的人数。裁判员等级分为国际裁判、国家级裁判、一级裁判、二级裁判、三级裁判。

体育场 指有400米跑道（中心含足球场），有固定道牙，跑道6条以上，并有固定看台的室外田径场地。体育场按看台容纳观众人数分为: 甲级25000人以上，乙级15000–25000人，丙级5000–15000人，丁级5000人以下。

体育馆 指有固定看台，可供篮球、排球、羽毛球、乒乓球、体操等项目训练比赛活动用的室内运动场地。体育馆按看台容纳观众人数分为: 甲级6000人以上，乙级4000–6000人，丙级2000–4000人，丁级2000人以下。

卫生机构 包括医院、疗养院、社区服务中心（站）、卫生院、门诊部、急救中心（站）、采供血机构、妇幼保健院（站、所）、专科疾病防治院（站、所）、疾病预防控制中心（防疫站）、卫生监督所、卫生监督检验（监测、检测）所（站）、医学科学研究机构、医学在职培训机构、健康教育所（站、中心）、诊所、卫生所、医务室、村卫生所。不包括卫生新闻出版社、卫生社会团体、卫生行政机关、教育部门登记注册的高中等医学（药）院校、军队编制内卫生机构、香港澳门特别行政区和台湾所属卫生机构。

医院 指设有固定床位，能收容病人住院并能为病人提供医疗、护理服务的医疗机构，包括县及县以上医院、农村乡卫生院和其他医院三部分。医院按所属性质不同分为卫生部门、工业及其他部门和集体经济单位三类。县及县以上医院按业务性质不同分为综合医院和专科医院。

卫生技术人员 包括执业（助理）医师、注册护士、药剂人员、检验和影像技师（士、员）等卫生专业人员。

社会福利事业单位 指集中收养社会孤老、残、幼的机构，包括由民政部门管理的社会福利院、儿童福利院、精神病人福利院和城镇集体举办的福利院及农村集体举办的敬老院。

社会福利事业单位收养人数 包括民政部门管理和城镇、农村集体举办的社会福利事业单位中收养的老人、少年儿童、缺乏生活自理能力的残疾人员和精神病人。

社会福利企业单位 指以安置城镇有一定劳动能力的盲、聋、哑和肢体残疾人员就业为目的，享受国家减免税待遇的国有或集体企业。包括福利工厂、福利商业和服务业、假肢厂和安置农场等单位。

律师 指受聘参加法律顾问处工作，担任法律顾问、刑（民）事代理人、刑事辩护人，办理非诉讼事件、解答法律询问，代写法律事务文书等主要从事律师业务的专职法律工作者和兼职律师。

公证人员 指在国家公证机关依法办理公证事务的司法人员，包括公证员、助理公证员和在公证处工作的其他人员。

办理公证文书 指公证处在一定时期内办结的公证文书件数。公证文书按司法部规定或批准的格式制作，包括国内公证和涉外公证两部分。国内公证分为经济合同公证和民事法律关系公证两大类。

调解人员 指在人民调解委员会担负调解民间一般民事纠纷和轻微违法行为引起纠纷的工作人员，包括调解委员会的委员和调解小组的调解员。

调解民间纠纷 指调解委员会依照法律规定，根据自愿原则，用说服教育的方法调解民间发生的有关民事权利和义务的争执，促成当事双方达到协议和谅解，解决纠纷。包括婚姻家庭纠纷，财产权益纠纷等，不包括法院受理调解的民事案件数。

受理劳动争议案件数 指劳动争议仲裁委员会根据国家有关规定，对劳动争议当事人的申请予以审查，符合受理条件而正式立案、准备处理的劳动争议案件数。

立案 指检察机关对犯罪线索进行初步调查后，认为存在职务犯罪事实并需要追究刑事责任时，依法决定作为刑事案件进行侦查的诉讼活动，是追究犯罪的开始。

Explanatory Notes on Main Statistical Indicators

Cultural Institutions refer to units which have their own organizational system and independent accounting system and specialize in or serve cultural development. They exclude other establishments run by these cultural institutions and amateur cultural groups established by various departments.

Art Troupe refers to the troupe which is engaged in drama, opera, music, dance, acrobatics or other art performance, opens independent accounts with banks and has self-supporting accounting system; excluding the troupes which are engaged partly in industrial or agricultural activities, partly in art performance and the professional troupes organized by the people.

Film Projection Units refer to units with film projection equipment, full or part time projectionists, permanent or non permanent places, approved by related administrative departments to show films regularly for certain groups of audience, including those film projection units which have been approved to give commercial shows and run business with independent accounting system as well as those film-renting units of the military system.

Number of Spectators at Art Performance refers to the number of attendants at commercial shows, completely booked shows or free shows given in minority national areas, and does not include the number of spectators at rehearsals for examination and internal shows for study.

Number of Athletes in Grades refers to the number of athletes who have been given titles through examination. The titles of athletes include international masters of sports, masters of sports, first-grade, second-grade and third-grade sportsmen and young athletes.

Number of Referees in Grades refers to the number of referees who have been given titles after examination. They are classified as international referees, national referees and referees of the first, second and third grades.

Stadiums refer to stadiums for track and field events with six lane 400-meter tracks around soccer fields, permanent track marks and permanent bleachers. Stadiums are classified according to seating capacity. they include: class a stadiums seating 25000 people each. class b stadiums seating 15000 to 25000 people each. Class C stadiums seating 5000 to 15000 people each, and Class D stadiums seating fewer than 5000 people.

Gymnasiums refer to indoor sports grounds with permanent seats in which basketball, volleyball. badminton, table tennis and gymnastics competitions can be held. Gymnasiums are classified according to seating capacity. They include Class A gymnasiums seating over 6000 people. Class B gymnasiums seating 4000 to 6000 people. Class C gymnasiums seating 2000 to 4000 people, and Class D gymnasiums seating fewer than 2000 people.

Health institution includes hospital, sanitarium, community service center (station), health center, emergency aid centers(station), blood gathering or supplying institution, maternity and child care center, disease prevention and control institution(epidemic prevention station), health supervision institution, health supervision and testing (monitory, detecting) institution, medical research institution, medical on-the-job training agency, health education center, clinic, health station, dispensary, health center in village. It excludes health news press, health social community, health administration, high-and-medium level medical (pharmic) college registered in educational administration, health institution in army, health institution belong to Hong Kong Special Administration Region or Taiwan.

Hospitals refer to medical institutions with permanent hospital beds, which are able to take in patients and provide them with medical and nursing services. Hospitals are classified into three categories: hospitals at or above the county level, hospitals of rural townships, and other hospitals. According to their ownership, hospitals can be classified into three categories: hospitals under the public health departments, hospitals under industrial and other departments and collective-owned hospitals. Hospitals at or above county level are divided into comprehensive and specialized hospitals.

Medical Technical Personnel includes practicing (assistant) doctor, certified nurse, pharmacist, laboratory and photographic technician, other technicians working in medical institution.

Social Welfare Institutions refer to institutions taking care of old people without children, handicapped people and orphans. They include social welfare institutions run by civil affairs departments, children welfare institutions, social welfare institutions for mental patients, and collective-owned old peoples homes in rural areas.

Number of People Taken in by Social Welfare Institutions refers to the number of old people, children, totally dependent handicapped people and mental patientsTaken in by social welfare institutions run by civil affairs departments and those run by collective units in urban and rural areas.

Social Welfare Enterprises are collective owned enterprises which employ the blind, deaf-mute, and other handicapped people who are able to work in cities and towns and enjoy exemption from state taxes, including welfare plants, welfare commercial services, artificial limb plants and farms, etc.

Lawyers are legal workers who are employed full time by legal counseling firms to act as legal advisers, agents in criminal or civil lawsuits, or defenders in criminal lawsuits, or to handle non-litigious legal affairs, to advise on matters of law or to write legal papers for others. Both full-time and part time lawyers are included.

Notary Personnel refers to judicial workers of the state notary offices handling notarization work according to law. They include notaries, assistant notaries, and other people working for notary offices.

Notarized Documents refer to the documents settled by notary offices in a year. The notary documents are drawn up in accordance with the regulations of the Ministry of Justice, including domestic documents and foreign-related documents. Domestic documents are divided into two major categories, documents on economic contracts and documents on civil legal relations.

Mediators refer to workers on peoples mediation committees responsible for mediating in civil disputes and cases of slight infraction of the law. They include members of the mediation committees and mediators of mediation groups.

Mediation of Civil Disputes refers to mediation committees work in mediating in civil disputes concerning civil rights and duties through persuasion and education in accordance with the provisions of law on a voluntary basis, so as to solve disputes by helping the parties involved come to an agreement and understanding. these disputes include divorce cases and disputes over property ownership, but exclude the civil cases to be handled by the court.

Number of Labour Dispute Cases Accepted refers to the number of cases of labour dispute submitted that, after being reviewed by the labour dispute arbitration committees in line with the relevant state regulations, are accepted and registered for treatment.

Acceptance of Case refers to the decision made by the procurators office to confirm the act of crime after initial investigation and to start legal proceedings of the case as criminal case.

20 企业调查

ENTERPRISES INVESTIGATION

资料整理：刘　艳
Data management:Liu Yan

第二十部分　企业调查

一、简要说明

本章资料主要包括各行业企业景气调查指数和企业家信心指数等，由国家统计局西安调查队提供。

二、主要指标

企业景气指数	139.6	比上年提高 4.1点
企业家信心指数	133.1	比上年提高 5.4点

20 ENTERPRISES INVESTIGATION

Ⅰ.Brief Introduction

Data in this chapter consists prosperity survey indices of various industries and Entrepreneur Expectation Indicator, provided by Enterprise Survey Crew of NBS Survey Office in Xi'an.

Ⅱ.Major Indicators

		Increase over Preceding Year
Business Climate Index	139.6	4.1 points
Entrepreneur Expectation Indicator	133.1	5.4 points

20-1 企业景气指数（2010年）

Business Climate Index（2010）

指 标	Item	一季度 First Quarter	二季度 Second Quarter	三季度 Third Quarter	四季度 Forth Quarter
企业景气指数	**Business Climate Index**	**123.9**	**131.5**	**130.1**	**133.1**
按行业门类分	Grouped by Sector				
工业	Industry	121.5	130.4	123.5	131.9
建筑业	Construction	133.5	144.8	139.4	142.3
交通运输、仓储及邮政业	Transport, Storage and Post	138.5	141.5	146.3	146.3
批发和零售业	Wholesale and Retail Sales	114.9	119.2	129.8	124.1
房地产业	Real Estate	135.0	125.0	136.8	136.8
社会服务业	Social Services	122.7	121.7	121.7	126.1
信息传输 、计算机服务和软件业	Information Transmission, Computer Service and Safeware Service	120.5	149.0	149.0	142.0
住宿和餐饮业	Hotels and Catering Services	114.9	129.9	123.9	123.9
按企业登记注册类型分	Grouped by Registration				
国有企业	State-owned Enterprises	122.7	125.1	126.4	130.5
集体企业	Collective-owned Enterprises	107.7	138.5	115.4	123.1
股份合作企业	Share-holding Cooperative Enterprises	116.7	140.0	160.0	120.0
联营企业	Joint Ownership Enterprises				
有限责任公司	Limited Liability Corporations	120.9	131.5	126.3	130.3
股份有限公司	Share-holding Corporations Ltd.	120.7	135.1	134.1	137.2
私营企业	Privately Owned Enterprises	100.0	0.0	0.0	200.0
港、澳、台投资企业	Enterprises Invested by Foreigners or Investors from Hongkong,Macro and Taiwan	139.4	155.9	128.5	176.9
外商投资企业	Enterprises Invested by Foreigners or Investors from Hongkong,Macro and Taiwan	138.2	129.2	140.1	126.9
按企业规模分	Grouped by Size of Enterprises				
大型企业	Large-size	169.6	176.5	165.1	175.1
中型企业	Medium-size	127.5	129.8	129.1	132.9
小型企业	Small-size	94.7	108.6	108.0	110.1
特殊分组	Special-Grouped				
国家重点企业	State Key Enterprises	122.8	135.3	122.5	133.6
国家试点企业集团成员	Member of State Experimental Enterprises Group	120.3	133.7	120.9	132.1
出口企业	Town and Township Enterprises	138.3	146.6	136.4	146.6
上市公司	Listed Companies	142.6	148.1	155.1	154.4
国有控股企业	State-holding Enterprises	130.9	135.1	135.9	137.1
生产总量	Total Production	101.9	135.4	131.0	132.0
盈利（亏损）变化	Change of Profits or Losses	102.6	119.2	115.6	121.7
流动资金	Circulating Funds	81.4	78.9	80.3	86.6
货款拖欠	Delinquent Loans	99.2	90.7	97.8	96.6
劳动力需求	Demand of Labor Force	102.1	120.3	117.4	116.6
固定资产投资	Investment of fixed Assets	106.6	113.9	109.8	114.6
产品订货	Product Order	101.2	115.3	113.8	118.1
企业融资	Accommodation	77.9	75.9	74.0	76.5

20-2　企业家信心指数（2010年）

Entrepreneur Expectation Indicator（2010）

指　标	Item	一季度 First Season	二季度 Second Season	三季度 Third Season	四季度 Fourth Season
企业家信心指数	**Entrepreneur Expectation Indicator**	**130.3**	**140.2**	**136.7**	**139.6**
按行业门类分	Grouped by Sector				
工业	Industry	131.5	143.2	131.9	139.8
建筑业	Construction	148.6	153.6	150.2	146.5
交通运输、仓储及邮政业	Transport, Storage and Post	150.4	148.0	151.1	135.2
批发和零售业	Wholesale and Retail Sales	101.6	126.9	126.6	130.8
房地产业	Real Estate	150.0	125.0	136.8	147.4
社会服务业	Social Services	118.2	139.1	147.8	152.2
信息传输、计算机服务和软件业	Information Transmission, Computer Service and Safeware Service	135.1	135.1	135.1	126.0
住宿和餐饮业	Hotels and Catering Services	117.9	127.0	120.9	123.9
按企业登记注册类型分	Grouped by Registration				
国有企业	State-owned Enterprises	126.9	141.9	137.9	141.5
集体企业	Collective-owned Enterprises	153.9	153.9	146.2	146.2
股份合作企业	Share-holding Cooperative Enterprises	100.0	140.0	160.0	140.0
联营企业	Joint Ownership Enterprises				
有限责任公司	Limited Liability Corporations	128.1	134.5	125.9	134.3
股份有限公司	Share-holding Corporations Ltd.	141.3	143.9	146.9	139.6
私营企业	Privately Owned Enterprises	100.0	200.0	100.0	200.0
港、澳、台投资企业	Enterprises Invested by Foreigners or Investors from Hongkong,Macro and Taiwan	110.2	161.5	130.4	153.9
外商投资企业	Enterprises Invested by Foreigners or Investors from Hongkong,Macro and Taiwan	135.5	140.9	132.8	136.5
按企业规模分	Grouped by Size of Enterprises				
大型企业	Large-size	162.3	180.9	153.8	176.9
中型企业	Medium-size	133.1	141.8	139.2	137.9
小型企业	Small-size	108.6	117.2	117.3	119.5
特殊分组	Special-Grouped				
国家重点企业	State Key Enterprises	129.9	121.6	111.6	111.6
国家试点企业集团成员	Member of State Experimental Enterprises Group	113.8	116.9	100.9	107.5
出口企业	Town and Township Enterprises	139.5	155.6	127.9	147.9
上市公司	Listed Companies	151.2	156.8	159.8	157.2
国有控股企业	State-holding Enterprises	136.9	146.7	139.3	143.4

主要统计指标解释

企业景气指数：是根据企业家对本企业综合生产经营情况所作的判断与预期（通常是对“良好”、“一般”、“不佳”的选择）而编制的指数，用以综合反映企业的生产经营状况。企业景气指数也称“企业综合生产经营景气指数”。

企业家信心指数：是根据企业家对企业外部市场经济环境与宏观政策的认识、看法判断和预期（通常是对“乐观”、“一般”、“不乐观”的选择）而编制的指数，用以综合反映企业家对宏观经济环境的感受与信心。企业家信心指数也称“宏观经济景气指数”。

景气指数的表示方式：景气指数的表示范围在0～200之间，其含义：100为景气指数的临界值，表明景气状况变化不大；100～200为景气区间，表明景气状况趋于上升或改善，越接近于200，状况越景气；0～100为不景气区间，表明经济状况趋于下降或恶化，越接近于0，状况越不景气。

国家重点企业：是指1999年10月经国务院批准确定的520户国家重点企业。

国家试点企业集团成员：是指由国务院批准组建的国家试点企业集团的成员单位。

上市公司：是指所发行的股票经国务院授权的中国证券监督管理委员会批准、在境内外证券交易所（包括上海、深圳、香港、纽约、东京等证券交易所）内上市买卖其有价证券的股份有限公司。

Explanatory Notes on Main Statistical Indicators

Business Climate Index it is an index worked out according to the judgment and anticipation (normally a choice from good , ordinary , not good) of entrepreneurs made based on synthetic productive and operational situation of the enterprise. It is used to reflect synthetically the productive and operational situation of the enterprise. It is also referred to as synthetic productive and operational prosperity index of enterprise .

Confidence index of entrepreneur it is an index worked out according to the judgment and anticipation (normally a choice from optimistic , ordinary , not optimistic) of entrepreneurs made based on their understandings and views of the market and economic environment outside the enterprise and the macro policies. It is used to reflect synthetically the confidence and feelings of the entrepreneurs to the macro economic environment. It is also referred to as macro-economy prosperity index .

The way to express prosperity index the range of prosperity index is from 0 to 200; 100 is the critical value, and means economic situation didn't change largely; from 100 to 200 is the interval of prosperity; and from 0 to 100 is the interval of not prosperity, meaning economic situation is going down or worse, the closer to 0, the worse the economic situation.

Key enterprise of the state it refers to the 520 key enterprises of the state authorized and confirmed by State Department in Oct., 1999.

Member of state experimental unit enterprise group refers to the members of state experimental unit enterprise groups authorized and formed by State Department.

Company on the market refers to the limited companies with stock authorized by China Securities Regulatory Commission which is authorized by State Department, and their securities can be deal on the market in stock exchanges (include exchanges of Shanghai, Shenzhen, Hong Kong, New York and Tokyo) inside and outside P.R. of China.

中国统计出版社最新资料书简目

（仅供参考，以最后出书为准）

统计资料

中国统计年鉴-2011　中国统计摘要-2011　国际统计年鉴-2011
2011中国发展报告　中国第三产业统计年鉴-2011　中国区域经济统计年鉴-2011
中国劳动统计年鉴-2011　中国社会统计年鉴-2011　中国城市统计年鉴-2009
中国建筑业统计年鉴-2011　中国人口和就业统计年鉴-2011　中国工业经济统计年鉴-2011
中国商品交易市场统计年鉴-2011　中国房地产统计年鉴-2011　中国能源统计年鉴-2011
中国民政统计年鉴-2011　中国贸易外经统计年鉴-2011　2011中国地区经济监测报告
中国科技统计年鉴-2011　中国农村统计年鉴-2011　中国农产品价格调查年鉴-2011
中国高技术产业统计年鉴-2011　中国教育经费统计年鉴-2010　中国农村贫困监测报告-2011
全国农产品成本收益资料汇编-2011　中国科学技术协会统计年鉴-2011　工业企业科技活动资料-2011
大中型批发零售和住宿餐饮企业统计年鉴-2011　中国城市(镇)生活与价格年鉴-2011
中国县（市）社会经济统计年鉴-2011　中国农村住户调查年鉴-2011（中、英文）　中国农村全面建设小康监测报告-2011
第二次全国R&D资源清查资料汇编－综合卷　第二次全国R&D资源清查资料汇编－工业企业卷　中国零售和餐饮连锁企业统计年鉴-2011
2010年中国第六次人口普查公报

2011年省级综合统计年鉴系列

北京　天津　河北　山西　内蒙古　辽宁　吉林　黑龙江　上海　江苏　浙江　安徽　福建　江西　山东
河南　湖北　湖南　广东　广西　海南　重庆　四川　贵州　云南　西藏　陕西　甘肃　青海　宁夏
新疆　新疆生产建设兵团

2011年市（县）级综合统计年鉴系列

天津滨海新区　石家庄　唐山　邯郸　太原　大同　长治　阳泉　晋城　朔州　晋中
运城　忻州　临汾　呼和浩特　包头　沈阳　大连　长春　吉林市　四平　哈尔滨　黑龙江垦区
上海浦东新区　苏州　无锡　常州　徐州　南通　盐城　镇江　江阴　丹阳
杭州　宁波　绍兴　台州　温州　金华　嘉兴　衢州　福州　福州经济技术开发区
厦门经济特区　南昌　上饶　济南　青岛　潍坊　郑州　洛阳　三门峡　南阳　武汉　宜昌
十堰　荆州　咸宁　长沙　广州　东莞　惠州　深圳　桂林　南宁　柳州　来宾　河池　海口　成都　绵阳
贵阳　昆明　庆阳　西安　兰州　银川　乌鲁木齐

“十一五”规划教材

非参数统计　医学统计学　概率论与数理统计　统计学　现代金融投资统计分析
多元统计分析　经济计量学教程　应用时间序列分析　统计指数理论及应用
统计数据处理概论　质量管理统计方法　社会统计学　多元统计分析实验
企业经营管理统计　市场调查与预测　统计学原理（非统计专业使用）
统计学:从数据到结论　国民经济核算教程（国民经济统计学）　概率论与数理统计（经济、管理类专业使用）

重点图书

挑大学选专业2011—高考志愿填报指南　挑大学选专业2011—考研择校指南

欲购以上图书请与中国统计出版社发行部联系

电话：（010）63376907,63376908　同榻行书店电话：68783171,68783172

通讯地址：北京市西城区三里河月坛南街57号　邮政编码：100826